GCSE MATHS LEVEL A

Jean Holderness

Causeway Press Ltd

Published by Causeway Press Ltd
P.O. Box 13, Ormskirk, Lancashire L39 5HP

First published 1993

British Library Cataloguing-in-Publication Data.
A catalogue record for this book is available from the British Library.

ISBN 1-873929-13-7

**The National Curriculum Series published by
Causeway Press:**
Mathematics: Levels 3 & 4 by David Alcorn
Mathematics: Level 5 by Jean Holderness
Mathematics: Level 6 by Jean Holderness
Mathematics: Level 7 by Jean Holderness
Mathematics: Level 8 by Jean Holderness
Mathematics: Levels 9 & 10 by Jean Holderness

Other titles by Jean Holderness:
GCSE Maths: Higher Level
GCSE Maths: Intermediate Level
GCSE Maths: Foundation Level
Pure Maths in Practice

Typesetting by Alden Multimedia, Northampton
Printed by Alden Press, Oxford

Preface

This book is planned for use on a 2-year or a 1-year course leading to the Higher level papers of the GCSE. It is based on the syllabuses published for use in 1994, which are all linked with the National Curriculum programme of study and attainment targets for Key Stage 4.

Students will have been learning Mathematics from an early age, so they will have already met many of the topics in this book. The earlier chapters will help to revise and consolidate the work of former years. A good understanding of the basic topics, leading to a sense of achievement, will form a firm foundation to build on when progressing through the syllabus.

The order of the book has been carefully planned, although, of course, it need not be followed rigidly. To some extent it follows the order of the topics in the National Curriculum. Chapters contain a mixture of straightforward questions for students who need to master the techniques, and more varied questions for others to do. Each chapter ends with a practice test.

After every 5 chapters there is a miscellaneous section which includes revision exercises, which could also be used as practice tests; and suggestions for activities to link with AT1, 'using and applying mathematics'. There are puzzle questions throughout the book. Also there are suggestions to students for study, revision and preparation for the examination.

I should like to thank my family and friends who have given me support and encouragement while I have been writing this book. I should also like to thank all those teachers, and others, who have provided helpful comments on the previous GCSE series.

Thanks also go to those who have helped with the production of the book, Sue and Andrew, and the staff at Alden Multimedia and Alden Press. From Causeway Press I have had great support from Mike and everyone else, and especially from David, who has given me a great amount of practical help and encouragement over several months.

I hope that you find this book useful and interesting.

Jean Holderness

To Jim

Acknowledgements

Artwork
Susan and Andrew Allen
Mark Andrews

Page design and cover
Susan and Andrew Allen

Copyright photograph
The Telegraph Colour Library — cover

Contents

Topics for Activities (included in the miscellaneous sections)

Tables

Time

60 seconds = 1 minute	52 weeks = 1 year
60 minutes = 1 hour	365 days = 1 year
24 hours = 1 day	366 days = 1 leap year
7 days = 1 week	12 months = 1 year

The Metric System   **British Units**

Length

1000 mm = 1 m	12 inches = 1 foot
100 cm = 1 m	3 feet = 1 yard
1000 m = 1 km	1760 yards = 1 mile

Area

$100 \text{ mm}^2 = 1 \text{ cm}^2$	144 sq. inches = 1 sq. foot
$10\,000 \text{ cm}^2 = 1 \text{ m}^2$	9 sq. feet = 1 sq. yard
$1\,000\,000 \text{ m}^2 = 1 \text{ km}^2$	
$1 \text{ hectare} = 10\,000 \text{ m}^2$	1 acre = 4840 sq. yards
$100 \text{ hectares} = 1 \text{ km}^2$	640 acres = 1 sq. mile

Volume

$1000 \text{ mm}^3 = 1 \text{ cm}^3$	1728 cu. inches = 1 cu. foot
$1\,000\,000 \text{ cm}^3 = 1 \text{ m}^3$	27 cu. feet = 1 cu. yard

The Metric System	British Units

Weight

100 mg = 1 g	16 ounces = 1 pound
100 cg = 1 g	14 pounds = 1 stone
1000 g = 1 kg	112 pounds = 1 hundredweight
1000 kg = 1 tonne	8 stones = 1 hundredweight
	2240 pounds = 1 ton
	20 hundredweights = 1 ton

Capacity

1000 ml = 1 ℓ	8 pints = 1 gallon
100 cl = 1 ℓ	
1000 ℓ = 1 kl	

1 litre = 1000 cm^3

1 litre of water weighs 1 kg   1 pint of water weighs $1\frac{1}{4}$ lb

1 cm^3 of water weighs 1 g   1 gallon of water weighs 10 lb

To change to the metric system

Length

1 inch = 2.54 cm
1 foot = 30.48 cm
1 yard = 91.44 cm = 0.9144 m
1 mile = 1.609 km

Weight

1 oz = 28.35 g
1 lb = 453.6 g
1 ton = 1016 kg = 1.016 tonne

Capacity

1 pint = 0.568 litre
1 gallon = 4.546 litre

To change from the metric system

Length

1 cm = 0.394 in
1 m = 39.37 in = 1.094 yd
1 km = 1094 yd = 0.621 mile

Weight

1 kg = 2.205 lb
1 tonne = 0.984 ton

Capacity

1 litre = 1.76 pints = 0.220 gallons

To the student : 1

Learning mathematics

Maths is not a new subject since you have been learning it all your life, but in this book are all the topics you need to learn for the Higher level of the GCSE in Maths.

We hope that you will enjoy studying Maths. Just think of some of the ways in which Maths is linked with our lives, for example:
Shapes in the natural world involving symmetry, curves, spirals, etc.
Shapes in architecture and design.
Management of our money.
Understanding of diagrams, graphs and maps.
Ability to think logically, so as to plan ahead.
You can think of many more examples of how Maths is essential in today's world.

Learn to think for yourself. Do not rely on being told how to do everything. The more things you can work out for yourself the better you will do.

Try to discover things for yourself. Look for patterns in numbers and shapes. From a particular result, could you deduce a general formula ? As an example, suppose you have a spare moment waiting for a lesson to begin and you put your ruler down on your exercise book and draw lines on either side of it, then you move the ruler and cross the lines with two others, getting a shape in the middle. Now you can discover many things about that shape: What is it ? Are there any equal lines or angles, or any point or lines of symmetry ? What is the sum of the angles ? What is its area ? By altering the angle at which the lines cross can you get a different area ? What is the least possible area ? Can you draw a sketch graph of the relationship between angle and area ? If you add more lines to the drawing you can make more discoveries.

As you work through this book, try to learn the important facts and methods of each chapter. If you do not understand the main ideas, ask someone to help you, either your teacher, someone else in your class or anyone else who can explain them to you. But when you have to answer an unusual question, before you ask for help, try to use your own commonsense and reason it out.

If you work steadily you can gain a good grade in GCSE Mathematics.

How this book is arranged

There are 25 main chapters. At the beginning of each chapter there is a list of topics included in that chapter. Then there are main facts or methods followed by worked examples, and an exercise to give you practice. The last exercise in each chapter has more varied questions. You may do them at this stage or you may leave them to return to later to give you more revision practice. Finally, there is a test on the ideas of the chapter.

There should be no need to do every part of every question in an exercise. More questions, rather than fewer, have been included for those students who need them. As soon as you have understood a topic you could go on to something else. Use your time wisely so that you complete the syllabus. Learn the important facts, methods and formulae as you go along.

After every 5 chapters there is a Miscellaneous Section. This can be used at any time. It includes revision questions and suggestions for activities or independent work.

There are puzzle questions fitted in at the ends of some chapters. Try some of these, and remember that some may have a catch in them ! Many puzzles do not form part of the examination course but they may be useful for independent work, and may suggest ideas for further investigation.

For Level 10 you have to explore independently a new area of Mathematics, so discuss with your teacher what you could choose. Some of the work of the later chapters may be suitable, if you work at it yourself before it is taught in class.

Now, get started and **enjoy your Maths**.

1 Arithmetic

The topics in this chapter include:

- multiplying mentally,
- using index notation,
- expressing positive integers as a product of prime numbers,
- using the rules of indices,
- calculating with fractions,
- using ratio and proportion,
- using unitary method and proportion,
- using compound measures,
- using percentages,
- calculating growth and decay rates.

Numbers

A calculator is an invaluable tool for saving time and doing accurate calculations, but there are basic arithmetical operations which you should be able to do mentally, quickly and accurately, and for which you should not waste time pressing calculator keys.

You may be asked to multiply and divide mentally in questions such as 80×0.2 and $600 \div 0.2$, so you will need to know the basic tables.

There will be many situations in your life when you need to work something out quickly and you will not have your calculator available. So make sure you are mentally alert.

To check your tables

On squared paper, or with columns drawn on lined paper, copy the chart at the top of the next page. You are going to fill in the results of multiplication, so the numbers in the first few squares down the first empty column are 12, 22, 10, 16, etc. You will work down each column in turn. Before you begin, note the time. You should complete the chart within 5 minutes. If you take longer, then repeat the exercise, using numbers in a different random

X	2	8	6	9	4	11	3	7	5	12
6										
11										
5										
8										
12										
3										
10										
4										
9										
7										

order, until you improve. Then check the accuracy of your work, which should be completely correct.

Exercise 1.1

These questions are intended to improve your speed and accuracy so concentrate and do them quickly.
Write down the answers only in questions 1 to 7.

1. Work out, working downwards in columns.

8×7	$30 + 90$	$21 - 6$	6×12	$100 \div 5$
6×4	$8 + 7$	$30 \div 5$	6×0	$99 + 7$
20×1	11^2	30×20	$\sqrt{64}$	99×0
20×3	$56 \div 7$	$20 - 8$	13×1	12^2

2. Work out

$32 \div 4$	$27 \div 9$	$55 \div 5$	$72 \div 12$	$15 \div 5$
$42 \div 7$	$132 \div 11$	$72 \div 9$	$30 \div 6$	$49 \div 7$
$96 \div 12$	$60 \div 6$	$36 \div 3$	$77 \div 11$	$45 \div 5$
$56 \div 8$	$144 \div 12$	$35 \div 7$	$60 \div 5$	$81 \div 9$

3. What is the remainder when

1   18 is divided by 5,
2   39 is divided by 7,
3   68 is divided by 11,

4   52 is divided by 4,
5   100 is divided by 8?

4. What must be added to

    1 8×7 to make 60,   **4** 7×11 to make 80,

    2 4×3 to make 20,   **5** 9×9 to make 100?

    3 5×9 to make 50,

5. Find the value of

    1 $5 \times 3 \times 1$ **5** $5000 \div 20$ **8** $(8 \times 12) - (7 \times 12)$

    2 $4 \times 2 \times 0$ **6** $89 + 99$ **9** $(6 \times 19) + (4 \times 19)$

    3 $10^2 - 9^2$ **7** $180 \div 5$ **10** $\frac{2}{3}$ of $36 + \frac{1}{3}$ of 36

    4 $10 \times 20 \times 40$

6. **1** How many more 4's than 5's are there in 40?

    2 How many more 8's than 12's are there in 96?

    3 Find two consecutive numbers whose squares differ by 11.

    4 Find two consecutive numbers whose squares add up to 181.

    5 Find three consecutive numbers whose squares add up to 50.

7. **1** Find one-half of each of these numbers

88	18	8	14	60	24	42	52	90	96

    2 Find one-third of each of these numbers

18	99	60	24	45	27	3	21	39	75

    3 Find one-quarter of each of these numbers

8	28	80	100	52	44	4	24	160	36

    4 Find one-fifth of each of these numbers

60	20	45	10	100	15	35	75	55	200

    5 Find two-thirds of each of these numbers

6	15	24	9	30	60	33	90	75	18

8. **1** Find two numbers whose sum is 13 and whose product is 36.

    2 Find two numbers whose sum is 11 and whose product is 30.

    3 Find two numbers whose sum is 52 and whose product is 100.

    4 Find two numbers whose sum is 16 and whose product is 15.

    5 Find two numbers whose sum is 16 and whose product is 48.

    6 Find three numbers whose product is 36 and whose sum is 11.

    7 Find three numbers whose product is 60 and whose sum is 12.

    8 Find two numbers whose product is 72 and which differ by 1.

    9 Find two numbers whose product is 24 and which differ by 5.

    10 Find two numbers whose product is 77 and which differ by 4.

9. **1** Start from 100 and count down in 6's until you reach a number less than 10. What number is this?

    2 Start from 1, then 2, then 4, and double the number every time until you reach a number greater than 1000. What number is this?

3 Start from 25 000 and keep dividing by 5 until you reach a number less than 10. What number is this?

4 Start with 1 and keep adding 7's until you reach a number greater than 100. What number is this?

5 Start from 0 and add 1, then 2, then 3, and so on until you reach a number greater than 100. What number is this?

10. **1** Write down any number between 1 and 10, multiply this by 3, then to the result add 8. Double this answer. Now subtract 3, multiply by 5, add 7. Subtract 2 and divide by 10. Add 17, divide by 3 and take away the number you started with. What is your answer?

2 Write down any number between 1 and 10, add 3 and multiply the result by 6. Then subtract 12, divide by 3, multiply by 10. Add 5, divide by 5 and add 7. Subtract 12 then divide by the number you started with. What is your answer?

3 Write down any number less than 5, double it and add 3. Square the result, add 3 and divide by 4. Subtract 1 and multiply by 2. Subtract 4, divide by the number you started with, add 14 and halve the result. Take away the number you started with. What is your answer?

Index notation

5^2 (five squared) means 5×5 and equals 25.
4^3 (four cubed) means $4 \times 4 \times 4$ and equals 64.
10^6 (ten to the sixth) means $10 \times 10 \times 10 \times 10 \times 10 \times 10$ and equals 1 000 000 (one million).

Square roots

$\sqrt{49} = 7$ since $7^2 = 49$.
$\sqrt{49}$ can be written in index form as $49^{\frac{1}{2}}$, so $49^{\frac{1}{2}} = 7$.

Cube roots

$\sqrt[3]{125} = 5$ since $5^3 = 125$.
$\sqrt[3]{125}$ can be written in index form as $125^{\frac{1}{3}}$, so $125^{\frac{1}{3}} = 5$.

Rules of indices

$3^2 \times 3^5 = 3 \times 3 \quad \times \quad 3 \times 3 \times 3 \times 3 \times 3 = 3^7$

This rule can be expressed generally as $a^m \times a^n = a^{m+n}$

$$\left(4^5\right)^3 = 4^5 \times 4^5 \times 4^5 = 4^{15}$$

This rule can be expressed generally as $\left(a^m\right)^n = a^{mn}$

$$6^5 \div 6^3 = \frac{6 \times 6 \times 6 \times 6 \times 6}{6 \times 6 \times 6} = 6^2$$

This rule can be expressed generally as $a^m \div a^n = a^{m-n}$, where $a \neq 0$.

(These rules have been used in cases where m and n are whole numbers, and in the third one, $m > n$. However, the rules are true for any values of m and n.)

Prime Numbers and Factors

A prime number has no factors (except itself and 1). The first few prime numbers are 2, 3, 5, 7, 11, 13, 17, ...
Other numbers can be expressed in prime factors.

Example

1     $240 = 2 \times 120$
           $= 2 \times 2 \times 60$
           $= 2 \times 2 \times 2 \times 30$
           $= 2 \times 2 \times 2 \times 2 \times 15$
           $= 2 \times 2 \times 2 \times 2 \times 3 \times 5$
           $= 2^4 \times 3 \times 5$

(A quicker way to split it up would be
$240 = 10 \times 24$
       $= 2 \times 5 \times 4 \times 6$
       $= 2 \times 5 \times 2 \times 2 \times 2 \times 3$
       $= 2^4 \times 3 \times 5)$

Tests of divisibility

Divisibility by 2

If the units figure is even, i.e. 2, 4, 6, 8, 0, the number divides by 2.

Divisibility by 3

Add up the digits in the number, and if the answer is more than 9 you can add up the digits of that answer, and repeat until you get a 1-figure number. If this number divides by 3 then 3 is a factor of the original number.

For example, for 2841, $2 + 8 + 4 + 1 = 15$ (and $15 \rightarrow 1 + 5 = 6$). This divides by 3 so 3 is a factor of 2841.

(Also, if the 1-figure number is 9, the original number divides by 9.)

Divisibility by 5

If the units figure is 5 or 0 the number divides by 5.

Divisibility by 7

There is no simple test.

Divisibility by 11

Alternate figures add up to the same total or there is a difference of 11 (or 22, 33, . . .) between the totals.
For example, for 28413, alternate figures are 2, 4, 3 with total 9; and 8, 1 also with total 9; so the number is divisible by 11. For 616, the totals of alternate figures are 12 and 1. There is a difference of 11 so the number is divisible by 11.

Square numbers

If a number is expressed in prime factors and its indices are even it is a perfect square.
Its square root can be found by dividing the indices by 2.

Example

2 $1936 = 2^4 \times 11^2$

   $\sqrt{1936} = 2^2 \times 11 = 4 \times 11 = 44$

Highest common factor (HCF)

This is the highest factor of two (or more) numbers.

Example

3 Find the HCF of 88 and 132.

  In prime factors, $88 = 2^3 \times 11$
          $132 = 2^2 \times 3 \times 11$
  Both numbers have a factor 2^2 and a factor 11.
  The HCF $= 2^2 \times 11 = 4 \times 11 = 44$.

Lowest common multiple (LCM)

This is the smallest number which is a multiple of two (or more) numbers.

Example

4   Find the LCM of 40 and 130.

$40 = 2^3 \times 5$
$130 = 2 \times 5 \times 13$
Any multiple of 40 must include 2^3 and 5.
Any multiple of 130 must include 2, 5 and 13.
So the lowest common multiple must include 2^3, 5 and 13.
The LCM $= 2^3 \times 5 \times 13 = 8 \times 5 \times 13 = 520$.

Rules of indices

$$a^m \times a^n = a^{m+n}$$

$$\left(a^m\right)^n = a^{mn}$$

$$a^m \div a^n = a^{m-n}$$

The rules above will be true for any values of m and n if the following meanings are given to numbers which do not have positive indices:

$$a^0 = 1$$

$$a^{-n} = \frac{1}{a^n}$$

$$a^{\frac{1}{n}} = \sqrt[n]{a}$$

$$a^{\frac{m}{n}} = \left(\sqrt[n]{a}\right)^m \text{ or } \sqrt[n]{(a^m)}$$

Examples

$$3^0 = 1, \quad 5^0 = 1, \quad 100^0 = 1$$

$$4^{-2} = \frac{1}{4^2} = \frac{1}{16}, \quad 5^{-1} = \frac{1}{5^1} = \frac{1}{5}, \quad 10^{-3} = \frac{1}{10^3} = \frac{1}{1000}$$

$$36^{\frac{1}{2}} = \sqrt{36} = 6, \quad 81^{\frac{1}{2}} = \sqrt{81} = 9$$

$$8^{\frac{1}{3}} = \sqrt[3]{8} = 2, \quad 125^{\frac{1}{3}} = \sqrt[3]{125} = 5$$

$$16^{\frac{3}{4}} = \left(\sqrt[4]{16}\right)^3 = 2^3 = 8$$

$$9^{1\frac{1}{2}} = 9^{\frac{3}{2}} = \left(\sqrt{9}\right)^3 = 3^3 = 27$$

$$25^{-\frac{1}{2}} = \frac{1}{25^{\frac{1}{2}}} = \frac{1}{\sqrt{25}} = \frac{1}{5}$$

$$64^{-\frac{2}{3}} = \frac{1}{64^{\frac{2}{3}}} = \frac{1}{\left(\sqrt[3]{64}\right)^2} = \frac{1}{16}$$

Exercise 1.2

1. Which of these numbers are prime numbers? 21, 23, 25, 27, 29.

2. What are the next two prime numbers after **1** 30 **2** 80?

3. Find the values of

   1 2^4

   2 7^3

   3 10^5

   4 $121^{\frac{1}{2}}$

   5 $64^{\frac{1}{3}}$

   6 $2^3 \times 3^2$

   7 $2^2 \times 5 \times 7$

   8 $2^3 \times 11$

   9 $3^3 \times 10^2$

   10 $2 \times 5^2 \times 13$

4. Express these numbers in prime factors.

1	48	**4**	60	**7**	70	**10**	100	**13** 121
2	99	**5**	180	**8**	96	**11**	39	**14** 81
3	52	**6**	24	**9**	64	**12**	80	**15** 150

5. Express these numbers in prime factors and hence find their square roots.

   1 225   **2** 1764   **3** 1089   **4** 256   **5** 5625

6. Express these numbers in prime factors and hence find
   (1) their highest common factor,
   (2) their lowest common multiple.

   1 28, 16

   2 10, 45

   3 66, 88

   4 210, 630

   5 144, 216

7. Simplify, leaving in index form.

1 $3^2 \times 3^4$ 6 $2^3 \div 2^5$

2 $5^6 \div 5^3$ 7 $5^5 \div 5$

3 $7^3 \times 7^3 \times 7^2$ 8 $\left(6^{-2}\right)^2$

4 $\left(2^4\right)^5$ 9 $\left(3^{\frac{1}{3}}\right)^6$

5 $3^8 \div 3^4$ 10 $\left(5^4\right)^{\frac{1}{2}}$

8. Find the value of

1 7^{-2} 6 $49^{\frac{1}{2}}$ 11 $81^{\frac{3}{4}}$

2 6^0 7 $1000^{\frac{2}{3}}$ 12 $4^{1\frac{1}{2}}$

3 2^{-3} 8 $32^{\frac{1}{5}}$ 13 $9^{-\frac{1}{2}}$

4 $\left(\frac{1}{3}\right)^{-1}$ 9 $\left(\frac{1}{4}\right)^{\frac{1}{2}}$ 14 $64^{-\frac{1}{3}}$

5 $2^3 \times 4^0 \times 6^{-1}$ 10 $8^{\frac{2}{3}}$ 15 $1000^{-\frac{2}{3}}$

9. From the numbers   8,   37,   50,   73,   81,   91,   360

1 Which number is a square number?
2 Which number is a cube number?
3 Which two numbers are prime numbers?
4 Which number is a multiple of 13?
5 Which number is a factor of 72?
6 Which number can be written in index form as $2^3 \times 3^2 \times 5$?
7 Which number is equal to the sum of two other numbers in the list?
8 Which number when divided by 9 leaves a remainder of 5?

10. Express 1728 in prime factors and hence find its cube root.

Fractions

Examples

1 Reduce $\frac{60}{75}$ to its lowest terms.

$$\frac{\overset{4}{\overset{12}{\cancel{60}}}}{\underset{5}{\underset{15}{\cancel{75}}}} = \frac{4}{5}$$

2   Change $3\frac{7}{8}$ to an improper fraction.

$$3\frac{7}{8}\left(=\frac{24}{8}+\frac{7}{8}\right)=\frac{31}{8}$$

3   Change $\frac{45}{7}$ to a mixed number.

$$\frac{45}{7}\left(=\frac{42+3}{7}\right)=6\frac{3}{7}$$

In **addition and subtraction** questions, do the whole number part and the fraction part separately.

4 $4\frac{11}{12}+2\frac{5}{8}=6\frac{22+15}{24}=6\frac{37}{24}=7\frac{13}{24}$

5 $3\frac{3}{8}-1\frac{4}{5}=2\frac{15-32}{40}=2-\frac{17}{40}=1\frac{23}{40}$

In **multiplication and division** questions, mixed numbers must be changed to improper fractions.

6 $5\frac{5}{6}\times2\frac{7}{10}=\dfrac{\overset{7}{\cancel{35}}}{\underset{2}{\cancel{6}}}\times\dfrac{\overset{9}{\cancel{27}}}{\underset{2}{\cancel{10}}}=\dfrac{63}{4}=15\frac{3}{4}$

7 $2\frac{5}{6}\div1\frac{1}{4}=\dfrac{17}{6}\div\dfrac{5}{4}$

(Instead of dividing by $\frac{5}{4}$, multiply by $\frac{4}{5}$.)

$$=\frac{17}{\underset{3}{\cancel{6}}}\times\frac{\overset{2}{\cancel{4}}}{5}=\frac{34}{15}=2\frac{4}{15}$$

Using a calculator

You may have a calculator which will calculate with fractions, and if so, you can learn how to use it. You must find out how to enter fractions or mixed numbers, and how to read the displayed answers. Do not rely on your calculator entirely. You still need to know the methods for working out fractions.

Ratio and Proportion

A ratio is a way of comparing the sizes of two quantities.
e.g. A quantity divided in the ratio 2 : 3 (read as 2 to 3)
means that the 1st share is $\frac{2}{3}$ of the 2nd share,

and the 2nd share is $\frac{3}{2}$ times the 1st share.

Ratios have no units, they are just numbers.

Here is a reminder of methods for using ratios.

Examples

8   Express 25 cm : $1\frac{1}{2}$ m as a ratio in its simplest form.

$$\frac{25\,\text{cm}}{1\frac{1}{2}\,\text{m}} = \frac{25\,\text{cm}}{150\,\text{cm}} = \frac{25}{150} = \frac{1}{6}. \text{ Ratio is } 1 : 6$$

9   Divide £24 in the ratio 3 : 5

3 : 5 gives 8 parts. 1 part is $\dfrac{£24}{8} = £3$.

Shares are 3 × £3 and 5 × £3, i.e. £9 and £15.

10   Increase 12 kg in the ratio 5 : 3

New weight is $\dfrac{5}{3}$ of 12 kg $= \dfrac{5}{3} \times 12\,\text{kg} = 20\,\text{kg}$.

11   Decrease £120 in the ratio 9 : 10

New amount is $\dfrac{9}{10}$ of £120 $= £\dfrac{9}{10} \times 120 = £108$.

Unitary method and proportion

Quantities which increase in the same ratio are in **direct proportion**.

Example

12   If 21 notebooks cost £7.56, what do 28 similar notebooks cost?

1st method, unitary method

21 notebooks cost £7.56
 1 notebook costs £0.36   (dividing by 21)
28 notebooks cost £10.08   (multiplying by 28)

2nd method, proportion

The prices are in direct proportion to the quantities.
Ratio of quantities, new : old $= 28 : 21 = 4 : 3$
Ratio of prices $= 4 : 3$

New price $= \dfrac{4}{3}$ of £7.56 $= £\dfrac{4}{3} \times 7.56 = £10.08.$

Quantities which vary so that one increases in the same ratio as the other decreases are in **inverse proportion**.

Example

13   If there is enough food in an emergency pack to last 12 men for 10 days, how long would the food last if there were 15 men?

1st method, unitary method

The food lasts 12 men for 10 days.

The food lasts 1 man for 120 days.   (multiplying by 12 because it would last twelve times as long)

The food lasts 15 men for 8 days.   (dividing by 15)

2nd method, proportion

As the number of men increases, the time the food will last decreases.
Ratio of number of men, new : old $= 15 : 12 = 5 : 4$
Ratio of times, new : old $= 4 : 5$

New time the food lasts for $= \dfrac{4}{5}$ of 10 days $= 8$ days.

Compound measures

The word **rate** is used in many real-life situations.

Examples

A woman is paid for doing a job at the rate of £6.75 per hour.
Grass seed is sown to make a lawn at the rate of 2 oz per square yard.
Income tax is paid at the standard rate of 25 p in the £ (or whatever the current rate is).
A car uses petrol at the rate of 40 miles to the gallon.
Wallpaper paste powder is added to water at the rate of 1 packet to 6 pints of water.

Speed

The rate at which distance is travelled is called **speed** and it is found from the formula

$$\text{Speed} = \frac{\text{distance}}{\text{time}}$$

It is measured in units such as miles per hour, kilometres per hour, metres per second. The abbreviation for metres per second is m/s or ms^{-1}.

The formula can be rearranged to give:

$$\text{Time} = \frac{\text{distance}}{\text{speed}}$$

$$\text{Distance} = \text{speed} \times \text{time}$$

The units have to correspond, e.g. metres, seconds, metres per second or km, hours, km per hour.

If the speed is variable, these formulae will give or use the **average speed**.

Velocity is a word used instead of speed when the direction of motion is included, so that if the direction from point A to point B is being regarded as positive, a speed in the opposite direction will have a negative velocity.

Examples

14   If a train travels 64 km in 40 minutes, what is its average speed?

$$\text{Speed} = \frac{\text{distance}}{\text{time}} = \frac{64}{\frac{2}{3}} \text{ km/h} = 64 \times \frac{3}{2} \text{ km/h} = 96 \text{ km/h}.$$

Note that to get the speed in km/h, the time 40 minutes had to be written as $\frac{40}{60}$ or $\frac{2}{3}$ hours.

15   A car travels 45 km at an average speed of 30 km/h and then travels 175 km at 70 km/h. What is the average speed for the whole journey?

(Do **not** just average the two speeds 30 and 70, getting 50, since this is wrong.)

$$\text{Average speed} = \frac{\text{total distance}}{\text{total time}}$$

The total distance is 220 km.
The time for the first part of the journey is $1\frac{1}{2}$ hours.
The time for the second part of the journey is $2\frac{1}{2}$ hours.
The total time is 4 hours.

$$\text{Average speed} = \frac{220}{4} \text{ km/h} = 55 \text{ km/h}.$$

Density

The density of a material = the mass per unit volume.
It is measured in units such as g/cm^3.

(In Physics it is important to use the exact word 'mass', but in Mathematics we often use the more everyday word 'weight' to mean mass.)

$$\text{Density} = \frac{\text{mass}}{\text{volume}}$$

The formula rearranged gives:

$$\text{Volume} = \frac{\text{mass}}{\text{density}}$$

$$\text{Mass} = \text{density} \times \text{volume}$$

Example

16   If copper has density of 8.9 g/cm^3, what will be the mass of a copper block with volume 45 cm^3?

$$\text{Mass} = 8.9 \times 45 \text{ g}$$
$$= 400.5 \text{ g}$$
$$= 401 \text{ g, to 3 sig. fig.}$$

Exercise 1.3

1.   Reduce these fractions to their lowest terms.

   1 $\dfrac{24}{88}$ **2** $\dfrac{18}{45}$ **3** $\dfrac{33}{132}$ **4** $\dfrac{75}{200}$ **5** $\dfrac{24}{54}$

   6 $\dfrac{60}{84}$ **7** $\dfrac{35}{56}$ **8** $\dfrac{21}{36}$ **9** $\dfrac{11}{110}$ **10** $\dfrac{26}{39}$

2.   Change these mixed numbers to improper fractions.

   1 $1\frac{3}{4}$ **2** $2\frac{1}{3}$ **3** $4\frac{5}{6}$ **4** $9\frac{1}{11}$ **5** $3\frac{1}{7}$

   6 $6\frac{5}{12}$ **7** $3\frac{7}{20}$ **8** $7\frac{7}{10}$ **9** $5\frac{7}{8}$ **10** $8\frac{2}{5}$

3. Change these improper fractions to mixed numbers.

   1 $\dfrac{23}{5}$ **2** $\dfrac{37}{10}$ **3** $\dfrac{11}{4}$ **4** $\dfrac{13}{5}$ **5** $\dfrac{100}{3}$

   6 $\dfrac{17}{6}$ **7** $\dfrac{25}{8}$ **8** $\dfrac{55}{9}$ **9** $\dfrac{40}{11}$ **10** $\dfrac{105}{12}$

Find the values of the following.

4. **1** $\frac{1}{2}+\frac{1}{3}+\frac{1}{4}$ **5** $2\frac{5}{12}+2\frac{1}{3}$ **8** $\frac{1}{2}+2\frac{5}{6}$

   2 $\frac{5}{8}+\frac{1}{6}$ **6** $4\frac{3}{8}+3\frac{1}{3}$ **9** $2\frac{3}{4}+1\frac{4}{5}$

   3 $2\frac{7}{10}+1\frac{3}{5}$ **7** $5\frac{5}{9}+\frac{1}{6}$ **10** $4\frac{1}{8}+1\frac{7}{12}$

   4 $3\frac{3}{8}+1\frac{4}{5}$

5. **1** $\frac{5}{8}-\frac{1}{6}$ **5** $1\frac{7}{20}-\frac{4}{5}$ **8** $\frac{1}{2}+\frac{1}{3}-\frac{1}{6}$

   2 $2\frac{11}{12}-\frac{7}{8}$ **6** $5\frac{5}{14}-3\frac{6}{7}$ **9** $2\frac{1}{2}+\frac{7}{10}-\frac{2}{5}$

   3 $2\frac{5}{6}-1\frac{1}{4}$ **7** $2\frac{2}{3}-2\frac{5}{9}$ **10** $1\frac{3}{4}-\frac{4}{5}+2\frac{7}{8}$

   4 $7\frac{5}{12}-5\frac{8}{9}$

6. **1** $\frac{3}{8}\times\frac{2}{3}$ **5** $2\frac{1}{6}\times\frac{9}{13}$ **8** $3\frac{3}{8}\times1\frac{1}{9}$

   2 $\frac{5}{6}\times\frac{7}{8}$ **6** $\frac{5}{6}\times\frac{9}{10}$ **9** $4\frac{1}{2}\times1\frac{5}{6}$

   3 $\frac{2}{3}\times1\frac{1}{8}$ **7** $1\frac{1}{7}\times10$ **10** $5\frac{5}{9}\times6\frac{3}{4}\times1\frac{1}{15}$

   4 $1\frac{3}{4}\times2\frac{2}{5}$

7. **1** $\frac{5}{6}\div\frac{7}{8}$ **5** $\frac{7}{12}\div\frac{14}{15}$ **8** $4\frac{4}{9}\div5\frac{5}{6}$

   2 $\frac{3}{10}\div1\frac{1}{6}$ **6** $2\frac{4}{5}\div7$ **9** $2\frac{1}{12}\div5\frac{5}{8}$

   3 $4\frac{1}{8}\div2\frac{3}{4}$ **7** $3\frac{3}{4}\div2\frac{2}{5}$ **10** $11\frac{1}{4}\div2\frac{3}{16}$

   4 $7\div1\frac{3}{4}$

8. **1** $6\frac{3}{4}-1\frac{2}{3}$ **5** $1\frac{5}{8}\times1\frac{3}{5}$ **8** $3\frac{1}{3}\times\frac{3}{10}$

   2 $5\frac{1}{12}\div7\frac{5}{8}$ **6** $4\frac{2}{3}-4\frac{1}{6}$ **9** $3\frac{1}{6}+1\frac{3}{4}$

   3 $2\frac{2}{3}\times2\frac{3}{4}$ **7** $2\frac{3}{5}\div1\frac{3}{10}$ **10** $3\frac{1}{7}\times\frac{4}{11}$

   4 $1\frac{3}{4}+2\frac{5}{12}+3\frac{5}{6}$

9. **1** $\left(\frac{15}{28}\times\frac{7}{30}\right)+\frac{7}{8}$ **5** $\left(3\frac{1}{7}\times8\frac{3}{4}\right)-2\frac{1}{3}$ **8** $12\frac{1}{5}-\left(2\frac{2}{9}\times4\frac{1}{2}\right)$

   2 $\left(2\frac{2}{3}-1\frac{3}{4}\right)\times4$ **6** $\left(\frac{2}{3}-\frac{1}{6}\right)^2$ **9** $2\frac{1}{4}-\left(1\frac{1}{2}\times\frac{2}{5}\right)$

   3 $\left(2\frac{1}{2}\div\frac{1}{4}\right)-6\frac{1}{2}$ **7** $1\frac{5}{12}\div\left(3\frac{1}{5}+1\frac{1}{3}\right)$ **10** $2\frac{1}{10}-1\frac{3}{5}+6\frac{1}{2}$

   4 $8\frac{3}{4}\times1\frac{3}{5}\div4\frac{2}{3}$

10. Express as ratios in their simplest forms

    1 13.2 cm : 16.5 cm
    2 75p : £1.80
    3 3 hours 20 minutes : 5 hours 20 minutes

11. **1** Divide £2.25 in the ratio 2 : 3
    2 Divide £1.54 in the ratio 4 : 7
    3 Divide 60p in the ratio 7 : 3

12. **1** Increase £270 in the ratio 5 : 3
    2 Increase £37.50 in the ratio 9 : 5
    3 Decrease £280 in the ratio 4 : 7

13. The edges of two cubes are 4 cm and 6 cm. Find the ratio of their volumes.

14. The angles of a quadrilateral are in the ratio 2 : 3 : 5 : 8. Find their sizes.

15. A line AB of length 9 cm is divided at P so that $AP : PB = 3 : 7$. Find the length of AP.

16. 28 bars of chocolate cost £6.16. What would be the cost of 35 similar bars?

17. If 20 boxes weigh 36 lb, what is the weight of 45 similar boxes?

18. If a car travels for 100 miles on fuel costing £4.80, what would the fuel cost be, at the same rate, for a journey of 250 miles?

19. If a store of emergency food would last 20 men for 36 days, how long would the same food last if there were 45 men?

20. 10 men can build a wall in 9 days. How long would 6 men take, working at the same rate?

21. A carpet to cover a floor of area 20 square yards costs £250. How much would it cost for a similar carpet to cover a floor of area 24 square yards?

22. In an hour 10 people can pick 40 kg of fruit. How much can be picked in an hour if there are 25 people?

23. A farmer has enough food for his 30 cows for 12 days. If he buys 6 more cows, how long will the food last then?

24. A pond can be emptied in 12 hours using 4 pumps. If the owner wants it emptied in 8 hours, how many extra pumps, which work at the same rate, will be needed?

25.   If grass seed is to be sown at the rate of 2 oz per square yard, how many lbs will be
      needed to make a rectangular lawn, 10 yards long by 8 yards wide? (16 oz = 1 lb)

26.   A main road through a village has a speed limit of 40 miles per hour. A motorist covers
      the $1\frac{1}{2}$ mile section in 2 minutes. Did he break the speed limit?

27.   A car passes a point A at 3.58 pm and reaches a point B $3\frac{1}{2}$ km distant at 4.03 pm. What
      is the average speed of the car?

28.   A train travels for 2 hours at 100 km/h and then for 1 hour at 85 km/h. Find its average
      speed for the whole journey.

29.   If petrol has a density of 0.8 g/cm^3 and the petrol in a can weighs 3.6 kg, how much
      petrol, in litres, does the can contain?

30.   If a piece of metal has a volume of 30 cm^3 and a mass of 267 g, what is its density?

31.   A motorist has to make a journey of 175 miles. She estimates that for 143 miles on the
      motorway she can maintain an average speed of 65 mph, but the last 32 miles is in a
      built-up area where her average speed will be 20 mph. How long will the total journey take?

32.   1   The costs of manufacture of an article are divided among labour, materials and
          overheads in the ratio 8 : 4 : 3. If the materials for 1000 articles cost £650, what is the
          total cost of these articles?

      2   Three men invest £2000, £3500 and £4500 respectively into a business and agree to
          share the profits in the ratio of their investments. The profits in the first year were
          £8000. How much did they each receive?

      3   A shade of paint is made up of 3 parts blue and 4 parts purple. How many litres of
          blue are needed to make up 10.5 litres of this paint?

Percentages

'Per cent' means 'per hundred', so 17% means $\dfrac{17}{100}$ or 0.17.

Here is a reminder of methods for percentage calculations.

Examples

1   Express $87\frac{1}{2}\%$ as a fraction.

$$87\tfrac{1}{2}\% = \frac{87\frac{1}{2}}{100} = \frac{175}{200} = \tfrac{7}{8}$$

2   Express $63\frac{1}{4}\%$ as a decimal.

$$63\tfrac{1}{4}\% = \frac{63\frac{1}{4}}{100} = \frac{63.25}{100} = 0.6325$$

To change a fraction or decimal to a percentage, multiply by 100 and write the % sign.

3 $\dfrac{5}{6} = \dfrac{5}{6} \times 100\% = \dfrac{250}{3}\% = 83\tfrac{1}{3}\%$

$0.575 = 0.575 \times 100\% = 57.5\%$

4   Find 24% of 60 cm, and find $16\frac{2}{3}\%$ of 9 litres.

24% of 60 cm $= 0.24 \times 60$ cm $= 14.4$ cm

$16\tfrac{2}{3}\%$ of $9\,\ell = \dfrac{16\frac{2}{3}}{100} \times 9\,\ell = \dfrac{50}{300} \times 9\,\ell = 1.5\,\ell$

5   What percentage is 34 g of 2 kg?

(First find what fraction 34 g is of 2 kg, then change this fraction to a percentage.)

$\dfrac{34\text{ g}}{2\text{ kg}} = \dfrac{34\text{ g}}{2000\text{ g}} = \dfrac{34}{2000} \times 100\% = 1.7\%$

6   Increase £50 by 15%.

The new amount will be $(100 + 15)\%$, i.e. 115% of £50.

115% of £50 $= £1.15 \times 50 = £57.50$

(Alternatively, you could find 15% of £50, i.e. £7.50, and then add this to the original £50, making £57.50.)

7   Decrease £900 by 12%.

The new amount will be $(100 - 12)\%$, i.e. 88% of £900.

88% of £900 $= £0.88 \times 900 = £792$

(Alternatively, you could find 12% of £900, i.e. £108, and then subtract this from the original £900, leaving £792.)

Profit and Loss

Examples

8   A dealer buys an article for £75 and sells it for £90. What is his percentage profit?

Percentage profit is always based on the cost price, unless otherwise stated.
Here the profit is £15 on a cost price of £75.

% profit $= \dfrac{15}{75} \times 100\% = 20\%$

9   A dealer buys an article, adds 30% to the cost price for his profit, and marks the selling price at £6.50. What did the article cost him?

The selling price is $(100 + 30)\%$, i.e. 130% of the cost price.

The cost price is $£\dfrac{100}{130} \times 6.50 = £\dfrac{6.50}{1.30} = £5.00$

The article cost £5.

VAT. Value Added Tax

This tax is added to the cost of many things you buy. In most shops the price marked includes the tax so you do not have to calculate it.

Occasionally, however, the prices are given without VAT and it has to be added to the bill. The present rate of this tax is $17\frac{1}{2}\%$ so the final price is $117\frac{1}{2}\%$ of the original price. To find the final price, multiply the original price by 1.175.

Examples

10   A builder says he will charge £80 for doing a small job. To this, VAT at $17\frac{1}{2}\%$ is added. What is the total cost?

The total cost is $£80 \times 1.175 = £94$.

If a price includes VAT, to find the original price divide by 1.175.

11   A video recorder costs £350. How much of this cost is tax?

The original price was $£\dfrac{350}{1.175} = £297.87$

The VAT is $£350 - £297.87 = £52.13$

The rate of tax might be changed. If it has, work out these examples using the up-to-date rate.

Income Tax

This is tax taken as a proportion of any money you earn. Most employees pay tax as PAYE which means 'Pay as you earn', so the tax is deducted from the pay by the employer, and the amount depends on how much is earned.

You are allowed a Personal Allowance, and maybe other Allowances. These give an amount you can earn on which no tax is paid, then any income above that is taxed at a Basic Rate. There is also a Higher Rate tax so that people with high incomes pay more.

Example

12   Mr Taylor earns £15 000 a year. How much income tax will he pay?

(We will imagine that the Personal Allowance is £3500 and the Basic rate of tax is 25%. The questions in this book use imaginary rates, since every year, on Budget Day, the tax rates can be altered and we cannot foresee what they will be when you are reading this book. Also, Allowances vary according to whether you are single or married.)

Income	£15 000
Personal Allowance	£3 500
Taxable Income	£11 500

Tax payable. 25% of £11 500 = £2875.

Mr Taylor pays £2875 income tax in that year. That leaves him with £12 125.
(The tax will be deducted in equal amounts each week, if he is paid weekly, or each month if he is paid monthly. In addition to having tax deducted from his earnings he will also have National Insurance contributions deducted.)

If you know the up-to-date tax rates, work out this example using them.

Growth and decay

Example

13   The numbers of insects in a colony are given in this table.

Time in days	0	1	2	3
Number of insects	1600	1840	2208	2760

Find the percentage increase in the 1st day, the 2nd day and the 3rd day.

In the 1st day,   increase $= 1840 - 1600 = 240$

$$\% \text{ increase} = \frac{240}{1600} \times 100\% = 15\%$$

In the 2nd day,   increase $= 2208 - 1840 = 368$

$$\% \text{ increase} = \frac{368}{1840} \times 100\% = 20\%$$

In the 3rd day,   increase $= 2760 - 2208 = 552$

$$\% \text{ increase} = \frac{552}{2208} \times 100\% = 25\%$$

Simple Interest

With Simple Interest, the interest is paid out each year, not added to the investment.

Example

14   £600 is invested and pays interest of £48 per year.
      What is the rate of interest?

      The rate of interest p.a. $= \dfrac{48}{600} \times 100\% = 8\%$

      p.a. means per annum, i.e. per year.

You may prefer to use the formula $I = \dfrac{PRT}{100}$ to find Simple Interest.

I is the simple interest.
P is the principal (the initial amount).
P and I are both in the same units, £'s, francs, etc.
T is the time, in years.
R is the percentage rate per annum.

Compound Interest

If the interest earned on money invested is added to the investment, then that money earns interest in future years. This is called Compound Interest. If money is invested at 8% per annum interest, and interest is added to the capital annually, then after 1 year the investment is increased by 8%, becoming 108% of the previous amount. So to find the new amount, multiply by 1.08.

Thus if £600 is invested at 8% per annum for 4 years,
After the 1st year the amount invested becomes £600 × 1.08   = £648
After the 2nd year the amount invested becomes £648 × 1.08   = £699.84
After the 3rd year the amount invested becomes £699.84 × 1.08 = £755.83
(to the nearest penny).
After the 4th year the amount invested becomes £755.83 × 1.08 = £816.30
(to the nearest penny).
Subtracting the original amount of £600 will give the interest earned.
The Compound Interest is £216.30.

If the rate of interest is $R\%$, the multiplying factor is $1 + 0.01R$.

Depreciation

Example

15   A machine was originally worth £4000. It depreciates in value by 10% each year. What will it be worth at the end of 3 years?

This is similar to Compound Interest in reverse. Every year the machine loses 10% of its value, so it is worth 90% of its previous value. To find its new value, multiply by 0.9.

After 1 year the machine is worth £4000 × 0.9 = £3600
After 2 years the machine is worth £3600 × 0.9 = £3240
After 3 years the machine is worth £3240 × 0.9 = £2916

If the rate of depreciation is $R\%$, the multiplying factor is $1 - 0.01R$.

Exercise 1.4

1. Express these percentages as fractions in their simplest forms.

    1 36%   **2** 45%   **3** $17\frac{1}{2}\%$ **4** $3\frac{1}{3}\%$ **5** $66\frac{2}{3}\%$

2. Express as decimals.

    1 47%   **2** 95%   **3** $22\frac{1}{2}\%$ **4** $6\frac{1}{4}\%$ **5** 99.9%

3. Change these fractions or decimals to percentages.

    1 $\frac{3}{4}$ **2** $\frac{5}{8}$ **3** 0.15   **4** $\frac{1}{3}$ **5** 0.875

4. Find

    1 48% of 3 m   **4** $62\frac{1}{2}\%$ of 2.4 cm
    2 30% of 2 kg   **5** 115% of £4
    3 $16\frac{2}{3}\%$ of $\frac{1}{2}$ hour

5. Find what percentage the 1st quantity is of the 2nd.

    1 £3.60, £5.00   **4** 750 g, 2 kg
    2 16 cm, 2 m   **5** 50p, 75p
    3 36 minutes, 1 hour

6. **1** Increase £6 by 4%   **4** Decrease £75 by 20%
   2 Increase £2.50 by 16%   **5** Increase £300 by 12%
   3 Decrease £120 by 10%

7. **1** Find the percentage profit if an article costing £2.50 to make is sold for £3.

   2 Find the percentage loss if an article costing £3 is sold for £2.50.

   3 A restaurant bill for £15 became £16.80 after a service charge was added. What was the percentage rate of the service charge?

8. 1 By selling a car for £980 a dealer made 40% profit on what he had paid for it. How much had he paid for it?

    2 To clear goods during a sale a shopkeeper reduced the price by 10% and sold them for £3.60. What was the original price?

    3 A bottle of shampoo was marked '10% extra' and contained 330 ml of liquid. What quantity should an ordinary bottle hold?

    4 The duty, £36, on a camera is 24% of its value. What is the value of the camera?

    5 After an 8% pay-rise Miss Scott earned £9720 per year. What was she earning before the rise?

9. Find the Simple Interest if

    1 £250 is invested for 3 years at 8% per annum,
    2 £600 is invested for 4 years at 11% p.a.,
    3 £840 is invested for 2 years at 10% p.a.

10. Using your calculator find the Compound Interest for the data of question 9.

11. Mr Parmar buys some DIY materials marked £24. VAT at $17\frac{1}{2}$% is added to this price. What is the total cost, including the tax?

12. Mr Kent employed a firm to do some repairs and the bill, including VAT at $17\frac{1}{2}$%, came to £423. How much of this was the price for the work, and how much was the tax?

13. Assuming that the income tax rates were: Personal Allowance £3600, Basic rate of tax 25%; find how much tax Miriam Kirby paid in the year if her salary was £9000. If this tax was paid in equal monthly instalments, how much tax did she pay per month?

14. A firm owns machinery which is judged to depreciate in value by 5% each year. If it was valued at £20 000 three years ago, what is it worth today, to the nearest £10?

15. £200 was invested for a child and left for 3 years, to gain Compound Interest. Here are the amounts in the account at the end of each year.

End of	Year 1	Year 2	Year 3
Amount	£218	£239.80	£257.79

Find the percentage rates of interest for the 1st year, the 2nd year and the 3rd year.

16. A grocer bought 10 cases of tinned fruit at £7.50 per case, each case containing 24 tins. He sold 200 tins at 42p each but the remainder were damaged and unfit for sale. Find his percentage profit.

Exercise 1.5 Applications

1. From the numbers 18, 19, 20, 23, 25, 27, write down

    1 the prime numbers,
    2 a square number,
    3 the numbers which are multiples of 3,
    4 a cube number,
    5 two numbers whose sum is 44.

2. Express 1080 in prime factors.
    If $1080 = 2^a \times 3^b \times 5^c$, state the values of a, b and c.
    State the smallest number by which 1080 must be multiplied to make a perfect square.

3. Express 360 and 405 in prime factors.
    Given that $360 \times 405 = 145\,800$, express $145\,800$ in prime factors.

4. Expressed in prime factors two numbers are $7^2 \times 11^3 \times 13$ and $7^3 \times 11 \times 17$.
    Find, expressed in prime factors

    1 the highest common factor of these numbers,
    2 the lowest common multiple of these numbers.

5. Find the values of 9^0, 9^2, $9^{\frac{1}{2}}$, 9^{-1}, $9^{-\frac{3}{2}}$.

6. **1** Find the value of 3^6.
    2 Find the least value of n for which 3^n is greater than $10\,000$.

7. Find the values of   **1** $\sqrt{25 \times 144}$ **2** $\sqrt{25 + 144}$ **3** $\sqrt{25} + \sqrt{144}$

8. $1\frac{1}{4}$ pints of milk are poured into an urn containing 10 pints of coffee. What fraction of the mixture is milk?

9. A plank of wood is $10\frac{1}{2}$ feet long. 3 pieces each $1\frac{3}{4}$ feet long are cut off. What length remains?

10. Mrs Carr wins some money in a competition. She gives $\frac{1}{3}$ of it to her husband and $\frac{2}{5}$ of the remainder to her daughter. She keeps the remaining money, £300, for herself. How much did she win?

11. Find   **1** $\sqrt{\frac{9}{25}}$ **2** $\sqrt{1\frac{11}{25}}$

12. $3\frac{1}{4}$ metres of material is needed for a loose cover for an armchair and $\frac{3}{4}$ metre for a small chair. Find the cost of the material for covering a suite of 2 armchairs and 6 small chairs with material costing £5.50 per metre.

13. Mrs Khan earns £3.40 per hour for a basic week of 40 hours. Overtime is paid at time-and-a-half. If she works 42 hours one week, what will she earn? If one week she earns £176.80, how many hours altogether did she work?

14. £900 is raised and is divided among 3 charities, *A*, *B* and *C* in the proportion 4 : 5 : 6. Find the amount each charity receives.
    If these amounts are represented on a pie chart, calculate the angle of each sector.

15. The insurance for the contents of a house is charged at £6.50 per £1000 of value. How much will the insurance cost for contents valued at £18 500?

16. A car journey takes 42 minutes when the average speed is 56 miles/hour. How long would it take if the average speed was 48 miles/hour?

17. The weekly wages paid by a firm to 5 workmen total £825. What will the weekly wages be if they employ two extra men, and pay them all at the same rate?

18. On a holiday journey the car mileage indicator readings and times were as follows:

Time	9.05 am	11.45 am	12.15 pm	2.00 pm
Mileage indicator reading	16335	16463	16463	16526

(I had stopped to visit a place of interest from 11.45 am to 12.15 pm.)
1 What was the average speed for the part of the journey up to 11.45 am?
2 What was the average speed for the part of the journey from 12.15 pm?
3 I estimate that my car used 5 gallons of petrol on the journey. What is the approximate fuel consumption in miles per gallon?

19. A firm buys petrol and diesel oil in the ratio 5 : 7, spending £2700 altogether per week. If the price of petrol is increased by 5% and the diesel oil by 3%, find the percentage increase in the total cost, correct to 1 decimal place.

20. The price of a camera is increased by 30%. Later, in a sale, the price is reduced by 20% of its new value. This final price is £78. What was the original price?

21. Jenny started work and earned £90 per week. Income tax during that year was based on a Personal Allowance of £3000 and income tax on income over that amount taxed at 25%. Jenny worked for only 30 weeks in that tax-year. How much did she earn? How much tax did she pay? In the following tax-year her wages were raised to £95 per week and she worked for the full year of 52 weeks. The income tax Personal Allowance was £3200 and the basic rate of tax remained at 25%. How much tax did she pay over the year, and how much was this per week, to the nearest penny?

22. £1560 was invested and after 1 year £124.80 interest was added. What was the percentage rate of interest?
If the total amount was left in the account for another year, and the same rate of interest applied, what would the money amount to at the end of the 2nd year?

Practice test 1

1. From the numbers 8, 12, 16, 19, 20
    1 Which number is a prime number?
    2 Which number is a square number?
    3 Which number is a multiple of 5?
    4 Which number is a factor of 84?
    5 Which two numbers have a sum which is a square number?
    6 Which two numbers have a sum which is a cube number?

2. Express in prime factors the numbers 378 and 441.
    Find
    1 the square root of 441,
    2 the highest common factor of 378 and 441,
    3 the lowest common multiple of 378 and 441, expressed in prime factors.

3. Mr Turner reckons that $\frac{1}{4}$ of his wages go in tax and insurance. Of the remainder, $\frac{1}{5}$ pays the rent and $\frac{1}{10}$ is put aside to pay the household fuel bills. This leaves him with £84 a week to spend. What is his weekly wage?

4. Two motorists, Mr Bowen and Mrs Crane, set off at 9 am to travel to a town 120 km away. Mr Bowen arrives there at 11.30 am and Mrs Crane arrives there at noon.
    1 What is the ratio of their times taken?
    2 What is the ratio of their average speeds?

5. 1250 cm^3 of a liquid weighs 1 kg.
    What is the density of the liquid, in g/cm^3?

6. Machinery which cost £5600 when new is judged to depreciate in value by 20% in its first year and by 10% each year in future years. What is its estimated value after the first 3 years?

2 *Geometry*

The topics in this chapter include:

- finding the locus of a point,

- using vector notation and methods,

- understanding the conditions for congruent triangles.

Locus

The locus of a point is the path traced by the point as it moves so as to satisfy certain conditions.

Examples

1   A flower-bed is to be made round the edge of a rectangular lawn, and every part of the flower-bed is not more than 1 m from the lawn. What is the locus of the outer edge of the flower-bed ?

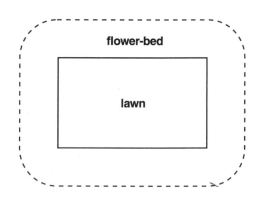

The locus is shown in the diagram. There are 4 straight lines 1 m from the edge of the lawn and 4 quarter-circles radius 1 m with centres at the corners of the lawn.

2   What is the locus of the path of a girl running across a field keeping as far from the hedge as from the fence ? (This path can be said to be 'equidistant from the hedge and the fence'.)

The locus is shown in the diagram. It is the line which bisects the angle between the hedge and the fence.

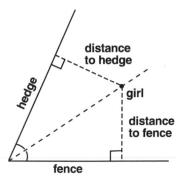

The distance measured from any point on the locus to the hedge (or fence) would be the shortest distance, and that is the length of the perpendicular line from the point to the hedge (or fence).

Special results

1. The locus of a point at a fixed distance r units from a given point A is a circle, centre A, radius r.

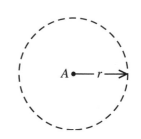

2. The locus of a point at a fixed distance r units from a given line AB is a pair of lines, each parallel to AB, and distance r from AB.

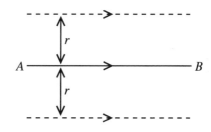

3. The locus of a point equidistant from two given points A and B is the perpendicular bisector of AB.

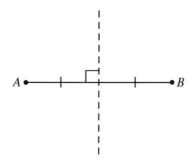

4. The locus of a point equidistant from two given lines AOB, COD is the pair of lines which bisect the angles at O.

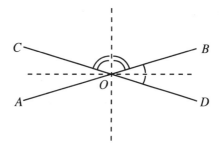

Constructions which may be needed.

To draw accurately a line a fixed distance from a given line

e.g. to draw a line 5 cm from AB.

Draw lines at right angles to AB at A and B
(or at any two points on AB).

Measure off 5 cm along these lines so that
$AD = 5$ cm and $BC = 5$ cm.

Join CD.
Then every point on CD is 5 cm from the
nearest point on AB.

Here is a reminder of two constructions using ruler and compasses. (You can also do these
constructions without compasses by using a ruler and a protractor.)

To find the perpendicular bisector of a line AB

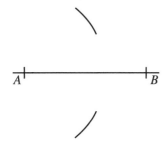

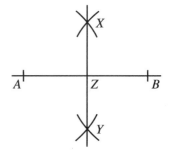

With centre A and a radius more than
half of AB, draw two arcs.

With centre B and the same radius,
draw two arcs to cut the first two arcs
at X and Y.

Join XY, cutting AB at Z.

Then Z is the mid-point of AB, and XZY
is the perpendicular bisector of AB.

To bisect an angle *ACB*

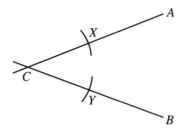

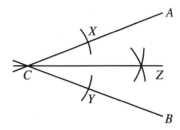

With centre *C*, draws arcs to cut *CA* and *CB* at *X* and *Y*.

With centres *X* and *Y* in turn, and a suitable radius, draw arcs to cut at *Z*.

Join *CZ*, which is the bisector of angle *ACB*.

Example

3 Draw a triangle *ABC* with *AB* = 9 cm, *AC* = 7 cm and ∠*BAC* = 66°.
Find
1 the locus of points inside the triangle which are 4.5 cm from *C*.
2 the locus of points inside the triangle which are equidistant from *AB* and *AC*.
Mark the point *P* inside the triangle which is 4.5 cm from *C* and is as far from *AB* as it is from *AC*.
How far is *P* from *B*?

First, draw the triangle accurately.

For **1**, the locus of the points 4.5 cm from a point *C* is a circle, centre *C*, radius 4.5 cm. In this question you only need the part of the circle which is inside the triangle. Draw this locus and label it (**1**).

For **2**, the locus of points inside the triangle which are equidistant from *AB* and *AC* is the bisector of ∠*A*.
You can construct the bisector using your protractor. Since ∠*A* = 66°, the bisector makes angles of 33° with *AB* and *AC*. Alternatively, you can use the method for bisecting an angle using ruler and compasses. Draw this locus and label it (**2**).

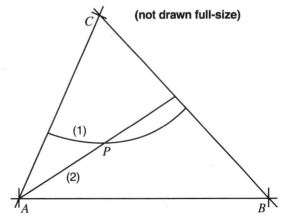

P is the point where the loci intersect.
Measure the distance *PB*.
(It should be 6.4 cm.)

Exercise 2.1

In questions 1 to 4 draw sketches showing the loci and describe each locus.

1. There are 2 rocks 100 m apart. A boat passes between the rocks keeping an equal distance from each. Show the locus of the boat.

2. Show the locus of the top of a child's head as the child sits on a slide and slides down.

3. Show the locus of a hand of a child who is swinging on a swing and holding onto the ropes.

4. A disc of radius 5 cm is fixed to a board. A disc of radius 3 cm is placed touching the first disc, and is moved to circle round it, always keeping in contact with it. Show the locus of the centre of the moving disc.

5. Draw a triangle ABC with $AB = 8$ cm, $BC = 9$ cm and $CA = 7$ cm. Draw the locus of points inside the triangle which are (1) 5 cm from B, (2) 6 cm from C.
    Mark a point P inside the triangle which is 5 cm from B and 6 cm from C.
    Measure PA.

6. Draw a triangle ABC with $AB = 7$ cm, $BC = 9.5$ cm and $\angle B = 90°$. Draw the locus of points inside the triangle which are (1) 2 cm from AB, (2) 3 cm from BC.
    Find a point P inside the triangle which is 2 cm from AB and 3 cm from BC.
    Measure PB.

7. P is a point which moves inside the rhombus $ABCD$ so that its distance from AB is less than its distance from AD and its distance from A is greater than its distance from C. Sketch the rhombus and shade the region in which P must lie.

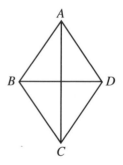

8. The diagram shows a rectangular field. Treasure is hidden in the field (1) 60 m from A, (2) equidistant from B and D. Draw a scale drawing of the field and draw loci for conditions (1) and (2). Mark with T the position of the treasure. How far is the treasure from corner B?

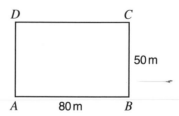

9.   The diagram shows an open space bounded by 2 walls
      of a building. It is planned to erect a safety barrier
      which will be 20 m from the walls. Copy the diagram
      and using a scale of 1 cm to represent 5 m show the locus
      of the barrier.
      At the corner where the 2 walls meet, a spotlight is fixed
      which lights up the area for a distance of 35 m. Show the
      locus of the boundary of the region lit by the spotlight.
      Shade the region which is the far side of the barrier from
      the walls but is lit by the spotlight.

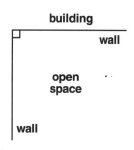

10.   As the minute hand of a clock rotates, an insect starts to move at a constant speed
      along the hand starting at the centre of the clock when the hand is pointing to 12 and
      moving towards the tip of the hand, reaching it when the hand again points to 12.
      Draw a circle of radius 6 cm to represent the clock face and draw 12 equally-spaced
      radii to represent the hand as it points to each number in turn. Mark the position the
      insect has reached on each one. Join these points with a curve to represent the path of
      the insect.

Vectors

A vector quantity has a size and a direction.

Examples:
Velocity. A plane overhead is travelling towards London at a speed of 600 mph.
Displacement. A boy is 400 m from home, and due South of it.
Force. Kick the ball as hard as you can in the direction of the goal.

The line *AB* can represent the vector of a displacement from *A* to *B*.

If *A* is (1, 2) and *B* is (5, 3) then the displacement is
4 units in the *x*-direction and 1 unit in the *y*-direction.

This vector can be represented by the matrix $\begin{pmatrix} 4 \\ 1 \end{pmatrix}$.

Any other line parallel to *AB* with the same length

also represents the vector $\begin{pmatrix} 4 \\ 1 \end{pmatrix}$.

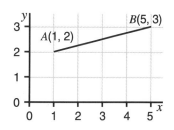

Notation

In printed books vectors are denoted by small letters in heavy type, e.g. **a**.
In writing, the letters are underlined instead, e.g. a̲.

If the vector is represented by a line AB this is written as $\overline{AB}$, $\overrightarrow{AB}$ or **AB**.

Numbers, which have size but no direction, are called scalars.
0 is the zero vector. It has no direction.

−**a** is a vector with the same length as **a** but in the opposite direction.

The lines on diagrams can be marked with arrows to show the directions of the vectors. In this diagram,

a is $\begin{pmatrix} 3 \\ 2 \end{pmatrix}$ and −**a** is $\begin{pmatrix} -3 \\ -2 \end{pmatrix}$.

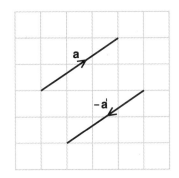

Addition of vectors

If $\mathbf{a} = \begin{pmatrix} 4 \\ 1 \end{pmatrix}$ and $\mathbf{b} = \begin{pmatrix} 3 \\ 5 \end{pmatrix}$ then $\mathbf{a} + \mathbf{b} = \begin{pmatrix} 4 \\ 1 \end{pmatrix} + \begin{pmatrix} 3 \\ 5 \end{pmatrix} = \begin{pmatrix} 4+3 \\ 1+5 \end{pmatrix} = \begin{pmatrix} 7 \\ 6 \end{pmatrix}$.

To find a + b from a diagram

1 Using a triangle

2 Using a parallelogram
   and its diagonal

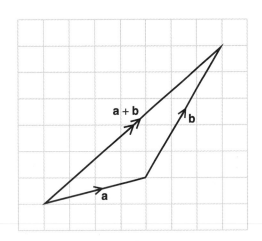

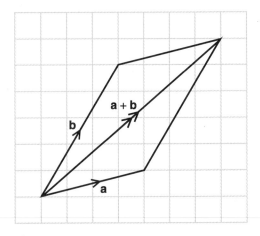

Subtraction of vectors

$$\mathbf{a} - \mathbf{b} = \begin{pmatrix} 4 \\ 1 \end{pmatrix} - \begin{pmatrix} 3 \\ 5 \end{pmatrix} = \begin{pmatrix} 4-3 \\ 1-5 \end{pmatrix} = \begin{pmatrix} 1 \\ -4 \end{pmatrix}$$

To find $\mathbf{a} - \mathbf{b}$ from a diagram

1 Using a triangle to add
   $\mathbf{a}$ and $-\mathbf{b}$

2 Using a parallelogram with
   $\mathbf{a}$ and $-\mathbf{b}$ and its diagonal

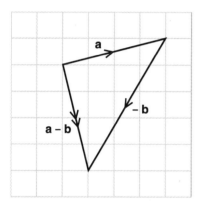

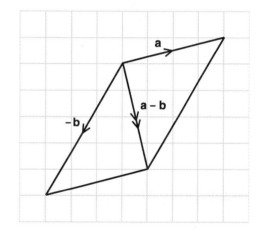

3 Using a triangle with $\mathbf{a}$ and $\mathbf{b}$.
   If $\overrightarrow{OA} = \mathbf{a}$ and $\overrightarrow{OB} = \mathbf{b}$ then
   $\overrightarrow{BA} = \mathbf{a} - \mathbf{b}$

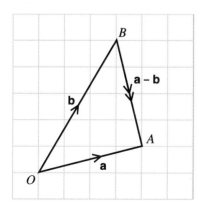

Multiplication by a number

$$2\mathbf{b} = 2 \times \begin{pmatrix} 3 \\ 5 \end{pmatrix} = \begin{pmatrix} 2 \times 3 \\ 2 \times 5 \end{pmatrix} = \begin{pmatrix} 6 \\ 10 \end{pmatrix}$$

The vector $k\mathbf{a}$ where k is a positive number has the same direction as $\mathbf{a}$ but it is k times as long as $\mathbf{a}$.

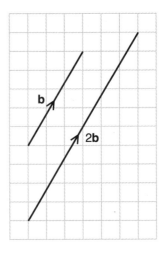

The vector $k\mathbf{a}$ where k is a negative number is in the opposite direction to $\mathbf{a}$ and it is $(-k)$ times as long as $\mathbf{a}$.

$$-3\mathbf{a} = -3 \times \begin{pmatrix} 4 \\ 1 \end{pmatrix} = \begin{pmatrix} -12 \\ -3 \end{pmatrix}$$

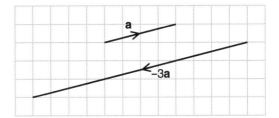

Translation

We can represent a translation by a vector.

Example

A (1, 1) is translated into A' (8, 2),
B (2, 5) is translated into B' (9, 6),
C (5, 3) is translated into C' (12, 4).

The translation is 7 units in the x-direction and 1 unit in the y-direction, and it can be represented by the vector $\begin{pmatrix} 7 \\ 1 \end{pmatrix}$.

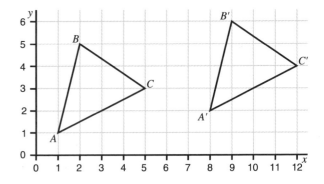

Every point on the line AB is translated into a point on the line $A'B'$.
Every point on BC is translated into a point on $B'C'$.
Every point on AC is translated into a point on $A'C'$.
Every point on $\triangle ABC$ is translated into a point on $\triangle A'B'C'$.

Exercise 2.2

In the diagrams, the lines are drawn on a unit grid.

1. **1** Write down the vectors **a, b, c, d, e, f** and **g** as column vectors.
    2 Which two vectors are equal ?
    3 Which vector is equal to **a** in size but not in direction?
    4 Which vector is equal to 2**b** ?

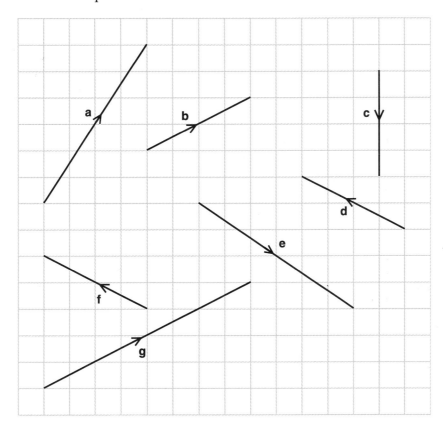

2. Write $\overrightarrow{AB}$ and $\overrightarrow{BC}$ in column form. D is a

    point such that $\overrightarrow{CD} = \begin{pmatrix} -2 \\ 1 \end{pmatrix}$, and E is a point such

    that $\overrightarrow{AE} = \begin{pmatrix} 0 \\ -1 \end{pmatrix}$.

    Show A, B, C, D, E on a diagram
    and find the length of $\overrightarrow{DE}$.

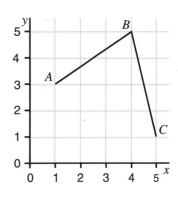

3.   Copy the diagrams on squared paper and for each one show a vector representing $\overrightarrow{AB} + \overrightarrow{BC}$.
     Write the vectors $\overrightarrow{AB}$ and $\overrightarrow{BC}$ in column form and find $\overrightarrow{AB} + \overrightarrow{BC}$. Thus check your answers in the diagrams.

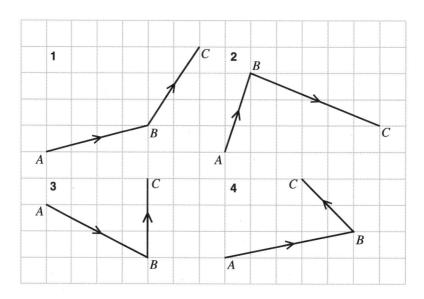

4.   Copy the diagrams and for each one show a vector representing $\overrightarrow{AB} + \overrightarrow{AD}$.
     Write the vectors $\overrightarrow{AB}$ and $\overrightarrow{AD}$ in column form and find $\overrightarrow{AB} + \overrightarrow{AD}$. Thus check your answers in the diagrams.

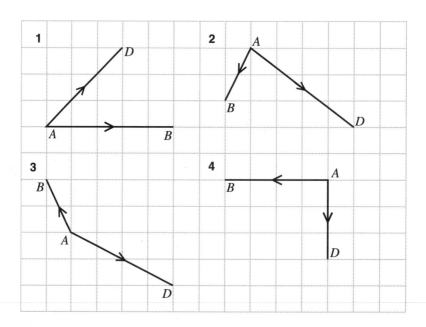

5. Copy the vectors of question 3 again. For each diagram show a vector representing $\overrightarrow{AB} - \overrightarrow{BC}$. Use the vectors in column form to find $\overrightarrow{AB} - \overrightarrow{BC}$, and thus check your answers in the diagrams.

6. Copy the vectors of question 4 again. For each diagram show a vector representing $\overrightarrow{AB} - \overrightarrow{AD}$. Use the vectors in column form to find $\overrightarrow{AB} - \overrightarrow{AD}$, and thus check your answers in the diagrams.

7. Draw $\overrightarrow{PQ} = \begin{pmatrix} 4 \\ 1 \end{pmatrix}$, and draw vectors representing $2\overrightarrow{PQ}$, $3\overrightarrow{PQ}$ and $-\overrightarrow{PQ}$.

8. If $\mathbf{a} = \begin{pmatrix} 3 \\ 4 \end{pmatrix}$ and $\mathbf{b} = \begin{pmatrix} 2 \\ -1 \end{pmatrix}$, find by calculation the vectors representing $\mathbf{a} + \mathbf{b}$, $\mathbf{a} - \mathbf{b}$, $3\mathbf{a}$, $\mathbf{a} + 4\mathbf{b}$, $2\mathbf{a} - 3\mathbf{b}$.

9. On squared paper plot the points A (3, 2), B (5, 6), C (0, 4) and D (−2, 0).
    Find $\overrightarrow{AD}$ and $\overrightarrow{BC}$.
    What kind of quadrilateral is $ABCD$?

10. Use squared paper for this question.
    A is the point with coordinates (3, 1). If $\overrightarrow{AB} = \begin{pmatrix} -2 \\ 4 \end{pmatrix}$ and $\overrightarrow{AC} = \begin{pmatrix} 2 \\ 3 \end{pmatrix}$, find the coordinates of B and C.
    D is a point such that $\overrightarrow{CD} = \frac{1}{2}\overrightarrow{AB}$ and E is a point such that $\overrightarrow{DE} = \overrightarrow{BD}$. Find $\overrightarrow{CE}$. What can be deduced about the points A, C and E?

Vector Geometry

Addition

$\overrightarrow{AC} = \overrightarrow{AB} + \overrightarrow{BC}$

$\overrightarrow{AC} = \mathbf{p} + \mathbf{q}$

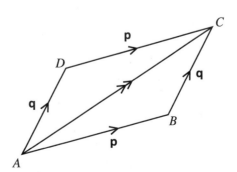

Equal vectors

If $\mathbf{a} = \mathbf{b}$ then the vectors are equal in length and parallel.
If $\mathbf{a} = k\mathbf{b}$ where k is a positive number then $\mathbf{a}$ and $\mathbf{b}$ are parallel and
length of $\mathbf{a} = k \times$ length of $\mathbf{b}$.
If $\mathbf{a} = k\mathbf{b}$ where k is a negative number then $\mathbf{a}$ and $\mathbf{b}$ are parallel but in opposite directions and
length of $\mathbf{a} = (-k) \times$ length of $\mathbf{b}$.

Position vectors

If O is the origin and $\overrightarrow{OA} = \mathbf{a}$, then $\mathbf{a}$ is called
the position vector of A.

If O is the origin and $\overrightarrow{OA} = \mathbf{a}$ and $\overrightarrow{OB} = \mathbf{b}$,
then $\overrightarrow{AB} = \overrightarrow{AO} + \overrightarrow{OB}$
$\qquad = -\mathbf{a} + \mathbf{b}$
$\qquad = \mathbf{b} - \mathbf{a}$

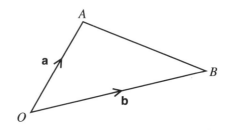

If M is the mid-point of AB, then
$\overrightarrow{AM} = \frac{1}{2}(\mathbf{b} - \mathbf{a})$,
so $\overrightarrow{OM} = \overrightarrow{OA} + \overrightarrow{AM}$
$\qquad = \mathbf{a} + \frac{1}{2}(\mathbf{b} - \mathbf{a}) = \frac{1}{2}(\mathbf{a} + \mathbf{b})$
i.e. the position vector of M is $\frac{1}{2}(\mathbf{a} + \mathbf{b})$.

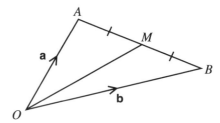

Length of a vector

The length of $\mathbf{a}$ can be called the magnitude or modulus
of $\mathbf{a}$ and this can be written using the notation $|\mathbf{a}|$.
If $\mathbf{a}$ is a vector $\begin{pmatrix} x \\ y \end{pmatrix}$ then the length of $\mathbf{a}$ is $\sqrt{x^2 + y^2}$.

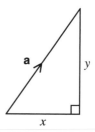

Example

A, B and C are points such that $\overrightarrow{OA} = \mathbf{a}$, $\overrightarrow{OB} = \mathbf{b}$ and $\overrightarrow{OC} = 2\mathbf{a} + \mathbf{b}$. The mid-point of AB is M and the mid-point of BC is N.

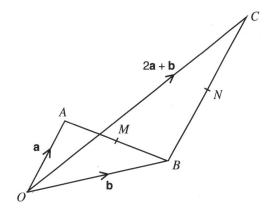

1 Find $\overrightarrow{OM}$ and $\overrightarrow{ON}$ in terms of $\mathbf{a}$ and $\mathbf{b}$.

2 Show that O, M and N lie on a straight line.

3 Show that $OANB$ is a parallelogram.

1 $\overrightarrow{AB} = \overrightarrow{AO} + \overrightarrow{OB} = \mathbf{b} - \mathbf{a}$

$\overrightarrow{AM} = \tfrac{1}{2}(\mathbf{b} - \mathbf{a})$

$\overrightarrow{OM} = \overrightarrow{OA} + \overrightarrow{AM} = \mathbf{a} + \tfrac{1}{2}(\mathbf{b} - \mathbf{a})$

$\qquad = \tfrac{1}{2}(\mathbf{a} + \mathbf{b})$

$\overrightarrow{CB} = \overrightarrow{CO} + \overrightarrow{OB}$

$\qquad = -(2\mathbf{a} + \mathbf{b}) + \mathbf{b} = -2\mathbf{a}$

$\overrightarrow{CN} = -\mathbf{a}$

$\overrightarrow{ON} = \overrightarrow{OC} + \overrightarrow{CN}$

$\qquad = 2\mathbf{a} + \mathbf{b} - \mathbf{a} = \mathbf{a} + \mathbf{b}$

2 So $\overrightarrow{OM} = \tfrac{1}{2}\overrightarrow{ON}$

Since these vectors have the same direction and both pass through O, the points O, M and N lie on the same line. (Also, $OM = \tfrac{1}{2}ON$ in length so M is the mid-point of ON.)

3 $\overrightarrow{AN} = \overrightarrow{AO} + \overrightarrow{ON}$

$\qquad = -\mathbf{a} + \mathbf{a} + \mathbf{b} = \mathbf{b}$

So AN is equal and parallel to OB.
$OANB$ is a parallelogram.

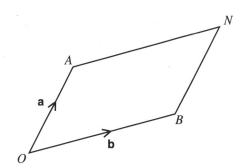

Exercise 2.3

1. If $\overrightarrow{AB} = \mathbf{a}$, $\overrightarrow{BC} = \mathbf{b}$ and $\overrightarrow{CD} = \mathbf{c}$, express in terms of $\mathbf{a}$, $\mathbf{b}$, $\mathbf{c}$,
    1 $\overrightarrow{AC}$,   **2** $\overrightarrow{AD}$.

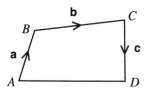

2. $\mathbf{a}$ and $\mathbf{b}$ are 2 vectors, not in the same direction. If $\overrightarrow{OC} = \mathbf{a} - \mathbf{b}$, $\overrightarrow{OD} = \mathbf{a} + 2\mathbf{b}$ and M is the mid-point of CD, find $\overrightarrow{OM}$.

3. Copy this sketch and show lines OP, where $\overrightarrow{OP} = \mathbf{a} + \frac{1}{2}\mathbf{b}$ and OQ, where $\overrightarrow{OQ} = \frac{1}{2}\mathbf{a} - \mathbf{b}$.

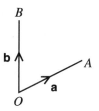

4. $\mathbf{a}$ and $\mathbf{b}$ are 2 vectors, not in the same direction.
    $\overrightarrow{OA} = \mathbf{a}$, $\overrightarrow{OB} = \mathbf{b}$, $\overrightarrow{OP} = \frac{3}{4}\mathbf{a} + \frac{1}{4}\mathbf{b}$ and $\overrightarrow{OQ} = \frac{1}{4}\mathbf{a} + \frac{3}{4}\mathbf{b}$.
    Show that P and Q lie on the line AB and find the ratio of lengths $AP : PQ : QB$.

Congruent triangles

Congruent triangles are the same shape and the same size.

(1)   (2)   (3)   (4)

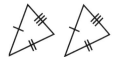 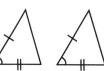 

We recognise that these triangles are congruent because …

In (1), 3 sides of the first triangle are equal in turn to 3 sides of the second triangle. (This reason is written as SSS.)

In (2), 2 sides of the first triangle are equal to 2 sides of the second triangle, also the angles included between the two sides are equal. (SAS)

In (3), 2 angles in the first triangle are equal to 2 angles of the second triangle, and a side of the first triangle is equal to a side of the second triangle, which is in a corresponding position in relation to the angles. (AAS)

In (4), the triangles are right-angled and their hypotenuses and one other pair of sides are equal. (RHS)

If one triangle can be reflected into the position of a second triangle, then the triangles are congruent.

If one triangle can be rotated into the position of a second triangle, then the triangles are congruent.

If one triangle can be translated into the position of a second triangle, then the triangles are congruent.

The symbol $\equiv$ means 'is congruent to'.

Examples

1 In the diagram it is given that $\angle BAC = \angle DAC$, and $AB = AD$.
   Explain why the triangles are congruent.

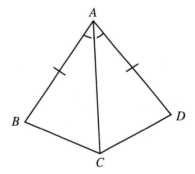

$$AB = AD \qquad \text{(given)}$$

$$\angle BAC = \angle DAC \qquad \text{(given)}$$

$$AC = AC \qquad \text{(same line)}$$

$$\triangle ABC \equiv \triangle ADC \qquad \text{(SAS)}$$

Because the triangles are congruent, we also know that

$$BC = DC$$

$$\angle B = \angle D$$

$$\angle ACB = \angle ACD$$

2 Prove that in a parallelogram the opposite sides are equal and opposite angles are equal.

$$a = c \qquad \text{(alternate angles)}$$

$$x = y \qquad \text{(alternate angles)}$$

$$AC = AC \qquad \text{(same line)}$$

$$\triangle ADC \equiv \triangle CBA \qquad \text{(AAS)}$$

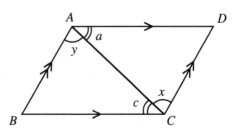

So $AD = CB$, $CD = AB$ and $\angle D = \angle B$, also $\angle DAB = \angle BCD$.

Exercise 2.4

1. In this figure,
   1 name 3 pairs of congruent triangles,
   2 name an angle equal to ∠*ABC*,
   3 name a line equal to *BX*.

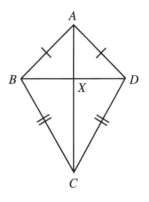

2. In this figure, if △*ABC* is rotated through 90°
   clockwise about point *C*, its new position is △*EDC*,
   so △*ABC* ≡ △*EDC*.

   1 Name lines equal to *BC* and *AB*.
   2 Name an angle equal to ∠*B*.

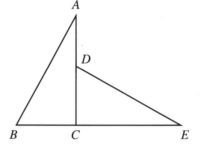

3. Are these pairs of triangles congruent? If so, give the vertices in corresponding order and
   give the reasons for congruence, and name the other pairs of equal sides or angles.

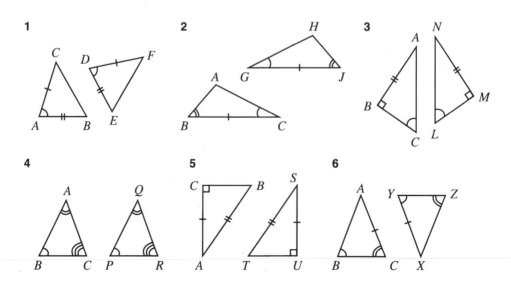

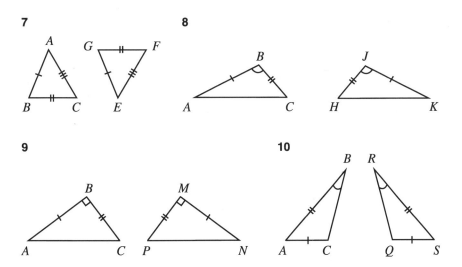

4. *TP* and *TQ* are tangents to the circle, centre *O*, touching it at *P* and *Q*. Assuming that the angles at *P* and *Q* are right angles, prove that triangles *PTO* and *QTO* are congruent, and hence prove that *TP* = *TQ*.

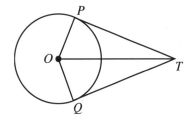

5. Use the diagram for constructing the bisector of an angle *ACB*, on page 31.

    1 Prove that triangles *CXZ*, *CYZ* are congruent.
    2 Hence prove that *CZ* is the bisector of ∠*ACB*.

6. Use the diagram for constructing the perpendicular bisector of a line *AB*, on page 30.

    1 Prove that triangles *AXY*, *BXY* are congruent.
    2 Name an angle equal to ∠*AXZ*.
    3 Prove that triangles *AXZ*, *BXZ* are congruent.
    4 Hence prove that *XY* is the perpendicular bisector of *AB*.

Exercise 2.5 Applications

1. Draw a triangle *ABC* with *AB* = 8 cm, *BC* = 10 cm and ∠*B* = 90°. Draw the locus of points inside the triangle which are (1) 1 cm from *BC*, (2) equidistant from *A* and *C*, (3) 9 cm from *A*.
    Using these loci, mark *P*, a point 1 cm from *BC* and equidistant from *A* and *C*, and shade the region of points inside the triangle which are more than 1 cm from *BC* and more than 9 cm from *A*.

2. **To construct the circumscribed circle of a triangle**

   Draw an acute-angled triangle *ABC*.
   Draw the perpendicular bisectors of *AC*
   and *BC* to meet at *O*.
   With centre *O*, radius *OA*, draw the
   circle.
   (This circle is also called the circumcircle
   of the triangle.)

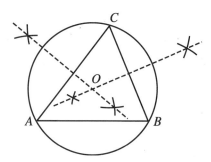

3. A camper pitches his tent equidistant from
   the farm, the shop and the cafe. Show on
   an accurate scale drawing where this is.
   How far is he from any of the three places ?

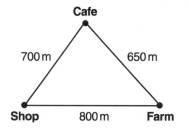

4. **To construct the inscribed circle of a triangle**

   Draw an acute-angled triangle *ABC*.
   Draw the bisectors of angles *A* and *B* to
   meet at *I*.
   Draw a line from *I*, perpendicular to *AB*,
   meeting *AB* at *X*.
   With centre *I*, radius *IX*, draw the circle.
   (This circle is also called the in-circle of
   the triangle.)

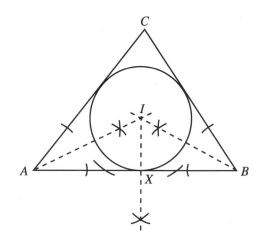

5. A camper pitches his tent equidistant from
   the beach, the river and the road. Show on
   an accurate scale drawing where this is.
   How far from the beach is it ?

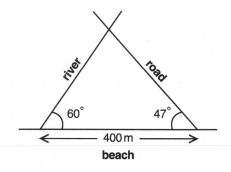

6. A ladder 6 m long is standing on horizontal ground, leaning against a vertical wall. As its foot slides along the ground, find the locus of the rung at the middle of the ladder. (Draw the ladder at various angles to the wall to find the locus.)

7.

The triangle is rotated clockwise about B until C lies on the table. Then it is rotated clockwise about the new position of C until A lies on the table. On an accurate drawing show the loci of C, B and A. Mark each locus clearly.

8. O is the origin, A is the point $(2, 3)$, B is $(-1, -2)$, C is $(4, 0)$ and D is the mid-point of BC. Find the vectors representing the lines

   1 $\overrightarrow{AB}$ 2 $\overrightarrow{AC}$ 3 $\overrightarrow{AD}$

9. O is the origin, A is the point $(9, 3)$ B is $(12, 7)$ and C is $(4, 5)$. D is the point such that $\overrightarrow{OD} = \overrightarrow{OA} + \frac{1}{2}(\overrightarrow{OB} + \overrightarrow{OC})$. Find the coordinates of D.

10. Find the values of the numbers a and b if $a\begin{pmatrix} 5 \\ 2 \end{pmatrix} + 3\begin{pmatrix} -1 \\ b \end{pmatrix} = \begin{pmatrix} 7 \\ -5 \end{pmatrix}.$

11. $\overrightarrow{OA} = \begin{pmatrix} 0 \\ 1 \end{pmatrix}$, $\overrightarrow{OB} = \begin{pmatrix} 3 \\ -2 \end{pmatrix}$ and $\overrightarrow{OC} = \begin{pmatrix} 4 \\ 3 \end{pmatrix}$, where O is the origin. Find $\overrightarrow{AB}$ and $\overrightarrow{BC}$.

12. If O is the origin and $\overrightarrow{OA} = \begin{pmatrix} 13 \\ -2 \end{pmatrix}$, $\overrightarrow{OB} = \begin{pmatrix} 22 \\ 1 \end{pmatrix}$, $\overrightarrow{OC} = \begin{pmatrix} 10 \\ -3 \end{pmatrix}$, find $\overrightarrow{AB}$ and $\overrightarrow{BC}$, and hence show that A, B and C lie on a straight line.

13. If $\overrightarrow{OA} = \mathbf{a}$ and $\overrightarrow{OB} = \mathbf{b}$, and D, E are the mid-points of OA and OB respectively, find in terms of $\mathbf{a}$ and $\mathbf{b}$,

    1 $\overrightarrow{AB}$,   2 $\overrightarrow{DE}$.
    What does this prove about the direction of $\overrightarrow{DE}$?

    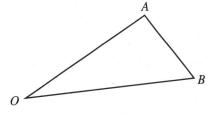

    What does this prove about the length of $\overrightarrow{DE}$?
    (This result is true for a line joining the mid-points of two sides in any triangle and is known as the **mid-point theorem.**)

14. *ABCD* is a quadrilateral and *P, Q, R* and *S* are
the mid-points of *AB, BC, CD, DA* respectively.
If $\overrightarrow{DB} = \mathbf{d}$, use the result of question 13
to find $\overrightarrow{SP}$ and $\overrightarrow{RQ}$ in terms of **d**.

What does this prove about the directions
of $\overrightarrow{SP}$ and $\overrightarrow{RQ}$?
What does this prove about the lengths
of $\overrightarrow{SP}$ and $\overrightarrow{RQ}$?
What sort of quadrilateral is *PQRS*?

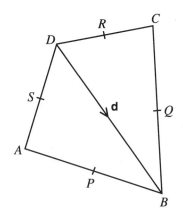

15. A boat has a speed in still water of 15 km/h
and the current has a speed of 8 km/h.
By scale drawing or by calculation, find
the resultant velocity of the boat and the
angle it makes with the direction in which
it is headed.

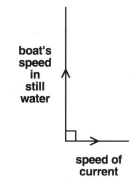

16. 2 forces of 20 N and 12 N act on a
particle at point *A*. Find the size
of the resultant force, by scale
drawing or by calculation.

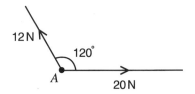

17. In this figure, *AX* is an axis of symmetry.

   1 Name triangles congruent to $\triangle ADN$,
      $\triangle ABN$, $\triangle ABE$.
   2 Name lengths equal to *BE* and *AD*.
   3 Name an angle equal to $\angle ABN$.

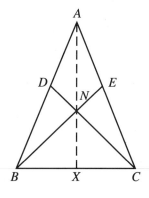

18. In the diagram the lines *AD*, *BE* and *CF* are parallel and equal.
Name a pair of congruent triangles and explain why they are congruent.
What angle is equal to $\angle ACB$?

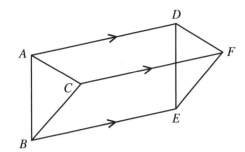

19. The points *D* and *E* are the mid-points of the sides *AB* and *AC* of the triangle *ABC*. The line *BE* is extended to *F* so that *BE = EF* and the line *CD* is extended to *G* so that *CD = DG*.

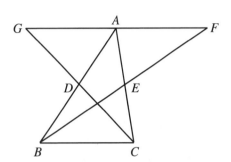

1 Explain why triangles *AEF* and *BEC* are congruent.
2 Which triangle is congruent to $\triangle ADG$?
3 Which angles are equal to $\angle FAE$ and $\angle GAD$?
4 Explain why *GAF* is a straight line.
5 Explain why *GF = 2BC* in length.

Practice test 2

1. Treasure is hidden in the triangular field *ABC* (1) equidistant from *AB* and *BC*, (2) 10 m from *AC*.
Draw a scale drawing of the field and draw loci for conditions (1) and (2). Mark with *T* the position of the treasure.
How far is it from corner *A* ?

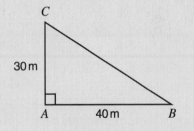

2. There are radio stations at 3 places, *A, B, C*. Broadcasts from *A* can be heard within a distance of 30 km, those from *B* within a distance of 40 km, and those from *C* within a distance of 45 km.
Draw an accurate scale drawing and mark the loci of the boundaries of the three broadcast receiving areas. Shade in the region where all three stations can be heard.

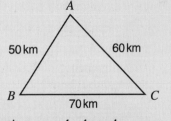

[Turn over]

3. **1** What vector would translate △*A* into △*B* ?

    2 What vector would translate △*B* into △*C* ?

    3 What vector would translate △*C* into △*A* ?

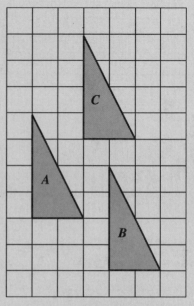

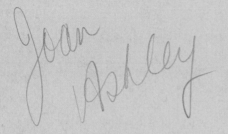

The lines are drawn on a
unit grid.

4.   *O* is the origin and $\overrightarrow{OA} = \begin{pmatrix} 2 \\ 2 \end{pmatrix}$, $\overrightarrow{OB} = \begin{pmatrix} 6 \\ 5 \end{pmatrix}$, $\overrightarrow{OC} = \begin{pmatrix} 2 \\ 0 \end{pmatrix}$, $\overrightarrow{OD} = \begin{pmatrix} -2 \\ -3 \end{pmatrix}$.

     Find $\overrightarrow{AB}$, $\overrightarrow{BC}$, $\overrightarrow{AD}$, $\overrightarrow{DC}$. Show that *ABCD* is a parallelogram.

5. $\overrightarrow{OA} = \mathbf{a}$ and $\overrightarrow{OB} = \mathbf{b}$. *E* is the point on *OA* such
that $OE : EA = 1 : 2$.   *F* is the point such
that $\overrightarrow{BF} = 2\mathbf{b}$.
Express in terms of **a** and **b**, $\overrightarrow{OE}$, $\overrightarrow{EB}$, $\overrightarrow{OF}$, $\overrightarrow{AF}$.
Show that *EB* is parallel to *AF*.
Find the ratio of lengths *EB* : *AF*.

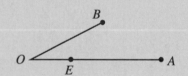

6.   In this figure, *ACD* and *BCE* are straight lines.

    1 Prove that triangles *ABC*, *DEC* are
       congruent.

    2 Name a length equal to *AB*.

    3 Name an angle equal to ∠*BAC*.

    4 What does this prove about the lines
       AB and *ED* ?

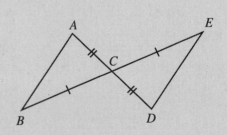

7. An explorer wants to estimate the width
    of a river. He stands at *A* directly opposite
    a tree, *T*, growing on the other bank,
    walks 50 m along the river bank
    to *B* where he places a stick, walks
    another 50 m to *C*, then walks at right
    angles to the river until he reaches
    a point *D* where the stick and the tree
    are in line.

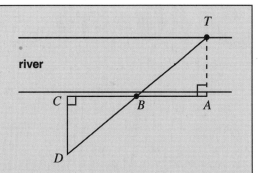

Prove that triangles *ABT*, *CBD* are congruent.
If *CD* = 80 m, how wide is the river ?

PUZZLES

1. A man has a wad of £5 notes numbered consecutively from 232426 to 232440. What is their total value ?

2. What is the next letter in this sequence ?
    N N N E N E E N E E E – – –

3. What is the next prime number after 113 ?

4. How many squares can be formed by joining 4 of these points ?

5. Five children were playing a game of cards.
    A set of cards numbered 1 to 10 are dealt so that they get two each. Paul has two cards which total 11, Mike has two cards which total 7, Laura has two cards which total 17, Kate has two cards which total 4 and Jane has two cards which total 16.
    In this game the winner is the person who has the card numbered 10. Who wins the game ?

6. If 1 m^3 of earth weighs 1600 kg, how much would there be in a hole 50 cm by 50 cm by 50 cm ?

7. Lorraine said 'Two days ago I was 13, next year I shall be 16'. What is the date today and when is her birthday ?

3 Algebra

The topics in this chapter include:

- substituting into formulae,

- manipulating algebraic formulae, equations or expressions,
  e.g.   multiplying out two brackets,
         finding common factors,
         understanding the relationship between powers and roots,
         transforming formulae,
         using formulae,
         understanding direct and inverse proportions,

- using rules of indices,

- using symbolic notation to express the rules of sequences,

- constructing and interpreting flow diagrams.

Simplifying expressions

Addition and subtraction

$$a + a = 2a$$
$$5b - 4b = b$$
$$3c - 3c = 0$$
$$3d + 4e + d - e = 4d + 3e$$

Multiplication and division

$$a \times a = a^2$$
$$2 \times b \times c = 2bc$$
$$d \times d \times d = d^3$$
$$e \div f = \frac{e}{f}$$
$$g \div g = 1$$

Expressions and formulae

If there are 8 parcels each weighing w kg, the total weight is $8w$ kg.

If a roll of ribbon b metres long is to be cut into 10 equal pieces, the length of each piece is $\dfrac{b}{10}$ metres.

The total cost of 5 kg of potatoes at p pence per kg and 3 kg of carrots at q pence per kg is $(5p + 3q)$ pence.

The formula for the perimeter of a rectangle, P cm, when the length is l cm and the breadth is b cm, is $P = 2(l + b)$.

The formula for the time taken, t seconds, to run 200 m at a speed of x m/s is $t = \dfrac{200}{x}$.

Further expressions

$$a^2 + a^2 = 2a^2$$

$$3b^2 \times 2b^3 = 6b^5$$

$$4c^3 \div 3c = \frac{4c^3}{3c} = \tfrac{4}{3}c^2$$

$$\sqrt{9d^2} = 3d$$

Removing brackets

$$3(a + 4b) = 3a + 12b$$

$$c(2c - 3d) = 2c^2 - 3cd$$

$$2e(3e + 5f - 1) = 6e^2 + 10ef - 2e$$

$$3(g + 4h) + 2(3g - h) = 3g + 12h + 6g - 2h = 9g + 10h$$

Rules for removing brackets

$$a + (b + c) = a + b + c$$

$$a + (b - c) = a + b - c$$

$$a - (b + c) = a - b - c$$

$$a - (b - c) = a - b + c$$

Note that the minus sign immediately in front of the bracket changes any signs inside the bracket when the bracket is removed.

Examples

$$5(x + 2y) + 2(x - 8y) = 5x + 10y + 2x - 16y = 7x - 6y$$

$$4(x + y) - (3x + 5y) = 4x + 4y - 3x - 5y = x - y$$

$$3(2x + y) - 2(3x - y) = 6x + 3y - 6x + 2y = 5y$$

Expanding brackets

Examples

1     $(x + 8)(x - 10) = x(x - 10) + 8(x - 10)$

$$= x^2 - 10x + 8x - 80$$

$$= x^2 - 2x - 80$$

You can work this out more quickly in this way.

$(x + 8)(x - 10)$ Multiply x by x. Answer x^2. Write this down.
                              Multiply $+8$ by -10. Answer -80. Write this down, leaving a
                              space between x^2 and -80 for two more terms.

$(x + 8)(x - 10)$ Multiply x by -10. Answer $-10x$.
                              Multiply $+8$ by x. Answer $+8x$.

The answer so far is $x^2 - 10x + 8x - 80$
$$= x^2 - 2x - 80$$

2     $(2x - 1)(x - 3) = 2x^2 - 6x - x + 3$

$$= 2x^2 - 7x + 3$$

3     $(x - 3y)(3x + y) = 3x^2 + xy - 9xy - 3y^2$

$$= 3x^2 - 8xy - 3y^2$$

4     $(3x + 2)^2 = (3x + 2)(3x + 2)$

$$= 9x^2 + 6x + 6x + 4$$

$$= 9x^2 + 12x + 4$$

Simplifying fractions

Reduction

Example

5   Simplify $\dfrac{3x^2y}{9xy^3}$

Divide the numerator and the denominator by 3, x and y.

$$\frac{\overset{x}{\cancel{3x^2y}}}{\underset{3\quad y^2}{\cancel{9xy^3}}} = \frac{x}{3y^2}$$

Addition and subtraction

Examples

6   $\dfrac{a}{6} + \dfrac{2a}{3} - \dfrac{a}{2} = \dfrac{a + 4a - 3a}{6} = \dfrac{2a}{6} = \dfrac{a}{3}$

7   $\dfrac{2}{15a} + \dfrac{5}{12a} = \dfrac{8 + 25}{60a} = \dfrac{33}{60a} = \dfrac{11}{20a}$

8   $\dfrac{a + 2}{3} - \dfrac{2a - 5}{12} = \dfrac{4(a + 2) - (2a - 5)}{12} = \dfrac{4a + 8 - 2a + 5}{12} = \dfrac{2a + 13}{12}$

Multiplication and division

Examples

9   $\dfrac{3ab^2}{5cd} \times \dfrac{10c^2}{7a^3} = \dfrac{3\cancel{a}b^2}{\cancel{5}\cancel{c}d} \times \dfrac{\overset{2\;\;c}{\cancel{10c^2}}}{\underset{a^2}{7\cancel{a^3}}} = \dfrac{6b^2c}{7a^2d}$

10   $\dfrac{2x}{y} \div \dfrac{3x^2}{y^2} = \dfrac{2\cancel{x}}{\cancel{y}} \times \dfrac{\overset{y}{\cancel{y^2}}}{\underset{x}{3\cancel{x^2}}} = \dfrac{2y}{3x}$

Substitution in expressions or formulae

Examples

11 If $x = \frac{1}{2}$ and $y = \frac{4}{5}$,

$$\frac{x}{3y-1} = \frac{\frac{1}{2}}{3 \times \frac{4}{5} - 1} = \frac{\frac{1}{2}}{\frac{7}{5}} = \frac{1}{2} \div \frac{7}{5} = \frac{1}{2} \times \frac{5}{7} = \frac{5}{14}$$

$$2x^2 + 5y^2 = 2 \times \left(\frac{1}{2}\right)^2 + 5 \times \left(\frac{4}{5}\right)^2 = \overset{1}{\cancel{2}} \times \frac{1}{\underset{2}{\cancel{4}}} + \overset{1}{\cancel{5}} \times \frac{16}{\underset{5}{\cancel{25}}}$$

$$= \frac{1}{2} + \frac{16}{5} = \frac{5+32}{10} = \frac{37}{10} = 3\frac{7}{10}$$

12 If $x = 3$ and $y = -5$,

$$5x + 10y = 5 \times 3 + 10 \times (-5) = 15 - 50 = -35$$

$$\frac{x+y}{xy-1} = \frac{3-5}{3 \times (-5) - 1} = \frac{-2}{-16} = \frac{1}{8}$$

13 A formula used to calculate distance is $s = ut + \frac{1}{2}ft^2$.
Find the value of s when $u = 5\frac{1}{3}$, $t = \frac{3}{5}$ and $f = -10$.

$$s = ut + \frac{1}{2}ft^2$$

$$= 5\frac{1}{3} \times \frac{3}{5} + \frac{1}{2} \times (-10) \times \left(\frac{3}{5}\right)^2$$

$$= \frac{16}{\underset{1}{\cancel{3}}} \times \frac{\overset{1}{\cancel{3}}}{5} - \frac{1}{\underset{1}{\cancel{2}}} \times \overset{1}{\cancel{10}} \times \frac{9}{\underset{5}{\cancel{25}}}$$

$$= \frac{16}{5} - \frac{9}{5} = \frac{7}{5} = 1\frac{2}{5}$$

Common factors

Examples

14   Factorise $6xy + 9xz$.

This is the opposite process to removing brackets.
The two terms have a common factor 3 and a common factor x.
Dividing $6xy$ by $3x$ gives $2y$.
Dividing $9xz$ by $3x$ gives $3z$.
So $6xy + 9xz = 3x(2y + 3z)$
This is the expression expressed in its factors.
It has factors 3, x and $(2y + 3z)$.

You can check that you have the correct factors by multiplying out the bracket.

15   Factorise $x^2 - x$.

The common factor is x.
$x^2 - x = x(x - 1)$

16   Factorise $6x^3 - 8x^2$.

$6x^3 - 8x^2 = 2x^2(3x - 4)$

Exercise 3.1

1.   **1**   What is the cost, in pence, of 5 kg of butter at a pence per kg?

   2   How many minutes are there in $2b$ hours?

   3   What is the total cost, in pence, of 3 lb of apples at e pence per lb and 2 lb of pears at f pence per lb?

   4   What is the change, in pence, from £1, after buying g packets of sweets at h pence each?

2.   **1**   If pencils cost k pence each, and k pencils cost £C, find a formula for C in terms of k.

   2   If a dozen eggs cost m pence and 4 eggs cost e pence, find a formula for e in terms of m.

   3   If m minutes is equivalent to $3n$ seconds, find a formula for m in terms of n.

3.   Simplify these expressions

1    $3c + 2c - 4c$ 10 $f^8 \div f^4$ 18 $3n^2 \div 2n^2$
2    $6d - 4d - 2d$ 11 $9a \times 5a$ 19 $ab + ba$
3    $5e + f + 3e - f$ 12 $8b \times 2c$ 20 $c^3 + c^3$
4    $2g - 3h + g - h$ 13 $4e \times 5e^2$ 21 $4d^2 + 4d^2$
5    $a \times a$ 14 $15f^3 \div 5f^2$ 22 $ef + 3ef - 2ef$
6    $b \times b \times b$ 15 $(3g)^2$ 23 $6ab \times 6ac \div 6bc$
7    $c \div c$ 16 $\sqrt{(25h^2)}$ 24 $(3g^2h^3)^2$
8    $d^3 \div d$ 17 $8m \div 2n$ 25 $\sqrt{(16j^2k^4)}$
9    $e^3 \times e^2$

4.   Simplify

1    $5a + (-2a)$ 6 $(-3f) - (-f)$
2    $b - (+2b)$ 7 $g + (-g)$
3    $(-4c) - (-9c)$ 8 $(+2h) - (-5h)$
4    $(-2d) + (-d)$ 9 $5x + (-6x) - (+2x)$
5    $7e + (+2e)$ 10 $(-7x) + (+9x) - (-3x)$

5.   Simplify

1    $8x \times 2y$ 5 $(-6x) \div 6x$ 8 $(-5) \div (-5x)$
2    $(-4x) \times 7y$ 6 $3 \times (-2xy)$ 9 $(-2x)^2$
3    $(+2x) \div (-3x)$ 7 $(-6) \times 4x^2$ 10 $0 \times (-3xy)$
4    $(-3x) \times (-9x)$

6.   Simplify

1    $2(a + 2b) + (a - b)$ 6 $5(p - 2q - r) + 3(p - q + 2r)$
2    $4(c - d) - 3(c + 2d)$ 7 $3(s + 8) - 4(2s - 5)$
3    $3(2e + f) + 2(e - 2f)$ 8 $x(x - 4) + 3(x - 2)$
4    $(g - h) - 4(g + 2h)$ 9 $x(2x + 3) - 4(3x - 1)$
5    $2j + 3k - (j - 3k)$ 10 $x(x^2 + 1) - x^2(x + 1)$

7.   Expand the following

1    $(x + 6)(x + 1)$ 11 $(3x - 4y)(x + 6y)$
2    $(x - 7)(x - 3)$ 12 $(2x + 5y)(x - y)$
3    $(x + 5)(x - 3)$ 13 $(3x + y)^2$
4    $(x + 4)^2$ 14 $(2x - 3y)(2x + 7y)$
5    $(x + 1)(2x + 5)$ 15 $(4x - 3y)(x + y)$
6    $(3x + 5)(2x - 1)$ 16 $(3x + 2)^2$
7    $(2x - 3)(x - 1)$ 17 $(4x - 3)(4x + 3)$
8    $(2x + y)(2x - y)$ 18 $(2x - y)^2$
9    $(15 - x)(4 + x)$ 19 $(x + 4y)(x - 4y)$
10   $(x - y)^2$ 20 $(3x + 2y)(3x - y)$

8. Simplify

   1 $\dfrac{12a^2b}{3ab}$
   2 $\dfrac{6c^2d}{54cd^2}$
   3 $\dfrac{25e^3f^2}{15ef}$

9. 1 $\dfrac{3a}{8} + \dfrac{a}{6}$
   2 $\dfrac{10b}{3} - \dfrac{2b}{9}$
   3 $\dfrac{d}{14} + \dfrac{3d}{7}$

10. 1 $\dfrac{a-1}{3} + \dfrac{a+1}{2}$
   2 $\dfrac{b-c}{2} - \dfrac{b+c}{4}$
   3 $\dfrac{3d-1}{3} + \dfrac{2-d}{4}$

11. 1 $\dfrac{8a}{15b} \times \dfrac{5c}{4a}$
   2 $\dfrac{3}{8b} \div \dfrac{15}{16b^2}$
   3 $\dfrac{3cd}{10ef} \times \dfrac{2e^3}{9d^2}$

12. If $a = 5$, $b = 3$ and $c = 1$, find the values of

   1 $4a + b$
   2 $a^2 + b^2$
   3 $2a^2$

   4 $\dfrac{a+c}{b-c}$

   5 $(3a - 5c)^2$

13. If $p = \frac{1}{2}$, $q = \frac{2}{3}$, $r = 1\frac{1}{4}$, find the values of

   1 $p + q$
   2 $4p - 3q$
   3 $r - q$
   4 $8pqr$
   5 $p^2 + 4r^2$
   6 $\dfrac{p}{q}$

   7 $4r - 3q$
   8 $4r^2 - 3q^2$
   9 $\dfrac{p+r}{7q}$
   10 $q(2p + r)$

14. If $x = 3$ and $y = -2$ find the values of

   1 $\dfrac{3x}{y}$
   2 xy^2
   3 $\dfrac{y}{x-4}$

   4 $x^2 - y^2$
   5 $(x - y)^2$

15. Factorise
   1 $10x - 15y$
   2 $3xy - 12yz$
   3 $4\pi a - 4\pi b$
   4 $20abc + 10a - 5b + 25c$
   5 $14x^2y - 21xy^2$

   6 $a^2 + a^3$
   7 $a^2 + 2ab - ac$
   8 $49 + 7x^3$
   9 $2\pi r^2 + 2\pi rh$
   10 $x^2y - xy^2$

16. A formula used to find gradients of lines is $m = \dfrac{a-b}{1+ab}$.

Find the values of m when
1 $a = \frac{1}{2}, b = \frac{3}{4}$,
2 $a = -2, b = -1$.

17. The formula for the sum of the squares of the numbers from 1 to n is $\frac{1}{6}n(n+1)(2n+1)$.

Use this formula to find the value of $1^2 + 2^2 + 3^2 + \cdots + 11^2 + 12^2$.

Equations

Example

1 Solve the equation $13x - 20 = 6x + 8$

Subtract $6x$ from both sides
$$7x - 20 = 8$$
Add 20 to both sides
$$7x = 28$$
Divide both sides by 7
$$x = 4$$

To check the equation, substitute $x = 4$ into both sides of the equation separately.
The two sides should be equal.
Left-hand side (LHS) $= 13x - 20 = (13 \times 4) - 20 = 52 - 20 = 32$.
RHS $= 6x + 8 = (6 \times 4) + 8 = 24 + 8 = 32$.
The two sides are both 32, so the equation checks.
If you are not required to do a check as part of the answer, do it at the side of your work, as rough working, or even mentally.

Equations involving fractions

Examples

2 $\dfrac{x}{4} + \dfrac{3x-2}{10} = 0$

By multiplying both sides by 20, the equation is simplified.
$$5x + 2(3x - 2) = 0$$
$$5x + 6x - 4 = 0$$
$$11x = 4$$
$$x = \tfrac{4}{11}$$

This equation could take too long to check by the usual method, so it might be better just to check through your working again.

3 $\quad \dfrac{x+11}{4} = 2 - \dfrac{x+3}{3}$

Multiply both sides by 12.

$$3(x+11) = 24 - 4(x+3)$$

$$3x + 33 = 24 - 4x - 12$$

$$7x = -21$$

$$x = -3$$

To check the equation, substitute $x = -3$ into both sides of the equation separately.

$$\text{LHS} = \frac{x+11}{4} = \frac{(-3)+11}{4} = \frac{8}{4} = 2$$

$$\text{RHS} = 2 - \frac{x+3}{3} = 2 - \frac{(-3)+3}{3} = 2 - 0 = 2$$

The two sides are both 2, so the equation checks.

Powers and roots

If $x^2 = a$ (where a is a positive number).
Take the square root of both sides.

$$x = \sqrt{a}$$

There is also a negative solution, $x = -\sqrt{a}$
The complete solution can be written $x = \pm\sqrt{a}$
This means x equals plus $\sqrt{a}$ or minus $\sqrt{a}$

Examples

4 $\quad$ If $x^2 = 36$

$$x = \sqrt{36} = 6 \quad \text{or} \quad x = -\sqrt{36} = -6$$

$$x = \pm 6$$

5 $\quad$ If $x^2 = 12$

$$x = \sqrt{12} \quad \text{or} \quad -\sqrt{12}$$

$$x = \pm 3.46, \text{ correct to 2 dec pl.}$$

If $x^3 = b$

Take the cube root of both sides.

$x = \sqrt[3]{b}$

6   If $x^3 = 125$

$x = \sqrt[3]{125} = 5$

(There is no negative solution.)

7   If $x^3 = 60$

$x = \sqrt[3]{60}$

$x = 3.91,$ correct to 2 dec pl.

If $\sqrt{x} = c$

Square both sides.

$x = c^2$

8   If $\sqrt{x} = 8$

$x = 64$

If $\sqrt[3]{x} = d$

Cube both sides.

$x = d^3$

9   If $\sqrt[3]{x} = 10$

$x = 1000$

Variation

In Chapter 1, questions involving proportion were worked out using arithmetical methods. Quantities which are in proportion can be linked by equations.

Direct Variation

If y is directly proportional to x, i.e. y varies directly as x,
then $y = kx$, where k is a positive constant number.

The word 'directly' need not be included as it is assumed that the variation is direct variation if
the word 'inverse' is not included.

The square law

If y varies as the square of x, then $y = kx^2$.

The cube law

If y varies as the cube of x, then $y = kx^3$.

If we know some corresponding values of x and y, we can find the value of k.

Example

10   If y varies as the cube of x and $y = 40$ when $x = 2$, find the equation connecting x and y,
      and find the value of y when $x = 3$.

$$y = kx^3$$

When $x = 2$, $y = 40$ so $40 = k \times 2^3$

$$40 = 8k$$
$$k = 5$$

The equation is $y = 5x^3$.
When $x = 3$, $y = 5 \times 3^3 = 135$.

Inverse Variation

If y is inversely proportional to x, i.e. y varies inversely as x, then $y = \dfrac{k}{x}$.

The inverse square law

If y varies inversely as the square of x, then $y = \dfrac{k}{x^2}$.

Example

11   If y varies inversely as the square of x, and $y = 5$ when $x = 3$, find the equation connecting x and y, and find the value of y when $x = 6$.

$$y = \frac{k}{x^2}$$

When $x = 3$, $y = 5$ so $5 = \dfrac{k}{3^2}$

$$5 = \frac{k}{9}$$

$$k = 45$$

The equation is $y = \dfrac{45}{x^2}$.

When $x = 6$, $y = \dfrac{45}{6^2} = 1\frac{1}{4}$.

Transformation of formulae

Examples

12   If $I = \dfrac{PRT}{100}$, find R in terms of the other letters.

$$I = \frac{PRT}{100}$$ Multiply both sides by 100

$$100I = PRT$$ Divide both sides by PT

$$R = \frac{100I}{PT}$$

13   If $a\sqrt{x} - b = c$, find x in terms of the other letters.

$$a\sqrt{x} - b = c$$ Add b to both sides

$$a\sqrt{x} = c + b$$ Divide both sides by a

$$\sqrt{x} = \frac{c + b}{a}$$ Square both sides

$$x = \frac{(c + b)^2}{a^2}$$ $\left(\text{Note that } x \text{ does not equal } \dfrac{c^2 + b^2}{a^2} \right)$

14 If $V = \frac{4}{3}\pi r^3$, find r in terms of V and π.

$V = \frac{4}{3}\pi r^3$ Multiply both sides by 3

$3V = 4\pi r^3$ Divide both sides by 4π

$\dfrac{3V}{4\pi} = r^3$ Take the cube root of both sides

$r = \sqrt[3]{\dfrac{3V}{4\pi}}$

15 If $ax + b = cx + d$, find x in terms of the other letters.

$ax + b = cx + d$ Subtract cx and b from both sides

$ax - cx = d - b$ Factorise $ax - cx$

$x(a - c) = d - b$ Divide both sides by $a - c$

$x = \dfrac{d - b}{a - c}$ $\left(x = \dfrac{b - d}{c - a} \text{ would also be correct} \right)$

Using formulae

Examples

16 If $T = 2\sqrt{l}$ and $T = 6$, what is the value of l?

Either transform the formula.

$T = 2\sqrt{l}$

$T^2 = 4l$

$l = \dfrac{T^2}{4}$

When $T = 6$, $l = \dfrac{6^2}{4} = \dfrac{36}{4} = 9$

Or use the formula directly.

$T = 2\sqrt{l}$

$6 = 2\sqrt{l}$

$3 = \sqrt{l}$

$l = 9$

17 If $V = \frac{4}{3}\pi r^3$ and $V = 80$, what is the value of r?

Either transform the formula as in example **14**

$$r = \sqrt[3]{\frac{3V}{4\pi}}$$

$$= \sqrt[3]{\frac{3 \times 80}{4\pi}}$$

$$= 2.67, \text{ to 3 sig. fig.}$$

Using your calculator, press 3 $\boxed{\times}$ 80 $\boxed{\div}$ 4 $\boxed{\div}$ $\boxed{\pi}$ $\boxed{=}$ $\boxed{\sqrt[3]{}}$

Or use the formula directly.

$$V = \frac{4}{3}\pi r^3$$

$$80 = \frac{4}{3}\pi r^3$$

$$240 = 4\pi r^3$$

$$r^3 = \frac{60}{\pi}$$

$$r = \sqrt[3]{\frac{60}{\pi}} = 2.67, \text{ to 3 sig. fig.}$$

Exercise 3.2

1. Solve these equations

    1 $3a + 1 = 13 - a$

    2 $16 - 4b = 0$

    3 $12c - 5 = 15 + 8c$

    4 $2d + 7 = 31 - 4d$

    5 $3(e + 2) - e = 26$

    6 $4(2f - 6) + 3(f + 5) = 35$

    7 $\frac{1}{4}(g - 2) = 6$

    8 $\frac{h + 7}{4} = 5$

    9 $\frac{1}{5}j - 6 = 8$

    10 $8k - 5 = 2k + 43$

2. Solve the equations

    1 $3(2x - 5) - 4(x + 7) = 13$

    2 $5(x + 3) + (x - 5) = 9$

    3 $2(5 + x) - 3(6 - x) = 42$

    4 $5(x - 1) + 3(x - 4) = -11$

    5 $22 - 5x - (x + 10) = 0$

3. Solve the equations

1 $\dfrac{2x-5}{3} = \dfrac{x-2}{2}$

2 $\dfrac{x-1}{3} = x - \dfrac{3(x+2)}{5}$

3 $\dfrac{x+1}{7} - 2 = \dfrac{x-1}{4}$

4 $\frac{3}{4}(2x-1) - \frac{2}{3}(4-x) = 2$

4. Solve the equations. If the solutions are not exact, give them correct to 2 decimal places.

1 $x^2 = 144$

2 $x^3 = 343$

3 $x^2 = 0.06$

4 $\sqrt{x} = 7$

5 $\sqrt[3]{x} = 6$

6 $x^2 = 3.61$

7 $\sqrt[3]{x} = 1.3$

8 $x^3 = 1.04$

9 $\sqrt{x} = 0.9$

10 $x^2 = 10$

5. 1 If $ax + by = c$, find y in terms of a, b, c and x.

2 If $E = \frac{1}{2}mv^2$, find v in terms of m and E, if v is a positive number.

3 If $v = u + at$, find a in terms of u, v and t.

4 If $C = \frac{5}{9}(F - 32)$, find F in terms of C.

5 If $s = \dfrac{n}{2}(a + l)$, find n in terms of s, a and l.

6. If y varies directly as x and $y = \frac{1}{2}$ when $x = 5$, find y when $x = 20$.

7. If y varies as the square of x and $y = 4$ when $x = 4$, find the equation connecting y with x and find the value of y when $x = 5$.

8. If y varies inversely as x and $y = 15$ when $x = 3$, find the value of y when $x = 5$.

9. If y varies inversely as the square of x and $y = 18$ when $x = 2$, find the value of y when $x = 3$.

10. If y varies as the cube of x and $y = 1000$ when $x = 5$, find the equation connecting y with x. What is the value of y when $x = 10$?

11. If y is inversely proportional to x and $y = \frac{1}{2}$ when $x = 3$, what is the value of y when $x = 6$?

12. A variable A is proportional to r^2. If $A = 20$ when $r = 2$, find the value of A when $r = 5$.

13. If w is directly proportional to d and $w = 24$ when $d = 6$, find the value of w when $d = 7$.

14. If y is inversely proportional to the square of x and $x = 3$ when $y = 4$, find the equation connecting y with x, and find the value of y when $x = 4$.

15. The weight W kg of a bar varies directly as ld^2, where l cm is its length and d cm its diameter. If $W = 5.6$ when $d = 3.5$ and $l = 48$, find the equation for W in terms of l and d. Hence find the weight of a bar of this type of length 42 cm and diameter 5 cm.

16. 20 paperback books are bought, some costing £1.80 each and the others costing £3.20 each. The total cost was £54.20. How many of the cheaper kind were there?
(Let there be x at £1.80 and $(20 - x)$ at £3.20.)

Indices

The rules are

$$a^m \times a^n = a^{m+n}$$

$$(a^m)^n = a^{mn}$$

$$a^m \div a^n = a^{m-n}$$

$$a^0 = 1$$

$$a^{-n} = \frac{1}{a^n}$$

$$a^{\frac{1}{n}} = \sqrt[n]{a}$$

$$a^{\frac{m}{n}} = (\sqrt[n]{a})^m \text{ or } \sqrt[n]{(a^m)}$$

Examples

$$x^5 \times x^3 = x^8$$

$$x^7 \div x^5 = x^2$$

$$(x^3)^4 = x^{12}$$

$$x^3 \times x^{-2} = x^{3+(-2)} = x$$

$$x \div x^{-5} = x^{1-(-5)} = x^6$$

$$(x^{-3})^2 = x^{-3\times 2} = x^{-6} \left(\text{or } \frac{1}{x^6} \right)$$

$$x^{-2} \times x^2 = x^{-2+2} = x^0 = 1$$

$$x^{\frac{1}{2}} \times x^{\frac{3}{2}} = x^{\frac{1}{2}+\frac{3}{2}} = x^2$$

$$(x^{\frac{1}{3}})^2 \times (x^{-2})^{\frac{1}{3}} = x^{\frac{2}{3}} \times x^{-\frac{2}{3}} = x^{\frac{2}{3}-\frac{2}{3}} = x^0 = 1$$

Sequences

By looking at the pattern of the numbers in a sequence we can find an expression for the nth term.

To find the expression for the nth term if the terms of the sequence increase by a constant number.

e.g. 3, 8, 13, 18, ... goes up by 5 each time.
The nth term will include a term $5n$.
In fact, it is $5n - 2$.

If the sequence decreases by a constant number:

e.g. 28, 25, 22, 19, ... goes down by 3 each time.
The nth term will include a term $-3n$.
In fact, it is $31 - 3n$.

For other sequences, look for patterns including squares, 1, 4, 9, 16; cubes, 1, 8, 27; powers, e.g. powers of 2; 2, 4, 8, 16, $(2, 2^2, 2^3, 2^4)$; and so on.

You can use the expression for the nth term to find any term of the sequence.

Example

The nth term of a sequence is $\dfrac{n}{2n + 1}$

The 1st term is $\dfrac{1}{(2 \times 1) + 1} = \frac{1}{3}$

The 2nd term is $\dfrac{2}{(2 \times 2) + 1} = \frac{2}{5}$

The 3rd term is $\dfrac{3}{(2 \times 3) + 1} = \frac{3}{7}$

The 10th term is $\dfrac{10}{(2 \times 10) + 1} = \frac{10}{21}$

and so on, for any term.

You can use a computer program to generate many such terms quickly, and perhaps make some discoveries about the patterns.

Flow diagrams

Instead of giving instructions in a simple list, they can be arranged in a **flow diagram**. You start by reading the box at the top, or sometimes at the left side, and follow the direction of the arrows, reading the boxes in turn, and carrying out the instructions or answering the questions in them.

You can put all the instructions in rectangular boxes, but if you use the other shapes shown it makes the flow diagrams clearer.

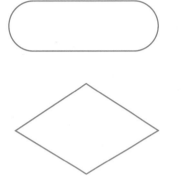

A rounded box is used at the beginning and end.

A diamond box is used for a question. The path you take from it will depend on the answer. In the example below the two paths are for the answers 'Yes' and 'No'. The path 'Yes' returns to a previous part of the diagram. This is called a **loop**.

Example

Here is a flow diagram which gives a sequence of numbers.

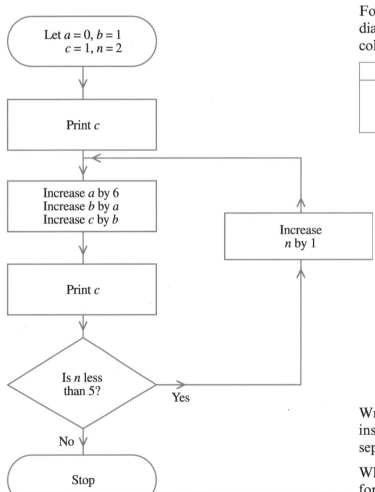

For working through the flow diagram, write down a, b, c, n in columns, which begin like this:

a	b	c	n
0	1	1	2
6	7	8	3
.	.	.	.

Write the numbers given by the instruction 'Print c' in a row, separated by commas.

What sequence of numbers is formed ?

Exercise 3.3

1. Simplify

    1 $a^3 \times a^4$

    2 $b^3 \times b^{-5}$

    3 $(c^5)^2$

    4 $(d^{\frac{1}{3}})^6$

    5 $(e^2)^{\frac{2}{3}} \times e^{\frac{2}{3}}$

    6 $(\sqrt{f})^3$

    7 $g^{-2} \div (g^{-1})^2$

    8 $h^{\frac{1}{3}} \times h^{\frac{1}{2}} \times h^{\frac{1}{6}}$

    9 $j^3 \times (j^{-1})^3$

    10 $k^0 \times k^{-\frac{4}{3}} \times (k^2)^{\frac{1}{3}}$

2. If $x = 10^p$ and $y = 10^q$, express as powers of 10

    1 xy **2** $\dfrac{x}{y}$ **3** $10x$ **4** x^2 **5** $\dfrac{y}{100}$

3. Find the value of x in these equations

    1 $2^x = 64$

    2 $3^x = 81$

    3 $4^x = \frac{1}{16}$

    4 $5^x = 1$

    5 $6^x = \dfrac{1}{\sqrt{6}}$

4. Here is a table of values connecting x and y which satisfy the equation $y = 4x^n$.
    Find the value of n.

x	-1	$\frac{1}{2}$	2
y	-4	$\frac{1}{2}$	32

5. Write down the next 2 terms in these sequences, and find an expression for the nth term.

    1 $3, 7, 11, 15, \ldots$

    2 $16, 15, 14, 13, \ldots$

    3 $10, 13, 16, 19, \ldots$

    4 $95, 90, 85, 80, \ldots$

    5 $1, \frac{1}{2}, \frac{1}{3}, \frac{1}{4}, \ldots$

    6 $2, 9, 28, 65, 126, \ldots$

    7 $15, 5, -5, -15, \ldots$

    8 $0, 2, 6, 12, 20, \ldots$

    9 $\frac{1}{3}, \frac{2}{4}, \frac{3}{5}, \frac{4}{6}, \ldots$

    10 $11, 14, 19, 26, \ldots$

6. These expressions are the nth terms of sequences. By putting $n = 1, 2, 3$ and 4 in turn,
    write down the 1st 4 terms of each sequence.

    1 $3n - 1$

    2 $100 - 10n$

    3 $n^2 + 1$

    4 10^n

    5 $n(n + 2)$

    6 3^n

    7 $\dfrac{n}{n + 1}$

    8 $n^3 - 1$

7.   This flow diagram will convert °C into °F.

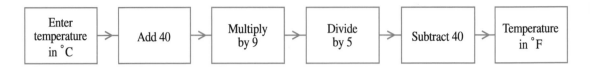

       Use the flow diagram to convert 41°C into °F.

8.   Here is a flow diagram.

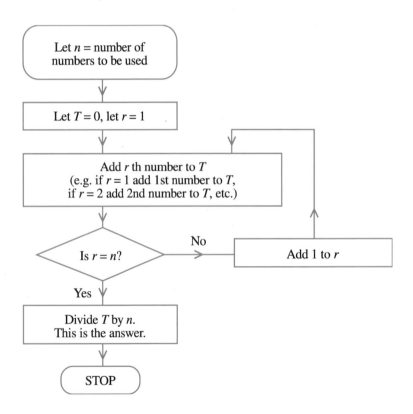

       Use the set of numbers 6, 8, 12, 15, 17 in this flow diagram.
       What is the answer ?
       What does the answer represent ?

9. Here is a flow diagram which gives a sequence of numbers.

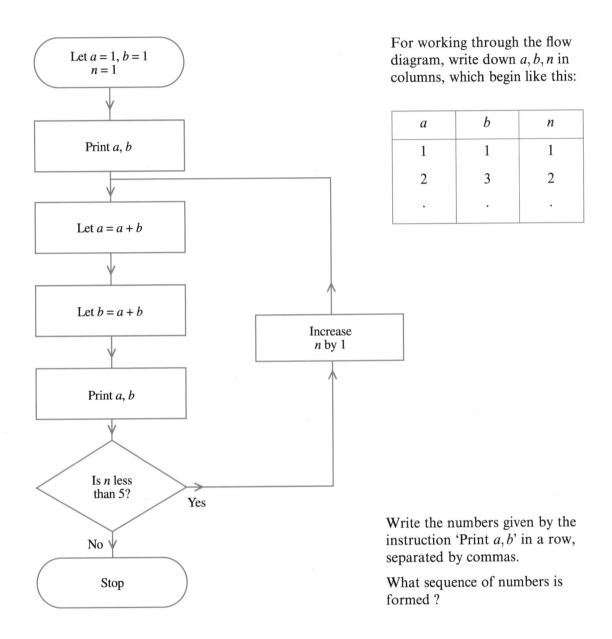

For working through the flow diagram, write down a, b, n in columns, which begin like this:

a	b	n
1	1	1
2	3	2
.	.	.

Write the numbers given by the instruction 'Print a, b' in a row, separated by commas.

What sequence of numbers is formed?

10. What is the nth term of the sequence 5, 25, 125, ... ?
     What is the least value of n for which the nth term $> 1\,000\,000$?

Exercise 3.4 Applications

1. If k lb of apples are bought for x pence per lb and sold for y pence per lb, what is the profit in £'s ?

2. The time taken to cook a chicken is given as 20 minutes per lb plus 20 minutes extra. Find a formula for the time, T hours, needed for a chicken weighing c lb.

3. Simplify   **1** $3a^3 + 4a^3$ **2** $3a^3 \times 4a^3$ **3** $3a^3 \div 4a^3$

4. Find the value of   **1** $\dfrac{b-a}{d-c}$,   **2** $\dfrac{a+b}{2}$,   **3** $(b-a)^2 + (d-c)^2$,

    when $a = -1$, $b = 2$, $c = 3$, $d = -4$.

5. If $s = \dfrac{n}{2}\left[2a + (n-1)d\right]$,

    1   find the value of s when $a = 38$, $n = 11$ and $d = -7$,
    2   find the value of d when $a = 3$, $n = 12$ and $s = -294$.

6. Find the value of $(x+y)^2 - (x^2+y^2)$ when $x = 5$ and $y = 3\frac{1}{2}$.

7. Simplify   **1** $\dfrac{3xy \times 4xy}{xy}$ **2** $\dfrac{1}{3xy} + \dfrac{1}{4xy}$ **3** $\dfrac{1}{3xy} \div \dfrac{1}{4xy}$

8. Simplify   **1** $5a^7 \times 4a^6$ **2** $27b^5 \div 9b$

9. Find the value of $\dfrac{a+b}{a-b}$ when $a = 2\frac{1}{2}$ and $b = 1\frac{1}{3}$.

10. If $x = 4y$, find the value of $\dfrac{x^2 - 4y^2}{x^2 + 4y^2}$.

11. Simplify $\dfrac{x-4}{3x} - \dfrac{x-5}{4x}$.

12. Start with any number between 1 and 10, double it, from the result subtract 20, then multiply by 3 and add 6.
Next divide by 6, subtract 1 and square the result.
Subtract 100, divide by the number you started with, and then add 20. Subtract the number you started with. What is your answer ?

Repeat the question beginning with the number n, checking that your previous answer is correct.

13. Factorise, and hence find the values of the following without using your calculator.

   1 $(24.3 \times 12.1) - (24.3 \times 11.1)$
   2 $(8.67 \times 16.9) + (1.33 \times 16.9)$
   3 $97^2 + (3 \times 97)$
   4 $(2 \times 3.142 \times 12.1) - (2 \times 3.142 \times 7.1)$
   5 $68^2 - (24 \times 68) + (56 \times 68)$

14. **1** Find the value of the number x if the ratio of $x : 3$ is the same as the ratio $4 : 5$.

   2 Find the value of the positive number x if the ratio of $4 : x$ is the same as the ratio $x : 25$.

15. Three regular polygons with a sides, b sides and c sides respectively meet at a point P.
What is the exterior angle of a polygon with a sides ?
What is the exterior angle of a polygon with b sides ?
What is the interior angle of a polygon with c sides ?

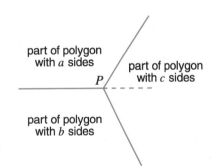

part of polygon with a sides

part of polygon with c sides

P

part of polygon with b sides

Find an equation connecting a, b and c, and simplify it to show that

$$\frac{1}{a} + \frac{1}{b} + \frac{1}{c} = \frac{1}{2}.$$

If $b = 12$ and $c = 6$, use this equation to find a.
If one polygon has 12 sides and another has 6 sides, what sort of polygon is the third one?

16. Carol's father was 24 years old when Carol was born. Now he is four times as old as Carol. How old is Carol now ?
(Let Carol be x years old, write down an equation and solve it.)

17. $(x+15)$ minutes past 7 o'clock is the same as $(2x-9)$ minutes to 8 o'clock. Find x.

18. **1** If $A = P\left(1 + \dfrac{R}{100}\right)$, find R in terms of A and P.

   2 If $T = 2\pi\sqrt{\dfrac{l}{g}}$, find l in terms of T, g and π.

   3 $S = \pi r l + \pi r^2$, find l in terms of S, r and π.

   4 If $3a = \sqrt{x+2}$, find x in terms of a.

   5 If $3a = \sqrt{x}+2$, find x in terms of a.

19. If $V = \frac{1}{6}x^2 h$, **1** find the value of h when $V = 50$ and $x = 4$, **2** find x in terms of V and h, where x is positive.

20. If $\dfrac{a}{b} = \dfrac{b}{c}$, where a, b and c are positive, find **1** c in terms of a and b,

   2 b in terms of a and c.

21. If $s = \dfrac{a}{1-r}$, find **1** s when $a = 10$ and $r = -\frac{1}{3}$, **2** r in terms of s and a.

22. The electrical resistance, R ohms, of two connected wires of lengths a cm and b cm varies directly as $\dfrac{ab}{a+b}$. When the length of each wire is 50 cm the resistance is 4 ohms.
   Find the resistance when the two wires are 25 cm and 75 cm long.

23. The load which can just be carried by a metal girder of a certain type varies inversely as its length. A load of 10 tonnes can just be carried by a girder 2 m long. What load can just be carried by a girder of the same type which is 1.6 m long ?

24. Simplify

   1 $a^{-\frac{1}{3}} \times a^{\frac{4}{3}}$ **2** $\dfrac{(b^2)^{\frac{1}{4}} \times b^{1\frac{1}{2}}}{b}$ **3** $\dfrac{c^{\frac{1}{2}} \times c^{\frac{2}{3}}}{c^{\frac{1}{6}}}$ **4** $d^{\frac{1}{2}}(d^{\frac{3}{2}} - d^{-\frac{1}{2}})$

25. Find the values of x if **1** $2^x = 1$ **2** $5^x = \frac{1}{5}$ **3** $8^x = 4$ **4** $3^x = \frac{1}{3}$ of 3^9

26. **1** The table shows some values of x and y which are linked by the equation $y = 6x^n$.

x	-2	-1	0	1	2
y	-48	-6	0	6	48

Find the value of n.
Find the value of y when $x = \frac{1}{2}$.
Find x when $y = 20.25$.

2 Here are some values of x and y which are linked by the equation $y = 10x^n$.

x	0	1	4	9
y	0	10	20	30

Find the value of n.
Find y when $x = 19.36$.
Find x when $y = 5$.

27. Write down the next 3 terms in these sequences, and find an expression for the nth term.

1 96, 48, 24, 12, ...
2 8, 5, 2, -1, ...
3 $\frac{1}{4}, \frac{2}{5}, \frac{3}{6}, \frac{4}{7}, \ldots$

28. The nth term of a sequence is $(-1)^n \, 3^{n+1}$. Write down the first 4 terms of the sequence.

29. Here are 2 flow diagrams for finding the size of each interior angle of a regular polygon.

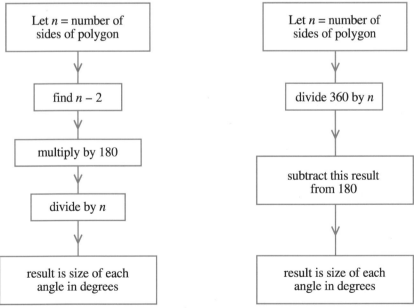

Use each flow diagram to find the size of an interior angle in

1 a hexagon, **2** a regular 20-sided polygon.

Which flow diagram do you prefer to use ?

30. To check whether a number (less than 275) is a prime number

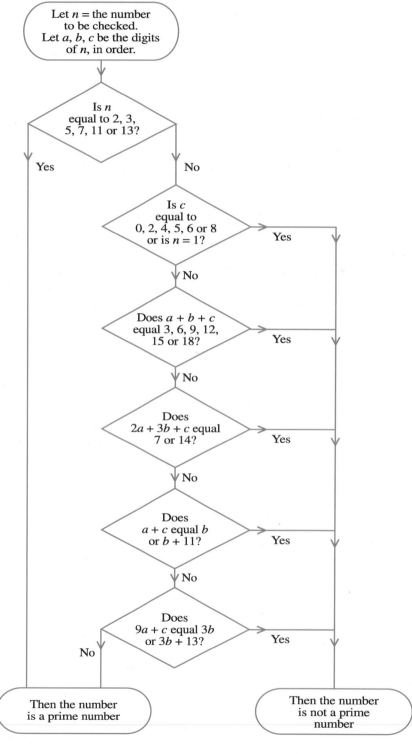

e.g. when $n = 231$, $a = 2$, $b = 3$, $c = 1$; when $n = 97$, $a = 0$, $b = 9$, $c = 7$.

Use the flow diagram to find whether or not these numbers are prime numbers.

1 119
2 151
3 165
4 221
5 257

For each answer, indicate the path taken by writing, e.g., no, no, yes.

Practice test 3

1. Simplify **1** $a + a$ **2** $a - a$ **3** $a \times a$ **4** $a \div a$ **5** $\sqrt{a^2}$

2. If $a = 1$ and $b = -1$, find the values of

   1 $5(a + b)$ **4** $a^3 - b^3$

   2 $6b - 4a$ **5** $2a^2 + 3b^2$

   3 $(a - b)^3$

3. If $a = \frac{1}{2}$, $b = \frac{1}{3}$ and $c = \frac{1}{5}$, find the values of

   1 $5c - (a + b)$ **2** $2a^2 + 3b^2$ **3** $a(b - c)$

4. A video recorder costs £60 deposit and then £25 per month for 12 months. Find a formula for the amount, £A, paid after n months, where $n \leqslant 12$. What is the total amount paid for the recorder ?

5. Remove the brackets and simplify the expression
   $(2x + 1)^2 - (x + 5)(x - 3)$.

6. Solve the equations

   1 $\dfrac{x}{2} - 6 = -10$ **4** $\frac{1}{2}(x - 3) = x + 6$

   2 $15x - 4 = 3x - 12$ **5** $\dfrac{x}{2} - \dfrac{x}{4} = 1$

   3 $6(x + 1) - 10(x + 2) + 16 = 0$

7. Factorise the expression $\pi r l + \pi r^2 + 2\pi r h$ and find its value, without using your calculator, when $l = 17$, $r = 5$ and $h = 9$, taking π as 3.14.

8. Find x in terms of the other letters.

   1 $ax + b = c$

   2 $a^2 = b^2 + x^2$, where $a > b$ and x is positive.

   3 $5 = \dfrac{2x}{x - a}$

   4 $b = 2\sqrt{x} + 5$

9. The weights of a set of similar articles are proportional to the cubes of their heights. One article is 15 cm high and weighs 10.8 kg. Find the height of the article which weighs 400 g.

[Turn over]

10.   Simplify

   1 $a^2 \times a^{-2}$ **2** $\dfrac{(b^4)^2 \times b^5}{b^{11}}$ **3** $c^0 \times (d^{-2})^{-1}$ **4** $\dfrac{(e^3)^{\frac{1}{4}} \times e^{1\frac{1}{4}}}{e}$

11.   Write down the next 3 terms in these sequences, and find an expression for the nth term.

   1   11, 19, 27, 35, ...
   2   1, 2, 4, 8, ...
   3   21, 17, 13, 9, ...

12.   Here is a flow diagram which gives a sequence of numbers.

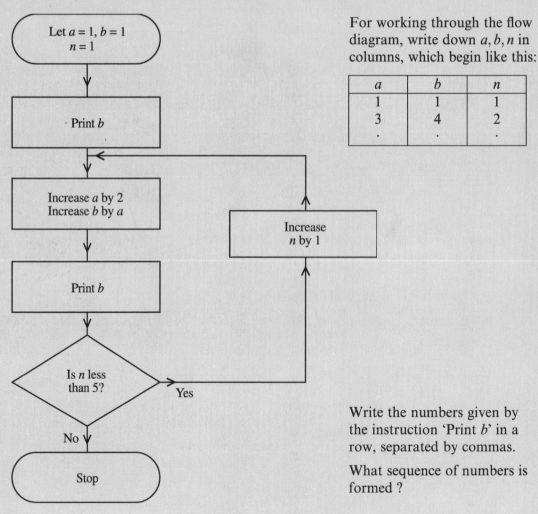

For working through the flow diagram, write down a, b, n in columns, which begin like this:

a	b	n
1	1	1
3	4	2
.	.	.

Write the numbers given by the instruction 'Print b' in a row, separated by commas.

What sequence of numbers is formed ?

PUZZLES

8.   How many mathematical words can you find reading horizontally, vertically or diagonally, in both directions ?

P	Y	R	O	T	C	E	V	R	H
E	E	S	H	A	R	E	A	P	Y
Q	M	R	T	N	A	F	A	Y	P
U	N	E	C	G	O	R	N	R	O
A	O	T	A	E	G	A	G	A	T
T	G	E	M	N	N	C	L	M	E
I	Y	M	E	T	I	T	E	I	N
O	L	A	X	I	S	I	A	D	U
N	O	I	T	A	R	O	C	G	S
E	P	D	O	H	E	N	O	C	E

9.   A ship in the harbour has a ladder with 12 rungs, each 30 cm apart, hanging over the side. At low tide 4 rungs are covered by the sea. If the tide rises at 40 cm per hour, how many rungs will be covered 3 hours later ?

10.   Copy the diagram on squared paper and fill in the answers to the clues on your copy.

Across

1   A cube number
3   A square number reversed
4   A multiple of the square root of 3 down
6   $2\frac{1}{2}$ times 8 across
8   The square root of 5 down
9   5 down − 8 down

Down

1   A factor of 4 across
2   $\frac{3}{4}$ of 3 across
3   A square number
5   The square of 8 across
7   A multiple of 8 down
8   (The cube root of 1 across) × (the centre digit of 1 across)

4 Numbers

The topics in this chapter include:

- multiplying and dividing mentally single digit multiples of any power of 10,

- using a calculator efficiently when solving problems,

- estimating and approximating to check that the results of calculations are of the right order,

- understanding the meaning of reciprocals and exploring relationships,

- expressing and using numbers in standard index form,

- recognising that measurement is approximate and choosing the degree of accuracy appropriate for a particular purpose,

- distinguishing between rational and irrational numbers.

Decimals

In the number 234.567 the figure 5 represents five-tenths because it is in the first decimal place, the 6 represents six-hundredths and the 7 represents seven-thousandths.

Working without a calculator

Addition, subtraction, easy multiplication and division

When adding, subtracting, or when multiplying or dividing by whole numbers, keep the figures in their correct positions relative to the decimal point.

Examples

1    $1.56 + 2.1 + 3.0075 + 14.834$

$$
\begin{array}{r}
1.56 \\
2.1 \\
3.0075 \\
+14.834 \\
\hline
21.5015 \\
\end{array}
$$

2    $12.1 - 3.0025$

$$
\begin{array}{r}
12.1000 \\
-3.0025 \\
\hline
9.0975 \\
\end{array}
$$

3 12.36×4 **4** $27.052 \div 8$

$$\begin{array}{r} 12.36 \\ \times \quad 4 \\ \hline 49.44 \end{array}$$

$$8\ )\overline{27.0520} \\ \quad\ \ 3.3815$$

Powers of 10

When multiplying by 10, 100, 1000, ... the numbers grow larger, so the figures move upwards (to the left), 1, 2, 3, ... places, assuming that the decimal point is fixed. Add 0's to fill any empty places between the figures and the decimal point.

Examples

5 $2.56 \times 10 = 25.6$
$3.5 \times 100 = 350$
$0.0041 \times 1000 = 4.1$

When dividing by 10, 100, 1000, ... the numbers become smaller, so the figures move downwards (to the right), 1, 2, 3, ... places, assuming that the decimal point is fixed. Add 0's to fill any empty places between the decimal point and the figures.

6 $31.8 \div 10 = 3.18$
$23 \div 100 = 0.23$
$5.56 \div 1000 = 0.00556$

7 $2.89 \times 20 = 28.9 \times 2 = 57.8$
$0.4261 \times 300 = 42.61 \times 3 = 127.83$
$45 \div 40 = 4.5 \div 4 = 1.125$
$31.92 \div 3000 = 0.03192 \div 3 = 0.01064$

Multiplication

To multiply two (or more) decimal numbers, first ignore the decimal points and multiply, then restore the decimals in the answer keeping as many decimal places in the answer as there were altogether in the question.

Examples

8 2.31×0.7 (3 decimal places altogether)
$(231 \times 7 = 1617)$
$2.31 \times 0.7 = 1.617$ (restoring 3 decimal places)

9 0.004×0.3 (4 decimal places)
$(4 \times 3 = 12)$
$0.004 \times 0.3 = 0.0012$ (including two 0's to restore 4 decimal places)

Division

Instead of dividing by a decimal, multiply both numerator and denominator by 10, 100, 1000, ... as necessary, to make the denominator into a whole number.

Examples

10 $0.07 \div 0.2 = \dfrac{0.07}{0.2} = \dfrac{0.7}{2}$ (multiplying both numerator and denominator by 10 to make 0.2 into 2)

$= 0.35$

11 $3.6 \div 0.04 = \dfrac{3.6}{0.04} = \dfrac{360}{4}$ (multiplying both numerator and denominator by 100 to make 0.04 into 4)

$= 90$

If the division is not exact, it will be necessary to stop after a suitable number of decimal places.

12   Find the value of $22 \div 7$, correct to 3 decimal places.

$7\,)\overline{22.0000}$
$\quad\ 3.1428$

Since the figure in the 4th decimal place is 8, the figure in the 3rd decimal place must be corrected up from 2 to 3.

$22 \div 7 = 3.143$, correct to 3 decimal places.

The rule for decimal places is:
Work to one more place than you need. If this extra figure is 5 or more, add 1 to the final figure of your answer.

13 3.2976	= 3.3	to 1 decimal place
	= 3.30	to 2 decimal places
	= 3.298	to 3 decimal places
0.8692	= 0.9	to 1 decimal place
	= 0.87	to 2 decimal places
	= 0.869	to 3 decimal places
0.0827	= 0.1	to 1 decimal place
	= 0.08	to 2 decimal places
	= 0.083	to 3 decimal places
0.00426	= 0.004	to 3 decimal places
	= 0.0043	to 4 decimal places

Significant figures

2.51, 25 100 and 0.0251 all have 3 significant figures, that is figures not counting 0's at the beginning or end of the number.
However, 0's in the middle of a number are counted, so 2.01, 20 100 and 0.0201 also have all got 3 significant figures.

To write a number to less significant figures than it has, use similar rules to those for changing to less decimal places.

Example

14   To 3 significant figures, $3\,657\,000 = 3\,660\,000$

$$9483 = 9480$$

$$587.9 = 588$$

$$4.962 = 4.96$$

To 2 significant figures, $3\,657\,000 = 3\,700\,000$

$$9483 = 9500$$

$$587.9 = 590$$

$$4.962 = 5.0$$

Multiplying and dividing mentally

Multiplying

Examples

15    $300 \times 60 = 3 \times 100 \times 6 \times 10$

$$= 18 \times 1000$$

$$= 18\,000$$

(In your head)

or

$$300 \times 60 = 300 \times 6 \times 10$$

$$= 1800 \times 10$$

$$= 18\,000$$

(In your head)

16 80×0.2 $80 \times 2 = 160$

                Restore 1 decimal place   } (In your head)

      $80 \times 0.2 = 16.0$

                  $= 16$

      or·

      $80 \times 0.2 = 0.2 \times 80$

                  $= 0.2 \times 10 \times 8$ } (In your head)

                  $= 2 \times 8$

                  $= 16$

17 0.04×0.9 $4 \times 9 = 36$

                Restore 3 decimal places   } (In your head)

      $0.04 \times 0.9 = 0.036$

Notice that when you multiply by a decimal which is a number less than 1, the answer will be smaller than the number you are multiplying.
e.g. 80×0.2 will be smaller than 80.
      0.04×0.9 will be smaller than 0.04 and also smaller than 0.9.

Dividing

Examples

18 $6300 \div 90 = 6300 \div 10 \div 9$

                  $= 630 \div 9$ } (In your head)

                  $= 70$

19 $40 \div 0.8 = 400 \div 8$

                  (making 0.8 into 8)   } (In your head)

                  $= 50$

20 $3 \div 0.05 = 300 \div 5$

                  (making 0.05 into 5)   } (In your head)

                  $= 60$

21 $0.06 \div 0.3 = 0.6 \div 3$

                  (making 0.3 into 3)   } (In your head)

                  $= 0.2$

Notice that when you divide by a decimal which is a number less than 1, the answer will be greater than the number you are dividing.

e.g. $40 \div 0.8$ will be greater than 40.
$3 \div 0.05$ will be greater than 3.
$0.06 \div 0.3$ will be greater than 0.06.

Exercise 4.1

In this exercise, do not use your calculator, except for checking.
Questions 6, 7, 8 and 10 should be done in your head, if possible.

1. 1 $1.32 + 2.5 + 3.792$
    2   $5.87 + 1.03 + 0.1$
    3   $0.004 + 0.08 + 0.157$

3. 1 3.87×4
    2   0.005×12
    3   0.208×7

2. 1 $21.03 - 0.017$
    2   $7.92 - 0.97$
    3   $0.0257 - 0.0163$

4. 1 $3.88 \div 4$
    2   $0.0056 \div 7$
    3   $0.208 \div 5$

5. Write as decimals.

    1   $\frac{2}{5}$
    2   $\frac{37}{100}$
    3   $\frac{4}{25}$

6. 1 1.32×10
    2   2.5×100
    3   $3.792 \div 10$
    4   1.03×1000
    5   $0.15 \div 100$
    6   $21.32 \div 1000$
    7   0.0272×100
    8   3.1×1000
    9   $3.1 \div 1000$
    10 0.0004×10

7. 1 30×0.5
    2   0.4×300
    3   0.005×60
    4   0.08×400
    5   2000×0.7

8. 1 0.8×0.09
    2   0.05×0.06
    3   0.2×0.03
    4   0.9×0.7
    5   0.004×0.5

9. 1   If $314 \times 28 = 8792$, find 3.14×2.8
    2   If $507 \times 131 = 66\,417$, find 0.507×0.131
    3   If $218 \times 91 = 19\,838$, find 21.8×9.1

10.   1 $80 \div 0.4$
      2   $9 \div 0.03$
      3   $0.4 \div 20$
      4   $270 \div 0.9$
      5   $0.002 \div 0.04$

11.   Write these numbers correct to 3 decimal places.

      1   29.7122   2   1.62815   3   202.9157   4   4.6798   5   0.003527

12.   Write the numbers of question 11 correct to 3 significant figures.

13.   Write these numbers correct to 3 significant figures.

      1   56 752   2   82.9804   3   253.312   4   206.789   5   1000.5

14.   By using approximate values, estimate answers for these questions.

      1   3.99×5.01 4 $0.0049 \div 0.096$
      2   $17.82 \div 5.82$ 5 395×0.12
      3   $(0.028)^2$

15.   Write down any even number between 1 and 11. Add 1.83 and multiply the total by 5.
      Now subtract 10.9 and then divide by 10. Add 0.675 and double the result. Subtract the
      number you started with. What is your answer?

Using your calculator

These instructions are for a scientific calculator.
With some calculators you may have to do some operations in a different way.

It is advisable to start every new calculation by pressing the $\boxed{C}$ key (for CLEAR), but you
may find that on your calculator this is unnecessary if you have just pressed the $\boxed{=}$ key.
This also works after pressing some of the other keys.

If your calculator does not seem to work in the ways shown here, read the instruction booklet
and try the examples shown there.

1.   When doing multiplication and division, it is better to multiply first and divide last if the
     division is not exact.
     e.g. For $\frac{2}{3}$ of 20, find $2 \times 20 \div 3$ instead of $2 \div 3 \times 20$.
     The answer is 13.333 ...

2.   If the answer is not exact, or has several figures, then round it up to a sensible degree
     of accuracy.
     Usually 3 significant figures will be sufficient for a final numerical answer.

3. If you have a question involving addition or subtraction together with multiplication, the calculator will read it as if there were brackets round the multiplication part, and do that part first. e.g. $25.1 + 76.2 \times 0.3$ is read as $25.1 + (76.2 \times 0.3)$ and the answer is 47.96.

    Similar rules work with addition or subtraction together with division. The calculator will do the division first. e.g. $5.93 - 0.86 \div 0.4$ is read as $5.93 - (0.86 \div 0.4)$ and the answer is 3.78.

4. If there are brackets then the part in brackets is worked out first.

    e.g. $(25.1 + 76.2) \times 0.3$

    Use the bracket keys on your calculator, or instead, you can press 25.1 $\boxed{+}$ 76.2 $\boxed{=}$ $\boxed{\times}$ 0.3 $\boxed{=}$ so that the calculator works out the addition before multiplying by 0.3. The answer is 30.39.

    For $(5.93 - 0.86) \div 0.4$, use the bracket keys or press 5.93 $\boxed{-}$ 0.86 $\boxed{=}$ $\boxed{\div}$ 0.4 $\boxed{=}$ The answer is 12.675.

    $\dfrac{5.93 - 0.86}{0.4}$ is the same question, written in a different way.

5. **Using the memory**

    $\dfrac{23.5 + 12.9}{18.1 - 6.9}$

    First find $18.1 - 6.9$ and put the answer (11.2) in the memory. Then press 23.5 $\boxed{+}$ 12.9 $\boxed{=}$ $\boxed{\div}$ $\boxed{\text{RM}}$ $\boxed{=}$ The answer is 3.25 RM stands for 'recall memory'.

    Alternatively, you could find $(23.5 + 12.9) \div (18.1 - 6.9)$, using brackets.

6. Make a rough check of your calculation to see if the calculator answer seems to be about the right size.

    e.g. $25.1 + 76.2 \times 0.3$
    A rough check for 76.2×0.3 is $80 \times 0.3 = 24$
    Then $25 + 24 = 49$
    The answer is 47.96 seems to be about the right size.

    $5.93 - 0.86 \div 0.4$

    For $0.86 \div 0.4$ use $\dfrac{0.8}{0.4} = \dfrac{8}{4} = 2$

    For 5.93 use 6
    $6 - 2 = 4$, so the answer 3.78 seems to be about the right size.

    $\dfrac{23.5 + 12.9}{18.1 - 6.9}$ is approximately $\dfrac{24 + 13}{18 - 7} = \dfrac{37}{11} = $ just over 3.
    The answer 3.25 seems to be about the right size.

7. **Keys** $\boxed{\sqrt{}}$ $\boxed{x^2}$ $\boxed{y^x}$ $\boxed{\sqrt[3]{}}$

$\boxed{\sqrt{}}$ is the square root key. It must be pressed after the number.

So for $\sqrt{6}$ press 6 $\boxed{\sqrt{}}$ and you will get 2.4494 . . .

To 3 significant figures this is 2.45.

$\boxed{x^2}$ is the squaring key.

For 3.2^2 press 3.2 $\boxed{x^2}$ and you will get 10.24

$\boxed{y^x}$ or $\boxed{x^y}$ is the key for getting cubes and other powers.

For 7^3 press 7 $\boxed{y^x}$ 3 $\boxed{=}$ and you will get 343.

For 2^6 press 2 $\boxed{y^x}$ 6 $\boxed{=}$ and you will get 64.

A different way to get 7^3 is to press 7 $\boxed{\times}$ $\boxed{x^2}$ $\boxed{=}$.

To get 8^4 press 8 $\boxed{x^2}$ $\boxed{x^2}$, and you will get 4096.

For cube roots, use the key $\boxed{\sqrt[3]{}}$

For the cube root of 125 press 125 $\boxed{\sqrt[3]{}}$ and you will get 5.

If there is not a cube root key, use the inverse key to $\boxed{y^x}$.

This is marked $\boxed{\sqrt[x]{y}}$.

For the cube root of 125 press 125 $\boxed{\sqrt[x]{y}}$ 3 $\boxed{=}$ and you will get 5. (The 3 is to show that you want the **cube** root.)

The quickest way to get a fourth root is to press $\boxed{\text{number}}$ $\boxed{\sqrt{}}$ $\boxed{\sqrt{}}$ e.g. for $\sqrt[4]{256}$ press 256 $\boxed{\sqrt{}}$ $\boxed{\sqrt{}}$ and you will get 4.

8. **The** $\boxed{\pi}$ **key**

π (pi) is the Greek letter which represents the special number 3.14159. . . used in circle formulae.

This number cannot be written exactly. For practical purposes it is usually sufficient to use 3.14 or 3.142 but if there is a $\boxed{\pi}$ key on your calculator it is quicker to use that. Do not leave more than 3 or 4 significant figures in the final answer.

e.g. For 6π press 6 $\boxed{\times}$ $\boxed{\pi}$ $\boxed{=}$ getting 18.849 . . .

To 3 significant figures this is 18.8

For $\dfrac{\pi}{2}$ press $\boxed{\pi}$ $\boxed{\div}$ 2 $\boxed{=}$ getting 1.5707 . . .

To 3 significant figures this is 1.57

9. **The** $\boxed{\text{sin}}$ $\boxed{\text{cos}}$ $\boxed{\text{tan}}$ **keys**

These are used in trigonometrical calculations. To find sin 24.5°, first make sure that
your calculator is set to work in degrees. Then press 24.5 $\boxed{\text{sin}}$ and you will get 0.4146...
(On some calculators you may have to press $\boxed{\text{sin}}$ 24.5)
The inverse function to sine is found by pressing the second function key and then the
sine key. It will be labelled $\sin^{-1}$ or arcsin. Thus to find the angle whose sine is 0.8, press
0.8 $\boxed{\text{inverse sine}}$ and you will get 53.13...
$\boxed{\text{cos}}$ and $\boxed{\text{tan}}$ keys work in a similar way.

10. **To find the remainder in a division sum**

e.g. Divide 961 by 23 and give the answer and remainder.

On your calculator, $961 \div 23 = 41.7826...$
From this, the whole number answer is 41.
Leaving the answer on your calculator, subtract 41 and press $\boxed{=}$.
This leaves 0.7826...
Multiply this decimal by 23 and it gives 18. This is the remainder.
Due to rounding errors on the calculator, instead of giving 18 exactly it might give
something like 18.00000001 or 17.99999999. Count either of these as 18.

Reciprocals

If x is a number (not 0) then $\dfrac{1}{x}$ is called the reciprocal of x.

A number multiplied by its reciprocal equals 1.

e.g. The reciprocal of 5 is $\frac{1}{5}$ since $5 \times \frac{1}{5} = 1$.

The reciprocal of $\frac{1}{3}$ is 3 since $\frac{1}{3} \times 3 = 1$.

The reciprocal of $\frac{4}{5}$ is $\frac{5}{4}$ since $\frac{4}{5} \times \frac{5}{4} = 1$.

The reciprocal of 0.7 is $\frac{10}{7}$ since 0.7 is $\frac{7}{10}$ and $\frac{7}{10} \times \frac{10}{7} = 1$.

In general, the reciprocal of $\dfrac{a}{b}$ is $\dfrac{b}{a}$.

There will be a reciprocal key on your calculator. It will be labelled $\dfrac{1}{x}$.

Press 8 $\boxed{\frac{1}{x}}$ and you will get 0.125 since $\frac{1}{8} = 0.125$

Press 1.1 $\boxed{\frac{1}{x}}$ and you will get 0.909090... since $\frac{1}{1.1} = \frac{10}{11} = 0.909090...$

Standard Index Form

A number is written in standard index form when it is written as $a \times 10^n$, where a is a number between 1 and 10 (not including 10) and n is an integer (positive or negative whole number, or 0).

Standard index form is often referred to as **standard form**. It can also be called **scientific notation**.

Examples

$$6579 = 6.579 \times 1000 = 6.579 \times 10^3$$
$$71\,800\,000 = 7.18 \times 10\,000\,000 = 7.18 \times 10^7$$
$$20 = 2 \times 10 = 2 \times 10^1$$
$$220.56 = 2.2056 \times 100 = 2.2056 \times 10^2$$

$$0.6423 = 6.423 \times \tfrac{1}{10} = 6.423 \times 10^{-1}$$
$$0.00912 = 9.12 \times \tfrac{1}{1000} = 9.12 \times 10^{-3}$$
$$0.00001 = 1 \times \tfrac{1}{100000} = 1 \times 10^{-5}$$

Your calculator will turn numbers into standard form. (Calculators do not all work in the same way so you may have to investigate to see how yours will do this.)

To turn 840 000 into standard form.
Press 840 000 $\boxed{=}$ $\boxed{\text{F} \leftrightarrow \text{E}}$ and it will show 8.4   05 which means 8.4×10^5.
Press $\boxed{\text{F} \leftrightarrow \text{E}}$ again and it will return to showing 840 000.

To enter a number which is already given in standard form, use the $\boxed{\text{EXP}}$ key.
To enter 8.4×10^5 press 8.4 $\boxed{\text{EXP}}$ 5 $\boxed{=}$ and it will work it out to 840 000.
You can get back to 8.4   05 by pressing $\boxed{\text{F} \leftrightarrow \text{E}}$
You can also find the value of 8.4×10^5 by pressing 8.4 $\boxed{\times}$ 10 $\boxed{y^x}$ 5 $\boxed{=}$

Press 0.0047 $\boxed{=}$ $\boxed{\text{F} \leftrightarrow \text{E}}$ and the calculator will show 4.7   −03 which means 4.7×10^{-3}.

To enter 4.7×10^{-3} press 4.7 $\boxed{\text{EXP}}$ 3 $\boxed{^+/_-}$ $\boxed{=}$ and it will work it out to 0.0047.
You can get back to 4.7   −03 by pressing $\boxed{\text{F} \leftrightarrow \text{E}}$.
You can also find the value of 4.7×10^{-3} by pressing 4.7 $\boxed{\times}$ 10 $\boxed{y^x}$ 3 $\boxed{^+/_-}$ $\boxed{=}$

If a number is too big or too small for the calculator to display it normally it cannot change it out of standard form.

For numbers already between 1 and 10, there is usually no need to express them in standard form, but if this is needed then the power of 10 is 10^0, (since $10^0 = 1$).
e.g. $8.3 = 8.3 \times 10^0$. A calculator would show 8.3   00

Examples

Use your calculator to find the values of:
$$(2.46 \times 10^7) \times (1.23 \times 10^2), \quad (3.92 \times 10^{-5}) \div (9.8 \times 10^{-3}), \quad (2.46 \times 10^7)^2, \quad \sqrt{4.9 \times 10^{-7}}.$$

For $(2.46 \times 10^7) \times (1.23 \times 10^2)$ press

2.46 $\boxed{\text{EXP}}$ 7 $\boxed{\times}$ 1.23 $\boxed{\text{EXP}}$ 2 $\boxed{=}$ and the calculator will show 3 025 800 000

If you press $\boxed{\text{F} \leftrightarrow \text{E}}$ this will change to 3.0258   09, which means 3.0258×10^9.

For $(3.92 \times 10^{-5}) \div (9.8 \times 10^{-3})$ press

3.92 $\boxed{\text{EXP}}$ 5 $\boxed{^+/_-}$ $\boxed{\div}$ 9.8 $\boxed{\text{EXP}}$ 3 $\boxed{^+/_-}$ $\boxed{=}$ and the calculator will show 0.004

If you press $\boxed{\text{F} \leftrightarrow \text{E}}$ this will change to 4. -03 which means 4×10^{-3}.

For $(2.46 \times 10^7)^2$ press 2.46 $\boxed{\text{EXP}}$ 7 $\boxed{x^2}$ and the calculator will show 6.0516   14

This means 6.0516×10^{14}, which is 605 160 000 000 000.

This number is too big to be shown on the calculator as an ordinary number.

For $\sqrt{4.9 \times 10^{-7}}$ press 4.9 $\boxed{\text{EXP}}$ 7 $\boxed{^+/_-}$ $\boxed{\sqrt{}}$ and the calculator will show 0.0007

If you press $\boxed{\text{F} \leftrightarrow \text{E}}$ this will change to 7. -04 which means 7×10^{-4}.

Exercise 4.2

1. Write these fractions as decimals, correct to 3 decimal places.

    1 $\frac{2}{3}$ **2** $\frac{5}{7}$ **3** $\frac{4}{9}$ **4** $\frac{1}{6}$ **5** $\frac{8}{11}$

2. By using approximate values estimate answers for these questions. Use your calculator to find the answers correct to 3 significant figures, and compare the answers with your estimates.

    1 $2 \times 3.14 \times 17$ **6** $\frac{4}{3} \times \pi \times 9.2^3$

    2 $\dfrac{0.002\,19}{7 \times 11}$ **7** $34.1 \div (19.3 - 10.02)$

    3 $(81.7 + 1.52) \div 62.8$ **8** $\sqrt[3]{0.0083}$

    4 $\dfrac{3.14 \times 0.782}{22.4 - 15.5}$ **9** $\sqrt{22.1^2 + 15.5^2}$

    5 $73.6^2 - 26.4^2$ **10** $\dfrac{23.48 + 19.76}{18.21 - 5.63}$

3.   Find the whole number answers and the remainders in these division questions.

   1 $2345 \div 7$ **2** $329 \div 23$ **3** $18\,000 \div 32$

4.   Find the reciprocals of the numbers from 2 to 16, as decimals. If they are not exact, write them as recurring decimals and also correct to 3 decimal places.

   1   Which of the numbers have reciprocals which are exact decimals ?
   2   Which of the numbers have reciprocals which have 1 recurring figure ?
   3   Which of the numbers have reciprocals which have 2 recurring figures ?
   4   Which of the numbers have reciprocals which have more than 2 recurring figures ?

5.   Express these numbers in standard index form. Try to do them first without using your calculator, then do them again with your calculator to check the answers.

1	506	**6**	0.027	**11**	93 070
2	2187	**7**	0.00051	**12**	0.00000013
3	15.07	**8**	0.000006	**13**	11.57
4	2300	**9**	0.345	**14**	0.1157
5	7 000 000	**10**	0.0208	**15**	0.0099

6.   These numbers are given in standard form. Write them as ordinary numbers. Try to do them first without using your calculator, then do them again with your calculator to check the answers.

1	1.05×10^2	**9**	2.93×10^2
2	9.6×10^4	**10**	1.1×10^6
3	4.12×10^{-1}	**11**	4.3×10^{-2}
4	5.2×10^3	**12**	8×10^5
5	2.89×10^{-2}	**13**	2.03×10^{-4}
6	7.5×10^5	**14**	9.9×10^3
7	4×10^{-3}	**15**	1.072×10^{-1}
8	6.11×10^{-1}		

7.   Use your calculator to work out these calculations. Express the answers in standard form.

1	$5.7 \times 10^3 \times (8.2 \times 10^4)$	**7**	$(3.4 \times 10^{-1}) \times (2.9 \times 10^{-2})$
2	$4.2 \times 10^5 \div (5.6 \times 10^3)$	**8**	$(4.06 \times 10^{-2}) \div (7 \times 10^{-4})$
3	$(4.7 \times 10^3)^2$	**9**	$(5.9 \times 10^{-3})^2$
4	$\sqrt{4.84 \times 10^6}$	**10**	$(1.3 \times 10^{-1}) \div (5.2 \times 10^5)$
5	$(5.4 \times 10^4) \div (1.8 \times 10^6)$	**11**	$\dfrac{8 \times 10^{-3}}{5 \times 10^3}$
6	$(1.1 \times 10^5) \times (2.4 \times 10^{-2})$	**12**	$\sqrt{6.4 \times 10^{-3}}$

8.   The mass of the Earth is 5.974×10^{21} tonnes. The Moon's mass is 0.0123 of the Earth's mass.
      Find the Moon's mass, giving your answer in standard form, correct to 3 significant figures.

Accuracy of measurements

There is a difference between counting, which is usually in whole numbers, but in any case goes up in jumps, and measurement, which goes up continuously.
We can never measure **exactly**, but by using appropriate instruments we can get measurements as accurately as they are needed for a particular purpose.

When measuring a line in Geometry, it is usual to give the length to the nearest mm.
In measuring the width of a desk, it is probably sufficient to measure to the nearest cm. In measuring larger distances the measurement would be taken to the nearest 10 cm, the nearest metre, the nearest 10 m or 100 m, or the nearest km.

With weighing, 1 gram is such a small weight that it would only be used for scientific or medical purposes or when an expensive substance was being bought. In cookery it is sufficient to weigh to the nearest 25 g. Heavier items can be weighed to the nearest kg, and very heavy objects are weighed in tonnes.

For capacity, medicines are often given using a 5 ml spoonful, and in the kitchen liquids are measured in a litre jug, with markings for every 50 ml. Larger quantities can be measured to the nearest 10 ℓ, 100 ℓ, etc.

Time can be measured to the nearest hour, to the nearest minute or to the nearest second. Athletes will want to measure their times in tenths or hundredths of a second.

If a measurement is 7 m, to the nearest metre, the actual measurement can be anything between 6.5 m and 7.5 m, i.e. it can be up to 0.5 m less or 0.5 m more.

If a weight is 8.3 kg, to the nearest 0.1 kg, the actual weight can be anything between 8.25 kg and 8.35 kg, i.e. it can be up to 0.05 kg less or 0.05 kg more.

Similar rules apply to measurements correct to 2 decimal places, 3 decimal places, to the nearest 10 units, etc.

If a length is given as 7 m, then you must assume that it has been measured to the nearest metre. If the length has been measured to the nearest 0.1 m, then it is better to write it as 7.0 m. In this case the length lies between 6.95 m and 7.05 m. If the length has been measured to the nearest cm (0.01 m) then it is better to write it as 7.00 m. The actual length lies between 6.995 m and 7.005 m. It could be up to 0.005 m (5 mm) less or 0.005 m more.

Exercise 4.3

1.   How many

1	mm in 5 cm	**11**	cm^2 in $1 m^2$
2	g in 3 kg	**12**	degrees in $1\frac{1}{2}$ right angles
3	pence in £10	**13**	mm in 2 m
4	cm in $\frac{1}{2}$ m	**14**	minutes in $2\frac{1}{2}$ hours
5	days in a year	**15**	centimes in 3 francs
6	m in 4 km	**16**	weeks in a year
7	cents in 2 dollars	**17**	mm^3 in $1 cm^3$
8	mg in 6 g	**18**	seconds in $\frac{1}{2}$ minute
9	cm^3 in 8 litres	**19**	m^2 in $1 km^2$
10	days in January	**20**	ml in 1 litre ?

2.   Give the readings shown on these instruments.

1   Weight in kg.

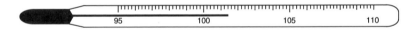

10   ↑   11

2   Temperature in °F.

95   100   105   110

3   Weighing scale in kg and g.   **4**   Measuring glass.

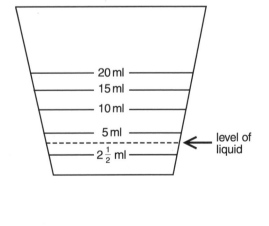

3. **1** Write 0.75 kg in g.
    2 Write 126 mm in cm.
    3 Write 2.6 m in cm.
    4 Write 400 ml in ℓ.
    5 Write 160 cm in m.

    6 Write 1520 g in kg.
    7 Write 0.7 ℓ in cl.
    8 Write 7.8 cm in mm.
    9 Write 1.2 m in cm.
    10 Write 3040 kg in tonnes.

4. Name a sensible metric unit for measuring or weighing

    1 the height of a tall tree,
    2 the amount of sugar in a bowl,
    3 the amount of water in a pond,
    4 the perimeter of a field,
    5 the height of a child.

5. Give the limits between which these measurements must lie.

    1 A line 6.5 cm long, measured to the nearest mm.
    2 A weight of 8.75 kg, weighed to the nearest 0.01 kg.
    3 A capacity of 4.2 ℓ, measured to the nearest 0.1 ℓ.
    4 A time of 2 hours 10 minutes, measured to the nearest 10 minutes.
    5 A time of 8 hours 5 minutes, measured to the nearest minute.

6. Write these measurements as stated.

    1 8.732 m, to the nearest 0.1 m,
    2 279.3 g, to the nearest 10 g,
    3 4160 ℓ, to the nearest 100 ℓ,
    4 5.51 m, to the nearest metre,
    5 156.92 cm, to the nearest mm,
    6 4.087 ℓ, to the nearest 0.1 ℓ,
    7 4.96 m, to the nearest 0.1 m,
    8 5.438 kg, to the nearest 10 g,
    9 2504 ℓ, to the nearest 10 ℓ,
    10 47.03 s, to the nearest 0.1 s.

7. Give limits between which these measurements must lie.

    1 A line 5.0 cm long, measured to the nearest mm.
    2 A weight of 200 g, weighed to the nearest 10 g.
    3 A time of 3 minutes, measured to the nearest minute.
    4 A capacity of 60 ml, measured to the nearest ml.
    5 An amount of £30, given to the nearest £1.

8. **1** Rob says that he is 1.62 m tall.
       How accurately do you think he has measured his height ?
       Using your answer, what are the limits between which his true height lies ?

    2 Rob says that his weight is 38 kg.
       To what accuracy do you think he has weighed himself ?
       Using your answer, what are the limits between which his true weight lies ?

Kinds of numbers

Integers

Positive integers   1, 2, 3, ...   (These are also called the Natural numbers.)
Zero, nought   0
Negative integers   −1, −2, −3, ...

Integers can be shown on a number line

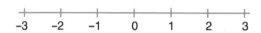

Rational numbers

These include integers, fractions and mixed numbers of the type $\dfrac{p}{q}$, where p and q are integers, and $q \neq 0$.

Fractions can be written as exact decimals, e.g. $\frac{5}{16} = 0.3125$, or as decimals which have a recurring pattern, e.g. $\frac{5}{9} = 0.55555\ldots$ and $\frac{5}{11} = 0.454545\ldots$, so all numbers which end in an exact decimal or a recurring decimal are rational numbers.

If you want to show that a decimal is a recurring one, then you write dots over the first and last number of the recurring pattern.

$0.\dot{7}$ means $0.77777\ldots$

$0.1\dot{6}$ means $0.166666\ldots$

$0.\dot{4}\dot{1}$ means $0.414141\ldots$

$0.\dot{2}9\dot{3}$ means $0.293293293\ldots$

$0.31\dot{2}8\dot{5}$ means $0.31285285285\ldots$

Rational numbers all have their places on the number line.

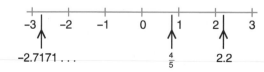

Irrational numbers

1   Square roots
Some numbers such as 4, 6.25, 0.0009 have exact square roots.

$\sqrt{4} = 2, \quad \sqrt{6.25} = 2.5, \quad \sqrt{0.0009} = 0.03$

Other numbers do not have exact square roots and these are irrational numbers.

For example, $\sqrt{2}$ is approximately 1.4142.
If you square 1.41421 on your calculator you will find the result is less than 2.
If you square 1.41422 on your calculator you will find the result is greater than 2.
So between 1.41421 and 1.41422 there is a number whose square is 2, but this number cannot be found exactly. We can find it to any suitable accuracy but it is not an exact decimal or one which repeats in a set pattern.

Here is an enlargement of the number line between 1.414 and 1.415.

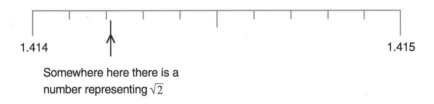

1.414   1.415

Somewhere here there is a
number representing $\sqrt{2}$

2   Cube roots of numbers which are not perfect cubes, e.g. $\sqrt[3]{4}, \quad -\sqrt[3]{7.3}$.

3 π and expressions involving π such as $\dfrac{\pi}{2}, \quad \pi^2, \quad \pi + 4$.

4   Most trig. functions where the angle is a rational number of degrees, e.g. $\sin 20°$, $\cos 85.1°$, $\tan 60°$.
(Certain trig. functions have exact values of 0, $\pm\frac{1}{2}$, or ± 1, and these are rational, e.g. $\sin 30° = \frac{1}{2}$.)

Surds

Irrational numbers such as $\sqrt{2}, \sqrt{3}, \sqrt{5}$ are also called surds.
These rules apply:

$$\sqrt{ab} = \sqrt{a} \times \sqrt{b} \qquad \sqrt{\frac{a}{b}} = \frac{\sqrt{a}}{\sqrt{b}}$$

Examples

$$\sqrt{28} = \sqrt{4 \times 7} = \sqrt{4} \times \sqrt{7} = 2\sqrt{7}$$

$$\sqrt{8} \times \sqrt{18} = \sqrt{8 \times 18} = \sqrt{144} = 12$$

$$\frac{\sqrt{50}}{\sqrt{2}} = \sqrt{\frac{50}{2}} = \sqrt{25} = 5$$

$$\tfrac{1}{2} \text{ of } \sqrt{20} = \tfrac{1}{2} \times \sqrt{4 \times 5} = \tfrac{1}{2} \times \sqrt{4} \times \sqrt{5} = \sqrt{5}$$

$$\sqrt{2\tfrac{1}{4}} = \sqrt{\frac{9}{4}} = \frac{\sqrt{9}}{\sqrt{4}} = \frac{3}{2} = 1\tfrac{1}{2}$$

$$\sqrt{18} + \sqrt{72} = 3\sqrt{2} + 6\sqrt{2} = 9\sqrt{2}$$

$$\sqrt{75} - \sqrt{27} = 5\sqrt{3} - 3\sqrt{3} = 2\sqrt{3}$$

Surds in the denominator of a fraction can be transferred to the numerator.

Examples

$$\frac{1}{\sqrt{2}} = \frac{1}{\sqrt{2}} \times \frac{\sqrt{2}}{\sqrt{2}} = \frac{\sqrt{2}}{2}$$

$$\frac{1}{\sqrt{3}+1} = \frac{1}{\sqrt{3}+1} \times \frac{\sqrt{3}-1}{\sqrt{3}-1} = \frac{\sqrt{3}-1}{(\sqrt{3}+1)(\sqrt{3}-1)}$$

$$= \frac{\sqrt{3}-1}{3-\sqrt{3}+\sqrt{3}-1} = \frac{\sqrt{3}-1}{2}$$

Exercise 4.4

1. Say whether the answers to these questions are natural numbers, integers, rational numbers or irrational numbers.

    1 $\left(1\tfrac{1}{2}\right)^2$ **2** $\sqrt{1\tfrac{1}{2}}$ **3** $(-6)^2$ **4** $(-6) \times 1\tfrac{1}{2}$ **5** $\sqrt{6 \times 1\tfrac{1}{2}}$

2. An integer n is such that $n < \sqrt{250} < n+1$. What is the value of n?

3. Say whether these numbers are rational or irrational.

    $2.\dot{7}, \quad \sqrt{3}, \quad \dfrac{1}{\sqrt{9}}, \quad 3\pi, \quad \sqrt[3]{27}.$

4. Write these numbers in order of size, smallest first, and say whether they are rational or irrational.

    $5\tfrac{1}{7}, \quad \pi + 2, \quad 5.1416, \quad \sqrt{27}, \quad 2.268^2.$

5. Express in the form $a\sqrt{b}$.

    1 $\sqrt{45}$ **2** $\sqrt{44}$ **3** $\sqrt{75}$ **4** $\sqrt{72}$ **5** $\sqrt{200}$

6. Simplify

    1 $\sqrt{\dfrac{9}{16}}$ **6** $\dfrac{\sqrt{500}}{\sqrt{20}}$

    2 $\sqrt{\dfrac{1}{81}}$ **7** $\sqrt{3} \times \sqrt{12}$

    3 $\sqrt{6\tfrac{1}{4}}$ **8** $\sqrt{15} \times \sqrt{10} \times \sqrt{6}$

    4 $\tfrac{1}{2}$ of $\sqrt{52}$ **9** $\sqrt{125} - \sqrt{20}$

    5 $\dfrac{\sqrt{28}}{\sqrt{7}}$ **10** $\sqrt{5}\left(\sqrt{5} - 1\right)$

7. If $a = 8$ and $b = 50$, say whether the numbers represented by these expressions are rational or irrational.

    1 $\sqrt{a}$ **5** $\sqrt{5a}$ **9** $b^{\frac{1}{2}}$

    2 $\sqrt[3]{a}$ **6** $\sqrt{2b}$ **10** $(3a + 1)^{\frac{1}{2}}$

    3 $\sqrt{ab}$ **7** $\sqrt[3]{20b}$ **11** b^{0}

    4 $\sqrt{\tfrac{a}{b}}$ **8** a^{-1} **12** πab

8. Simplify these numbers, expressing them in the form $a\sqrt{b}$ or $a\sqrt{b} + c$.

    1 $\dfrac{1}{\sqrt{5}}$ **4** $\dfrac{8}{\sqrt{5} + 1}$

    2 $\dfrac{3}{\sqrt{6}}$ **5** $\dfrac{12}{\sqrt{6} - 2}$

    3 $\dfrac{8}{\sqrt{2}}$

Exercise 4.5   Applications

1. Work out the answers to these questions in your head, just writing down the answer.

    1 600×50 **5** 8×0.05 **8** $630 \div 90$

    2 70×0.2 **6** $4500 \div 50$ **9** $8.8 \div 0.8$

    3 0.8×0.6 **7** $33 \div 0.3$ **10** $0.3 \div 0.5$

    4 40×0.9

2. Divide 1720 by 0.8, without using your calculator.

Do not use your calculator, except for checking, in questions 3 to 11.

3.   What is the square root of 0.16 ?

4.   Simplify $0.1 \times 0.2 \times 0.3$.

5. 0.0035×8000

6.   Express $\frac{9}{250}$ as an exact decimal.

7.   Subtract 0.006 from 0.06.

8.   Find the exact value of $4.2752 \div 0.4$.

9.   Find the exact value of $\dfrac{1.4 \times 0.05}{0.07}$.

10.   What fraction, in its simplest form, is equivalent to 0.075 ?

11.   If $A = 5.14$, $B = 3.709$ and $C = 13.3$, find

   1 $A + B + C$ **2** $A \div 100$ **3** $10(C - A)$

12.   Express 9876.524 correct to
   1   the nearest whole number,
   2   2 decimal places,
   3   3 significant figures.

13.   How many packets of sweets, each containing 110 g, can be made up from $5\frac{1}{2}$ kg of sweets ?

14.   How many lengths of wood 0.4 m long can be cut from a piece 2.8 m long ?

15.   Two tourists, Alan and Bill, returned to England, each with 300 francs to change back into British money. When Alan changed his the rate was 12.0 francs to the £, and a week later when Bill changed his the rate was 12.5 francs to the £. Who got more British money, and how much more ?

16.   If a car travels 12 km on a litre of petrol, how much will petrol cost for a journey of 270 km, if the price is 60p per litre ?

17.   500 sheets of paper weigh 3 kg. What is the weight, in g, of 1 sheet ? The pile of sheets is 7 cm thick. What is the thickness, in mm, of 1 sheet ?

18. If $v^3 = \dfrac{64P}{wA}$, find the value of v, correct to 3 significant figures, when $P = 1450$, $w = 62.3$
and $A = 0.0105$.

19. A formula for the area of a triangle is $A = \sqrt{s(s-a)(s-b)(s-c)}$.
    If $a = 2.5$, $b = 3.2$ and $c = 4.1$,
    1   find the value of s, where $s = \frac{1}{2}(a + b + c)$,
    2   find the value of A.

20. Name a sensible metric unit for measuring or weighing
    1   the weight of a loaded lorry,
    2   the capacity of a car's fuel tank,
    3   the weight of a letter, to be sent by air-mail,
    4   the distance between two towns,
    5   the width of a piece of paper.

21. Tara says that it takes her 20 minutes to cycle to school.
    How accurately do you think she has stated this time ?
    Using your answer, what are the limits between which the true time lies ?

22. Find the reciprocals of the numbers from 30 to 40, writing them to 4 decimal places if
    they are not exact decimals.
    Say which of the numbers have reciprocals which
    1   are exact decimals,
    2   are decimals with 1 recurring figure,
    3   are decimals with 2 recurring figures,
    4   are decimals with 3 recurring figures,
    5   are decimals with more than 3 recurring figures.

23. Express in standard index form.
    1   15 000   2   364   3   0.000 952   4   0.5276   5   23.2

24. Find the values of
    1   1.86×10^3 4 $(8.64 \times 10^4) \div (4.32 \times 10^{-1})$
    2   7.65×10^{-3} 5 $\sqrt{8.1 \times 10^{-5}}$
    3   $(9.34 \times 10^{-2}) \times (1.35 \times 10^5)$

25. The Earth is approximately 93 million miles from the Sun. Taking 1 mile as equivalent to
    1.6 km, find this distance in km, to 2 significant figures, expressing your answer in
    standard form.

26. The weight of a litre of hydrogen is 0.0899 g. Find the weight of 1 cm^3 of hydrogen, expressing your answer in standard form.

27. From this list of irrational numbers,

$$\sqrt{3}, \quad 2+\sqrt{3}, \quad \sqrt{5}, \quad 5-\sqrt{5}, \quad \sqrt{10}, \quad 10+\sqrt{10}, \quad \sqrt{12},$$

give examples of two numbers
1 whose sum is irrational,
2 whose sum is rational,
3 whose product is irrational,
4 whose product is rational.

28. Write down two examples of

1 rational numbers between 2 and 4,
2 irrational numbers between 2 and 4.

29. 0.111213141516... is an example of a decimal which has a non-recurring pattern. Is it a rational or an irrational number?

30. Simplify

1 $\sqrt{\frac{49}{64}}$

2 $\sqrt{1\frac{7}{9}}$

3 $\frac{1}{3}$ of $\sqrt{18}$

4 $\frac{\sqrt{48}}{\sqrt{3}}$

5 $\sqrt{5} \times \sqrt{45}$

6 $\sqrt{6} \times \sqrt{2} \times \sqrt{12}$

7 $\sqrt{8} \times \sqrt{5} \times \sqrt{10}$

8 $\sqrt{98} + \sqrt{8} + \sqrt{2}$

9 $(\sqrt{2}+1)(\sqrt{2}-1)$

10 $\left(\frac{\sqrt{3}}{2}\right)^2 + \left(\frac{1}{2}\right)^2$

Practice test 4

1. Work out the answers to these questions in your head, just writing down the answers.

1 60×30
2 0.7×0.1
3 40×0.9
4 0.6×8
5 10×0.1

6 $4.2 \div 0.7$
7 $0.56 \div 0.08$
8 $270 \div 0.9$
9 $0.36 \div 0.6$
10 $10 \div 0.1$

2. Write down the reciprocal of 22
1 as a recurring decimal,
2 correct to 3 significant figures,
3 correct to 3 decimal places.

3. Using your calculator, find the value of $\sqrt[4]{\dfrac{360}{0.0738 \times 92.1^3}}$, giving the answer correct to 3 significant figures.

4. Find the value of n if

   1   $0.0064 = 6.4 \times 10^n$ 2 $3280 = 3.28 \times 10^n$

5. Work out $(9 \times 10^{-2}) \times (1.2 \times 10^3)$, and express your answer in standard index form.

6. Give limits between which these measurements must lie.

   1   A weight of 60 kg, weighed to the nearest 10 kg.
   2   A weight of 56 kg, weighed to the nearest kg.
   3   A capacity of 250 ml, measured to the nearest 10 ml.
   4   A length of 4.6 m, measured to the nearest 0.1 m.
   5   An amount of £700, given to the nearest £100.

7. Write these numbers in order of size, smallest first, and say which are rational and which are irrational.

   $1.\overset{..}{4}\overset{}{1}$, $\sqrt{2}$, 1.4142, 1.19^2, $\dfrac{9\pi}{20}$.

8. If the rates of exchange are as follows: £1 = 1.75 dollars, and £1 = 11.9 francs, how many francs are equivalent to 10 dollars?

PUZZLES

11. Copy this long division sum and fill in the missing figures.

$$
\begin{array}{r}
2\ * \\
*\,3\,\overline{)1\ 2\ 4\ *} \\
*\ 6 \\
\hline
3\ *\ * \\
3\ *\ * \\
\hline
\end{array}
$$

12. Down the corridor next to the school hall there are five classrooms, numbered from 1 to 5, and these are occupied by the five forms, 7A, 7B, 7C, 7D and 7E.
7A is not in room 1, 7B is not in room 5, 7C is not in room 1 or room 5.
7D is in a room with a lower number than 7B. 7C's room is next to 7B's room.
7E's room is not next to 7C's room. Which class is in room 1?

5 Statistical investigations

The topics in this chapter include:

- specifying and testing a hypothesis,
- designing and using a questionnaire,
- analysing results,
- using sampling to investigate a population,
- using diagrams, graphs or computer packages to analyse a set of complex data.

Statistics

Statistics involves numerical data.

Firstly, the data must be collected. Sometimes you carry out an investigation or experiment and collect data for yourself. Sometimes you can use data which someone else has collected. This includes data in government publications, newspapers, scientific textbooks, etc.

Secondly, the data is displayed in the form of a list, a table or a diagram.

Thirdly, it is studied, in order to make conclusions from it, often involving decisions for the future.

A statistical investigation

To carry out a statistical investigation, first of all decide what is the **aim** of the investigation. Then you can decide where to obtain the data you need, whether you will collect it for yourself or whether you will find it elsewhere.
If you are collecting data for yourself, you will probably need to make a tally table on which to record it.

When you have carried out the investigation, you should then display your information in an interesting way, so that other people can read about it. Make neat lists or tables, and include statistical diagrams.

Here are the kinds of diagrams you can use.

Bar charts, pie charts, pictograms.
For frequency distributions, bar-line graphs, histograms, frequency polygons. You may also need to draw a cumulative frequency graph.
For trends, straight-line graphs (time series graphs).
For correlation or lines of best fit you would draw scatter graphs.

From a set of data, you can find the 3 main averages, mean, median and mode.
You can find a measure of dispersion, either the range, the interquartile range or the standard deviation.

Using a computer program

Nowadays there are many types of spreadsheet programs which you can use to present and analyse your data. After you have entered your data, many programs produce a variety of diagrams to illustrate the data, and will work out averages and dispersion. This is very useful, especially if you have a large amount of data.

Collecting data

There are several ways in which you could collect data. Having collected it, present it in a list or a table, or in a statistical diagram. Then study it to see if you can find any interesting conclusions from it.

1   You can collect data from yourself, your friends or your family. You can conduct a survey in the street, getting data from the people there. You can collect data by observation, for example, making a traffic survey. You will probably do experiments in Science, or in other subjects, with data which can be analysed statistically.

2   You can find data from books, newspapers and other sources and use that.

Questionnaires

To conduct a survey amongst a group of people one way is to ask them to answer a questionnaire. You can either give them the questionnaire to fill in themselves or you can ask the questions and write down their answers.
Decide exactly what information you want and how you are planning to use the answers.
Keep the questionnaire as short as possible, and keep the questions short, clear and precise.
Avoid questions which people may not be willing to answer because they are embarrassing or offensive.

The best questions can be answered by categories, such as the ones below, where you can put a tick in one of the boxes.

Age

Under 20	
20–under 40	
40–under 60	
60 or over	

No	
Yes	
Don't know	

Strongly agree	
Agree	
Don't know/no opinion	
Disagree	
Strongly disagree	

'How long do you spend watching TV ?' This is a very vague question, and will produce equally vague answers, so you will find it difficult to analyse the data.

'How long did you spend watching TV yesterday ? Tick one of the following:'

Not at all	
Up to 1 hour	
Between 1 and 3 hours	
Between 3 and 5 hours	
Over 5 hours	

This is much more precise, and you have only to count the ticks in each category to have some useful data about viewing habits.

It is a good idea to try out your questionnaire on a few people first to see if it is clear enough and likely to give you the data you need, or whether it needs improving. This is called a **pilot survey**.

If you are asking members of the public for their views, you have not the resources, time or authority to make a proper sample. You will probably have to question people in the street or shopping area, and your sample will have to consist of people in that area at that time. (But a survey on where people shop could be biased if you select your sample from outside the largest supermarket in the area.) Try to make your sample representative by including people of different ages, and equal numbers of men and women. Be very polite when you approach people, and thank them afterwards for their help. Remember that some people will be in too much of a hurry to stop to talk to you. Before you do such a survey, discuss your plans with your teacher and with your parents.

Analysing a questionnaire

A hypothesis

A theory that you are putting to a test is called a **hypothesis**.
For example, you may wish to test people's opinion on a particular matter and your hypothesis would be that most people had a certain preference.
To test your hypothesis, you could question a sample of people and analyse the results.

Now, if you asked 100 people and 90 of them agreed with the preference, then you could consider that you have proved your hypothesis.
If only 30 agreed with it, then you would decide that you had not proved your hypothesis. The difficulty is knowing whether to say you have proved your hypothesis if only about 55 people out of 100 agreed with it. With a slightly different sample of people you could have got different results, so if the result is near 50–50 you cannot be sure that your hypothesis is proved. A statistician would have further tests to use in deciding when to accept a hypothesis, but as a rough rule, for a sample of 100, only accept the hypothesis when you get at least 60 people agreeing with it.

Multiple responses

In a more detailed questionnaire, people may be asked to put items in order of merit, order of preference, or some other order.
You have to decide how to analyse such results.

Example

Here 10 people, identified by the letters A to J, have put 5 drinks in order of preference.

$1 = $ 1st choice, $2 = $ 2nd choice, etc.

	A	B	C	D	E	F	G	H	I	J
Poppo	2	3	3	3	4	3	4	5	3	3
Quencho	4	2	4	1	2	1	5	1	2	2
Ribbo	3	5	5	5	5	5	2	3	5	4
Squasho	5	4	2	2	1	4	1	4	4	1
Tisso	1	1	1	4	3	2	3	2	1	5

How would you analyse these results ?

This is a complicated process and you might use one of several methods.

1st idea

You can see how many 1's there are for each product.

Drink	Number of 1st choices
Poppo	0
Quencho	3
Ribbo	0
Squasho	3
Tisso	4
	10

Tisso has 4 1's and this is the most popular.

However, only 4 out of 10 people voted for Tisso so you may think that this is not sufficient to say it is the best. You might have been more sure if more than half the people had voted for it.

So you might go on to another method.

2nd idea

Count the 1st and 2nd choices.

Drink	Number of 1st choices	Number of 2nd choices	Total 1st and 2nd choices
Poppo	0	1	1
Quencho	3	4	7
Ribbo	0	1	1
Squasho	3	2	5
Tisso	4	2	6
	10	10	20

It now looks as if Quencho is the most popular, using this way of analysing the results.

3rd idea

You may think that all the choices should be taken into consideration.

You can add up all the 'scores' for each drink from the 1st table of choices.
e.g. For Poppo, $2 + 3 + 3 + 3 + 4 + 3 + 4 + 5 + 3 + 3 = 33$
This gives a table like this:

Drink	Total of scores
Poppo	33
Quencho	24
Ribbo	42
Squasho	28
Tisso	23
	150 ←

Since each column adds up to 15, this should add up to 10×15, and is a useful check.

Since 1 is best and 5 is worst, it is the drink with the lowest total (not the highest) which is best, so using this method it seems that Tisso is the most popular, although Quencho is a close second. If you had asked people to give 5 marks for the best, 4 for the next best, and so on, or you had done this yourself when tabulating the results, then it would be the item with the highest total which would be considered the most popular.
You can change all the results in the table to marks in this way, and check this.
This method of scoring would be useful if, for instance, there were 10 products and you only asked for the 1st five to be put in order. After scores of 5, 4, 3, 2 and 1, the rest would be given marks of 0.

These methods have been suggested as possible ways in which you can come to a conclusion. Choose whichever way you want.
Perhaps you will invent your own rules to decide which item is best.

Sampling

When we need data about a certain population we often just take a sample.
e.g. If you wanted to find out the views of pupils in a school about a particular matter, you might not want to ask everyone, so you would select certain people and ask them.

If a manufacturer of electric light bulbs wanted to know how long his bulbs last, he could not test all of them or he would have no bulbs left to sell. He would just test a sample. Here the population is the whole batch of light bulbs. In statistics the word 'population' does not need to refer to people. It is used to describe the whole set of items which are involved, and a sample involves some of those items.

It is no use choosing a sample if it is biased, that means likely to give unfair results, which do not represent the results which apply to the whole population. For a school matter, you could not just ask your friends whose views are the same as yours. The light bulb manufacturer should not just test the bulbs produced by one particular machine, as bulbs made by other machines may not be of the same quality.
In a survey about poeple's incomes, names were chosen at random out of the telephone directory, and those people questioned. The sample was biased because people with low incomes are less likely to have telephones.

A random sample

The best kind of sample to take is a random sample. In this, every member of the population has the same chance of being chosen for the sample as every other member.
One way to select the members for the sample is to give each one a number, and then draw numbers out of a hat, or use random number tables or random numbers generated by a computer.

It is not always possible or easy to get a random sample so you may have to use other methods. For example, if you wanted the views of people in your town, you might just have to select your sample by asking people in the street.

The sample should be **large enough** to represent fairly all the varieties in the population.

The sample should **represent fairly**, in the right proportions, all categories in the population.

e.g. In a survey about a school matter which affects the whole school the sample should include all age groups and, if it is a mixed school, girls and boys.

A stratified sample

For this, the population is divided into different groups called strata (layers), and then samples are taken from each group, in numbers in proportion to the relative sizes of the groups. This method is particularly useful if the population is quite large.

In a school survey, pupils are already divided into groups called forms, classes or tutor groups. If there are roughly equal numbers in each tutor group then you could select a stratified sample by choosing two (or more) pupils from each group. These pupils could be chosen at random.

If you are doing a survey in the street, rather than just stopping people at random, you could choose a stratified sample by choosing equal numbers of men and women, and people of different ages.

The size of the sample

You would have to decide how many items or people you need in your sample. If there are 1000 pupils in a school, a 10% sample would use a sample of 100 pupils and a 5% sample would use a sample of 50 pupils. A smaller sample might not represent the views of the whole school, and a larger sample would make the data collection process take too long.

Systematic sampling

Another way to choose a sample is to list the population in some sort of order, for instance alphabetical order, and then take every 10th or 20th name on the list to form a 10% or 5% sample.
Pupils in a school are already listed in order on class registers. Put the registers in class order and use them as if the names were in one long list. Instead of always starting with the 10th name, choose a random number from 1 to 10 to start with, and then take every 10th name after that.

A survey of school leavers chose a sample by selecting those people whose birthdays were on the 5th, 15th or 25th of the month. This produced a 10% sample.

Exercise 5.1

1. Here are some questions which might be used in surveys.
    In each case, re-write the question, or the answer categories, so that the answers will be more useful for the survey.

    1 How much water do you think your household uses ?

    | More than average | |
    | About average | |
    | Less that average | |

    (A survey about water meters.)

2   How often do you drink our product ?

Daily	
Weekly	
Monthly	
Other (please specify)	

(A health-food drink.)

3   Which figure best describes your annual household income ?

Less than £25 000	
£25 001–£30 000	
£30 001–£40 000	
£40 001–£50 000	
More than £50 000	

(A holiday survey given to a group of friends.)

4   How many times do you eat out at restaurants ?

Seldom/never	
Once a month	
2–4 times a month	
More than 4 times a month	

(Market research survey.)

5   Do you read your newspaper chiefly for:

General news	
Sport	
TV/Entertainment	
Finance/business	

(Market research survey.)

2.   Imagine that you are running a pre-school playgroup.
Design a questionnaire which you could ask the parents of the children to fill in, to give you their views on how well the playgroup meets their needs and those of their children.
(Include about 4 to 8 questions.)

3.   Certain community leaders thought that there ought to be a swimming pool and other
      community amenities in the local area. They sent questionnaires to 500 households.
      One question was: Do you think a local swimming pool is needed ?

Highly desirable	
Desirable	
Not needed	

      Replies were received from 160 households and of these
      72 ticked 'Highly desirable',
      20 ticked 'Desirable',
      63 ticked 'Not needed',
      15 did not answer that question.

      On the basis of these replies, do you think that the community leaders should approach
      the Council saying that there is a good local demand for a swimming pool ?

Questions 4 to 8
Here are some (fictitious) results in which people A, B, C, ... have put some products P, Q,
R, ... in order of preference.
1 = 1st choice, 2 = 2nd choice, etc.

If these were the results of surveys that you had carried out, analyse them and write down
your conclusions, including saying which product you would decide is the most popular.

(Choose for yourself the methods you will use. There are no definite correct answers although
some answers may be more acceptable than others.)

4.

	Person				
Product	A	B	C	D	E
P	4	3	2	3	1
Q	3	1	1	4	4
R	2	4	4	1	3
S	1	2	3	2	2

5.

	Person				
Product	A	B	C	D	E
P	1	1	3	3	2
Q	3	2	1	2	1
R	2	3	2	1	3

6.

	Person					
Product	A	B	C	D	E	F
P	1	3	1	2	4	2
Q	2	1	2	4	3	4
R	4	2	4	1	2	1
S	3	4	3	3	1	3

7.

	Person				
Product	A	B	C	D	E
P	3	2		1	1
Q			1		2
R				2	3
S	2	3	2		
T	1	1	3	3	

(People only asked for 1st 3 preferences.)

8.

	Person							
Product	A	B	C	D	E	F	G	H
P		1		4	2		1	1
Q	2	4		1	3	1		2
R	1		1	2		4	3	3
S		3	2		4		2	
T	4	2	3			3		
U	3		4	3	1	2	4	4

(People only asked for 1st 4 preferences.)

9.   Give reasons why you may not achieve a random sample of students in your school or college if you choose your sample by asking students in the dining room or canteen, in the dinner hour.

10.   The P.E. teacher in a mixed 6th form college of 600 students wants to find out the relative popularity of various sporting activities, e.g. soccer, rugby, hockey, netball, swimming, badminton, etc.
To get the opinions of students she decides to ask a sample of 100 students.
Describe 4 different methods of choosing the sample and for each method state any bias which could occur.
Say which you think is the best method.

Exercise 5.2 Applications

1. Imagine that you are the manager of a seaside caravan park.
   Design a questionnaire which you could ask your customers to fill in, to give you some
   idea of whether the amenities on the site are satisfactory, and whether certain extra ones
   would be welcomed.

2. The owners of a local radio station wish to obtain information on any improvements that
   could be made to increase the listening figures. They decide to send out a questionnaire,
   asking the following questions:

   1 What is your name ?
   2 Do you enjoy listening to our station ?
   3 What type of programme do you enjoy most ?
   4 Do you listen in the mornings ?
   5 Do you like quizzes and competitions ?
   6 What kind of work do you do ?
   7 How much do you earn ?

   Are the questions suitable ? Where necessary, replace them by more useful ones,
   including categories of answers.

3. You are trying to test whether people prefer a certain brand of a product rather than any
   other brand.
   You ask a sample of people whether they prefer this brand.

   'Do you like this brand in preference to other brands ?'

	Number of replies
Strongly prefer	52
Prefer	81
Don't know	21
Prefer some other brand	67

   On the basis of these results, assuming that the sample was correctly chosen, would you
   say that this brand is preferred ?

4. A survey was made to find out how workers in a certain firm travelled to work (by car,
   bus, walking, etc). The sample was chosen by stopping workers on their way into work in
   the road leading from the nearest bus stop.
   Explain why this sample was likely to be unsatisfactory, and suggest how a more
   satisfactory sample could be chosen.

Questions 5 to 8

Here are the results of some (fictitious) surveys in which people were given a list of activities they could take part in, and they were asked to give their 1st 3 choices for what they wanted to do. Here are the results.

If these were surveys that you had carried out, analyse the results and write down your conclusions, including saying which one of the activities you would choose as being the one most people wanted to do.

5.

Activity	Number putting it		
	1st	2nd	3rd
P	11	7	10
Q	11	8	8
R	6	11	12
S	9	10	8
T	8	9	7

6.

Activity	Number putting it		
	1st	2nd	3rd
P	8	7	6
Q	7	7	14
R	9	9	7
S	8	9	5

7.

Activity	Number putting it		
	1st	2nd	3rd
P	2	5	7
Q	6	8	8
R	8	7	4
S	4	3	3
T	5	2	3
U	5	5	5

8.

Activity	Number putting it		
	1st	2nd	3rd
P	7	8	5
Q	7	3	10
R	6	9	5

9. In a certain firm there were 4 workshops, with 175 workers in workshop A, 50 in
    workshop B, 250 in workshop C and 125 in workshop D. In each workshop, 40% of the
    workers were men and 60% were women.
    The management decided to consult the workers about a proposal to change the hours of
    work, and decided to select a 10% sample to interview.
    Explain how they could choose the sample so that men and women and workers from all
    the workshops were fairly represented.

10. It is said that 'Children spend too much time watching television'.
    To test this hypothesis, imagine you are going to carry out a survey among Year 7 pupils
    in a school. There are 5 forms with 30 pupils in each, including equal numbers of boys
    and girls.

    1   State 2 different ways in which you could select a 10% sample.
    2   Design a questionnaire which you could use to find out how much television the
        children watch.
    3   Design a questionnaire which you could use to get opinions from adults or your own
        age-group on what should be regarded as 'too much time' in the above statement.

11. **A statistical investigation**
    Choose a topic that interests you, or has some practical purpose, and carry out an
    investigation.
    First of all, decide what is the **aim** of the investigation. It is no use spending time
    collecting data without knowing whether it will be of any use.
    You need not collect the data for yourself. You may use data that someone has already
    collected, or you may use data from books, magazines, etc.

    Here are some brief notes which may give you ideas for choosing what to do.

    1   Investigations into heights of people, shoe sizes, heights of teenagers compared with
        parents' heights, etc.

    2   Financial matters, e.g. children's spending money, family budgets, money spent on
        leisure, transport, etc.

    3   Television, e.g. amount of time devoted to different kinds of programmes, comparing
        different channels. Time taken by advertising, kinds of advertising.
        Time people spend watching TV or videos. Favourite types of programme.
        Percentage of people who have satellite or cable television.

    4   Sports, e.g. football results, goals scored, differences between home and away
        matches, comparisons with other years. Similar analysis of other sports.
        Popularity of various sports by people taking part, by spectators or by watching them
        on television.

    5   Leisure interests, e.g. costs of a hobby, time needed for it.

6   Holidays, e.g. destinations, type, cost, length of time, method of travel.

7   Traffic, e.g. surveys, number of people in each car. Ages of cars. Traffic flow at different times. Distances travelled. Use of public transport or taxis. Travel costs.

8   School or college issues, e.g. any plans to alter existing arrangements for uniform, meals, homework. Survey of attendance and punctuality. Distances from homes to school. Examination results.

9   Local issues, e.g. whether people want a new by-pass built and their views for and against. Council spending. Ages of local population.

10   Employment, e.g. types of work and numbers of jobs available locally. Pay and prospects.

11   National issues, e.g. whether people support Government proposals on some matter and their views for or against.

12   Health issues, e.g. healthy eating, types of exercise.

13   International problems such as third world famine. Ecological issues.

14   Work linked with other school or college subjects such as experiments in Biology and other Sciences, links with Geography fieldwork, plans in technology.

Practice test 5

1.   Here is a question included in a holiday survey, to be answered by the father who is holidaying with his family.
     Please rate the facilities in the hotel (e.g. bar, lounge, etc.).

Excellent	
Good	
Average	
Poor	

     Give reasons why it may be difficult to answer this question fairly.

2.   Imagine that you are the cook at an adventure holiday centre for teenagers.
     Design a questionnaire which you could give to a group of teenagers at the end of their stay, to see whether the meals you are providing are satisfactory, or whether any improvements should be made.
     (Include about 4 to 8 questions.)

     [Turn over]

3.   Here are the results of a (fictitious) survey in which people were given a list of activities they could take part in, and they were asked to give their 1st 3 choices for what they wanted to do. Here are the results.
      Analyse the results of the survey and write down your conclusions, including saying which one of the activities you would choose as being the one most people wanted to do.

Activity	Number putting it		
	1st	2nd	3rd
P	6	7	8
Q	6	11	5
R	8	7	10
S	10	7	10
T	10	8	7

4.   An interviewer carried out a door-to-door survey one week, on each morning from Monday to Friday, to ask for people's views on whether mothers with young children should go out to work.
      Explain why the sample is likely to be biased.

5.   A survey is to be made in a school about the pupils' views on changing the school uniform. The school has 180 pupils in each of 5 year groups with 6 forms in each year group. There are roughly equal numbers of boys and girls in each form.
      The method of collecting data is to issue a questionnaire to a 10% sample of pupils.
      Explain 3 different methods for obtaining the sample, and say which method you would prefer to be used.

PUZZLES

13.   How many triangles are there in this figure ?

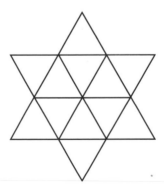

14. Here is the final table in the local league. Every team has played every other team once. What was the score in the match between the Allsorts and the Dribblers ?

	played	won	drawn	lost	goals for	goals against	points
Allsorts	3	3	0	0	4	0	6
Buskers	3	1	1	1	4	4	3
Cobblers	3	0	2	1	3	4	2
Dribblers	3	0	1	2	0	3	1

15. How many squares are there in this figure, and how many contain the dot ?

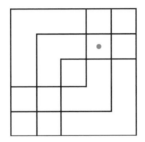

16. Start from *, going horizontally or vertically (not diagonally), and spell out the names of 7 plane figures.

T	A	N	T	R	I	X	A
N	G	O	R	T	A	E	G
E	G	O	A	E	N	H	O
P	R	L	P	L	G	M	N
M	A	E	E	Z	I	U	Q
A	L	L	A	R	E	A	U
R	A	*P	L	S	T	D	R
E	R	A	U	Q	A	L	I

17. Seasonal greetings. On graph paper, label the x-axis from 0 to 12 and the y-axis from 0 to 8, using the same scale on both axes. Mark these points. Join each point to the next one with a straight line, except where there is a cross after the point.
(5, 6)   (4, 6)   (4, 8)   (5, 8)×   (8, 6)   (8, 8)   (8.8, 8)   (9, 7.8)
(9, 7.2)   (8.8, 7)   (8, 7)   (9, 6)×   (1, 2)   (3, 4)×   (1, 6)   (1, 8)
(2, 7)   (3, 8)   (3, 6)×   (11, 7)   (12, 8)×   (6, 6)   (6, 8)   (6.8, 8)
(7, 7.8)   (7, 7.2)   (6.8, 7)   (6, 7)   (7, 6)×   (10, 8)   (11, 7)   (11, 6)×
(4, 7)   (4.8, 7)×   (3, 2)   (1, 4)×
Complete the diagram.

Miscellaneous Section A

Exercise A1   Revision

1. 35 packets of sweets cost £6.30. What will be the cost of 42 similar packets ?

2. If $a = \frac{1}{2}$, $b = \frac{1}{4}$ and $c = 0$, find the values of

    1 $ab + 2bc$

    2 $2b^2 + a^3$

    3 $3c(a + b)$

    4 $\dfrac{2a + 3b + 4c}{2a - b}$

3. $ABCD$ is a square and CDE is an equilateral triangle. Find the sizes of

    1 $\angle ADE$,
    2 $\angle AED$,
    3 $\angle AEC$.

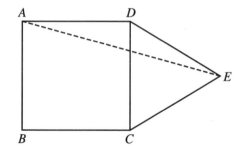

4. The internal dimensions of the base of a rectangular tank are 2 m by 1 m and it can contain water to a depth of 80 cm. How long will it take to fill the tank by means of an inlet pipe delivering water at the rate of 50 litres per minute ?

5. This pie chart represents the expenses of a catering firm. The total expenses were £54 000. If the angles at the centre of each sector were Wages, 150°; Food, 120°; Fuel, 40°; Extras, 50°; find the cost of each item.
    In the following year the cost of food rose by 6%, fuel increased by 10% and wages increased by 8%.
    The cost of the extras decreased by 10%.
    Find the new total cost.

6. On a stretch of straight coastline there is a coastguard station at A. Their rescue boats patrol a region within 10 km of the coast, and there is a lookout at the station who can see a distance of 15 km through a telescope.
    Using a scale 1 cm to 2 km, copy the diagram and mark in
    (1) the boundary of the patrolled region, and
    (2) the boundary of the region at sea that the lookout can see.
    Shade the region of the sea which is not patrolled, but is visible to the lookout.

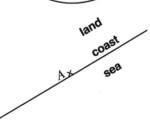

7. $C = \dfrac{1000P}{V}$, where P is power in kilowatts, V is voltage in volts, C is current in amps.

If the local voltage is 240 volts, what is the current for a 2 kW fire, to the nearest amp ?

8. Find the values of

    1 $1\frac{3}{4} + 4\frac{5}{6}$ **3** $2\frac{2}{3} \times 2\frac{1}{4} \times \frac{5}{6}$ **5** $(3\frac{1}{4} + 1\frac{1}{3}) \times 1\frac{1}{5}$

    2 $3\frac{1}{10} - 2\frac{3}{5}$ **4** $2\frac{1}{12} \div 1\frac{1}{4}$

9. Triangle ABC is equilateral. D is a point on AC such that $AD : DC = 3 : 1$. Triangle ADE is equilateral. Name a triangle congruent to $\triangle\,ACE$. Which line is equal to CE ?

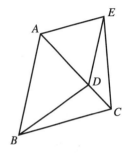

10. If 1 metre $= 1.094$ yards, find the number of km^2 in a square mile, correct to 3 significant figures. (1 mile $= 1760$ yards.)

11. Rearrange these formulae to give x in terms of the other letters.

    1 $y = mx + c$
    2 $y = 2\sqrt{x} - 3$
    3 $ax = b - cx$
    4 $y = x^2 + 4$, where x is positive.

12. If O is the origin and $\overrightarrow{OA} = \begin{pmatrix} 3 \\ 2 \end{pmatrix}$, $\overrightarrow{OB} = \begin{pmatrix} 5 \\ 6 \end{pmatrix}$, $\overrightarrow{OC} = \begin{pmatrix} 4 \\ -4 \end{pmatrix}$, $\overrightarrow{OD} = \begin{pmatrix} 2 \\ -8 \end{pmatrix}$, find $\overrightarrow{AB}$, *omit* $\overrightarrow{BC}$, $\overrightarrow{AD}$, $\overrightarrow{DC}$.
    What kind of quadrilateral is $ABCD$?

13. The number of insects in a colony doubles each week. If there were 100 insects initially, how many would there be after 5 weeks ?

14. **1** If 1 franc is worth p pence, how many pence will f francs be worth ?
    2 If x kg of potatoes are bought for y pence, what is the price per kg ?
    3 The sum of two numbers is 12. One of them is x. What is the other ? What is their product ?
    4 Elaine is 3 years younger than Eric. If Eric is x years old, how old will Elaine be next year ?
    5 A man earned £x per month and his wife earned £y per week. What were their total earnings in a year ?

15.   A man buys a painting as an investment. He pays £2000 for it and estimates that its value should increase by 10% each year. He plans to sell it in 3 years time. How much profit does he expect to gain on this investment ?

Exercise A2   Revision

1.   A floor 12 m long and 7.5 m wide is to be covered by tiles 30 cm square. How many tiles will be needed ?

2.   The angles of a quadrilateral, in order, are $(x + 5)°$, $(x - 25)°$, $(2x - 95)°$ and $(175 - x)°$. Find the value of x. What sort of quadrilateral is it ?

3.   The air service between London and Kereva, together with connecting train services to Veefield, are given in a time-table as follows:

London dep.	23.00	10.20	11.20	15.25	16.55
Kereva airport arr.	00.30	11.40	12.50	16.45	18.10
Kereva station dep.	04.30	13.31	15.17	17.55	20.01
Veefield arr.	06.13	14.43	16.25	19.03	21.09

   1   What is the time of departure from London of the fastest service to Kereva ?
   2   What is the time taken for the slowest journey from London to Veefield ?
   3   The single fare from London to Kereva is £190, and the distance is 760 km. How much is the cost per km ?
   4   From Kereva to Veefield is 84 km. What is the average speed of the 13.31 train ?

4.   1   What is the bearing of B from A ?
     2   What is the bearing of C from B ?
     3   What is the bearing of B from C ?

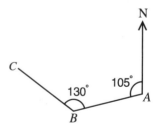

5.   1   Express 96 in its prime factors.
     2   A number expressed in its prime factors is $2^6 \times 3^4 \times 5^2$. What is the square root of this number ?
     3   Which numbers between 40 and 50 are prime ?

6. A group of 6 children held a money-raising event and raised £90, which they decided to split between 2 charities, X and Y.
They each wrote down the amounts they wanted to send to each, (in £'s).

Child	Adam	Ben	Claire	Donna	Edward	Farida
To charity X	50	85	20			
To charity Y	40	5		55		

Edward wanted to send equal amounts to each charity. Farida wanted to send twice as much to charity X as to charity Y.
Copy and complete the table.
Plot the data on a scatter diagram with charity X on the horizontal axis and charity Y on the vertical axis.
The children found the mean of the amounts they wished to send to X, and this was the money they sent, with the rest going to Y. Draw a line on your graph and represent these amounts by a point on the line. How much did each charity receive ?

7. If $y = \dfrac{16}{x} - x$, for what values of x is $y = 0$?

8. Simplify, without using your calculator,

   1 5.32×100 **4** $55 \div 0.11$

   2 0.07×0.5

   3 $2.8 \div 70$ **5** $\dfrac{6.3 \times 0.8}{0.56}$

9. In $\triangle ABC$, with $AB = AC$, AD is drawn perpendicular to BC.
By using congruent triangles, prove that

   1 $\angle B = \angle C$,

   2 D is the mid-point of BC.

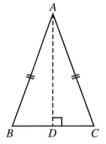

10. A plumber does three repair jobs as follows:– the first from 9.35 am to 11.15 am, the second from 11.45 am to 12.50 pm and the third from 2.05 pm to 3.50 pm. Find the average time taken for a job.

11. Imagine that you have decided to carry out a survey among Year 11 pupils in a school, to find out their views on some school matter. There are 4 forms with 30 pupils in each, including equal numbers of boys and girls.
State 3 different ways in which you could select a 10% sample. Mention any advantages or disadvantages of each method.

12.   1   If $s = ut + \frac{1}{2} ft^2$, what is the value of s when $u = 9, f = 10, t = 4$?

      2   If $I = \dfrac{PRT}{100}$, what is the value of I when $P = 750, R = 8, T = 4$?

      3   If $g = \dfrac{v - u}{t}$, find t when $v = 90, u = 20$ and $g = 10$.

      4   If $S = 90(2n - 4)$, find n when $S = 720$.

      5   If $a = \dfrac{b(100 + c)}{100 - c}$, find b when $a = 9$ and $c = 20$.

13.   Find the size of angle a.

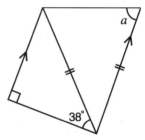

14.   Round a bend on a railway track of given radius the height to which the outer rail is raised above the inner rail varies as the square of the maximum speed permitted. When the permitted speed was 32 km/h the outer rail was raised 3.2 cm. What height should it have been raised for a maximum permitted speed of 40 km/h?

15.   This diagram shows the geometrical illustration of $(3x + 2)^2$.
      Total area $= (3x + 2) \times (3x + 2) = (3x + 2)^2$
      4 separate areas $= 9x^2 + 6x + 6x + 4$
      $\qquad\qquad\qquad = 9x^2 + 12x + 4$
      So $(3x + 2)^2 = 9x^2 + 12x + 4$

      Illustrate geometrically these identities.
      1   $x(x + y) = x^2 + xy$
      2   $(x + 4)(2x + 1) = 2x^2 + 9x + 4$
      3   $(2x + y)(x + 2y) = 2x^2 + 5xy + 2y^2$
      4   $(2x + 5)^2 = 4x^2 + 20x + 25$
      5   $(x + 3y)^2 = x^2 + 6xy + 9y^2$

PUZZLES

18.   A weighty problem. Which would you rather have, half a tonne of 10 pence coins or a tonne of 5 pence coins?

19.   An equilateral triangle and a regular hexagon have equal perimeters. If the triangle has an area of 4 cm^2, what is the area of the hexagon?

To the student : 2

Activities

As part of your Mathematics course, you should choose and make use of knowledge, skills and understanding of Mathematics in practical tasks, in real-life problems and to investigate within Mathematics itself.

You may be tested on this section by doing practical work during your course, or you may be tested by taking an extra examination paper which includes suitable practical tasks.

Some suggestions are given here for activities. If you are being tested by coursework, you should discuss with your teacher the sort of activities which will be acceptable. As well as the activities suggested here, you may gain ideas from other sources. There may be cross-curricular activities, school or locally-based projects, national or international current affairs which may suggest suitable investigations. You can also get ideas from other textbooks, library books, worksheets, etc.

If you are being tested in an extra examination paper you should use some of the activities here for practice in doing the investigational type of questions.

The organisation of an activity

First of all, decide what is to be the **aim** of the activity or investigation, and write this down. Decide how much time you have available for it, and then make a detailed plan of what you are actually going to do.
Decide where you are going to find any further information you need. Sources can include library books, newspapers, magazines, or asking other people.
Carry out the activity. Work methodically and check information and results. Write a logical account of your work. Give reasons for any choices made. Examine and comment on any results and justify any solutions.
You may choose to present your work in a booklet, on a poster or by another form of display, including drawings or photographs.
After doing an activity you may be able to extend your investigations and make further discoveries. (See the examples on page 225.)

Exercise A3 Activities

1. **A holiday abroad**

   Plan a holiday abroad for your family, or for you and your friends. Decide on the type of holiday you want and how much you want to spend on it. Include details of travel, destination, plans and costs.

2. **Banking**

   Many people have a bank account nowadays. Many firms pay wages directly into employees' bank accounts as this is safer and quicker than paying by cash.
   Find out from the main banks in your district full details of how to open an account and how to manage it.

3. **Moebius bands**

   These are long strips of paper glued together at the ends to form a loop. Some of the strips have a twist, or several twists, put in them before they are glued. Make one each with 0 twists, 1 twist, 2 twists, etc. For each loop, investigate whether it is one-sided or two-sided, and how many edges it has. Continue your investigations by seeing what happens when you cut each strip lengthwise down a centre line. It is interesting to try to predict the result in advance. Investigate sides and edges again, and the lengths of the new strips in comparison with the original. Finally, make new strips which you can cut lengthways by a cut which is $\frac{1}{3}$ of the width across. Investigate the results.

   Moebius was a mathematician who lived in the 19th century. Can you find out anything about him ?

4. **A guess-the-number trick**

   Ask a friend to:
   (1) Write down a 4-digit number, e.g. 7291,
   (2) then multiply it by 100,
   (3) and subtract the original number;
   (4) then add up the figures of the answer.
   $\qquad (7 + 2 + 1 + 8 + 0 + 9 = \ldots)$

   $$
   \begin{array}{r}
   729100 \\
   -\quad 7291 \\
   \hline
   721809 \\
   \hline
   \end{array}
   $$

   Now say you can guess the total, if you are allowed 3 guesses.
   What numbers must you use for your 3 guesses ?

5. **Inconsistencies in proofs**

Find the mistake in each of these proofs.

1 **To prove that 1 equals 2**

Let $x = y$
Then multiply both sides by x.
$x^2 = xy$
Subtract y^2 from both sides.
$x^2 - y^2 = xy - y^2$
Factorise both sides.
So $(x + y)(x - y) = y(x - y)$
Divide both sides by $x - y$.
$x + y = y$
Let $x = 1$, then $y = 1$ also.
$1 + 1 = 1$
i.e. $2 = 1$

2 **To prove that all triangles are isosceles**

Let $\triangle ABC$ be any triangle.
Let K be the point where the bisector of
$\angle A$ meets the perpendicular bisector of BC.
M is the mid-point of BC.
Perpendiculars from K meet AB at L and
AC at N.

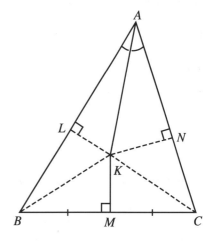

Proof

$\triangle ALK \equiv \triangle ANK$ (AAS)
So $AL = AN$ and $LK = NK$

$\triangle BKM \equiv \triangle CKM$ (SAS)
So $BK = CK$

$\triangle BLK \equiv \triangle CNK$ (RHS)
So $BL = CN$

Then $AL + BL = AN + CN$
i.e. $AB = AC$
$\triangle ABC$ is isosceles.

6. **Magic squares**

Here is a 4 by 4 magic square, used by the German artist Albrecht Durer in an engraving 'Melancholia' to show the date, 1514.

16	3	2	13
5	10	11	8
9	6	7	12
4	15	14	1

What are the totals of each row, each column and the two main diagonals ?

Make a 3 by 3 magic square using the numbers 1 to 9.

If a 5 by 5 magic square uses numbers 1 to 25, what is the number to which all rows and columns should add up ?

Try to find a general formula for the totals of rows and columns for an n by n magic square using numbers 1 to n^2.

One way of constructing a magic square with an odd number of rows or columns is:
(1) Put 1 in the middle of the top row.
(2) Put each following number above and to the right of the preceding number. If this is above the top row go to the bottom row and if it is to the right of the right-hand column go to the left-hand column.

The 1st 5 numbers are shown.

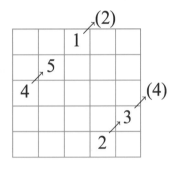

(3) If a number cannot be placed because its square has already been filled (as 6 cannot be placed because 1 is there), put the number below the last number written. (Thus put 6 below 5 and continue as before.)

Copy and complete this magic square according to this method.
Check that the rows, columns and main diagonals all add up to the same number.

Make a 7 by 7 magic square using the same method.

Here is an 8 by 8 magic square.
Check that the rows, columns and main diagonals
all add up to the same number.

7	53	41	27	2	52	48	30
12	58	38	24	13	63	35	17
51	1	29	47	54	8	28	42
64	14	18	36	57	11	23	37
25	43	55	5	32	46	50	4
22	40	60	10	19	33	61	15
45	31	3	49	44	26	6	56
34	20	16	62	39	21	9	59

What happens if you replace each number by
its square ?

Look for other patterns in the square.
For instance, copy the square just writing in
the odd numbers and leaving the other squares
blank, or just writing in the numbers 1 to 32
and leaving the other squares blank.

7. **Motoring**

How much does it cost to run a car (or, if you prefer, a motor bike) ?
Before buying a car (or a motor bike) you should estimate how much it will cost you.
Make a list of all the necessary expenses and find the total annual cost, and hence the
weekly cost.

8. **Cardioids and other designs from circles**

Draw a circle and divide the circumference into 72 equals parts. (If you choose a radius
just larger than that of your protractor you can mark off points every 5° along the
protractor edge.)
Number the points from 1 to 72 in order.
Join 1 to 2, 2 to 4, 3 to 6, 4 to 8, and so on, with straight lines. After joining 36 to 72
imagine the numbering continues past 72, or continue numbering, so that the point
numbered 2 is also number 74. Continue joining 37 to 74, 38 to 76, etc. Number 72 will
join to 144, which is the same point, so just make a dot there.

You can investigage similar ideas by joining 1 to 3, 2 to 6, 3 to 9 etc., then 1 to 4, and so
on. You can also number points in a positive direction and a negative direction and join
1 to −2, 2 to −4, etc.

The curves in the first group are called epicycloids.
The one joining k to $2k$ is a cardioid, and the one joining k to $3k$ is a nephroid.
The second group, joining k to $-2k$, k to $-3k$, etc. are called hypocycloids. For these,
do not draw the circle, only mark the points, and manage without numbering them.
Draw another concentric circle with a radius 3 cm larger. When you join 2 points extend
the line in both directions until it meets the outer circle.

6 Lengths, areas and volumes

The topics in this chapter include:

- using Pythagoras' theorem,
- calculating distances in solid figures, using plane sections,
- length, area and volume calculations,
- calculating lengths of arcs and areas of sectors, surface areas of cylinders and volumes of cones and spheres,
- distinguishing between formulae by considering dimensions.

A theorem is a mathematical statement which can be proved to be true.

Pythagoras' theorem

Pythagoras' theorem states that:

In a right-angled triangle, the area of the square on the hypotenuse is equal to the sum of the areas of the squares on the other two sides.

$$a^2 = b^2 + c^2$$

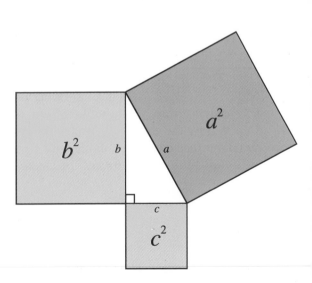

Here, because it is simpler, we have labelled the sides, using small letters, instead of labelling the vertices of the triangle.

a^2 means the area of the square with side a, and in this diagram, side a is the hypotenuse (the side opposite to the right angle).
b^2 means the area of the square with side b.
c^2 means the area of the square with side c.

Although the theorem is about areas of squares on the sides of the triangles, we use it mainly for calculating lengths of sides of right-angled triangles.

Examples

1 To find a

$$a^2 = b^2 + c^2$$

$$= 8^2 + 5^2 \quad (a \text{ in cm})$$

$$= 64 + 25 = 89$$

$$a = \sqrt{89} \text{ cm}$$

$$= 9.4 \text{ cm, to the nearest mm.}$$

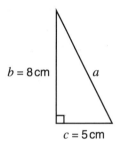

You can find the square root using your calculator. Since you know that $9^2 = 81$ and $10^2 = 100$, you know that $\sqrt{89}$ is a number between 9 and 10, so you can make a rough check of your answer.

(If you do not have to set down your working, you can do the whole calculation in one step on your calculator.
Press $8 \boxed{x^2} \boxed{+} 5 \boxed{x^2} \boxed{=} \boxed{\sqrt{}}$ and you will get 9.43 ...)

We can use the result of Pythagoras' theorem to find the length of one of the other sides.

2 Find b.

Notice that c is the hypotenuse.

$$c^2 = a^2 + b^2$$

$$30^2 = 10^2 + b^2 \quad (b \text{ in cm})$$

$$900 = 100 + b^2$$

$$b^2 = 800$$

$$b = \sqrt{800} \text{ cm}$$

$$= 28.3 \text{ cm, to the nearest mm.}$$

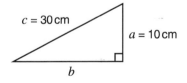

Triangle ABC

A triangle can have the vertices labelled by capital letters, as usual.
In this triangle, BC is the hypotenuse.

$$BC^2 = AB^2 + AC^2$$

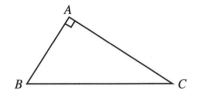

Example

3   If, in this triangle, $AB = 2.6$ cm and $BC = 3.5$ cm, calculate AC.

Notice that the hypotenuse is BC.

$$BC^2 = AB^2 + AC^2$$

$$3.5^2 = 2.6^2 + AC^2 \quad (AC \text{ in cm})$$

$$12.25 = 6.76 + AC^2$$

$$AC^2 = 5.49$$

$$AC = \sqrt{5.49} \text{ cm}$$

$$= 2.3 \text{ cm, to the nearest mm.}$$

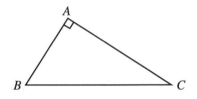

If we want to use small letters for sides, we use
a for the side opposite $\angle A$ (the side BC),
b for the side opposite $\angle B$ (the side AC), and
c for the side opposite $\angle C$ (the side AB).

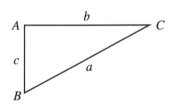

There are certain groups of numbers which give exact answers, and it is useful to learn the ones which involve small numbers.

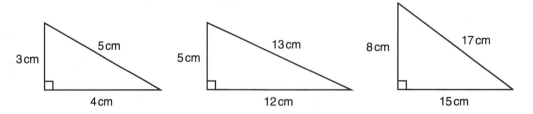

There are many others, including multiples of these numbers such as 6, 8, 10;   10, 24, 26;
30, 40, 50;   ...

Using Pythagoras' theorem in a solid figure

4 The cuboid $ABCDEFGH$ has $AB = 12$ cm, $BC = 9$ cm and $CG = 8$ cm.
Calculate the length of the diagonal line from A to G.

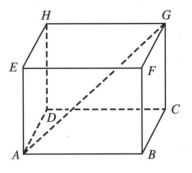

The base is a rectangle and AC can be found using $\triangle ABC$ and Pythagoras' theorem.

$AC^2 = AB^2 + BC^2$

$\qquad = 12^2 + 9^2 \quad (AC \text{ in cm})$

$\qquad = 225$

$AC = 15$ cm

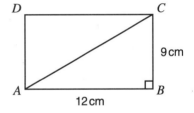

The plane section $ACGE$ is a rectangle.
(Since CG is perpendicular to BC and to DC it is perpendicular to all lines on the base, including AC.)

AG can be found using $\triangle ACG$ and Pythagoras' theorem.

$AG^2 = AC^2 + CG^2$

$\qquad = 15^2 + 8^2 \quad (AG \text{ in cm})$

$\qquad = 289$

$AG = 17$ cm

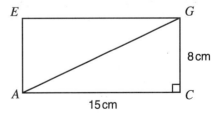

Exercise 6.1

Give answers which are not exact correct to the nearest mm.

1. Find the hypotenuse, a, in these triangles.

    1 $b = 5$ cm, $c = 10$ cm
    2 $b = 6$ cm, $c = 8$ cm
    3 $b = 1$ cm, $c = 2$ cm
    4 $b = 7$ cm, $c = 4$ cm
    5 $b = \sqrt{7}$ cm, $c = 3$ cm

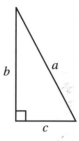

2. Find the third side in these triangles.

    1 $b = 8$ cm, $a = 17$ cm
    2 $b = 6$ cm, $a = 9$ cm
    3 $c = 24$ cm, $a = 25$ cm
    4 $c = 5$ cm, $a = 6$ cm
    5 $c = 7$ cm, $a = 11$ cm

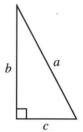

3. Find the lengths of sides x and y.

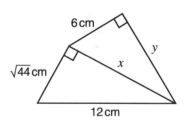

4. Find the lengths of

    1 AB,
    2 BC,
    3 AC.

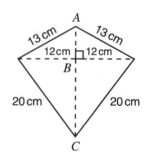

5. Find the lengths of

    1 BD,
    2 BC,
    3 AC.

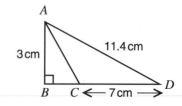

6.   A cylindrical tin has radius 7 cm and height 48 cm. What is the length of the longest stick
     which will just fit into the tin ?

7.   In this cuboid find

     1   the length of AC,
     2   the length of AD.

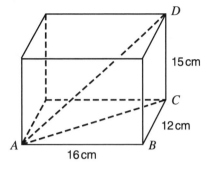

Perimeters

The perimeter of a plane figure is the total length of the edges.

> The perimeter of a rectangle $= 2 \times$ (length $+$ breadth)
> $$= 2(l+b)$$

The perimeter of a circle is called the circumference.

> Circumference $= \pi \times$ diameter $= 2 \times \pi \times$ radius
> $$C = \pi d$$
> $$C = 2\pi r$$

An arc of a circle

The length of an arc where the angle is $\theta°$
is $\dfrac{\theta}{360}$ of the circumference.

> Length of arc $= \dfrac{\theta}{360} \times 2\pi r$

θ is the Greek letter theta.

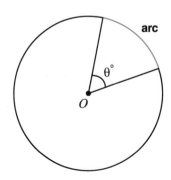

Areas

Area of a rectangle = length × breadth = lb

Area of a square = $(\text{length})^2 = l^2$

Area of a triangle = $\frac{1}{2}$ × base × perpendicular height = $\frac{1}{2}bh$

Area of a parallelogram = base × perpendicular height = bh

Area of a trapezium = $\frac{1}{2}$ × sum of the parallel sides × the perpendicular distance between them

$$= \frac{1}{2}(a+b)h$$

Area of a circle = π × $(\text{radius})^2$ $A = \pi r^2$

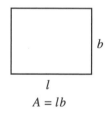

$A = lb$

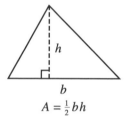

$A = \frac{1}{2}bh$

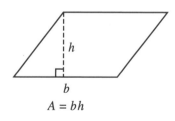

$A = bh$

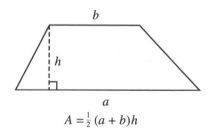

$A = \frac{1}{2}(a+b)h$

A sector of a circle

The area of a sector = $\dfrac{\theta}{360}$ of the area of the circle.

Area of sector = $\dfrac{\theta}{360} \times \pi r^2$

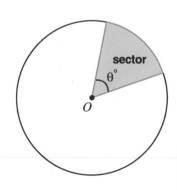

Examples

1   Rectangle

Perimeter $= 2(l + b)$

$\qquad = 2 \times (10 + 8)$ cm

$\qquad = 2 \times 18$ cm $= 36$ cm

Area $= lb$

$\qquad = 10 \times 8$ cm^2

$\qquad = 80$ cm^2

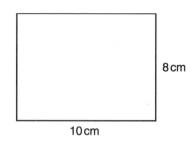

8 cm

10 cm

2   Triangle

Area $= \frac{1}{2}bh$

$\qquad = \frac{1}{2} \times 10 \times 6$ cm^2

$\qquad = 30$ cm^2

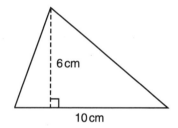

6 cm

10 cm

3   Parallelogram

Area $= bh$

$\qquad = 9 \times 5$ cm^2

$\qquad = 45$ cm^2

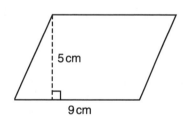

5 cm

9 cm

4   Trapezium

Area $= \frac{1}{2}(a + b)h$

$\qquad = \frac{1}{2} \times (11 + 7) \times 8$ cm^2

$\qquad = \frac{1}{2} \times 18 \times 8$ cm$^2 = 72$ cm^2

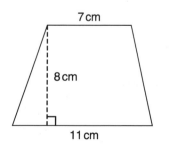

7 cm

8 cm

11 cm

5   **Circle**

Find the circumference of a circle with radius 25 cm.

$C = 2\pi r$

$\quad = 2 \times \pi \times 25 \text{ cm}$

$\quad = 157.07\ldots \text{ cm}$

$\quad = 157 \text{ cm, to 3 sig. fig.}$

6   Find the area of a circle with radius 4 cm.

$A = \pi r^2$

$\quad = \pi \times 4^2 \text{ cm}^2$

$\quad = 50.26\ldots \text{ cm}^2$

$\quad = 50.3 \text{ cm}^2, \text{ to 3 sig. fig.}$

7   The circle has centre O and radius 5 cm. $\angle AOB = 36°$.
Find the length of the arc AB and the area of the sector AOB.

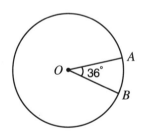

Length of arc $AB = \dfrac{\theta}{360} \times 2\pi r$

$\qquad\qquad = \dfrac{\overset{1}{\cancel{36}}}{\underset{10}{\cancel{360}}} \times 2 \times \pi \times 5 \text{ cm}$

$\qquad\qquad = 3.14 \text{ cm, to 3 sig. fig.}$

Area of sector $= \dfrac{\theta}{360} \times \pi r^2$

$\qquad\qquad = \dfrac{\overset{1}{\cancel{36}}}{\underset{10}{\cancel{360}}} \times \pi \times 5 \times 5 \text{ cm}^2$

$\qquad\qquad = 7.85 \text{ cm}^2, \text{ to 3 sig. fig.}$

Exercise 6.2

Take π as 3.142 or use the π key on your calculator, and give approximate answers correct to 3 significant figures.

1.   Find the areas of these figures.

1

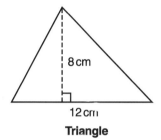

8 cm

12 cm

Triangle

2

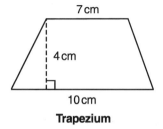

7 cm

4 cm

10 cm

Trapezium

2.   Find the lengths of the circumferences and the areas of these circles.

    1   Radius 14 cm.   **3**   Diameter 2 m.

    2   Radius 6 cm.   **4**   Radius 4.5 cm.

3. O is the centre of the circle.

    1   Find the length of the arc AB if the radius is 6.3 cm
        and $\angle AOB = 40°$.
    2   Find the length of the arc AB if the radius is 4.8 cm
        and $\angle AOB = 110°$.
    3   Find the area of the sector AOB if the radius is 3.2 cm
        and $\angle AOB = 70°$.
    4   Find the area of the sector AOB if the radius is 6 cm
        and $\angle AOB = 144°$.
    5   If $\angle AOB = 108°$ and the length of the arc $AB = 4.2$ cm, find the radius of the circle.

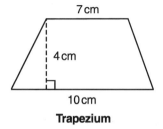

4.   **1**   Find the area of this parallelogram.
     2   Find the value of x.

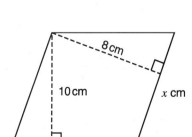

8 cm

10 cm

x cm

12 cm

5.　This quarter-circle (quadrant) has a radius of 7 cm.

Find
1　the length of the arc AB,
2　the perimeter of the figure,
3　the area of the figure,
4　the area of $\triangle AOB$,
5　the area of the shaded segment.

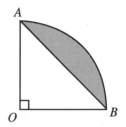

6.　$ABCD$ is a square.
Find the areas of
1　$\triangle ABE$,
2　$\triangle CEF$,
3　$\triangle ADF$,
4　$\triangle AEF$.

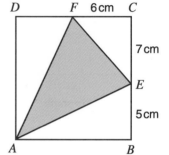

Solid figures

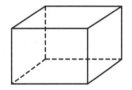

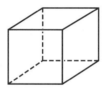

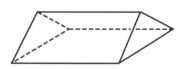

Cuboid, or rectangular block　　　　**Cube**　　　　**Triangular prism**

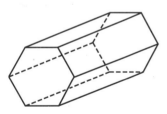

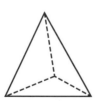

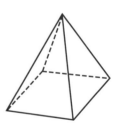

Hexagonal prism　　**Triangular pyramid, or tetrahedron**　　**Pyramid with square base**

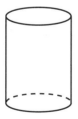

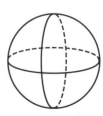

Cylinder　　　　**Cone**　　　　**Sphere**

Volumes

Volume of a cuboid = length × breadth × height = lbh

Volume of a cube = (length)^3 = l^3

Volume of a solid of uniform cross-section = area of cross-section × height

Volume of a pyramid = $\frac{1}{3}$ × area of base × height

Volume of a cylinder. $V = \pi r^2 h$

Volume of a cone. $V = \frac{1}{3}\pi r^2 h$

Volume of a sphere. $V = \frac{4}{3}\pi r^3$

Cones

In the formula for the volume of a cone, $V = \frac{1}{3}\pi r^2 h$,
h is the perpendicular height.
The slant height is denoted by l.
If you are given r and l, you must first calculate h using Pythagoras'
theorem.

e.g. If $r = 5$ cm and $l = 13$ cm,

$$l^2 = r^2 + h^2$$
$$13^2 = 5^2 + h^2 \quad (h \text{ in cm})$$
$$h^2 = 13^2 - 5^2$$
$$h = 12 \text{ cm}$$

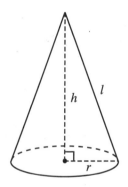

Surface areas

Cylinders

The area of the curved surface of a cylinder

  = 2 × π × radius × height
$S = 2\pi r h$

The total surface area of a **closed** cylinder includes two circular ends.
Total surface area of a closed cylinder = $2\pi r^2 + 2\pi r h$
$$= 2\pi r(r + h)$$

If a cylinder is an **open** cylinder, e.g. a cylinder with a base but without a lid, then there is only one circular end.

Total outside surface area of an open cylinder $= \pi r^2 + 2\pi r h$
$$= \pi r(r + 2h)$$

Cones

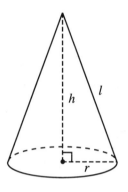

The area of the curved surface of a cone

　$= \pi \times \text{radius} \times \text{slant height}$

$S = \pi r l$

Spheres

The surface area of a sphere $= 4 \times \pi \times (\text{radius})^2$

$S = 4\pi r^2$

Examples

1　**Prism**

Find the volume of this prism.

Area of triangle $= \frac{1}{2} bh$

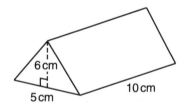

　　　　$= \frac{1}{2} \times 5 \times 6 \text{ cm}^2$

　　　　$= 15 \text{ cm}^2$

Volume of prism $=$ area of triangle $\times$ length

　　　　$= 15 \times 10 \text{ cm}^3$

　　　　$= 150 \text{ cm}^3$

2　**Cone**

Find the volume of a cone of radius 4 cm, perpendicular height 6 cm.

$V = \frac{1}{3} \pi r^2 h$

　$= \frac{1}{3} \times \pi \times 4^2 \times 6 \quad \text{cm}^3$

　$= 101 \text{ cm}^3$, to 3 sig. fig.

3   **Sphere**

Find the volume of a sphere of radius 6 cm.

$V = \frac{4}{3}\pi r^3$

$\quad = \frac{4}{3} \times \pi \times 6^3 \quad cm^3$

$\quad = 905 \ cm^3$, to 3 sig. fig.

4   **Cylinder**

Find the curved surface area of a cylinder, radius 4 cm, height 10 cm.

Curved surface area $= 2\pi rh$

$\quad\quad\quad\quad\quad = 2 \times \pi \times 4 \times 10 \quad cm^2$

$\quad\quad\quad\quad\quad = 251 \ cm^2$, to 3 sig. fig.

Exercise 6.3

Take π as 3.142 or use the π key on your calculator, and give approximate answers correct to 3 significant figures.

1.   Find the volume of this prism.

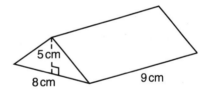

2.   This sketch shows the side of a shed.

   1   Find its area.
   2   Find the volume of the shed, if it is
        4 m long.

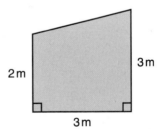

3.   **1**   Find the volume of a cylinder with radius 3 cm, height 7 cm.
   2   Find the area of the curved surface of a cylinder with radius 15 cm, height 40 cm.
   3   Find the volume of a cylinder with diameter 5.6 cm, height 10 cm.
   4   Find the area of the curved surface of a circular metal pipe with length 1 m and diameter 10 cm.
   5   Find the total surface area of a closed cylinder with radius 3.6 cm and height 4.4 cm.

4.   1   Find the volume of a cone with radius 4 cm and perpendicular height 12 cm.
     2   Find the volume of a cone with radius 3.1 cm and perpendicular height 6.3 cm.
     3   Find the volume of a sphere with radius 10 cm.
     4   Find the volume of a sphere with diameter 22.8 cm.
     5   If a sphere has a volume of 972π cm^3, what is its radius ?

5.   A room is 4 m wide, 3 m long and $2\frac{1}{2}$ m high. What is the total area of the four walls ?

6.   1   If a large rectangular room has length 9 m, breadth 8 m and its volume is 360 m^3, what is its height ?

     2   What is the surface area of a solid cube whose volume is 27 cm^3 ?

     3   A box measures 10 cm by 6 cm by 4 cm.
         (1) Find its volume.
         (2) How many cubes of edge 2 cm will fit in the box ?

     4   A rectangular tank is 4 m long, $2\frac{1}{2}$ m wide and 3 m deep. How many cubic metres of water does it contain when it is half-full ?

     5   How many cubic metres of concrete will be needed to make a path 25 metres long, $1\frac{1}{2}$ metres wide, if the concrete is to be laid to a depth of 8 cm ?

7.   A cone has perpendicular height 24 cm and slant height 25 cm.

     Find
     1   the radius of the base,
     2   the volume of the cone.

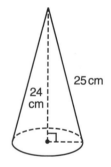

Units in formulae

To find a length, e.g. a perimeter, you use **length** units such as cm, m or km.
Any formula to find a length only involves units of length, and **has** to involve units of length.
Such formulae are said to be of dimension 1.

Examples are
$P = 2(l + b)$
$C = 2\pi r$

To find an area you use area units such as cm^2, m^2, km^2.
Any formula to find an area involves units of length × units of length.
Area formulae are of dimension 2.

Examples are
$A = lb$
$A = \pi r^2$
$S = 2lb + 2lh + 2bh$

To find a volume you use volume units such as cm^3, m^3.
Any formula to find a volume involves units of length × units of length × units of length,
or units of area × units of length.
Volume formulae are of dimension 3.

Examples are
$V = lbh$,
$V =$ area of base × height,
$V = \frac{4}{3}\pi r^3$

Formulae which involve combinations of these units such as $2\pi r + \pi r^2$, $lbh + 5r$, are not giving
either lengths, areas or volumes.
$2\pi r$ is a length formula because it involves r, in length units. It is of dimension 1.
πr^2 is an area formula because it involves r^2, in area units. It is of dimension 2.
$2\pi r + \pi r^2$ does not represent length or area.

lbh is a volume formula because it involves l, b, h, all lengths. It is of dimension 3.
$5r$ is a length formula because it involves r, in length units. It is of dimension 1.
$lbh + 5r$ does not represent volume or length.

A formula which involves area units ÷ length units will give a length.

e.g. Height of triangle $= \dfrac{2 \times \text{area}}{\text{base}}$

A formula which involves $\sqrt{\text{area units}}$ will give a length.

e.g. Radius of circle $= \sqrt{\dfrac{A}{\pi}}$

A formula which involves volume units ÷ area units will give a length.

e.g. Height $= \dfrac{\text{volume of cylinder}}{\text{area of base}}$

A formula which involves $\sqrt[3]{\text{volume units}}$ will give a length.

e.g. Radius of sphere $= \sqrt[3]{\dfrac{3V}{4\pi}}$

A formula which involves volume units ÷ length units will given an area.

e.g. Area of cross-section $= \dfrac{\text{volume}}{\text{height}}$

Exercise 6.4

1.   For these formulae, decide if X represents a length, area or volume.
     a, l, b, h, r are all lengths. A is an area and V is a volume.

     1 $X = 4\pi r^3$ **6** $X = \frac{1}{3}\pi r^2 h$ **11** $X = \dfrac{A}{h}$

     2 $X = \dfrac{A}{\pi h}$ **7** $X = Ah$

                                          8 $X = \pi ab$ **12** $X = \dfrac{V}{A}$

     3 $X = 2\pi r^2$ **9** $X = \dfrac{V}{\pi r h}$ **13** $X = \dfrac{l^3}{a}$

     4 $X = b + h$ **14** $X = \sqrt{2A}$

     5 $X = lb + \frac{1}{2}\pi r^2$ **10** $X = \dfrac{l^2 b}{A}$ **15** $X = \sqrt[3]{8V}$

2.   Look at the list of expressions below, where b, r, h are lengths.

     $b + 2\pi r$

     $\frac{1}{2}b^2 + \pi r^2 h$

     $b^2 + \pi r h$

     $b^3 + \pi b r$

     $\frac{1}{3}b^3 + \pi r^2 h$

     Write down the expression which represents

     1 a length,   **2** an area,   **3** a volume.

3.   In this list of formulae, each one has an error.
     Explain how you can tell, by considering dimensions, why each one is wrong.
     r, b, h are lengths, A is an area.
     Write down the correct formulae.

     1 The volume of a cylinder. $V = \pi r^3 h$
     2 The height of a triangle. $h = 2Ab$

     3 The radius of a circle. $r = \dfrac{A}{\pi}$

     4 The volume of a prism. $V = Ah^2$
     5 The total surface area of a closed cylinder. $S = 2\pi(h + r)$

Exercise 6.5   Applications

1.   The longer side of a rectangular field is 52 m and a footpath crossing the field along a
     diagonal is 65 m long. Find the length of the shorter side of the field.

2.   A patrol boat goes 7 km South, then 8 km East, then 8 km South. Find how far it is, in a direct line, from its starting point.

3.   A gardener is making a rectangular concrete base for a greenhouse 7 feet wide and 24 feet long. Having measured out the edges he checks that it is truly rectangular by measuring both diagonals. How long should these diagonals be ?

4.   Find

   1   the area of $\triangle ABC$,
   2   the length of AC,
   3   the length of BX.

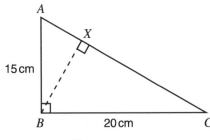

5. $ABCDEFGH$ is a cuboid with $AB = 16$ cm, $AD = 12$ cm and $AE = 5$ cm.

   Calculate the length of
   1 GB,
   2 AC,
   3 AG.

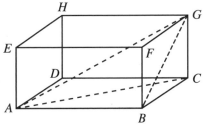

6.   **The converse of Pythagoras' theorem**

   > If, in a triangle, $a^2 = b^2 + c^2$, then the angle opposite side a is a right angle.

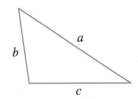

   Which of these triangles are right-angled ?

   1   The sides have lengths 3.5 cm, 12 cm, 12.5 cm.
   2   The sides have lengths 4 cm, 5 cm, 6 cm.
   3   The sides have lengths 2.4 cm, 7.0 cm, 7.4 cm.
   4   The sides have lengths 5 cm, 11 cm, 14 cm.
   5   The sides have lengths 9.1 cm, 9.1 cm, 12.8 cm.

7. $ABCD$ is a square of side 8 cm. Find the areas of the four triangles, and hence find the area of the quadrilateral $PQRS$.

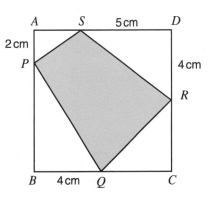

8.   *AOB* is a sector of a circle centre *O*, radius 8 cm with $\angle AOB = 135°$.

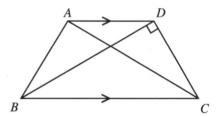

Find, leaving your answers in terms of π.
1   the length of the arc *AB*,
2   the area of the sector *AOB*.

The sector is cut out and bent round with *OA* and *OB* joined to
make a hollow cone.
3   What is the circumference of the base of the cone ?
4   Find the radius of the base of the cone.
5   Find the curved surface area of the cone using the formula $A = \pi r l$.
     Does this agree with the area of the sector it was made from ?

9.   *ABCD* is a trapezium with *AD* parallel to *BC*.

1   Name a triangle equal in area to $\triangle ABC$.

If *BC* = 17 cm, *CD* = 8 cm and $\angle BDC = 90°$, find
2   the length of *BD*,
3   the area of triangle *BDC*,
4   the area of triangle *ABC*.

10.   A circular pond of radius 18 metres is surrounded by a circular path of width 2 metres.
      Find the area of the path.

11.   1   If a circle has a circumference of 100 m, what is its radius ?
      2   If a circle has an area of 100 m², what is its radius ?

12.   What fraction of the circle is the sector *AOB* ?

If the radius of the circle is 10 cm, find
1   the length of the arc *AB*,
2   the area of the sector *AOB*.

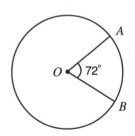

13.   *O* is the centre of the circle.

1   Find the size of $\angle AOB$ if the length of the arc *AB* is $5\frac{1}{2}$ cm
     and the radius of the circle is 7 cm.
2   Find the size of $\angle AOB$ if the area of the sector *AOB* is
     12.56 cm² and the radius of the circle is 6 cm.

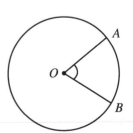

14. Ice 10 cm thick covered a pond whose surface area is 300 m². Find the weight of the ice, if 1 m³ of ice weighs 920 kg.

15. Find the outside curved surface area of a cylindrical storage tank with diameter 5.8 m and height 3.2 m.

16. The diagram shows the side of a swimming pool which slopes steadily from a depth of 1 m to 3 m. It is 25 m long.

   1 Find the area of the side.
   2 The pool is 10 m wide. Find its volume.

17. Some cylindrical tins have radius $3\frac{1}{2}$ cm and height 10 cm. Find the volume of a tin. The tins are packed in a rectangular box of length 28 cm, width 21 cm and height 10 cm. How many tins will fit in the box ?

18. If a cone has a radius of 4 cm and a volume of 200 cm³, what is its perpendicular height ?

19. 6 spheres with radius 5 cm are packed in a rectangular box with measurements 30 cm by 20 cm by 10 cm. The space around the spheres is filled with sawdust for packing. What is the volume of the space to be filled with sawdust?

20. For these formulae, decide if X represents a length, area, volume or none of these. a, b, c, h, r, s are lengths, A is an area and V is a volume.

   1 $X = \frac{1}{2}(a+b+c)$

   2 $X = \sqrt{s(s-a)(s-b)(s-c)}$

   3 $X = \dfrac{a^2 + b^2 + c^2}{abc}$

   4 $X = a^2 h$

   5 $X = \sqrt{\dfrac{V}{\pi h}}$

   6 $X = A + \pi bh$

   7 $X = \dfrac{V}{ab}$

   8 $X = \pi ab + h^3$

   9 $X = 2\pi r + 2r$

   10 $X = \dfrac{5(a+b)^2}{3a}$

Practice test 6

1. **1** Find the length of AC.
   2 Find the length of DC.
   3 Find the perimeter of $ABCD$.
   4 Find the area of $ABCD$.

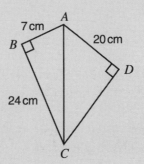

[Turn over]

2. Find the total area of the quadrilateral *ABCD*.

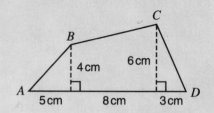

3. The circle is inscribed in a square of side 6 cm.
   Find the total shaded area.

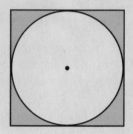

4. *O* is the centre of the circle.

   1 Find the length of the arc *AB* if the radius is 4.5 cm
     and $\angle AOB = 40°$.
   2 Find the area of the sector *AOB* if the radius is 3 cm
     and $\angle AOB = 150°$.

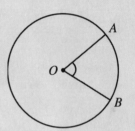

5. The perpendicular height of a cone is 16 cm.
   The slant height of the cone is 16.4 cm.
   Find the radius of the base of the cone, and hence find
   the area of the base of the cone.

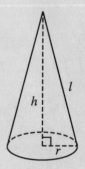

6. The end of this prism is a right-angled triangle.

   1 Find the area of the triangle.
   2 Find the volume of the prism.

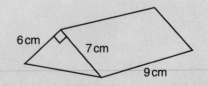

7.   From this list of expressions, where p, q, r are lengths,

$$p^2 + 4pqr,$$

$$\frac{pq}{r} + \sqrt{\pi r^2},$$

$$\pi p^3 + 2q^2 r,$$

$$\frac{3pr}{q^3},$$

$$\frac{3pqr}{\sqrt{p^2 + q^2}},$$

write down the expression which represents
1   a length,   2   an area,   3   a volume.

8.   A container consists of a cylinder radius 20 cm, height 18 cm
     with a conical top of height 30 cm. What is the total volume ?

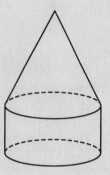

PUZZLE

20. Six girls went on a shopping trip. Afterwards they discussed what they had spent.
     Altogether they had spent £60.
     Rabia's and Susie's spending totalled £37.20.
     Tania spent as much as Ursula and Valerie combined.
     Susie spent three times as much as Ursula.
     Wendy spent twice as much as Valerie.
     Tania and Valerie together spent just half as much as Rabia.
     How much had each girl spent ?

7 Probability

> **The topics in this chapter include:**
>
> - understanding and using relative frequency as an estimate of probability,
> - making subjective estimates,
> - finding probabilities from equally likely events,
> - adding probabilities for mutually exclusive events.

Probability

Probability or chance is the likelihood of an event happening.
It is measured on a numerical scale from 0 to 1 and can be given as a fraction, a decimal or a percentage.

A probability of 0 means that there is no chance of the event happening.
A probability of 1 means that it is certain that the event will happen.
A probability of $\frac{1}{2}$ means that there is a 50–50 chance of the event happening. In the long run, $\frac{1}{2}$ of the trials will give successful results.
A probability of $\frac{2}{3}$ means that in the long run $\frac{2}{3}$ of the trials will give successful results.
The nearer the value of the probability is to 1, the more chance there is of successful outcome.
The nearer the value of the probability is to 0, the less chance there is of a successful outcome.

When we know the probability of an event happening we can use its value to predict the likelihood of a future result. That is why Probability is linked to Statistics. Government departments, business firms, industrialists, scientists, medical researchers and many other people and organisations use the figures from past events to predict what is likely to happen in the future, and thus they can plan ahead. For example, insurance companies use their knowledge of past claims to predict future ones, and they can then decide what premiums they must charge. If you want to gamble on a sporting event it is useful to estimate the probability of winning. You might then realise that you are unlikely to win in the long run and decide not to waste your money on the bet.

Relative frequency

If we have trials with different outcomes, some of which are successful, then

the relative frequency of a successful outcome $= \dfrac{\text{number of successful outcomes}}{\text{total number of trials}}$.

The relative frequency gives an estimate of the probability of a successful outcome.

e.g. There are a number of beads in a bag, some red and some blue, and to find the probability of picking a red bead out if picking a bead at random, a large number of trials are made. A bead is picked out, its colour noted, and the bead is replaced. This experiment is repeated 1000 times altogether, and the number of red beads noted was 596.

So, the probability of a red bead $= \dfrac{\text{number of trials giving a red bead}}{\text{total number of trials}}$

$$= \frac{596}{1000} = 0.60, \text{ to 2 dec. pl.}$$

We can only use this method for estimating probability if we do enough trials to show that the fraction is settling down to a steady value. Some events are completely unpredictable and in those cases the fraction would not settle down and we could not find a value for the probability.

Exercise 7.1 includes suggestions for experiments.
All the trials should be done randomly and fairly. Toss a coin properly. Give a die (dice) a good shake before rolling it out onto a flat surface. Shuffle a pack of cards properly and for most experiments you should take out the jokers first so that the pack contains the 52 cards of the 4 suits. If you have not got proper equipment it is often possible to think of a substitute. If you can combine other people's results with yours to give more trials, do so. Keep a record of your results to use again later.

Using random numbers to simulate results

Instead of actually doing the experiments, you may prefer to use a graphics calculator or a computer to produce random numbers.
To simulate the throwing of a die, on the graphics calculator, press

| Int | (| Ran# | × | 6 | + | 1 |) | EXE | EXE | EXE | ...

and you will get a sequence of random numbers between 1 and 6.
By changing 6 into 2 in the instructions, you will get a sequence of 1's or 2's which you can use as the results of tossing coins, with 1 for heads and 2 for tails.

You can produce similar results on a computer using a simple basic program.
However, you may have commercial computer programs available which will do these and other simulated experiments.

Subjective estimates

Probability may be worked out using the formula

$$\text{Probability} = \frac{\text{number of successful outcomes}}{\text{number of equally likely outcomes}}$$

If it is not possible to use that formula the probability can be estimated by finding the relative frequency.

$$\text{Probability} = \frac{\text{number of successful trials}}{\text{total number of trials}}$$

provided that the number of trials is large, and the fraction settles down to a steady value.

But there are many times in life when we have to estimate the probability or chance of something happening, and we cannot use calculation.
e.g. What is the probability that this year there will be a White Christmas ?
(This means that there will be snow on Christmas Day.)
Now if you live in Northern Canada, you might estimate the probability as 1 (certain to happen), and if you live in the Sahara Desert you might estimate the probability as 0 (certain not to happen). If you live in Southern England, and there has never been snow on Christmas Day for many years, you may think that there is a very slight chance, and estimate the probability as 0.1, or 0.05. If you live in the Scottish Highlands, and most years there has been snow, you might estimate the probability as 0.8, 0.9 or 0.95.
For other parts of Britain you might make estimates at some other point on the probability scale. If you think there is an even chance, the probability will be 0.5. If it is more likely to snow than not, the probability will be over 0.5. And so on ...

Some people may have a bet on an outcome such as this. For other people, the result is more serious. Shepherds have to make sure the sheep are safe. Transport authorities have to keep their vehicles running, and people planning journeys may have to change their plans.

You learn about probability by doing simple experiments with coins, dice, cards, etc. but probability is an important subject, and affects all our lives.

Exercise 7.1

1. Toss a coin 200 times. Record your results in order, in a grid of 10 columns by 20 rows. Put H for head and T for tail.

   The grid starts like this:

H	H	T	H	T	T	H			

   Before you begin, estimate how many heads you are likely to get.

   If the total number of tosses is n and the number of heads is h, find the fraction $\frac{h}{n}$, to 2 decimal places.
   This gives the estimated probability of a toss showing a head.

2. Instead of tossing coins again, use the results of question 1 in pairs, as if you had tossed two coins together, so that the possible results are HH, HT, TH, TT. If you had 200 single results you will have 100 results for pairs. Count the number of heads in each pair and put your results on a tally chart. Before you begin estimate how many of each you will get.

Heads	Tally marks	Frequency (f)
0		
1		
2		
		100

What is the most likely result ?
What are your estimates for the probabilities of 0 heads, 1 head, 2 heads ?

3. Throw a die 400 times. Record the number which lands face upwards, in a grid of 20 columns by 20 rows.
If the total number of throws is n and the number of sixes is s, find the fraction $\frac{s}{n}$, to 2 decimal places.
This gives the estimated probability of a throw showing a six.

Work out the probabilities of getting the other numbers, 1 to 5.
Is the die a fair one ?

4. Put 10 similar drawing-pins into a cup and holding it approximately 20 cm above a table, gently tip the drawing-pins out so they land on the table. They come to rest point upwards, like this ⊥ , or on their side, like this ⋌ . Count and record how many land point upwards. Repeat the experiment 50 times.

If the total number of drawing-pins tipped out is n, and the number which rest point upwards is s, find the fraction $\frac{s}{n}$, to 2 decimal places, after 5, 10, 20, 30, 40 and 50 repetitions.

If the results are settling down to a certain value this gives the value of the probability that a drawing-pin in this type of experiment will land point upwards. (There is no theoretical way of checking this result.)
The height through which the drawing-pins fall may affect the result. You could investigate this by repeating the experiment from different heights. Different makes of drawing-pins may also give different results.

5.   Shuffle a pack of cards and pick out 3 cards. Record as P if they contain at least one
     picture-card (i.e. Jack, Queen or King). Record as N if there is no picture card.
     Replace the cards, shuffle and repeat 100 times altogether.
     Before you begin, estimate how many times P will occur.

     Find the fraction $\dfrac{\text{number of times P occurs}}{\text{total number of trials}}$ as a decimal to 2 decimal places.

     From your results, what value would you give for the probability that of three cards
     drawn at random, at least one card is a picture-card ?

6.   Collect 200 single-figure random numbers by taking the last figure of a list of phone
     numbers out of a random page of a directory. (If a firm has consecutive numbers listed,
     only use the first one.) Record these numbers in a grid, as in question 1.
     Before you begin, estimate how many of each number 0 to 9 you expect to get.

     Count up your results and show them in a table.

     Now add up the frequencies of the odd numbers.

     Find the fraction $\dfrac{\text{number of odd numbers}}{\text{total number of numbers}}$ as a

     decimal to 2 decimal places.
     From your results, what value would you give for
     the probability that a number picked at random
     from the numbers 0 to 9 is odd ?

Number	Frequency
0	
1	
2	
3	
4	
5	
6	
7	
8	
9	

7.   Here are some statements. Some of them may not apply to you, or they may be
     certainties. Choose 5 statements from the rest and put them in order of likelihood. Then
     decide which probabilities are less than 0.5 and which are greater than 0.5. Finally, give
     estimated probabilities for them.

     (a) Tomorrow will be wet.
     (b) You will give some useful help at home this evening.
     (c) You will be late for school/college one day next week.
     (d) You will go to the cinema next weekend.
     (e) During the next fortnight, you will get some new clothes.
     (f) During the next month, you will win a prize in a competition.
     (g) For your next holiday you will go to the USA.
     (h) When you take GCSE Maths you will achieve a satisfactory result.
     (i) Next year, you will continue your education (at school or college).
     (j) When you take your driving test, you will pass at the first attempt.
     (k) Make up your own statement.

8.   Imagine a young couple, Mr and Mrs Kaye, who are going to spend 10 days holiday in Greece.
      Give estimated probabilities for these statements.

      1   The plane's departure will be delayed.
      2   There will be fine, sunny weather every day during the holiday.
      3   The hotel accommodation will be satisfactory.
      4   The couple will spend more money than they expected to.
      5   They will make new friends.
      6   Mrs Kaye will buy some new clothes.
      7   Mr Kaye will go water-skiing.
      8   One of them will need medical treatment during the holiday.
      9   They will buy some duty-free goods on the plane coming home.
      10   They will go again to the same place next year.

9.   A bag contains 6 coloured discs. One disc is pulled out, its colour noted and then it is returned to the bag. After 120 draws the results are Yellow 44 times, Red 19 times, Blue 57 times. How many counters of each colour do you think are in the bag ?

Equally likely outcomes

If a trial has a number of **equally likely outcomes** and of these certain ones are successful then:

$$\text{Probability (or chance) of a successful outcome} = \frac{\text{number of successful outcomes}}{\text{total possible outcomes}} = \frac{s}{n}$$

Examples

1   Find the probability of a tossed coin showing heads.

     There are 2 equally likely outcomes, heads or tails, and of these 1 outcome, heads, is successful.

     Probability of heads $= \dfrac{s}{n} = \dfrac{1}{2}$

2   Find the probability of a number picked at random from the numbers 1 to 10 being exactly divisible by 4.

     There are ten equally likely outcomes of which two (4 and 8) are successful.

     Probability of picking a number exactly divisible by $4 = \dfrac{s}{n} = \dfrac{2}{10} = \dfrac{1}{5}$

Use of sample spaces

Example

3   Five discs numbered 1 to 5 are placed in a bag and one is drawn out at random and not replaced. A second disc is then drawn out at random.
   (1) What is the probability that the second disc has a number higher by at least 2 than the first disc ?
   (2) What is the probability that the total of the two numbers is 6 ?

Set down the possible equally likely results in a diagram called a sample space.

		1st disc				
		1	2	3	4	5
2nd	1		·	·	·	·
disc	2	·		·	·	·
	3	·	*a* ·		·	·
	4	·	·	·		·
	5	·	·	·	·	

A dot represents one of the equally likely outcomes, e.g. dot (*a*) represents the outcome that the first disc is 2 and the second disc is 4. There are 20 dots so there are 20 equally likely outcomes. (It might be more useful to write the actual outcomes e.g. (2, 4), or the total score, instead of just dots.)

We will mark in some way all the outcomes where the second disc has a number higher by at least 2 than the first disc, and in a different way where the total of the two numbers is 6. (Normally these would go on the original diagram but here to make it clearer we have two new diagrams.)

(1)

		1st disc				
		1	2	3	4	5
2nd	1		·	·	·	·
disc	2	·		·	·	·
	3	⊡	·		·	·
	4	⊡	⊡	·		·
	5	⊡	⊡	⊡	·	

(2)

		1st disc				
		1	2	3	4	5
2nd	1		·	·	·	⊙
disc	2	·		·	⊙	·
	3	·	·		·	·
	4	·	⊙	·		·
	5	⊙	·	·	·	

⊡   represents a successful outcome.
There are 6 successful outcomes.

⊙   represents a successful outcome.
There are 4 successful outcomes.

(1)   The probability that the 2nd disc has a number higher by at least 2 than the first disc
$$= \frac{s}{n} = \frac{6}{20} = 0.3$$
(2)   The probability that the total of the two numbers is 6 $= \dfrac{s}{n} = \dfrac{4}{20} = 0.2$

Exercise 7.2

1. A fair die is thrown once. What is the probability of getting

   1 a three,
   2 a square number ?

2. 100 discs, numbered from 1 to 100, are placed in a bag and one is drawn out at random. What is the probability of getting a disc with

   1 a number greater than 70,
   2 a number which includes the digit 1,
   3 a number whose digits add up to 9 ?

3. In a fairground game a pointer is spun and you win the amount shown in the sector where it comes to rest. Assuming that the pointer is equally likely to come to rest in any sector, what is the probability that

   1 you win some money,
   2 you win 20p ?

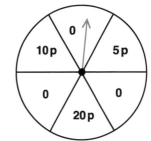

4. In a tombola game, $\frac{7}{8}$ of the counters are blank. The rest have a number on them and they win a prize. If you take a counter out of the drum at random what is the probability that you win a prize ?

5. If you choose a card at random from a pack of 52 playing-cards, what is the probability that it is

   1 an ace,
   2 a diamond,
   3 a red card with an even number ?

6 A letter is chosen at random from the 11 letters of the word MATHEMATICS. What is the probability that it is

   1 the letter M,
   2 a vowel,
   3 a letter from the second half of the alphabet ?

7. In a pack of playing-cards, the 2 of diamonds and the 2 of hearts have been removed. If you choose a card at random from the remaining cards, what is the probability that it is

   1 a diamond,
   2 a two,
   3 the 2 of diamonds ?

8. A box contains 2 red, 3 yellow and 5 green sweets. One is taken out at random, and eaten. A second sweet is then taken out.

    1   If the 1st sweet was green, what is the probability that the 2nd sweet is also green ?
    2   If the 1st sweet was not red, what is the probability that the 2nd sweet is red ?

9. Two dice are thrown together. Make a sample space diagram of the equally likely results.

    What is the probability
    1   that the sum of the two numbers is greater than 10,
    2   that the sum of the two numbers is 7,
    3   of a double (the two dice showing the same number),
    4   of both dice showing numbers less than 3 ?

10. There are six cards numbered 1 to 6. One card is selected at random and not replaced, and then a second card is selected. Make a sample space diagram of the equally likely results.
    What is the probability
    1   that the sum of the two numbers is greater than 10,
    2   that the sum of the two numbers is 7,
    3   that the product of the two numbers is odd ?

11. Five cards marked A, B, C, D, E are placed in a bag. One card is drawn out and replaced and then a second card is drawn out. Make a sample space diagram of the equally likely results.

    Find the probability of getting
    1   A first and then B,
    2   A and B in either order.
    3   Repeat the questions if the second card is drawn out without the first card being replaced.

Mutually exclusive events

When there are two or more outcomes of an event and at each time only one of the outcomes can happen (because if one outcome happens, this prevents any of the other outcomes happening), then the outcomes are called mutually exclusive events.

The sum of the probabilities of all possible mutually exclusive events is 1, because it is certain that one of them will occur.

If the probability of an event happening is p, then the probability of the event not happening is $1 - p$.

The OR rule

If there are two mutually exclusive events A or B, then the probability of A or B occurring
= the probability of A occurring + the probability of B occurring.
i.e.

$$P(A \text{ or } B) = P(A) + P(B)$$

If there are 3 events, A or B or C, then

$$P(A \text{ or } B \text{ or } C) = P(A) + P(B) + P(C)$$

The rule is similar if there are more than 3 events.

Examples

1   In the last year in a certain school, pupils must study one of the subjects music, or art, or
Latin.
25% of the pupils study music and 60% of the pupils study art.
If a pupil from that year is chosen at random, what is the probability that the pupil
studies music, art, music or art, Latin ?

$P(\text{music}) = \frac{25}{100} = \frac{1}{4}, \quad P(\text{art}) = \frac{60}{100} = \frac{3}{5}$

$P(\text{music or art}) = \frac{25}{100} + \frac{60}{100} = \frac{85}{100} = \frac{17}{20}$

$P(\text{Latin}) + P(\text{music or art}) = 1$

so $P(\text{Latin}) = 1 - \frac{17}{20} = \frac{3}{20}$

2   In a pack of 52 cards one card is drawn at random. What is the probability that it
is   **1**   a heart,   **2**   an ace,   **3**   an ace or a heart ?

1 $P(\text{heart}) = \dfrac{13}{52} = \frac{1}{4}$

2 $P(\text{ace}) = \dfrac{4}{52} = \frac{1}{13}$

3   It would be wrong to use the OR rule because the two events, ace and heart, can
occur together with the ace of hearts. They are not mutually exclusive events. Instead,
find the number of successful outcomes. There are 13 hearts, including the ace, and
the other 3 aces, making 16 successful outcomes altogether.

$P(\text{ace or heart}) = \dfrac{s}{n} = \dfrac{16}{52} = \frac{4}{13}$

Exercise 7.3

1. A biscuit tin contains 7 shortbread biscuits, 8 cream biscuits, 10 chocolate biscuits and 15 wafer biscuits.
    If a biscuit is picked out at random, what is the probability that
    1 it is either a cream biscuit or a chocolate biscuit,
    2 it is not a wafer biscuit ?

2. 6 men, 4 women, 3 girls and 7 boys enter for a contest.
    If they each have an equal chance of winning, what is the probability that the winner is
    1 a man,
    2 a child,
    3 a female ?

3. In a raffle, Mrs Andrews buys 10 tickets and Mr Andrews buys 5 tickets. There are 200 tickets sold altogether.
    What is the probability that the 1st price is won by either Mr or Mrs Andrews ?

4. A bag contains a number of sweets, some red and some green. The probability of taking a red sweet, at random, is $\frac{7}{12}$.
    1 What is the probability of taking out a green sweet ?
    2 If 35 of the sweets are green sweets, how many red sweets are there ?

5. A box contains cartons of orange juice, grapefruit juice and pineapple juice.
    If a drink is taken out at random the probability that it is orange or pineapple is $\frac{5}{8}$.
    1 What is the probability that it is grapefruit ?
    2 The probability that it is orange is $\frac{3}{8}$. What is the probability that it is pineapple ?

6. A number of beads are placed in a bag. Most beads are marked with a number 1, 2, 3, 4 or 5. If a bead is picked out at random the probabilities of the different scores are:

    $P(1) = 0.05$
    $P(2) = 0.3$
    $P(3) = 0.25$
    $P(4) = 0.2$
    $P(5) = 0.15$

    What is the probability of getting
    1 a bead marked 4 or 5,
    2 a bead marked with an odd number,
    3 a bead which is not marked with a number ?

7.   When 6 coins are tossed, the probabilities of different numbers of heads and tails are as follows:

P(6 heads) $= \frac{1}{64}$

P(5 heads, 1 tail) $= \frac{6}{64}$

P(4 heads, 2 tails) $= \frac{15}{64}$

P(3 heads, 3 tails) $= \frac{20}{64}$

P(2 heads, 4 tails) $= \frac{15}{64}$

P(1 head, 5 tails) $= \frac{6}{64}$

P(6 tails) $= \frac{1}{64}$

If you toss 6 coins once, what is the probability of getting

1   at least 4 heads,
2   at least 3 heads,
3   at least 1 tail ?

Exercise 7.4   Applications

1.   Use a set of dominoes going up to double six. (If you have no dominoes, label cards 0–0, 0–1, up to 0–6; then 1–1, 1–2, up to 1–6; then 2–2, etc., ending 6–6. There are 28 cards altogether.)
Pick out a domino at random and record the total score. Replace and repeat 200 times. The scores range from 0 to 12. Make a tally chart of the results.
What is the estimated probability of getting a score of 6 if a domino is picked at random ?

2.   Ask as many people as you can on what day of the week their birthday falls this year. Tally the results. What is the estimated probability that if a person is chosen at random, his/her birthday is on a Saturday ?

3.   Think of some situations which may possibly or probably occur, but are not certain to occur, in the next few days, and estimate how likely each one is to occur.
Write down a statement which has a probability of occurring of

1   0.8 or higher,
2   0.2 or lower,
3   approximately 0.5,
4   slightly over 0.5,
5   slightly under 0.5.

4.   200 discs numbered 1 to 200 are placed in a bag and one is drawn out at random. What is the probability of getting a disc with a number which is a square number ?

5.   There are 12 marbles in a bag of which x are red ones. What is the probability that a marble drawn at random is red ?
     When 3 more red marbles are added to those in the bag the probability of getting a red marble is doubled. Write down an equation and solve it to find how many red marbles there were originally.

6.   Find the theoretical results for the experiments you carried out in Exercise 7.1, questions 1, 2, 3, 5 and 6, and compare your experimental results with these.

7.   If 100 discs labelled 1 to 100 are put in a bag and one is drawn out at random, what is the probability that

     1   it is a multiple of 9,
     2   it is a square number,
     3   it is either a multiple of 9 or a square number,
     4   it is a multiple of 9 and a square number,
     5   it is not a multiple of 9 nor a square number ?

8.   In a survey of 36 boys, the numbers playing football, cricket and rugby are given in the diagram.
     If a boy is picked at random from this group what is the probability that he plays
     1   football,
     2   cricket and football but not rugby,
     3   only rugby ?

     4   If a boy who plays cricket is chosen at random, what is the probability that he also plays football ?

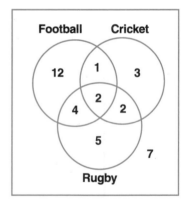

9.   Two cards are drawn from a pack of 52 cards. What is the probability that the second card is from the same suit as the first
     1   if the 1st card is replaced before the 2nd card is drawn,
     2   if the 1st card is not replaced before the 2nd card is drawn ?

10. Write down a list of all possible results if a coin is tossed 4 times in succession, e.g. HHHH, HTHH, HHHT, ...

     What is the probability of getting
     1   4 heads,
     2   3 or more tails,
     3   exactly 2 heads and 2 tails ?

11. This table shows the numbers of boys and girls in 200 families.

		Number of boys				
		0	1	2	3	4
	0	45	6	7	8	3
Number	1	7	15	25	12	1
of girls	2	5	23	13	1	0
	3	10	9	2	0	0
	4	2	3	0	2	1

e.g. There are 45 families with no children, and 6 families with 1 boy but no girls.

Find the probability that in a family chosen from these at random, there are

1   two boys and one girl,
2   an equal number of boys and girls (at least one of each),
3   more than two boys.

12. A bag contains 6 cards numbered 1 to 6. Two cards are selected at random. Show the outcomes in a sample space diagram.
Find the probability that

1   there is a difference of 2 between the numbers on the two cards,
2   the two cards have a sum of 6,
3   the two cards have a difference of 2 and a sum of 6.

13. Alex and Bryan each choose independently and at random a number from the numbers 10, 11, 12, 13, 14 or 15. Draw a sample space diagram to show the possible choices.
Find the probability that

1   Alex has chosen a prime number,
2   Alex and Bryan have chosen the same number,
3   the two numbers chosen have a sum of 24,
4   the sum of the two numbers chosen is divisible by 5.

14. Raffle tickets are sold from books of three different colours, blue, green and pink. The probability that the winning ticket is blue is $\frac{1}{3}$ and the probability that the winning ticket is green is $\frac{2}{5}$. What is the probability that the winning ticket is pink ?

15. At a certain set of traffic lights,
    the probability of the lights showing red = 0.3,
    the probability of the lights showing red and amber = 0.04,
    the probability of the lights showing green = 0.6,
    the probability of the lights showing amber = x.

    1 What is the value of x ?
    2 A motorist passes through the junction every day. Unless the lights are showing green he has to stop.
    What is the probability that he has to stop ?
    3 A pedestrian crosses the road at the junction every day. He can cross safely when the lights are showing red. Unless the lights are showing red, he has to wait.
    What is the probability that he has to wait ?

16. In a batch of components the probabilities of the number of faults per component are as follows:

    P(0 faults) = 0.8,

    P(1 fault) = 0.12,

    P(2 faults) = 0.06.

    The other components have more than 2 faults.

    What is the probability that a component picked at random has
    1 1 or 2 faults,
    2 more than 2 faults,
    3 at least 1 fault ?

Practice test 7

1. In an experiment with a biased die, the following results were obtained for the number facing uppermost when the die was thrown 400 times.

Number	1	2	3	4	5	6
Number of times	39	72	57	111	25	96

   Using these results, find the probability of throwing
   1 number 6,
   2 an odd number,
   3 a number greater than 3.

2.   The students in a school club belong to two forms 11X and 11Y.

	11X	11Y
Girls	12	16
Boys	8	14

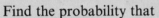

If from this club one member is chosen at random, what is the probability that it is

1   a boy,
2   a member of 11Y,
3   a girl from 11X ?
4   If a girl has to be chosen at random what is the probability that she is from 11X ?

3.   A regular triangular pyramid (tetrahedron) has its four faces numbered 1, 2, 3, 4 and it is used as a die by counting as the score the number on the bottom face. Draw up a sample space showing the outcomes when this die is thrown twice.

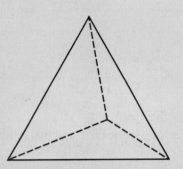

Find the probability that
1   in each of the two throws the score is 4,
2   in the two throws the sum of the scores is 4,
3   in the two throws the product of the scores is 4.

4.   Jan estimates that the probability of the bus being early is 0.1, of it being on time is 0.7, and otherwise it will be late.
1   What is the probability that the bus will be late ?
2   If the bus is early, Jan will miss it, and thus be late for school. If the bus is late, Jan will also be late for school.
      What is the probability that Jan will be late for school ?

5.   Seeds are planted with 5 in each pot. The probabilities of 0, 1, 2, 3, 4 or 5 seeds in a pot germinating are as follows:

Number of seeds germinating	0	1	2	3	4	5
Probability	0.002	0.008	0.02	0.14	0.39	0.44

What is the probability of having a pot in which
1   less than 2 seeds germinate,
2   at least 1 seed germinates,
3   4 or 5 seeds germinate ?

Inequalities and equations

> **The topics in this chapter include:**
>
> • solving inequalities,
>
> • solving equations by trial and improvement methods,
>
> • using algebraic methods to solve simultaneous equations.

Inequalities

$<$ is the symbol for 'is less than', so $3 < 4$ means '3 is less than 4'.
$>$ is the symbol for 'is greater than'.
$\leqslant$ is the symbol for 'is less than or equal to'.
$\geqslant$ is the symbol for 'is greater than or equal to', so $x \geqslant 3$ means 'x is greater than or equal to 3'.

Examples

1   If x is an integer, what are the possible values of x if $-1 \leqslant x < 5$?

x is greater than or equal to -1.
x is less than 5.
The possible values of x are $-1, 0, 1, 2, 3, 4$.

Inequalities on the number line

2    $x > 1$

$x \leqslant 2$

$-2 < x < 4$

$x \leqslant -1$ or $x \geqslant 6$

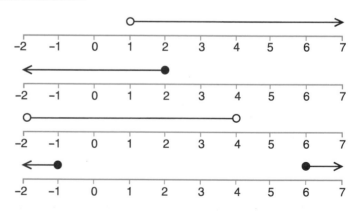

We have used the symbol ● if the end point is included and the symbol ○ if the end point is not included.

To solve simple inequalities, use the same methods as for solving simple equations.

You can add equal numbers to both sides,
you can subtract equal numbers from both sides,
you can multiply both sides by the same **positive** number,
you can divide both sides by the same **positive** number,

and the inequality remains true.

If you multiply or divide both sides by a **negative** number, the inequality sign must be reversed at the same time.

Examples

3   Find the values of x which satisfy the inequality $13x - 20 > 6x + 8$.

$13x - 20 > 6x + 8$ Subtract $6x$ from both sides.
$7x - 20 > 8$ Add 20 to both sides.
$\qquad 7x > 28$ Divide both sides by 7.
$\qquad x > 4$

4   Find the values of x which satisfy the inequality $8 - 3x \geqslant 14$.

$8 - 3x \geqslant 14$ Subract 8 from both sides.
$\qquad -3x \geqslant 6$ Divide both sides by -3, reversing the inequality sign.
$\qquad x \leqslant -2$

Other inequalities

Examples

5   Solve the inequality $6x^2 < 54$.

Divide both sides by 6.
$x^2 < 9$

First, think of the **equation** $x^2 = 9$.
There are two solutions, $x = -3$ and $x = 3$.

Now, if x has any value between -3 and 3, then x^2 is less than 9.
If x has any value less than -3 or greater than 3, x^2 is greater than 9.

So the solution to $x^2 < 9$ is 'x lies between -3 and 3'. This is written as $-3 < x < 3$.
It is shown here on a number line.

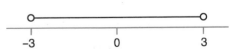

6   Solve the inequality $x^2 \geqslant 25$.

This means $x^2 = 25$ or $x^2 > 25$.
$x^2 = 25$ when $x = -5$ or $x = 5$.
If x has any value less than -5 or greater than 5 then $x^2 > 25$.

So the solution to $x^2 \geqslant 25$ is $x \leqslant -5$ or $x \geqslant 5$.

This cannot be written any simpler as it is
represented by two distinct regions on the
number line.

Exercise 8.1

1.   Show these inequalities on a number line. Draw a separate number line for each part,
labelling each line from -4 to 4.

1	$x > -3$	**5**	$-2 < x < -1$
2	$x < -1$	**6**	$-3 \leqslant x \leqslant 4$
3	$x \geqslant 0$	**7**	$x < -3$ or $x > 2$
4	$x \leqslant 3$	**8**	$x \leqslant 1$ or $x \geqslant 2$

2.   If x is an integer such that $-4 \leqslant x \leqslant 4$, write down the possible values for x, for the
inequalities of question 1.

3.   Find the values of x which satisfy these inequalities.

1 $6(x - 7) < 6$ **5** $5(x + 1) \leqslant x + 8$

2 $x - 1 > 2x + 5$ **6** $3(x - 4) < 5(x - 7)$

3 $5 - x \geqslant 6 - 3x$ **7** $\dfrac{x - 2}{3} \geqslant -1$

4 $\dfrac{x}{2} - 8 \leqslant -10$ **8** $\dfrac{x}{3} - \dfrac{x}{4} \geqslant 1$

4.   Find the values of x which satisfy these inequalities.

1 $x^2 > 36$ **4** $x^2 < 1$

2 $x^2 > 2.25$ **5** $x^2 \geqslant \frac{1}{16}$

3 $x^2 \leqslant 100$

5.   Find the values of x which satisfy these inequalities.

1 $2x^2 \leqslant 98$ **2** $x^2 + 4 \geqslant 85$ **3** $\frac{1}{2}x^2 < 72$

6. If x is a positive whole number such that $1 \leqslant x \leqslant 10$, state the values of x satisfied by these inequalities.

   1 $x^2 \geqslant 45$ **3** $5x^2 > x^2 + 320$

   2 $2x^2 + 1 \leqslant 20$ **4** $35 < x^2 < 65$

7. The values of x satisfy the inequality $4x + 3 \leqslant 40 \leqslant 6x - 4$.

   1 Find the largest possible value of x.
   2 Find the smallest possible value of x.
   3 If x is an integer, write down all the possible values of x.

8. Mrs Taylor wants to buy some oranges and lemons to make marmalade. If she decides to buy x oranges and y lemons, write down 4 inequalities to represent these statements. She decides to buy at least 2 oranges and 3 lemons, and not more than 9 fruits altogether. Oranges cost 20p each, and lemons 24p each, and Mrs Taylor has only £2 to spend.

   If she buys 3 oranges, what is the greatest number of lemons she can buy ?

Solving equations by trial and improvement methods

An equation such as $5x - 8 = 22$ is called a **linear** equation.

Equations can include powers of x, such as x^2, x^3 or higher powers.

An equation such as $x^2 - 5x + 3 = 0$, with highest power x^2, is called a **quadratic** equation. A quadratic equation can have 2, 1 or 0 solutions.

An equation such as $x^3 - 5x^2 + 3x + 7 = 0$, with highest power x^3, is called a **cubic** equation. A cubic equation can have 3, 2 or 1 solutions.

Example

1 Solve the equation $x^3 - 3x = 52$, given that the solution is a positive number.

Write this as $x^3 - 3x - 52 = 0$.
Make a table of values.

x	0	1	2	3	4	5	6
x^3	0	1	8	27	64	125	216
$-3x$	0	-3	-6	-9	-12	-15	-18
-52	-52	-52	-52	-52	-52	-52	-52
$x^3 - 3x - 52$	-52	-54	-50	-34	0	58	146

The solution is $x = 4$.

From looking at the table it seems unlikely that there will be another solution with x positive.

Equations whose solutions are not whole numbers

Examples

2   Solve the equation $2x^2 = 5x + 10$, correct to 1 decimal place, finding the positive solution.

Rewrite the equation as $2x^2 - 5x - 10 = 0$.
Make a table of values.

x	0	1	2	3	4	5
x^2	0	1	4	9	16	25
$2x^2$ $-5x$ -10	0 0 -10	2 -5 -10	8 -10 -10	18 -15 -10	32 -20 -10	50 -25 -10
$2x^2 - 5x - 10$	-10	-13	-12	-7	2	15

When $x = 3$, $2x^2 - 5x - 10 = -7$ (negative)
When $x = 4$, $2x^2 - 5x - 10 = 2$ (positive)
So the value of $2x^2 - 5x - 10$ will be 0 somewhere between 3 and 4 (and probably nearer to 4 than to 3).

We now use trial and improvement methods to find the solution correct to 1 decimal place.
Find the value of the function when $x = 3.7$, using your calculator. (We chose 3.7 because we think the solution is greater than 3.5.)
We can set the working down in the table of values, but it is probably just as easy to work it out in one stage.
Press 2 $\boxed{\times}$ 3.7 $\boxed{x^2}$ $\boxed{-}$ 5 $\boxed{\times}$ 3.7 $\boxed{-}$ 10 $\boxed{=}$ and you will get -1.12, which is negative.
Now we know that the solution is between $x = 3.7$ and $x = 4$.

Try $x = 3.8$ next.
Using your calculator, you will get -0.12, still negative.
Now we know that the solution is between $x = 3.8$ and $x = 4$, and seems quite near to $x = 3.8$.

Trying $x = 3.9$ gives the value 0.92, which is positive.
So now we know that the solution is between $x = 3.8$ and $x = 3.9$.
Since we want the answer correct to 1 decimal place, we want to know whether it is nearer to 3.8 or to 3.9. So we find the value of the function for x halfway between 3.8 and 3.9, i.e. for $x = 3.85$.
The value is found to be 0.395, which is positive.

So the solution is between $x = 3.8$ and $x = 3.85$, and correct to 1 decimal place it is $x = 3.8$.

If you wanted the solution correct to 2 decimal places you would have to continue using this method, trying (say) 3.82 next. To 2 decimal places the solution is $x = 3.81$.

3   Solve the equation $x^3 + 3x - 20 = 0$, correct to 1 decimal place, given that the solution is a positive number.

Make a table of values.

x	0	1	2	3	4	5
x^3	0	1	8	27	64	125
$3x$	0	3	6	9	12	15
-20	-20	-20	-20	-20	-20	-20
$x^3 + 3x - 20$	-20	-16	-6	16	56	120

The table shows that there will be a value 0 somewhere between $x = 2$ and $x = 3$, and probably nearer to 2 than to 3.

Find the value of the function when $x = 2.3$.

Press 2.3 $\boxed{y^x}$ 3 $\boxed{+}$ 3 $\boxed{\times}$ 2.3 $\boxed{-}$ 20 $\boxed{=}$ and you will get -0.933, which is negative.
Try $x = 2.4$ and you will get 1.024, which is positive.
So the solution is between $x = 2.3$ and $x = 2.4$.

Since we want the answer correct to 1 decimal place, we find the value of the function when $x = 2.35$. This is 0.028, which is positive.

So the solution lies between $x = 2.3$ and $x = 2.35$, and correct to 1 decimal place it is $x = 2.3$.

Exercise 8.2

1.   Solve these quadratic equations by trial, finding solutions which are positive whole numbers.

    1 $x^2 - x = 30$
    2 $x^2 + 4x = 21$
    3 $x^2 - 7x + 6 = 0$ (2 solutions)
    4 $x^2 = 8x - 15$ (2 solutions)
    5 $3x^2 + 8 = 14x$

2.   Solve these cubic equations by trial, finding solutions which are positive whole numbers.

    1 $x^3 - x^2 - x = 95$
    2 $x^3 = 10x - 3$
    3 $x^3 = x^2 + 5x - 6$
    4 $x^3 - x^2 = 14x + 30$
    5 $(x + 1)(x + 2)(x - 2) = 60$

3.   Solve these equations by trial and improvement, finding solutions which are positive numbers, correct to 1 decimal place.

    1 $x^2 - 2x = 18$
    2 $2x^2 + x = 5$
    3 $x^2 - 4x - 3 = 0$
    4 $x^3 - x^2 = 56$
    5 $x^3 + x = 59$
    6 $x^3 - x - 2 = 0$
    7 $x^3 = 2x + 100$
    8 $2x^2 = x + 85$
    9 $x^3 + 6x = 29$
    10 $x^2 - 10 = 8x$

4.   Ann is 4 years older than Bobby. The sum of the squares of their ages is 400. Find their ages.

5.   If a stone is thrown vertically upwards with a velocity of u m/s, its height above the ground after t seconds is given by the formula $s = ut - 5t^2$.
How long does it take, to the nearest 0.1 s, for a stone thrown upwards with a velocity of 20 m/s to reach a height of 17.5 m above the ground ?

Simultaneous Equations

'Simultaneously' means 'at the same time'. To solve simultaneous equations means we must find a solution for x and y which satisfies both equations.

Examples

1   Solve the simultaneous equations $3x + 5y = -1$, $2x - 3y = 12$.

$$3x + 5y = -1 \quad (1)$$
$$2x - 3y = 12 \quad (2)$$
Multiply (1) by 3 and (2) by 5.
$$9x + 15y = -3 \quad (1a)$$
$$10x - 15y = 60 \quad (2a)$$
Add these together.
$$19x \quad = 57$$
$$x \quad = 3$$
Substitute $x = 3$ in (1).
$$9 + 5y = -1$$
$$5y = -10$$
$$y = -2$$
The solution is $x = 3$, $y = -2$.

You can check these equations in the same way as you checked linear equations.
Check both equations.
In (1), LHS $= 3x + 5y = 3 \times 3 \ + \ 5 \times (-2) = 9 - 10 = -1$; RHS $= -1$.
Both sides are the same, so the equation checks.
In (2), LHS $= 2x - 3y = 2 \times 3 \ - \ 3 \times (-2) = 6 + 6 = 12$; RHS $= 12$.
Both sides are the same, so this equation also checks.

2   Solve the simultaneous equations $7x + 2y = 19, \quad 4x + 3y = 22.$

$$7x + 2y = 19 \quad (1)$$
$$4x + 3y = 22 \quad (2)$$

Multiply (1) by 3 and (2) by 2.

$$21x + 6y = 57 \quad (1a)$$
$$8x + 6y = 44 \quad (2a)$$

Subtract (2a) from (1a).

$$13x \quad\quad = 13$$
$$x \quad\quad = 1$$

Substitute $x = 1$ in (1).

$$7 + 2y = 19$$
$$2y = 12$$
$$y = 6$$

The solution is $x = 1$, $y = 6$.

Check for yourself that this solution is correct.

Be very careful if subtracting numbers or terms with negative signs.
e.g. in a case like $3x - 6y = 6 \quad (1)$
$$3x - 5y = 11 \quad (2)$$
When subtracting (2) from (1), $(-6y) - (-5y) = (-6y) + 5y = -y$
When subtracting (1) from (2), $(-5y) - (-6y) = (-5y) + 6y = y$

Solving by substitution

This method is useful when we have a term containing x (i.e. not $2x$, $3x$, etc.) or y.

Example

3   Solve the equations $x - 8y = 3 \quad (1)$
$$3x - 10y = 2 \quad (2)$$

(1) can be written as $x = 3 + 8y \quad (1a)$
Substitute this expression for x in (2).
$$3(3 + 8y) - 10y = 2$$
Remove the bracket and solve in the usual way.
$$9 + 24y - 10y = 2$$
$$9 + 14y = 2$$
$$14y = -7$$
$$y = -\tfrac{1}{2}$$

Use (1a) again, substituting $y = -\tfrac{1}{2}$.

$$x = 3 + 8 \times \left(-\tfrac{1}{2}\right)$$
$$= 3 - 4$$
$$= -1$$

The solution is $x = -1$, $y = -\tfrac{1}{2}$.

Exercise 8.3

Solve the simultaneous equations

1. $4x + 3y = 34$
   $x - 3y = 1$

2. $3x - 4y = 5$
   $2x + y = -4$

3. $3x + 4y = 10$
   $2x + 3y = 8$

4. $x + 5y = 7$
   $3x - y = -11$

5. $3x + 8y = 7$
   $5x - 6y = 2$

6. $7x - 3y = 26$
   $9x - 5y = 30$

7. $2x + 3y = -10$
   $4x - y = 15$

8. $2x - 3y = -1$
   $4x - y = -2$

9. $3x + 4y = 6$
   $4x - y = -11$

10. $3x + 4y = 0$
    $2x + 5y = -7$

11. $3x - 2y = 1$
    $5x - 6y = 3$

12. $x + 3y = 3x - 5y = 7$

13. $5x - 2y = 7x + 2y = x - 5$

14. $10x + y = 7x - y + 18 = 77$

15. At a snack-bar, 5 cups of tea and 3 cups of coffee cost £2.30, and 3 cups of tea and 2 cups of coffee cost £1.45. What is the price of a cup of tea, and of a cup of coffee? (Let a cup of tea cost x pence and a cup of coffee cost y pence. Write down two equations and solve them simultaneously.)

16. Write down two equations connecting x and y, simplify them, and solve them simultaneously. Hence find the numerical values of the lengths of the sides of this parallelogram.

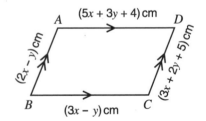

Exercise 8.4 Applications

1. Find the range of values of x for which

   1 $3 - 2(4 - x) \geqslant 3x$ **2** $x - 3 < 7 < 5x + 2$

2. Find the smallest integer n such that $n + 9 \leqslant 3n - 4$.

3. Find all pairs of positive integers (x, y) such that $3x + 2y \leqslant 11$.

4. A coach firm has to carry 300 people on an outing. It has 5 coaches which can carry up to 50 passengers each and 7 minibuses which can carry up to 20 passengers each. There are 10 drivers available.
    If x coaches and y minibuses are used, write down 4 inequalities satisfied by x and y.
    By trial, find how many coaches and how many minibuses should be used, so as to use the least number of drivers.

5. A polygon with n sides has $\dfrac{n(n-3)}{2}$ diagonals. How many sides has a polygon with 65 diagonals ?

6. The perimeter of a rectangular field is 220 m. Find an expression for the breadth in terms of the length x m.
    If the area of the field is 2800 m^2, find its length.

7. The sum s of the first n square numbers, $1^2, 2^2, 3^2, \ldots, n^2$, is given by the formula $s = \frac{1}{6}n(n+1)(2n+1)$.

    If $s = 204$, find the value of n.

8. There are 12 containers of cuboid shape with length and width x m and height 5 m, and one cubical container of edge x m. Find the value of x, to 1 decimal place, if the total capacity of the containers is 360 m^3.

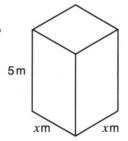

5 m x m x m

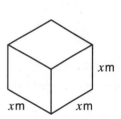

x m x m x m

9. Entrance fees to a show for 3 adults and 2 children total £6.80; for 2 adults and 5 children it costs £8.20. How much is the cost for an adult, and for a child ?

10. Write down two equations connecting x and y, simplify them, and solve them simultaneously. Hence find the numerical values of the three angles.

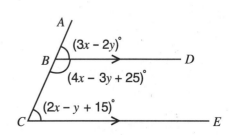

11. If this triangle is equilateral, write down an
equation connecting x and y and simplify it.
Write down a second equation connecting
x and y and simplify it.
Solve the equations simultaneously to find
x and y.
What is the numerical value of the perimeter
of the triangle ?

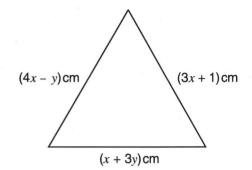

$(4x - y)$ cm

$(3x + 1)$ cm

$(x + 3y)$ cm

12. The law of a machine is given by $E = aR + C$. When $R = 10$, $E = 5.5$ and when $R = 40$,
$E = 7$. Find the values of a and C.

13. An employer pays some of his workers £50 per day, and others £40 a day. Altogether he
has 30 workers and the daily wages amount to £1440. How many workers get the £40
wage ?

14. Two rolls of carpet are together worth £1200. The first roll costs £20 per metre. The
second, which is 12 m longer than the first, costs £16 per metre. How many metres were
there in each roll ?

15. If $y = ax + b$, and x and y satisfy this table of values, what are the values of a and b ?

x	1	2	3
y	-1	2	5

16. $7x + 5y = 47$
$5x + 7y = 49$.
Find the values of   **1** $x + y$,   **2** $x - y$.
Hence find the values of x and y.

17. Solve the equations

$$5a - 2b = 19$$
$$4a + 9b = -6.$$

Hence solve the equations

$$\frac{5}{c} - \frac{2}{d} = 19$$

$$\frac{4}{c} + \frac{9}{d} = -6.$$

Practice test 8

1. Solve the inequalities

    1 $3(1 - 2x) \geqslant 12$
    2 $3x - 5 < x + 6$
    3 $5x^2 + 11 \leqslant 256$

2. Solve these equations by trial, finding solutions which are positive numbers.

    1 $(x + 3)(x - 2) = 104,$
    2 $x^3 + 8x = 29$, correct to 1 decimal place.

3. Solve the simultaneous equations

    1 $5x - 2y = 17$ **2** $8x - 2y = 10$
        $6x + 7y = 11$ $6x - y = 6$

4. Patrick buys a bunch of 10 roses and 5 carnations for his wife, and they cost £3.50.
    At the same stall, Margaret buys a bunch of 8 roses and 10 carnations for her
    mother, and they cost £4.
    Find the cost of 1 rose, and 1 carnation

PUZZLES

21. A firm sells stationery in packets as follows:
     A notebook and 2 biros cost 48p, a notebook and 4 pencils cost 58p, a notebook,
     a pencil and 3 felt-tipped pens cost 64p.
     How much should you pay for a package containing a notebook, a pencil, a biro and
     a felt-tipped pen ?

22. The ages of my father, my son and myself total 85 years. My father is just twice my
     age, and the units figure in his age is equal to the age of my son. How old am I ?

23. A GSCE Maths target !
     Replace every letter by a number in this addition sum,
     where S = 3 and 0 is not used. Then find the word for 72851.

     ```
       A G C S E
     + M A T H S
     ─────────────
       T A R G E T
     ```

24. See how many of the numbers from 1 to 100 you can represent using three 9's, and
     mathematical signs.   e.g. $78 = (9 \times 9) - \sqrt{9}$.
     Then try to represent all the others using four 9's.

Averages and frequency distributions

The topics in this chapter include:

- organising and analysing data,

- finding the mean, median, mode

    1   of a set of data,

    2   of a frequency distribution,

- using grouped data,

- drawing frequency polygons, comparing two frequency polygons.

Averages

When statistical data has been collected, we often need to find an average measurement. There are several kinds of average. Here we will use the mean, the median and the mode.

1   **The mean** $= \dfrac{\text{the total of the items}}{\text{the number of items}}$.

The formula is written as

$$\bar{x} = \frac{\Sigma x}{n},$$

where $\bar{x}$ (read as x bar) is the symbol for the mean;

   Σ, the Greek capital letter sigma, means 'the sum of', so Σx means the sum of the x-values;

   n is the number of items.

2   **The median.** When the items are arranged in order of size, the median is the value of the middle item, or the value halfway between the middle two if there is an even number of items.

3   **The mode** is the value which occurs most often. (Sometimes a set of values will not have a mode, as there may not be any value which occurs more often than any of the others.)

Example

1   **Numbers of members of a club attending the meetings**

Week number	1	2	3	4	5	6	7	8	9	10	Total
Attendance	20	19	24	22	20	23	20	28	24	20	220

Find the mean, median and mode attendances.

The mean attendance

$$\bar{x} = \frac{\Sigma x}{n} = \frac{220}{10} = 22$$

The median

(Arrange the items in order of size.)

19   20   20   20   20   22   23   24   24   28
                                                          ↑
                                                       middle

The median is halfway between 20 and 22, i.e. 21.
(Half the values are less than 21 and half are greater than 21.)

The mode

The value which occurs most often is 20 (as there were 4 weeks when 20 members were present), so the mode is 20.

Summary:- Mean = 22, median = 21, mode = 20.

All these averages can be used in different circumstances, although the most usual one is the mean, as this is the one which involves all the values. If one of the values is very high or low compared to the others, this will affect the mean and in this case the median might be a better average to use. The mode is the simplest average to find, but generally it is not as useful as the other two.

Example

2   In a class test, the marks were

5   10   25   25   25   30   30   30   30   35

The mean mark is 24.5, the median mark is 27.5 and the mode mark is 30.

Comment about the averages.

The fairest average to quote here is the median. Half the students have less than 27.5 and half have more.
The mean has been distorted by the two low values, and only two students have marks less than the mean.
The mode is not a representative average, as only 1 student has a better mark.

If the word 'average' is used without specifying which one in an arithmetical question, it refers to the mean.

In your answers, remember to give the unit of measurement, e.g. cm, kg. Check that your answer seems to be reasonable. Do not give too many decimal places. If the data is accurate to the nearest whole number then it is reasonable to give the averages to 1 decimal place.

Example

3   After 5 tests Kevin has an average of 13 marks. In a 6th test he scores 19 marks. What is his new average mark ?

In the 1st 5 tests Kevin scored a total of $13 \times 5 = 65$ marks
In the 6th test he scored   19 marks
Total marks scored in 6 tests $= 84$ marks

Average mark $= \dfrac{\Sigma x}{n} = \dfrac{84}{6} = 14$ marks

Using a statistical calculator to find the mean

e.g. To find the mean of 23, 24, 28, 29, 31.

Set the calculator to work in statistical mode, then press

23 $\boxed{\text{DATA}}$ 24 $\boxed{\text{DATA}}$ 28 $\boxed{\text{DATA}}$ 29 $\boxed{\text{DATA}}$ 31 $\boxed{\text{DATA}}$

When you have entered all the data, pressing
$\boxed{n}$ will tell you the number of items entered, 5,
$\boxed{\Sigma x}$ will tell you the sum of the items entered, 135,
$\boxed{\bar{x}}$ will tell you the mean of the items entered, 27.

Dispersion

The average (mean, median or mode) gives us a general idea of the data, but two sets of numbers can have the same mean but be very different in other ways. The other main statistic we find is a measure of dispersion (or spread).

There are several measures of dispersion, of which we will use three:
1   the range,
2   the interquartile range (used in Chapter 13),
3   the standard deviation (used in Chapter 18).

The range is the simplest measure of dispersion to find.

> Range = highest value − lowest value

The range only uses the extreme values so it is not always very representative.

Exercise 9.1

1. Find the mean, median and range of these sets of numbers.

    1 4   5   5   7   7   8   9   10   12   15   17
    2 12   20   31   35   39   48   55   71   85
    3 2   14   5   12   7
    4 25   53   37   17   62   93   41   27   33   19
    5 1.5   1.7   1.8   1.9   2.0   2.0   2.1   2.2

2. Find the median, mode and range of these sets of numbers.

    1 4   5   5   7   7   7   8   9   9   10   12   12   12   12   13
    2 26   27   29   25   31   33   27   32   28   27   33
    3 3   5   1   6   2   5   4   8   1   5   2   5   7   2   1   5   4   3   6   9   4   1   6   7

3. Find the mean of

    1 59.2,   90.0,   75.8,   32.6.
    2 £985,   £863,   £904,   £967,   £868.
    3 1 hr 20 min,   2 hr 30 min,   1 hr 45 min,   3 hr 10 min,   2 hr 8 min,   1 hr 13 min.
    4 $1\frac{1}{4}$, $2\frac{1}{3}$, $3\frac{1}{2}$.
    5 2.5 kg,   3.4 kg,   2.7 kg,   1.9 kg,   4.0 kg.

4. **1** The weights in kg of 10 children are
            54,   52,   62,   49,   61,   56,   51,   64,   54,   67.
            Find the mean and the median weights.

    2 The ages of 5 boys are
            12 y 1 m,   12 y 5 m,   13 y 7 m,   11 y 2 m,   11 y 7 m.
            Find the mean age.

    3 The weights of 10 helpings of potatoes (to the nearest 10 g) are
            150 g,   170 g,   190 g,   160 g,   180 g,   140 g,   170 g,   170 g,   150 g,   160 g.
            Find the mean weight.

5. The 1971 census recorded 7.45 million people living in Greater London in 2.65 million households. Find the mean number of people per household.
    The figures for the North-west region of England were 6.74 million people and 2.27 million households. Were there more people per household in London or in the North-west region ?

6. A cricketer had an average of 30 runs (per innings) after playing 10 innings. In his next innings he was out after scoring 52 runs. What was his new average ?

Frequency Distributions

Discrete data (i.e. the variables are numbers, not measurements)

Formula for the mean

$$\bar{x} = \frac{\Sigma fx}{\Sigma f}$$

where Σf is the total of the frequencies,
Σfx is the total of the fx values.

Example

1 The numbers of children in 50 families (with at least 1 child) are as follows:

4 5 2 2 3 4 4 3 5 4 7 3 3 4 2 2 2 2 2 6 3 2 3 3 1
2 3 2 2 6 5 5 3 2 4 4 2 4 1 2 2 2 1 3 3 2 2 4 5 3

Tally chart

Number of children	Number of families	
	Tally	f
1	III	3
2	𝍸 𝍸 𝍸 III	18
3	𝍸 𝍸 II	12
4	𝍸 IIII	9
5	𝍸	5
6	II	2
7	I	1
		50

(Remember the 5th tally mark goes through the other 4.)

The most suitable diagram to represent the data is a bar-line graph, but a histogram is sometimes used.

Bar-line graph

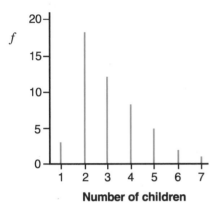

Children in 50 families

Histogram

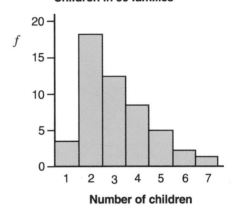

Children in 50 families

Averages and Range

Mode. There are most families with 2 children (18), so the mode is 2 children per family.

Median. If the numbers were arranged in order of size
1 1 1 2 2 2 . . . 5 6 6 7
the middle value would be halfway between the 25th and 26th numbers, and these are both 3, so the median is 3 children per family.
(This is easier to find by making a cumulative frequency table as explained in Chapter 13.)

Mean. Write down a frequency table. x is the number of children, f is the frequency. Add a column for fx. Find the sums of the columns f and fx.

x	f	fx
1	3	3
2	18	36
3	12	36
4	9	36
5	5	25
6	2	12
7	1	7
	50	155

(1×3)
(2×18)

$$\bar{x} = \frac{\Sigma fx}{\Sigma f} = \frac{155}{50} = 3.1$$

The mean is 3.1 children per family.

The range = highest value − lowest value = 7 − 1 = 6 children.

Combining means

Examples

2   If the mean amount spent on travelling to work by 6 girls was 40 p, and the mean
     amount spent on travelling to work by another 4 girls was 50 p, what was the mean
     amount for the 10 girls together ?

     Do **not** just average 40 p and 50 p, because 45 p is not the correct answer.
     Always find the total amount, then find the mean.
     The total amount for the 1st 6 girls is $40 \text{ p} \times 6 = 240 \text{ p}$
     The total amount for the other 4 girls is $50 \text{ p} \times 4 = \underline{200 \text{ p}}$
     The total amount for the 10 girls is 440 p

     The mean amount is $\dfrac{440 \text{ p}}{10} = 44 \text{ p}.$

3   There are 60 workers in a firm and their mean wage was £160 per week. If everyone
     received a £10 per week pay-rise what would the new mean wage be ?

     (You would probably guess that it would be £170 and this is correct.)

     The previous total of wages was $£160 \times 60 =$ £9600
     The extra total of wages is $£10 \ \times 60 = \underline{\ \ £600}$
     The new total of wages is   £10200

     The new mean wage $= \dfrac{£10200}{60} = £170$ per week.

     If, instead, everyone received a 7% pay-rise, what would the new mean wage be ?

     You might guess that this is 107% of £160 = £171.20, and this is correct.

     The previous total of wages was £160 × 60 = £9600
     The extra total of wages is 7% of £9600 = $\underline{\ \ £672}$
     The new total of wages is   £10272

     The new mean wage $= \dfrac{£10272}{60} = £171.20$ per week.

Exercise 9.2

For the frequency distributions in questions 1 to 5,
1   draw a bar-line graph of the distribution,
2   find the mean, median and mode of the distribution.

1.   Number of people per household in a sample of 50 households.

Size of household, x	1	2	3	4	5	6
Number of households, f	10	18	9	7	4	2

2.   Number of goals scored by 30 teams in a league.

Goals	0	1	2	3	4	5
f (number of teams)	8	9	5	4	2	2

3.   Number of heads when 8 coins were tossed together 60 times.

Number of heads	0	1	2	3	4	5	6	7	8
f		1	2	7	15	17	11	5	2	0

4.   Number of pupils per class in 30 classes in a school.

Number in class	29	30	31	32	33
f	6	10	5	5	4

5.   Apexa plays a computer game in which she can score from 0 to 10 in each game. The scores she achieved in several games are shown here.

Score	0	1	2	3	4	5	6	7	8	9	10
Frequency	2	3	0	4	3	8	5	9	3	1	2

6.   A dealer bought 90 cases of goods at £10 per case and a second lot of 70 cases at £6 per case. What is the average price per case ?

7.   The average age of 6 boys is 8 years 2 months, and the average age of 5 girls is 9 years 1 month. Find the average age of the 11 children.

8.   In a year-group of 60 pupils, the number of subjects each pupil passed in an examination was as follows:

```
5  8  8  7  8  7  6  4  8  7  8  7  7  8  5  6  6  3  6  6
8  7  9  5  7  8  7  7  8  6  7  9  4  7  8  9  6  5  9  8
3  8  7  4  5  8  4  5  6  9  9  9  9  7  8  8  5  6  7  6
```

Tally the results to form a frequency distribution. Draw a histogram or a bar-line graph of the distribution. Find the mean, median and mode of the number of subjects passed.

Grouped data

If the range of data is wide we can put it into convenient groups, called classes.

Example

1   The distribution of examination marks of 120 students.

Mark	0–9	10–19	20–29	30–39	40–49	50–59	60–69
f (number of students)	5	14	22	29	27	19	4

The data can be represented by a histogram.

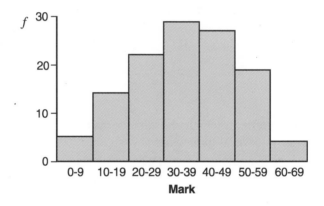

In a histogram, the **area** of each block represents the frequency.
In the histograms in this chapter, the class intervals are of equal width, so the heights of the columns are in proportion to their frequencies, and can be labelled to represent the frequencies. If the class intervals are unequal then the heights do not represent the frequencies. This is explained in Chapter 18.

The modal class is the class which includes most students, here it is the class 30–39 marks.

The median mark is best found using a cumulative frequency table (see Chapter 13).

To find the mean mark we assume that each student has the mark corresponding to the centre of the class interval in which it lies, e.g. the centre of the marks 0–9 is 4.5, of 10–19 is 14.5, and so on. Of the 14 students who got between 10 and 19 marks, some probably got less than 14.5 marks and some more, so 14.5 is the best estimate we can make.

Use the formula $\bar{x} = \dfrac{\Sigma fx}{\Sigma f}$, taking x as the value at the centre of the interval.

If you are using your calculator to find the numbers in the *fx* column, add them into the memory as you go along, then to get the total you only have to press the 'recall memory' key.

If you do not need to show the separate totals you may be able to add them up directly. But it is advisable to do a check in case you have missed out some. Does the answer **look** right ? Anything above 69 is bound to be wrong. Looking at the distribution we would make a rough estimate that the average mark is between 30 and 39 marks.

Mark	f	x centre of interval	fx	
0–9	5	4.5	22.5	$\bar{x} = \dfrac{\Sigma fx}{\Sigma f}$
10–19	14	14.5	203.0	
20–29	22	24.5	539.0	$= \dfrac{4260}{120}$
30–39	29	34.5	1000.5	
40–49	27	44.5	1201.5	$= 35.5$ marks.
50–59	19	54.5	1035.5	
60–69	4	64.5	258.0	
	120		4260.0	

Using a statistical calculator

Set the calculator to work in statistical mode then press

4.5 $\boxed{x}$ 5 $\boxed{\text{DATA}}$ 14.5 $\boxed{x}$ 14 $\boxed{\text{DATA}}$ and so on.

When you have entered all the data,
$\boxed{n}$ will tell you the number of items, Σf, and gives 120,
$\boxed{\Sigma x}$ will tell you the sum of the items, Σfx, and gives 4260,
$\boxed{\bar{x}}$ will tell you the mean, and gives 35.5.

Continuous data

(i.e. the variables are measurements, such as lengths, weights, times, which go up continuously, not in jumps.)

Example

2   The lengths of leaves from a bush, using a sample of 60 leaves.

Length in cm	5.0–5.4	5.5–5.9	6.0–6.4	6.5–6.9	7.0–7.4	7.5–7.9
f	2	12	20	15	8	3

Measurements in the 1st class interval will include lengths from 4.95 to 5.45 cm, in the 2nd class interval from 5.45 to 5.95 cm, and so on.
The centre of the 1st class interval is 5.2 cm, of the 2nd one is 5.7 cm, and so on.

In the histogram, since the measurements are continuous, we can label the edges of the intervals,

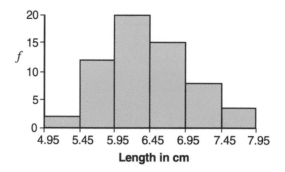

The modal class is the class interval from 6.0 to 6.4 cm. (This actually includes measurements from 5.95 to 6.45 cm.)

To find the mean length of leaf, copy and complete this table.

x centre of interval	f	fx
5.2	2	10.4
5.7	12	
6.2		
6.7		
7.2		
7.7		
	60	

$$\bar{x} = \frac{\Sigma fx}{\Sigma f}$$

$$= \frac{\cdots}{60} \text{ cm}$$

$$= \cdots \text{ cm}$$

Give your answer to 1 decimal place.
(The correct answer is 6.4 cm.)

Age distributions

Ages are usually given in completed years so in a table such as this a child who has not quite reached the age of 10 years will be included in the 5–9 class interval. Thus the class interval is from 5 years to 10 years and the centre of the interval is 7.5 years. A child is included in the 10–14 class interval if he has had his 10th birthday but not his 15th, and the class interval is from 10 years to 15 years, with centre of interval 12.5 years.

Age in years	f
5–9	2
10–14	3
15–19	5

Compare this with a table for weight
Weights are usually measured to the nearest kg so a
weight of 9.7 kg will go in the 10–14 class interval. But
the 5–9 class interval can also include weights over
4.5 kg. So the class intervals are 4.5–9.5 kg, 9.5–14.5 kg,
14.5–19.5 kg, and the centres of intervals are 7 kg, 12 kg
and 17 kg respectively.

Weight in kg	f
5–9	2
10–14	3
15–19	5

Histograms

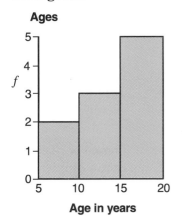

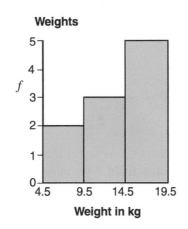

Exercise 9.3

1. The marks of 40 children in a test were as follows:

Mark	0–2	3–5	6–8	9–11	12–14	15–17	18–20
Number of children	4	3	5	7	10	6	5

   1 What is the modal class of this distribution ?
   2 Draw a histogram of the distribution.
   3 Find the mean mark.

2. The heights of 40 plants, given to the nearest cm, are as follows:

Height in cm	3	4	5	6	7	8
Number of plants	1	7	10	12	8	2

   1 Draw a histogram of this distribution.
   2 Find the mean of the distribution.

3. The weights of 120 men are as follows:

Weight in kg	60–	65–	70–	75–	80–	85–90
Number of men	4	18	36	50.	10	2

(The 1st class includes weights between 60 and 65 kg, and the centre of interval is 62.5 kg, and so on.)

1 What is the modal class of the distribution ?
2 What is the centre of interval of this class ?
3 Draw a histogram of the distribution.
4 Find the mean weight.

4. The ages of 100 cars in a survey are as follows:

Age in years	0–2	2–4	4–6	6–8	8–10	10–12	12–14
Number of cars	16	23	24	17	12	7	1

(The 1st class includes cars up to just under 2 years old, the centre of interval is 1 year. The 2nd class includes cars from 2 years to just under 4 years old, the centre of interval is 3 years; and so on.)

1 What is the modal class ?
2 Draw a histogram of the distribition.
3 Find the mean age of the cars in the survey.

5. The lengths of 60 leaves on a plant.

Length in cm	7–9	10–12	13–15	16–18	19–21
Number of leaves	4	16	24	13	3

1 What are the boundaries of the length measurements in the 1st class interval ? What is the centre of this interval ?
2 Find the mean length of the leaves.
3 Draw a histogram of the distribution.

6. The histogram shows the times taken by a group of boys to run a race.

1 How many boys were there altogether ?
2 What percentage of boys took less than 7 minutes ?
3 What is the modal class of the distribution ?
4 What is the centre of interval of the modal class ?
5 Find the mean time taken by the boys.

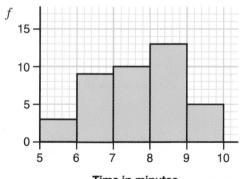

Frequency Polygons

A frequency polygon is an alternative diagram which is sometimes used instead of a histogram. One use is for when two or more frequency distributions with the same total frequencies have to be compared. It is possible to draw their frequency polygons on the same graph, whereas this is not possible with histograms.

The simplest way to see how to draw a frequency polygon is to draw one on the same diagram as a histogram. It is constructed by joining the mid-points of the top lines of the histogram.

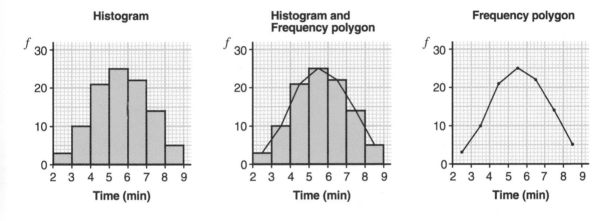

You can see that the word 'polygon' was chosen because it consists of a series of straight lines.

Some people say that the polygon should be closed, by meeting the horizontal axis on both sides.

You cannot do this if you are drawing the frequency polygon on the same diagram as a histogram, as you will not have left an empty class interval.

If you are drawing a separate frequency polygon, you can add an extra class interval on each side. These have frequency 0. Join the polygon to the mid-point of each.

Frequency polygon with extra intervals added.

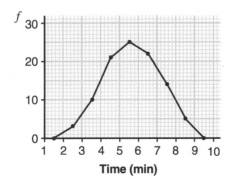

Exercise 9.4

Questions 1 to 5

For the questions 1 to 5 of Exercise 9.3, page 193, either add a frequency polygon to the histogram that you have already drawn, or draw a separate frequency polygon of the data.

6. The distributions of examination marks in two examinations are shown in this table. Draw frequency polygons for these distributions on the same graph and comment on them.

Mark	0–9	10–19	20–29	30–39	40–49	50–59	60–69	70–79	80–89	90–99
1st exam	3	8	7	11	14	18	21	10	6	2
2nd exam			1	3	6	8	15	38	22	7

Exercise 9.5   Applications

1. The average of the numbers x, 30, 32, 40, $2x$ is 34.2. Find the value of x.

2. The times taken by 6 girls on a training run were
    10 min 20 sec,   9 min 5 sec,   11 min 45 sec,   12 min 0 sec,   8 min 30 sec,   10 min 50 sec.
    Find the mean time taken.

3. The average weight of 5 packages is 8.6 kg. The average weight of 4 of them is 9.6 kg. What does the 5th package weigh ?

4. A school had 1029 pupils and 70 teachers. What was the mean number of pupils per teacher ? The next year the school increased its intake and had an extra 60 pupils. To keep approximately the same mean number of pupils per teacher, how many extra teachers were needed ?

5. The goals scored by 20 football teams were as follows:
    8 teams scored no goals, 4 teams scored 1 goal each, 3 teams scored 2 goals, 1 team scored 3 goals, 3 teams scored 4 goals, 1 team scored 5 goals.
    What is the average number of goals scored per team, by the 20 teams ?

6. The number of seeds germinating in 40 pots when 6 seeds were planted in each pot was as follows:

Number of seeds	0	1	2	3	4	5	6
Number of pots	0	1	3	12	10	11	3

Draw a bar-line graph of the distribution.
Find the mean, median and mode of the distribution.
If you pick a pot at random from this batch what is the probability that it will have 4 or more germinating seeds ?

7. In a class there are 8 boys in Set 1 and 12 boys in Set 2. In a test the Set 1 boys' average mark is 65 and the Set 2 boys' average mark is 60. Find the average mark for the whole class.

8. The marks of 25 children in an examination were as follows:

68 78 64 67 73 94 69 86 62 67 82 79 61
87 71 81 79 82 77 73 81 84 74 76 66

Tally these data in classes 60–64, 65–69, 70–74, etc.
Draw a histogram of the grouped distribution.
Find the mean of the distribution.

In questions 9 and 10, draw histograms of the distributions. Find the mean of the distribution, and state the modal class.

9. The weekly wages of 30 women.

Wage (to nearest £20)	60	80	100	120
Number of women	3	7	15	5

(The 1st class includes women whose wages are between £50 and £70, the 2nd class £70 to £90, and so on.)

10. Heights of 60 men.

Height in cm	168–170	171–173	174–176	177–179	180–182	183–185	186–188	189–191
Number of men	2	4	8	13	14	9	7	3

In question 11, 12 and 13, draw histograms of the distributions. Find the mean of the distribution, and state the modal class.

11. Ages of children in a club.

Age (in completed years)	11	12	13	14	15
Number of children	8	10	6	4	2

12. Length of 30 leaves.

Length in cm	6.0	6.5	7.0	7.5	8.0	8.5
Number of leaves	1	5	7	11	4	2

13. Times taken by 100 children to travel to school.

Time in minutes	0–5	5–10	10–15	15–20	20–25	25–30
Number of children	3	15	27	34	19	2

14. The weights of a group of children are given in this frequency distribution.

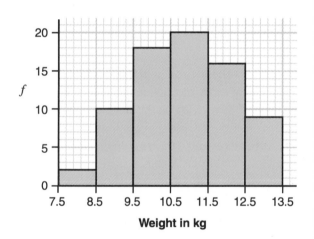

   1 How many children are there altogether ?
   2 What is the modal class ?
   3 Find the mean weight.
   4 What percentage of the children weigh less than 9.5 kg ?

15. 30 students were asked in a survey to say how many hours they spent watching television in the previous week. Their answers, in hours to the nearest hour, are as follows:

12   20   13   15   22   3   6   24   20   15   9   12   5   6   8
30   7   12   14   25   2   6   12   20   20   18   3   18   8   9

Tally these data in classes 1–5, 6–10, 11–15, etc.
(The class 1–5 includes actual times from 0.5 to 5.5 hours and the centre of interval is 3 hours, the class 6–10 includes times from 5.5 to 10.5 hours and the centre of interval is 8 hours; and so on.)
Calculate the mean of the grouped distribution.
Draw a histogram of the distribution.

Questions 16 to 20

Draw frequency polygons of the data of questions 9 to 13 above.

21. The table shows the age distribution of the population of the UK in 1901 and 1981. Draw frequency polygons on the same graph to represent the data, and comment on them.
(Figures in 100 000's.)

Age (years)	Population	
	1901	1981
0–9	85	70
10–19	78	90
20–29	70	78
30–39	53	76
40–49	40	62
50–59	28	64
60–69	18	56
70–79	8	40
80–89	2	15

(A few people in the last group are over 89 years old.)

22. The number of words per sentence in the first 50 sentences of two books are recorded below.
Draw frequency polygons on the same graph to represent the data.
Find the mean number of words per sentence for each book.
Compare the two sets of data and comment on them.

(1) 'The Children of the New Forest'
(2) 'The Adventures of Tom Sawyer'

Number of words	Number of sentences	
	(1)	(2)
1–10	2	27
11–20	9	11
21–30	14	9
31–40	7	0
41–50	4	3
51–60	8	0
61–70	3	0
71–80	2	0
81–90	1	0

Practice test 9

1.   The temperature in a city each day of a summer week was (in °C)
     22 22 23 24 23 20 20

     Find the mean temperature.

2.   At a seaside resort there was a mean amount of 3 hours of sunshine per day for
     the 6 days Monday to Saturday of a certain week. On the Sunday there were
     10 hours of sunshine. What was the mean amount of sunshine per day for the
     whole week ?

3.   The number of goals scored in 84 football matches were written down in order
     as they were heard on the radio.
     Results:
     0 2 0 2 2 2 0 3 1 4 1 0 1 0 2 1 4 1 5 1 5 0 3
     2 2 1 1 4 2 0 3 0 1 1 2 1 0 1 1 2 2 1 2 0 1 1
     1 2 0 0 2 2 1 2 0 3 2 0 1 0 0 0 1 0 1 2 1 0 2
     2 3 0 2 0 3 1 1 2 1 2 2 2 1 3

     Make a frequency table to show these results.
     Draw a bar-line graph of the distribution.
     Find the mean, median and mode number of goals scored, and the range.

4.   12 kg of pet food at 14p per kg are mixed with 18 kg of pet food at 20p per kg.
     What is the cost of 1 kg of the mixture ?

5.   The heights of 80 students are as follows:

Height in cm	150–154	155–159	160–164	165–169	170–174	175–179	180–184	185–189
Number of students	3	4	9	16	18	17	7	6

     1   What is the modal class of the distribution ?
     2   What are the actual limits of heights of students in this modal class ?
     3   What is the centre of interval of this modal class ?
     4   Draw a histogram of the distribution.
     5   Draw a frequency polygon of the distribution.
     6   Find the mean height of the students.

PUZZLES

25. In the 'Tower of Hanoi' puzzle, there are 8 discs of different sizes on 1 peg, with two empty pegs.

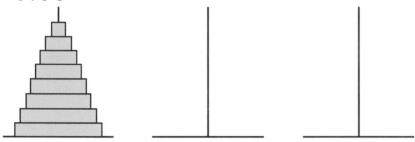

The game is to transfer all the discs to one of the empty pegs.
Only one disc can be moved at a time. A disc can only be placed on an empty peg or onto a larger disc, never onto a smaller one.
Make your own version of this game using circles of cardboard, and see how many moves are needed. You may prefer to discover the pattern of moves by starting with less than 8 discs. Notice the moves of the smallest disc.
The legend has it that there is such a peg with 64 discs on it. At the rate of 1 move per second, how long will it take to move all 64 discs ?

26. Mine cost 52p, my neighbour's cost 26p and I got some for my friend who lives at the far end of the road, and they cost 78p. What was I buying in the hardware shop ?

27. Colin, David, Peter, Richard and Susan took a Maths test, and after Colin had been told his mark he asked the teacher how the others had done.
'Well, I can't tell you anything about Susan's mark as I have not marked her paper yet, but I can tell you about the other three. Peter did better than David though not as well as Richard. The sum of their three marks is equal to three times your mark, and when their marks are multiplied together they make 540.'
So Colin went away to find a pencil and some paper, and later he returned to point out that he still had not got enough information to find out the marks of the three boys.
'Yes, that is correct, but I have now marked Susan's work, and she is top with 26 marks more than David, so now you will be able to sort out everyone's scores.'
What are the marks of the five students ?
(All the marks are whole numbers.)

10 Coordinates and straight-line graphs

The topics in this chapter include:

- drawing and interpreting the graphs of linear functions,
- interpreting and using m and c in $y = mx + c$,
- using graphical methods to solve simultaneous equations,
- using straight-line graphs to locate regions given by linear inequalities,
- using coordinates to locate position in 3-D.

Coordinates

A point on a graph can be specified by giving its coordinates, i.e. its x-value and its y-value.

Example

1 Point A has x-value 1 and y-value 2.
   This can be written as the point (1,2).
   A is (1, 2),
   B is (−2, 1),
   C is (0, −3).
   Copy this diagram and plot the
   point D (3, −2).
   Join AB, BC, CD and DA.
   What sort of figure is $ABCD$?

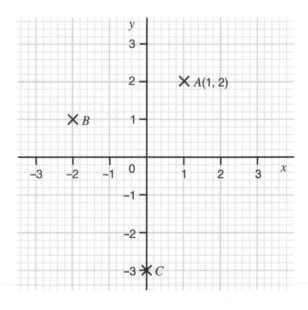

To find the gradient of a line drawn on a graph

Choose 2 points A and B on the line, a reasonable distance apart.

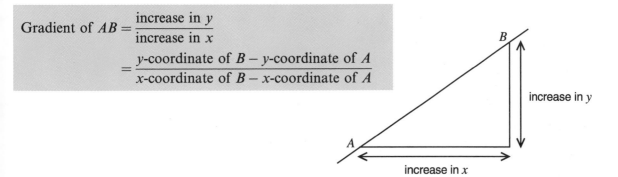

$$\text{Gradient of } AB = \frac{\text{increase in } y}{\text{increase in } x}$$

$$= \frac{y\text{-coordinate of } B - y\text{-coordinate of } A}{x\text{-coordinate of } B - x\text{-coordinate of } A}$$

If A is (1, 2.2) and B is (8.6, 7.9),

gradient of $AB = \dfrac{7.9 - 2.2}{8.6 - 1} = \dfrac{5.7}{7.6} = 0.75$

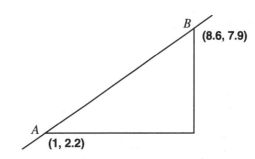

If the line slopes the other way the gradient will be negative.

To find the distance between A and B

Using Pythagoras' theorem,

$$AB^2 = AC^2 + BC^2$$

$$= (8.6 - 1)^2 + (7.9 - 2.2)^2$$

$$= 7.6^2 + 5.7^2$$

$$= 90.25$$

$$AB = 9.5 \text{ units}$$

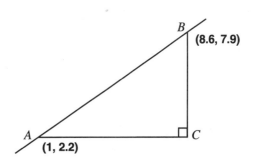

Straight-line graphs

Examples

2 For this question, use graph paper with x from -1 to 3 and y from -3 to 9 using scales of 1 cm to 1 unit on both axes.

(1) This is a table connecting values of x and y.

x	-1	0	1	2	3
y	-1	0	1	2	3

To represent this table on graph paper, plot the points $(-1, -1)$, $(0, 0)$, $(1, 1)$, $(2, 2)$, $(3, 3)$.
These points lie on a straight line. Draw it.
The connection in the table between y and x is $y = x$.
So $y = x$ is the equation of the line.

(2) Here is another table.

x	-1	0	1	2	3
y	-2	0	2	4	6

To represent this, plot the points $(-1, -2)$, $(0, 0)$, $(1, 2)$, $(2, 4)$, $(3, 6)$ on the same graph as before, and draw the straight line through these points.
The equation of this line is $y = 2x$.

It is a steeper line than the first one.
The gradient (or slope) of $y = x$ is 1.
The gradient of $y = 2x$ is 2.

(3) Make similar tables for $y = 3x$, and $y = \frac{1}{2}x$, and plot these lines on your graph.

3 For this question use graph paper with x from -1 to 3 and y from -4 to 5, using equal scales on both axes.
Plot the points given in this table, and draw the line.

x	-1	0	1	2	3
y	1	2	3	4	5

The equation of this line is $y = x + 2$.
Draw the line $y = x$ on the same graph.
These lines are parallel, both with gradient 1. $y = x + 2$ cuts the y-axis at $(0, 2)$, but $y = x$ passes through the origin $(0, 0)$.
Make a table of values for the line $y = x - 3$, and plot this line on the same graph.

In general, the graph with equation $y = mx + c$, where m and c are numbers, is a straight line with gradient m, and it cuts the y-axis at the point $(0, c)$.

Examples

4   Draw the graph of $y = 5 - 2x$.
    This is a straight line. Its gradient is -2 and it cuts the y-axis at the point $(0, 5)$.
    When $x = 3$, $y = 5 - (2 \times 3) = 5 - 6 = -1$.
    When $x = -1$, $y = 5 - (2 \times (-1)) = 5 + 2 = 7$.
    Draw axes with x from -1 to 3 and y from -1 to 7.
    Plot the points $(-1, 7)$, $(0, 5)$, $(3, -1)$ and draw the line.
    It slopes downwards as x increases because its gradient is negative.

    It is unnecessary to plot many points when you know the graph is a straight line. Two
    points are sufficient but a third point is also useful as a check on accuracy.

5   A line crosses the y-axis at $(0, -2)$ and has gradient $3\frac{1}{2}$. What is its equation ?

    The general equation of a straight line is $y = mx + c$.
    Here, $m = 3\frac{1}{2}$ and $c = -2$.
    The equation of the line is $y = 3\frac{1}{2}x - 2$.
    This can be written as $2y = 7x - 4$.

6   A line passes through the points $A(-1, 5)$ and $B(4, 2)$. Find its equation.

    The gradient of the line

    $= \dfrac{\text{increase in } y}{\text{increase in } x}$

    $= \dfrac{2 - 5}{4 - (-1)} = -\frac{3}{5}$

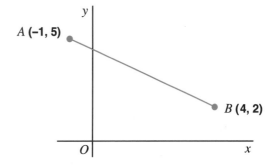

    The equation of the line is $y = -\frac{3}{5}x + c$, where $(0, c)$ is the point where the line crosses
    the y-axis.
    If the line is drawn accurately on graph paper then you can find the value of c from the
    graph. Alternatively, find c from the equation.

    Since the line passes through $B(4, 2)$, the equation is satisfied by the values $x = 4$, $y = 2$.
    So
    $2 = -\frac{3}{5} \times 4 + c$
    $c = 4\frac{2}{5}$

    The equation is $y = -\frac{3}{5}x + 4\frac{2}{5}$.
    This can be written as $5y = 22 - 3x$.

    You can use the coordinates of A to check this equation.

Lines of best fit

If variables satisfy a straight line law, then results obtained experimentally may have slight errors so that plotted values may not exactly lie on a line. In that case, a line may be drawn to fit as nearly as possible to the plotted points, and this is called the line of best fit. Further readings may be made from that line.

Example

7   The following values of the speed y m/s of an object at times t seconds are obtained by experiment. Plot the values of y against t and show that they lie approximately on a straight line. Use the line to estimate the value of y when $t = 3.5$.

t	1	2	3	4	5	6
y	2.05	2.75	3.6	4.45	5.3	5.9

Draw an accurate graph and draw a line of best fit. Find the gradient of the line. It is approximately 0.8.

The graph meets the y-axis at approximately 1.2, so the equation of the line is $y = 0.8t + 1.2$.

Using the line on the graph, or using its equation, when $t = 3.5$, $y = 4.0$.

Sketch graph

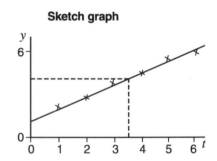

Exercise 10.1

1.   Draw the x-axis from 0 to 10 and the y-axis from 0 to 8 using equal scales on both axes.

   1   Plot points $A\,(6, 3)$ and $B\,(10, 5)$.
       Draw the line OAB (where O is the origin). What is the equation of this line ?
   2   Plot the point $C\,(9, 7)$ and join BC.
       Find the point D such that $ABCD$ is a rectangle. Join AD and DC.
       What are the coordinates of D ?
   3   What is the equation of the line BD ?

2.   Find the gradients of the lines (1), (2), (3), (4), (5).

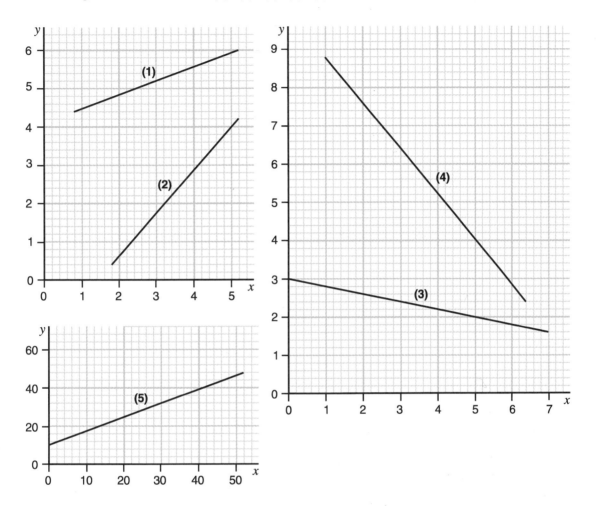

3.   Draw the x-axis from -2 to 6 and the y-axis from -10 to 20.
      If $y = 3x - 2$, find the values of y when $x = -2$, 0 and 5.
      For the graph of $y = 3x - 2$ plot 3 points and join them with a straight line.
      What is the gradient of this line ?
      Where does the line cut the y-axis ?

4.   Draw the x-axis from -6 to 8 and the y-axis from -8 to 8.
      Plot the points $A(5, 3)$ and $B(2, 6)$. Join AB and find the gradient of this line.
      Plot the points $C(-4, -2)$ and $D(-2, 4)$. Join CD and find the gradient of this line.
      Plot the point $E(2, -6)$. Through E draw a line with gradient 3.
      Plot the point $F(-6, 2)$. Through F draw a line with gradient -1.

5. State the gradients of these lines, and also give the coordinates of the points where the
    lines cut the y-axis.

    1 $y = 4x - 1$ **4** $y = 2 - 5x$
    2 $y = 3 - x$ **5** $3y = x + 3$
    3 $y = \frac{1}{2}x + 7$

6. Find the length of the line AB, where

    1 A is $(1, 0)$, B is $(8, 24)$,

    2 A is $(-5, 7)$, B is $(7, 2)$,

    3 A is $(-12, 1)$, B is $(0, -8)$.

7. On graph paper, label the x-axis from -2 to 6 and the y-axis from -8 to 12.
    Draw these graphs and label them. Show as much of each graph as fits on the graph
    paper.

    1 $y = 2x + 2$ **4** $y = 3x - 6$
    2 $y = 8 - 4x$ **5** $5y = 50 - 2x$
    3 $y = -x - 4$

8. The diameter and circumference of different-sized circular objects were measured, with
    the following results:

Diameter, d, in cm	2.6	5.4	8.2	13.2	15.8
Circumference, c, in cm	7.8	17.5	26.2	41.0	49.5

    Plot the values of c (vertical axis) against d (horizontal axis), and show that the points lie
    approximately on a straight line.
    Draw a line of best fit for these points. This line should pass through the origin. Find the
    gradient of this line.
    What is the equation connecting c and d ?

9. Use small scales so that 3 separate graphs fit on one page. Label the x and y axes from
    -4 to 4, using the same scales on both axes.
    On the 1st graph draw the lines $y = 4x$ and $y = -\frac{1}{4}x$. What are the gradients of these
    lines ?
    On the 2nd graph draw the lines $y = -3x$ and $y = \frac{1}{3}x$. What are the gradients of these
    lines ?
    On the 3rd graph draw the lines $y = 1\frac{1}{2}x$ and $y = -\frac{2}{3}x$. What are the gradients of these
    lines ?
    What do you notice about these pairs of lines ?
    What is the product of the gradients of each of these pairs of lines ?

Simultaneous equations

Example

Use a graphical method to solve the simultaneous equations $x - 3y = -9$ and $8x + 6y = 3$.

$x - 3y = -9$ can be rearranged as $3y = x + 9$, and then as $y = \frac{1}{3}x + 3$.
$8x + 6y = 3$ can be rearranged as $6y = -8x + 3$, and then as $y = -\frac{4}{3}x + \frac{1}{2}$.
Find the y-values when $x = -3, 0, 3$.

For $y = \frac{1}{3}x + 3$

x	-3	0	3
y	2	3	4

For $y = -\frac{4}{3}x + \frac{1}{2}$

x	-3	0	3
y	$4\frac{1}{2}$	$\frac{1}{2}$	$-3\frac{1}{2}$

Draw the x-axis from -3 to 3 and the y-axis from -4 to 5.
Plot the points for each line and draw the lines on the graph.
Label each one with its equation.

The equations are satisfied simultaneously at the point which lies on both lines.
Draw dotted lines from this point to both axes, to read off the coordinates. The point is $(-1\frac{1}{2}, 2\frac{1}{2})$.
The solution of the equations is $x = -1\frac{1}{2}, y = 2\frac{1}{2}$.

Sketch graph

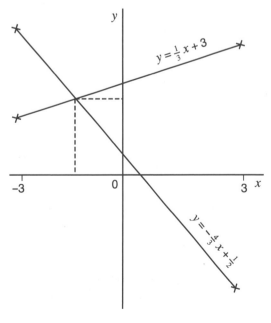

Exercise 10.2

Use a graphical method to solve the simultaneous equations in questions 1 to 5.

1. $2y = 12 - x$ Draw the x-axis from 0 to 16 and the y-axis from -2 to 6.
    $3y = x - 2$

2. $3y = 4x - 14$ Draw the x-axis from 0 to 12 and the y-axis from -6 to 10.
    $4y = 3x$

3. $3x + y + 1 = 0$ Draw the x-axis from -4 to 4 and the y-axis from -20 to 20.
    $2y = 20 + 5x$

4. $3y = 2x + 8$ Draw the x-axis from -1 to 6 and the y-axis from 0 to 8.
    $6y = 30 - 5x$

5. $2y = 3 - x$ Draw the x-axis from -4 to 4 and the y-axis from -5 to 5.
    $2y = 4x - 7$

6. Draw x and y axes from 0 to 8.

    1 To draw the graph of $2x + 3y = 6$.

    If $x = 0$, what is the value of y ? Mark the point corresponding to these values on the graph.
    If $y = 0$, what is the value of x ? Mark the point corresponding to these values on the graph.
    Join these two points.

    In a similar way, draw the graphs of

    2 $5x + 4y = 20$,
    3 $8x + 5y = 40$,
    4 $6x + 7y = 42$.

    From your graphs find the solution of the simultaneous equations $6x + 7y = 42$, $8x + 5y = 40$.

7. A bag contains £2.80 in ten-pence and five-pence coins. If there were x ten-pence and y five-pence coins, write down an equation connecting x and y, and simplify it.
    If there were half as many ten-pence coins and twice as many five-pence coins, the total amount would be £3.20. Write down another equation connecting x and y, and simplify it.
    Draw axes with x from 0 to 70 and y from 0 to 60.
    Draw the lines represented by the equations and hence solve the equations simultaneously.
    How many of each kind of coin were there originally ?

Linear inequalities

A line divides the plane into two regions.

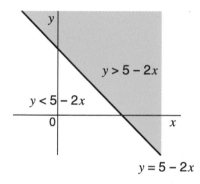

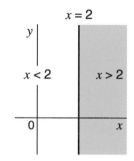

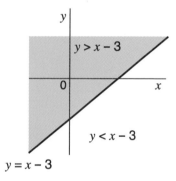

Example

On a graph, draw the lines $x = 3$, $y = 4$,
$5y = 30 - 6x$.
Identify the regions where
1   $x \leqslant 3$, $y \leqslant 4$ and $5y \geqslant 30 - 6x$,

2   $0 \leqslant x \leqslant 3$, $0 \leqslant y \leqslant 4$ and $5y \leqslant 30 - 6x$.

In the diagram, the shaded region is where
$x \leqslant 3$, $y \leqslant 4$ and $5y \geqslant 30 - 6x$.

The pentagon A is where $0 \leqslant x \leqslant 3$,
$0 \leqslant y \leqslant 4$ and $5y \leqslant 30 - 6x$.

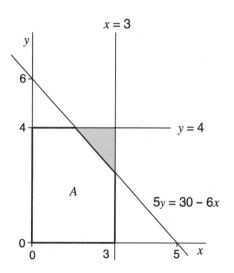

If the region does **not** include the boundary line then this line can be drawn as a dotted line.

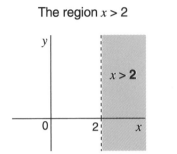

The region $x > 2$

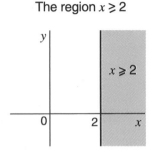

The region $x \geqslant 2$

A region can be identified by shading it, but sometimes it is better to shade the unwanted parts and leave the required region unshaded.

The region where $x \geqslant 0$, $y \geqslant 0$, $x + y \leqslant 5$, is the region left unshaded.

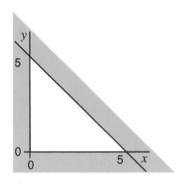

Exercise 10.3

1. Draw x and y axes from 0 to 10. Draw the lines $x = 2$, $y = 3$ and $y = 10 - x$.
   Identify the region where $x \geqslant 2$, $y \geqslant 3$ and $y \leqslant 10 - x$.

2. Draw x and y axes from 0 to 6, and draw the lines $y = 2$, $y = 2x$ and $x + y = 6$.
   Identify the region where $y \geqslant 2$, $y \leqslant 2x$ and $x + y \leqslant 6$.

3. Draw x and y axes from 0 to 8, and draw dotted lines for $y = x$, $2y = 8 + x$ and $2y = 8 - x$.
   Identify the regions A, B, C, where
   for A, $x \geqslant 0$, $y > x$ and $2y < 8 - x$;
   for B, $y \geqslant 0$, $y < x$ and $2y < 8 - x$;
   for C, $y > x$, $2y > 8 - x$ and $2y < 8 + x$.

4. Sketch on a graph the line $y = x$. Identify on your graph the region where $x \geqslant 0$, $y \geqslant x$ and $y \leqslant 10$.

5. Draw the graph of $y = 10 - 3x$.
    If x and y are positive integers, mark on the graph the points whose coordinates satisfy
    the inequality $3x + y \leqslant 10$. How many such points are there ?

6. Draw the x-axis from -2 to 2 and the y-axis from -2 to 10.
    Draw the lines $y = -2$, $y = -x$ and $y = 3x + 4$.
    Identify the region A where $y \geqslant -x$, $y \leqslant 3x + 4$ and $x \leqslant 0$, and the region B where
    $x \geqslant 0$, $y \leqslant -x$ and $y \geqslant -2$.
    Describe in a similar way the region bounded by 4 lines containing the point $(-1, -1)$.

7. A trainee is tested on two pieces of work. In order to pass the test he must spend at least
    1 minute on the first piece of work but complete it within 5 minutes, and take between
    2 and 7 minutes on the second piece of work. In addition he must not take longer than
    9 minutes to complete both pieces.
    If the time in minutes taken for the 1st piece is represented by x and the time in minutes
    taken for the 2nd piece is represented by y, write down the inequalities which must be
    satisfied by x and y.
    Draw x and y axes from 0 to 9 and draw the lines representing the boundaries of these
    inequalities. Identify the region representing the times which are satisfactory.

Coordinates in 3-dimensions

Coordinates are used to indicate position.
By introducing another axis (the z-axis) we can represent
positions in 3-dimensions.
If the x and y axes are in a horizontal plane (such as on
a level table), the z-axis goes vertically upwards.
The origin is the point $(0, 0, 0)$. The axes are all at right
angles to each other.

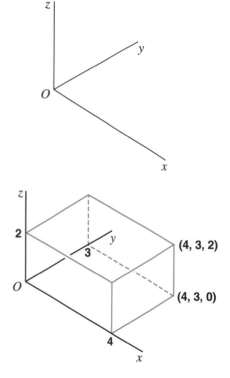

To find the point $(4, 3, 2)$, first find the point $(4, 3)$ as
usual, using the axes Ox, Oy.
Then move upwards (i.e. in the direction of the z-axis)
for 2 units.

Example

A cuboid has one vertex at the origin and three of its edges on the x, y and z axes.
One vertex is at the point $(3, 1, 2)$.
What are the coordinates of the other vertices ?

These are shown on the diagram.
Notice that all the points on the base of the cuboid
have z-coordinate 0, the others have
z-coordinate 2.
Notice which vertices have x-coordinate 0, and which
have x-coordinate 3.
Notice which vertices have y-coordinate 0, and which
have y-coordinate 1.

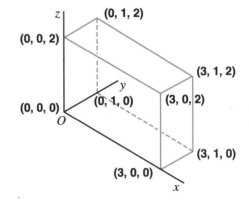

Exercise 10.4

1. $ABCDEFGH$ is a cuboid.
   A is the point $(2, 1, 0)$.
   B is the point $(8, 1, 0)$.
   D is the point $(2, 4, 0)$.
   E is the point $(2, 1, 6)$.
   Find the coordinates of the
   points C, F, G and H.

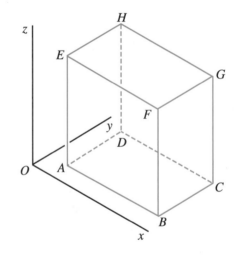

2. $ABCDEFGH$ is a cuboid.
   A is the point $(1, 4, 5)$.
   G is the point $(12, 7, 9)$.
   If AB, AD and AE are parallel to the x, y and z
   axes respectively, find the coordinates of
   B, C, D, E, F and H.

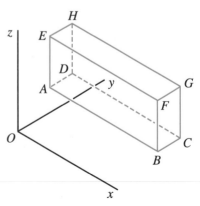

3. *ABCDEFGH* is a cuboid.
    A is the point $(2, 3, 4)$.
    AB has length 7 units and is parallel to the *x*-axis.
    AD has length 1 unit and is parallel to the *y*-axis.
    AE has length 3 units and is parallel to the *z*-axis.
    Find the coordinates of the points *B, C, D, E, F,*
    G and *H*.

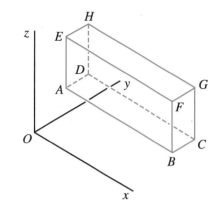

4. *ABCDEFGH* is a cuboid.
    G is the point $(7, 9, 4)$.
    HG has length 15 units and is parallel to
    the *x*-axis.
    FG has length 13 units and is parallel to
    the *y*-axis.
    CG has length 7 units and is parallel to the
    z-axis.
    Find the coordinates of the points *A, B, C,*
    D, E, F and *H*.

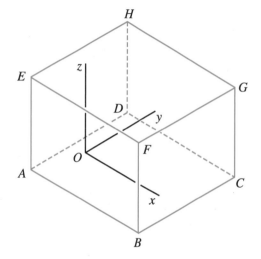

Exercise 10.5 Applications

1   If *A* is $(3, 0)$, *B* is $(4, 1)$, *C* is $(1, 3)$ and *D* is $(0, 2)$, find the gradients of the lines *AB, BC,*
    AD and *DC*.
    Show that *ABCD* is a parallelogram.

2. If *A* is $(3, -1)$, *B* is $(8, 4)$ and *C* is $(7, 11)$, find the lengths of *AB, AC* and *BC* in surd
    form.
    What sort of triangle is $\triangle ABC$?

3. Find the equations of these lines:

    1   With gradient -1 and passing through the point $(1, 7)$.
    2   With gradient 2 and passing through the point $(2, -5)$.
    3   With gradient $\frac{1}{3}$ and passing through the point $(-1, 0)$.

4.   The line $y + 4x = 8$ meets the x-axis at A. Find the coordinates of A. Find the equation of the line with gradient 4 passing through A.

5.   A straight line with gradient 4 passes through $(-1, -2)$ and $(3, a)$. Find the value of a.

6.   An experiment is carried out with readings of values of x and y. Here are the results.

x	8	17	30	42	54	66	78
y	46	71	94	118	142	176	190

Plot these values on a graph and draw the line of best fit.
Find the equation of the line.
Find an approximate value for y when $x = 60$.

7.   An object moves from rest so that its distance, y m, travelled in time t seconds is satisfied by an equation of the form $y = at^2$.
These results were recorded.

t	0	0.5	1	1.5	2	2.5	3
y	0	0.8	3.3	7.4	13.2	20.6	29.7

Plot y against t^2 and show that the points lie approximately on a straight line $y = a(t^2)$.
Find the value of a from your graph.

8.   The diagram shows two lines with equations $y = 2x - 3$ and $x + 2y = 7$.

1   State the coordinates of P and R.
2   Find the distance between Q and S.
3   Which equations are solved by finding the coordinates of T?
4   Solve these equations by another method and hence find the coordinates of T.

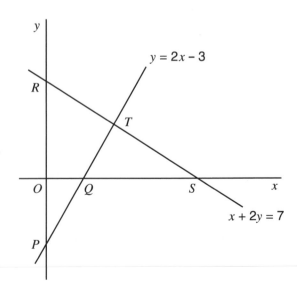

9.   Draw axes with x from -4 to 4 and y from -12 to 24. Draw the graph of $y = 3x + 2$, by
finding values of y when $x = -4$, 0 and 4 and plotting the three points.
Also draw the graph of $y = 16 - 2x$ in a similar way.
Using your graphs, solve the simultaneous equations $y = 3x + 2$ and $y = 16 - 2x$.
Solve these equations by another method, to check your solution.

10.   For prizes for a children's party Mrs Davies decides to buy packets of sweets at 16p each
and bars of chocolate at 32p each.
If she buys x packets of sweets and y bars of chocolate, what is the total cost ?
She needs 25 prizes altogether. Write down an equation using this fact.
On graph paper draw x and y axes from 0 to 40. Draw the graph of the equation.
Mrs Davies decides to spend £6.40 on the prizes. Write down another equation using this
fact and draw its line on your graph.
How many packets of sweets and bars of chocolate does she buy ?

11.   The diagram shows 3 lines whose equations
are $x = 3$, $y = 2$ and $x + 2y = 11$.
Write down the inequalities satisfied by all
points inside $\triangle ABC$.

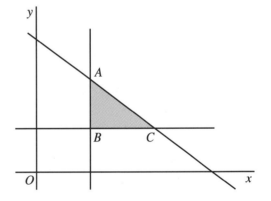

12.   Mrs Jones makes toy animals, dogs and elephants, to sell. She can make not more than
10 of these animals in a week. There is more demand for elephants so she always makes
at least twice as many elephants as dogs, although she makes at least two dogs.
If in one week she makes x dogs and y elephants, write down inequalities satisfied by x
and y.
On graph paper, draw x and y axes from 0 to 10 and draw the lines giving the
boundaries of these inequalities. Identify the region containing sets of points (x, y)
satisfying all these inequalities.
List the possible combinations of animals she could make.
If she makes £6 profit on each dog and £4 profit on each elephant, consider the possible
combinations and decide what she should make to get most profit. How much profit will
this be ?

13. *ABCDEFGH* is a cuboid.
     A is the point $(2, 3, 5)$.
     B is the point $(6, 3, 5)$.
     D is the point $(2, 6, 5)$.
     E is the point $(2, 3, 17)$.
     Find the coordinates of the points *C*, *F*, *G* and *H*.

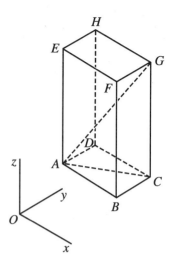

     State the lengths of *AB* and *BC* and use Pythagoras'
     theorem to find the length of *AC*.
     State the length of *CG*.
     What is the size of $\angle ACG$?
     Find the length of *AG*.

Practice test 10

1.   If *A* is $(-3, 1)$ and *B* is $(5, 3)$, find
     1 the gradient of *AB*,
     2 the length of *AB*,
     3 the coordinates of the mid-point of *AB*.

2.   Find the gradient of the line *AB*.
     Find the equation of the line *AB* in the
     form $ax + by = c$, where *a*, *b* and *c* are
     integers.

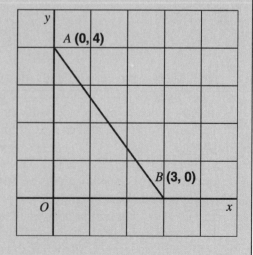

3. An experiment is carried out and readings of x and y are made.
    Here are the results:

x	6	8	10	12	14	20
y	13.5	17.5	19.5	22	26.5	36

    Plot these values on a graph and draw the line of best fit.
    Find the equation of the line.
    Use the equation or the graph to find an approximate value for y when $x = 17.5$.

4. Use a graphical method to solve these simultaneous equations:

    $y = 6 - 2x$
    $3y = 4x - 17$

    Draw the x-axis from 0 to 8 and the y-axis from -10 to 6.

5. $ABCDEFGH$ is a cuboid.
    A is the point $(-1, -4, -2)$.
    AB has length 10 units and is parallel to
    the x-axis.
    BC has length 9 units and is parallel to
    the y-axis.
    AE has length 6 units and is parallel to the
    z-axis.
    Find the coordinates of the points
    B, C, D, E, F, G and H.

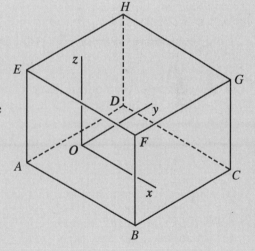

6. Draw axes for x and y from -3 to 9 using equal scales on both axes.
    Draw the lines AB, $2y = x + 8$; CD, $2y = x - 2$ and EF, $2y = 6 - x$.
    What are the coordinates of the points where EF meets AB, and CD ?
    Identify the region on the graph where $y \geqslant 0$, $2y \leqslant x - 2$ and $2y \leqslant 6 - x$.
    What shape is this region ?

Miscellaneous Section B

Exercise B1   Revision

1. From this list of numbers:

   15   21   24   27   31   34   44   47   51   57

   1 Find the largest prime number.
   2 Find two numbers whose product is 765.
   3 Find two numbers whose sum is 104.
   4 Find two numbers which as numerator and denominator of a fraction reduce to $\frac{2}{3}$.
   5 Find two numbers which as numerator and denominator of a fraction simplify to 1.8.

2. Show that these triangles are congruent to each other.

   (1) 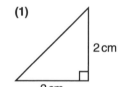   **(2)** 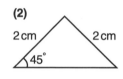   **(3)**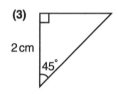

3. Find the positive value of $\sqrt{b^2 - 4ac}$ when $a = 3$, $b = -5$ and $c = -8$.

4. A bag contains 10 coloured discs. One disc is pulled out, its colour noted, and then it is returned to the bag. After 200 draws the results are:
   Red, 104; Yellow, 62; Green 34.
   How many discs of each colour do you think there are in the bag ?

5. The marks of 12 students in a test are 5, 5, 6, 6, 6, 7, 8, 8, 10, 10, 14, 17.

   Find
   1 the mode,
   2 the median,
   3 the mean,
   4 the range, of the marks.

6. **1** Find the largest integer n where $\dfrac{n}{12} < \dfrac{5}{7}$.

   2 List the positive integers n such that n is less than 25% of $(2n + 11)$.

7.   If O is the origin and $\overrightarrow{OA} = \begin{pmatrix} 1 \\ 3 \end{pmatrix}$, $\overrightarrow{OB} = \begin{pmatrix} 9 \\ 15 \end{pmatrix}$, $\overrightarrow{OC} = \begin{pmatrix} 5 \\ 7 \end{pmatrix}$,

     find $\overrightarrow{OD}$, where D is the mid-point of BC.

     Find $\overrightarrow{AD}$. What is the length of AD ?

8.   Find the values of the following, without using your calculator.

     1 $0.07 + 0.05$
     2 0.07×0.05
     3 $0.07 \div 0.05$

9.   A cone-shaped container, radius 15 cm, height 50 cm, is full of oil. The oil is poured into cylindrical tins, radius 5 cm, height 20 cm. How many tins can be filled ?

10. Find the values of $49^{\frac{1}{2}}$, 3^0, $8^{\frac{2}{3}}$, 5^{-2}, $9^{1\frac{1}{2}}$, $16^{-\frac{1}{4}}$.

11. Mary and Ann are hoping to be chosen for the position of shooter in the netball team. The probability that Mary will be chosen is 0.5 and the probability that Ann will be chosen is 0.3.
     1   What is the probability that Mary or Ann will be chosen ?
     2   What is the probability that someone else will be chosen ?

12. The free end of a pendulum is pulled aside from the vertical and then released. It swings through an arc of length 1.5 m and then swings backwards and forwards, the length of each arc being 3% less than that of the preceding one.
     Find the length of the fifth arc.

13. The points A and B have coordinates $(1, -1)$ and $(4, -5)$.

     Find
     1   the length of the line AB,
     2   the gradient of the line AB.

14. Use your calculator to find the price of fuel in pence per litre, to the nearest penny, when it is £3 per gallon. (Take 1 gallon as equivalent to 4.55 litres.)

15. Solve these equations by trial, finding solutions which are positive whole numbers.

     1 $x^2 + x = 56$
     2 $x^2 - 2x = 120$
     3 $(x + 3)(x - 2) = 104.$

Exercise B2   Revision

1. Which diagram represents the locus of points inside the triangle PQR which are

    1   equidistant from PQ and QR,
    2   equidistant from P and R ?

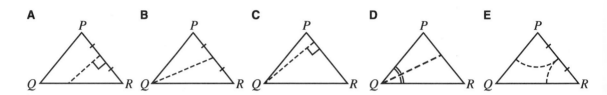

2. A spherical wire cage for holding a plant pot is formed by fastening together 3 circular hoops of diameter 30 cm and one smaller hoop of diameter 20 cm. Find the total length of wire needed, giving the answer to the nearest 0.1 m.

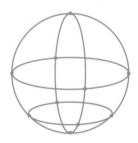

3. A hair shampoo is sold in two sizes costing 92p and £1.34. The cheaper bottle is marked as holding 110 ml and the other one holds 150 ml. Which bottle is the better value for money ?

4. If $f(x) = x^2 + 5x + 10$, find the largest integer which is a common factor of f(2) and f(5).

5. This table shows the number of children in 100 families.

Children in family	0	1	2	3	4	5	6
Number of families	15	20	30	21	8	5	1

    Draw a bar-line graph to illustrate the data.
    Find the mean, median and mode number of children per family.

6. Find the approximate value (to the nearest whole number) of $\sqrt{3.92 \times 9.08}$.
    Now use your calculator to find its value correct to 3 significant figures.

7. Write down any number less than 10, add 3 to it and square the result. Then add 1 and multiply by 10. Subtract 100 and divide by the number you started with. Add 5 and then divide by 5. Subtract 9 and halve the result. Subtract the number you started with. What is your answer ?

    Repeat the question beginning with the number x and show that your previous answer is correct.

8. In the following lists, where values are given for $x = -2, 0, 1$ and 3, find the connection between y and x, in the form $y = mx + c$, where m and c are numbers.

1

x	y
-2	2
0	0
1	-1
3	-3

2

x	y
-2	-1
0	0
1	$\frac{1}{2}$
3	$1\frac{1}{2}$

3

x	y
-2	-3
0	-1
1	0
3	2

4

x	y
-2	5
0	3
1	2
3	0

5

x	y
-2	-3
0	1
1	3
3	7

On graph paper, draw axes for x from -2 to 3 and for y from -3 to 7.
For each list, plot the points on the graph and join them with a straight line.
Label each line with its equation.

9. Here is a sequence of sets of numbers:

$(3, 4, 5)$, $(5, 11, 13)$, $(7, 24, 25)$, $(9, 40, 41)$, $(11, 60, 61)$,   . . .

   1 These numbers are connected with the sides of right-angled triangles. With which mathematician are they associated ?

   2 One number in the sequence above is incorrect. Which one is incorrect, and what is the correct number ?

   3 By finding the connection between the first number of a set and the **sum** of the other two, deduce the next set of numbers in the sequence.

10. Solve the simultaneous equations
$$\tfrac{1}{2}x - \tfrac{1}{5}y = 3$$
$$\tfrac{3}{4}x + \tfrac{2}{3}y = 19.$$

11. Here are some (fictitious) results where people A, B, C, D, E, have put products P, Q, R, S, T, in order of preference.
$1 = $ 1st choice, $2 = $ 2nd choice, etc.

Analyse the results and write down your conclusions, including saying which product you would decide is the most popular.

Product	Person				
	A	B	C	D	E
P	5	2	1	1	4
Q	4	4	4	2	3
R	3	5	2	3	2
S	1	3	5	5	5
T	2	1	3	4	1

12. Find the values of

    1 $1\frac{1}{6} + \left(\frac{2}{3} \times 2\frac{1}{4}\right)$ **2** $\left(1\frac{1}{6} \div \frac{2}{3}\right) + 2\frac{1}{4}$ **3** $1\frac{1}{6} - \frac{2}{3} + 2\frac{1}{4}$

13. One quantity W varies as the cube of another quantity a. Given that $W = 4$ when $a = 2$, find the value of W when $a = 5$, and find a when $W = 108$.

14. If $x = 3$ and $y = -5$, find the values of

    1 $\dfrac{2y + 2}{4x}$ **2** $2x^2 - y$ **3** $\sqrt{y^2 - x^2}$

15. Several discs with numbers 1 to 7 are placed in a bag. One disc is pulled out, its number noted and then it is returned to the bag. After 500 draws the results were:

Number	1	2	3	4	5	6	7
Frequency	154	95	80	74	44	28	25

    On the basis of these results, if another disc is drawn out, what is the probability that it will be
    1 number 3,
    2 a number less than 3,
    3 an odd number ?

Exercise B3   Activities

1. **Pentominoes and hexominoes**
   Pentominoes are arrangements of 5 equal squares which join together with edges of adjacent squares fitting exactly together, such as

   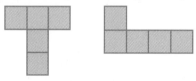

   Pieces which would be identical if turned round or turned over are counted as the same.
   Thus 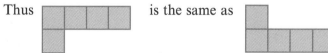 is the same as

   There are 12 different pieces. Find them. Some of them will form the net of an 'open' cube. Which ones ? The 12 pieces can be fitted together to form various rectangles. Make some cardboard pieces and investigate.

   Hexominoes consist of 6 squares joined together. Investigate these shapes and see how many you can find. Some of them will form the net of a cube. Which ones ? Which pieces can be used to make tessellations ?

2.   **Probability of winning in competitions**

There are many competitions in newspapers, magazines and leaflets available in shops. Other competitions such as raffles are organised to raise money for Charities.

Examples:

1   If there are 8 items which you have to put in order of merit, find how many different entries are possible. Often the winning entry depends on the judge's opinion, so assume that all entries are equally likely to win. What is the probability that your entry is the correct one ?

2   If there are 8 questions each with possible answers, A, B, C, D, how many possible combinations of answers are there ? If you choose answers at random, what is the probability that your entry is the correct one ?

3   Premium Bonds are a form of gambling where you do not lose your original investment, but instead of earning interest on it the interest is paid out in prizes to the winners. You can get a leaflet from the Post Office which gives details about how the scheme works, and from this you can work out your chances of winning a prize.

4   You may like to try to work out the probability of winning on various 'fairground' games, or other forms of gambling such as the football pools, poker or roulette. But note that the promoter arranges things so that he makes a profit in the long run.

3.   **Following new lines of enquiry**

When you are doing a mathematical activity, you may be able to extend your investigation and make further discoveries.
Here are some examples of how **you** could think of extending an investigation.

1   After investigating diagonals of polygons and finding a formula for the number of diagonals of a polygon with n sides, you could decide to investigate diagonals of solid figures such as the 5 regular solid figures (tetrahedron, cube, octahedron, dodecahedron and icosahedron). You could find a formula for the number of diagonals in terms of the numbers of vertices and edges.

2   After investigating the possible units digits of square numbers, decide to investigate the tens digits of the same numbers. Depending on what the units digit is, what can you discover about the tens digit ?

3   Having found a formula for the nth triangular number, decide to find a formula for the sum of the first n triangular numbers. Investigate any links between the numbers, the sums and Pascal's triangle. (In the song 'On the 12th day of Christmas', how many gifts were there altogether ?)

4   Having learnt Pythagoras' theorem, decide to see if a similar result is true for areas of semicircles or equilateral triangles drawn on the sides of a right-angled triangle.

You could, of course, carry out the above activities if you have not already done so, even though they are not your own ideas. Maybe you can extend them still further.

4.   Using a computer

If you have the use of a computer and a selection of computer programs then there are many investigations or activities which you can do.

The choice of activities will depend on the programs available, but here are a few general suggestions. If you have not got suitable software, it is often possible to do some investigations using simple programs which you can write yourself.

1   Statistical investigations, using spreadsheets to produce graphs and diagrams, and to calculate averages and measures of dispersion.

2   Probability investigations, using computer-generated random numbers to simulate throws of dice, tosses of coins, selections of discs, etc. (When throwing a die, how many throws are needed, on average, to get a six ?)

3   To investigate prime numbers and prime factors of numbers.

4   To investigate sequences, number chains, etc.

5   To draw graphs of algebraic or trig. functions, and compare related functions. To draw graphs of growth, e.g. Compound Interest, or decay.

6   To solve equations by trial and improvement methods or by iterative techniques.

7   To do calculations using mathematical formulae, e.g. solving quadratic equations using the general formula, multiplying matrices, finding areas and volumes, finding lengths and angles using trig. formulae, finding areas under curves of functions using the trapezium rule with many thin strips.

The computer is a very powerful tool. Do make use of it.

5.   Pythagoras' theorem

State the theorem.
One way to prove the theorem is to use
similar triangles *ABC*, *DBA* and *DAC*.
See if you can discover this proof.
Can you find other ways of proving the theorem ?

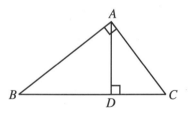

Dissections

1   Find the centre *X* of the square *BCRS*.
Draw lines through *X* parallel to *AC* and to *CT*.
This divides the square into 4 sections which you
can cut out. Also cut out square *ABPQ*.
Rearrange these 5 pieces to make the square *ACTU*.

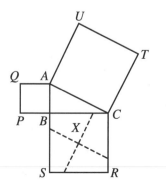

2   **Tangrams**. Use thin cardboard to
    make this.
    Start with two equal squares and cut
    into 7 pieces as shown.
    Rearrange these 7 pieces to make
    one large square.
    This is an ancient puzzle. The pieces
    make many more shapes, using all
    7 pieces each time. The pieces can be
    turned over.

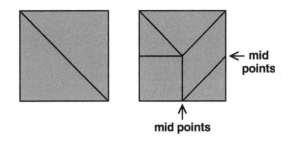

← mid
points

↑
mid points

Make a parallelogram, an isosceles trapezium, a rectangle, an isosceles right-angled
triangle and a trapezium with 2 adjacent right angles. Here are some other designs to
make, and you can invent others.

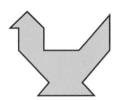 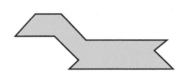

Problem

If you had a long piece of rope, divided by knots into 12 equal parts, how could you use
it to make a right angle on the ground, e.g. to mark out a rectangular playing-area ?

Sets of numbers

The ones you probably know are 3 : 4 : 5, 5 : 12 : 13 and 8 : 15 : 17.
Investigate these and similar patterns to find others.

hypotenuse	1 other side	sum	difference	3rd side
5	4	9	1	3
13	12	25	1	5
. . .	. . .	. . .	1	7
5	3	8	2	4
17	15	32	2	8
. . .	. . .	72	2	12

Pythagoras

Consult library books and try to find out something about him. When did he live ?
Where ? Like you, he tried to investigate patterns in numbers.

6.   **The Sieve of Eratosthenes and prime numbers**

Write down the numbers 2 to 50 inclusive. Draw a circle round 2 and then cross out all other numbers which divide by 2. The 1st number not circled or crossed out is 3. Draw a circle round 3 and then cross out all other numbers which divide by 3. The next number not crossed out or circled is 5. Draw a circle round 5 and then cross out all other numbers which divide by 5. The next number not crossed out is 7. Draw a circle round 7 and then cross out all other numbers which divide by 7. Now draw a circle round all the remaining numbers which are not crossed out. The circled numbers are the prime numbers. Write them down in a list.
Why was it sufficient to stop at 7 ? If we had made a list up to 125 what other number would need to be crossed out ?

This method can be used to find the prime numbers up to any large number. It is useful to set the numbers down on squared paper in neat columns and then a pattern can be seen as you cross out the numbers.

Set out in columns of 10,   1   2   3   4   5   6   7   8   9   10
                            11   12   13   14   15   16   17   18   19   20
                            21   22   .   .   .

or try other columns, especially columns of 6.   1   2   3   4   5   6
                                                  7   8   9   10   11   12
                                                  13   14   15   16   17   18
                                                  19   20   .   .   .

1 is a special number, so mark it in a different way. It is not counted as a prime number although it has no factors other than itself.
This method is known as 'The Sieve of Eratosthenes'. See if you can find out anything about Eratosthenes who lived a long time ago.

Carry out further investigations with prime numbers.
First, get a list of more prime numbers, up to 500 or 1000.
Does the number of prime numbers in a range of 100 numbers decrease as the numbers get larger ? E.g. Are there fewer prime numbers between 400 and 500 than between 300 and 400 ?
Prime numbers with a difference of 2 are called **prime pairs**. Examples are 29, 31; 41, 43. Make a list of these for numbers less than 200. It is thought that the number of prime pairs is infinite.
However, there is sometimes a sequence of consecutive numbers which are not prime, for example, between the prime numbers 113 and 127 there are 13 numbers which are not prime. Can you find a longer run of numbers which are not prime ?

With modern computers, searches can be made for larger prime numbers. The largest one found (in 1992) was $2^{756839} - 1$. By now, a larger one may have been discovered. But it can be proved that the number of prime numbers is infinite, so there is no such thing as the largest prime number, only the largest one **known**.

To the student : 3

Improving your work

Check your handwriting and if necessary, improve it. It must be legible even when you are working quickly. Badly written work means that you confuse 6 with 0 or b, 2 with z, 5 with s, and so on. Show minus signs clearly. Do not alter figures, e.g. a 2 into a 3, by overwriting. Cross the 2 out and write the 3 nearby. Do not change $+$ into $-$ except by crossing it out and re-writing clearly. $+$ which might mean either $+$ or $-$ cannot be marked as correct because you have not made it clear which it is. Altered figures which are not clear cannot be marked as correct. So always make clear alterations.

Try to work at a reasonable speed. If you tend to work slowly, try to speed up, because in an examination you must give yourself a reasonable chance of completing the paper to gain good marks. When you are doing a question, concentrate completely on it so that you immediately think about the method, start it quickly, and continue working it out without a pause until you finish it. Work out any simple arithmetic in your head so that you do not break your concentration, and waste time, by pressing calculator keys. (You could do a check later, using the calculator, if you want to.)

Make sure that you use brackets correctly. $180 - 30 + 40$ is not the same as $180 - (30 + 40)$. The first expression equals 190, the second one equals 110. Be careful when you work out algebraic expressions or equations, especially those involving brackets.

Sketch diagrams, or rough plans of what you are going to do, are very useful even if they are not required as part of the answer.

When you have found an answer, consider if it is reasonable, especially if you have pressed calculator keys to get it. Look at the relative sizes of lengths or angles on the diagram, which should give a general idea even if the diagram is not drawn to an exact scale. A man earning £12 000 per year would not pay £30 000 per year in tax! It would also be rather unlikely for him to pay only £30 in tax. A circle with radius 10 cm cannot have a chord of length 24 cm. (Why ?) If the answer to a simple algebraic equation is an awkward number such as $x = -3\frac{10}{71}$, this **could** be correct, but it is more likely that you have made a mistake. When you have found an answer, give it correct to a suitable degree of accuracy. e.g. to 3 significant figures, and do not forget the units, e.g. £, cm, m^2, kg, where necessary.

11 *Enlargement and similar figures*

The topics in this chapter include:

- enlarging a shape,
- using similarity,
- using the relationships between areas and volumes of similar figures.

Enlargements

A figure and its enlargement have the same shape.
The **scale factor** of the enlargement is the number of times the original has been enlarged.
e.g. If the scale factor is 2, all lines on the enlargement are twice as long as corresponding lines on the original.
If the scale factor is 3, all lines on the enlargement are three times as long as corresponding lines on the original.

Examples

1   Enlargement with scale factor 2

2   Enlargement with scale factor 3

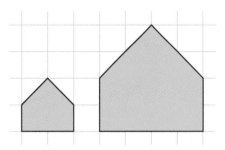

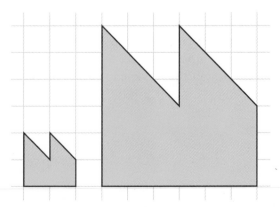

> Length of line on enlargement = scale factor × length of line on original
>
> Scale factor = $\dfrac{\text{length of line on the enlargement}}{\text{length of line on the original}}$

The scale factor need not be a whole number.

e.g. If the scale factor is $1\frac{1}{2}$, all lines on the enlargement are $1\frac{1}{2}$ times as long as the corresponding lines on the original.

Since $1\frac{1}{2} = \frac{3}{2}$, this is equivalent to the ratio $3:2$.

The length on the enlargement : length on original = $3:2$.

Enlargement with scale factor $1\frac{1}{2}$.

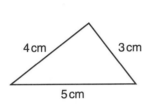
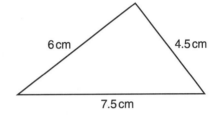

Example

3   Trapezium *PQRS* is an enlargement of trapezium *ABCD*.
Find the scale factor of the enlargement, and the lengths of *QR*, *RS* and *SP*.

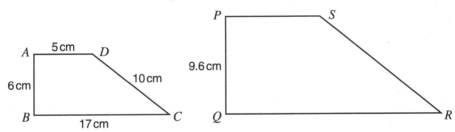

Scale factor = $\dfrac{\text{length of } PQ}{\text{length of } AB} = \dfrac{9.6 \text{ cm}}{6 \text{ cm}} = 1.6$ (or $1\frac{3}{5}$)

Length of QR = scale factor × length of BC

$\quad\quad\quad\quad = 1.6 \times 17$ cm

$\quad\quad\quad\quad = 27.2$ cm

Length of $RS = 1.6 \times 10$ cm

$\quad\quad\quad\quad = 16$ cm

Length of $SP = 1.6 \times 5$ cm

$\quad\quad\quad\quad = 8$ cm

Reduction

If you 'enlarge' a shape by a scale factor less than 1, then you are actually making a reduction of the figure.

e.g. Enlargement by a scale factor $\frac{3}{4}$.

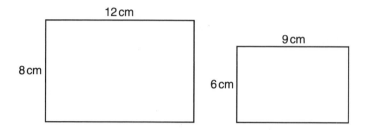

Exercise 11.1

1. This rectangle is enlarged with a scale factor $2\frac{2}{3}$.
    What are the measurements of the enlarged rectangle ?

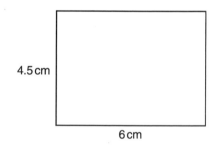

2. $\triangle DEF$ is an enlargement of $\triangle ABC$.

    1 What is the scale factor of the enlargement ?

    2 What is the length of DF ?

    3 What is the length of BC ?

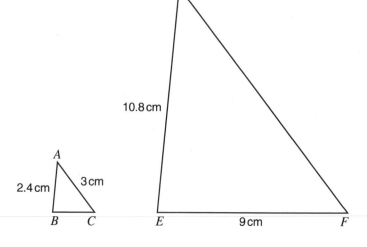

3. Copy this drawing of a box, on squared paper, and then draw an enlarged box using a scale factor of $1\frac{1}{2}$.

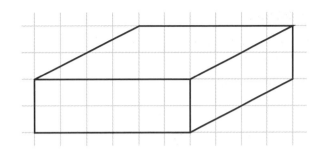

4. Each figure consists of a semicircle above a rectangle.
   B is a reduction of A.

   1 By what scale factor must the lengths of A be multiplied to give the corresponding lengths of B?

   2 If the perimeter of A is 72 cm, what is the perimeter of B?

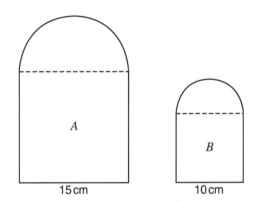

Similar figures

Similar figures have the same shape.
All corresponding angles are equal.
All corresponding lengths are in proportion, i.e. they are in the same ratio as all other corresponding lengths.

The **areas** of similar plane figures are proportional to the **squares** of corresponding lengths.

The **surface areas** of similar solid figures are proportional to the **squares** of corresponding lengths.

The **volumes** of similar solid figures are proportional to the **cubes** of corresponding lengths.

Lengths	$l : L$
Areas	$l^2 : L^2$
Volumes	$l^3 : L^3$

Examples

1 The lengths of these rectangles are in the
ratio $4 : 10 = 2 : 5$
The breadths of these rectangles are
in the ratio $3 : 7.5 = 6 : 15 = 2 : 5$
(All angles are 90°.)
The rectangles are similar.

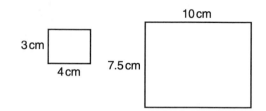

The ratio of the areas of the rectangles is $2^5 : 5^2 = 4 : 25$,
i.e. the area of the smaller rectangle is $\frac{4}{25}$ of the area of the other rectangle.

2 Two similar cylinders have heights of 9 cm and 12 cm.

Ratio of heights $= 9 : 12 = 3 : 4$
Ratio of radii $= 3 : 4$
Ratio of areas of curved surfaces $= 3^2 : 4^2 = 9 : 16$
Ratio of areas of circular ends $= 9 : 16$
Ratio of total surface areas $= 9 : 16$
Ratio of volumes $= 3^3 : 4^3 = 27 : 64$

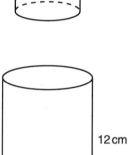

If the volume of the larger cylinder is 960 cm³,
what is the volume of the smaller one ?

Ratio of volumes is $27 : 64$
Volume of smaller cylinder $= \frac{27}{64}$ of 960 cm³ $= 405$ cm³.

3 Two containers are similar in shape. The larger one is 20 cm high and holds 10 ℓ of
liquid. How high is the smaller one, which holds 3.43 ℓ of liquid ?

Ratio of volumes $= 10\,000$ cm³ $: 3430$ cm³

$= 1000 : 343$

$= 10^3 : 7^3$

Ratio of heights $= 10 : 7$

Height of smaller container $= \frac{7}{10}$ of 20 cm $= 14$ cm.

Scale drawing

Scales can be given in various ways, such as

   1 cm represents $\frac{1}{2}$ m,

or, 2 cm represents 1 m,

or, Scale 1 : 50,

or, $\frac{1}{50}$ scale.

In any scale drawing, the scale should be stated.

The scale of a map can be called the Representative Fraction, or R.F.

Thus R.F. $= \frac{1}{100\,000}$ or R.F. $= 1 : 100\,000$ means that 1 unit represents $100\,000$ units, so 1 cm represents $100\,000$ cm, which is 1 km.

Areas and volumes

If the scale of a map or model is $a : b$,
then corresponding areas will be in the ratio $a^2 : b^2$
and volumes will be in the ratio $a^3 : b^3$.

e.g. The scale of a map is '1 cm represents 5 km'.

Then an area of 1^2 cm^2 represents 5^2 km^2,
i.e. 1 cm^2 represents 25 km^2.

Exercise 11.2

1.   These pairs of figures are similar. State the ratios of corresponding lengths. Calculate the lengths of the unknown, marked sides.

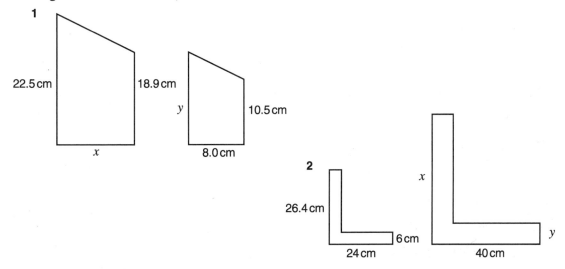

1. (These pairs of figures are similar. State the ratios of corresponding lengths. Calculate the lengths of the unknown, marked sides.)

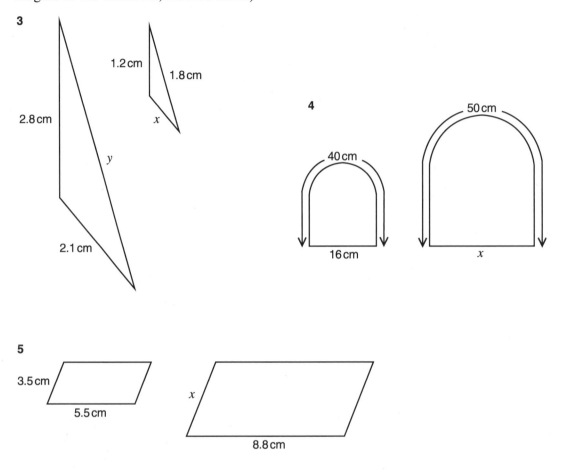

2. State the ratios of the areas of the figures in question 1, parts **1** to **5**.

3. These pairs of solid figures are similar. State the ratios of corresponding lengths. Calculate the unknown, marked lengths.

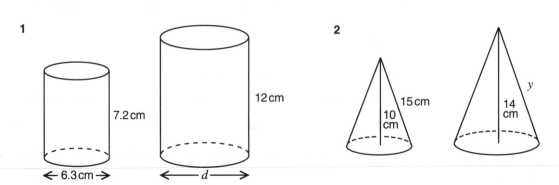

3

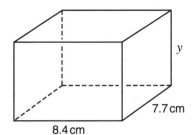

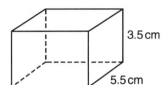

4

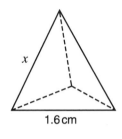

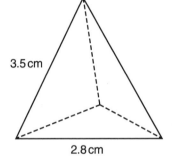

5

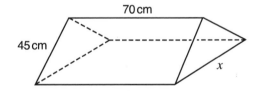

4. State the ratios of the surface areas, and the ratios of the volumes, of the figures in question 3.

5. A map has a scale of 2 cm to represent 1 km. What is the scale in ratio form ?
   If two villages are 8.4 cm apart on the map, what is the actual distance between them ?

6. A hall is 20 m long and 13.5 m wide. What measurements should be used on a plan to a scale of 1 : 250 ?

7. These concentric circles have radii 3 cm and 4 cm.
    Without substituting any numerical value for π,
    find

    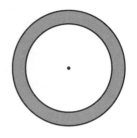

    1   the ratio of the lengths of their circumferences,
    2   the ratio of their areas.
    3   What fraction of the whole area is shaded ?

8. Two containers are similar in shape, and one is 12 cm high, the other 16 cm high. If the
    smaller one holds 1.35 litres of liquid, how much does the larger one hold ?

Similar triangles

Similar triangles have the same shape.
(If they have the same size also, they are called congruent triangles.)

(1)   (2)   (3)

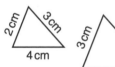   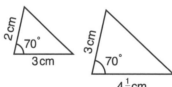   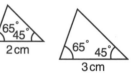

We recognise that the triangles are similar because:

In (1), the three sides of the first triangle are proportional to the three sides of the second
         triangle.

In (2), two sides of the first triangle are proportional to two of the sides of the second triangle,
         and the angles included between the two sides are equal.

In (3), the three angles of the first triangle are equal to the three angles of the second triangle,
         (i.e. the triangles are equiangular).
         (The 3rd angle in each triangle is $180° - (65° + 45°) = 70°$.)

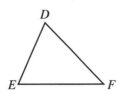

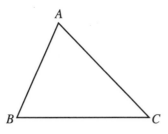

If two triangles ABC, DEF are similar, then we know

1    $\angle A = \angle D$, $\angle B = \angle E$, $\angle C = \angle F$.

2    $\dfrac{AB}{DE} = \dfrac{AC}{DF} = \dfrac{BC}{EF}$,   i.e. corresponding sides are proportional.

3    $\dfrac{\text{Area } \triangle ABC}{\text{Area } \triangle DEF} = \dfrac{AB^2}{DE^2}$ $\left(\text{or } \dfrac{AC^2}{DF^2} \text{ or } \dfrac{BC^2}{EF^2} \right)$

     i.e. areas of similar triangles are proportional to **squares** of corresponding sides.

Examples

1   Triangles ABD, ACE are similar because

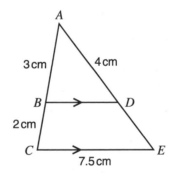

$\qquad \angle A = \angle A$ (same angle)

$\qquad \angle ABD = \angle C$ (corresponding angles)

$\qquad \angle ADB = \angle E$ (corresponding angles)

So $\dfrac{AB}{AC} = \dfrac{AD}{AE} = \dfrac{BD}{CE}$

So $\dfrac{3}{5} = \dfrac{4}{AE}$, $3AE = 20$ cm

$\qquad\qquad AE = 6\frac{2}{3}$ cm

$\qquad\qquad DE = 2\frac{2}{3}$ cm

$\dfrac{BD}{7.5} = \dfrac{3}{5}$, $BD = \dfrac{3 \times 7.5}{5}$ cm $= 4.5$ cm.

$\dfrac{\text{Area } \triangle ABD}{\text{Area } \triangle ACE} = \dfrac{AB^2}{AC^2} = \dfrac{3^2}{5^2} = \dfrac{9}{25}$.

i.e. area $\triangle ABD = \frac{9}{25}$ of area $\triangle ACE$.

It is also true that $\dfrac{AB}{BC} = \dfrac{AD}{DE}$, i.e. a straight line parallel to one side of a triangle divides

the other sides proportionally.

2 Triangles ABC, DEC are similar because

$\dfrac{AC}{DC} = \dfrac{BC}{EC}$ $(= \frac{2}{3})$ and $\angle ACB = \angle DCE$.

So $\angle A = \angle D$ and $\angle B = \angle E$.

$\dfrac{AB}{DE} = \dfrac{AC}{DC} = \dfrac{2}{3}$,   i.e. AB is $\frac{2}{3}$ of DE.

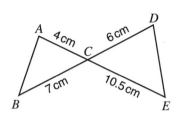

$\dfrac{\text{Area } \triangle ABC}{\text{Area } \triangle DEC} = \dfrac{AC^2}{DC^2} = \dfrac{2^2}{3^2} = \dfrac{4}{9}$.

If area $\triangle ABC = 10$ cm^2, then area $\triangle DEC = \frac{9}{4} \times 10$ cm$^2 = 22.5$ cm^2.

Exercise 11.3

1. In these questions, equal angles are marked in the same way.
    Say why the triangles are similar and name the 3 pairs of corresponding sides, and any other equal angles.

1

2

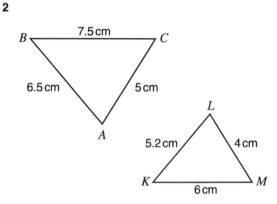

3

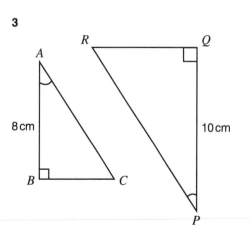

4

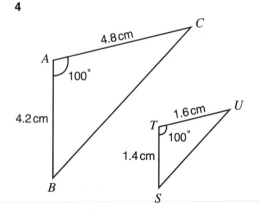

2. **1** Explain why these triangles are similar.

   2 What is the ratio $BC : EF$?

   3 What is the ratio area $\triangle ABC$: area $\triangle DEF$?

   4 Which angle is equal to $\angle C$?

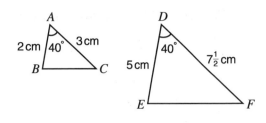

3. **1** Explain why these triangles are similar.

   2 Name an angle equal to $\angle B$.

   3 What is the ratio area $\triangle ABC$: area $\triangle DEF$?

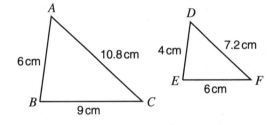

4. **1** What are the values of $\dfrac{AD}{AC}$ and $\dfrac{AE}{AB}$?

   2 Are triangles ADE, ACB similar?

   3 What angle is equal to $\angle ADE$?

   4 What is the ratio $DE : CB$?

   5 What is the ratio area $\triangle ADE$: area $\triangle ACB$?

   6 If the area of $\triangle ADE = 6$ cm^2, what is the area of $\triangle ACB$?

   7 What is the area of quadrilateral $DECB$?

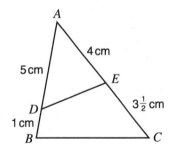

5. **1** Are triangles AXB, DXC similar?

   2 Find the length of AB.

   3 What is the ratio of areas of $\triangle AXB$ and $\triangle DXC$?

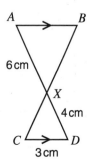

6. A stick 2 m long is placed vertically so that its top is in line with the top of a cliff, from a point A on the ground 3 m from the stick and 120 m from the cliff. How high is the cliff ?

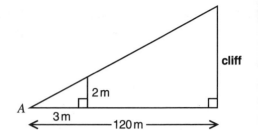

7. A triangle of area 5 cm^2 is transformed by enlargement into a similar triangle of area 45 m^2.
   What is the scale factor of the enlargement ?
   One side of the new triangle has length 4.5 cm. What is the length of the corresponding side of the original triangle ?
   One angle of the new triangle has size 66°. What is the size of the corresponding angle of the original triangle ?

Exercise 11.4   Applications

1. On graph paper draw the x-axis from -4 to 8 and the y-axis from 0 to 8.
   Plot these points and join them in order, to make a letter Z, $(-4, 6)$, $(-1, 6)$, $(-4, 3)$, $(-1, 3)$.
   Enlarge this letter Z, starting with the top left-hand point at $(1, 8)$ and using a scale factor of $2\frac{1}{3}$.

2. These cylinders are similar.
   What is the ratio of corresponding lengths ?
   What is the height of the 2nd cylinder ?
   What is the ratio of their total surface areas ?
   What is the ratio of their volumes ?

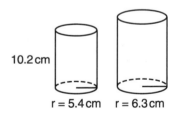

3. A model of a hall is made to a scale of 2 cm to 1 m. The height of the model is 16 cm, its floor area is 800 cm^2 and its volume is 12 800 cm^3. Find the height, floor area and volume of the hall.

4. Two similar solid statues weigh 560 g and 1890 g. The lighter one has a height of 10 cm. If they are made of similar material, what is the height of the other one ?

5. The scale of a map is 5 cm to 1 km. What is the distance between two places which are 17.5 cm apart on the map ?
   What is the actual area of a region which is represented on the map by an area of 5 cm^2 ?

6. A line AB is of length 8 cm and P is a point on AB such that $AP : PB = 1 : 2$.
    With centre P two circles are drawn, radii PA and PB. What fraction of the area of the
    larger circle is the area of the smaller circle ?

7. Two similar cones have volumes in the ratio $27 : 125$.

    1 What is the ratio of their radii ?
    2 What is the ratio of the areas of their bases ?

8. The length of the shadow of a vertical post 2.4 m high is 3.3 m. At the same time and
    place the length of the shadow of a vertical flagpole is 17.6 m. Find the height of the
    flagpole.

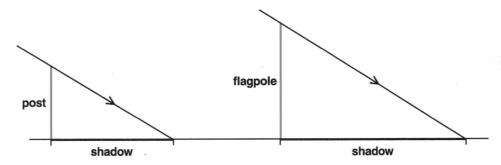

(The sun is so far away that its rays form parallel lines.)

9. In $\triangle ABC$, $AB = 16$ cm, $BC = 12$ cm. D is
    the mid-point of AC and DE is perpendicular
    to AC.

    1 Find the length of AC.
    2 Show that triangles ADE, ABC are similar.
    3 Find the length of DE.

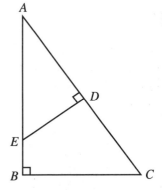

10. **1** What fraction of the area of $\triangle ABC$ is
          the area of $\triangle BDE$?
    2 What fraction of the area of $\triangle ABC$ is
          the area of $\triangle CDF$?
    3 Hence, what fraction of the area of
          $\triangle ABC$ is the area of the parallelogram
          $AEDF$?

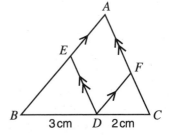

11. 1 Name two similar triangles.
     2 Find the ratio $AX : XC$.
     3 Find the ratio of areas of $\triangle AXD : \triangle DXC$.
     4 Find the ratio of areas of $\triangle AXD : \triangle BXC$.

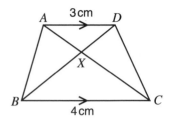

Practice test 11

1. The cylinders are similar.

    1 What is the scale factor of the
       enlargement to turn the small cylinder
       into the large one ?
    2 The radius of the small cylinder is 1.8 cm.
       What is the radius of the large one ?

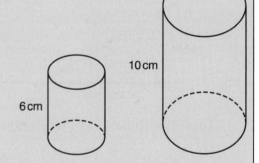

2. 1 Are these rectangles similar ?
    2 What is the ratio of the lengths
       of their diagonals ?

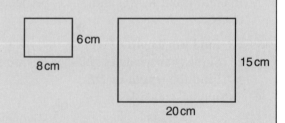

3. The scale of a map is 1 : 25 000. What is the actual distance in km between two places
    which are 8 cm apart on the map ?

4. Two spheres have radii 15 cm and 20 cm. What is the ratio of
    1 their diameters,
    2 their surface areas,
    3 their volumes ?

5. 1 Explain why triangles *ABC*, *ADE* are similar.
    2 What is the ratio *AD* : *AB* ?
    3 What is the ratio *ED* : *CB* ?
    4 What is the ratio area △*ADE* : area △*ABC* ?
    5 If *DE* = $4\frac{1}{2}$ cm, what is the length of *BC* ?
    6 Calculate the areas of △*ADE* and △*ABC*
       and verify that your ratio of areas is correct.

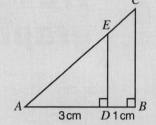

6. *ACD* and *BCE* are straight lines.
    Show that these triangles are similar
    and name the equal angles.
    What does this prove about the
    lines *AB* and *ED* ?

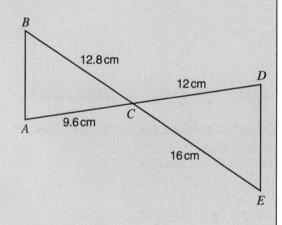

PUZZLES

28. How many squares of side 24 cm can be cut from a piece of paper 65 cm square ?

29. Write in figures: eleven thousand, eleven hundred and eleven.

30. When Katie and Roger were married, they hadn't much money, and on their first
     wedding anniversary Roger was unable to buy his wife a decent present. So he gave
     her 1p, and said that it was all he could afford, but he would try to double the amount
     each year from then on. Sure enough, the next year he gave her 2p, and the following
     year 4p. Katie was quite pleased to get £5.12 this year, and says she is looking forward
     to their Silver Wedding anniversary when they will have been happily married for 25
     years. Roger, however, doesn't seem quite so enthusiastic about this. Why ?

12 Travel graphs and other graphs

The topics in this chapter include:

- travel graphs,

- graphs which represent relationships.

Distance-time graphs

On a distance-time graph, the horizontal axis is the time axis and the vertical axis is the distance axis.

The graph is a straight line when the speed is steady. If the speed is not steady, the graph will not be a straight line.

When the speed is steady, its value is given by the gradient of the line. The greater the speed, the greater the gradient of the line.

If the gradient is negative, the object is travelling in the opposite direction to that in which the distance is measured.

Velocity is a word used instead of speed when the direction of motion is included.

Example

This graph represents a boy's journey from a town P.

He leaves at 12 noon and walks for 30 minutes at a steady speed. This is represented by the line AB. The gradient of the line gives the speed. At what speed does he walk ?

The line BC represents the next stage, where he cycles.
For how long does he cycle ?
What distance does he cycle ?
At what speed does he cycle ?

The line CD represents a rest of 30 minutes.
How far is he away from P ?

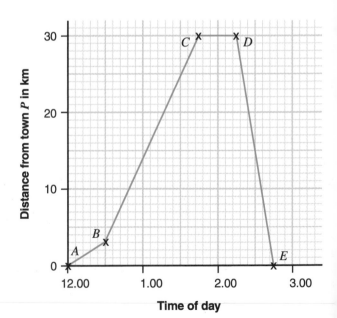

The line *DE* represents his journey home by bus.
What time does the bus journey begin ?
How long is the bus journey ?
What is the speed of the bus ?
(The gradient of the line *DE* gives the velocity which is negative because the direction of motion is in the opposite direction to that at first.)

The **average speed** from *A* to *C* can be found by joining *A* and *C* with a straight line and finding its gradient. It is $\dfrac{30}{1\frac{3}{4}}$ km/h $= 17.1$ km/h.

Exercise 12.1

1. The graph represents the journey
    of a cyclist.
    What is the cyclist's speed ?

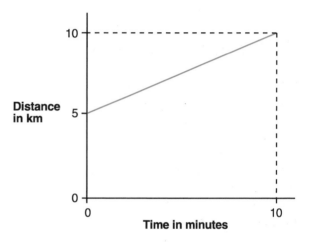

2. The diagram represents the journeys of 4 trains, 3 of them travelling from town *A* to town *B*, 100 km away, and one going in the opposite direction.

    1 Which two trains
    travel at the same
    speed ? What speed
    is it ?

    2 Which train has the
    slowest speed ?
    What speed is it ?

    3 Train (2) should have
    been travelling at a
    speed of 40 km/h.
    How many minutes
    late was it on reaching
    town *A* ?

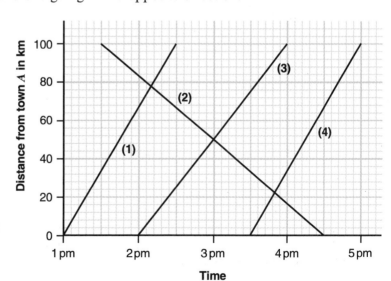

3.   The graph shows the journeys of 2 girls, Pam and Ruth.
      Pam cycles from town A to village B, stopping for a rest on the way. Ruth cycles from
      village B to town A.

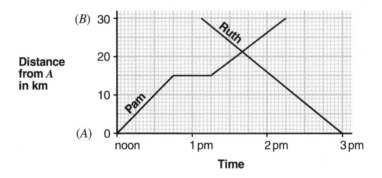

1   For how long did Pam rest ?
2   What was Pam's average speed on the part of her journey after her rest ?
3   When did the two girls pass each other and how far from B were they at this time ?
4   What was Ruth's average speed ?
5   How far apart were the girls at 2.00 pm ?

4.   Paula leaves home to go to school. She walks at a steady speed of 5 km/h to her friend's
      home, which is $2\frac{1}{2}$ km away. There she waits for 20 minutes until her friend is ready to
      leave. The two girls are then taken by car to the school, which is 5 km away. The car
      travels at a steady speed of 30 km/h.
      Draw a graph to represent Paula's journey.

5.   Two cars start at 9 am, one from place A and the other from place B, which is
      60 miles from A. They move towards each other, the first car travelling at 30 mph
      and the other one at 40 mph.
      Show these journeys on a graph.
      At what time do the cars meet, and how far are they from A when they meet ?

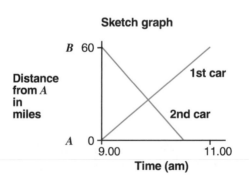

6. John cycled from home to a friend's house. He stayed for a while and then cycled home, stopping on the way to buy some sweets at a shop.
    The graph shows his journeys.

    1 How long did it take John to cycle to his friend's house ?
    2 How long did he stay at his friend's house ?
    3 How far from his friend's house was the shop ?
    4 How long did he spend in the shop ?
    5 After leaving the shop, what was John's speed on the homeward journey ?

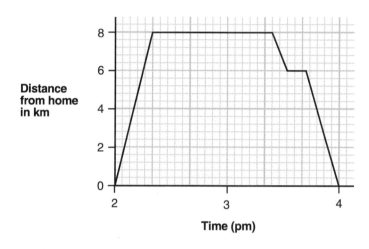

7. A plane flies from Airport A to Airport B and after a short stop for refuelling flies on to Airport C. The speed from A to B is constant, and the speed from B to C is also constant, though greater than that from A to B.
    The table gives details of the flight.

Time after start, in hours	0	1	2	$2\frac{1}{2}$	3	4	5	6
Distance from A, in km	0	800	1600	2000	2000	2900	3800	4700

Draw a graph to represent the journey of the plane, using scales of 2 cm to represent 1 hour, and 500 km.

1 How far was the plane from A after $1\frac{1}{2}$ hours ?
2 How long did the plane spend at Airport B ?
3 How long after the start did the plane reach a place 4000 km from A ?
4 What was the speed of the plane on the part of the journey from B to C ?

8.   The table gives the distances travelled by a car at various times.

Time after start, in seconds	0	1	2	3	4	5	6	7	8
Distance from start, in metres	0	0.6	2.5	5.5	9.8	15.3	20.7	22.6	23.2

Draw a distance-time graph, joining the points with a smooth curve.

Use the graph to estimate
1   the distance from the starting point after 3.5 s,
2   the time taken to travel a distance of 20 m.

Other graphs

Example

A Gas Company makes a standing charge of £10 a quarter plus a cost of 1.5 p for every kilowatt hour (kWh) of gas used.
What would be the total bill if 8000 kWh were used ?
What would be the total bill if 4000 kWh were used ?
If no gas was used, there would still be the £10 standing charge to pay.

Draw an accurate graph, with the number of kWh on the horizontal axis, from 0 to 8000, using a scale of 2 cm to represent 1000 kWh, and with cost in £'s on the vertical axis, from 0 to 130, using a scale of 2 cm to £20.
Plot the 3 points corresponding to 0 kWh, 4000 kWh and 8000 kWh used, and join them with a straight line.

Use your graph to find the amount of the bill when 2800 kWh were used. Also find the number of kWh used if a gas bill was for £88.

(This sketch graph shows how your accurate graph will look, and how it can be used.)

8000 kWh cost £130,
4000 kWh cost £70,
2800 kWh cost £52,
£88 is the cost of 5200 kWh.

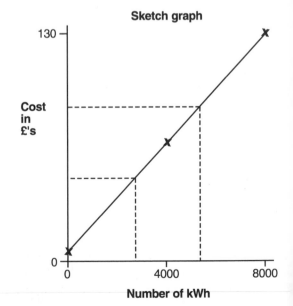

Exercise 12.2

1. When a local firm is called out to service machinery, it charges £40 for coming out plus an amount for time spent on the job, at the rate of £30 per hour.

    Draw a graph of the costs for jobs taking up to 5 hours.

    Use the graph to find
    1   the cost for a job taking $2\frac{1}{4}$ hours,
    2   the time spent, if the bill was for £175.

2. The quantities, w grams, of a salt which can be dissolved in a given volume of water at different temperatures, $t\,°C$, are given in the table.

t (°C)	10	20	25	30	40	50	55	60
w (g)	41	44	45.5	47	50	53	54.5	56

    Draw a graph to show this information using a scale of 2 cm to 10 units on both axes. Draw a line of best fit.

    Use the graph to find
    1   the amount of the salt which will dissolve in the given volume of water at a temperature of 34°C,
    2   the temperature at which 52 g of the salt will dissolve in the given volume of water.

3. Draw a graph to convert temperature from °F to °C.
    Draw the °F axis horizontally, labelling it from 0 to 240, and draw the °C axis vertically, labelling it from 0 to 120.
    When the temperature is 32°F, it is 0°C. (Freezing point.)
    When the temperature is 212°F, it is 100°C. (Boiling point.)
    Plot these two points on the graph, and join them with a straight line.
    Use your graph to convert 70°F into °C, and to convert 80°C into °F.
    A person's 'normal' temperature is 98.4°F. What is the approximate value in °C ?

4. These times are taken from a table of 'lighting-up times for vehicles', on the Sunday of each week.

Week number	1	2	3	4	5	6	7	8
Time of day	16.32	16.40	16.50	17.02	17.14	17.26	17.39	17.52

    Plot these values on a graph. Draw the 'week number' axis horizontally with 2 cm to each unit. Draw the 'time of day' axis vertically, from 16.00 hours to 18.00 hours taking 1 cm to 10 minutes. Join the plotted points with a smooth curve.

Sketch graphs

These can show the general relationship between two variables, without showing exact details. Often, one of the variables is time, and that usually goes on the horizontal axis.

Examples

Distance-time graphs

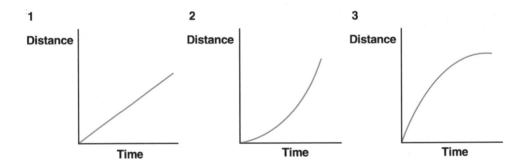

1   shows an object moving with a steady speed.
2   shows an object moving with an increasing speed (i.e. it is accelerating).
3   shows an object moving with a decreasing speed (i.e. it is slowing down).

Profits of a firm

4   shows that there is a steady increase in profits.
5   shows that there is a steady decrease in profits.
6   shows that for the first few months of the year, profits increased, but the rate of increase slowed down and profits reached a maximum, and then slowly fell. (If these profits were plotted every month, then the graph would not be a curve, because the readings are not continuous. It would be a line-graph (time-series graph), with points joined by a series of straight lines. However, in a sketch graph which shows the general relationship, it is reasonable to draw a curve.)

Other graphs

7

A wave graph

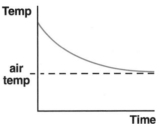

8

A cooling graph

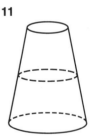

7   E.g. the height of the tide in a harbour.

8   The hot liquid cools quickly at first, then more slowly as it gets nearer to air temperature.

Filling containers

9   **10**   **11**

If liquid is poured into these containers at a steady rate of volume per second, then the rate at which the height of liquid increases depends on the shape of the container.

9   **10**   **11**

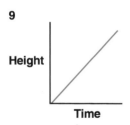
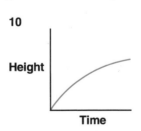
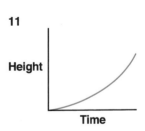

In **9**, the height will increase steadily.

In **10**, the height will increase quickly when there is a small area of cross-section, and increase more slowly as the area of cross-section increases.

In **11**, the height will increase slowly at first and increase more quickly as the area of the cross-section decreases.

Special relationships

Direct proportion

When two quantities x, y are in direct proportion then
the connection between them is $y = kx$, where k is
a constant number, and the graph is a straight line
passing through the origin.

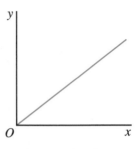

Examples

Time and distance, when the speed is steady.
Conversion graphs for foreign currency, British and metric units, etc. (The graph of
temperature conversion from °C to °F is a straight line but it does not go through the origin.)

Inverse proportion

When two quantities x, y are in inverse proportion
then the connection between them is $y = \dfrac{k}{x}$,
and the graph looks like this.

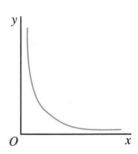

Examples

Length and breadth of a rectangle when the area is constant.
Pressure and volume of a gas when temperature is constant.

Quadratic functions

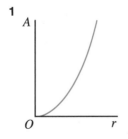

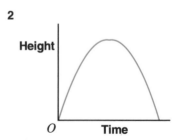

1   The connection between radius and area of a circle is $A = \pi r^2$, so the graph is the same
     shape as $y = \pi x^2$.
2   The height of a cricket ball at different times after it is thrown into the air obeys a
     quadratic equation law and the graph is of this form.

Exercise 12.3

1. These sketch graphs show the amount of water in a storage tank, during a day when it was being filled.
    Identify which sketch matches each of these statements.

    1 The tank has been filling all day at a steady rate,
    2 The tank has been filling all day, and at an increasing rate as the day progressed.
    3 This morning the tank was gradually filled until it was full and since then it has been kept topped up.
    4 The tank was filled gradually this morning until it was full. Since then some water has been taken out and not yet replaced.

A

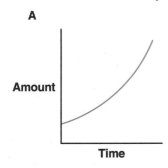

B

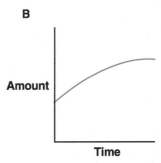

C

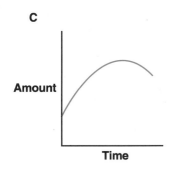

D

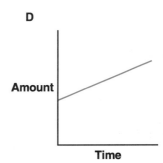

2. **Speed-time graphs**

    (Do not confuse these with distance-time graphs.)

    Draw sketch graphs to show the relationships between time and speed under these conditions.

    1 The speed is kept constant, at 15 m/s.
    2 The speed increases at a steady rate, from rest to 30 m/s over 10 seconds.
    3 The speed decreases at a steady rate, from 30 m/s to 10 m/s in 10 seconds.

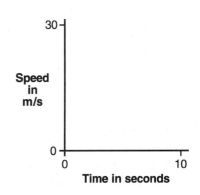

3.   The graph shows the temperature
     recorded in the room of a house
     between 6 am and 6 pm.
     Describe the changes in temperature
     and suggest likely reasons for them.

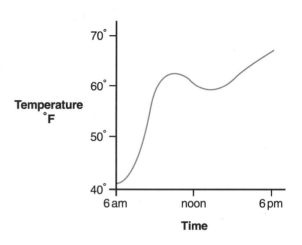

4.   Draw sketch graphs to show the general relationships between these variables.
     It may help you to make a table of values first, in some cases.
     If the relationship is represented by a straight line, draw it using a ruler, not freehand.

   1   The connection between the number of trees bought and their cost, if they cost
       £8 each.
       (Number on the horizontal axis, cost in £'s on the vertical axis.)

   2   The connection between the time taken and the speed, to go a distance of 60 miles at
       various average speeds.
       (Time in hours on the horizontal axis, speed in mph on the vertical axis.)

   3   The connection between the diameter and area of a circle.
       (Diameter in cm on the horizontal axis, area in cm^2 on the vertical axis.)

   4   The height h m above ground reached by a stone thrown upwards, after various times
       t seconds. The equation connecting h and t is $h = 20t - 5t^2$.
       (t on the horizontal axis, h on the vertical axis.)

   5   The distance-time graph of a runner in a race, who starts off quickly and gradually
       reduces speed until he is running very slowly, until the last quarter of the race where
       he makes a final burst of speed.
       (Time on the horizontal axis, distance on the vertical axis.)

Exercise 12.4 Applications

1. Karen walks from school to a bus stop and then catches a bus which takes her to the village. She then walks the remaining distance home. The journey is shown by the graph.

    1 How long does Karen wait at the bus stop ?
    2 At what speed does the bus travel ?
    3 How far does Karen walk after getting off the bus ?

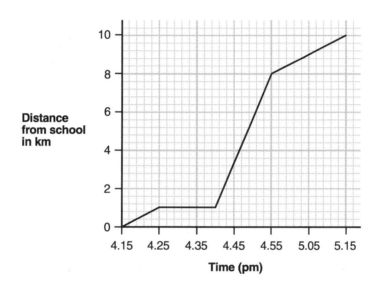

2. Dhiren leaves village A on his bicycle at noon and cycles at a speed of 15 km/h towards a town B. After an hour he has 30 minutes rest and then continues at a speed of 12 km/h, reaching B at 3 pm. His father leaves town B by car at 1.45 pm, driving towards A at a steady speed, and arrives at A at 2.30 pm.

    Represent this information on a distance-time graph, drawing the time axis from noon to 3 pm and the distance axis showing distances from A from 0 to 40 km.

    1 How far apart are A and B ?
    2 How far from B, and at what time, did his father pass Dhiren ?

3. A train leaves town A for town B at 1 pm and maintains a steady speed of 60 km/h. At 2 pm another train leaves B for A maintaining a steady speed of 72 km/h. The distance between A and B is 180 km.

    Draw the distance-time graphs for these two trains using the same axes.
    When do the trains pass one another and how far are they from A at this time ?

4. The table shows the distances reached by a train at different times after leaving a station.

Time in minutes	0	10	20	30	40	50	60
Distance in km	0	4	13	15	22	33	50

Show the data on a distance-time graph, joining the points by a curve.

Find from your graph
1   the distance travelled in the first 45 minutes,
2   the time when the train was 10 km from the station.

5. In a motor race car *B* gives car *A* 10 minutes start, travels at 100 mph and overtakes *A* 60 miles from the start.
Draw graphs to represent the journeys of *A* and *B*. Take scales of 2 cm to represent 10 minutes, and 20 miles.
A completes the course in 69 minutes. Use the graph to find the length of the course.

Also find
1   the number of minutes by which *B* won,
2   how far *A* was from the finishing post when *B* completed the race,
3   the speed of *A*, in mph.

6. At noon a motorist travelling at 40 km/h and a cyclist riding at 20 km/h both leave a point *A*, going in the same direction. At 12.15 pm the motorist overtakes a pedestrian, also going the same way, walking at $7\frac{1}{2}$ km/h.

Draw graphs to represent the journeys of the motorist, the cyclist and the pedestrian.
Take scales of 2 cm to represent 10 minutes, and 5 km.
Use the graph to find at what time the cyclist will overtake the pedestrian, and how far they both will be from *A* at that time.

7. A tank contains water, and when it is drained by means of a tap the water level falls by 2.5 cm each second. At the start, the depth of the water is 50 cm.
Show on a graph the relationship between the depth of water and the time after opening the tap.

Use the graph to find
1   the depth of water in the tank after 12 seconds,
2   the time taken for the tank to empty.

8. The table gives the total length, y cm, of a spring when a weight, w kg is hanging on one end.

w (kg)	0.1	0.2	0.3	0.4	0.5	0.6
y (cm)	27.2	31.7	36.2	40.7	45.2	49.7

Plot the results on a graph.

Find from the graph
1   the weight to be attached for the length of the spring to be 30 cm,
2   the length of the spring when no weight is attached,
3   how much the spring is extended when a weight of 0.45 kg is attached.

9. The graph shows a man's weight at different ages.
    Describe the changes in weight and suggest possible reasons for them.

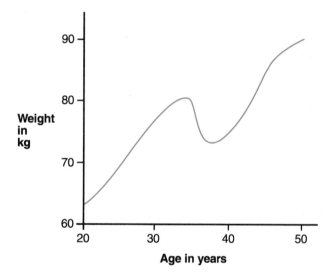

10. The graph shows how the depth
     of water in a harbour varies
     throughout the day.

1   At what times were high tide ?
2   At what times were low tide ?
3   Estimate the time of the next high
    tide.

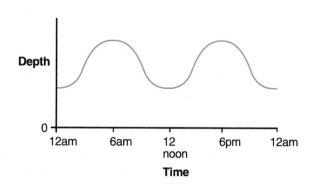

11. Draw sketch graphs showing the relationship between time and height of water when these containers are being filled with water which is being poured in at a steady rate of volume per second.

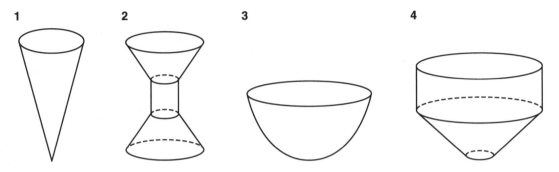

12. These sketch graphs show these relationships. Identify which is which.

   1   The diameter, x cm, of a circle, and the circumference, y cm.

   2   The length, x cm, and the breadth, y cm, of a rectangle of constant area 48 cm².

   3   The distance travelled by a young child over several seconds when running to meet his mother who is waiting for him 100 m away.

   4   The amount £y in a savings account after x years when the rate of interest is 10%.

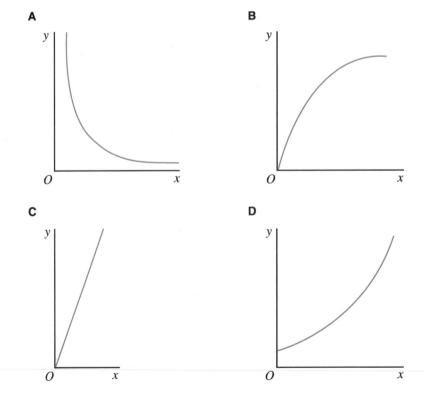

13. Draw a sketch graph to show the height above the central point A of a boy on a circular fairground wheel rotating at a steady rate of 1 revolution per minute, at various times during the first minute.

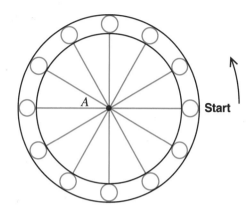

Start

14. Draw a sketch graph to show the value of a piece of machinery at various times. It was originally worth £20 000 and depreciates in value at the rate of 10% each year.

Practice test 12

1. The graph represents the journeys of two motorists, one in a car and one in a van.

   1 At what time did the car reach *B* ?
   2 What was the speed of the van ?
   3 At what time, and how far from *A*, did the car pass the van ?
   4 How far apart were the car and the van at 2 pm ?
   5 What was the average speed of the car over the whole journey from A to B ?

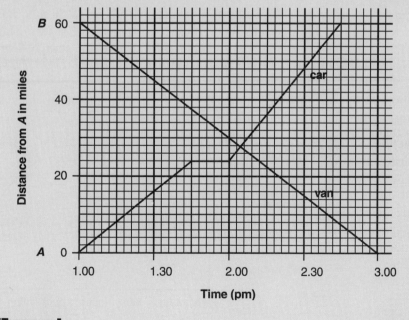

[Turn over]

2.   Two cars start at 8 am from a town and travel by the same route towards a city
     60 miles away. The first one travels at 48 mph for $\frac{3}{4}$ hour, stops for $\frac{1}{4}$ hour and then
     proceeds at 20 mph only. The second car goes steadily at 30 mph.
     Draw graphs to represent these journeys. Use scales of 2 cm to $\frac{1}{2}$ hour, and to 10 miles.
     Find the time when the second car overtakes the first one and find how far they are
     from the town at that time.

3.   A rocket is fired vertically into the air from ground level, and its height h metres after
     t seconds is given in the table.

t	0	5	10	15	20	25	30
h	0	625	1000	1125	1000	625	0

     Draw a distance-time graph, joining the points with a smooth curve.

     1   What is the greatest height achieved by the rocket ?
     2   At what times is the rocket at half of its greatest height ?
     3   For how many seconds is the rocket 900 m or more above the ground ?

4.   The cost, £C, of making n articles in a certain factory is given by the formula
     $C = 160 + 20n$.
     Draw a graph showing the cost for making up to 30 articles.
     From the graph find how many articles can be made for £500.

5.   Draw a graph to convert metres/second into km/h for speeds up to 50 m/s. Label the
     horizontal axis from 0 to 50 (m/s) and the vertical axis from 0 to 180 (km/h). Use the
     information that 0 m/s = 0 km/h and 50 m/s = 180 km/h to draw the straight-line graph.
     What speed is equivalent to   1   13 m/s,   2   100 km/h ?

6.   The graph shows how the temperature varied with time during a day in a certain
     tropical country.

     1   What was the
         minimum temperature
         and at what time of
         day did it occur ?
     2   What was the hottest
         time of day and what
         was the maximum
         temperature ?

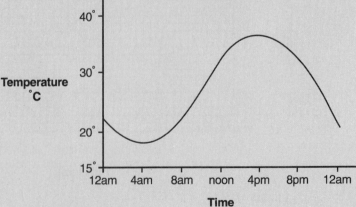

7. These sketch graphs show the costs of running a business over several months.
    Identify which sketch graph matches each of these statements.
    1 The costs are rising steadily.
    2 The costs are falling after having reached a peak.
    3 The costs are rising at an increasing rate.
    4 The costs have been rising but now seem to have levelled out.

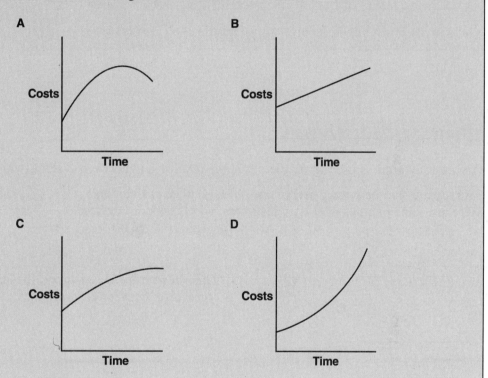

PUZZLE

31. Mary is the eldest of five children and she is responsible for bringing her brothers,
    Tony and James, and her sisters, Patricia and Wendy, home from school. This journey
    includes crossing a river by a small rowing-boat, which only holds two of them at a
    time, and only Mary and Tony can row this. Usually they all get across quite quickly,
    but one particular afternoon the children were quarrelsome and Mary did not want to
    leave the two boys together, or the two girls together, unless she was with them to
    keep them in order. She usually sent Wendy across the river first, with Tony, but on
    this afternoon Wendy refused to go with Tony and insisted she would only go in the
    boat with Mary. Then James said it was his turn to go across before Wendy did.
    How did Mary get them all across the river peacefully ?

13 Further Statistics

The topics in this chapter include:

- drawing a line of best fit on a scatter diagram,
- constructing and interpreting a cumulative frequency curve.

Scatter diagrams

A scatter diagram is used when there is some relationship between 2 sets of variables.

The relationship between 2 sets of variables is called **correlation**.
Here are some pictures of scatter diagrams, with axes not labelled.

This shows that there is good (positive) correlation between the variables.

Here there is an exact relationship. This can be described as perfect correlation.

There is some correlation but it is not very close.

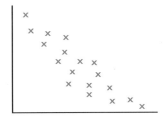

This is a relationship where as one variable increases, the other decreases.
This is said to be inverse or negative correlation.

Perfect inverse correlation.

There does not seem to be any relationship.
There is no correlation, or there is zero correlation.

To draw a line of best fit

You just draw the best line you can, deciding by putting your ruler (or your set-square may be better) on the graph and trying it in various positions, until you have a slope which matches the general slope of the points, and an average position where the points are balanced with some on both sides of the line.

Diagrams showing lines of best fit

(Scales are not shown.)

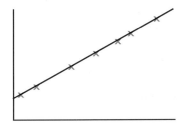 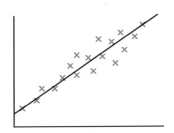 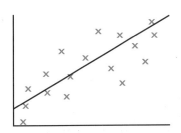

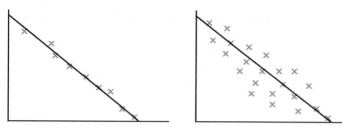

With a suitable computer program, a scatter diagram can be plotted on a computer screen. This is very useful if you have a large amount of data, because it is much quicker than drawing your own graph and plotting the points on it. You can see if there seems to be evidence of correlation, and the program will also draw a line of best fit (called a regression line of y on x in more advanced work).

Example

The length and width of 10 leaves from a bush.

| Length (in cm) | 6.4 | 7.5 | 6.7 | 7.3 | 6.8 | 5.6 | 5.1 | 4.7 | 5.5 | 6.2 |
| Width (in cm) | 2.6 | 3.9 | 2.8 | 3.4 | 3.7 | 2.1 | 2.3 | 1.5 | 2.2 | 2.6 |

Scatter diagram of the lengths and widths of 10 leaves

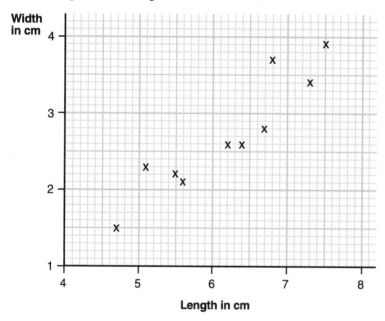

Note that the labelling on the axes need not start at 0.

The 1st set of data is usually plotted on the horizontal axis.

The diagram shows that there is some relationship between length and width. Longer leaves tend to be wider, although the relationship is not exact. We can draw a line of best fit, although we may not all agree on what is the 'best' line.

This line can be used to estimate the likely width of a leaf with a certain length, but the result will only be a 'best estimate', not a fixed measure.

For a leaf of length 7 cm the estimate for the width is 3.3 cm.

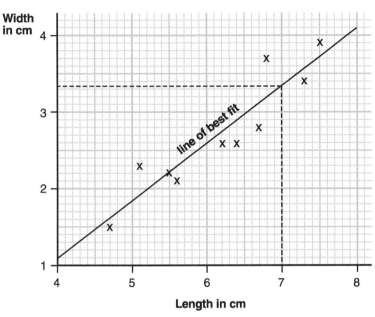

Exercise 13.1

Questions 1 to 5

Sets of two related variables x and y are given in the tables. Plot the values on scatter diagrams, with x on the horizontal axis, from 10 to 70, and y on the vertical axis, from 0 to 50.

Say whether the correlation is positive or negative.

Draw a line of best fit.

Use your line to estimate a y-value which would correspond with an x-value of 45.

1.

x	10	20	30	40	50	60	70
y	2	3	12	25	33	36	47

2.

x	10	15	20	25	30	40	50	55	60	70
y	44	40	39	32	31	25	17	15	9	7

3.

x	15	20	25	30	40	50	60	70
y	8	17	20	19	24	39	41	46

(For questions 4 and 5 see the general instructions on the previous page.)

4.

x	15	20	25	30	35	40	50	55	60	70
y	45	31	35	25	22	12	15	8	5	6

5.

x	10	15	20	25	30	40	50	55	60	65	70
y	6	7	18	17	25	26	42	39	43	49	48

6.   8 plots were treated with different amounts of fertilizer and the crop yield recorded.

Amount of fertilizer (units/m^2)	1	2	3	4	5	6	7	8
Yield (in kg)	36	41	58	60	70	76	75	92

Plot a scatter diagram of these results and draw a line of best fit.

7.   The marks of 10 students in a Maths exam were as follows:

Paper 1	32	38	42	45	48	51	57	62	70	72
Paper 2	45	44	49	51	50	55	60	60	68	70

Plot the points on a scatter diagram and draw a line of best fit.
Another student scored 55 marks on Paper 1 but was absent for Paper 2. Use your diagram to estimate what he might have scored on Paper 2.

8.   The heights of 10 boys and their fathers are given in this table.

Height of father (in cm)	167	168	169	171	172	172	174	175	176	182
Height of son (in cm)	164	166	166	168	169	170	170	171	173	177

Plot the points on a scatter diagram and draw a line of best fit. Use your diagram to estimate the height of a boy of this age if his father is 1.7 m tall.

9.   Draw 5 sketch diagrams, with 10 crosses shown on each, to show examples of pairs of variables which have
    1   good positive correlation,
    2   positive correlation which is fairly good,
    3   good negative correlation,
    4   perfect negative correlation,
    5   no correlation.
    (Do not label axes or show scales.)
    In diagrams 1 to 4, add a line of best fit to your sketch.

Averages and Dispersion

When statistical data has been collected, we often need to find an average measurement.

The median. When the items are arranged in order of size, the median is the value of the middle item, or the value halfway between the middle two if there is an even number of items.

The range is the simplest measure of dispersion to find.

Range = highest value − lowest value

The range only uses the extreme values so it is not always very representative.

The interquartile range is a measure of the middle half of the data, so it is more representative.

Quartiles are the quarter-way divisions in the data, found in a similar way to finding the median.

The interquartile range = upper quartile value − lower quartile value

Example

1   The numbers of members of two clubs attending meetings in different weeks are as shown.
     The numbers have been arranged in order of size.

     Club A.   19, 20, 20, 20, 20, 22, 23, 24, 24, 28.
     Club B.   8, 11, 13, 15, 18, 23, 30, 32, 34, 36.

     The mean in each case is 22 but there is a much bigger dispersion in Club B.

     Range in Club A = 18 − 19 = 9.
     Range in Club B = 36 − 8 = 28.

     In Club A.

| 19 | 20 | 20 | 20 | 20 ↓ 22 | 23 | 24 | 24 | 28 |

     ↓ (under second 20): lower quartile (centre of lower half)
     median (under 20 22)
     ↓ (under first 24): upper quartile (centre of upper half)

     Interquartile range = 24 − 20 = 4.

     Verify for yourself that the interquartile range in Club B = 19.

Cumulative Frequency

To find the median and the interquartile range of a grouped frequency distribution, it is useful to find the cumulative frequency and draw a cumulative frequency graph.

Examples

2 The frequency table shows the exam marks of 300 students. Make a cumulative frequency table and draw the cumulative frequency graph.
Find the median mark and the interquartile range of marks.

Frequency table

Mark	f
1–10	3
11–20	7
21–30	13
31–40	29
41–50	44
51–60	65
61–70	70
71–80	49
81–90	14
91–100	6
	300

Cumulative frequency table

Mark	Cum. freq.
0	0
10 or less	3
20 or less	10
30 or less	23
40 or less	52
50 or less	96
60 or less	161
70 or less	231
80 or less	280
90 or less	294
100 or less	300

← A useful beginning to the table
←i.e. $3 + 7$
←i.e. $3 + 7 + 13$
←i.e. $3 + 7 + 13 + 29$

The points are plotted on a graph, with cumulative frequency on the vertical axis.

If the points are joined to each other by straight lines, this is called a **cumulative frequency polygon.**

If the points are joined by a smooth curve, this is called a **cumulative frequency curve** or **ogive.**

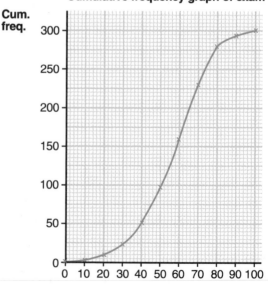

Cumulative frequency graph of exam marks

Median mark. The line to find the median mark is drawn at half the total frequency, that is at 150.

Quartiles. The line to find the lower quartile is drawn at one-quarter of the total frequency, that is at 75, and the line to find the upper quartile is drawn at three-quarters of the total frequency, that is at 225.

Sketch graphs

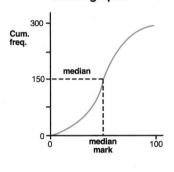 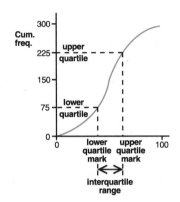

Reading from the actual graph:

The median mark is 59.
The lower quartile is 45, the upper quartile is 69.
The interquartile range = upper quartile − lower quartile = 69 − 45 = 24.

If the measurements are **continuous** then use the words 'less than x' instead of 'x or less' in the cumulative frequency table.

3   The frequency table shows the lifetimes of a sample of 140 light bulbs. Make a cumulative frequency table and draw the cumulative frequency graph.
Find the median lifetime and the interquartile range of lifetimes.
Find how many bulbs last for more than 1500 hours.

Frequency table

Lifetime in hours (to the nearest 100 hours)	Frequency
800	3
900	9
1000	14
1100	23
1200	46
1300	26
1400	9
1500	6
1600	4
	140

Cumulative frequency table

Lifetime in hours	Cum. freq.
less than 750	0
less than 850	3
less than 950	12
less than 1050	26
less than 1150	49
less than 1250	95
less than 1350	121
less than 1450	130
less than 1550	136
less than 1650	140

(The 3 bulbs whose lifetimes are given as 800 hours to the nearest 100 hours have actual lifetimes between 750 and 850 hours. So there are no bulbs with lifetimes less than 750 hours and 3 bulbs with lifetimes less than 850 hours. Another 9 bulbs making 12 altogether have lifetimes less than 950 hours. All 140 bulbs have lifetimes less than 1650 hours.)

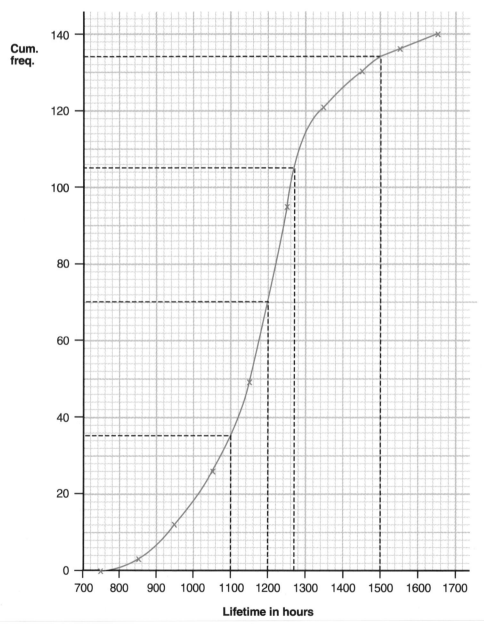

Cumulative frequency graph of lifetimes of bulbs

Cum. freq.

Lifetime in hours

Using the graph, the median lifetime is found by drawing a line at 70.
The median lifetime is 1200 hours.

The quartile lifetimes are found by drawing lines at 35 and 105.
Lower quartile lifetime = 1100 hours.
Upper quartile lifetime = 1270 hours.
The interquartile range is (1270 − 1100) hours = 170 hours.

Drawing a line at 1500 hours shows that 134 bulbs last for less than 1500 hours, so
6 bulbs last longer.

Exercise 13.2

1. Use the frequency distribution of the heights of 60 men given in question 10,
    Exercise 9.5, page 197, to make a cumulative frequency distribution which will begin
    like this:

Height (in cm)	Cum. freq.
less than 167.5	0
less than 170.5	2
less than 173.5	6

    Draw the cumulative frequency graph. Find the median height, the upper and lower
    quartile heights and the interquartile range. How many men are taller than 1.8 m ?

2. Use the frequency distribution of the ages of children in a club given in question 11,
    Exercise 9.5, to make a cumulative frequency distribution which will begin like
    this:

Age (in years)	Cum. freq.
less than 11	0
less than 12	8
less than 13	18

    Draw the cumulative frequency graph. Find the median age, the upper and lower
    quartile ages and the interquartile range of ages.

3. Use the frequency distribution of the lengths of leaves given in question 12, Exercise 9.5,
    to make a cumulative frequency distribution.
    Draw the cumulative frequency graph and find the median length, the quartile lengths
    and the interquartile range of lengths.
    (There are no leaves less than 5.75 cm, the 1st class interval has 1 leaf less than
    6.25 cm.)

4.   Use the frequency distribution of the times children take to travel to school given in question 13, Exercise 9.5, to make a cumulative frequency distribution, which will begin like this:

Time (in minutes)	Cum. freq.
0	0
less than 5	3
less than 10	18

Draw the cumulative frequency graph and find the median time, the quartile times and the interquartile range of times.

5.   Use the data given in the histogram in question 14, Exercise 9.5, to make a cumulative frequency distribution, which will begin like this:

Weight (in kg)	Cum. freq.
less than 7.5	0
less than 8.5	2
less than 9.5	12

Draw the cumulative frequency graph, find the median weight, the upper and lower quartile weights and the interquartile range of weights.
How many children weigh less than 10 kg ?

Exercise 13.3   Applications

1.   A manufacturing company gives these figures for each quarter in a two-year period.

Quarter	1	2	3	4	1	2	3	4
Output units	10	20	40	25	30	40	50	45
Total cost (in £1000's)	41	48	67	53	61	70	79	73

Draw a scatter diagram for the data, with output units on the horizontal axis and total cost on the vertical axis. Draw a line of best fit. What is the estimate for the total cost likely to be incurred at an output level of 35 units ?

2.   The heights and weights of 8 young men are given in this table.

Height (in cm)	168	170	173	178	181	182	183	185
Weight (in kg)	68	70	70	74	75	76	78	79

Plot the points on a scatter diagram and draw a line of best fit.
Estimate the likely weight of a young man if he is 1.75 m tall.

3. The marks gained by 10 students in each of two papers of a Maths examination were as follows:

Student	A	B	C	D	E	F	G	H	J	K
Marks for Paper 1	30	39	44	60	28	64	70	56	32	46
Marks for Paper 2	48	55	56	75	35	78	86	70	46	56

Draw a scatter diagram for the data, putting the marks for Paper 1 on the horizontal axis. Draw a line of best fit.

Another student got 52 marks on Paper 1 but was absent for Paper 2. Use the line of best fit to estimate a mark for this student for Paper 2.

4. A test was carried out on seven fields by treating them with different amounts of nitrogen fertilizer and measuring the percentage of protein in the grass.
Here are the results.

Units of fertilizer applied	0	1	2	3	4	5	6
Percentage of protein	14.0	15.2	17.0	19.4	21.4	22.6	23.2

Plot a scatter diagram of these results and draw a line of best fit.

5. Eight paintings were entered for a competition and were examined by two judges, who marked them out of 100.
The marks are shown in the table.

Painting	1	2	3	4	5	6	7	8
1st Judge	45	55	65	40	25	45	35	65
2nd Judge	50	65	80	50	35	60	40	75

Plot a scatter diagram of the data and draw a line of best fit.
Another painting arrived unavoidably late, and was given a mark of 50 by the 1st judge, but it was not possible for the 2nd judge to examine it. Use the line of best fit to estimate the mark it might have gained from the 2nd judge.

Questions 6 to 10. Use the data given in questions 2 to 6, respectively, of Exercise 9.3, page 193, for these questions.

Make a cumulative frequency table for the data and draw the cumulative frequency graph. Find the median value, the upper and lower quartile values and the interquartile range of values.

11. This cumulative frequency table shows the distribution of times of arrival of 50 children who were late for school on one particular day.

Minutes late	Cum. freq.
less than 5	22
less than 10	30
less than 15	43
less than 20	47
less than 25	49
less than 30	50

Draw a cumulative frequency graph.

Find the median number of minutes late, the upper and lower quartile values and the interquartile range of values.

12. The amounts spent by 120 customers in a shop were as follows:

Amount (£'s)	f
0 to under 5	10
5 to under 10	12
10 to under 20	27
20 to under 40	37
40 to under 60	22
60 to under 100	12

Make a cumulative frequency table for the data and draw the cumulative frequency graph.
Find the median amount, the upper and lower quartile amounts and the interquartile range of amounts.

Practice test 13

1. The exam marks for 10 students for Maths and Physics are as follows:

Maths mark	63	89	53	45	47	74	69	79	64	37
Physics mark	44	65	38	32	35	53	50	59	51	26

Plot these marks on a scatter diagram and draw a line of best fit.
Another student scored 56 in Maths but was absent for the Physics exam. Use your diagram to give an estimated mark for Physics.

2. 80 workers were tested on a particular piece of work and the times they took are recorded in the table.

Time in minutes	Number of workers
4.0–4.5	6
4.5–5.0	10
5.0–5.5	17
5.5–6.0	24
6.0–6.5	15
6.5–7.0	5
7.0–7.5	3

Make a cumulative frequency table for the data.
Draw the cumulative frequency graph.
Find the median time, the upper and lower quartile times and the interquartile range of times.
The management had planned that the maximum time needed for this piece of work was 6.3 minutes. What percentage of the workers took longer than this to complete the work ?

PUZZLES

32. The rail journey from Ashfield to Beechgrove takes exactly 4 hours and trains leave each way on the hour and on the half-hour. If you were on a train going from Ashfield to Beechgrove, how many trains going from Beechgrove to Ashfield would you pass during the journey ?

33. Copy the diagram and starting in the top left-hand square, draw a continuous line passing through each square once only, so that the sum of the numbers in each group of four squares is 24.

6	6	3	15	5	3
6	9	3	10	6	3
3	3	3	8	8	5
5	10	4	2	3	10
3	6	11	2	3	9
5	8	4	7	10	9

14 Trigonometry in right-angled triangles

The topics in this chapter include:

- using sine, cosine and tangent ratios in right-angled triangles,
- calculating distances and angles in solid figures using plane sections and trig. ratios.

Sine, cosine and tangent ratios

$$\sin A = \frac{\text{opp}}{\text{hyp}}$$

$$\cos A = \frac{\text{adj}}{\text{hyp}}$$

$$\tan A = \frac{\text{opp}}{\text{adj}}$$

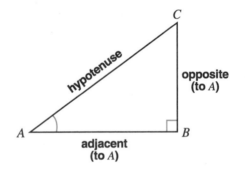

To find a side

Examples

1   To find AB.

$$\cos A = \frac{\text{adj}}{\text{hyp}}$$

$$\cos 32° = \frac{x}{8}$$

$$x = 8 \times \cos 32°$$

$$= 6.784$$

$$AB = 6.78 \text{ cm, to 3 sig. fig.}$$

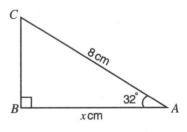

To use your calculator, make sure it is set to work in degrees, then press
8 $\boxed{\times}$ 32 $\boxed{\cos}$ $\boxed{=}$ and you will get 6.784...
(On some calculators you may have to press $\boxed{\cos}$ 32 instead of 32 $\boxed{\cos}$.)

For practical uses you would probably give the answer to the nearest mm. However, to check that you have done a correct calculation your answer may be wanted to 3 significant figures.

Make a rough check of the size of the answer. Here, it should be less than 8 cm, and 6.78 cm seems about right.

2 To find AC.

Use the tangent ratio. Also use the angle opposite to AC, i.e. angle B, which is 54°.

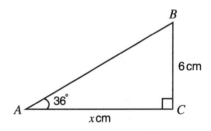

$$\tan B = \frac{\text{opp}}{\text{adj}}$$

$$\tan 54° = \frac{x}{6}$$

$$x = 6 \times \tan 54°$$

$$= 8.258$$

$$AC = 8.26 \text{ cm, to 3 sig. fig.}$$

On your calculator, make sure it is set to work in degrees than press 6 $\boxed{\times}$ 54 $\boxed{\tan}$ $\boxed{=}$

If you prefer to use $\angle A$, the working goes like this:

$$\tan A = \frac{\text{opp}}{\text{adj}}$$

$$\tan 36° = \frac{6}{x}$$

$$x = \frac{6}{\tan 36°}$$

$$= 8.258$$

$$AC = 8.26 \text{ cm, to 3 sig. fig.}$$

3   To find AC.

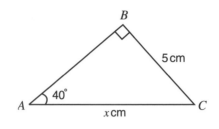

$$\sin A = \frac{\text{opp}}{\text{hyp}}$$

$$\sin 40° = \frac{5}{x}$$

$$x = \frac{5}{\sin 40°}$$

$$= 7.779$$

$AC = 7.78$ cm, to 3 sig. fig.

On your calculator press 5 $\div$ 40 $\boxed{\sin}$ $\boxed{=}$

To find an angle, given two sides

If one of the sides is the hypotenuse, use the sine or cosine ratio. Otherwise use the tangent ratio.

Examples

4   To find $\angle A$.

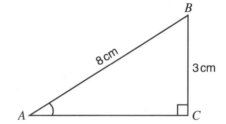

$$\sin A = \frac{\text{opp}}{\text{hyp}}$$

$$= \frac{3}{8} \ (= 0.375)$$

$$\angle A = 22.0°$$

(Give the answer in degrees correct to 1 decimal place. On your calculator, make sure it is set to work in degrees. Find the key for the inverse of the sine function. It might be labelled $\sin^{-1}$, or arcsin. You will probably have to press the second function key and then the sine key to get it.
Press 3 $\div$ 8 $\boxed{=}$ $\boxed{\text{inverse sine}}$)

You can now find $\angle B$ by subtraction.
$\angle B = 90° - 22.0° = 68.0°$

5   To find $\angle A$

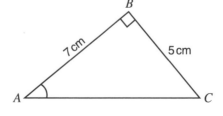

$$\tan A = \frac{\text{opp}}{\text{adj}}$$

$$= \frac{5}{7} \ (= 0.7143)$$

$$\angle A = 35.5°$$

On your calculator press 5 $\div$ 7 $\boxed{=}$ $\boxed{\text{inverse tan}}$

An isosceles triangle can be split into two congruent right-angled triangles.

Example

6   To find BC.

$$\sin \angle DAB = \frac{\text{opp}}{\text{hyp}}$$

$$\sin 20° = \frac{x}{6}$$

$$x = 6 \times \sin 20°$$

$$BC = 2x \text{ cm}$$

$$= 4.10 \text{ cm, to 3 sig. fig.}$$

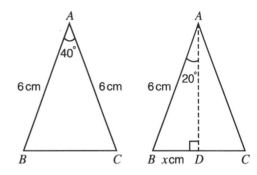

Exercise 14.1

1.   Calculate the length of the side AC in these right-angled triangles, giving the answers to 3 significant figures.

1
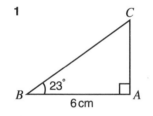

2
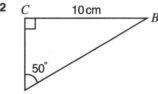

3
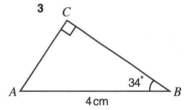

4
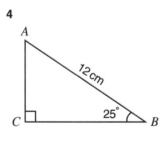

5
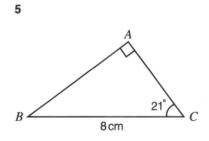

6
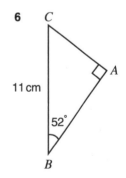

7
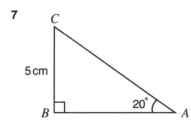

8
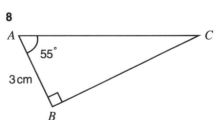

9
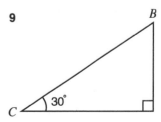

2.   Sketch this isosceles triangle and draw the axis of symmetry. Use the right-angled triangles formed to calculate the length of *BC*, to 3 significant figures.

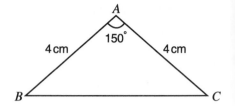

3.   Calculate ∠*A* in these right-angled triangles, in degrees, to 1 decimal place.

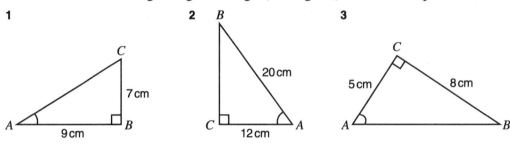

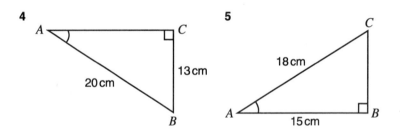

4.   Calculate *AB*, and write down, as fractions, the ratios for sin *A*, cos *A*, tan *A*, sin *B*, cos *B*, tan *B*.

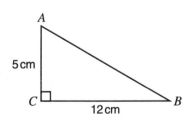

5.   When a kite is flying, the string makes an angle of 22° with the horizontal, and the string is 200 m long. How high is the kite ?

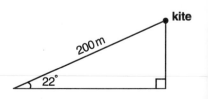

6. A speedboat travels 8 km North and then 3 km East. On what bearing must it be steered to go directly back to the starting point ?

7. From a point *A* on top of a cliff 70 m high two boats *B* and *C* have angles of depression of 33° and 42°, and both boats are due East of *A*.
Find the lengths of *BD* and *CD* and hence find out how far apart the boats are.

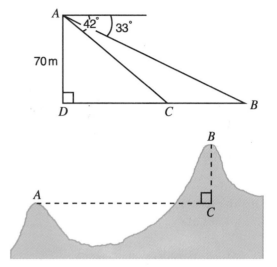

8. *A* and *B* are points on two mountain peaks. The distance between *A* and *B* on a map is 12 cm. The scale of the map is 1 : 50 000. Find the horizontal distance *AC*, in km.
The heights of *A* and *B* are given as 2900 m and 3650 m respectively.
Find the angle of elevation of *B* from *A*.

Calculating in solid figures

Plane sections

You can use trig. ratios to calculate lengths or angles in solid figures, by taking **plane sections** which can include right-angled triangles.

Here are some examples.

Plane sections of a cuboid

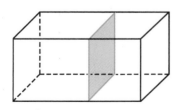

A section parallel to a face

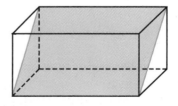

A section diagonally through two parallel edges

Plane sections of a pyramid

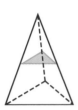

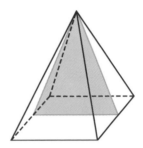
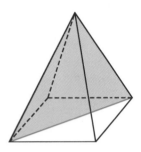

The angle between a line and a plane

The line meets the plane at point A.
B is another point on the line.

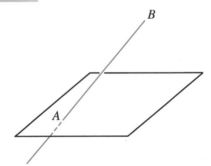

Draw a line from B, perpendicular to
the plane, to meet the plane at C.
Join AC.

AC is called the **projection** of AB on the plane.
The angle that the line AB makes with
the plane is $\angle BAC$.

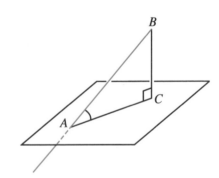

The angle between two planes

From a point on the line of intersection of the
planes, draw two lines, one in each plane,
perpendicular to the line of intersection.
The angle between the two planes is given by $\theta°$,
the angle between the two lines.

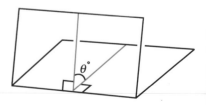

In **3-dimensional diagrams** it is important to decide which angles are right angles.
Draw all vertical lines upright. Right angles will not necessarily look like right angles on the drawing.

Examples

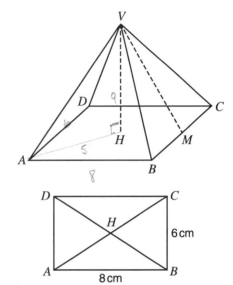

1   *VABCD* is a pyramid with vertex *V*
     vertically above the centre *H* of the
     horizontal rectangular base *ABCD*.
     M is the mid-point of *BC*. If *AB* = 8 cm,
     AD = 6 cm and *VH* = 9 cm, find
     (1) the angle *VA* makes with the base,
     (2) the angle the plane *VBC* makes
         with the base.

     (1) Since *VH* is vertical and *ABCD* is
         horizontal the angle that *VA* makes
         with the base is $\angle VAH$.
         In the rectangle, diagonal *AC* = 10 cm
         (by using Pythagoras' theorem,
         3, 4, 5 triangle) and *H* is the mid-point
         of *AC*, so *AH* = 5 cm.

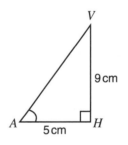

         In the right-angled triangle *VAH*,

         $$\tan \angle VAH = \frac{\text{opp}}{\text{adj}} = \frac{VH}{AH} = \frac{9}{5}$$

         $$\angle VAH = 60.9°$$

         VA makes an angle of 60.9° with the
         base.

     (2) The plane *VBC* and the base *ABCD*
         meet along the line *BC*.
         MV and *MH* are both perpendicular to
         BC, one line in each plane.
         The angle the plane *VBC* makes with
         the base is $\angle VMH$.
         MH = 4 cm since it is half the length
         of *AB*.

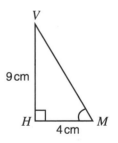

         $$\tan \angle VMH = \frac{\text{opp}}{\text{adj}} = \frac{VH}{MH} = \frac{9}{4}$$

         $$\angle VMH = 66.0°$$

         The plane *VBC* makes an angle of 66.0°
         with the base.

2   A tower, AT, 30 m high, stands at a point A.
At a point B due South of A on level ground
the angle of elevation of the top of the tower
is 28°, and at a point C due West of B on
level ground the angle of elevation of the top
of the tower is 15°.
Find the distances of B and C from A and the
bearing of C from A.

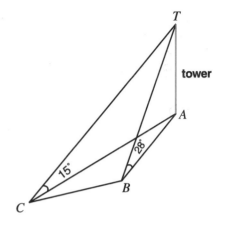

To find AB use $\triangle ABT$. $\angle TAB$ is a right angle
since AT is vertical and AB is horizontal.

To find AB use $\angle BTA$, which is 62°.

$$\tan \angle BTA = \frac{\text{opp}}{\text{adj}}$$

$$\tan 62° = \frac{x}{30}$$

$$x = 30 \times \tan 62°$$

$$= 56.42$$

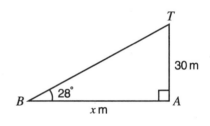

B is 56 m from the tower, to the nearest m.

To find AC use $\triangle ACT$.
$\angle TAC$ is a right angle since TA is vertical
and AC is horizontal.
To find AC use $\angle CTA$ which is 75°.

$$\tan \angle CTA = \frac{\text{opp}}{\text{adj}}$$

$$\tan 75° = \frac{y}{30}$$

$$y = 30 \times \tan 75°$$

$$= 111.96$$

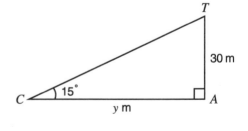

C is 112 m from the tower, to the nearest m.

To find the bearing of C from A use $\triangle ABC$.
$\angle ABC$ is a right angle since A is North of
B and C is West of B.

$$\cos \angle CAB = \frac{\text{adj}}{\text{hyp}}$$

$$= \frac{AB}{AC}$$

$$= \frac{56.42}{111.96}$$

$$\angle CAB = 59.7°$$

$$= 60°, \text{ to the nearest degree.}$$

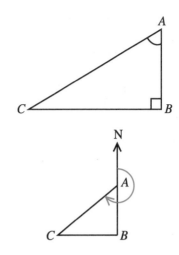

The bearing of C from A is $180° + 60° = 240°$

It is better to use more accurate values for the lengths of AB and AC here, rather than
the corrected-up lengths of 56 m and 112 m. In fact you could use the values given on
your calculator for $30 \times \tan 62°$ and $30 \times \tan 75°$.

Exercise 14.2

In questions 1 to 4 give approximate lengths correct to the nearest mm and angles correct to
1 decimal place.

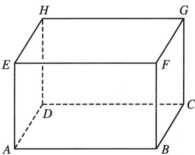

1.   In the diagram, $ABCDEFGH$ is a cuboid.
     $AB = 50$ cm, $BC = 30$ cm, $CG = 20$ cm.

     1   Find the lengths of AC and AG.
     2   Find the angle which AF makes
         with the base $ABCD$.
     3   Find the angle which AG makes
         with the base.

2.   In the diagram, $VABCD$ is a pyramid
     on a horizontal square base $ABCD$,
     with vertex V vertically above N.
     $AB = 10$ cm, $VN = 8$ cm. M is the
     mid-point of AB.

     1   Find the length of VM.
     2   Find the angle which VM makes with
         the base.
     3   Find the length of VA.
     4   Find the angle which VA makes with
         the base.

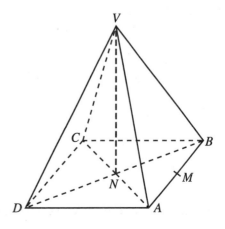

3. *VABCD* is a pyramid on a square base
    of side 4 cm with *VA*, *VB*, *VC* and *VD*
    equal in length and *V* vertically above
    H, the centre of the square. *M* is
    the mid-point of *BC* and $\angle VMH = 50°$.

    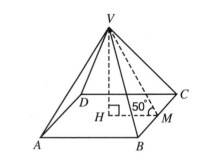

    Find the lengths of

    1 *HM*,   **2** *VH*,   **3** *HB*.

    4 Find the size of $\angle VBH$.

4. The diagram shows a prism with a
    rectangular base *BCFE* which is on
    a horizontal plane, and with vertical
    ends *ABC* and *DEF*, which are congruent
    equilateral triangles. *BC* = 14 cm and
    CF = 20 cm. *M* is the mid-point of *EF*.

    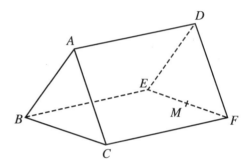

    Find
    1 the length of *DM*,
    2 the length of *DC*,
    3 the angle between the line *DC* and the base.

5. *ABCD* is a rectangular lawn, on level
    ground, and *CE* is a vertical flagpole.
    AB = 48 m and *BC* = 36 m. The angle
    of elevation of the top of the flagpole
    from *A*, $\angle EAC$, is 12°.

    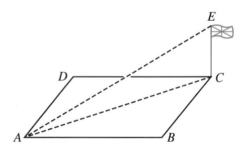

    Find
    1 the length of *AC*,
    2 the height, *CE*, of the flagpole,
    3 the angle of elevation of the
        top of the flagpole from *D*.

6. From a point *A* on the top of a cliff
    120 m high two boats, *B* and *C*, can be
    seen. *B* is due East at an angle of
    depression of 26°, and *C* is due South
    at an angle of depression of 40°. *D* is the
    point vertically below *A* at the edge
    of the sea.
    Find the lengths of *DB* and *DC*, and hence
    find the distance between the boats.

    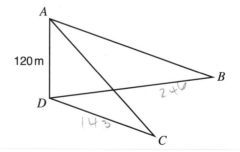

Exercise 14.3   Applications

1.   A surveyor who wishes to find the
width of a river stands on one bank
at point *X* directly opposite a tree *T*.
He then walks 80 m along the river bank to
a point *C*. The angle *XCT* is found to be 72°.
Find the width of the river.

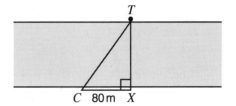

2.   A man walks 10 km North-East and then 7 km South-East. How far is he from
his starting-point, and on what bearing must he walk to go directly back to his
starting-point ?

3.   Triangle *ABC* is isosceles with $AB = AC$.
$BC = 10$ cm.

   1   Find the height *AD*.
   2   Find the area of $\triangle ABC$.

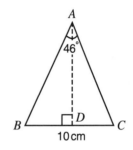

4.   *AB* and *CD* are walls of two blocks
of flats, which are 200 m apart. From
E, the mid-point of *AC*, the angle of
elevation of *B* is 12° and the angle of
elevation of *D* is 24°.

   Find   **1**   *AB*,   **2**   *CD*.
   3   If a person is standing on the roof at
       B what is the angle of elevation of *D* ?

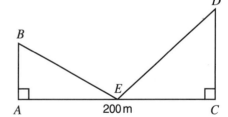

5.   A plane flies due East from *A* to *B*.
C is a town 80 km from *A* on a bearing
of 038°.

   1   Find the distance of the plane from
       C when it is at *D*, the nearest point to *C*.
   2   Find the distance of the plane from *C*
       when it is at *B*, where $AB = 80$ km.

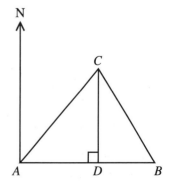

6.   **1**   Find the height of $\triangle AOB$, and hence find the area of $\triangle AOB$.

2 O is the centre of a circle of radius 10 cm. Find the area of sector AOB. Hence, using your answer to **1**, find the shaded area.

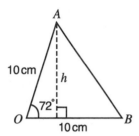

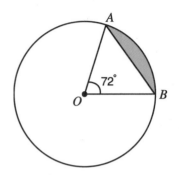

7.   A cone has vertex A and O is the centre of the base. $AO = 6$ cm and a slant line AB makes an angle of $35°$ with OA.

Find
1   the radius of the base,
2   the area of the base.

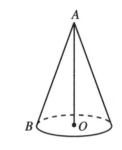

8. $ABCD$ is a rectangular courtyard by the side of a block of flats and E is a window 60 m vertically above A. From D the angle of elevation of E is $45°$ and from B it is $35°$. Calculate

1 AD,   **2** AB,   **3** AC.

4   Find the angle of elevation of E from C.

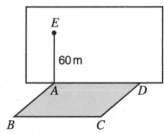

9.   Helen is 200 m due East from the foot of a tall tower, and on level ground. She measures the angle of elevation of the top of the tower as $38°$. Calculate the height of the tower.
Helen walks due South, still on level ground, for 150 m. How far is she from the foot of the tower now? What is the angle of elevation of the top of the tower from this point? (Ignore Helen's height.)

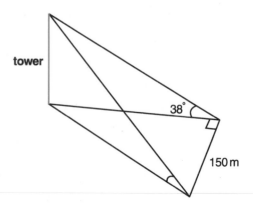

Practice test 14

1. A ladder 6 m long is placed against a wall so that the foot of the ladder is 2.5 m from the wall. What angle does the ladder make with the ground ?

2. The angle of elevation of the top of a church steeple from a point on the ground 120 m away is 32°.
Find the height of the steeple.

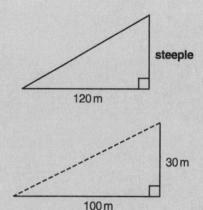

3. From a point at the top of a tower 30 m high, what is the angle of depression of a landmark on the ground 100 m away from the foot of the tower ?

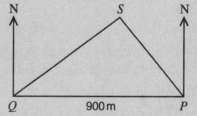

4. P and Q are places 900 m apart on a coastline running East–West.
A ship S is at sea on a bearing of 341° from P, and on a bearing of 071° from Q.

 1 What size is $\angle QSP$?
Find
 2 SP,
 3 SQ,
 4 the distance of S from the nearest point on the coast.

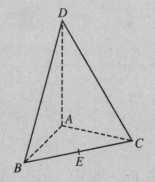

5. $ABCD$ is a pyramid which has a horizontal base and its vertex at D.
DA is perpendicular to the base ABC.
$AB = AC = 12$ cm and $\angle BAC = 90°$.
$AD = 16$ cm. E is the mid-point of BC.

Find

 1 the length of DB,
 2 the length of BC,
 3 the length of DE,
 4 the angle between DB and the base,
 5 the angle between the plane DBC and the base.

15 Functions and their graphs

Topics in this chapter include:

- knowing the form of graphs of simple functions,
- solving equations using graphical methods,
- finding the sine, cosine and tangent of angles of any size,
- sketching the graphs of sine, cosine and tangent functions,
- generating trig. functions and interpreting them.

Functions

If a set of values, x, is connected to another set of values, y, and for each value of x there is only one value of y, then y is said to be a function of x.

The symbol $f(x)$ means 'function of x' so $y = f(x)$.
Other functions can be identified as $g(x)$, $h(x)$, etc.

A function can be represented by ordered pairs of numbers.
e.g. (1, 1), (2, 4), (3, 9), (4, 16).
The 1st number of each pair is the value of x, the 2nd number is the value of y.

A function can be represented by a mapping diagram.
e.g.

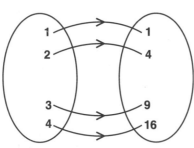

A function can be represented by a table.

e.g.

x	1	2	3	4
y	1	4	9	16

A function can be represented by an equation. The equation for this function is $y = x^2$.
It could also be written as $f(x) = x^2$.
The notation $f: x \mapsto x^2$ can also be used. This is read as 'the function f such that x is mapped onto x^2'.

Using f(x) notation

$f(-1)$ means the value of $f(x)$ when $x = -1$.
e.g. If $f(x) = x^2 + 1$, $f(-1) = (-1)^2 + 1 = 2$
$$f(0) \quad = 0^2 + 1 = 1$$
$$f(5) \quad = 5^2 + 1 = 26$$
and so on.

$f(2x)$ means the function related to $f(x)$, with x replaced by $2x$.
If $f(x) = x^2 + 1$, $f(2x) = (2x)^2 + 1 = 4x^2 + 1$

$f(x - 3)$ means the function related to $f(x)$ with x replaced by $x - 3$.
If $f(x) = x^2 + 1$, $f(x - 3) = (x - 3)^2 + 1 = x^2 - 6x + 10$

Graphs of functions

If the values of x are continuous, the function can be represented by its graph.

This is the graph of $y = x^2$.

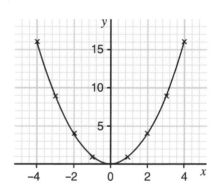

Using a computer or graphics calculator

If you have the use of a computer then you probably have a graph-plotting program which you can use to plot graphs of various functions. You could also use a graphics calculator, although the graphs are shown much smaller than on a computer screen.
One use of plotting the graphs on the computer screen or calculator is so that you can see the general shape of the graph. If you need to find roots of equations from the points of intersection of 2 graphs, you can see where these roots are, approximately.
By zooming into an area around a root, or by re-scaling axes to draw that area to a larger scale, you can get a more accurate value for the root. The trace facility will help you to find approximate values of x and y at a point of intersection. This is equivalent to using trial and improvement methods algebraically.
It is also useful to use a computer or calculator to check graphs you have drawn, and the roots of equations you have found.

Some basic functions

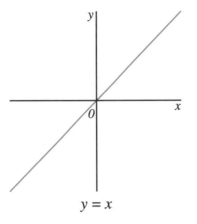

$y = x$

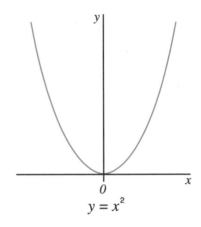

$y = x^2$

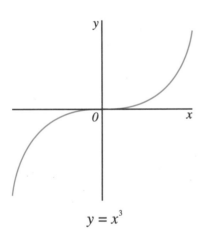

$y = x^3$

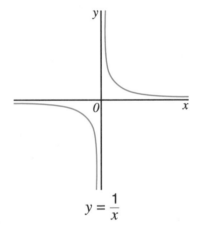

$y = \dfrac{1}{x}$

Linear functions

The general equation of a straight line is $y = mx + c$.
The gradient is m and the line cuts the y-axis at $(0, c)$.
c is called the **intercept** on the y-axis.

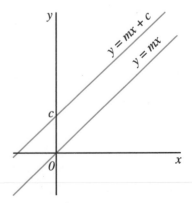

Quadratic functions

The general equation of a quadratic function is $y = ax^2 + bx + c$.
The shape of the graph is a parabola.

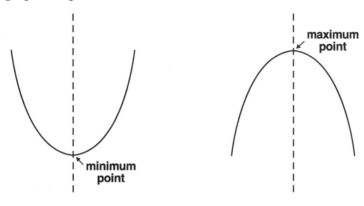

curve when a is positive   curve when a is negative

The graph cuts the x-axis at the points where x satisfies the equation $ax^2 + bx + c = 0$.
The graph cuts the y-axis at $(0, c)$.
The line of symmetry is the line $x = -\dfrac{b}{2a}$.

Graphs of quadratic functions

Examples

1   Draw the graph of $y = x^2 - 5x + 2$, for values of x from -1 to 6.

Make a table of values, working out x^2 and $-5x$, and then $x^2 - 5x + 2$, for each value of x.

x	-1	0	1	2	3	4	5	6
x^2	1	0	1	4	9	16	25	36
$-5x$	5	0	-5	-10	-15	-20	-25	-30
2	2	2	2	2	2	2	2	2
y	8	2	-2	-4	-4	-2	2	8

Since the y-values are symmetrical about $x = 2\frac{1}{2}$, it is useful to find the value of y when $x = 2\frac{1}{2}$, as we can then plot the minimum point.
When $x = 2\frac{1}{2}$, $y = \left(2\frac{1}{2}\right)^2 - 5 \times 2\frac{1}{2} + 2 = -4\frac{1}{4}$.

On the graph we draw the x-axis from -1 to 6 and the y-axis from -5 to 8.
Plot the points and join them with a smooth curve.

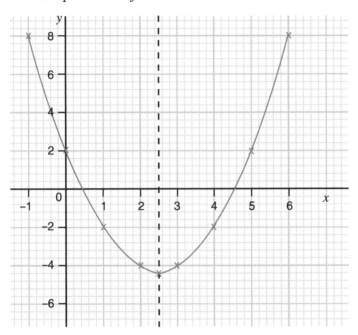

To solve the equation $x^2 - 5x + 2 = 0$, we must find where $y = 0$, i.e. where the curve
crosses the x-axis. The solution (to 1 decimal place) is $x = 0.4$ or $x = 4.6$.

2   Draw the graph of $y = (x + 2)(3 - x)$ for values of x from -3 to 4.

Make a table of values, working out $x + 2$, $3 - x$ and then the product $(x + 2)(3 - x)$
for each value of x.

x	-3	-2	-1	0	1	2	3	4
$x + 2$	-1	0	1	2	3	4	5	6
$3 - x$	6	5	4	3	2	1	0	-1
y	-6	0	4	6	6	4	0	-6

An extra value which might be plotted is when $x = \frac{1}{2}$, $y = 2\frac{1}{2} \times 2\frac{1}{2} = 6\frac{1}{4}$.

Complete the question. Draw the x-axis from -3 to 4 and the y-axis from -6 to 7.
Plot the points and join them with a smooth curve.
From your graph find the axis of symmetry, and the maximum point on the curve.

We can use the graph to solve an equation such as $(x + 2)(3 - x) = 2$.
For this, $y = 2$.
Draw the line $y = 2$ on your graph and find the two points where it crosses the curve.
Draw dotted lines to the x-axis at these points to read the values of x.
The solution is $x = -1.6$ or 2.6.

Graphs of cubic functions

Example

3 Draw the graph of $y = x^3 - 3x - 5$ for values of x from -2 to 3.
Find an approximate solution of the equation $x^3 - 3x - 5 = 0$.

Make a table of values.

x	-2	-1	0	1	2	3
x^3	-8	-1	0	1	8	27
$-3x$	6	3	0	-3	-6	-9
-5	-5	-5	-5	-5	-5	-5
y	-7	-3	-5	-7	-3	13

To solve $x^3 - 3x - 5 = 0$.

$y = 0$ at some point between
$x = 2$ and $x = 3$.
From an accurate graph the
solution is $x = 2.3$

Sketch graph

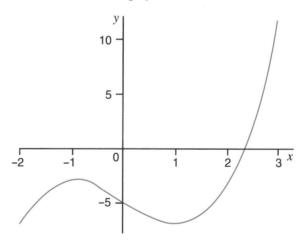

You can use trial and improvement methods with your calculator to get a closer approximation.
When $x = 2.3$, $y = 0.267$ which is positive, when $x = 2.27$, $y = -0.113$, which is negative, so the solution lies between 2.27 and 2.3.
When $x = 2.28$, $y = 0.012$, which is positive, so the solution lies between 2.27 and 2.28.
When $x = 2.275$, $y = -0.050$, which is negative, so the solution lies between 2.275 and 2.28.
The solution is 2.28, to 2 decimal places.

Another graphical method for solving $x^3 - 3x - 5 = 0$ is to draw the graphs of $y = x^3$ and $y = 3x + 5$.

Where these intersect, $x^3 = 3x + 5$,
i.e. $x^3 - 3x - 5 = 0$.

Sketch graph

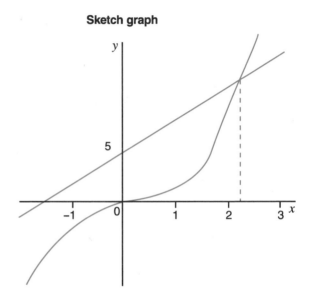

The same equation could also be solved by drawing the graph of $y = x^3 - 3x$, and finding where it crosses the line $y = 5$.

At this point, $x^3 - 3x = 5$, i.e. $x^3 - 3x - 5 = 0$.

Exercise 15.1

1. Draw axes with x from -2 to 5 and y from -4 to 10.
    Copy and complete this table of values for the function $y = x^2 - 3x$.

x	-2	-1	0	1	$1\frac{1}{2}$	2	3	4	5
x^2	4				$2\frac{1}{4}$		9		
$-3x$	6				$-4\frac{1}{2}$		-9		
y	10				$-2\frac{1}{4}$		0		

Draw the graph of $y = x^2 - 3x$.
What is the equation of the axis of symmetry of the curve ?
Use your graph to solve the equation $x^2 - 3x = 6$.

2. Draw axes with x from -4 to 4, and y from -4 to 12.
    Copy and complete this table of values for the function $y = 12 - x^2$.

x	-4	-3	-2	-1	0	1	2	3	4
12	12							12	
$-x^2$	-16							-9	
y	-4							3	

Draw the graph of $y = 12 - x^2$.
What is the greatest value of y on the curve ?
Use your graph to estimate the value of $\sqrt{12}$.

3. Draw axes with x from -3 to 5 and y from -7 to 9.
    Copy and complete this table of values for the function $y = 8 + 2x - x^2$.

x	-3	-2	-1	0	1	2	3	4	5
8	8					8			
$2x$	-6					4			
$-x^2$	-9					-4			
y	-7					8			

Draw the graph of $y = 8 + 2x - x^2$.
What are the coordinates of the point on the graph where y has its greatest value ?

Use your graph and the line $y = 3$ to solve the equation $x^2 - 2x = 5$.

4. Draw axes with x from -1 to 5 and y from -4 to 5.
    Make a table of values for the function $y = x^2 - 4x$ for values of x from -1 to 5.
    Draw the graph of $y = x^2 - 4x$.
    For the line with equation $y = x - 3$, find the values of y when $x = -1, 0, 5$, and draw
    the line on the same graph. Find the values of x at the two points where the line cuts the
    curve.
    This is a graphical method for solving the equation $x^2 - 4x = x - 3$, i.e. $x^2 - 5x + 3 = 0$.

5. Draw axes with x from -3 to 4 and y from -5 to 25. Make a table of values for the
    function $y = (2x + 1)(x - 2)$, for values of x from -3 to 4.
    Draw the graph of $y = (2x + 1)(x - 2)$.
    Draw also the line $y = 10 - 3x$ on the same graph.
    Find the values of x at the two points where the line cuts the curve.
    Write down the equation satisfied by these solutions, and simplify it.

6. Copy and complete this table of values for the function $y = x^3 - 4x$.

x	-4	-3	-2	-1	0	1	2	3	4
x^3 $-4x$	-64 16								
y	-48								

Draw axes with x from -4 to 4, and y from -50 to 50.
Plot the points given by the table and also the points $(-3.5, -28.9)$, $(-0.5, 1.9)$, $(0.5, -1.9)$ and $(3.5, 28.9)$.
Draw the graph.
Comment on its shape.

7. Draw the graph of $y = x(x - 2)(x - 4)$ for values of x from -1 to 5.
Use the graph to find approximate solutions of the equation $x^3 - 6x^2 + 8x - 2 = 0$.

8. Copy and complete the table of values for the function $y = 2^x$.

x	-4	-3	-2	-1	0	1	2	3	4
y	$\frac{1}{16}$	$\frac{1}{8}$							

Draw the graph of $y = 2^x$ for values of x from -4 to 4.
Use your graph to solve the equation $2^x = 10$.

9. The graph of $y = \dfrac{18}{x}$.

Copy and complete this table of values.

x	-4	-3	-2	-1	1	2	3	4
y	$-4\frac{1}{2}$	-6						

$x = 0$ has been omitted from the table because y does not exist when $x = 0$.
Draw axes with x from -4 to 4 and y from -30 to 30.
Plot the points on your graph. Find y when $x = 0.6$ and when $x = -0.6$ and plot these two points.
The positive values of x give one part of the graph and the negative values give another part. Draw the graph.
This curve (which is in two parts) is called a rectangular hyperbola.

10. A rectangular block has height 6 cm and a square base of side x cm. The total surface area is 160 cm^2.

Find an equation satisfied by x.

Draw the graphs of $y = x^2$ and $y = 80 - 12x$ for values of x from 0 to 8, labelling the y-axis from -20 to 80.

Show that the value of x at the point of intersection of the graphs gives the length of a side of the base of the box.

Find this length, to the nearest mm.

Trigonometrical functions

You have used the trigonometrical ratios, $\sin \theta°$, $\cos \theta°$ and $\tan \theta°$ in right-angled triangles. However, these functions have uses other than in right-angled triangles, and we need to define them for angles of any size.

We will give the definitions later, but for now we will use a calculator to find the values of the functions.

Examples

$$\sin 100° = \ \ \ 0.9848$$

$$\cos 150° = -0.8660$$

$$\tan 220° = \ \ \ 0.8391$$

$$\sin(-70°) = -0.9397 \qquad \text{Press 70 } \boxed{^+/_-} \ \boxed{\sin}$$

$$\cos 500° = -0.7660$$

$$\tan 600° = \ \ \ 1.7321$$

All these have been written to 4 decimal places.

In a similar way you can find the values of the trigonometrical functions of any sizes of angles, except for $\tan \theta°$ when θ is 90 or any odd multiple of 90, positive or negative.

You cannot do the operations in reverse. If you know that $\sin \theta° = 0.9848$ and use the inverse sine key on your calculator it will give you an acute angle.

You may think that it is strange to have a negative angle.
Think of a machine which rotates. If it goes one way you can measure the angle of turning as positive, and the other way as negative.

In Mathematics we measure the angles from the x-axis and we take the anticlockwise direction as positive and the clockwise direction as negative.
(Do not confuse this with bearings which do not follow the mathematical system. There the direction is clockwise and the angles are measured from the North.)

To draw the graph of $y = \sin x°$
for values of x from 0 to 360.

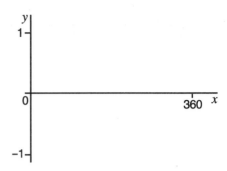

On the x-axis, label from 0 to 360,
using a scale of 2 cm to 45.
On the y-axis, label from -1 to 1
using a scale of 4 cm to 1 unit,
so that each small 2 mm square
represents 0.05.

First, plot the points for x from 0 to 90, finding the y-values on your calculator. y-values
for $x = 9, 18, 27, \ldots , 90$ will do. Draw this part of the curve.
Now continue finding y-values for $x = 99, 108, 117, \ldots ,$ to 180.
What do you notice ?
Draw this part of the curve.

Now continue finding y-values for $x = 189, 198, \ldots ,$ to 270, and then to 360.
What do you notice ?
Draw the rest of the curve.
Describe the curve you have drawn and describe some of the things you notice about it.

You can draw the graph of $y = \cos x°$, in a similar way.

To draw the graph of $y = \tan x°$

The graph of $y = \tan x°$ is rather different.

Use the same scale as before for x, from 0 to 360.
On the y-axis, label from -5 to 5 using a scale of 2 cm to 1 unit, so that each small square
represents 0.1.
Again, plot the points for x from 0 to 90 first, using values 0, 9, 18, ... You can get as
far as 72, and then 76.5, before the y-values get too big to plot. Draw this part of the
curve.
Next, it is best to go to $x = 180$, and draw the part of the curve between $x = 180$ and
270.
Then, start at 180 and go backwards with $x = 171, 162, \ldots$ until, again, the y-values go
off the graph.
Finally, start at 360 and go backwards towards 270, and draw the rest of the curve.
It is not a continuous curve. It has breaks at 90 and 270.
Describe some of the things you notice about the curve.

Sketch graphs of trig. functions

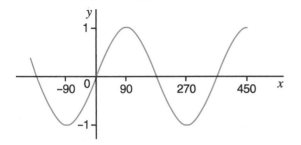

$$y = \sin x°$$

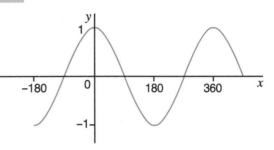

$$y = \cos x°$$

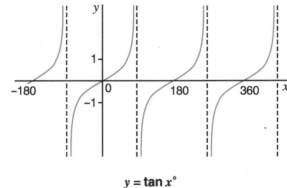

$$y = \tan x°$$

You can see these graphs on a graphics calculator by pressing

graph sin EXE ,   graph cos EXE ,   graph tan EXE .

However, if you want to plot graphs of other trig. functions you must first specify the ranges and scales.

Definitions of the trig. functions

$$\sin \theta = \frac{y\text{-coordinate}}{r}$$

$$\cos \theta = \frac{x\text{-coordinate}}{r}$$

$$\tan \theta = \frac{\sin \theta}{\cos \theta}$$

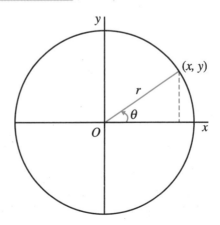

Sketch graphs of related functions

Here is a sketch graph of $y = \cos x°$ for x from 0 to 360.

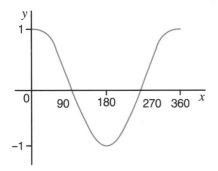

To draw the graph of $y = 1 + \cos x°$, every y-value of the graph of $y = \cos x°$ will have 1 added on.

Make a table of values to help you.

x	$\cos x°$	$1 + \cos x°$
0	1	2
90	0	1
180	−1	0
270	0	1
360	1	2

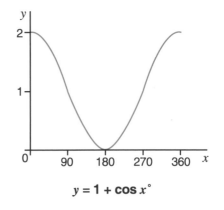

$y = 1 + \cos x°$

The graph of $y = -\cos x°$ is the reflection of the graph of $y = \cos x°$ in the x-axis.

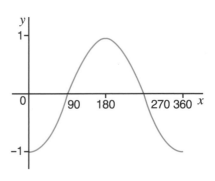

$y = -\cos x°$

To draw the graph of $y = 1 - \cos x°$,
first draw the graph of $y = -\cos x°$,
then add 1 to every y-value.

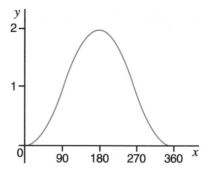

$y = 1 - \cos x°$

x	$\cos x°$	$1 - \cos x°$
0	1	0
90	0	1
180	−1	2
270	0	1
360	1	0

To draw the graph of $y = 2 \cos x°$,
every y-value of the graph of
$y = \cos x°$ will be multiplied
by 2.

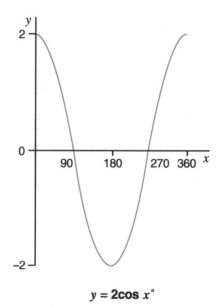

$y = 2\cos x°$

x	$\cos x°$	$2 \cos x°$
0	1	2
90	0	0
180	−1	−2
270	0	0
360	1	2

Exercise 15.2

1. Use the flow chart for the function $f(x) = 2 \tan x° + 1$ to find $f(0)$, $f(45)$, $f(135)$ and $f(180)$.

    enter x ⟶ find tan x ⟶ multiply by 2 ⟶ add 1

2. Using the sketch graph of $y = \sin x°$ to help you,
    1 sketch the graph of $y = -\sin x°$ for $0 \leqslant x \leqslant 360$,
    2 sketch the graph of $y = 2 - \sin x°$ for $0 \leqslant x \leqslant 360$.

3. 1 Sketch the graph of $y = 3 \cos x°$ for $0 \leqslant x \leqslant 360$.
    2 Find the value of y when $x = 200$, using your calculator.
    3 Find the possible values of x when $y = 1.4$.

4. The diagram shows part of the graph of
    the function $y = 1 - \sin x°$.
    What are the coordinates of the points
    A, B, C, D ?

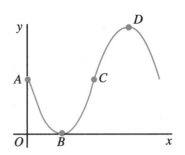

5. Use this flow chart

    | enter x | $\longrightarrow$ | multiply by 2 | $\longrightarrow$ | find cos function |

    to find the values of $\cos 2x°$ for $x = 0, 30, 45, 90, 135, 150, 180$.
    Sketch the graph of $y = \cos 2x°$ for $0 \leqslant x \leqslant 180$.

6. Draw accurately using the same scales and axes the graphs of $y = \sin x°$ and $y = \dfrac{x}{150}$,
    for values of x from 0 to 180. On the x-axis take 2 cm to 20 units, on the y-axis take
    10 cm to 1 unit.

    Use your graphs to solve the equations
    1 $\sin x° = 0.4$,

    2 $x = 150 \sin x°$.

7. The height, y m, of the tide in a harbour above the lowest level is given by the equation
    $y = 5 - 5 \cos 30t°$, where t is the time in hours after low tide.

    Sketch a graph showing this height
    for 12 hours after low tide.

    What is the increase in depth
    of the water between low and
    high tides ?

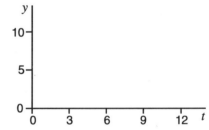

    A boat can only enter the harbour when
    there is a depth of 2.5 m of water above the lowest level.
    Draw a line on your graph which shows this depth of water.
    Mark the point which represents the earliest time after low tide when the boat can enter
    the harbour.
    Use your calculator to find this time.

Exercise 15.3   Applications

1. Draw the graph of $y = x^2 - 7x + 10$ for values of x between 0 and 7. (Draw the x-axis
    from 0 to 7 and the y-axis from -4 to 10.)
    Use your graph to solve the equation $x^2 - 7x + 2 = 0$.
    By drawing another line on the graph, solve the equation $x^2 - 8x + 10 = 0$.

2. Draw the graph of $y = x^3 - 3x^2$ for values of x from -1 to 4.
    On the same axes, draw the graph of $y = 2x - 2$.

    Hence solve the equation $x^3 - 3x^2 = 2x - 2$.

3. Draw the graph of $y = 4\sqrt{x}$ for values of x from 0 to 9.
    On the same axes draw the graph of $x + y = 8$.
    For what value of x is $8 - x = 4\sqrt{x}$?

4. Copy and complete this table of values for the function $y = 2x - \dfrac{3}{x}$.

x	$\frac{1}{4}$	$\frac{1}{2}$	1	$1\frac{1}{2}$	2	$2\frac{1}{2}$	3
$2x$							
$\dfrac{3}{x}$							
y							

    Draw the graph of $y = 2x - \dfrac{3}{x}$.
    Draw the x-axis from 0 to 3 and the y-axis from -12 to 6.
    Plot the points and draw the graph from $x = \frac{1}{4}$ to $x = 3$.
    By drawing a line on your graph, find the value of x at the point on the curve where the x and y coordinates are equal.

5. The graph of $y = x^3 - 7x^2 + 9$ crosses the x-axis between $x = 1$, where y is positive, and $x = 2$, where y is negative.
    Use your calculator and a trial and improvement method to find a solution of $x^3 - 7x^2 + 9 = 0$ between $x = 1$ and $x = 2$, correct to 1 decimal place.

6. Draw the graphs of $y = x^2$ and $y = 2x + 2$ for x from -4 to 4. Label the y-axis from -6 to 16.
    Find approximate solutions of the equation $x^2 - 2x - 2 = 0$.
    By drawing another straight-line graph on the same axes find approximate solutions of the equation $x^2 + x - 10 = 0$.

7. Draw the graph of $y = x^2(x - 5)$ for values of x from -2 to 6.
    A storage tank is in the form of a cuboid with a square base of side x m and a height of $(5 - x)$ m.
    Use the graph to find the possible values of x if its volume is 15 m^3.

8. Sketch the graph of $y = \cos x°$ for values of x from 0 to 90.
On the same diagram sketch the graph of $y = \sin 2x°$ for values of x from 0 to 90.
Show that there is a solution of the equation $\cos x° = \sin 2x°$ for x between 0 and 45.
Draw accurately the parts of the graphs between $x = 0$ and $x = 45$, using a scale of 1 cm to 5 units on the x-axis and 1 cm to 0.1 units on the y-axis.
Find a value of x for which $\cos x° = \sin 2x°$.

9. Copy and complete the table of values for $x = 0$ to 90 for the function $y = \sin x° + \cos x°$, working to 3 decimal places and giving the values of y to 2 decimal places.

x	0	10	20	30	40	50	60	70	80	90
$\sin x°$	0									
$\cos x°$	1									
y	1									

Draw an accurate graph of $y = \sin x° + \cos x°$.
1   What is the value of x when y has its maximum value ?
2   What is the maximum value of y ?

10. Copy and complete the table of values for $x = 0$ to 90 for the function $y = (\cos x°)^2$.

x	0	15	30	45	60	75	90
$\cos x°$	1						
$(\cos x°)^2$	1						

Sketch the graph of $y = (\cos x°)^2$
1   for x from 0 to 90,   2   for x from 0 to 180.

11. *P* is a point on the rim of a disc of radius 1 unit which is rotating about its centre *O* in an anticlockwise direction at the rate of $1°$ per second.
Initially *P* is at P_0 and after time t seconds it is at height h units above its initial position.
Find by drawing or calculation the values of h when $t = 0, 30, 60, 90, \ldots, 360$.
(When $t > 180$, h will be negative since *P* is below its initial position.)
Sketch the graph of h as a function of t.
What is the equation of this function ?
As *P* moves, another simple function, k, of t is described. Can you say which this is, and show which length represents k on the diagram ?
For what range of values of t is k negative ?

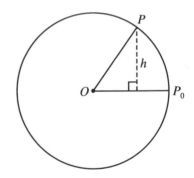

Practice test 15

1. Draw axes with x from -3 to 4 and y from -6 to 8.
   Copy and complete this table of values for the function $y = x^2 - x - 5$.

x	-3	-2	-1	0	1	2	3	4
x^2	9				1			
$-x$	3				-1			
-5	-5	-5	-5	-5	-5	-5	-5	-5
y	7				-5			

   Draw the graph of $y = x^2 - x - 5$.
   Write down the equation of the line about which the curve is symmetrical.
   Use your graph to solve the equation $x^2 - x - 5 = 0$.

2. **Graph of the positive part of $y = \dfrac{1}{x}$**

   Draw the x and y axes from 0 to 10, using the same scale on both axes.
   Copy and complete this table of values, using your calculator where necessary, and giving values correct to 1 decimal place.

x	0.1	0.2	0.3	0.4	0.5	0.6	0.8	1	2	3	4	5	6	8	10
y	10	5													

   Plot the points on your graph. Two extra points to help you are $(0.15, 6.7)$ and $(0.125, 8)$.
   Join the points with a smooth curve.

3. If $y = \sin x°$, for $0 \leqslant x \leqslant 360$,
   1 sketch the graph of the function,
   2 state the greatest and least values of y,
   3 find y when $x = 100$, using your calculator,
   4 find the values of x such that $y = 0.5$,
   5 find the values of x such that $y = -0.5$.

4. A particle is moving such that t seconds after it started its distance along a straight line from a point O is y m, where $y = 1 - \cos 6t°$.
   Sketch the graph of y against t, for t from 0 to 60.
   During the 1st minute, what is the furthest distance the particle is from O, and at what time is it at this point?

Miscellaneous Section C

Exercise C1   Revision

1.   If $a = 9.5$, $b = 11.2$ and $c = 7.3$, find the values of

   1 s, where $s = \frac{1}{2}(a + b + c)$,

   2 $\sqrt{\dfrac{s(s - a)}{bc}}$.

2.   This cone has radius 7 cm and slant height 25 cm.

   1   Find its perpendicular height.
   2   Find its volume.

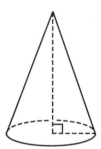

3.   Find the values of x which satisfy these inequalities.

   1 $3x^2 + 5 \leqslant 113$
   2 $5x^2 - 6 \geqslant x^2 + 94$

4. $ABCD$ is a parallelogram.
    $BC = 10$ cm, $\angle ABC = 57°$ and $\angle BAC = 90°$.
    Calculate
   1 AB,
   2 AC,
   3   the area of the parallelogram.

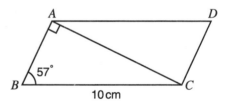

5.   What numbers are these ?

   1   It is less than 100, it is a prime number, it is one less than a multiple of 7 and its digits add up to 5.
   2   It is less than 100, it is 2 more than a square number and it is a multiple of 11. When divided by 9 there is a remainder of 3.
   3   It is a factor of 180, it is 4 less than a square number, and when it is divided by 7 there is a remainder of 3.

6.   Solve the simultaneous equations

   1 $4x - 3y = 11$
          $2x + \ y = 13$

   2 $3x + 2y = \ 5$
          $7x + 3y = 15$

7. Imagine that you decide to do a statistical investigation about pocket money of young children. For example, you might like to find out how much pocket money they get, what it is spent on, and whether any is regularly saved in a savings account.
    Write a brief questionnaire (about 4 to 8 questions) which you could use to give you suitable information.

8. These windows are similar in shape, consisting of a semicircle above a rectangle. What is the ratio of their perimeters ?

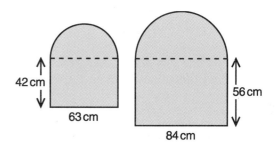

9.

Share	Price in pence	
	Lowest	Highest
A	250	400
B	550	670
C	310	530
D	130	290
E	380	510
F	280	460
G	470	650
H	100	140
I	120	270
J	310	440

The price of shares changes according to the state of the Market.
Here are the lowest and highest prices for 10 selected shares in 1992. (Prices are to the nearest 10p.)

Draw a scatter diagram, with lowest price on the horizontal axis and highest price on the vertical axis.
Draw a line of best fit.

If the lowest price of another share was £2.20, estimate from the line of best fit what its highest price was likely to have been.

10. Which statement best describes this graph, showing profits of a firm over several months.

   A The profits of the firm show a steady increase.

   B The firm's profits are increasing at an increasing rate.

   C Although the profits are increasing, the rate of increase is slowing down.

   D The firm is making a steady profit.

   E After an initial decrease the profits then increased.

   Draw similar sketch graphs to describe the other four statements, and label them.

11. In a certain school, students must learn either French or Spanish, or both languages. The numbers studying each subject are shown in the diagram.

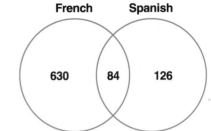

1   If a student of the school is chosen at random, what is the probability that this student studies both French and Spanish ?

2   If a student is chosen at random from those who study Spanish, what is the probability that this student also studies French ?

12. The line $y = mx + c$ has gradient -2 and it passes through the point $(3, -2)$. Find the values of m and c.

13. A is the point $(1, 5)$. If $\overrightarrow{AB} = \begin{pmatrix} 2 \\ -4 \end{pmatrix}$ and $\overrightarrow{AC} = \begin{pmatrix} 4 \\ 1 \end{pmatrix}$, write down the coordinates of the points B and C.

E and F are points such that $\overrightarrow{CE} = \frac{1}{2}\overrightarrow{AB}$ and $\overrightarrow{CF} = \overrightarrow{AC}$. Show that $\overrightarrow{BE} = \overrightarrow{EF}$ and state what can be deduced about the points B, E, F.

14. Expand the following:

1   $2x^2(3x^3 + x)$ 4 $(3x + y)(2x - 5y)$

2   $(x - 1)(x - 7)$ 5 $(2x + y)^2$

3   $(x + 3)(2x + 5)$

15. Make a table of values for the graph of $y = 2x - \dfrac{12}{x}$, for values of x from 1 to 6. Draw the x-axis from 0 to 6 and the y-axis from -10 to 10. Draw the graph for $1 \leqslant x \leqslant 6$. Write down the x-value of the point where the curve crosses the x-axis. Show why this solution is equal to the value of $\sqrt{6}$.

Exercise C2 Revision

1.   Calculate the length of AB and state as fractions the values of $\sin A$, $\cos A$ and $\tan A$.

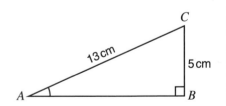

2.   On a map with a scale of 3 inches to 1 mile a region has an area of $13\frac{1}{2}$ square inches. What is the actual area of the region ?

3. The circle centre O, radius 5 cm, has a regular hexagon inscribed in it.

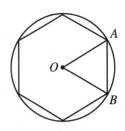

1 What is the length of the chord AB ?
2 Find the length of the arc AB, to the nearest mm.
3 Find the area of the sector AOB.

4. A baby was weighed at the Health Clinic every month and the weights recorded for the first year were as follows:

Age in months	1	2	3	4	5	6	7	8	9	10	11	12
Weight in kg	4.5	5.0	6.0	6.5	7.0	7.5	8.0	8.5	9.0	9.2	9.4	9.5

Show this information on a graph, joining the points with a series of straight lines. In which month was there the greatest gain in weight ?

5. The equation $x^2 - 6x + 7 = 0$ has a solution for x between $x = 4$ and $x = 5$.
    Use your calculator and a trial method to find this solution correct to 1 decimal place.

6. A triangular field has sides 900 m, 700 m, 600 m. Treasure is hidden in the field (1) 200 m from the longest side, (2) equidistant from the two other sides.
    Draw a scale drawing using a scale of 1 cm to represent 100 m, showing the loci for (1) and (2). Mark the position of the treasure. Find its distance from the nearest corner of the field, to the nearest 10 m.

7. Write down the next two numbers in each sequence, and find an expression for the nth term.

1 1, 9, 25, 49,
2 1, 3, 6, 10, 15,
3 2, 4, 8, 16,
4 100, 93, 86, 79, 72,
5 $1, \frac{1}{2}, \frac{1}{3}, \frac{1}{4}, \frac{1}{5},$

8. The diagram shows a pyramid with a horizontal rectangular base 12 cm by 6 cm and vertical height 8 cm.

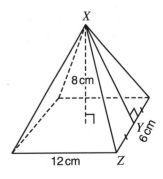

Find
1 the area of the base,
2 the length of the slant height XY,
3 the angle which XY makes with the base,
4 the angle which XZ makes with the base.

9. **1** Multiply 3.8×10^4 by 5×10^{-2}, giving the answer in standard index form.

2 Divide 3.8×10^4 by 5×10^{-2}, giving the answer in standard index form.

10. The histogram shows the distances from home to school of a group of children. What is the probability that a child chosen at random from this group lives within 1 mile of the school ?

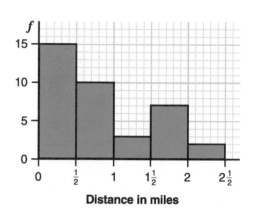

Distance in miles

11. In this triangle PQR, the perimeter is 60 cm, and QR is 5 cm longer than PQ. Write down two equations involving x and y, simplify them and solve them. Find the numerical values of the sides of the triangle.

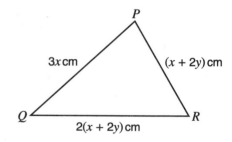

12. **1** If 20 fence-posts cost £48, what would be the cost of 25 posts ?

2 It is estimated that 5 men can lay a pipeline in 16 days. To do the work in 10 days, how many extra men should be used (assuming that all men work at the same rate) ?

13. Copy and complete the following table of values for the function $y = x^2 - 2x - 2$.

x	-2	-1	0	1	2	3	4
x^2	4		0				
$-2x$	4		0				
-2	-2		-2				
y	6		-2				

On graph paper, draw the graph of $y = x^2 - 2x - 2$ for values of x from -2 to 4.

1 What is the equation of the line about which the curve is symmetrical ?

2 Use your graph to estimate the solutions of $x^2 - 2x - 2 = 0$.

3 Use your graph to estimate the solutions of $x^2 - 2x = 6$.

14.   The diagram represents an octagon formed by
      cutting equal isosceles triangles from the corners
      of a square of side 12 cm.
      Find, in terms of x, the total area of the four corners.
      If the area of the octagon is $\frac{7}{8}$ of the area of the
      original square, find the value of x.
      Find the perimeter of the octagon, correct to the nearest mm.

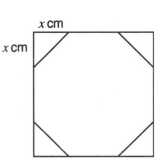

15.   The percentages of the total male population in each age-group are given in the table.
      (Figures for UK, 1989.)

Age (years)	%
0–9	13.7
10–19	13.7
20–29	16.9
30–39	14.0
40–49	13.2
50–59	10.7
60–69	9.9
70–79	5.7
80–89	2.2

Make a cumulative frequency table of the data and draw a
cumulative frequency graph.

Find the median age and the interquartile range of ages.

What percentage of the male population is over 65 years old ?

(A small number of the last
group are 90 or over.)

Exercise C3   Revision

1.   Given the set of numbers

      4, $\sqrt{25}$, $\sqrt[3]{6}$, π, $0.\dot{3}$, $\frac{3}{4}$, $3\frac{1}{7}$,   3.142, -5,

      write down

      1   the positive integers,
      2   the integers,
      3   the rational numbers which are not integers,
      4   the irrational numbers.

2.   Copy this sketch graph and identify these
     regions on it.

     A $y < x, \quad x < 3, \quad y > 3 - x$

     B $y > -1, \quad x > 3, \quad y < 3 - x$

     C $y > 0, \quad y < x, \quad y < 3 - x$

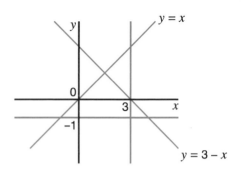

3.   If $\overrightarrow{BD} = 2\overrightarrow{DC}$, show that $\mathbf{b} + 2\mathbf{c} = 3\mathbf{d}$.

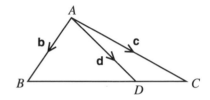

4.   Find the values of 4^{-1}, $4^{-\frac{1}{2}}$, 4^0, $4^{\frac{1}{2}}$, $4^{1\frac{1}{2}}$.

5.   There are two tins of similar shape, one is 8 cm high and the other is 12 cm high.
     If the smaller one holds 2 litres of liquid, how many litres will the larger one hold ?

6.   The graph represents the
     journey of a boy who
     cycles from a town A to a
     town B, and after a rest
     there, cycles back to A.

     1   For how long did the
             boy stay in town B ?
     2   What was his speed on
             the outward journey ?
     3   What was his speed
             on the return journey ?

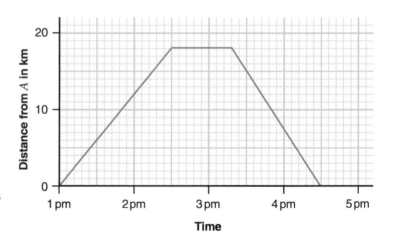

7.   There are 7 discs in a bag numbered from 1 to 7. A disc is drawn (and not replaced) and
     a second disc is drawn. Show the sample space of all possible pairs of results and find the
     probability that
     1   the sum of the numbers drawn is odd,
     2   the product of the numbers drawn is odd.

8. 1 Simplify $\dfrac{x-3}{3} - \dfrac{x+1}{6}$

    2 Solve the equation $\dfrac{x+3}{6} - \dfrac{x}{5} = 1$

9. Sketch the graphs, for x from 0 to 360, of
    1 $y = \sin x°$
    2 $y = -\sin x°$
    3 $y = 1 - \sin x°$

10. Draw the x-axis from -6 to 10 and the y-axis from -4 to 11 using equal scales on both axes. Draw triangles labelled A to F by plotting and joining the 3 points given in each case.

    Triangle A (2, 6), (2, 9), (3, 10)

    Triangle B (5, 3), (6, 6), (7, 6)

    Triangle C (9, 0), (6, −2), (6, −3)

    Triangle D (−5, 7), (−3, 10), (−2, 10)

    Triangle E (−5, 4), (−2, 4), (−1, 5)

    Triangle F (−4, −2), (−4, −3), (−1, −1)

    Which pairs of triangles are congruent ?

11. Rectangular plots of land of area 600 m² are to be sold.
    If the length of a plot is x m and the width is y m, express y in terms of x.
    Draw axes for x and y from 0 to 60. Plot the corresponding values of x and y for $x = 10, 15, 20, 30, 40, 50, 60$. Join the points with a curve.
    If the perimeter of a plot is 120 m, by drawing a straight line on the graph find the measurements of the plot.

12. An explorer setting out from his base camp C walks due West for 8 km and then due North for 5 km. Use trigonometry to find on what bearing he must now travel to go directly back to camp.

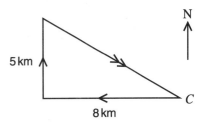

13. A closed cylinder has a radius of 14 cm. Find the area of one end.
    If its volume is 10 000 cm², find its height, to the nearest mm.
    Hence find the total surface area.

14. In the sunshine, a stick which is 1 m high
     has a shadow of length 0.8 m on the
     horizontal ground. At the same time a
     flagpole has a shadow which is 4.8 m long.
     How high is the flagpole ?

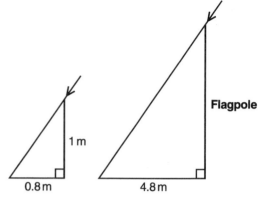

15. The time spent on homework by 30 students in a certain week was as follows:

     (Times in hours, to the nearest hour.)

8	3	3	6	9	5	20	7	12	14	25	2	6	12	20
20	18	18	12	9	20	15	24	5	3	22	15	13	16	20

     Make a frequency distribution table of the data using class intervals 1–5, 6–10, 11–15,
     16–20, 21–25.
     Draw a histogram of the distribution.
     What is the modal class ?
     Find the mean of the grouped distribution, to the nearest 0.1 hour.

Exercise C4   Activities

1.   **A scale model**

     Design a study-bedroom suitable for a teenager and make a scale model of the room,
     showing the door, windows and heating source. Make scale models of the furniture and
     include those. Show where the lighting is and where the power points are. Paint your
     model to show the colour scheme.
     A more ambitious project would be to make a model of a house, a famous building or a village.

2.   **Planning for a wedding**

     This is a most important occasion in a couple's life and deserves proper planning.
     You can imagine it is your own wedding in a few years' time or the wedding of
     imaginary friends.
     Decide what type of wedding. Church, other place of worship, Registry Office ? It can be
     a very simple wedding with just two witnesses or a very grand one. Plan all the details of
     the wedding, and make a list of costs involved, with a separate note of who pays for
     each. Traditionally the bride's father paid for most things but that is not always the case
     nowadays. There are many small details to include, for instance, transport to the
     wedding, legal costs, wedding ring or rings.
     Plan the timetable for the day, so that the ceremony begins on time, and the couple leave
     for their honeymoon on time, especially if they have a train or plane to catch.
     Illustrate your booklet with pictures, e.g. of the bride's dress.

3.   **Investigating π**

Measure the circumference C and diameter D of circles of different sizes from a penny to a large wheel and find the value of π from $\dfrac{C}{D}$.

Show that the area of a circle is πr^2 by cutting a circle into small sectors and rearranging them into the shape of an approximate parallelogram with length πr and height r.

Write π to as many decimal places as are shown on your calculator. See if you can find a list giving more decimal places. People have invented phrases to help them to remember the first few decimal places of π. One of these is 'Sir, I have a number.' The number of letters in each word gives π as 3.1416. Can you invent a phrase of your own, or even a rhyme ?

There are various infinite series which give π, such as
$$\pi = 4 - \frac{4}{3} + \frac{4}{5} - \frac{4}{7} + \frac{4}{9} - \frac{4}{11} + \frac{4}{13} - \frac{4}{15} + \cdots$$
Use your calculator to work out several terms of this.

Archimedes, who lived about 200 BC, found a value for π by considering a pattern for the perimeters of regular polygons with 6, 12, 24, 48 and 96 sides inscribed in a circle, and then polygons outside and touching a circle. (The circumference is greater than the perimeter of polygons inside, and less than the perimeter of polygons outside the circle.) He gave π as a number between $3\frac{1}{7}$ and $3\frac{10}{71}$. Write these numbers as decimals to see how close he was.

Make a list of all the formula you know which involve π.

Find π using probability and by tossing sticks. If you toss sticks over a set of parallel lines then the sticks may either land touching or across a line, or land completely between the lines. The probability that a stick will touch a line is $\dfrac{2s}{\pi d}$, where the sticks are s cm long and the lines are d cm apart.
Use the floorboards of the room if they form parallel lines, otherwise draw lines on the floor. Find 10 thin sticks with length about $\frac{3}{4}$ of the distance between the lines. Toss the sticks randomly 50 times, and find the total number n, out of 500, which land touching or across a line. Then $\dfrac{n}{500}$ is an estimate of the probability. Put $\dfrac{n}{500} = \dfrac{2s}{\pi d}$ and rearrange this equation to find an experimental value for π. Find the percentage error.

Find π using probability and random numbers.
If you choose 2 numbers at random they can either have a common factor, e.g. 40 and 75 have a common factor 5, or they can be prime to each other, i.e. have no factor in common, e.g. 40 and 63 have no common factor although they both have factors.

The probability that 2 numbers are prime to each other is $\dfrac{6}{\pi^2}$.

Get 500 pairs of random numbers from random number tables, a computer, or using the numbers from a phone directory. Numbers less than 100 will do. Find how many pairs are prime to each other. If there are n pairs, then $\dfrac{n}{500}$ is an estimate of the probability. Put $\dfrac{n}{500} = \dfrac{6}{\pi^2}$, and rearrange this equation to find an experimental value for π. Find the percentage error.

4.   **Using mathematics**

Here are some practical problems. There are several possible solutions. See how many
you can think of. Make up similar problems to solve.

1   An explorer in unknown territory discovers a deep gorge.
     He needs to report on its width but it is too wide to get
     across to measure it. How can he estimate its width ?

2   He can see the bottom and wants to estimate its depth.
     How can he do this ?

3   On the other side of the gorge is a very tall unusual tree.
     How can he estimate its height ?

4   He has been travelling from his base camp in a
     north-easterly direction so he knows he has to go in a
     south-westerly direction to return to camp. Unfortunately,
     he has dropped his compass down the gorge. How can he find out which direction to go in ?

5.   **History of numbers and calculation**

Counting can be traced back to very ancient times, and yet it is only a few years ago that
modern calculators and computers were invented. You could make a topic booket about
this, including early methods of writing numbers in different parts of the world, and
methods of calculation such as the abacus, Napier's bones and logarithms, and ending
with a section on the development of the computer.

6.   **Using a counter-example in disproving statements**

Prove that these statements are not always true, by finding an example where the
statement is not true.

1    $2x^2$ is always greater than x.

2   If $\theta°$ is an angle in a triangle and $\sin \theta° = \frac{1}{2}$, then $\theta = 30$.

3   If two triangles have equal areas then they have equal perimeters.

4   If the probability of event A happening is $\frac{1}{3}$ and the probability of event B happening
     is $\frac{1}{2}$ then the probability of either A or B happening is $\frac{1}{3} + \frac{1}{2} = \frac{5}{6}$.

5    $\triangle ABC$, $\triangle DEF$ have $AB = DE = 8$ cm, $BC = DF = 6$ cm and $\angle A = \angle D = 20°$.
     Therefore the triangles are congruent.

PUZZLE

34.   There are two discs; one is red on both sides, the other is red on one side and green on
       the other, but they are otherwise identical. Without looking, one is picked at random
       and placed flat on the table. If the top side of this disc is red, what is the probability
       that the hidden side is also red ? Is it $\frac{1}{4}$, $\frac{1}{3}$, $\frac{1}{2}$, $\frac{2}{3}$ or $\frac{3}{4}$?

To the student : 4

Making plans for revision

As the time of the examination draws nearer you should look back over your progress and see if you are satisfied with it, and make a plan of action for the future. If you have been working steadily from the beginning of the course, you may not need to make any extra effort. If you enjoy the challenge of Maths you are probably working well and learning everything as you go along. But if you find some of the work difficult and are feeling discouraged, perhaps a little extra effort at this stage, and perhaps a change in the way you approach your work, will help to improve your standard, and you will feel more confident.

In addition to lessons and set homework you should spend some time each week on individual study. Make a plan for this depending on how much time you have available and what you need to learn or practise. In addition to Maths, you will have work to do in all your other subjects, so take these into consideration. If you have to do a 'Project' in any subject, then start it in good time or you will find yourself at the last minute spending all your time on it, and your other work is neglected.

You must plan how you are going to revise the work. You could work through this book again in order, spending so much time on each chapter. Choose a suitable selection of questions to do, either straightforward ones if you need practice in these, or the more challenging questions if you are more confident with the topic. Alternatively, you could use the revision exercises in the miscellaneous sections A to E of the book. You might prefer to revise all the arithmetic, then the algebra, then the geometry, and so on. The important thing is that **you** should decide for yourself what **you** need to do, and then plan how you are going to do it.

Sort out your difficulties as you go along. Try to think things out for yourself as far as possible, rather than having to be shown how to do everything. But if you need extra help, then **ask** someone to help you, either your teacher, someone in your class or a higher class, a parent or a friend.

Keep a list of what you are doing. At first there will be a lot to do and not much done, but you will find it encouraging when after a few weeks you can see that you are making real progress.

16 Probabilities of combined events

Independent events

Two events, where the outcome of the second event does not depend on the outcome of the first event, are called independent events.

The AND rule

If there are two independent events A and B, then the probability of both A and B occurring = the probability of A occurring × the probability of B occurring.

$$P(A \text{ and } B) = P(A) \times P(B)$$

If there are 3 independent events, A, B and C, then

$$P(A \text{ and } B \text{ and } C) = P(A) \times P(B) \times P(C)$$

The rule is similar if there are more than 3 events.

(Compare this with the OR rule for mutually exclusive events on page 163.)

Examples

1   If two dice are thrown, find the probability of getting two sixes.

The 1st experiment is tossing the 1st die. $P(\text{six}) = \frac{1}{6}$

The 2nd experiment is tossing the 2nd die. $P(\text{six}) = \frac{1}{6}$

$P(\text{two sixes}) = P(\text{six}) \times P(\text{six}) = \frac{1}{6} \times \frac{1}{6} = \frac{1}{36}$

(This result can also be found using a sample space diagram.)

2   A playing card is drawn from a pack of 52 cards and after replacing it and shuffling the pack, a second card is drawn.
What is the probability that both cards drawn are aces ?
What is the probability that the 1st card is a heart and the 2nd card is not a heart ?

These events are independent because the 1st card is replaced before the 2nd card is drawn.

$P(\text{1st card an ace}) = \frac{1}{13}$

$P(\text{2nd card an ace}) = \frac{1}{13}$

$P(\text{both cards are aces}) = P(\text{1st an ace and 2nd an ace}) = \frac{1}{13} \times \frac{1}{13} = \frac{1}{169}$

$P(\text{1st card a heart}) = \frac{1}{4}$

$P(\text{2nd card not a heart}) = \frac{3}{4}$

$P(\text{1st card a heart and 2nd not a heart}) = \frac{1}{4} \times \frac{3}{4} = \frac{3}{16}$

3   A seed manufacturer guarantees that 90% of a particular type of flower seed will germinate.
If 5 seeds of this type are sown, what is the probability that they will all germinate ?
What is the probability that none of them will germinate ?

$P(\text{one seed germinates}) = 90\% = 0.9$

$P(\text{all seeds germinate}) = P(\text{1st, 2nd, 3rd, 4th and 5th seeds germinate})$
$= 0.9 \times 0.9 \times 0.9 \times 0.9 \times 0.9$
$= 0.59049$
$= 0.59,\ \text{to 2 dec pl.}$

$P(\text{one seed does not germinate}) = 0.1$

$P(\text{no seeds germinate}) = P(\text{1st, 2nd, 3rd, 4th and 5th do not germinate})$
$= 0.1 \times 0.1 \times 0.1 \times 0.1 \times 0.1$
$= 0.00001$

(These answers assume that the results are independent and that the conditions are satisfactory. If the seeds were not planted in the right soil, not kept at a suitable temperature or not watered properly, it is much more probable that none of the seeds would germinate.)

Tree-diagrams

When there are two or more independent events we can show the combined results on a tree-diagram or in a table.

Example

4   Emily goes to school by bus or car, or she walks. The probability of going by bus is $\frac{1}{2}$, of going by car is $\frac{1}{3}$, and of walking is $\frac{1}{6}$.

When she comes home from school, she either walks, with probability $\frac{1}{2}$, or goes by bus, with probability $\frac{2}{5}$, or occasionally gets a lift home in a friend's car, with probability $\frac{1}{10}$. This is regardless of which way she travelled to school in the morning.

Here is a tree-diagram showing the combined outcomes.
W = walk, B = by bus, C = car.

Going	Coming	Outcome	Probability
	$\frac{1}{2}$ W	WW	$\frac{1}{6} \times \frac{1}{2} = \frac{1}{12}$
W	$\frac{2}{5}$ B	WB	$\frac{1}{6} \times \frac{2}{5} = \frac{1}{15}$
$\frac{1}{6}$	$\frac{1}{10}$ C	WC	$\frac{1}{6} \times \frac{1}{10} = \frac{1}{60}$
	$\frac{1}{2}$ W	BW	$\frac{1}{2} \times \frac{1}{2} = \frac{1}{4}$
$\frac{1}{2}$ B	$\frac{2}{5}$ B	BB	$\frac{1}{2} \times \frac{2}{5} = \frac{1}{5}$
	$\frac{1}{10}$ C	BC	$\frac{1}{2} \times \frac{1}{10} = \frac{1}{20}$
	$\frac{1}{2}$ W	CW	$\frac{1}{3} \times \frac{1}{2} = \frac{1}{6}$
$\frac{1}{3}$ C	$\frac{2}{5}$ B	CB	$\frac{1}{3} \times \frac{2}{5} = \frac{2}{15}$
	$\frac{1}{10}$ C	CC	$\frac{1}{3} \times \frac{1}{10} = \frac{1}{30}$

Write all the results as fractions with denominator 60 to check that the total probability is 1.

We can also show the outcomes and the probabilities in a table.

		Going		
		W $\left(\frac{1}{6}\right)$	B $\left(\frac{1}{2}\right)$	C $\left(\frac{1}{3}\right)$
Coming home	W $\left(\frac{1}{2}\right)$	WW $\frac{1}{6} \times \frac{1}{2}$	BW $\frac{1}{2} \times \frac{1}{2}$	CW $\frac{1}{3} \times \frac{1}{2}$
	B $\left(\frac{2}{5}\right)$	WB $\frac{1}{6} \times \frac{2}{5}$	BB $\frac{1}{2} \times \frac{2}{5}$	CB $\frac{1}{3} \times \frac{2}{5}$
	C $\left(\frac{1}{10}\right)$	WC $\frac{1}{6} \times \frac{1}{10}$	BC $\frac{1}{2} \times \frac{1}{10}$	CC $\frac{1}{3} \times \frac{1}{10}$

What is the probability of Emily walking either to or from school, or both ways ?

Look at all the results in the diagram or table which include W. These are mutually exclusive events and must be added.

$$P(\text{walks at least one way}) = P(WW) + P(WB) + P(WC) + P(BW) + P(CW)$$
$$= \tfrac{1}{12} + \tfrac{1}{15} + \tfrac{1}{60} + \tfrac{1}{4} + \tfrac{1}{6}$$
$$= \frac{5 + 4 + 1 + 15 + 10}{60}$$
$$= \tfrac{35}{60} = \tfrac{7}{12}$$

What is the probability of Emily using transport both ways ?

This can be found in a similar way.
However, either Emily walks at least one way **or** she uses transport both ways.
So you can find this answer by subtraction.

$$P(\text{using transport both ways}) = 1 - P(\text{walks at least one way})$$
$$= 1 - \tfrac{7}{12} = \tfrac{5}{12}$$

5   **The outcomes when 3 coins are tossed**

1st coin	2nd coin	3rd coin	Outcome	Probability
		$\tfrac{1}{2}$ H	HHH	$\tfrac{1}{2} \times \tfrac{1}{2} \times \tfrac{1}{2} = \tfrac{1}{8}$
	$\tfrac{1}{2}$ H	$\tfrac{1}{2}$ T	HHT	$\tfrac{1}{8}$
H	$\tfrac{1}{2}$ T	$\tfrac{1}{2}$ H	HTH	$\tfrac{1}{8}$
$\tfrac{1}{2}$		$\tfrac{1}{2}$ T	HTT	$\tfrac{1}{8}$
	$\tfrac{1}{2}$ H	$\tfrac{1}{2}$ H	THH	$\tfrac{1}{8}$
$\tfrac{1}{2}$		$\tfrac{1}{2}$ T	THT	$\tfrac{1}{8}$
T	$\tfrac{1}{2}$ T	$\tfrac{1}{2}$ H	TTH	$\tfrac{1}{8}$
		$\tfrac{1}{2}$ T	TTT	$\tfrac{1}{8}$

Since there are 3 events, we canot show the outcomes in a table, but we can show them in a list.

HHH
HHT
HTH
HTT   P(3 heads) $= \frac{1}{8}$
THH
THT   P(2 heads and 1 tail) $= \frac{1}{8} + \frac{1}{8} + \frac{1}{8} = \frac{3}{8}$
TTH   P(1 head and 2 tails) $= \frac{3}{8}$
TTT   P(3 tails) $= \frac{1}{8}$

(The probability of 2 heads and 1 tail involves the 3 possible orders, either HHT, HTH or THH, each with probability $\frac{1}{8}$. These are mutually exclusive events and their probabilities are added.)

6   The probabilities of 3 independent events taking place are $\frac{1}{3}$, $\frac{3}{4}$ and $\frac{2}{5}$, respectively. What is the probability that at least one of these events takes place ?

The simplest way to find this is to first find the probability that none of the events takes place.
The probabilities that the events do not happen are $\frac{2}{3}$, $\frac{1}{4}$ and $\frac{3}{5}$.

P(no event takes place) $= \frac{2}{3} \times \frac{1}{4} \times \frac{3}{5} = \frac{1}{10}$
P(at least one event takes place) $= 1 - \frac{1}{10} = \frac{9}{10}$

You can also solve this question by using a tree-diagram.

Two events are less likely to happen that one of the events

When finding the probability of two or more independent events, the probabilities of the separate events are **multiplied**.
Since these probabilities are numbers less than 1, the result is smaller than any of the separate probabilities.
(This is assuming that neither probability is 0 or 1.)

Exercise 16.1

1.   A bag contains 3 red discs and 5 white discs. A disc is taken out and replaced. Another disc is then taken out. Find the probability that both discs are red.

2.   The probability that Gavin wins the 100 m race is $\frac{2}{5}$. The probability that Frank wins the 400 m race is $\frac{4}{15}$.
What is the probability that
1   both of them win their races,
2   neither of them wins their race ?

3. If 3 dice are thrown, what is the probability that
   1 all three show a six,
   2 all three show the same number ?

4. A tin contains 2 red, 1 orange and 4 yellow counters, and another tin contains 1 green, 2 blue and 3 violet counters.
   If two counters are taken at random, one from each tin, what is the probability that they are
   1 red and violet,
   2 orange and green ?

5. The chances of four walkers completing a long-distance walk are, respectively $\frac{1}{4}$, $\frac{2}{5}$, $\frac{1}{2}$ and $\frac{2}{3}$.
   What is the probability that at least one of them will complete it ?

6. In a large batch of seed, 80% of the plants which can be grown from it will have red flowers and the rest will have pink flowers.
   Using a tree-diagram or otherwise, find the probability that two plants grown from this batch of seed will have flowers of the same colour.

7. There is a bag containing a large number of marbles, of which 25% are red and the rest are white.
   Using a tree-diagram, find the probability that if two marbles are taken at random from the bag,
   1 both will be red,
   2 both will be white,
   3 there will be one of each colour.

8. The probability of a marksman hitting a target is 0.7.
   1 What is the probability of him missing the target ?

   Show the results of 3 shots (hit or miss) on a tree-diagram, and, assuming that the results are independent, find the probability that, out of 3 shots,
   2 the marksman hits the target each time,
   3 the marksman hits the target twice,
   4 the marksman hits the target at least twice.

9. On the way to work Mrs Cole passes through three sets of traffic lights. The probability that the first set is green when she gets to them is $\frac{2}{3}$, the probability that the second set is green is $\frac{3}{4}$ and the probability that the third set is green is $\frac{1}{2}$. Show the probabilities (for green or not green) on a tree-diagram.

   What is the probability that
   1 she finds all three sets of lights green as she gets to them,
   2 she has to stop at at least two of the three sets of lights ?

Conditional probabilities

To find the combined probability of 2 events A, B which are not independent:
If A is the 1st event and B the 2nd then the probability of B will depend on the outcome of the 1st event.
The multiplication rule still holds.

$$P(A \text{ and } B) = P(A) \times P(B \mid A)$$

where $P(B \mid A)$ is the probability of B, given that event A has occurred.

If B is the 1st event and A the 2nd then the probability of A will depend on the outcome of the 1st event.

$$P(A \text{ and } B) = P(B) \times P(A \mid B)$$

where $P(A \mid B)$ is the probability of A given that event B has occurred.

If there are 3 events, in order A, B, C, then

$$P(A \text{ and } B \text{ and } C) = P(A) \times P(B \mid A) \times P(C \mid A \text{ and } B)$$

where $P(B \mid A)$ is the probability of B, given that event A has occurred,
and $P(C \mid A \text{ and } B)$ is the probability of C, given that events A and B have occurred.

There is a similar rule for more than 3 events.

If the events occur simultaneously, e.g. 3 discs are picked out of a bag, imagine that they occur in order one after another, i.e. the 3 discs are picked out one at a time.

Examples

1   If a card is drawn from a pack of 52 cards, and then before it is replaced a second card is drawn, what is the probability that they are both hearts ?

$$P(\text{1st one is a heart}) = \frac{13}{52} = \tfrac{1}{4}$$

$$P(\text{2nd one is a heart}) = \frac{12}{51} = \tfrac{4}{17} , \text{ provided that the 1st card was a heart.}$$

$$P(\text{both cards are hearts}) = P(\text{1st a heart}) \times P(\text{2nd a heart})$$

$$= \tfrac{1}{4} \times \tfrac{4}{17} = \tfrac{1}{17}$$

2   In a bag there are 5 red discs and 3 blue ones. If two discs are picked out at random (and not replaced), what is the probability of getting one of each colour ?

1st disc drawn	**2nd disc drawn**	**Outcome**	**Probability**

$$\frac{5}{8} \times \frac{4}{7} = \frac{20}{56} \qquad (RR)$$

$$\frac{5}{8} \times \frac{3}{7} = \frac{15}{56} \qquad (RB)$$

$$\frac{3}{8} \times \frac{5}{7} = \frac{15}{56} \qquad (BR)$$

$$\frac{3}{8} \times \frac{2}{7} = \frac{6}{56} \qquad (BB)$$

Note as a check that the total probabilities add up to 1.
Probability of one of each colour:
P(red then blue **or** blue then red) = P(red then blue) + P(blue then red)
$$= \tfrac{15}{56} + \tfrac{15}{56} = \tfrac{15}{28}$$

3   A man has four possible routes home from work. For the 1st part of the journey he can either go by train or by bus. The probability that he will go by train is $\frac{2}{3}$.
After he gets off the train he can either walk or catch a bus. The probability that he will walk is $\frac{3}{4}$.
If the 1st part of his journey is by bus then he completes his journey by taxi, with probability $\frac{1}{5}$, or by walking.
What is the probability that he walks part of the way home ?

1st part	**2nd part**	**Probability**

$$\frac{2}{3} \times \frac{1}{4}$$

$$\frac{2}{3} \times \frac{3}{4} \qquad \text{(walks part of the way)}$$

$$\frac{1}{3} \times \frac{1}{5}$$

$$\frac{1}{3} \times \frac{4}{5} \qquad \text{(walks part of the way)}$$

The probability that he walks part of the way home $= \left(\tfrac{2}{3} \times \tfrac{3}{4}\right) + \left(\tfrac{1}{3} \times \tfrac{4}{5}\right) = \tfrac{23}{30}$

Exercise 16.2

1. A bag contains 5 red discs and 6 white discs. Two discs are to be taken out at random, without replacing the first one before the second one is taken out.
   Find the probability that the first disc taken out is red and the second one is white.

2. Two cards are drawn from a pack of 52 cards.
   What is the probability that
   1 both cards are diamonds,
   2 neither card is a diamond,
   3 at least one of the cards is a diamond ?

3. A box of chocolates contains 4 with soft centres and 5 with hard centres. If 2 chocolates are taken out of the box and eaten, and then another 2 are taken out, what is the probability that the first 2 will have soft centres and the second 2 will have hard centres ?

4. A bag contains 9 discs numbered from 1 to 9. If 3 discs are drawn out at random, and not replaced, what is the probability that the numbers on the discs drawn are
   1 all odd numbers,
   2 all even numbers,
   3 all less than four ?

5. A box contains 5 white and 4 blue counters. If counters are drawn in succession, without replacement, until a blue one appears, what is the probability that the first blue one is the 5th counter drawn out ?

6. A bag contains 8 blue marbles and 2 red marbles. Two marbles are drawn at random. Show the probabilities on a tree-diagram.

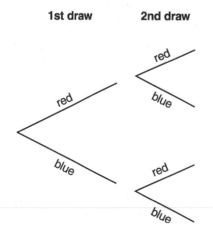

1st draw   **2nd draw**

What is the probability of getting
1 2 red marbles,
2 1 marble of each colour,
3 2 blue marbles ?

7.   A bag contains 1 red marble and 2 green ones. One is drawn out and not replaced, and a second one is drawn out.
     What is the probability that
     1   both marbles are green,
     2   one marble is red and one is green ?

8.   A box contains 3 red, 5 white and 4 blue discs, and 2 discs are drawn out without replacement.
     What is the probability that both discs are the same colour ?

9.   A bag contains 3 red discs and 4 blue ones. If 3 discs are taken out, without replacement, show the outcomes on a tree-diagram, and find the probability that
     1   all 3 discs taken out are red ones,
     2   2 discs are red ones and 1 is blue,
     3   1 disc is red and 2 are blue,
     4   all 3 discs are blue.

10. A pile of cards consists of 5 hearts and 7 clubs. 3 cards are drawn from these at random, without replacement.
     Show the outcomes on a tree-diagram, and find the probability that
     1   all 3 cards are hearts,
     2   2 cards are hearts and 1 is a club,
     3   1 card is a heart and 2 are clubs,
     4   all 3 cards are clubs.

Exercise 16.3   Applications

1.   Two cards are drawn, one from each of two packs.
     What is the probability they they are
     1   a club from the 1st pack and a diamond from the 2nd pack,
     2   a red ace from the 1st pack and a black ace from the 2nd pack,
     3   an even numbered card from the 1st pack and a picture card, Jack, Queen or King, from the 2nd pack ?

2.   Two fuses in a circuit have independent probabilities of $\frac{1}{4}$ and $\frac{1}{3}$ respectively of failing during an experiment.
     What are the probabilities of
     1   both fuses failing,
     2   only one fuse failing,
     3   neither fuse failing ?

3.   Two girls are to be chosen out of a group of 7 girls by drawing two names out of a hat.
     What is the probability that Jane and her friend Kate will both be chosen ?

4. Three competitors Alan, Bob and Charles enter for the high jump and the long jump in the school sports. The chances of each of them winning these events are estimated as follows:

	Alan	Bob	Charles
High jump	$\frac{2}{5}$	$\frac{3}{10}$	$\frac{1}{10}$
Long jump	$\frac{1}{3}$	$\frac{1}{2}$	$\frac{1}{12}$

What is the probability that
1   Alan wins both events,
2   Bob wins the high jump and Charles wins the long jump,
3   both events are won by other competitors ?

5. Find the probability that in a random group of 4 people,
1   all their birthdays are in the same month of the year,
2   all their birthdays are in different months.

6. When three marksmen shoot at a target their chances of hitting it are $\frac{1}{3}$, $\frac{1}{4}$ and $\frac{1}{5}$, respectively.
If they all shoot at the same target simultaneously, what is the probability that the target will be hit ?

7. Two cards are drawn from a pack of cards. What is the probability of drawing two aces,
1   if the 1st card is replaced before the 2nd card is drawn,
2   if the 1st card is not replaced before the 2nd card is drawn ?

8. A circuit includes three valves. The probabilities, which are independent, of the valves being defective are 0.1, 0.2 and 0.25, respectively.
Find the probability that
1   all three valves work properly,
2   two valves work properly and one does not.

9. In a packet of sweets there are 5 red ones, 6 yellow ones and 7 orange ones. If a child takes 2 sweets without looking, what is the probability that
1   they are both red ones,
2   they are both the same colour ?

10. Out of a batch of 10 batteries inspected, 3 were found to be defective. If 2 batteries are taken at random from the batch, what is the probability that
1   both batteries are defective,
2   just one battery is defective,
3   at least one battery is defective ?

11. James has 6 keys, of which one will open the office door. If he does not know which key this is, and tries them in turn, find the probability that

    1   the 1st key he tries is the right one,
    2   the 1st key does not open the door, but the 2nd key he tries is the right one,
    3   the 3rd key he tries opens the door,
    4   the 4th key he tries opens the door,
    5   the 5th key he tries opens the door,
    6   the 6th key he tries opens the door.

12. Tom has 3 goes on an amusement machine. At each go, the probability of him winning a prize is $\frac{1}{4}$.

    What is the probability of him winning
    1   no prizes,
    2   1 prize,
    3   2 prizes,
    4   3 prizes ?

13. Two dice are thrown together. The 1st die is marked from 1 to 6 in the normal way, the 2nd one has faces marked 1, 2, 3, 4, 4, 4.
    Find the probability that
    1   both dice show 4's,
    2   neither die shows a 4,
    3   both dice show even numbers.

14. Alex has 2 coins and Chris has 3. If they both toss their coins, what is the probability that
    1   Alex gets 2 heads and Chris gets 3 heads,
    2   both of them get 2 heads,
    3   both of them get 1 head ?

15. Two dice are thrown together. Draw up a sample space showing the total scores.

    1   List in a table the probability of scoring each total from 2 to 12.
    2   What is the most likely total score ?
    3   What is the chance of getting this score three times in successive throws ?

16. Yasmin and Zelda play two sets of tennis. The probability of Yasmin winning the 1st set is $\frac{2}{3}$. If she wins the 1st set, the probability of her winning the 2nd set is $\frac{2}{3}$, but if she loses the first set the probability of her losing the 2nd set is $\frac{1}{2}$. (There are no drawn sets.)

    What is the probability of
    1   Yasmin winning both sets,
    2   Zelda winning both sets,
    3   the girls winning one set each ?

17. A darts player reckons that he can score 20 on his first throw with probability $\frac{3}{4}$. If he scores 20 with one throw, then the probability of scoring 20 with his next throw is $\frac{4}{5}$, but if he misses with one throw, the probability of scoring 20 with his next throw is $\frac{1}{2}$. Assuming that he aims for 20 each time, find the probability that in three throws he scores
    1 20 each time,
    2 only one 20,
    3 no 20's.

18. A coin and a die are tossed together. What is the probability of getting
    1 a head on the coin and a six on the die,
    2 a head on the coin or a six on the die (or both) ?

Practice test 16

1. A biased coin is tossed 4 times. At each toss the probability of heads is 0.6. What is the probability of getting heads, heads, tails, tails, in that order ?

2. Three table-tennis players, Nasir, Bilal and Sundip play in different matches. Their probabilities of winning are respectively $\frac{1}{2}$, $\frac{1}{4}$ and $\frac{1}{5}$.
    What is the probability that
    1 Nasir and Bilal win their matches, but Sundip loses his match,
    2 all three boys win their matches ?

3. A box contains 6 red and 4 white counters and another box contains 7 yellow and 3 green counters. If two counters are taken at random, one from each box, what is the probability that they are a red one and a green one ?

4. If 5% of a large batch of light bulbs manufactured by a certain firm are defective, and a sample of 4 bulbs is chosen from the batch at random, what is the probability that
    1 there will be no defective bulbs in the sample,
    2 there will be at least one defective bulb ?

5. All the hearts are removed from a pack of cards. From the remainder of the pack three cards are drawn. What is the probability that they are all diamonds ?

6. 4 red and 7 green marbles are placed in a bag. If two are taken out at random, what is the probability that they are
    1 both red,
    2 both green ?

7.   A box contains 4 red, 5 green and 6 yellow counters. Two counters are taken out
     together, at random. Find the probability that
     1   they are both the same colour,
     2   they are of different colours.

8.   A die is thrown 3 times. Draw a tree-diagram showing 'six' or 'not six' and find
     the probabilities that there will be
     1   no sixes,
     2   1 six only,
     3   2 sixes,
     4   3 sixes.

PUZZLES

35. Alan, Bob and Charles are allowed to pick apples in an orchard. Alan picks 7 sackfuls
     containing 16 kg each, Bob picks 7 sackfuls containing 14 kg each, Charles has smaller
     sacks and he picks 10 sackfuls holding 9 kg each. They had agreed beforehand that they
     would share the fruit equally. How can they do this without opening any of the sacks ?

36. This map shows the roads where Jenny lives. How many
     different routes are there for her to cycle from home to
     school, (never going Northwards, of course) ?

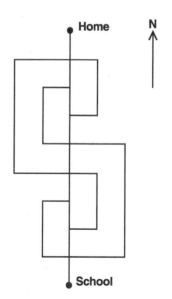

37. There are three married couples having dinner together.
     George is older than Michelle's husband.
     Frank's wife is older than Nadia.
     Lynnette's husband is older than George.
     Michelle is not Edward's wife.
     The oldest man is married to the youngest woman.
     The oldest woman paid the bill. Who was this ?

Further algebraic methods

The topics in this chapter include:

- expressing general laws in symbolic form,
- factorising algebraic expressions,
- simplifying fractional expressions,
- completing the square,
- investigating sequences.

Laws of connected variables

If there are two variables x and y, and y is a function of x, then it is often possible to find the equation for the function from a table or ordered pairs of numbers.

e.g.

x	1	2·	3	4
y	5	2	-1	-4

The equation connecting y and x is $y = 8 - 3x$.

The first functions to consider are linear functions, i.e. functions with equations of the form $y = mx + c$, where m and c are numbers. Their graphs are straight lines.

The table above represents a linear function because as x increases by 1 unit, y decreases by 3 units.
So the equation involves $-3x$, and you can soon discover that it is $y = 8 - 3x$, checking that all the pairs of values satisfy this equation.

There are other equations connecting x and y. One of these is
$y = x^4 - 10x^3 + 35x^2 - 53x + 32$. You can check that the values above satisfy this equation. If we had been given more than 4 pairs of values, we might find that this second equation is no longer satisfied.
However, when you find a simple equation connecting y and x, do not look for a more complicated one.

If the function is not linear, other functions to consider are
$y = x^2$, and related functions such as $y = x^2 + 3$, $y = x^2 - x$.

$y = x^3$, and related functions such as $y = x^3 - 5$, $y = x^3 + 2x$.

$y = \dfrac{1}{x}$, and related functions such as $y = \dfrac{20}{x}$, $y = \dfrac{1}{x+2}$.

$y = 2^x$, and related functions such as $y = 3^x$, $y = 10^x$, $y = 2^x - 1$.

Example

Find the equation connecting y and x for the function of which these are pairs of values.

x	-1	0	1	2	3
y	$-\frac{1}{2}$	0	1	3	7

This is not a linear function as when x increases by 1 unit, y does not increase or decrease by a constant number. The increases are $\frac{1}{2}$, 1, 2, 4, which is the doubling sequence. This suggests that 2^x is involved.

Here is the table for the function $y = 2^x$.

x	-1	0	1	2	3
y	$\frac{1}{2}$	1	2	4	8

Comparing these tables shows that the first function is $y = 2^x - 1$.

Exercise 17.1

Pairs of values of simple functions are given in these tables.
Find the equations connecting y and x.

1.
x	-2	0	2	4
y	-11	-3	5	13

2.
x	0	1	2	3
y	0	1	8	27

3.
x	-1	0	1	2	3
y	0.1	1	10	100	1000

4.
x	1	2	4	6	16
y	48	24	12	8	3

Pairs of values of simple functions are given in these tables.
Find the equations connecting y and x.

5.

x	1	4	7	10
y	1	-11	-23	-35

6.

x	1	2	3	4
y	4	16	64	256

7.

x	0	1	2	3	4
y	-2	-1	2	7	14

8.

x	1	2	3	4
y	$\frac{3}{4}$	$\frac{4}{5}$	$\frac{5}{6}$	$\frac{6}{7}$

9. The table shows the connection between the weight hung from a spiral spring and the length of the spring.

Weight, w kg	0	0.5	1	1.5	2
Length, l cm	10	10.8	11.6	12.4	13.2

Find the equation for l in terms of w.

10. An object is dropped and falls through the air. The distance, s metres, it has fallen at various times, t seconds, is as given.

t	0	1	2	3	4	5
s	0	4.9	19.6	44.1	78.4	122.5

Find the equation for s in terms of t.

Factorising

Common factors

Examples

1    $x^3 + 4xy^2 = x(x^2 + 4y^2)$

2    $12x^2y - 18xy^2 = 6xy(2x - 3y)$

Difference of two squares

$$a^2 - b^2 = (a+b)(a-b)$$

Examples

3    $x^2 - 16 = (x+4)(x-4)$

4    $4x^2 - 9y^2 = (2x+3y)(2x-3y)$

5    $12x^2 - 3 = 3(4x^2 - 1)$ (taking out the common factor 3, first)
           $= 3(2x+1)(2x-1)$

Note that $a^2 + b^2$ has no factors, unless a and b have a common factor.

Factors by grouping

Examples

6    $ax^2 + ay^2 - bx^2 - by^2 = a(x^2 + y^2) - b(x^2 + y^2)$
                   $= (x^2 + y^2)(a - b)$ (since $(x^2 + y^2)$ is a common factor)

7    $px - 6p - qx + 6q = p(x-6) - q(x-6)$
                  $= (x-6)(p-q)$

If the 1st and 2nd terms have no common factor, then pair the 1st and 3rd terms together, and then the 2nd and 4th terms will pair together.

8    $21ab + 4 - 28b - 3a = 21ab - 28b - 3a + 4$
                   $= 7b(3a-4) - (3a-4)$
                   $= (3a-4)(7b-1)$

Easy trinomials

Examples

9    $x^2 + 7x + 10 = (x\ldots\ldots)(x\ldots\ldots)$
                ↑   ↑——signs both the same, both positive or both negative
                └————————signs same as this, so both positive
                        $(x+\ldots)(x+\ldots)$
       $x^2 + 7x + 10$
                ↑   ↑——factors of 10, so 10 and 1 **or** 5 and 2
                └————————which add up to 7, so 5 and 2
       $x^2 + 7x + 10 = (x+5)(x+2)$

10　$x^2 - 10x + 25 = (x\ldots)(x\ldots)$

　　　　　　└─────signs both the same, both positive or both negative
　　　　　　└─────signs same as this, so both negative
　　　　　　　　　$(x - \ldots)(x - \ldots)$

　　$x^2 - 10x + 25$

　　　　　　└─────factors of 25 so 25 and 1 **or** 5 and 5
　　　　　　└─────which add up to 10, so 5 and 5

　　$x^2 - 10x + 25 = (x - 5)(x - 5) = (x - 5)^2$

11　$x^2 + 5x - 36 = (x\ldots)(x\ldots)$

　　　　　　└─────signs are: one + and one −
　　　　　　　　　$(x + \ldots)(x - \ldots)$

　　$x^2 + 5x - 36$

　　　　　　└─────factors of 36 so 36 and 1, or 18 and 2, or 12 and 3,
　　　　　　　　　or 9 and 4, or 6 and 6
　　　　　　└─────with a difference of 5, so 9 and 4
　　　　　　└─────to get $+5x$ we need $+9$ and -4

　　$x^2 + 5x - 36 = (x + 9)(x - 4)$

12　$x^2 - 5x - 36$

　　　　　　└─────to get $-5x$ we need $+4$ and -9

　　$x^2 - 5x - 36 = (x + 4)(x - 9)$

　　Also $x^2 - 5xy - 36y^2 = (x + 4y)(x - 9y)$

Other trinomials

Examples

13　$2x^2 - 8x + 6$

　　Since there is a common factor, deal with this first.
　　$2x^2 - 8x + 6 = 2(x^2 - 4x + 3)$
　　　　　　　　　$= 2(x - 3)(x - 1)$

14　$3x^2 - 11x + 6 = (3x\ldots)(x\ldots)$

　　　　　　└─────signs both the same, both positive or both negative,
　　　　　　└─────signs same as this so both negative
　　　　　　　　　$(3x - \ldots)(x - \ldots)$

　　$3x^2 - 11x + 6$

　　　　　　└─────try possible factors of 6, i.e. 6 and 1 or 3 and 2.

　　　　　　There are 4 possibilities
　　　　　　(a)　$(3x - 6)(x - 1)$
　　　　　　(b)　$(3x - 1)(x - 6)$
　　　　　　(c)　$(3x - 3)(x - 2)$
　　　　　　(d)　$(3x - 2)(x - 3)$

(a) and (c) can be rejected because there is a common factor 3 in one bracket yet there was no common factor in the original expression.

(b) when multiplied out gives $3x^2 - 19x + 6$.
(d) when multiplied out gives $3x^2 - 11x + 6$, so these are the correct factors.

$$3x^2 - 11x + 6 = (3x - 2)(x - 3)$$

15 $2x^2 - 7x - 9 = (2x.....)(x.....)$
signs are: one $+$ and one $-$
Either $(2x + ...)(x - ...)$ or $(2x - ...)(x + ...)$

$2x^2 - 7x - 9$
Possible end factors are 9 and 1 or 3 and 3.
There are 6 possibilities. Find the middle term when these are worked out.

$(2x + 9)(x - 1)$ Middle term is $+7x$
$(2x - 9)(x + 1)$ middle term is $-7x$, so these are the correct factors.
$(2x + 1)(x - 9)$ middle term is $-17x$
$(2x - 1)(x + 9)$ middle term is $+17x$
$(2x + 3)(x - 3)$ middle term is $-3x$
$(2x - 3)(x + 3)$ middle term is $+3x$

$$2x^2 - 7x - 9 = (2x - 9)(x + 1)$$

Methods for factorising

1	Common factors
2	Difference of two squares
3	Factors by grouping
4	Trinomials

1   Always find common factors first.
2   Recognise the difference of two squares, an expression of the form $a^2 - b^2$.
The factors are $(a + b)(a - b)$.
3   If there are 4 terms they can often be factorised by being grouped in pairs.
4   Trinomials can be factorised into two brackets.

Exercise 17.2

Factorise the following:

1. **1** $5x + 15y$
    2 $3x^2 - 6x$
    3 $4ab - 12bc$

    4 $6x^3 + 12$
    5 $x^3 + xy$

2. **1** $9x^2 - y^2$
    2 $x^2 - 16y^2$
    3 $x^2 - 1$
    4 $25x^2 - 49y^2$
    5 $1 - 36x^2$

    6 $100x^2 - 9$
    7 $x^2 - 169$
    8 $64 - x^2$
    9 $3x^2 - 12y^2$
    10 $x^2 - 100$

    11 $x^3 - x$
    12 $81x^2 - 25$
    13 $\pi a^2 - \pi b^2$
    14 $5x^2 - 125$
    15 $4x^2 - 36y^2$

3. **1** $px + qx + py + qy$
    2 $ax + bx - ay - by$
    3 $1 + x + y + xy$
    4 $2ax - 4ay - 3bx + 6by$
    5 $3ax + ay + 6bx + 2by$

    6 $2xy + 6y - x - 3$
    7 $3ay - a - 6y + 2$
    8 $pq + 2p - 2q - 4$
    9 $1 + x + x^2 + x^3$
    10 $a^2 + ab - ac - bc$

4. **1** $x^2 + 11x + 10$
    2 $x^2 - 8x + 12$
    3 $x^2 + 4x - 12$
    4 $x^2 - 2x - 15$
    5 $x^2 + x - 30$
    6 $x^2 - 17x + 30$
    7 $x^2 + 9x + 20$

    8 $x^2 + 2x - 8$
    9 $x^2 - 7x - 8$
    10 $x^2 + 5x - 14$
    11 $x^2 + 8x + 16$
    12 $x^2 + 19x + 18$
    13 $x^2 + x - 6$
    14 $x^2 - 7x + 6$

    15 $x^2 + 8x + 15$
    16 $x^2 - 2x + 1$
    17 $x^2 - 10x + 21$
    18 $x^2 - 2x - 24$
    19 $x^2 + 8x - 33$
    20 $x^2 + 14x + 49$

5. **1** $3x^2 + 6x - 9$
    2 $2x^2 + 9x + 7$
    3 $2x^2 - 11x + 5$
    4 $2x^2 - 11x + 12$
    5 $2x^2 - 2x - 12$
    6 $3x^2 - 11x - 20$
    7 $3x^2 + 2x - 1$

    8 $3x^2 + 14x + 11$
    9 $3x^2 - 31x + 10$
    10 $3x^2 + 33x + 30$
    11 $2x^2 - 3x - 5$
    12 $2x^2 - 3x - 9$
    13 $2x^2 + 4x - 30$
    14 $3x^2 - 17x - 6$

    15 $2x^2 - 4x - 6$
    16 $2x^2 + 12x + 10$
    17 $2x^2 - x - 3$
    18 $3x^2 - 5x - 8$
    19 $4x^2 + 8x - 12$
    20 $4x^2 - 16$

6. **1** $a^2b - 4ab^2$
    2 $x^2 + x - 12$
    3 $4\pi a^2 - 4\pi b^2$
    4 $ap + 2bp - 5a - 10b$
    5 $1 - 5x + 6x^2$
    6 $1 - 9x^2$
    7 $x^2 - 14xy - 15y^2$

    8 $2x^2 - 10x + 12$
    9 $x^3 + x^2 - 30x$
    10 $4ax - ay + 8bx - 2by$
    11 $2 - 5x - 3x^2$
    12 $45x^2 - 5y^2$
    13 $x^2 - 5x - 24$
    14 $3x^2 - ax - 9xy + 3ay$

    15 $2x^2 + 5x - 18$
    16 $x^2 + 23x + 60$
    17 $1 - x - 20x^2$
    18 $x^2 + 6x + 9$
    19 $x^4 - 81$
    20 $6x^2 + 12x + 6$

7.   If the area of a square is $(4x^2 + 20x + 25)$ cm^2, find an expression for its perimeter.

8.   Factorise $n^2 + n$ and explain why the value of this expression is always even, if n is any positive integer.
      Factorise $n^3 - n$ and explain why the value of this expression is always divisible by 6, if n is any positive integer greater than 1.

Completing the square

This is a process which we will use later when solving quadratic equations.
It involves an expression such as $x^2 + 12x$ and the aim is to add a number so that the whole expression can be written as a square.

Diagramatically:

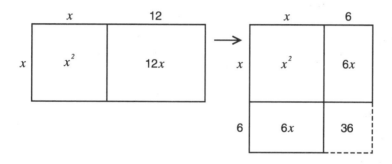

The number to be added is 36.
i.e. $x^2 + 12x + 36 = (x + 6)^2$
36 came from (half of 12) squared.

Similarly, $x^2 - 10x + \ldots$
(Half of 10) squared $= 5^2 = 25$
$x^2 - 10x + 25 = (x - 5)^2$

$x^2 + x + \ldots$
(Half of 1) squared $= \left(\frac{1}{2}\right)^2 = \frac{1}{4}$
$x^2 + x + \frac{1}{4} = \left(x + \frac{1}{2}\right)^2$

Maximum and minimum values

Using the method of completing the square, $x^2 + 2x + 14$ can be written as $(x + 1)^2 + 13$.
The first term of this expression is always positive, except when $x = -1$, when it is 0.
Thus the value of the complete expression is always greater than 13, except when $x = -1$, when it is 13.
So the minimum value of the expression is 13.

For $15 + 10x - x^2$, this can be written as
$-(x^2 - 10x) + 15$
$= -(x^2 - 10x + 25) + 25 + 15$
$= 40 - (x - 5)^2$

$(x - 5)^2$ is always positive, except when $x = 5$, when it is 0.
Thus the value of the complete expression is always less than 40, except when $x = 5$, when it is 40.
So the maximum value of the expression is 40.

Fractions

Remember that you use the same methods for algebraic fractions as you use for numerical fractions.

Examples

1   Simplify $\dfrac{x^2 - x}{x^2 + 3x - 4}$

Do not cancel until you have factorised. You can only cancel factors.

$$\frac{x^2 - x}{x^2 + 3x - 4} = \frac{x(x - 1)}{(x + 4)(x - 1)} = \frac{x}{x + 4}$$

(There is no other common factor so this is in its simplest form.)

2   $\dfrac{3x}{4} + \dfrac{x - 2}{6} - \dfrac{2x - 1}{12} = \dfrac{9x + 2(x - 2) - (2x - 1)}{12}$

$$= \frac{9x + 2x - 4 - 2x + 1}{12}$$

$$= \frac{9x - 3}{12}$$

$$= \frac{\overset{1}{3}(3x - 1)}{\underset{4}{12}}$$

$$= \frac{3x - 1}{4}$$

3   $\dfrac{5}{2x - 3} - \dfrac{3}{3x + 5} = \dfrac{5(3x + 5) - 3(2x - 3)}{(2x - 3)(3x + 5)}$

$$= \frac{15x + 25 - 6x + 9}{(2x - 3)(3x + 5)}$$

$$= \frac{9x + 34}{(2x - 3)(3x + 5)}$$

(The denominator is usually left in factor form.)

4 $\dfrac{4x+2}{4x^2-9} \div \dfrac{6x+3}{4x-6} = \dfrac{2(2x+1)}{(2x+3)(2x-3)} \div \dfrac{3(2x+1)}{2(2x-3)}$

$\qquad\qquad = \dfrac{2(2x+1)}{(2x+3)(2x-3)} \times \dfrac{2(2x-3)}{3(2x+1)}$

$\qquad\qquad = \dfrac{4}{3(2x+3)}$

5 $\dfrac{1-x-2x^2}{y} \times \dfrac{2y^2}{2x-1} = \dfrac{(1+x)\,(1-2x)^{-1}}{\cancel{y}} \times \dfrac{2\cancel{y}^{\,y^2}}{2x-1}$

$\qquad\qquad = -2y(1+x)$

Note that $2x-1$ cancels into $1-2x$, giving -1, since $1-2x = -(2x-1)$.

6   Solve the equation $\dfrac{3}{2x+1} = \dfrac{2}{3x-4}$.

Multiply both sides by $(2x+1)(3x-4)$.

$3(3x-4) = 2(2x+1)$

$9x - 12 = 4x + 2$

$5x = 14$

$x = 2\frac{4}{5}$

Exercise 17.3

1.   Add a number to complete the square in these expressions, and write the complete expression as a square.

   1 $x^2 + 16x$ $\qquad\qquad\qquad$ **4** $x^2 + x$
   2 $x^2 - 24x$ $\qquad\qquad\qquad$ **5** $x^2 - 11x$
   3 $x^2 + 3x$

2.   Find the maximum or minimum values of these expressions.
   1 $x^2 - 12x + 4$ $\qquad\qquad$ **2** $6 + 2x - x^2$

3.   If $9x^2 + 12x + a$ is a perfect square, find the value of a.

4.   Simplify these fractions

   1 $\dfrac{3a^2 + 6ab}{2ab + 4b^2}$ $\qquad\qquad$ **3** $\dfrac{5e^2 - 10e}{10ef - 30e}$

   2 $\dfrac{c^2 + cd}{c^2 - d^2}$ $\qquad\qquad$ **4** $\dfrac{h^2 - 4}{h^2 + 5h + 6}$

5. Simplify these fractions.

1 $\dfrac{1}{x-3} - \dfrac{2}{2x-3}$ 3 $\dfrac{x+2}{x-1} - \dfrac{x}{x-2}$

2 $\dfrac{2(x-1)}{2x+3} + \dfrac{1}{x}$ 4 $\dfrac{2}{x+2} - \dfrac{x-6}{x^2-4}$

6. Factorise where possible then simplify these fractions.

1 $\dfrac{2b}{4a^2 - 8ab + 3b^2} \div \dfrac{4}{2a - 3b}$

2 $\dfrac{x+5}{x^2 - 2x - 3} \times \dfrac{x-3}{x^2 + 6x + 5}$

7. Solve the equations.

1 $\dfrac{3}{6x+1} = \dfrac{2}{6x-1}$ 2 $\dfrac{3}{x-2} = \dfrac{4}{2x+1}$

8. A bill of £40 is intended to be shared among x people. How much should they each pay ?
    If two of the people refuse to pay, how much will each remaining person have to pay ?
    Write down an expression for the extra amount each person has to pay, and simplify it.

Convergent and divergent sequences

The sequence 4, 2, 1, 0.5, 0.25, ... gets closer and closer to the value 0 as the number of terms increases.
We could show this on a sketch graph.

The crosses show the values of the terms.
It is useful to draw the curve, but the other points on the curve have no meaning.

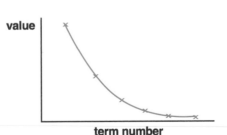

The sequence $2+\frac{1}{2}, 2-\frac{1}{4}, 2+\frac{1}{8},$ $2-\frac{1}{16}, 2+\frac{1}{32}, \ldots$ gets closer and closer to the value 2 as the number of terms increases. Alternate values are greater and less than 2 and the diagram looks like this:

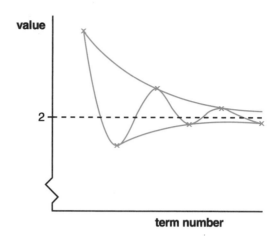

If a sequence gets closer and closer to a certain value, called the **limit**, as the number of terms increases, then the sequence is called a **convergent sequence**. The numbers converge onto the limit.

Any sequence which does not converge to a limit is called a **divergent sequence**.

Here are sketch graphs for two divergent sequences.

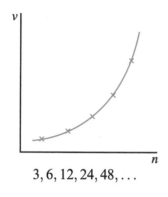

$3, 6, 12, 24, 48, \ldots$

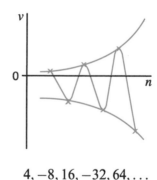

$4, -8, 16, -32, 64, \ldots$

Iterative sequences

These are sequences where every term can be found using the preceding term or terms. The terms of the sequence are denoted by u_1, u_2, u_3, u_4, $\ldots$ the nth term is u_n and the one after u_n is u_{n+1}.
Other letters can be used instead of u.

Examples

1   The sequence where $u_1 = 1$, $u_2 = 1$ and $u_{n+1} = u_{n-1} + u_n$

$u_3 = u_1 + u_2 = 1 + 1 = 2$
$u_4 = u_2 + u_3 = 1 + 2 = 3$
$u_5 = u_3 + u_4 = 2 + 3 = 5$
and so on.

The sequence is 1, 1, 2, 3, 5, 8, ... and this is the Fibonacci sequence.
It is a divergent sequence.

You can use your calculator, or a computer program, to find further terms of the sequence.

2   The sequence where $u_1 = 1$ and $u_{n+1} = 1 + \dfrac{1}{u_n}$

$u_1 = 1$

$u_2 = 1 + \dfrac{1}{u_1} = 1 + 1 = 2$

$u_3 = 1 + \dfrac{1}{u_2} = 1 + \frac{1}{2} = 1\frac{1}{2} = \frac{3}{2}$

$u_4 = 1 + \dfrac{1}{u_3} = 1 + \frac{2}{3} = 1\frac{2}{3} = \frac{5}{3}$

$u_5 = 1 + \dfrac{1}{u_4} = 1 + \frac{3}{5} = 1\frac{3}{5} = \frac{8}{5}$

and so on.

Notice that this sequence is formed from the Fibonacci sequence.

If the successive terms are written as decimals, to 3 decimal places, they are

$u_1 = 1$
$u_2 = 2$
$u_3 = 1.5$
$u_4 = 1.667$
$u_5 = 1.6$
$u_6 = 1.625$
$u_7 = 1.615$
$u_8 = 1.619$
$u_9 = 1.618$
$u_{10} = 1.618$
$\ldots$

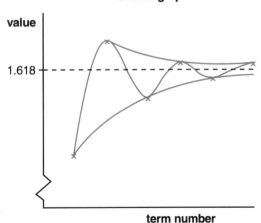

Sketch graph

The sequence is a convergent sequence.
The limit is approximately 1.618.

Using a graphics calculator you can find the values of $u_2, u_3, u_4, \ldots$ by pressing

1 EXE   This enters $u_1 = 1$.

1 + 1 ÷ Ans EXE   This calculates u_2.

EXE   This calculates u_3.

and press EXE again and again to find $u_4, u_5, \ldots$

(Your calculator may use ENTER instead of EXE .)

Exercise 17.4

1. Say what the next 2 terms are in each of these sequences, and explain the rule for generating each sequence.
   Say whether the sequence is convergent or divergent, and if it is a convergent sequence, state the limit of the sequence.

   1 4, 8, 12, 16, 20, ...   **6** $\frac{1}{9}, \frac{1}{3}, 1, 3, 9, \ldots$

   2 4, 1, −2, −5, −8, ...   **7** 128, 96, 72, 54, 40.5, ...

   3 4, 1, $\frac{1}{4}$, $\frac{1}{16}$, ...   **8** 3, −6, −12, −24, 48, ...

   4 2, 4, 8, 16, ...   **9** $3 + \frac{1}{2}, 3 - \frac{1}{4}, 3 + \frac{1}{8}, 3 - \frac{1}{16}, 3 + \frac{1}{32}, \ldots$

   5 $\frac{3}{5}, \frac{4}{6}, \frac{5}{7}, \frac{6}{8}, \frac{7}{9}, \ldots$ **10** 5, 0.5, 0.05, 0.005, 0.0005, ...

2. Work out the first 8 terms of these sequences and say whether the sequence is convergent or divergent. For those which are convergent, say what the limit is. If the limit cannot be found exactly, give it correct to 2 decimal places.
   (Keep as many figures as are available on your calculator but record each term to 4 decimal places. If you use a computer program or graphics calculator you can record the terms to more decimal places, and maybe work out more terms.)

   1 $u_{n+1} = 4u_n - 5$. $u_1 = 3$ **5** $u_{n+1} = u_n - 3n - 1$. $u_1 = 7$

   2 $u_{n+1} = \dfrac{2}{u_n} + 3$. $u_1 = 1$ **6** $u_{n+1} = \dfrac{u_n}{n}$. $u_1 = 80$

   3 $u_{n+1} = \sqrt{2u_n + 4}$. $u_1 = 2.5$ **7** $u_{n+1} = 4u_n - 3u_{n-1}$. $u_1 = 2, u_2 = 5$

   4 $u_{n+1} = \dfrac{9}{u_n + 2}$. $u_1 = 2$ **8** $u_{n+1} = \dfrac{u_n + u_{n-1}}{2}$. $u_1 = 4, u_2 = 3$

3. This sequence can be used to find an approximation for the square root of a number N. The limit of the sequence is $\sqrt{N}$.

   $$u_{n+1} = \tfrac{1}{2}u_n + \frac{N}{2u_n}$$

   Starting with $u_1 = 2$, find $\sqrt{80}$, correct to 4 decimal places.

Exercise 17.5 Applications

1. Pairs of values of related variables are given in these tables. Find the equations connecting the variables.

    1 The weight W g of a set of discs of different radii r cm but with the same thickness.

r cm	0	1	2	3	4	5
W g	0	12	48	108	192	300

    2 A light bar with a fixed load at one end is pivoted near that end and balanced by different weights W kg hung in turn from different distances d cm along the bar from the pivot.

W kg	1	2	2.5	4	5
d cm	30	15	12	7.5	6

    3 There is a drop in temperature from that at sea-level as the height above sea-level increases. Here is the approximate relationship between the height h m and temperature $t°C$, when the temperature at sea-level was 12°C.

h m	0	100	200	300	400	500
$t°C$	12	11.4	10.8	10.2	9.6	9.0

    4 The weight W g of a set of similar solid model pyramids of different heights h cm.

h cm	0	10	20	30	40
W g	0	100	800	2700	6400

2. **1** Factorise $x^2 - 9$. By putting $x = 20$, find the prime factors of 391.

    2 Factorise $3x^2 + 7x + 2$. Hence find two factors of 372 and then express 372 in its prime factors.

3. Factorise $c^2 - b^2$. If $a^2 = c^2 - b^2$ find the value of a when

    1 $c = 25, b = 24$ **2** $c = 37, b = 35$ **3** $c = 20, b = 16$.

4. If a rectangle has an area of $(2x^2 + 5x - 3)$ cm^2 and one side is $(2x - 1)$ cm, what is the length of the other side ?

5. Find a common factor of $3x^2 + x - 2$ and $3x^2 - 5x + 2$.

6. Simplify $(x+y)^2 + x(x-2y) - 9y^2$ and factorise your answer.

7. Find the maximum or minimum values of these expressions.
    1   $x^2 - 8x + 20$
    2   $6 - x - x^2$
    3   $2x^2 - 12x + 1$, i.e. $2(x^2 - 6x) + 1$

8. Simplify $\dfrac{6}{(x-6)^2} + \dfrac{1}{x-6}$.

9. Solve the equation $\dfrac{x}{2x-9} = \dfrac{2x-6}{4x-21}$.

10. A train travels 60 miles at an average speed of x mph and then 80 miles at an average speed of $(x+10)$ mph.
    Find an expression for the total time taken, and simplify it.

11. Write down the next 2 terms in each of these sequences.
    Say whether each sequence is convergent or divergent.
    For those which are convergent, say what the limit is.

    1   $\frac{36}{1}, \frac{36}{2}, \frac{36}{3}, \frac{36}{4}, \ldots$
    2   $\frac{5}{1}, \frac{9}{2}, \frac{13}{3}, \frac{17}{4}, \frac{21}{5}, \ldots$
    3   $1+1, 3+1, 9+1, 27+1, \ldots$
    4   $\frac{1}{64}, \frac{1}{32}, \frac{1}{16}, \frac{1}{8}, \ldots$

12. Work out the 1st 8 terms of this sequence and say whether the sequence is convergent or divergent. If it is convergent, say what the limit is, correct to 2 decimal places.

    $$u_{n+1} = \frac{1}{1+u_n}, \quad u_1 = 0.1$$

13. The limit of the sequence given by this iterative formula is an approximation for a solution of the equation $x^3 - 5x + 3 = 0$.

    $$u_{n+1} = \tfrac{1}{5}(u_n^3 + 3).$$

    Starting with $u_1 = 1$, find a solution of the equation, correct to 2 decimal places.

Practice test 17

1. The table shows the greatest weights which can be held by certain ropes.

Diameter, d cm	1	2	3	4	5
Weight, w kg	14	56	~~136~~	224	350

   126

   Find the equation connecting w and d.

2. Factorise

   1 $3a^2 - 12ab$
   2 $x^2 - 16x + 15$
   3 $\pi x^2 h - \pi y^2 h$
   4 $3x^2 - 19x - 14$
   5 $8ab - 6ac + 12b - 9c$

3. What must be added to $x^2 - 20x$ to make a perfect square ?
   Write the complete expression as a square.

4. Factorise where possible, then simplify these expressions.

   1 $\dfrac{3x + 15y}{4x + 20y}$ **2** $\dfrac{x^2 - x}{3x} \times \dfrac{2xy}{4x - 4}$ **3** $\dfrac{2x^2 + x}{10x + 5} \div \dfrac{x}{15}$

5. Express $\dfrac{x}{x + 4} + \dfrac{4}{x - 4}$ as a single fraction.

6. Solve the equation $\dfrac{x + 10}{x - 2} = \dfrac{x + 14}{x - 1}$.

7. Work out the 1st 10 terms of the sequence given by the iterative formula $u_{n+1} = u_n + n + 1$, $u_1 = 1$, and say whether it is convergent or divergent.
   Give the name of the sequence.

8. This sequence can be used to find an approximation for the cube root of a number N. The limit of the sequence is $\sqrt[3]{N}$.

   $u_{n+1} = (Nu_n)^{\frac{1}{4}}$.

   For $x^{\frac{1}{4}}$, enter x then press the square root key twice in succession.
   Use the sequence to find the cube root of 220, correct to 3 decimal places, starting with $u_1 = 10$.

PUZZLES

38.   A friend offered £100 to provide prizes for a Charity Tombola on condition that exactly 100 prizes were bought. The committee running the Tombola wanted to buy prizes costing £10, £2 and 50 pence, with more than one at each price. How could they fulfil the conditions of the gift ?

39.   Mark, the racing driver, did his first practice lap at 40 miles per hour. What speed would he have to average on his second lap if he wanted to produce an average for the two laps of 80 miles per hour ?

40.   A practical test. You are given 27 packages and told that 26 of them are of equal weight but 1 is slightly lighter. You are also given a balance-type weighing scale so that you can weigh some on one side against some on the other. However, you are only allowed to make 3 weighings. How can you find the lighter one ?

41.   Arrange (a) three 1's, (b) three 2's, (c) three 4's, without using any mathematical signs, so that you represent the highest possible number in each case.

42.   A group of six children have to send a team of four of them to take part in a quiz. But they all have their own views on whether they will take part or not.
Laura won't be in the team unless Michelle is also in it.
Michelle won't be in the team if Oliver is.
Naomi won't be in the team if both Laura and Michelle are in it.
Oliver won't be in the team if Patrick is.
Patrick will be in the team with any of the others.
Robert won't be in the team if Laura is, unless Oliver is in it too.
Which 4 took part in the quiz ?

43.   Decode this division sum. Every letter stands for a different figure.

```
                    M E T R E
        O D ) L A T W M U E
                L E L
                D E W
                D U E
                  M M M
                  M M U
                      D U E
                      D U E
                      R R R
```

Data and distributions

The topics in this chapter include:

- constructing and interpreting a histogram with understanding of the connection between area and frequency,
- calculating the standard deviation of a set of data,
- considering different shapes of histograms.

Histograms

The most suitable diagram for representing a frequency distribution with grouped data is a histogram.

In a histogram, the **area** of each block represents the frequency.

Histograms with class intervals of equal width

Some of these were used in Chapter 9.

In these histograms, the class intervals are of equal width, so the heights of the columns are in proportion to their frequencies, and can be labelled to represent the frequencies.

Histograms with unequal class intervals

A histogram can have unequal class intervals. In such cases the heights of the columns must be adjusted so that the areas of the blocks are in proportion to their frequencies.

To calculate the heights of the columns, which are rectangles,

Area = height × width of class interval

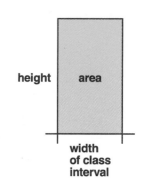

height   area

The area represents the frequency, so

$$\text{Height} = \frac{\text{frequency}}{\text{width of class interval}}$$

width
of class
interval

This height can be labelled 'frequency density', so

$$\text{Frequency density} = \frac{\text{frequency}}{\text{width of class interval}}$$

Example

A check was made of the number of hours overtime worked by 400 employees in a certain firm. Here are the figures:

Annual overtime (hours)	0 to < 5	5 to < 10	10 to < 20	20 to < 30	30 to < 40	40 to < 60	60 to < 100
Frequency (number of employees)	14	22	73	137	95	43	16

In the histogram

Area (frequency)	14	22	73	137	95	43	16
Class width	5	5	10	10	10	20	40
Height $= \dfrac{\text{frequency}}{\text{width}}$	2.8	4.4	7.3	13.7	9.5	2.15	0.4

Histogram

Draw the horizontal axis from 0 to 100, labelling the values for the edges of the blocks at 0, 5, 10, 20, 30, 40, 60, 100.

Draw the vertical axis from 0 to 14.
Draw each block to the height given in the table.

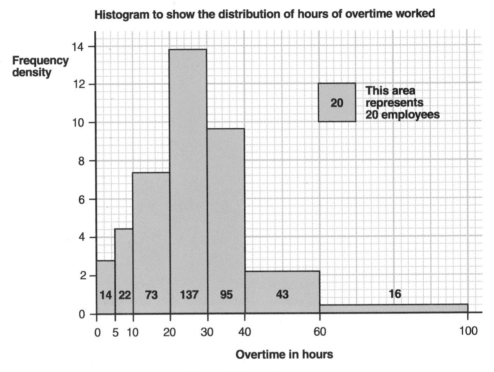

Complete the histogram with a title and label the axes.
It is helpful to write the actual frequencies in the blocks as they cannot be read from the vertical axis.
You should also give a key to show how much a certain area represents. Here we have made the block in the key 10 units wide as that is the width of 3 of the central blocks in the histogram. We have drawn it with a height of 2 units, so that in this case it represents a frequency of 20, but we could have made it any suitable height.

Exercise 18.1

1. The amounts spent by 120 customers in a shop were as follows:

Amount in £'s	0–5	5–10	10–20	20–40	40–60	60–100
f	10	12	27	37	22	12

1 Work out the heights of the columns for a histogram.
2 Draw the histogram.

2.   The times spent on homework by a year-group of 150 pupils are shown in the table.

Time in minutes	Number of pupils
0 to < 30	21
30 to < 40	6
40 to < 50	24
50 to < 55	17
55 to < 60	19
60 to < 70	30
70 to < 80	21
80 to < 100	12

1 Work out the heights of the columns for a histogram.

2 Draw the histogram.

3.   The age distribution of the population of a village was as follows:

Age (in years)	under 5	5–9	10–14	15–24	25–34	35–44	45–64	65–84
Number of people	35	42	44	76	72	59	115	57

Draw a histogram of the distribution. (The boundaries of the class intervals are
0, 5, 10, 15, 25, 35, 45, 65 and 85 years.)

4.   The histogram shows the distribution of the ages of cars in a survey.
Show the data in a frequency distribution table, including the total number of cars.

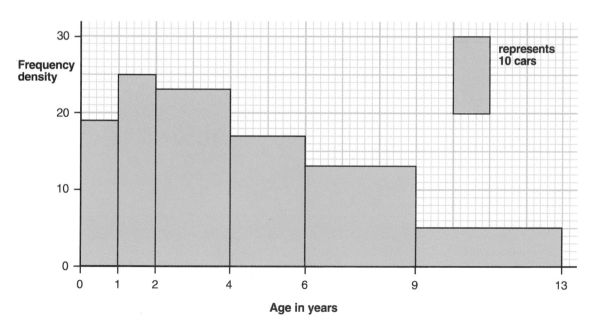

represents 10 cars

Frequency density

Age in years

Dispersion

You already know two measures of dispersion, the range and the interquartile range.

The range = highest value − lowest value.

The interquartile range = value of upper quartile − value of lower quartile.

Standard deviation

This is another measure of dispersion. In advanced methods of statistics it is much more useful than the range or the interquartile range.

To find the standard deviation of a set of numbers

Find the mean.
Find the deviation of each variable from the mean.
(Check that the sum of the deviations is 0.)
Square the deviations, and find the sum of the squares.
Find the average of the squares.
Take the square root of the average.

Here is the formula for the standard deviation of a set of numbers.

$$s = \sqrt{\frac{\Sigma(x - \bar{x})^2}{n}}$$

Example

The lengths of 6 rods are 55 cm, 56 cm, 57 cm, 63 cm, 67 cm, 68 cm.
Find the mean and standard deviation of the lengths.

x	$x - \bar{x}$	$(x - \bar{x})^2$
55	−6	36
56	−5	25
57	−4	16
63	2	4
67	6	36
68	7	49
366	0	166

check that this total is 0

$\bar{x} = \dfrac{\Sigma x}{n} = \dfrac{366}{6}$ cm = 61 cm

The mean length is 61 cm.

$s = \sqrt{\dfrac{\Sigma(x - \bar{x})^2}{n}} = \sqrt{\dfrac{166}{6}}$ cm

$ = \sqrt{27.666\ldots}$ cm

$ = 5.26$ cm, to 2 dec. pl.

The standard deviation of the lengths is 5.26 cm.

Remember to give the units, in this case, cm.

When the data is given in whole numbers, work out the mean to 1 decimal place and the standard deviation to 2 decimal places.

If the mean is not exact, it is easier to use an alternative formula for the standard deviation.

$$s = \sqrt{\frac{\Sigma x^2}{n} - \left(\frac{\Sigma x}{n}\right)^2}$$

It can be proved algebraically that this formula is correct.

We will do the previous example using this formula.

x	x^2
55	3025
56	3136
57	3249
63	3969
67	4489
68	4624
366	22492

$$s = \sqrt{\frac{\Sigma x^2}{n} - \left(\frac{\Sigma x}{n}\right)^2}$$

$$= \sqrt{\frac{22492}{6} - \left(\frac{366}{6}\right)^2} \text{ cm}$$

$$= \sqrt{27.666\ldots} \text{ cm}$$

$$= 5.26 \text{ cm, to 2 dec. pl.}$$

In using this formula for standard deviation, we can measure the x-numbers from any chosen number, not necessarily from 0. The chosen number is called an assumed mean and it is written as x_0.

In this example, suppose the readings were all taken from an assumed mean of 60 cm. Then 55 cm would be written as -5 cm, 68 cm would be $+8$ cm, etc. This will simplify the working, which now looks like this:

Old x	New x with $x_0 = 60$	x^2
55	-5	25
56	-4	16
57	-3	9
63	$+3$	9
67	$+7$	49
68	$+8$	64
	$+6$	172

To find the mean, add x_0 to the formula.

$$\bar{x} = x_0 + \frac{\Sigma x}{n}$$

$$= \left(60 + \tfrac{6}{6}\right) \text{ cm}$$

$$= 61 \text{ cm}$$

$$s = \sqrt{\frac{\Sigma x^2}{n} - \left(\frac{\Sigma x}{n}\right)^2}$$

$$= \sqrt{\frac{172}{6} - \left(\frac{6}{6}\right)^2} \text{ cm}$$

$$= \sqrt{27.666\ldots} \text{ cm}$$

$$= 5.26 \text{ cm, to 2 dec. pl.}$$

If you are asked to find the standard deviation of a set of data, **showing your working**, then you should use one of the above methods, setting down the values in columns as shown. You can use your calculator, as usual, to work out any calculations needed.

At other times, or for checking answers, you can use a statistical calculator or a computer program. You enter the data, and the program will calculate the values of the mean and the standard deviation.

To do the last example using a statistical calculator:
Set the calculator to work in statistical mode.

Press 55 DATA 56 DATA 57 DATA 63 DATA 67 DATA 68 DATA

Then if you press $\boxed{\Sigma x}$ you will get 366.

If you press $\boxed{\Sigma x^2}$ you will get 22 492.

If you press $\boxed{\bar{x}}$ you will get 61.   (This is the mean.)

If you press $\boxed{\sigma}$ you will get 5.2599...   (This is the standard deviation.)

σ is the small Greek letter sigma. Do not use the key $\boxed{s}$ for standard deviation as the calculator will give a slightly different answer.
(σ may be labelled σ_n or $x\sigma_n$.)

The mean and standard deviation of a frequency distribution

Here is an example using the heights of a group of children.
For the standard deviation we need a column fx^2. Note that fx^2 is not the same as $(fx)^2$. It is the fx column multiplied by the x column.

Height in cm	Frequency	x centre of interval	fx	fx^2
110 to < 120	6	115	690	79350
120 to < 130	17	125	2125	265625
130 to < 140	32	135	4320	583200
140 to < 150	26	145	3770	546650
150 to < 160	19	155	2945	456475
	100		13850	1931300

$$\bar{x} = \frac{\Sigma fx}{\Sigma f} = \frac{13850}{100} \text{ cm} = 138.5 \text{ cm}$$

To find the standard deviation use the formula

$$s = \sqrt{\frac{\Sigma fx^2}{\Sigma f} - \left(\frac{\Sigma fx}{\Sigma f}\right)^2}$$

$$= \sqrt{\frac{1931300}{100} - \left(\frac{13850}{100}\right)^2} \text{ cm}$$

$$= \sqrt{130.75} \text{ cm}$$

$$= 11.43 \text{ cm}$$

To do this example using a statistical calculator, set the calculator to work in statistical mode then press

115 $\boxed{\times}$ 6 $\boxed{\text{DATA}}$ 125 $\boxed{\times}$ 17 $\boxed{\text{DATA}}$ (etc.)

When you have entered all the data, if you press
$\boxed{\Sigma x}$ you will actually get Σfx, 13850,
$\boxed{\Sigma x^2}$ you will get Σfx^2, 1931300,
$\boxed{n}$ you will get Σf, 100,
$\boxed{\bar{x}}$ you will get the mean, 138.5,
$\boxed{\sigma}$ you will get the standard deviation, 11.43.

It is also possible to use an assumed mean x_0. This reduces the size of the numbers used and makes the calculations simpler.

Here is the same example. We use one of the centres of interval as the assumed mean, usually one near the middle of the list. Here we are choosing 135.

Height in cm	f	C of I	New x $x_0 = 135$	fx	fx^2
110–120	6	115	−20	−120	2400
120–130	17	125	−10	−170	1700
130–140	32	135	0	0	0
140–150	26	145	+10	+260	2600
150–160	19	155	+20	+380	7600
	100			+350	14300

$$\bar{x} = x_0 + \frac{\Sigma fx}{\Sigma f} = \left(135 + \tfrac{350}{100}\right) \text{ cm}$$

$$= (135 + 3.5) \text{ cm}$$

$$= 138.5 \text{ cm}$$

$$s = \sqrt{\frac{\Sigma fx^2}{\Sigma f} - \left(\frac{\Sigma fx}{\Sigma f}\right)^2}$$

$$= \sqrt{\frac{14300}{100} - \left(\frac{350}{100}\right)^2} \text{ cm}$$

$$= \sqrt{143 - 12.25} \text{ cm}$$

$$= \sqrt{130.75} \text{ cm}$$

$$= 11.43 \text{ cm, to 2 dec. pl.}$$

It is useful as a check to work out the values of 3 standard deviations below and above the mean, as most of the data should lie in that range.
Here, those values are approximately 104 cm and 173 cm, and all the data lies between those values.

Exercise 18.2

For the following sets of data, find the mean and the standard deviation.
In questions 1 to 6 you can use either the basic formula or the alternative formula to find the standard deviation. In questions 7 to 10 use the alternative formula.
If you have a statistical calculator, check your answers using it.

1. The weights, in kg, of 6 young children.
    28, 22, 24, 26, 23, 27.

2. The number of policies issued each week by an insurance company, for 13 weeks.
    23, 62, 54, 53, 36, 44, 47, 39, 17, 24, 54, 55, 38.

3. The heights, in cm, of 12 girls.
    164, 148, 166, 156, 173, 163, 164, 171, 156, 161, 158, 152.

4. The distances travelled by a projectile, in metres, when launched into the air, 10 times.
    51, 55, 48, 60, 62, 66, 40, 47, 51, 55.

5. The total amounts from sales of a product each week over 5 weeks. Figures in £100's.
    88, 99, 102, 93, 103.

6. The fuel consumption, in miles/litre, of 8 cars.
    9.9,   7.3,   8.5,   6.8,   9.2,   7.5,   8.4,   6.4.

7. The temperatures, in °F, over 7 days.
    72,   68,   65,   60,   53,   49,   47.

8. The marks of 9 students in an examination.
    64,   56,   53,   44,   41,   20,   19,   46,   41.

9. The times taken to run a race on 5 occasions, in seconds.
    47.5,   50.2,   51.0,   48.0,   47.8.

10. The sales of ice-cream on 12 days, amounts in kg.
    310,   290,   350,   310,   410,   390,   210,   330,   340,   210,   250,   380.

Find the mean and standard deviation of the data in these frequency distributions.

11. The number of people per household in 50 households.

Size of household	1	2	3	4	5	6
f (Number of households)	9	20	7	7	5	2

12. Heights of 40 Christmas trees.

Height (cm)	165–175	175–185	185–195	195–205	205–215
f	6	11	12	6	5

13. Ages of 200 cars in a survey.

Age in years	0–2	2–4	4–6	6–8	8–10	10–12
Number of cars	60	51	34	27	20	8

14. The heights of 100 students.

Height in cm	153–157	158–162	163–167	168–172	173–177
f	9	23	35	27	6

Shapes of histograms

We often draw a histogram because we can deduce things from its general shape.
Here are some examples.

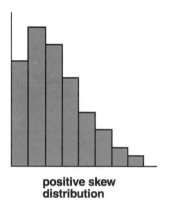

**positive skew
distribution**

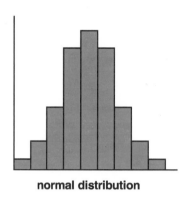

normal distribution

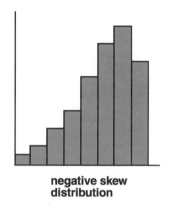

**negative skew
distribution**

If we replace the histogram with a smooth curve, which encloses the same area between the
curve and the *x*-axis as is enclosed by the histogram, then these histograms can be replaced by
these frequency curves.

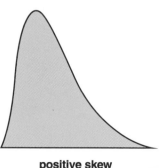

**positive skew
distribution**

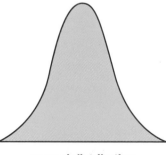

normal distribution

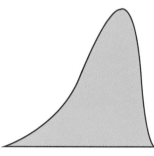

**negative skew
distribution**

On these distributions, the positions of the mean, median and mode are roughly as shown:
The mode is at the peak of the curve.
The median divides the curve into two equal areas.

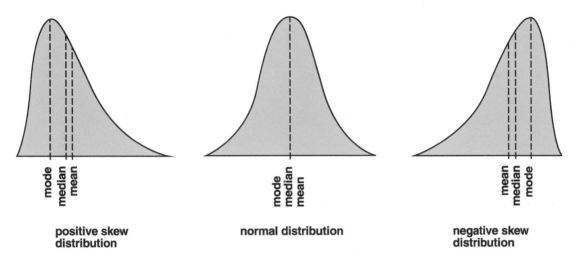

positive skew distribution   **normal distribution**   **negative skew distribution**

If the distribution is skewed, the median is often a better average to use than the mean, as the mean is affected by extreme values.

Examples of a positively skewed distribution:
The number of children in families,
the number of goals scored in football matches,
exam marks when the exam was too hard.

Examples of a negatively skewed distribution:
Exam marks when the exam was too easy,
speed of traffic on a motorway.

The Normal Distribution

The word 'normal' here implies a distribution with this bell-shaped curve.
It is symmetrical about the line through its peak, which gives the position of the mean, median and mode.

Many observations are normally distributed, or nearly so.
Examples are:
Heights of people,
lengths of leaves from a tree,
exam marks when the exam is set to match the ability of the pupils,
lifetimes of light bulbs,
weights of manufactured products, e.g. bags of sugar,
estimates of length.

Another property of the normal distribution curve is the relationship between the curve, the mean and the standard deviation.

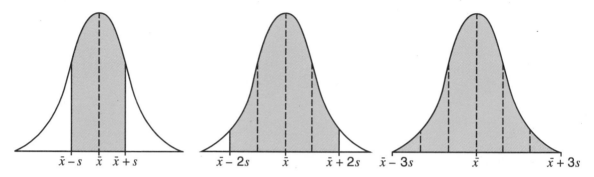

The curve is symmetrical about the mean so there is 50% of its area on either side of the mean.

About 68% $\left(\text{roughly } \frac{2}{3}\right)$ of its area lies within 1 standard deviation of the mean on either side.

About 95% of its area lies within 2 standard deviations of the mean.

About 99.8% of its area lies within 3 standard deviations of the mean.
(This is **nearly all**,—only 0.2% of the area lies outside this range, 0.1% on either side.)

The curve tails off at both ends.

We can use these facts to estimate the percentage of the population in each part.

Example

The weights of a large number of pupils in the same age-group have been recorded, and the weights are found to be normally distributed. The mean weight is 46 kg and the standard deviation is 3 kg.

Using the properties of the normal distribution curve, here are the estimated percentages of pupils whose weights are within various ranges.

The distribution is symmetrical about the mean.

50% of the pupils weigh less than 46 kg and
50% weigh more than 46 kg.

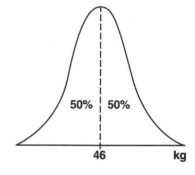

68% of the weights lie within
1 standard deviation on either
side of the mean.

This leaves 16% of the pupils
weighing less than 43 kg and
16% weighing over 49 kg.

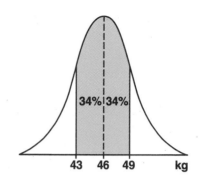

95% of the weights lie within
2 standard deviations on either
side of the mean.

This leaves $2\frac{1}{2}$% of the pupils
weighing less than 40 kg and
$2\frac{1}{2}$% weighing over 52 kg.

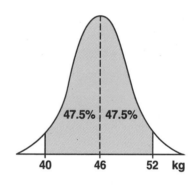

Nearly all the weights are within
3 standard deviations on either
side of the mean.

Only 1 pupil out of 1000 would weigh less
than 37 kg, and only 1 pupil out of 1000
would weigh more than 55 kg.

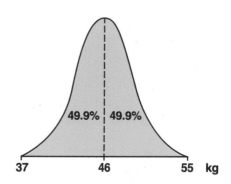

Exercise 18.3

For the frequency distributions in questions 1 to 5, sketch (roughly) the histograms or the frequency distribution curves and describe the shape of each distribution.

1. The birth weights of 80 babies.

Weight in lb	Number of babies
4.5 to just under 5.5	3
5.5 to just under 6.5	9
6.5 to just under 7.5	22
7.5 to just under 8.5	28
8.5 to just under 9.5	16
9.5 to just under 10.5	2

2. The runs scored by 40 batsmen in matches on a Sunday.

Runs	0–19	20–39	40–59	60–79	80–99	100–119
Number of batsmen	40	21	11	3	2	3

3. The ages, in completed years, of children in a Youth Organisation.

Age	Number of members
5 or 6	590
7 or 8	2130
9 or 10	1930
11 or 12	1120
13 or 14	430
15 or 16	50

4. The number of letters in surnames of 137 people.

Number of letters in surname	2	3	4	5	6	7	8	9	10
Frequency	1	4	14	28	35	22	17	12	4

5.   The number of seeds germinating in pots, when 6 seeds were planted in each pot, for 150 pots.

Number of seeds	0	1	2	3	4	5	6
Number of pots	1	0	3	3	15	50	78

6.   The girths of trees in a plantation, measured at a fixed height above ground, are as shown.

Girth in cm	f
40–45	17
45–50	57
50–55	99
55–60	66
60–65	35
65–70	24
70–75	2
	300

Draw a histogram of the distribution.

The mean, median and mode are, respectively, 54.6 cm, 53.8 cm, 52.8 cm. Mark the positions of these on the histogram.

7.   The lifetime of an electronic component is found to be normally distributed, with a mean lifetime of 2000 hours and a standard deviation of 300 hours.

Approximately what percentage of a large batch of these components will last for
1   less than 2000 hours,
2   between 1700 and 2300 hours,
3   between 1400 and 2600 hours,
4   longer than 2300 hours ?

8.   In an examination taken by 2000 candidates the marks were found to be normally distributed with a mean of 54 marks and a standard deviation of 8 marks.

1   What was the approximate range of marks ?
2   What was the approximate number of candidates who gained marks between 38 and 70 ?
3   What was the approximate number of candidates who gained more than 70 marks ?

Exercise 18.4 Applications

1. The time that elapses between successive cars passing a road checkpoint is given in the table.

Time (in seconds)	0–5	5–10	10–20	20–30	30–40	40–60	60–90
Number of cars	16	14	25	19	15	18	12

Draw a histogram of the distribution.

2. The distribution of ages of men and women getting married is shown in this table. (Figures for UK, 1987, in 1000's.)

Age (in years)	Men	Women
16–20	24	69
21–24	118	140
25–29	120	91
30–34	51	37
35–44	49	37
45–54	20	15
55 and over	16	9

Work out the heights of the columns for separate histograms for men and for women. The boundaries of the class intervals are 16, 21, 25, 30, 35, 45, 55, and assume the last interval ends at 70.
Draw the histograms.
Compare the histograms and comment about them.

3. The histogram on the next page shows the weights of some parcels.
Copy and complete the frequency distribution table, including the total number of parcels.

Weight in kg	Number of parcels
0 to less than 4	. . .
4 to less than 6	. . .
. . .	

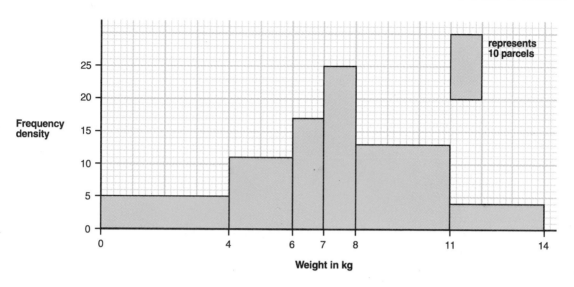

For questions 4 to 10, find the mean and standard deviation of the data. If you have a statistical calculator, check your answers using it.

4. The weights, in kg, of 8 bags of sugar.
   1.03,   1.02,   0.99,   1.01,   1.03,   1.01,   1.03,   1.04.

5. The lengths of 12 leaves, in mm.
   38,   44,   41,   26,   55,   31,   32,   23,   28,   59,   35,   56.

6. The number of matches in 10 boxes.
   46,   51,   55,   53,   49,   48,   47,   52,   48,   53.

7. The times taken, in minutes, by a plumber to do 5 jobs.
   56,   65,   46,   60,   75.

8. The weekly amounts earned by a self-employed person in 6 weeks.
   £157,   £215,   £189,   £148,   £160,   £132.

9. The number of sixes when 5 dice were thrown together 50 times.

Number of sixes	0	1	2	3	4	5
f	19	20	8	2	1	0

10. Heights of 40 plants, measured to the nearest 0.5 cm.

Height in cm	6.5	7.0	7.5	8.0	8.5	9.0
f	2	7	9	13	6	3

11. Times taken by 100 workers to travel to work.

Time in minutes	f
0–10	2
10–20	18
20–30	35
30–40	28
40–50	14
50–60	3

Find the mean time, and the standard deviation of times.

Work out the values of 3 standard deviations below and above the mean, verifying that all the data lies within that range.

In questions 12 to 14, sketch (roughly) the histograms or frequency distribution curves of the data. Describe the shapes of the distributions.

12. The number of emergency calls received by a local exchange on 200 days.

Number of calls	0	1	2	3	4	5 or more
Number of days	60	77	48	12	3	0

13. The heights of 150 girls.

Height in cm	f
135 to < 140	4
140 to < 145	9
145 to < 150	17
150 to < 155	42
155 to < 160	46
160 to < 165	23
165 to < 170	6
170 to < 175	3
	150

14. The number of heads when 8 coins are tossed 250 times.

Number of heads	0	1	2	3	4	5	6	7	8
f	1	7	29	55	73	53	25	7	0

15. A survey of distances travelled by a particular type of tyre gives these results:

Distance (in 1000 km)	Number of tyres
0 to 20	11
20 to 30	18
30 to 40	38
40 to 50	52
50 to 60	42
60 to 90	39
	200

Work out the heights of the columns for a histogram.
Draw the histogram.
Find the mean distance.
The median distance travelled is 46 300 km and the mode distance is 45 800 km. Mark the mean, median and mode positions on the histogram.

16. The distribution of weights of powder packed in bags labelled 1 kg is found to be normal, with mean weight 1020 g and standard deviation 8 g.

Approximately, what percentage of a large batch of these bags will weigh
1   more than 1028 g,
2   more than 1004 g ?
3   Between which limits of weight do nearly all the bags lie ?

Practice test 18

1. The earnings of 120 workers in a certain industry are shown in this frequency table.

Earnings (£)	f
80–100	3
100–110	8
110–120	16
120–130	15
130–140	17
140–160	19
160–180	15
180–200	9
200–250	18
	120

Work out the heights of the columns for a histogram.

Draw the histogram.

Comment briefly on its shape.

[Turn over]

2. The diagram shows a histogram representing the lengths of some planks of wood. If there were 28 planks measuring between 2 m and 3 m, copy and complete the frequency distribution table, including the total number of planks.

Length in metres	Number of planks
0 to 2	. . .
2 to 3	28
. . .	

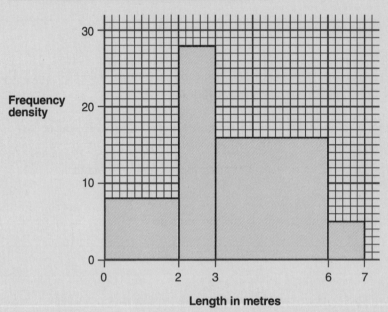

In questions 3 to 5, find the mean and standard deviation of the data.

3. The attendances of a class on 10 days.
    28, 29, 26, 25, 24, 26, 26, 29, 28, 29.

4. The weights, in grams, of a sample of 6 apples.
    90, 86, 98, 92, 101, 106.

5. The numbers of goals scored by 20 teams in a league.

Number of goals	0	1	2	3	4	5
Number of teams	6	7	3	2	1	1

6. Here are three distributions of examination marks, in each case for 60 students. Sketch (roughly) the histograms or frequency distribution curves and describe the shapes of the distributions. Compare the distributions and comment about them.

Mark	Group A f	Group B f	Group C f
0– 9			9
10–19	1		18
20–29	4	1	13
30–39	5	2	10
40–49	13	4	6
50–59	15	5	2
60–69	12	9	1
70–79	6	13	1
80–89	3	15	
90–99	1	11	

7. For a normally distributed population approximately 68% of the population lies within ± 1 standard deviation from the mean, and approximately 95% of the population lies within ± 2 standard deviations from the mean.

A piece of radioactive materal emits particles which when counted have a normal distribution with mean 100 particles/second and standard deviation 10 particles/second.
In 2000 separate counts, each of length 1 second, how many approximately will have counts of
1 between 90 and 110 particles,
2 between 80 and 120 particles,
3 between 80 and 100 particles ?

PUZZLE

44. A group of people on a coach outing went into a cafe for a snack. The party leader ordered a cup of tea and a sandwich for everyone, and the total bill came to £18.49. How many people were on the coach ?

19 **Gradients and areas**

The topics in this chapter include:

- calculating growth and decay rates and displaying them graphically,
- constructing tangents to graphs to find the gradient,
- finding the approximate area between a curve and the horizontal axis and interpreting the result.

Gradients

Gradient of a chord

A line joining two points on a curve is called a chord of the curve.

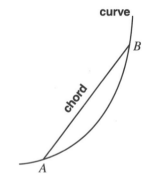

$$\text{Gradient of chord } AB = \frac{y\text{-coordinate of } B - y\text{-coordinate of } A}{x\text{-coordinate of } B - x\text{-coordinate of } A}$$

E.g. If A is (0.7, 1.2) and B is (5.2, 15.6),

$$\text{gradient of chord } AB = \frac{15.6 - 1.2}{5.2 - 0.7}$$

$$= \frac{14.4}{4.5}$$

$$= 3.2$$

The average rate of increase or decrease of y between two points on a graph, can be found from the gradient of the **chord** joining these points.

Gradient of a curve at a point

Draw the tangent to the curve at the point. (The tangent is the line which touches the curve at that point.)
Find the gradient of the tangent, by taking any two points on it and using their coordinates.
The gradient of the curve = the gradient of the tangent to the curve.

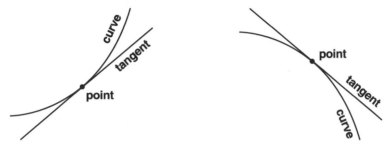

In the 1st diagram the gradient is positive, in the 2nd diagram it is negative.

The gradient of the curve shows the **rate of change**, which can be a rate of increase or decrease.

Example

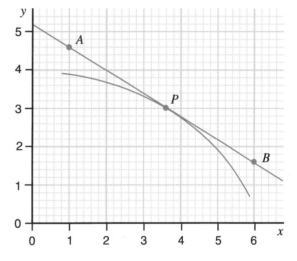

1   In the diagram, find the gradient of the curve at the point $P(3.6, 3)$.

Draw the tangent to the curve at P. Choose 2 points on the tangent and call them A and B. Find their coordinates. (It simplifies the calculation if you choose points with integer x-values.)

Here, A is $(1, 4.6)$, B is $(6, 1.6)$.

Gradient of the curve at P
= gradient of the tangent at P

$$= \frac{y\text{-coordinate of } B - y\text{-coordinate of } A}{x\text{-coordinate of } B - x\text{-coordinate of } A}$$

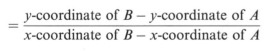

$$= \frac{1.6 - 4.6}{6 - 1} = \frac{-3.0}{5} = -0.6$$

The gradient of the curve at P is -0.6.
It is negative because the curve is sloping downwards.
At the point P the curve is decreasing at the rate of 0.6 units of y per unit of x.

Maximum and minimum points

At these points the gradient of the tangent is 0.

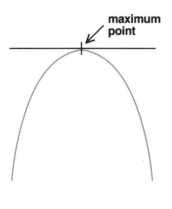 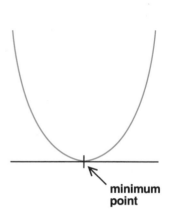

Distance-time graphs

The rate at which distance is travelled is called **speed**.
Velocity is a word used instead of speed when the direction of motion is included, so that if one direction is regarded as positive, a speed in the opposite direction will have a negative velocity.

To find velocity from a distance-time graph

The average velocity from *A* to *B* is given by the gradient of the chord *AB*.

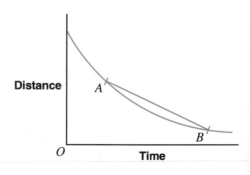

The actual velocity at C is given by the gradient of the tangent of the curve, at C.

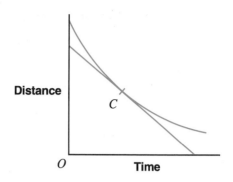

On this diagram the velocity is negative. This means that the object is travelling in the opposite direction to that in which the distance is measured.
The speed has the same numerical value as the velocity, but it is positive.
e.g. If the velocity is -5 m/s, the speed is 5 m/s.

On a distance-time graph, if at any point the gradient of the tangent to the curve is 0, the velocity at that point is 0, so at that time the object is at rest, possibly just for an instant.

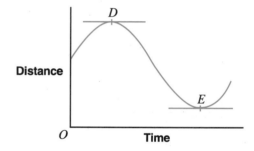

On the sketch graph the velocity is 0 at D and E.

Example

2   Here is the distance-time graph of a particle moving along a straight line.
   (1)   Find the average velocity between times $t = 1$ and $t = 3$.
   (2)   Find the actual velocity at time $t = 2$.

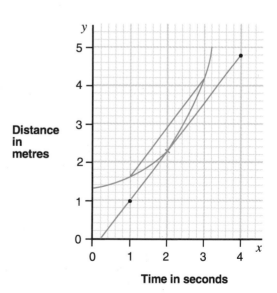

(1) Average velocity

   $=$ gradient of chord

   $= \dfrac{\text{increase in distance}}{\text{increase in time}}$

   $= \dfrac{4.1 - 1.6}{3 - 1}$ m/s $= 1.3$ m/s

(2) Velocity at time $t = 2$,

   $=$ gradient of tangent

   $= \dfrac{4.8 - 1.0}{4 - 1}$ m/s

   $= 1.3$ m/s

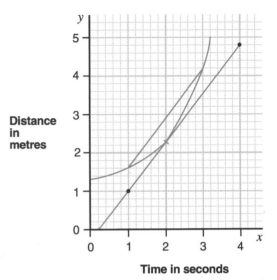

Distance in metres

Time in seconds

Velocity-time graphs

The rate at which velocity increases with time is called **acceleration**.
A negative acceleration is called a retardation or deceleration.

   Acceleration $= \dfrac{\text{increase in velocity}}{\text{increase in time}}$

If velocity is given in m/s and time in seconds then the acceleration is measured in metres per second, per second, which is written in symbols as m/s^2 or ms^{-2}.

To find acceleration from a velocity-time graph

The acceleration at A is given by the gradient of the tangent at A.

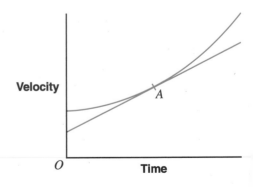

Velocity

O **Time**

On a velocity-time graph, if at a point
the gradient of the tangent is 0, at that
time the object has no acceleration.

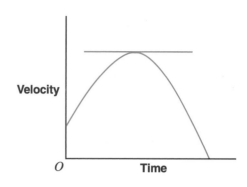

Example

3   Here is a velocity-time graph
     of a particle moving along a
     straight line.
     Find the acceleration at time
     $t = 3$.

     Acceleration = gradient of tangent

     $$= \frac{\text{increase in velocity}}{\text{increase in time}}$$

     $$= \frac{38 - 11}{4 - 2} \text{ cm/s}^2$$

     $$= 13.5 \text{ cm/s}^2$$

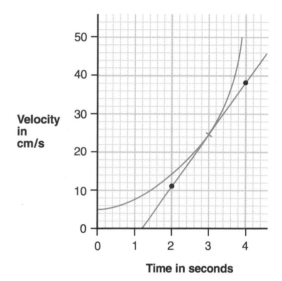

Curves of growth

For curves with an equation of the form $y = a^t$, where t is the time
and a is a positive constant number, the graph looks like this.

The rate of increase of y at any time is given by the gradient of the
tangent to the curve at that time.
It is proportional to the value of y at that time.

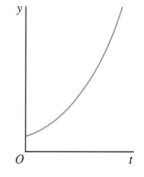

1   The growth of a population of bacteria which increases at
     any time by a constant percentage of the number present at
     that time has a graph of this form.

2   The amount of money at any time when compound interest at a fixed rate of interest is
     added to the amount at fixed intervals of time has a graph which approximates to this
     curve. (The true graph would go up in steps since interest is not added continuously but
     only at fixed intervals, such as once a year or once a month.)

Curves of decay

For curves with an equation of the form $y = a^{-t}$, where t is the time, the graph looks like this.

The rate of decrease at any time is given by the gradient of the tangent to the curve at that time, ignoring the negative sign, and it slows down as time increases.
It is proportional to the value of y at that time.

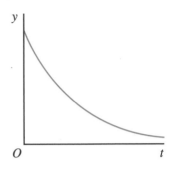

1   The amount of radioactivity in a radioactive substance has a graph of this form.
The **half-life** of a radioactive substance is the time it would take from any instant to lose half of its radioactivity.

2   The value of an article which depreciates in value at any time at a constant rate of its value at that time has a similar graph. (If the depreciation is subtracted at fixed intervals, not continuously, the graph goes down in steps but approximates to the curve.)

Exercise 19.1

1.   Draw the graph of $y = x^2$ for values of x from 0 to 8, labelling the y-axis from 0 to 70.
Draw the tangents to the curve at the points with x-coordinates 2, 4, 6, and calculate their gradients.
Copy and complete this table.

x-coordinate of the point	0	2	4	6	8
Gradient of the curve at the point	0				16

Is there a pattern in the results ?
At what point would the curve have gradient 10 ?

2.   Draw the x-axis from 0 to 8 and the y-axis from 0 to 16.
Make a table of values for the graph of $y = (x - 4)^2$ for x from 0 to 8.
Draw the graph.
What is the gradient of the curve at the point where $x = 4$?
Find the gradient of the curve at the points where $x = 2$ and $x = 5$.
By symmetry, what are the gradients of the curve at the points where $x = 6$ and $x = 3$?
Make a table of your results.
Is there a pattern in the results ? If so, can you deduce a value for the gradient of the curve at the point where $x = 7$?

3. Draw the graph of $y = x^3$ for values of x from -2 to 3.
    Draw tangents to the curve at $x = 1$ and $x = 2$ and calculate their gradients.
    Estimate the gradients of the tangents at $x = 0$, $x = -1$ and $x = -2$.
    Copy and complete this table, where the gradients of the tangents to the curve at $x = 3$
    and $x = 4$ have also been given.

x	-2	-1	0	1	2	3	4
Gradient of curve						27	48

Can you discover a pattern in the results ?

4. The table gives the heights of an object projected vertically upwards from ground level.

Time in seconds	0	1	2	3	4	5
Height in metres	0	20	30	30	20	0

Draw a horizontal axis from 0 to 5 (for time, in seconds) and a vertical axis from 0 to
40 (for height, in metres). Plot the points and join them with a smooth curve.
Estimate the maximum height the object attains. At what times is the object 10 m above
the ground ?
By drawing a tangent to the curve and calculating its gradient, find an estimate of the
speed of the object at time $1\frac{1}{2}$ seconds.

5. A particle leaves a point O and moves in a straight line so that its distance, s metres,
    from O at time t seconds after leaving O is as given in the table.

t	0	$\frac{1}{2}$	1	2	3	4	5	$5\frac{1}{2}$	6
s	0	2.5	4	5	4.5	4	5	6.5	9

1   Draw the distance-time graph for t from 0 to 6, joining the points with a smooth curve.
2   At what times after leaving O is the particle's velocity zero ?
3   Find the velocity 5 seconds after leaving O.

6. A train starts from a rest at a station A and increases speed at a steady rate for
    2 minutes until it reaches a speed of 100 km/h. It maintains this steady speed for
    12 minutes, and then slows down at a steady rate of 20 km/h per minute until it comes
    to a stop at station B.
    Represent this information graphically on a speed-time graph.

1   How far does the train travel at its highest speed ?
2   What is its speed after $\frac{1}{2}$ minute, and at what time is it next travelling at this speed ?

7. The table shows the speed of a train at various times as it travels between two stations.

Time from start, in seconds	0	15	30	45	60	75	90	105	120
Speed, in m/s	0	9	14	18	21	21	18	11	0

Draw a speed-time graph, joining the points with a smooth curve.

Find from the graph
1   the greatest speed of the train,
2   the two times when the train was travelling at half its greatest speed.
3   By drawing a tangent to the curve, find the retardation 105 seconds after the start.

8. An open metal tank is to be made with a horizontal square base of side x m and volume 18 m^3. Find the height of the tank in terms of x. Show that the total area of metal used is $\left(x^2 + \dfrac{72}{x} \right)$ m^2.

Make a table of values for the graph of $y = x^2 + \dfrac{72}{x}$ for $x = 1, 2, 3, 4, 5, 6$.

Draw the x-axis from 0 to 6 and the y-axis from 0 to 80, and draw the graph of $y = x^2 + \dfrac{72}{x}$.

Find the approximate value of x for which y is a minimum.
Hence find the measurements of the tank for which the area of metal used is a minimum.

9. The temperature of water in a jug is shown in this table.

Time in minutes	0	2	4	6	8	10	12
Temperature in °C	100	60	40	30	25	23	21

Plot the points on a graph, with time on the horizontal axis, and join them with a smooth curve.
Find the average rate of cooling in the first 10 minutes (in degrees per minute).
By drawing a tangent to the curve, estimate the rate of cooling at time 2 minutes.

10. A certain population of bacteria increases continuously at such a rate that it doubles every hour.
If the initial population is 1000, make a table showing the population every hour for the next 5 hours.
Draw a graph with time on the horizontal axis and number in the population on the vertical axis.
Find the approximate time when the population will be 10 000.
By drawing tangents to the graph find the rates of growth per hour at times 2 hours and 4 hours.

To find the area under a curve

When we refer to the area under a curve we mean the area between the curve and the x-axis. So the area under the curve between the lines $x = a$ and $x = b$ is shown shaded in the sketch.

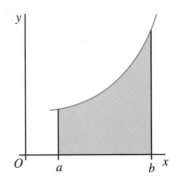

The area under this straight line is in the shape of a trapezium.
If the heights are y_0 and y_1 and the width is $b - a$,

> Area $= \frac{1}{2}$ (sum of parallel sides)
> $\quad\quad \times$ distance between them
>
> $\quad = \frac{1}{2}(y_0 + y_1)(b - a)$

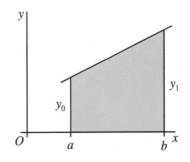

Example

1   Find the area under the line $y = 2x + 5$ between the points $(2, 9)$ and $(6, 17)$.

The heights (parallel sides) are 9 and 17.
The distance between them $= 6 - 2 = 4$
Area $= \frac{1}{2} \times (9 + 17) \times 4$
$\quad\quad = 52$ unit^2

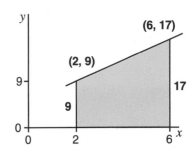

The area under a curve can be estimated.

Finding the area by counting squares

Count the number of squares on the grid.
For part squares, if the area included is half or
more of a square, count it as a whole square,
and if the area included is less than half of a
square, ignore it. The errors by taking these
approximations should balance each other
fairly well.
This is a rather tedious method.
Here there are approximately 150 small squares.
25 of these make 1 unit square.

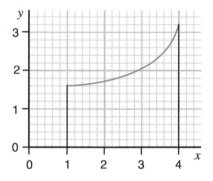

Area $= \frac{150}{25} = 6.0$ unit^2 approximately.

Finding the area by using the trapezium rule

If we divide the total area into thin vertical strips
of equal widths, each strip has approximately
the shape of a trapezium. We can calculate the
areas of these trapeziums.
The more strips we use, the more accurate will
be the result.

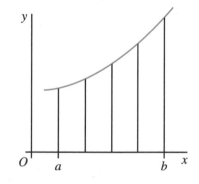

1st strip is nearly a trapezium.
Find the total width $b - a$ and hence find the value of x_1.
Find the y-values when $x = a$ and when $x = x_1$.

Area of trapezium $= \frac{1}{2}(y_0 + y_1)(x_1 - a)$

Similarly, find the other areas and add them
together to find the total area.

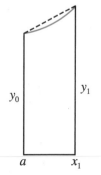

The areas all added together give the general formula for n strips:

> The area under curve $\approx \dfrac{h}{2}(y_0 + 2y_1 + 2y_2 + 2y_3 + \cdots + 2y_{n-1} + y_n)$

where h = width of a strip = $\dfrac{b-a}{n}$

and the y-values in order are $y_0, y_1, y_2, y_3, \ldots, y_{n-1}, y_n$.

$\approx$ means 'is approximately equal to'.

Example

2   Find the area under this curve between $x = 1$ and $x = 9$, by dividing it into 4 trapeziums.

1st method. Working out the area of each trapezium separately.

Each strip is 2 units wide.
Read off the y-values from the graph.

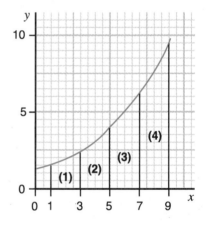

x	1	3	5	7	9
y	1.6	2.4	4.0	6.2	9.5

1st trapezium. Area = $\frac{1}{2} \times (1.6 + 2.4) \times 2 = 4.0$
2nd trapezium. Area = $\frac{1}{2} \times (2.4 + 4.0) \times 2 = 6.4$
3rd trapezium. Area = $\frac{1}{2} \times (4.0 + 6.2) \times 2 = 10.2$
4th trapezium. Area = $\frac{1}{2} \times (6.2 + 9.5) \times 2 = \underline{15.7}$
$\qquad\qquad\qquad\qquad\qquad\qquad\qquad\qquad = 36.3$

Total area = 36.3.
The area under the curve is approximately 36 unit^2.

2nd method. Using the formula.

$h = 2, \quad y_0 = 1.6, \quad y_1 = 2.4, \quad y_2 = 4.0, \quad y_3 = 6.2, \quad y_4 = 9.5.$

Area under curve $\approx \dfrac{h}{2}(y_0 + 2y_1 + 2y_2 + 2y_3 + y_4)$
$\qquad\qquad\qquad = \frac{2}{2} \times (1.6 + 2 \times 2.4 + 2 \times 4.0 + 2 \times 6.2 + 9.5)$
$\qquad\qquad\qquad = 36.3 \text{ unit}^2$

Why will the approximate area, in this case, be slightly **greater** than the actual area ?

To find distance from a velocity-time graph

The area under the graph (i.e. between the graph and the time axis) gives the **distance** travelled between the two times.

If the velocity is in m/s and the time in seconds then the distance will be in metres.

Graphs showing steady velocity or steady acceleration

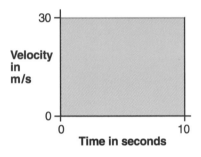

An object moving at 30 m/s for 10 seconds will have travelled 300 metres.
This is represented by the area of the rectangle.

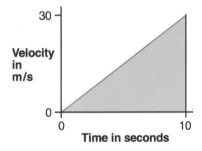

An object starting from rest and increasing speed steadily over 10 seconds to 30 m/s will have travelled 150 metres.
This is represented by the area of the triangle.

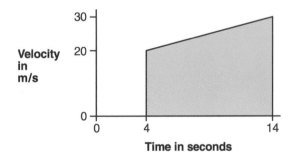

An object moving with steadily increasing speed from 20 m/s at time 4 seconds to 30 m/s at time 14 seconds will have travelled between those times a distance represented by the area of the trapezium.

Area $= \frac{1}{2}$ (sum of parallel sides)
$\qquad \times$ distance between them
$\qquad = \frac{1}{2} \times (20 + 30) \times (14 - 4)$
$\qquad = 250$
Distance $= 250$ m

Graphs with variable velocity and acceleration

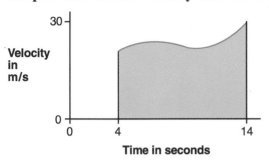

The distance travelled between times 4 seconds and 14 seconds is represented by the area under the curve between these times. This area can be estimated.

Examples

3   A car increases velocity at a steady rate from 50 km/h to 70 km/h over 6 seconds. What is the distance travelled during this time ?

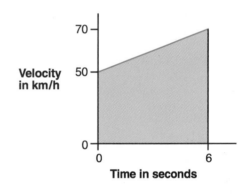

Distance = shaded area

$$= \tfrac{1}{2}(y_0 + y_1)h$$

$$= \tfrac{1}{2} \times (50 + 70) \times \frac{6}{60 \times 60} \text{ km}$$

$$= \tfrac{1}{10} \text{ km} = 100 \text{ m}$$

(Since the velocity was given in km/h, to correspond, the time had to be given in hours,

so it was $\dfrac{6}{60 \times 60}$ hours, and then the distance was given in km.

Alternatively, the velocities could have been changed into km/s and the time left in seconds.)

4   The speed of a racing car during the first minute after starting from rest is given in this table.

Time in seconds	0	10	20	30	40	50	60
Speed in m/s	0	28	46	51	47	43	46

Draw the velocity-time graph, joining the points with a smooth curve. By dividing the area under the graph into 6 trapeziums of equal width, estimate the distance travelled in the first minute.

Width of each trapezium or triangle $= 10$

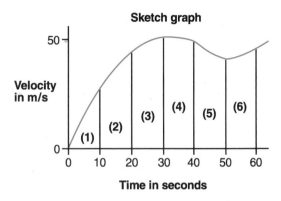

Sketch graph

Triangle (1).   Area $= \frac{1}{2} \times 28 \times 10$ $= \;$ 140
Trapezium (2).   Area $= \frac{1}{2} \times (28 + 46) \times 10 = \;$ 370
Trapezium (3).   Area $= \frac{1}{2} \times (46 + 51) \times 10 = \;$ 485
Trapezium (4).   Area $= \frac{1}{2} \times (51 + 47) \times 10 = \;$ 490
Trapezium (5).   Area $= \frac{1}{2} \times (47 + 43) \times 10 = \;$ 450
Trapezium (6).   Area $= \frac{1}{2} \times (43 + 46) \times 10 = \;$ <u>445</u>
                                                                                2380

Total area $= 2380$.
Estimated distance travelled $= 2400$ m $= 2.4$ km, to 2 significant figures.

Or, using the formula,

$$\text{Area under curve} \approx \frac{h}{2} \left(y_0 + 2y_1 + 2y_2 + 2y_3 + 2y_4 + 2y_5 + y_6 \right)$$

$$= \tfrac{10}{2} \times (0 + 2 \times 28 + 2 \times 46 + 2 \times 51 + 2 \times 47 + 2 \times 43 + 46)$$

$$= 2380$$

Estimated distance travelled $= 2400$ m $= 2.4$ km, to 2 sig. fig.

Other graphs of rates of change

If you have a graph showing acceleration against time, then since acceleration is the rate of change of velocity, the area under the curve between two times gives the increase in velocity during that time interval.

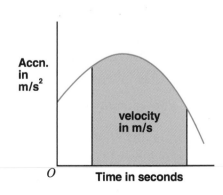

Similarly with other graphs.

From a graph showing rate of change of volume against time, the area under the curve between two times gives the increase in volume during that time interval.

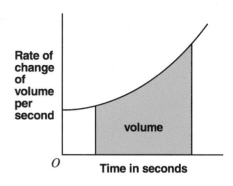

Exercise 19.2

1. A train starts from rest and for the first 70 seconds its speed increases steadily until it reaches 15 m/s. Then the speed immediately decreases at a constant rate until the train stops in a further 50 seconds.
    Sketch the speed-time graph for the train and find the distance travelled.

2. The graph shows the speed of an object over 10 seconds.

    Find
    1 the total distance travelled,
    2 the average speed over the 10 seconds,
    3 the retardation over the last 4 seconds.

    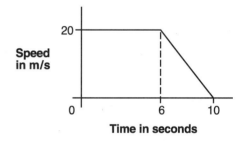

3. A cyclist starts from rest and after t seconds has a velocity of v m/s where $v = \frac{1}{4} t^2$.
    Sketch a graph of his velocity against time for the 1st 4 seconds.
    Use the trapezium rule with 4 strips of equal width to find the approximate distance he has travelled in the 1st 4 seconds.

4. The velocity, v m/s, after time t seconds of a particle moving in a straight line is given by the equation $v = 3t^2 + 2t + 4$.
    Draw a velocity-time graph for the 1st 5 seconds.

    1 Find the acceleration when $t = 3$.
    2 Use the trapezium rule with 5 strips of equal width to find the approximate distance travelled in the 1st 5 seconds.

5. A car starts from rest and increases its speed steadily for 12 seconds, travelling 96 m in this time.
    Sketch a speed-time graph of its motion.
    Calculate the speed at the end of 12 seconds.
    How far does the car travel in the first 6 seconds ?

6. A scale drawing of a field is shown here. It is bounded by straight fences on 3 sides and the 4th side is bounded by a stream.
    Find an approximate value for the area of the field.

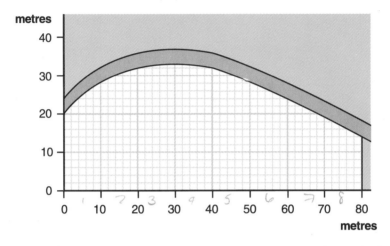

7. Copy and complete the table of values for the function $y = 2 + 2x - \frac{1}{2}x^2$ and draw the graph of the function for x from 0 to 4.

x	0	$\frac{1}{2}$	1	$1\frac{1}{2}$	2	$2\frac{1}{2}$	3	$3\frac{1}{2}$	4
y	2	$2\frac{7}{8}$		$3\frac{7}{8}$		$3\frac{7}{8}$		$2\frac{7}{8}$	

An archway is designed so that it has the shape shown. $OA = 4$ m, $OC = AB = 2$ m and OC and AB are vertical. The top of the arch is part of the curve $y = 2 + 2x - \frac{1}{2}x^2$, with x and y in metres.

1   Find the greatest height of the archway.
2   A door is to be made for the archway. Using the trapezium rule and dividing it into 4 strips of equal width, find the area of the door (the shaded area).

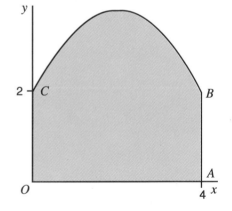

8. Oil is poured into a container at the rate of R ml/s, such that, at time t seconds, $R = 150 - 5t$.

1   Draw the graph of R against t, for t from 0 to 30.
2   At what rate is oil entering the container after 2 seconds ?
3   At what time is oil entering the container at the rate of 40 ml/s ?
4   The container is initially empty. Find the volume of oil in the container after 10 seconds. (The volume is given by the area under the graph.)
5   If the container is filled in 30 seconds, what volume does it hold ?

Exercise 19.3 Applications

1. A particle starts from a point A and moves in a straight line so that t seconds later its distance from A is s metres, as shown in the table.

t	0	$\frac{1}{2}$	1	2	3	4	5	6
s	0	15.4	26	36	36	32	30	36

   1 Draw the distance-time graph for the particle, joining the plotted points by a smooth curve.
   2 Find the velocity of the particle when $t = \frac{1}{2}$.
   3 Find the times when the velocity is zero.

2. A water tank contains 40 gallons of water. Water is taken from the tank and, after a certain time, a tap is turned on to refill it. The table shows the number of gallons, n, of water in the tank at time t minutes after the water was first taken from the tank.

t	0	1	2	3	4	5	6
n	40	35	29	18	15	23	40

   1 Draw a graph showing the amount of water in the tank at times up to 6 minutes, joining the plotted points with a smooth curve.
   2 Estimate the time at which the tap was turned on.
   3 At what times were there 20 gallons of water in the tank ?
   4 Find the rate at which the water was flowing out of the tank when $t = 1\frac{1}{2}$.

3. The graph shows the population of an island between the years of 1960 and 1990.

   1 What was the percentage increase in population between 1960 and 1970 ?
   2 What was the population in 1975 ?
   3 What was the rate of growth of the population (per year) in 1975 ?

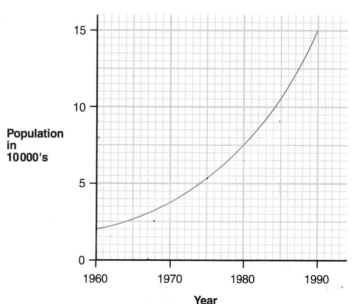

4. The graph is the speed-time graph of a train.

Find
1 the acceleration of the train during the first 3 minutes (in km/min^2),
2 the distance travelled in the first 6 minutes.

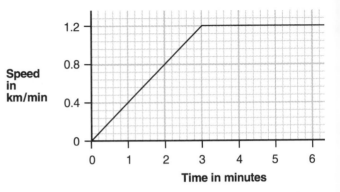

5. Two vehicles A and B start from rest at the same time, and A's speed for the first 20 seconds is given in this table.

Time in seconds	0	4	8	12	16	18	20
Speed in m/s	0	1	3	7	13	15	16

The speed of B increases steadily at the rate of 0.75 m/s^2 for the first 20 seconds. Draw the speed-time graphs for A and B for the first 20 seconds.

From the graphs
1 find the time when A and B are moving at the same speed,
2 estimate the times when A has the same acceleration as B,
3 find the distance travelled by B in the first 20 seconds,
4 estimate the distance travelled by A in the first 20 seconds, by dividing the area under the curve into 5 strips of equal width.

6. A spring is stretched so that the rate of increase of its length, R cm/s, after t seconds is given by the equation $R = 0.4 - 0.01\,t$.
The unstretched length of the spring is 10 cm.

1 Draw the graph of R against t, for t from 0 to 30.
2 At what rate is the spring being stretched after 5 s ?
3 At what time is the spring being stretched at the rate of 0.3 cm/s ?
4 Find the increase in length in the first 6 s. (This is given by the area under the graph.)
5 The stretching continues for 30 s. What is the final length of the spring ?

7. A piece of land has one straight boundary, 200 m long and one continuous irregular boundary. Perpendicular offsets are taken from the straight boundary to the irregular boundary at 25 m intervals and the distances measured are shown in the table.

Offset number	1	2	3	4	5	6	7	8	9
Length in metres	0	13	29	37	50	45	30	9	0

Sketch a plan with the straight boundary drawn horizontally and the offsets drawn upwards from it.
Find the area of the land by using the trapezium rule.

Practice test 19

1. Draw axes with x and y from 0 to 8 and equal scales on both axes.
   With compasses, centre at the origin, radius 6 units, draw the quarter-circle which lies within the graph.
   Let A, B and C be points on the circumference of the quarter-circle where $x = 1$, 3 and 5 respectively.
   Draw the tangents to the circle at A, B and C and find their gradients.

2. Use the quarter-circle you have drawn for question 1.
   Find the approximate area between the curve and the axes, by dividing it vertically into 6 strips of equal width and using the trapezium rule. (Read the y-values from your graph.)
   Check your answer by using the formula for the area of a circle.
   Is the approximate answer slightly less, or slightly greater, than the true value ? Explain why this is so.

3. A particle leaves a point O and moves in a straight line so that after t seconds its distance, s cm, from O is as given in the table.

t	0	$\frac{1}{2}$	1	$1\frac{1}{2}$	2	$2\frac{1}{2}$	3	$3\frac{1}{2}$	4
s	0	3.1	4	3.4	2	0.6	0	0.9	4

   1 Draw the distance-time graph for t from 0 to 4, joining the points with a smooth curve.
   2 At what times is the velocity zero ?
   3 Find the velocity of the particle when $t = 2.2$.

4. Draw a graph to represent the journey of a car which starts from rest and increases its speed uniformly for 10 seconds, reaching a speed of 30 m/s. It maintains this speed for 30 seconds and then decreases its speed uniformly at the rate of 2 m/s per second until it comes to rest.

   Put time on the horizontal axis, from 0 to 55 s.
   Put speed on the vertical axis, from 0 to 30 m/s.

   1 What is the acceleration during the 1st part of the journey ?
   2 What is the speed of the car at time 45 s ?
   3 What is the total distance travelled when the car comes to rest ?

20 Accuracy and error

The topics in this chapter include:

- understanding upper and lower bounds of numbers,
- calculating the upper and lower bounds in the addition, subtraction, multiplication and division of numbers,
- determining the possible effects of error on calculations.

Upper and lower bounds of numbers

Examples

Number	expressed to	lower bound of number	upper bound of number
8	nearest whole number	7.5	8.5
9	nearest whole number	8.5	9.5
12	nearest whole number	11.5	12.5
20	nearest whole number	19.5	20.5
3.4	1 decimal place	3.35	3.45
6.9	1 decimal place	6.85	6.95
8.0	1 decimal place	7.95	8.05
2.01	2 decimal places	2.005	2.015
4.56	2 decimal places	4.555	4.565
8.00	2 decimal places	7.995	8.005
20	nearest ten	15	25
300	nearest whole number	299.5	300.5
300	nearest ten	295	305
300	nearest hundred	250	350

The number 8.5 is exactly halfway between 8 and 9. It is the upper bound of 8, and the lower bound of 9. It could be corrected down to 8, or corrected up to 9. You should normally correct it up. This is a rule made for convenience, and to make it clear, we repeat it here.

> Work to one more figure than you need.
>
> If that figure is 5 or more, correct up.
>
> If that figure is 4 or less, do not correct up.

However, considering the procedure in reverse, we have to **include the upper and lower bounds** as possible original numbers.

Notice the differences with the boundaries for 8 (to the nearest whole number), 8.0 (to 1 decimal place) and 8.00 (to 2 decimal places).

If you correct a number to 1 decimal place, and the number in this decimal place is 0, you should still write it in the answer to show that you are working correct to 1 decimal place.
e.g. $16.1 \div 4 = 4.025$
$\qquad\qquad = 4.0$, correct to 1 dec. pl.
If you correct a number to 2 decimal places and the number in the 2nd decimal place is 0, you should still write it in the answer to show that you are working correct to 2 decimal places.
e.g. $3 \times \tan 25° = 1.3989\ldots$
$\qquad\qquad = 1.40$, correct to 2 dec. pl.
By writing 1, 2 or more decimal places we can tell how accurate we have made the number.

With numbers of tens, i.e. 10, 20, 30, etc. it is not possible to tell whether they have been corrected to the nearest whole number, with a units figure which just happens to be 0, or corrected to the nearest ten.

20 to the nearest whole number can represent a number lying anywhere between 19.5 and 20.5 inclusive.
20 to the nearest ten can represent a number lying anywhere between 15 and 25 inclusive.

There are similar difficulties for hundreds, thousands, etc.

Significant figures

The boundaries when correcting to 1, 2, 3, ... significant figures are similar to those for correcting to whole numbers or to so many decimal places.

Accuracy of measurements

Since measurements are continuous, i.e. they go up gradually, not in jumps, all measurements are approximations.
e.g. If the length of a line is given as 10.8 cm then this has been measured to the nearest mm and the actual length can lie anywhere between 10.75 cm and 10.85 cm.
If the length was measured more accurately and given as 10.77 cm, the actual length could lie between 10.765 cm and 10.775 cm.

Calculations involving approximate numbers

Addition

If you add two approximate numbers then the total is also approximate.

Example

2.75 and 3.17 are each given to 2 decimal places.

$2.75 + 3.17 = 5.92$

Normally, we give the answer as 5.92, and you should continue to do this in most questions.

However, it is sometimes important to realise that the answer may differ from 5.92, and you may be asked to find the lower and upper bounds of the answer.

Lower bound.   2.75 has a lower bound of 2.745
                  3.17 has a lower bound of 3.165
                                             5.910

The lower bound of the sum is 5.91, written to 2 dec. pl.

Upper bound.   2.75 has an upper bound of 2.755
                  3.17 has an upper bound of 3.175
                                              5.930

The upper bound of the sum is 5.93, written to 2 dec. pl.

Subtraction

Using the same numbers as above, for $3.17 - 2.75$,

3.17	3.165	3.175
2.75	2.755	2.745
0.42	0.410	0.430

The usual answer would be 0.42, but the answer can range from 0.41 (lower bound) to 0.43 (upper bound).

Notice that to find the least difference, we take the lower bound of the larger number and the upper bound of the smaller number.
To find the greatest difference, we take the upper bound of the larger number and the lower bound of the smaller number.

Multiplication

$3.17 \times 2.75 = 8.7175 = 8.72$, to 2 dec. pl.

Lower bound:
$3.165 \times 2.745 = 8.687925 = 8.69$, to 2 dec. pl.
Upper bound:
$3.175 \times 2.755 = 8.747125 = 8.75$, to 2 dec. pl.

The usual answer would be 8.72, to 2 dec. pl., or 8.7, to 1 dec. pl.
2 decimal places would be suitable as the original numbers are given to 2 decimal places, but 1 decimal place might be better, considering that the possible answers can range from 8.69 to 8.75.

Division

$3.17 \div 2.75 = 1.1527\ldots = 1.153$, to 3 dec. pl.
$3.165 \div 2.755 = 1.1488\ldots = 1.149$, to 3 dec. pl.
$3.175 \div 2.745 = 1.1566\ldots = 1.157$, to 3 dec. pl.

The usual answer would be 1.153, to 3 dec. pl. For the possible answers the lower bound is 1.149 and the upper bound is 1.157.

3 decimal places would be suitable for a division question as the original number to be divided was given to 2 decimal places, but 2 decimal places might be better, considering the possible range of answers.

Notice that to find the lowest possible answer, divide the lower bound of the first number by the upper bound of the second number.
To find the highest possible answer, divide the upper bound of the first number by the lower bound of the second number.

Multiplication or division of an approximate number by an exact number

Examples

1   28.3×100

If 28.3 is a number correct to 1 decimal place then the lower bound is 28.25 and the upper bound is 28.35.
If 100 is an exact number, then
$28.3 \ \times 100 = 2830$
$28.25 \times 100 = 2825$
$28.35 \times 100 = 2835$

The usual answer is 2830, the lower bound is 2825 and the upper bound is 2835.

Notice that the possible error in 28.3 is ± 0.05, and when this is multiplied by 100 the possible error in the result is 100 times as large.
$\pm 0.05 \times 100 = \pm 5$.

Error used here does not mean mistake, it means the difference between the stated result and the true result.

2 $63 \div 5$

If 63 is a number correct to the nearest whole number then the lower bound is 62.5 and the upper bound is 63.5.
If 5 is an exact number, then
$63 \div 5 \;\; = 12.6$
$62.5 \div 5 = 12.5$
$63.5 \div 5 = 12.7$

The usual answer is 12.6, the lower bound is 12.5 and the upper bound is 12.7.

Notice that the possible error in 63 is ± 0.5, but when this is divided by 5, the possible error is $\frac{1}{5}$ of this.
$\pm 0.5 \div 5 = \pm 0.1$

Exercise 20.1

1.   Correct the numbers in these statements to the accuracy stated.

   1   The girl's height is 1.623 m. (To the nearest cm)
   2   The time taken to fill a tank was 2 h 43 min. (To the nearest 5 minutes)
   3   The attendance at a show was 2591 people. (To the nearest 100)
   4   The mean distance of the Moon from the Earth is 233 813 miles. (To the nearest 1000 miles)
   5   The capacity of a car's fuel tank is 40.914 ℓ. (To the nearest 5 ℓ)

2.   Give the lower and upper bounds of these numbers.

1	2.96	**6**	620 (given to the nearest ten)
2	0.607	**7**	21.0
3	5.226	**8**	8700 (given to the nearest hundred)
4	63	**9**	24.00
5	2.05	**10**	8300 (given to 3 significant figures)

3.   Work out these calculations, where each number is given to 2 decimal places. Give the usual answer, and also the lower and upper bounds of the possible answers, all to 2 decimal places.

1	$1.73 + 7.04$	**4**	33.45×3.52
2	$6.01 - 3.62$	**5**	6.61^2
3	68.34×8.76		

4.   Work out these calculations, where each number is given to the nearest whole number. Give the usual answer, and also the lower and upper bounds of the possible answers, all to 2 significant figures.

1	$23 + 38$	**4**	$37 \div 80$
2	$66 - 16$	**5**	$82 \div 16$
3	13×6		

5. Work out these calculations, where each number is given to 1 decimal place. Give the usual answer, and also the lower and upper bounds of the possible answers, all to 3 significant figures.

    1 62.9 + 6.3   **4** 91.6 ÷ 2.4
    2 69.0 − 2.7   **5** 20.9 ÷ 8.7
    3 15.5 × 2.2

6. Work out these calculations, where the first number is given correct to 3 significant figures, and the second number is an exact number. Give the usual answer and also the lower and upper bounds of the possible answers, all to 3 significant figures.

    1 1.27 × 12   **4** 5.88 ÷ 7
    2 32.5 ÷ 20   **5** 23 800 ÷ 5
    3 0.194 × 16

7. The population of a region per km^2 is given as 58 to the nearest whole number. The area of the region is given as 6320 km^2, to the nearest 10 km^2.
    What are the lower and upper bounds for the actual population of the region ?

8. 4 sample packages were weighed, each to the nearest gram, and their weights were 395 g, 401 g, 426 g and 399 g.

    What are the lower and upper bounds for
    1 the total weight,
    2 the average (mean) weight, of the packages ?

Approximations in terms of error

If a number is given to the nearest whole number, e.g. 12, then the lower bound is 11.5 and the upper bound is 12.5.
The number can be written as 12 ± 0.5. The maximum error is 0.5.
Similarly, 2.8, correct to 1 decimal place, can be written as 2.8 ± 0.05.

Calculations can be carried out with numbers in this notation.
e.g. In the example on page 398, the numbers are 2.75 and 3.17. These can be written as 2.75 ± 0.005 and 3.17 ± 0.005.

Addition

Usual answer	lower bound	upper bound
2.75	2.75 − 0.005	2.75 + 0.005
3.17	3.17 − 0.005	3.17 + 0.005
5.92	5.92 − 0.01	5.92 + 0.01

The answer could be given as 5.92 ± 0.01

Subtraction

Usual answer	lower bound	upper bound
3.17	$3.17 - 0.005$	$3.17 + 0.005$
2.75	$2.75 + 0.005$	$2.75 - 0.005$
0.42	$0.42 - 0.01$	$0.42 + 0.01$

The answer could be given as 0.42 ± 0.01.

Multiplication

We use the rules for multiplying out brackets, and ignore the term 0.005×0.005 as it is so small.

Usual answer: $3.17 \times 2.75 = 8.7175$

Lower bound: $(3.17 - 0.005)(2.75 - 0.005)$

$$= 8.7175 - (0.005 \times 3.17) - (0.005 \times 2.75)$$
$$= 8.7175 - 0.0296$$

Upper bound: $(3.17 + 0.005)(2.75 + 0.005)$

$$= 8.7175 + (0.005 \times 3.17) + (0.005 \times 2.75)$$
$$= 8.7175 + 0.0296$$

The answer could be given as 8.72 ± 0.03, to 2 dec. pl.

It is not so easy to adapt this method for division.

Absolute error and percentage error

The error, or **absolute error**, is the difference between the estimated value and the true value.

e.g. If the true value is £82.55 and the estimated value is £80, the absolute error is £82.55 − £80 = £2.55.
The absolute error is in the same units as the true value, and it is always positive.

The relative error $= \dfrac{\text{absolute error}}{\text{true value}}$

e.g. If the true value is £82.55 and the estimated value is £80, the relative error is $\dfrac{2.55}{82.55} = 0.031$, to 2 significant figures.

The relative error is often expressed as a percentage and this is called a percentage error.

$$\textbf{Percentage error} = \frac{\text{absolute error}}{\text{true value}} \times 100\,\%$$

In the example above, the percentage error $= 3.1\,\%$, to 1 dec. pl.

Example

If you measure a line to the nearest mm, and get 7.8 cm, then the upper bound is 7.85 cm and the lower bound is 7.75 cm.
The maximum absolute error is 0.05 cm.

Since we do not know the true length, we use the measured length as an approximation for the true length in the formula for the percentage error.

$$\text{Approximate maximum percentage error} = \frac{0.05}{7.8} \times 100\,\% = 0.6\,\%, \text{ to 1 dec. pl.}$$

Error given as a percentage

e.g. If a length is given as 50 m with a possible 3% error then the possible actual error is 3% of 50 m $= 1.5$ m, and the bounds of the length are (50 ± 1.5) m.

In general, if a value is v and the possible percentage error is $p\,\%$, then the possible actual error is $\dfrac{pv}{100}$ and the upper and lower bounds of the value are $v \pm \dfrac{pv}{100} = v\left(1 \pm \dfrac{p}{100}\right)$.

Exercise 20.2

Repeat some of the questions 3, 4, 5, 6 of Exercise 20.1, page 400, except for the division questions, using numbers in the form $a \pm$ error, and compare your answers with those obtained by using the other method.

1. Find the maximum absolute error and the approximate value for the maximum percentage error in these estimations.

   1 A length of 5.3 cm, correct to the nearest mm.
   2 A weight of 1.72 kg, to 2 dec. pl.
   3 £310, correct to the nearest £10.
   4 7 months, correct to the nearest month.

2. Find the percentage error in these estimations.

   1 A measured length was 6.7 cm; the true length was calculated as 6.56 cm.
   2 A measured weight was 4.1 kg; the true weight was calculated as 4.25 kg.
   3 π was estimated as 3.1. Use the value given by your calculator as the true value.

3.   A side of a field was 360 m long, to the nearest 10 metres. Find the maximum absolute
      error and the approximate maximum percentage error for this length.
      The length was divided into 30 equal parts, for building plots. How long was one plot ?
      Find the maximum absolute error and the approximate percentage error for the lengths
      of the plots.
      Comment on the answers.

4.   The capacity of a storage tank was given as 75 400 litres, with a possible percentage error
      of 5%. What are the lower and upper bounds of the capacity ?

Exercise 20.3   Applications

1.   A square courtyard has sides of length 27 m, correct to the nearest metre.
      What are the lower and upper bounds for
      1   the perimeter,
      2   the area of the courtyard ?

2.   The weight of 1 cm^3 of gold is stated to be 19.3 g, to 3 significant figures.
      What are the lower and upper bounds for the weight of 20 cm^3 of gold ?

3.   David tried to find the value of π by measuring the circumference and diameter of a
      wheel. To the nearest cm these lengths were 163 cm and 52 cm respectively.
      What are the lower and upper bounds for the experimental value he obtained for π ?

4.   A metal rod was measured as 142.1 cm. After a length was cut off, its new length was
      58.4 cm. The measurements were made to the nearest mm.
      What are the least and greatest values of the reduction in length ?

5.   The average daily rainfall for a month of 30 days was given as 0.42 cm, to 0.01 cm. What
      are the lower and upper bounds of the total rainfall for the month ?

6.   A formula is given as $t = \dfrac{p}{4d - a}$. If $p = 6.9$, $d = 3.4$ and $a = 5.0$, all these values being
      correct to 1 decimal place, find the lower and upper bounds for the value of t.

7.   Small components each weighed 3.8 g. Find the maximum absolute error and the
      approximate maximum percentage error for one component.
      20 components were packed together. What is their total weight ? What is the maximum
      absolute error and the approximate maximum percentage error of this total weight ?
      Comment on the answers.

8. $\sqrt{3}$ was estimated as 1.7. Use the value given by your calculator as the true value, and find the percentage error in the approximation.

9. Two sides of a rectangular lawn are measured as 15.1 m and 12.8 m, both with a maximum percentage error of 2%.
   Find the lower and upper bounds of
   1 the length of the lawn,
   2 the width,
   3 the perimeter,
   4 the area.

Practice test 20

1. Correct the numbers in these statements to the accuracy stated.

   1 The average weight of 7 children was 50.1429 kg. (To the nearest kg)
   2 The amount of wine produced was 716.583 litres. (To the nearest litre)
   3 The population of the town was 261 704. (To the nearest 1000)
   4 The length of the race (3 miles) is 4828.032 m. (To the nearest 10 m)
   5 The speed of light is 299 792.458 km/s. (To the nearest 1000 km/s)

2. Find the value of $\dfrac{65.3 + 14.9}{85.0}$ to 3 significant figures.

   If all the numbers are correct to 1 decimal place, find the lower and upper bounds of the answer.

3. An empty jar weighs 285 g and when it is full of jam it weighs 872 g. If each measurement is correct to the nearest gram, what are the lower and upper bounds for the weight of the jam ?

4. If 25 marbles weigh 730 g, correct to the nearest 10 g, what are the lower and upper bounds for the average weight of one marble ?

5. Two sides of a rectangle were measured to the nearest mm, as 6.3 cm and 4.1 cm.

   1 Find the least and greatest possible values of the perimeter.
   2 Find the least and greatest possible values of the area.

6. An exact distance of 24.8 m is estimated incorrectly as 25 m. What is the percentage error in the estimate ?

Miscellaneous Section D

Exercise D1   Revision

1. If $AX = 4$ cm and $XB = 3$ cm, what are the ratios of

    1 $XY : BC$,
    2 area $\triangle AXY$: area $\triangle ABC$?

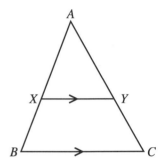

2. Factorise

    1 $x^2 + 16x$
    2 $x^2 - 16$
    3 $x^2 + 16x - 80$
    4 $x^2 - 16x + 60$

3. A parallelogram has base 8×10^{-2} m and height 6.5×10^{-2} m. Find its area in m^2, giving your answer in standard form.

4. Draw a triangle ABC with $BC = 10$ cm, $AB = 6$ cm and $\angle B = 55°$. Draw the locus of points inside the triangle which are (1) equidistant from AB and AC, (2) 2.5 cm from the mid-point of BC. Find a point P which lies on (1) and (2), and measure PA.

5. Here are the results of a (fictitious) survey in which people were given a list of activities they could take part in, and they were asked to give their 1st 3 choices for what they wanted to do. Here are the results.

    Analyse the results and write down your conclusions, including saying which one of the activities you would choose as being the one most people wanted to do.

Activity	Number putting it		
	1st	2nd	3rd
P	4	2	0
Q	3	5	1
R	5	1	1
S	0	2	3
T	0	2	7

6. £100 was invested for a child and left for 5 years, to gain Compound Interest, until the child was older.

During the 1st 2 years the rate of interest was 6% per annum, then the rates for the next 3 years were 7%, 8% and 9% respectively.

Use your calculator to find how much money was in the account at the end of the 5 years, to the nearest 10p.

7. The table shows the heights of 120 seedlings.

Height in cm	0–2	2–4	4–6	6–8	8–10	10–12
Number	14	34	22	30	18	2

1 Draw a histogram of the distribution and describe its shape.
2 Make a cumulative frequency table and draw a cumulative frequency graph.
   From the graph find the median height and the interquartile range of heights of the seedlings.

8. The sides of a rectangle, each measured to the nearest cm, are 6 cm and 4 cm.

Find
1 the largest possible length of the perimeter,
2 the smallest possible length of the perimeter,
3 the largest possible area of the rectangle,
4 the smallest possible area.

9. Make a table of values for the graph of $y = 2^x$ for integer values of x from -4 to 4. Draw the x-axis from -4 to 4 and the y-axis from 0 to 20. Draw the graph of $y = 2^x$. Draw tangents to the curve at $x = -3, -1, 1, 3$ and find the gradients of these tangents. Copy and complete this table where the values of the gradients for $x = -4, -2, 0, 2, 4$ have been filled in.

x	-4	-3	-2	-1	0	1	2	3	4
y									
gradient of curve	0.04		0.17		0.69		2.8		11.1
$\dfrac{\text{gradient}}{y}$									

Fill in the results of $\dfrac{\text{gradient}}{y}$.

Are these results approximately constant ? If so, this shows that the gradient at any point is proportional to y.

10. Three boys, Paul, Quentin and Robert enter for a job selection test, and their chances of
     passing it, independently, are $\frac{1}{2}, \frac{4}{5}$, and $\frac{2}{3}$ respectively.

     What is the probability that
     1   all 3 boys pass,
     2   none of the boys passes,
     3   2 of the boys pass and the other one does not ?

11. A pyramid stands on a square base $ABCD$ of side 5 cm
     and its vertical height $VO = 7$ cm, where O is the centre
     of $ABCD$.

     Calculate
     1   the length of AO, to the nearest mm,
     2   the size of $\angle VAO$,
     3   the size of $\angle VMO$, where M is the mid-point of AB.

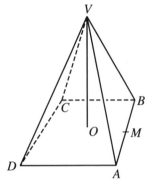

12. Say whether the roots (solutions) of these equations are rational or irrational.
     1   $13x - 7 = 2x + 3$
     2   $2x^2 + 3 = 28$
     3   $x^3 - 2 = 62$
     4   $\pi x = 50$

13. Find the mean, median, mode and standard deviation of this set of numbers.

     1   2   2   2   5   7   8   10   14   17   20

14. Work out the 1st 8 terms of this sequence, recording them to 3 decimal places. Say
     whether the sequence is convergent or divergent. If it is convergent, give the limit, correct
     to 2 decimal places.

     $u_{n+1} = \sqrt{u_n + 3}$, $u_1 = 2$.

15. 5 oranges and 2 lemons cost £1.05. 9 oranges and 1 lemon cost £1.37. Find the cost of
     1 orange, and of 1 lemon.

Exercise D2   Revision

1.   Three men weigh 60 kg, 58 kg and 68 kg. What is their average weight ? A fourth man
     joins them and the average weight of all four is 64 kg. What does the fourth man weigh ?

2. *ABCDEFGH* is a cuboid.
   A is the point $(2, 2, 0)$.
   B is the point $(18, 2, 0)$.
   D is the point $(2, 14, 0)$.
   E is the point $(2, 2, 15)$.
   Find the coordinates of the points *C*, *F*, *G* and *H*.
   Find the lengths of *AC* and *AG*.

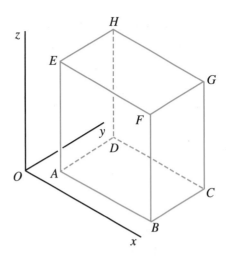

3. When a certain biased die is thrown, the probabilities of getting numbers 1 to 6 are as follows:

Number	1	2	3	4	5	6
Probability	$\frac{1}{24}$	$\frac{1}{6}$	$\frac{1}{12}$	$\frac{1}{4}$	$\frac{1}{8}$	$\frac{1}{3}$

   What is the probability of getting
   1 a 5 or a 6,
   2 a number less than 6,
   3 an even number ?

4. From a point on horizontal ground 700 m away from the base of a very tall tower, the angle of elevation of the top of the tower is $15°$. Find the height of the tower, to the nearest 10 m.

5. Pairs of values of simple functions are given in these tables. Find the equations connecting *x* and *y*.

1

x	-1	0	1	2	3
y	0	0	2	6	12

2

x	1	2	3	4	5
y	2	10	30	68	130

6. The graph shows the speed of a train which starts from A and increases speed steadily until it reaches 20 m/s. After keeping a steady speed for some time it then decreases its speed steadily until it stops at B.

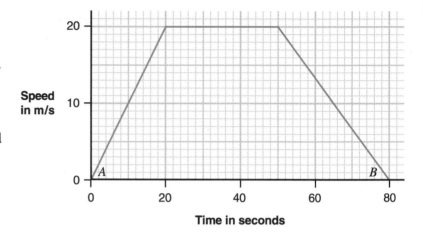

Speed in m/s

Time in seconds

1 For how long altogether was its speed greater than 12 m/s ?

2 What was the total distance travelled ?

7. Draw the graph of $y = x^2 + x - 3$ for values of x from -4 to 3.

1 What is the least value of y ?

2 Use your graph to solve the equation $x^2 + x - 3 = 0$, correct to 1 decimal place.

8. The heights of 200 plants are given in this table.

Height in cm	f
3–7	4
7–9	8
9–11	25
11–12	27
12–13	31
13–14	35
14–15	28
15–17	32
17–19	4
19–23	6
	200

Work out the heights of the columns for a histogram.

Draw a histogram of the distribution.

Comment on its shape.

9. The weight of a load of gravel was given as 5.4 tonnes, with a possible error of 2%. What are the lower and upper bounds of the weight ?

10. Solve these quadratic equations by trial, finding solutions which are positive integers.

1 $2x^2 - 5x - 88 = 0$

2 $(2x + 1)(x - 4) + 10 = 0$

11. A box contains 10 discs. 3 are red, 2 are yellow and 5 are green.
     Two discs are drawn out. (The first disc is not replaced before the second one is drawn out.)
     Show the results of the two drawings on a tree-diagram.

     Find the probability that
     1 both discs are red,
     2 both discs are the same colour,
     3 the discs are of different colours.

12. This figure is called a Reuleaux curve. It is constructed
     by drawing an equilateral triangle *ABC*. Then with
     centre *A*, radius *AB*, the arc *BC* is drawn.
     With centre *B*, arc *AC* is drawn and with centre *C*,
     arc *AB* is drawn.
     1 If $AB = l$ cm, find the length of the arc *AB*
     in terms of π and l.
     2 Prove that the figure has the same perimeter
     as that of a circle with diameter *AB*.

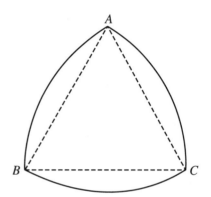

13. Find the lengths of *DE* and *DF* and state
     the ratio of area $\triangle ABC$: area $\triangle DEF$ in
     its simplest form.

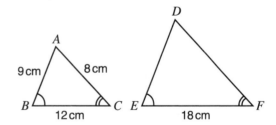

14. Copy and complete this table showing the size of an interior angle of a regular polygon.

Number of sides	3	4	5	6	8	9	10
Size of each interior angle (in degrees)	60						144

     On graph paper, label the horizontal axis for 'number of sides' from 3 to 10, and label
     the vertical axis for 'size of angle in degrees' from 0 to 180.
     Plot the values in the table on the graph.
     Join the points with a smooth curve. (Note that intermediate points on the curve have no
     meaning, except where the number of sides is 7.)
     Estimate the size of an interior angle of a regular polygon with 7 sides.

15.   The Council Tax payable by 6 householders is as follows:

Value of the property (£1000's)	30	50	65	80	120	150
Tax (to nearest £10)	430	510	580	650	800	940

Draw a scatter diagram of the data, with the value of the property on the horizontal axis and tax on the vertical axis.
Draw a line of best fit.
Use the line of best fit to determine how much tax a householder with a house worth £100 000 should pay.
In fact, the prices are calculated in bands, not as gradual increases, and that householder will pay the same as the one with a house worth £120 000. How much extra is this above your previous answer ?

Exercise D3   Revision

1.   On a small photograph, a building is 4 cm high and its area is 12 cm^2. On an enlargement, if the building is 10 cm high, what is its area ?

2.   The distributions of examinations marks in two examinations are shown in this table. Draw frequency polygons for these distributions on the same graph and comment on them.

Mark	20–29	30–39	40–49	50–59	60–69	70–79	80–89	90–99
1st exam	4	14	38	30	11	3		
2nd exam		5	18	25	31	15	4	2

3.   Simplify

1 $x^{\frac{1}{2}} \times x^{2\frac{1}{2}}$ **2** $\left(x^3\right)^{\frac{2}{3}}$

Find the values of

3 $27^{\frac{1}{3}}$ **4** $16^{\frac{3}{4}}$ **5** $49^{-\frac{1}{2}}$

4.   Draw the x-axis from -1 to 3 and the y-axis from -8 to 13.
Draw the lines AB, $y = 3x - 5$ and CD, $y = 9 - 4x$.
Use your graph to solve the simultaneous equations $y = 3x - 5$, $y = 9 - 4x$.

5. This table gives the lengths of time of 80 phone calls.

Time (in minutes)	0–2	2–4	4–6	6–8	8–10	10–12
Number of calls	18	22	16	14	8	2

Draw a histogram of this distribution.
Find the mean time per call and the standard deviation of times.

6. Simplify these expressions.

1 $\dfrac{x}{6} - \dfrac{x-6}{12}$

2 $\dfrac{x^2 - 4x}{2x + 1} \times \dfrac{1}{x^2 - 16} \times \dfrac{2x^2 + 9x + 4}{x}$

7. **a** and **b** are two vectors not in the same direction. If $\overrightarrow{AB} = 4\mathbf{b}$, $\overrightarrow{AC} = 3\mathbf{a} + 6\mathbf{b}$ and $\overrightarrow{AD} = 12\mathbf{a} + 12\mathbf{b}$, find $\overrightarrow{BC}$ and $\overrightarrow{CD}$ in terms of **a** and **b**.
Show that B, C and D lie on a straight line and find the ratio of lengths $BC : CD$.

8. In this right-angled triangle, AB is measured correct to the nearest 0.1 m and $\angle A$ is measured to the nearest degree.
Find the lower and upper bounds for the length of BC.

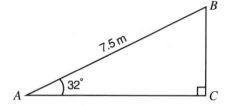

9. Alan plays a game where he can either win, draw or lose. The probability of him winning is $\frac{1}{3}$, the probability of him drawing is $\frac{1}{2}$. What is the probability of him losing ?
Show the results of two games on a tree-diagram and find the probability that he wins at least one of the two games.

10. Draw axes as shown and show the journey of a boy on his bicycle and his father in the car.
The boy starts from A at 1 pm and cycles at a steady speed of 10 km/h for 2 hours. He then rests for $\frac{1}{2}$ hour and then continues cycling to B, which is 40 km from A, and he arrives at 6 pm.

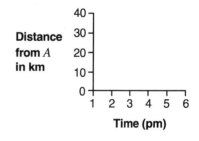

His father starts from A at 4 pm and arrives at B at 5.20 pm, travelling at a steady speed.

1 On the second part of the journey the boy travelled at a steady speed. What was his speed ?
2 What was his father's speed ?
3 When and where did the father overtake his son ?

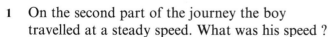

11. The perimeter of this triangle is 28 cm. The side *BC*
    is 5 cm longer than the side *AB*. Write down
    two equations, simplify them, and solve them
    simultaneously.
    Hence find the numerical values of the lengths
    of the sides of the triangle.

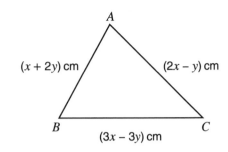

12. *ABCD* is a rectangle.

    Find
    1   the length of *DE*,
    2   the area of △ *ADE*,
    3   the length of *AB*.

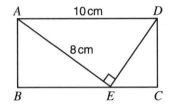

13. A kite is flying at the end of a string 50 m long and the string makes an angle of $x°$ with
    the ground. The vertical height of the kite is y m.

    Express y in terms of x.

    Sketch the graph of y for $0 \leqslant x \leqslant 90$.

14.

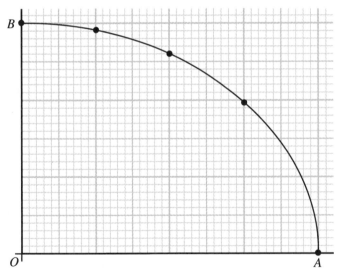

The diagram is a quadrant *OAB* of an ellipse, with *OA* = 8 units.
Find the approximate area of the quadrant by using the trapezium rule and dividing the
area into 4 strips of equal width, taking all readings from the diagram.
Check your answer by using the formula
Area of quadrant $= \frac{1}{4}\pi ab$,
where a = the length of *OA* and b = the length of *OB*.

15. A bag contains a number of fruit drops, some red, some yellow and some green.

The probability of taking a red sweet, at random, is $\frac{1}{3}$.

The probability of taking a yellow sweet, at random, is $\frac{1}{5}$.

What is the probability of taking
1   a red sweet or a yellow sweet,
2   a green sweet ?

3   If 28 of the sweets are green ones, how many sweets are there altogether ?

Exercise D4   Activities

1.   **My house**

Imagine that it is a few years into the future and you are about to buy a house.
Design the house and draw a plan of each floor.
Then draw the plan of each room, showing where the doorways and windows are, and
where each item of furniture will go.
Find the approximate cost of each item of furniture (by looking in shops, catalogues or
advertisements).
For each room make a list of the furniture and fittings you will need and find the total
cost. Find the total cost for all the rooms in the house.
If you intend to have a garden you could include a plan for this, and add on the costs of
garden tools and garden furniture.
Find the up-to-date price of a similar house by looking at advertisements, and find the
total cost of everything.
Cut pictures from magazines and catalogues to illustrate your booklet, and make an
attractive cover for it.
This is your dream house so you need not be too practical about being able to afford it,
if you wish to design a really luxurious one, on the other hand you may prefer to be
practical and plan for an inexpensive one. You may prefer to choose a flat, or a
bungalow, instead of a house.

2.   **Shapes in everyday life**

Make a display about these, with drawings, pictures, postcards, photographs and models.

Ideas:
symmetry in nature, and in man-made objects,
triangles: pylons, etc.
circles: wheels, drainpipes,
tins and boxes of different solid shapes,
shapes in nature: spirals in snails, jellyfish, pattern on a sunflower centre, cone of a
volcano,
shapes in building: unusual modern designs, bridges, the Pyramids, radio telescopes
(paraboloid), cooling towers (hyperboloid), spheres of an early warning system.

3.   **History of measurement**

It is interesting to find out about the measures which were used long ago in Britain. Land is still measured in acres. An acre is the area of land that could be ploughed in a day, in the days when oxen were used for ploughing.

If you have an interest in another country, maybe you could find out about how its system developed.

In France at the time of the Revolution, the old measures were abolished and the Metric System adopted. This is now used worldwide for scientific work and is being introduced gradually into Britain.

You could make a topic booklet about measurements. You could include weights as well. You could also find out about the measurement of time, and about coinage, or these could be topics in themselves.

4.   **Geometrical models**

There are 5 regular solids so you could begin by making these.

Equilateral triangles stuck together, 3 at a point, will make a regular tetrahedron.

Equilateral triangles stuck together, 4 at a point, will make a regular octahedron.

Equilateral triangles stuck together, 5 at a point, will make a regular icosahedron.

Why are these the only regular solids which can be made with equilateral triangles ? Another regular solid is made with squares. What is it ?

The 5th regular solid is made by sticking together regular pentagons. It is a dodecahedron.

If you have the plans of the nets of these solids you can make them from their nets. Put a tab on each alternate edge of the net. Score all lines before you bend them.

There are 13 semi-regular solids, made with combinations of regular polygons. You could try to make these.

With 6 squares and 8 equilateral triangles, with the same length of edge, putting 2 of each alternately at each point, you get a cuboctahedron. With 18 squares and 8 triangles, with 3 squares and 1 triangle meeting at a point, you can make a rhombicuboctahedron. With 6 squares and 32 triangles, with 4 triangles and a square meeting at a point, you can make a snub cube. Other solids use different combinations of equilateral triangles, squares and regular pentagons, hexagons, octagons and decagons. Can you discover them all ?

There are 4 other regular solids called the Kepler-Poinsot Polyhedra, which are interesting models.

To make the great stellated dodecahedron, first make a regular icosahedron as a base. Then make 20 triangular pyramids to stick on the 20 faces of the icosahedron. The long slant edges of these pyramids must be 1.62 times the length of the base edges, which are the same length as the edges of the icosahedron.

If you are interested in making mathematical models you can find details of many others from library books.

5. **Cubes**

Work out the cubes from 1^3 to 10^3.

Copy and complete this pattern.

natural numbers	sum	cubes of natural numbers	sum
1	1	1^3	1
$1 + 2$	3	$1^3 + 2^3$	9
$1 + 2 + 3$	6	$1^3 + 2^3 + 3^3$	36
$\cdots$		$\cdots$	
$1 + 2 + \cdots + 10$	55	$1^3 + 2^3 + \cdots + 10^3$	

What do you notice about the connection between the 2nd and 4th columns ?
Double the numbers in column (2) and divide each by the largest number of the same
row in column (1). What do you notice ? Can you use this to find a formula for
(1) $1 + 2 + 3 + \cdots + n$.
(2) $1^3 + 2^3 + 3^3 + \cdots + n^3$?

It is not so easy to find a formula for $1^2 + 2^2 + 3^2 + \cdots + n^2$, but using a similar method,
finding 1^2, $1^2 + 2^2$, $1^2 + 2^2 + 3^2$, $\ldots$, and multiplying the sums by 6, you may discover
the formula.

6. **The arrangement of red cards in a pack of cards**

If a pack of cards has been shuffled properly, then when you turn up the top card it is
equally likely to be a red card (heart or diamond) or a black one (club or spade). In this
experiment you should investigate how many cards are turned over before a red card
appears.
Shuffle the pack of cards and turn over the cards one-by-one, counting until a red card
appears. If it is the first card it counts as 1. If it is only the second card it counts as 2,
and so on. Record the result. Then continue turning the cards over, beginning the count
again at 1, and carrying on until another red card appears. Repeat until you have 10 results.

Before you go any further, make two guesses:
1   What is the mode number of the results ?
2   What is the mean of the results ?

To continue the experiment, shuffle all the cards again properly and begin again using the
full pack.
Carry on in this way. After every 10 results shuffle the cards and begin again with a full pack.
Repeat until you have got 100, or more, results.
Make a frequency table of the results and show them in a bar-line graph. Comment on
the shape of the graph.
Find the mode. Does it agree with your guess ?
Find the mean. Does it agree with your guess ?
Find the standard deviation of the distribution.

7.   The Fibonacci Sequence

1,   1,   2,   3,   5,   8,   13,   21,   . . .

Discover how each number in the sequence is linked to the previous numbers and continue the sequence for several terms. (As a check, 377 is a member of the sequence.)

Fibonacci was an Italian who lived in the 13th century. See if you can find out more about him.

1   His sequence is usually linked to 'the rabbit problem'.
'How many pairs of rabbits can be produced from a single pair in a year assuming that every month each pair gives birth to a new pair, which starts breeding from the second month ?'

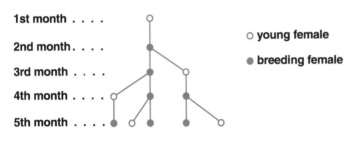

1st month . . . .

2nd month. . . .

3rd month . . . .

4th month . . . .

5th month . . . .

o young female

● breeding female

. . .

2   Divide each number of the sequence by the preceding number, and then divide each number by the next one.

$\frac{1}{1} = 1$ $\frac{1}{1} = 1$

$\frac{2}{1} = 2$ $\frac{1}{2} = 0.5$

$\frac{3}{2} = 1.5$ $\frac{2}{3} = 0.667$

$\frac{5}{3} = 1.667$ $\frac{3}{5} = 0.6$

         . . .   . . .

Continue for about 20 terms. What do you notice ?
Investigate the relationships between each number and the next alternate number.

3   Number patterns

Take every three consecutive numbers of the sequence. Multiply the two outside ones and square the middle one. What do you notice ?
Investigate consecutive numbers 4 at a time, then 5 at a time.
Find the sums of 1, $1 + 1$, $1 + 1 + 2$, $1 + 1 + 2 + 3$, etc. What do you notice if you add 1 to each ?
Investigate sums of squares of 2 consecutive numbers, and differences of squares of alternate numbers.
See if you can find other number patterns connected with the sequence.

4   Many natural objects have links with Fibonacci numbers. Count the numer of petals on a daisy-type flower. Count the spirals on a pine cone, a pineapple or the centre part of a sunflower, and then count the spirals in the opposite direction.

5   Draw a regular pentagon and draw its diagonals.

Find the ratios $\dfrac{AB}{BC}$, $\dfrac{AC}{AB}$ and $\dfrac{AD}{AC}$, by measuring.

By using similar triangles or trig. you could show that these equal 1.618, or $\dfrac{\sqrt{5}+1}{2}$ exactly.

Find the ratios $\dfrac{BC}{AB}$, $\dfrac{AB}{AC}$ and $\dfrac{AC}{AD}$.

$\left(\text{These equal 0.618, or } \dfrac{\sqrt{5}-1}{2} \text{ exactly.}\right)$

Is there a link with the Fibonacci Sequence ?
The ratio 1.618 : 1 or 1 : 0.618 is known as The Golden Section.
It is often used in Art and Architecture.

6   **Golden section spiral**

Start with a large rectangle with sides in the ratio 1.62 : 1.
Mark off a square.
Starting from A, with centre A_1, draw a quarter circle, going to B.
Now join XY and A_1Z as guidelines, as a corner of each following square lies on one of these lines.
Mark off a square including point B.
Starting from B, with centre B_1, which is on A_1B and on XY, draw a quarter circle, going to C.
Mark off a square including point C.
Starting from C, with centre C_1, which is on B_1C and on A_1Z, draw a quarter circle going to D.
Continue until the squares get too small to go any further. Where does it end ?

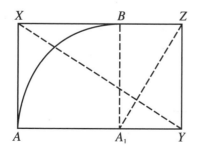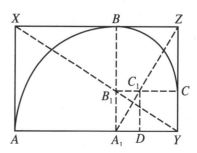

8. **Compound Interest**

Investigate how money grows at different rates of interest. Illustrate this by drawing graphs.

How long would it take to 'double your money' at different rates of interest ? A magazine article quoted this as 'the rule of 72'. If the rate is $R\%$ per annum then the number of years needed to double the money is found by dividing 72 by R. You can check to see how reliable this rule is.

If money is invested at 12% per annum and interest is added twice a year instead of annually, then 6% is added every 6 months. If interest is paid monthly, this is 1% added at the end of every month. Does it make any difference how often the interest is added, in the long run ?

You could link this investigation with (1) what happens to a population which increases at a constant rate, and (2) what happens when the value of an object depreciates at a constant rate.

PUZZLES

45. You have applied for a good job and you and two other equally clever applicants, Harry and Jane, have to take a selection test. You are sitting on chairs as at the corners of an equilateral triangle, facing each other. You are told that someone is going to hold up a board behind you and above your head, which will be either green or red. These three boards will all be put into view at the same time. None of you will be able to see the board behind yourself, but you can each see the other two. If you see at least one green board you must stand up. When the boards are held up, the boards above Harry and Jane are both green, so you stand up. Harry and Jane also stand up.

Now you are given the next instruction. 'As soon as you know the colour of your own board, raise your hand.' So there is a long wait while you each try to decide whether your board is red or green, and no-one raises a hand.

Is your board red or green ?

46. The shaded areas are squares, and one triangle has an area of 10 cm^2. What is the area of the other triangle ?

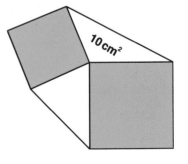

To the student : 5

Learning formulae

There are certain formulae which you will need to know by heart. The best way to learn a formula is to know where it comes from.

There is a formula checklist on page 522. Copy the list, completing each formula, then check your answers from the relevant chapters of the book. Learn those you do not know.

Learning formulae in isolation is not very useful. You need to link this with learning methods, so that you can use the formulae correctly.

Practice exams

You may have a practice exam at school. This will give you some idea of your present standard. It will show you that you can do well if you have learnt the work. It will give you practice in working to time and working under pressure.

After the exam, you will be told your marks or grade and given back your paper. Perhaps your teacher will go through all the questions with the class or you may have to correct them yourself. Ask about anything you do not understand.

If you get a low mark, do not be too discouraged if you know that you can do better next time. But decide what you are going to do to improve your standard.

In an exam it is the marks which count. Could you have got more marks if you had spent less time on some questions and more on others ? Should you have revised some topics more thoroughly ?

Did you throw away any marks by:
not reading a question carefully enough,
not showing the necessary working with the answer,
writing so badly that the marker could not read it,
writing so badly that **you** could not read it and copied it wrongly on the next line,
not checking an answer that was obviously wrong,
not giving an answer to the accuracy asked for, e.g. to the nearest cm ?

Since this was a practice exam, having made some of these mistakes, you can see that by avoiding them in future you can gain more marks.

Make a list of topics you still need to revise, and plan how you will use the remaining time before the proper examination.

Your teacher may given your further practice papers to do at home. If not, you may like to give yourself some. You can use the practice test questions or the revision exercises in this book. Try to do them as in a proper exam, spending the correct time on them and working in a quiet room without referring to books or notes.

21 Circle properties

> **The topics in this chapter include:**
>
> • knowing and using angle and tangent properties of circles.

A circle

A circle is the locus of a point which moves at a constant distance from a fixed point.

In the diagram, A is the fixed point, and is the centre of the circle. r units is the constant distance, and is the radius of the circle.

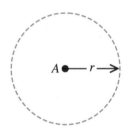

Some symmetrical properties of chords and tangents

Chord property

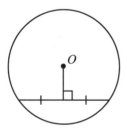

The line from the centre
to the mid-point of a chord
is perpendicular to the chord.

Tangent property

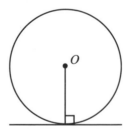

The radius to the point of contact
is perpendicular to the tangent.

Equal chords   **Tangents from an external point**

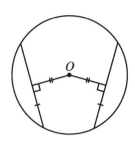

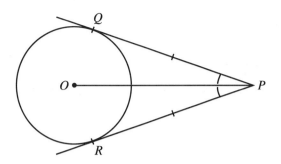

Chords of equal length are
equidistant (the same distance)
from the centre.

They are equal, i.e. $PQ = PR$.
Also OP bisects $\angle QPR$.

Angle properties

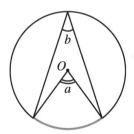

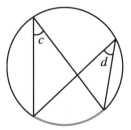

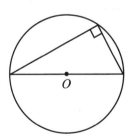

The angle at the centre is
twice as big as the angle at
the circumference (standing
on the same arc).

$$a = 2b$$

Angles at the circumference
(standing on the same arc)
are equal.
(There are sometimes called
angles in the same segment.)

$$c = d$$

The angle in a semicircle
is a right angle.

Cyclic quadrilaterals

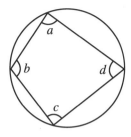

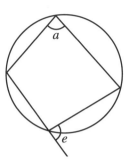

Opposite angles add up to 180°.

$$a + c = 180°$$
$$b + d = 180°$$

An exterior angle is equal to the opposite interior angle.

$$e = a$$

The alternate segment theorem

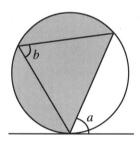

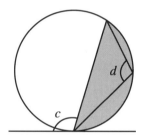

The angle between a tangent and a chord is equal to any angle made by that chord in the alternate segment of the circle.

$$a = b \qquad\qquad\qquad c = d$$

Examples

1   Find the marked angles. O is the centre of the circle.

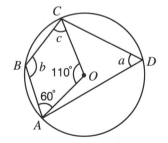

$a = 55°$ (angle at centre = twice angle at circumference; both on arc AC)

$b = 125°$ (opposite angles of cyclic quadrilateral $ABCD$)

$c = 65°$ (angle sum of quadrilateral $OABC = 360°$)

2   Find the marked angles. *TP* is a tangent
touching the circle at *P*.

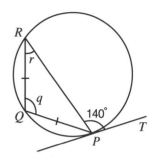

$q = 140°$ (angle between tangent and
                       chord = angle in the
                       alternate segment)

$r = 20°$ (angle in isosceles triangle,
                       sum of angles = 180°)

Exercise 21.1

1.   *AB* is a chord 30 cm long, in a circle
centre *O*. The radius is 17 cm.
Find the length of *OC*.

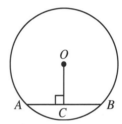

2.   Circles centres *A* and *B* intersect at *C*
and *D*. The radius of the circle centre *A*
is 13 cm, the radius of the circle centre
B is 15 cm, and the length of *CD* is
24 cm.

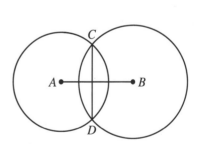

   1   Name an axis of symmetry of the
figure.
   2   Find the distance *AB*.

3.   *O* is the centre of the circle.
OAP is a straight line with *OA* = 4 cm and
AP = 4.5 cm.
Find the length of the tangent *PT*.

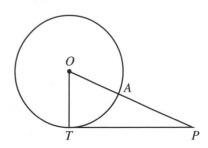

4.   Find the marked angles. O is the centre of the circle.

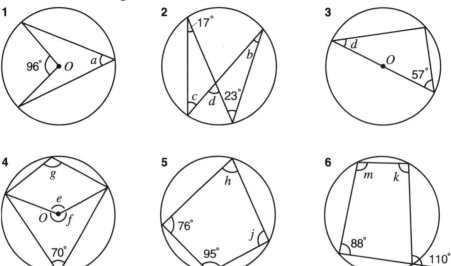

5.   Find the marked angles. O is the centre of the circle. TP and TQ are tangents touching the circle at P and Q.

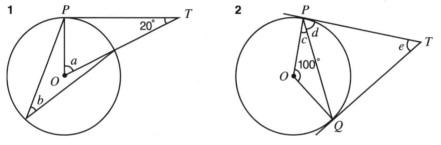

6.   Find the marked angles. O is the centre of the circle.

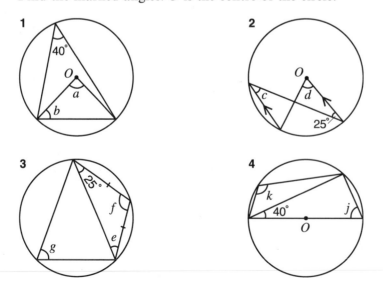

7. The sides of the triangle *ABC* touch the circle at *P*, *Q*, *R*. Find the angles of triangle *PQR*.

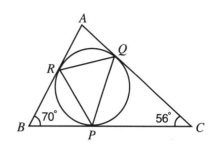

8. Find the marked angles. *O* is the centre of the circle. *TP* and *TQ* are tangents touching the circle at *P* and *Q*.

1

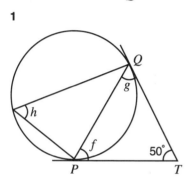

2

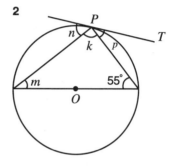

9. The two circles each have centre *O*. *AB* is a tangent to the smaller circle, touching at *X*.
What is the size of ∠*AXO* ?
Explain why *AX* = *XB*.
If the circles have radii 7.2 cm and 12 cm, find the length of *AB*.

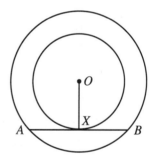

10. In the diagram, *O* is the centre of the circle, *PT* is a tangent touching the circle at *T*, and the line *PQR* bisects ∠*TPB*. ∠*PTB* = 28°.

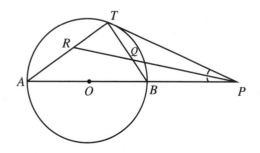

1 Find the sizes of ∠*TAB*, ∠*TBA*, ∠*TPB*, ∠*TQR*.
2 Prove that *TR* = *TQ*.
3 Prove that triangles *PQT*, *PRA* are similar.

Exercise 21.2   Applications

1. *AB* is a chord of length 24 cm, which moves in
    a circle centre *O*, radius 15 cm. *M* is the mid-point
    of *AB*.

    1   Find the distance *OM*.
    2   As the chord moves, what is the locus of *M* ?

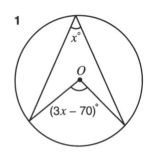

2. In the diagram, *OD* is a radius and is 13 cm long.
    AB = 10 cm, *CD* = 24 cm and *AB* is parallel
    to *CD*.
    Find the distance between *AB* and *CD*.

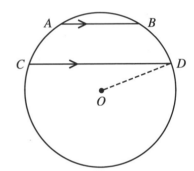

3. *AOB* is a diameter of a circle, centre *O*.
    $\angle ABC = 52°$.

    1   Prove that *OD* bisects $\angle AOC$.
    2   If *AD* and *AC* were joined, what is the
        size of $\angle CAD$?

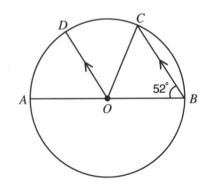

4. *O* is the centre of the circle. *TD* is a
    tangent touching the circle at *T*.
    $\angle ABT = 67°$.
    Find the size of $\angle ODT$.

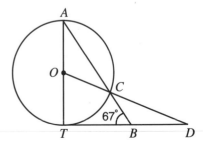

5. Find the value of x in these figures. O is the centre of the circle.

1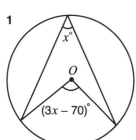

2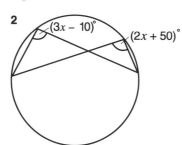

3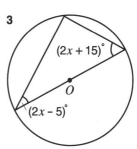

4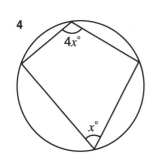

5 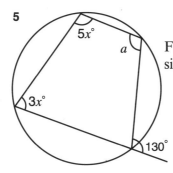 Find also the size of angle a.

6. The circle touches the sides of the triangle
    ABC at P, Q, R.
    Find the size of angle C.

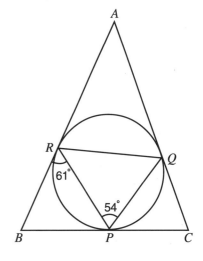

7. TP, TQ are tangents touching the circle,
    centre O, at P and Q.
    Find the size of angle T.

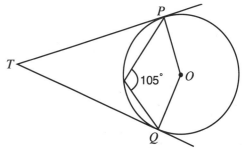

8. In the diagram, O is the centre of the
   circle. $\angle OPR = x°$, $\angle PQR = y°$.

   Find, in terms of x,
   1 $\angle POR$,
   2 $\angle PSR$.
   3 Show that $y = 90 + x$.

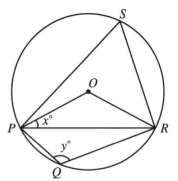

9. Draw a line OT 14 cm long, with mid-point M.
   With centre M, draw a circle passing through O and T.
   With centre O, draw a circle radius 5 cm to cut the first circle at P and Q.
   Join TP and TQ.
   Explain why TP and TQ are tangents to the circle with centre O.

10. A regular pentagon $ABCDE$ is inscribed in a
    circle centre O.

    1 Find the size of $\angle AOB$.
    2 Find the size of $\angle ADB$.
    3 What fraction of $\angle CDE$ is $\angle ADB$?

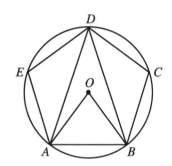

11. AC and BD are straight lines.
    1 Prove that triangles AXB, DXC are similar, and
       hence show that $XA \times XC = XB \times XD$.
    2 If $XA = 7.5$ cm, $XB = 4.2$ cm and $XC = 5.6$ cm,
       find the length of XD.

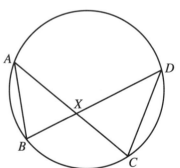

12. **1** Name an angle equal to $\angle XAB$.
    2 Prove that $\triangle XAB$, $\triangle XDC$ are similar, and
       hence show that $XA \times XC = XB \times XD$.
    3 If $XA = 7.5$ cm, $AC = 9.3$ cm and
       $XB = 8.4$ cm, find the length of BD.

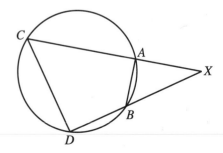

Practice test 21

1. *ABCD* is a cyclic quadrilateral in which
   $\angle ABC = 67°$ and $\angle DCA = 39°$.
   Find the size of $\angle DAC$.

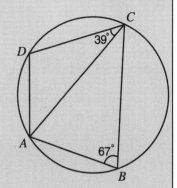

2. *O* is the centre of the circle. The tangent
   PT is 15 cm long. The radius is 8 cm.
   Find the length of *OP* and hence find the
   length of *AP*.

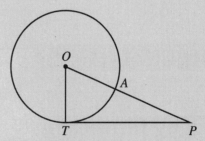

3. Find the angles of the triangle *ABC*. *O* is
   the centre of the circle.

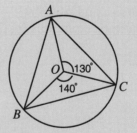

4. In the diagram, *AB* is a tangent to the circle,
   $AC = BC$ and $AB = BE$. $\angle ABC = 38°$ and
   BCED is a straight line.

   Find the sizes of the angles *BAC*, *ADE*,
   AEB and *DAE*.

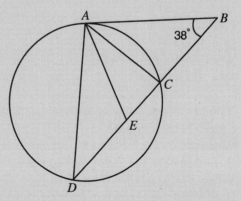

22 *Quadratic equations*

> **The topics in this chapter include**
>
> - solving quadratic equations by using factors, the formula, completing the square or iteration,
> - interpreting and using coefficients in quadratic functions.

Quadratic Equations

Solving by factorising

If there are two numbers a and b, and $ab = 0$, then either $a = 0$ or $b = 0$. This fact leads to the method of solving quadratic equations by factorising.

Examples

1   Solve the equation $x^2 + 5x = 84$.

Make the right-hand side zero.
$$x^2 + 5x - 84 = 0$$
Factorise the left hand side.
$$(x + 12)(x - 7) = 0$$
$$x + 12 = 0 \text{ or } x - 7 = 0$$
$$x = -12 \text{ or } x = 7$$

You can check these equations in the same way as you checked linear equations.
Check both solutions.
When $x = -12$, LHS $= x^2 + 5x = (-12)^2 + (5 \times -12) = 144 - 60 = 84$, RHS $= 84$.
Both sides are the same, so the equation checks when $x = -12$.
When $x = 7$, LHS $= 7^2 + (5 \times 7) = 49 + 35 = 84$, RHS $= 84$.
Both sides are the same, so the equation checks when $x = 7$.

The answers to an equation may be called the **roots** of the equation.
Here the roots are -12 and 7.

2   Solve the equation $3x^2 + 10x - 8 = 0$.

Factorise.
$(3x - 2)(x + 4) = 0$
$3x - 2 = 0$ or $x + 4 = 0$
$3x = 2$ or $x = -4$
$x = \frac{2}{3}$ or $x = -4$

Equations of the type $a^2x^2 - b^2 = 0$

Example

3   Solve the equation $4x^2 - 9 = 0$.

$4x^2 = 9$
Take the square root of both sides.
$2x = \pm 3$
(This means $2x = +3$ or -3.)
$x = 1\frac{1}{2}$ or $-1\frac{1}{2}$

This equation could also be solved by factorising.
$(2x + 3)(2x - 3) = 0$
$2x + 3 = 0$ or $2x - 3 = 0$
$2x = -3$ or $2x = 3$
$x = -1\frac{1}{2}$ or $x = 1\frac{1}{2}$

Solving equations by using the general formula

Consider the equation $ax^2 + bx + c = 0$, where a, b and c are numbers, and $a \neq 0$.
The formula for the solution to this equation is

$$x = \frac{-b \pm \sqrt{b^2 - 4ac}}{2a}$$

Examples

4   Solve the equation $3x^2 + 10x - 8 = 0$.
(This is the same equation as in example **2**.)

Comparing with $ax^2 + bx + c = 0$, we have $a = 3$, $b = 10$ and $c = -8$.

The solution is $x = \dfrac{-b \pm \sqrt{b^2 - 4ac}}{2a}$

$$= \dfrac{-10 \pm \sqrt{10^2 - 4 \times 3 \times (-8)}}{2 \times 3}$$

You can use your calculator at this stage to work out $\sqrt{10^2 - 4 \times 3 \times (-8)}$.

$$= \dfrac{-10 \pm 14}{6}$$

$$= \dfrac{-10 + 14}{6} \quad \text{or} \quad \dfrac{-10 - 14}{6}$$

$$x = \tfrac{2}{3} \quad \text{or} \quad -4$$

Since the number under the square root is a perfect square, the square root is exact and the answers are rational numbers. In this case they are often given in fractional form, rather than as approximate decimals.
An equation where the number under the square root is a perfect square could have been solved by factorising.

5   Solve the equation $2x^2 - 7x + 4 = 0$, giving your solution correct to 2 decimal places.

$2x^2 - 7x + 4$ cannot be factorised so you have to use the general formula.
Comparing $2x^2 - 7x + 4 = 0$ with $ax^2 + bx + c = 0$; $a = 2$, $b = -7$ and $c = 4$.

The solution is $x = \dfrac{-b \pm \sqrt{b^2 - 4ac}}{2a}$

$$= \dfrac{7 \pm \sqrt{(-7)^2 - 4 \times 2 \times 4}}{2 \times 2}$$

Use your calculator to work out $\sqrt{(-7)^2 - 4 \times 2 \times 4}$.
Since the result is not exact, save it in the memory of the calculator.

$x = \dfrac{7 \pm \sqrt{17}}{4}$

$= \dfrac{7 + \sqrt{17}}{4} \quad \text{or} \quad \dfrac{7 - \sqrt{17}}{4}$ Press   7 $\boxed{+}$ $\boxed{\text{RM}}$ $\boxed{=}$ $\boxed{\div}$ 4 $\boxed{=}$
                                                  then   7 $\boxed{-}$ $\boxed{\text{RM}}$ $\boxed{=}$ $\boxed{\div}$ 4 $\boxed{=}$

$x = 2.780\ldots \quad \text{or} \quad 0.719\ldots$

$= 2.78 \text{ or } 0.72$, correct to 2 dec. pl.

Exercise 22.1

1. Solve the equations

   1 $(x+1)(x-2) = 0$
   2 $(x+2)(3x+1) = 0$
   3 $(x-3)(2x-1) = 0$

   4 $(3x+4)(2x-3) = 0$
   5 $(4x+1)(3x-2) = 0$

2. Solve these equations by using factorising.

   1 $x^2 + 7x + 10 = 0$
   2 $x^2 - 13x + 12 = 0$
   3 $x^2 + x - 12 = 0$
   4 $x^2 - 13x - 30 = 0$
   5 $x^2 - 13x + 30 = 0$
   6 $x^2 - 8x + 16 = 0$
   7 $x^2 - 2x - 8 = 0$

   8 $x^2 - x - 42 = 0$
   9 $x^2 + 24x - 25 = 0$
   10 $x^2 - 11x + 24 = 0$
   11 $x^2 - 5x = 0$
   12 $x^2 + 9x = 36$
   13 $x^2 + 13x + 40 = 0$
   14 $x^2 + 6x = 0$

   15 $x^2 + 20 = 12x$
   16 $x^2 = x$
   17 $x^2 + 6x + 9 = 0$
   18 $x^2 - 8x = 33$
   19 $x^2 + 29x + 100 = 0$
   20 $x^2 + 48 = 14x$

3. Solve the equations.

   1 $x^2 = 1$
   2 $x^2 - 25 = 0$
   3 $9x^2 = 4$

   4 $4x^2 - 1 = 0$
   5 $(x-2)^2 = 1$
   6 $(x+3)^2 = 25$

4. Solve these equations using factorising or using the general formula, giving non-integer answers in fractional form.

   1 $2x^2 - 15x + 7 = 0$
   2 $2x^2 + 7x + 5 = 0$
   3 $3x^2 + 2x - 1 = 0$
   4 $3x^2 + 8 = 14x$

   5 $2x^2 = x + 10$
   6 $2x^2 - 5x - 3 = 0$
   7 $3x^2 + x = 10$

   8 $2x^2 + 11x + 12 = 0$
   9 $3x^2 - 10x + 3 = 0$
   10 $2x^2 - 18x + 40 = 0$

5. Using your calculator, find the two values for each of these expressions, correct to 2 decimal places.

   1 $\dfrac{4 \pm \sqrt{8}}{2}$

   2 $\dfrac{-5 \pm \sqrt{12}}{4}$

   3 $\dfrac{-1 \pm \sqrt{10}}{2}$

6. Solve these equations by using the general formula, giving the roots correct to 2 decimal places.

   1 $x^2 + 4x - 9 = 0$
   2 $2x^2 - 5x + 1 = 0$
   3 $x^2 - 2x - 6 = 0$
   4 $3x^2 + 2x - 6 = 0$

   5 $2x^2 + 6x + 3 = 0$
   6 $3x(x-1) = 5$
   7 $2x^2 + 1 = 6x$

   8 $x^2 - 5x = 3$
   9 $(x+3)^2 = 2$
   10 $x^2 = 12x - 5$

7. When 17 times a certain number is subtracted from twice its square, 55 remains. Find the number.

8. A paddock is rectangular in shape with width x m and it is 3 times as long as it is wide. Find an expression for its area.
    It is enlarged by making it 20 m longer and 10 m wider. This doubles its area. Write down an equation and solve it to find the value of x.

9. Solve the equation $2x^3 + x^2 - 3x = 0$. (This is a cubic equation and there are 3 solutions.)

Solving equations by completing the square

In Chapter 17 you learnt about completing the square. This technique can be used in solving quadratic equations. It is the method from which the general formula is obtained.

Example

1   Solve the equation $2x^2 - 7x + 4 = 0$.
    (This equation was solved using the formula on page 434.)

Subtract 4 from both sides.

$2x^2 - 7x = -4$

Divide both sides by 2.

$x^2 - \frac{7}{2}x = -2$

Complete the square by adding $\left[\frac{1}{2}\text{ of }\left(-\frac{7}{2}\right)\right]^2$ to both sides.

$x^2 - \frac{7}{2}x + \frac{49}{16} = -2 + \frac{49}{16}$

$\left(x - \frac{7}{4}\right)^2 = \frac{17}{16}$

Take the square root of both sides.

$$x - \frac{7}{4} = \pm \frac{\sqrt{17}}{4}$$

Add $\frac{7}{4}$ to both sides.

$$x = \frac{7 \pm \sqrt{17}}{4}$$

$= 2.78$ or 0.72, to 2 dec. pl.

Completing the square is a good method to use when the equation starts with x^2 and the term in x has an even number, i.e. $a = 1$ and b is even.

Example

2   Solve the equation $x^2 + 6x + 7 = 0$.

$x^2 + 6x = -7$

Add $\left(\frac{1}{2} \text{ of } 6\right)^2$ to both sides.

$x^2 + 6x + 9 = 2$

$(x + 3)^2 = 2$

Take the square root of both sides.

$x + 3 = \pm\sqrt{2}$

$x = -3 \pm \sqrt{2}$

$\quad = -3 + \sqrt{2} \text{ or } -3 - \sqrt{2}$

$\quad = -1.585\ldots \text{ or } -4.414\ldots$

$\quad = -1.59 \text{ or } -4.41, \text{ to 2 dec. pl.}$

Solving equations by iteration

Examples

3   To solve the equation $x^2 + 2x - 2 = 0$.

Rewrite it as $x^2 + 2x = 2$

$$x(x + 2) = 2$$

$$x = \frac{2}{x + 2}$$

Use the iteration formula $x_{n+1} = \dfrac{2}{x_n + 2}$

If you begin with $x_1 = 5$,

$x_2 = \dfrac{2}{x_1 + 2} = \dfrac{2}{5 + 2} = \frac{2}{7} = 0.2857\ldots$

Put the answer in the memory of the calculator.

$x_3 = \dfrac{2}{x_2 + 2} = 0.875$

Press 2 $\boxed{\div}$ $\boxed{(}$ $\boxed{\text{RM}}$ $\boxed{+}$ 2 $\boxed{)}$ $\boxed{=}$ and put the answer in the memory to use next.

$x_4 = \dfrac{2}{x_3 + 2} = 0.6957$

$x_5 = \dfrac{2}{x_4 + 2} = 0.7419$

Using a graphics calculator you can find the values of $x_2, x_3, x_4, \ldots$ by pressing

5 $\boxed{\text{EXE}}$ This enters $x_1 = 5$.

2 $\boxed{\div}$ $\boxed{(}$ $\boxed{\text{ANS}}$ $\boxed{+}$ 2 $\boxed{)}$ $\boxed{\text{EXE}}$ This calculates x_2.

$\boxed{\text{EXE}}$ This calculates x_3.

$\boxed{\text{EXE}}$ This calculates x_4.

and press $\boxed{\text{EXE}}$ again and again to find $x_5, x_6, \ldots$

Here are the first 12 terms of the sequence.

$x_1 = 5$	$x_7 = 0.7328$
$x_2 = 0.2857$	$x_8 = 0.7319$
$x_3 = 0.875$	$x_9 = 0.7321$
$x_4 = 0.6957$	$x_{10} = 0.7320$
$x_5 = 0.7419$	$x_{11} = 0.7321$
$x_6 = 0.7294$	$x_{12} = 0.7320$

The sequence converges to 0.732, correct to 3 decimal places, and this is the approximate value for a root of the equation.

Try this method again, starting with different values for x_1.

You will find that it is not possible to get any further if you get any value of x_n to be -2, since the denominator of the fraction would then be zero.

A different iteration formula can be used to solve the same equation, $x^2 + 2x - 2 = 0$.

Rewrite it as $2x = 2 - x^2$

$$x = \frac{2 - x^2}{2}$$

Use the iteration formula $x_{n+1} = \dfrac{2 - x_n^2}{2}$

If you begin with $x_1 = 5$, you will not get a convergent sequence.

If you begin with $x_1 = 0.5$, you will need more terms, but the sequence also converges to 0.732.

Another way of arranging the equation is $x = \dfrac{2}{x} - 2$, so you can use the iteration formula $x_{n+1} = \dfrac{2}{x_n} - 2$.

If you begin with $x_1 = -3$, you will get the second root of the equation, -2.732.

4   What quadratic equation can be solved by using the iteration formula $x_{n+1} = \dfrac{2}{10 - x_n}$?

At the limiting value, $x_{n+1} = x_n = x$.

The equation is $x = \dfrac{2}{10 - x}$

$$x(10 - x) = 2$$
$$10x - x^2 = 2$$

i.e. $x^2 - 10x + 2 = 0$

Roots of quadratic equations

A quadratic equation can be written in the form $ax^2 + bx + c = 0$.
e.g. $2x^2 = 5x + 3$ can be written as $2x^2 - 5x - 3 = 0$.
Comparing it with $ax^2 + bx + c = 0$, $a = 2$, $b = -5$ and $c = -3$.

If you work out the value of $b^2 - 4ac$ you can find whether the roots (solutions) of the equation are rational or irrational, when a, b and c are rational numbers.

If $b^2 - 4ac$ is a perfect square, the roots are rational.
If $b^2 - 4ac$ is positive, but not a perfect square, the roots are irrational.
If $b^2 - 4ac = 0$, there is one repeated root, which is rational.
If $b^2 - 4ac$ is negative, there are no real roots.

In the equation above,
$b^2 - 4ac = (-5)^2 - 4 \times 2 \times (-3) = 25 + 24 = 49$
This is a perfect square, so the roots are rational.
(In fact, they are $x = -\frac{1}{2}$ or $x = 3$.)

Exercise 22.2

1.   Find out if there are real roots in these equations, and if so, whether they are rational or irrational.

   1 $x^2 + 10x + 21 = 0$ **4** $5x^2 + 12x + 15 = 0$
   2 $4x^2 + 49 = 28x$ **5** $3x^2 - 16x + 5 = 0$
   3 $10x^2 = 4x + 1$

2.   Solve these equations using the method of completing the square, giving answers correct to 2 decimal places.

   1 $x^2 - 12x - 6 = 0$ **4** $x^2 - 9x + 12 = 0$
   2 $x^2 + 2x = 7$ **5** $2x^2 - 5x = 1$
   3 $x^2 - 18x + 10 = 0$

3.   The roots of the equation $2x^2 + ax + 2a = 0$ are real and equal. Find the value of a.

4. In these questions, show that the limiting values of the iteration formulae will give roots
    of the corresponding quadratic equations.
    Solve the equations, finding one root of each, correct to 2 decimal places.

    1 $x^2 - 9x - 19 = 0$.   Use $x_{n+1} = \dfrac{19}{x_n - 9}$ and let $x_1 = 1$.

    2 $x^2 - 7x + 9 = 0$.   Use $x_{n+1} = \dfrac{x_n^2 + 9}{7}$ and let $x_1 = 1.8$.

    3 $2x^2 + 8x - 5 = 0$.   Use $x_{n+1} = \dfrac{5}{8 + 2x_n}$ and let $x_1 = 5$.

    4 $3x^2 + 5x - 1 = 0$.   Use $x_{n+1} = \dfrac{1 - 3x_n^2}{5}$ and let $x_1 = -0.2$.

    5 $2x^2 = 5x + 4$.   Use $x_{n+1} = \dfrac{2}{x_n} + 2.5$ and let $x_1 = -4$.

5. A rectangular lawn is 44 m by 36 m and it is surrounded by a path of constant width.
    The total area of the lawn and the path is 2288 m^2.

    1 If the path is x m wide, show that the value of x can be found by solving the
    equation $x^2 + 40x = 176$.
    2 Show that this equation has real roots which are rational and unequal.
    3 Solve the equation by completing the square and hence find the width of the path.
    4 Check your solution by using the iteration formula $x_{n+1} = \dfrac{176}{x_n + 40}$ and putting
    $x_1 = 6$.

Exercise 22.3 Applications

1. Solve the equations

    1 $x(x + 4) - (x - 2) = 20$ **3** $(x + 2)(x + 3) - 5 = (x + 1)^2$
    2 $5 + x = (7 - x)^2$ **4** $(3x + 1)^2 - x(x + 40) - 4 = 3(2x - 1)$

2. Solve the equations

    1 $\dfrac{x + 3}{x - 1} = \dfrac{x + 5}{x - 7}$ **2** $\dfrac{8}{x + 3} = 6 - x$ **3** $\dfrac{6}{x} - \dfrac{5}{2x - 1} = 1$

3. P is a point on the side AB of a rectangle $ABCD$
    and $AP = 2x$ cm, $PC = x$ cm, $AB = 13$ cm
    and $AD = 4$ cm.
    What is the length of PB, in terms of x ?
    Write down an equation involving x and solve it.
    What is the area of the trapezium $APCD$?

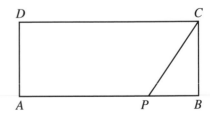

4. A train travels 80 km at an average speed of x km/h and then 45 km at an average speed of $(x - 10)$ km/h.
   Find an expression for the total time taken for the journey.
   If the total time was $3\frac{1}{2}$ hours, write down an equation and solve it to find the value of x.

5. A gardener wishes to enclose a rectangular plot which will have an area of 160 m². If he makes the length of the plot x m long, what will be the width of the plot ?
   If the plot requires 60 m of fencing to surround it, write down an equation and solve it to find the measurements of the plot, in metres, correct to 1 decimal place.

6. Solve the equation $x + \dfrac{27}{x} = 28$.

   Hence find 2 solutions of the equation $y^3 + \dfrac{27}{y^3} = 28$.

7. Show that the cubic equation $x^3 - 13x + 9 = 0$ can be rearranged as $x = \dfrac{9}{13 - x^2}$.

   Use the iteration formula $x_{n+1} = \dfrac{9}{13 - x_n^2}$ with $x_1 = 4$ to find a solution of the equation, correct to 3 decimal places.

Practice test 22

1. Solve the equations
   1 $x^2 - 9 = 0$
   2 $x^2 - 9x = 0$
   3 $x^2 - 8x - 9 = 0$
   4 $x^2 - 8x + 8 = 0$, using the method of completing the square,
   5 $x^2 - 9x - 8 = 0$, using the general formula.
   Give the answers to **4** and **5** correct to 2 decimal places.

2. A farmer has 70 m of fencing available and he wants to enclose a rectangular area of 300 m². What measurements will his rectangle have ?
   (Let the length be x m.)

3. The lengths of the sides of a right-angled triangle are x cm, $2x$ cm and $(2x + 1)$ cm. Find the length of the shortest side, correct to the nearest mm.

4. Show that the equation $2x^2 - 7x + 4 = 0$ can be arranged in the form $x = 3.5 - \dfrac{2}{x}$.

   Use the iteration formula $x_{n+1} = 3.5 - \dfrac{2}{x_n}$ with $x_1 = 3$ to find a root of the equation, correct to 2 decimal places.

23 Sine and cosine rules

The topics in this chapter include:

- using sine and cosine rules to solve problems, including simple cases in 3-D.

The sine and cosine rules can be used to calculate lengths or angles in any triangle. They are particularly useful when the triangle is not right-angled or isosceles.

Labelling a triangle

The small letter a refers to the side opposite angle A,
the small letter b refers to the side opposite angle B,
the small letter c refers to the side opposite angle C.

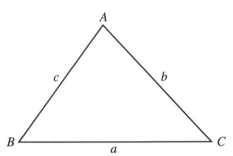

(Write C and c clearly so that you can tell which is which. Capital letters refer to angles, small letters refer to sides, so C refers to the angle C, c refers to the side opposite angle C.)

Sine rule

$$\frac{a}{\sin A} = \frac{b}{\sin B} = \frac{c}{\sin C}$$

This can be rearranged as

$$\frac{\sin A}{a} = \frac{\sin B}{b} = \frac{\sin C}{c}$$

Cosine rule

$$a^2 = b^2 + c^2 - 2bc \cos A$$

$$\text{or } b^2 = a^2 + c^2 - 2ac \cos B$$

$$\text{or } c^2 = a^2 + b^2 - 2ab \cos C$$

These can be rearranged as

$$\cos A = \frac{b^2 + c^2 - a^2}{2bc}$$

$$\cos B = \frac{a^2 + c^2 - b^2}{2ac}$$

$$\cos C = \frac{a^2 + b^2 - c^2}{2ab}$$

These rules can be used in any triangle, but you would not use them in a right-angled triangle, in which the usual ratios, $\sin \theta = \dfrac{\text{opp}}{\text{hyp}}$, $\cos \theta = \dfrac{\text{adj}}{\text{hyp}}$, $\tan \theta = \dfrac{\text{opp}}{\text{adj}}$, are simpler and easier to use.

The usual method of calculating sides or angles in an isosceles triangle is to split it into two congruent right-angled triangles, rather than using the rules given here.

Using the sine rule to find the length of a side

You must know the length of one other side, and the sizes of two of the angles.

Example

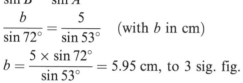

1   To find side b.

$\angle A = 180° - (55 + 72)° = 53°$

Use the part of the sine rule involving a and b.

$$\frac{b}{\sin B} = \frac{a}{\sin A}$$

$$\frac{b}{\sin 72°} = \frac{5}{\sin 53°} \quad \text{(with } b \text{ in cm)}$$

$$b = \frac{5 \times \sin 72°}{\sin 53°} = 5.95 \text{ cm, to 3 sig. fig.}$$

Unless told otherwise, give lengths correct to 3 significant figures.

To use your calculator, make sure it is set to work in degrees, then press

5 ⊠ 72 $\boxed{\sin}$ ÷ 53 $\boxed{\sin}$ $\boxed{=}$ getting 5.954 ...

On some calculators you may have to press

5 ⊠ $\boxed{\sin}$ 72 ÷ $\boxed{\sin}$ 53 $\boxed{=}$

If you want to find side c, use $\dfrac{c}{\sin C} = \dfrac{a}{\sin A}$.

Check that this gives $c = 5.13$ cm.

You could use $\dfrac{c}{\sin C} = \dfrac{b}{\sin B}$ instead since you have previously found b, but it is safer to use a in case you have made a mistake in calculating b.

Check if your answers seem reasonable. In this triangle, $\angle B$ is the largest angle so b will be longer than a. $\angle C$ is only slightly larger than $\angle A$, so side c will be just greater than 5 cm.

Obtuse angles

Sometimes one of the angles in the triangle will be greater than 90°. If you are using a calculator there will be no problem, e.g. find sin 100° and you will get the correct value of 0.9848.

Using the sine rule to find an angle

You must know the lengths of two sides and an angle opposite one of these sides.

Example

2   To find $\angle C$.

$$\frac{\sin C}{c} = \frac{\sin A}{a}$$

$$\frac{\sin C}{3} = \frac{\sin 123°}{5}$$

$$\sin C = \frac{3 \times \sin 123°}{5}$$

$$\angle C = 30.2°$$

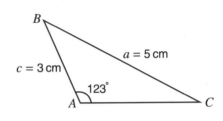

Give angles in degrees correct to 1 decimal place.

To use your calculator, make sure it is set to work in degrees, then press

3 $\boxed{\times}$ 123 $\boxed{\sin}$ $\boxed{\div}$ 5 $\boxed{=}$ $\boxed{\text{inverse sine}}$ getting 30.2 ...

Note that $\angle C$ is definitely an acute angle as $\angle A$ is obtuse. There could be complications if you did not know whether $\angle C$ was an acute angle or an obtuse angle. (You should not be asked to solve such questions.)
Now that you know the sizes of angles A and C, you can find $\angle B$ by subtraction.

$$\angle B = 180° - (123 + 30.2)° = 26.8°$$

You can now use the sine rule to find the length of side b, if needed.

Using the cosine rule to find the length of a side

You must know the lengths of the other two sides and the size of the angle included between them.

Example

3   To find side a.

Use $a^2 = b^2 + c^2 - 2bc \cos A$
$$= 4^2 + 3^2 - (2 \times 4 \times 3 \times \cos 70°)$$
$$= 16 + 9 - 8.2085 = 16.7915$$
$$a = 4.10 \text{ cm, to 3 sig. fig.}$$

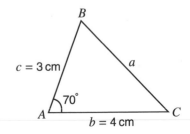

You must work out the whole of $2 \times 4 \times 3 \times \cos 70°$
before you subtract it from the 1st two terms.

You can do the complete calculation on your calculator.

Press 4 $\boxed{x^2}$ $\boxed{+}$ 3 $\boxed{x^2}$ $\boxed{-}$ 2 $\boxed{\times}$ 4 $\boxed{\times}$ 3 $\boxed{\times}$ 70 $\boxed{\cos}$ $\boxed{=}$ $\boxed{\sqrt{\ }}$

Now that you know the length of side a you can use the sine rule if you need to find $\angle B$ or $\angle C$, and then find the remaining angle by subtraction.

Obtuse angles

The cosine of an obtuse angle has a negative value. If you are using a calculator it will give the value directly, e.g. $\cos 110° = -0.3420$.

Example

4   To find side c.

$$c^2 = a^2 + b^2 - 2ab\cos C$$
$$= 4^2 + 3^2 - (2 \times 4 \times 3 \times \cos 110°)$$
$$= 16 + 9 + 8.2085 = 33.2085$$
$$c = 5.76 \text{ cm, to 3 sig. fig.}$$

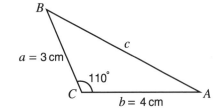

(The minus sign from $\cos 110°$ combined with the minus sign in the formula gives $+8.2085$.)

You can do the complete calculation on your calculator.

Press 4 $\boxed{x^2}$ $\boxed{+}$ 3 $\boxed{x^2}$ $\boxed{-}$ 2 $\boxed{\times}$ 4 $\boxed{\times}$ 3 $\boxed{\times}$ 110 $\boxed{\cos}$ $\boxed{=}$ $\boxed{\sqrt{\ }}$

The calculator will automatically add the last term, $-2 \times 4 \times 3 \times \cos 110°$ to the 1st two terms by changing $- \times -$ into $+$.

Using the cosine rule to find an angle

You must know the lengths of all three sides.

Example

5   To find $\angle A$.

Use $\cos A = \dfrac{b^2 + c^2 - a^2}{2bc}$

$$= \dfrac{9^2 + 8^2 - 11^2}{2 \times 9 \times 8}$$
$$= 0.1667$$
$$\angle A = 80.4°$$

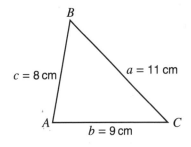

You can do the complete calculation on your calculator.

Press 9 $\boxed{x^2}$ $\boxed{+}$ 8 $\boxed{x^2}$ $\boxed{-}$ 11 $\boxed{x^2}$ $\boxed{=}$ $\boxed{\div}$ 2 $\boxed{\div}$ 9 $\boxed{\div}$ 8 $\boxed{=}$ $\boxed{\text{inverse cos}}$

If you need to find all three angles, find the largest one first, i.e. the angle opposite the largest side, using this method. Then you know that the other two angles must be acute angles and you can use the sine rule to find one of them, and find the third angle by subtraction. (You can use the cosine rule again to find the second angle if you prefer it.)

Example

6   To find the angles of $\triangle ABC$.

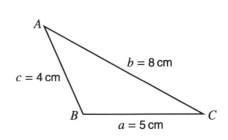

Use $\cos B = \dfrac{a^2 + c^2 - b^2}{2ac}$

$$= \dfrac{5^2 + 4^2 - 8^2}{2 \times 4 \times 5}$$

$$= -0.575$$

$$\angle B = 125.1°$$

$$\dfrac{\sin A}{a} = \dfrac{\sin B}{b}$$

$$\dfrac{\sin A}{5} = \dfrac{\sin 125.1°}{8}$$

$$\sin A = \dfrac{5 \times \sin 125.1°}{8}$$

$$\angle A = 30.8°$$

$$\angle C = 180° - (125.1 + 30.8)° = 24.1°$$

Area of a triangle

There is a trig. formula for the area of a triangle.

> Area $\triangle ABC = \frac{1}{2}\, bc \sin A$
>
> $\qquad\quad = \frac{1}{2}\, ac \sin B$
>
> $\qquad\quad = \frac{1}{2}\, ab \sin C$

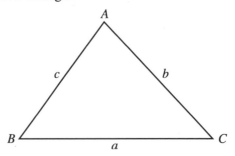

Example

7   To find the area of $\triangle ABC$.

Area $\triangle ABC = \frac{1}{2}\, ac \sin B$

$$= \frac{1}{2} \times 8 \times 5 \times \sin 117°$$

$$= 17.8 \text{ cm}^2, \text{ to 3 sig. fig.}$$

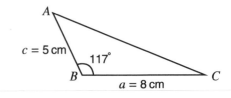

Exercise 23.1

1.   Use the sine rule to find the stated side in these triangles, giving answers correct to 3 significant figures.

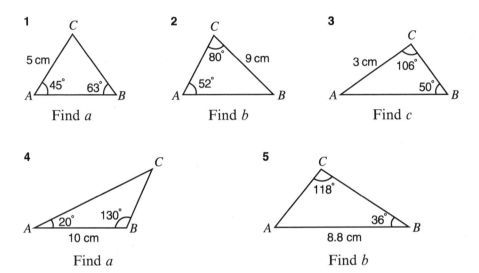

1	2	3
Find *a*	Find *b*	Find *c*

4	5
Find *a*	Find *b*

2.   Use the sine rule to find the stated angle in these triangles, in degrees, correct to 1 decimal place. (In each case the angle is an acute angle.)

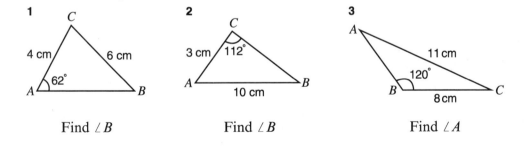

1	2	3
Find ∠B	Find ∠B	Find ∠A

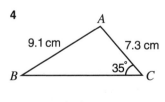

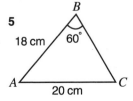

Find ∠B   Find ∠C and hence find ∠A

3.   Use the cosine rule to find the 3rd side of these triangles, giving answers correct to
      3 significant figures.

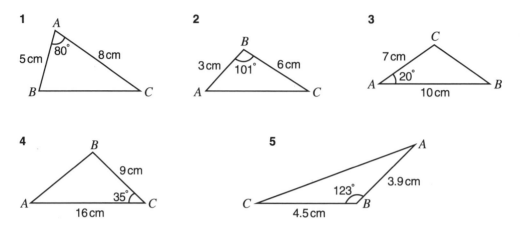

4.   Use the cosine rule to find the stated angle in these triangles, in degrees, correct to
      1 decimal place.

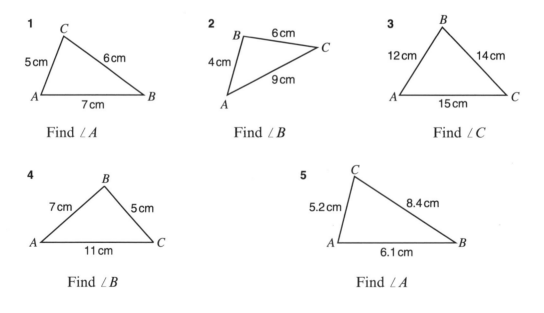

5.   Find the areas of the triangles in question 3, giving answers correct to 3 significant
      figures.

6.   Use the sine or cosine rule as appropriate, to find the stated sides or angles in these triangles. Give lengths correct to 3 significant figures and angles in degrees correct to 1 decimal place.

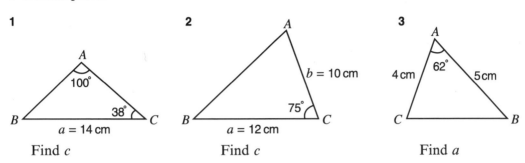

1

Find *c*

2

Find *c*

3

Find *a*

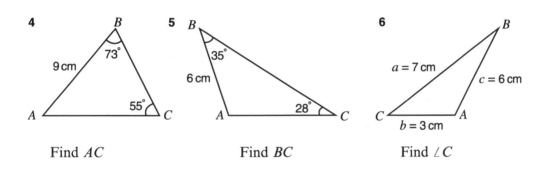

4

Find *AC*

5

Find *BC*

6

Find ∠*C*

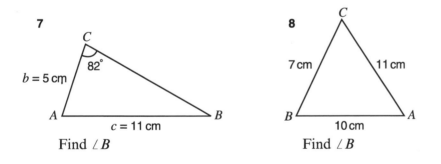

7

Find ∠*B*

8

Find ∠*B*

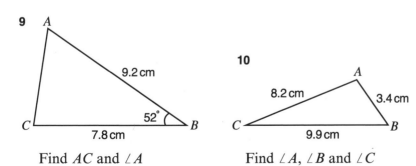

9

Find *AC* and ∠*A*

10

Find ∠*A*, ∠*B* and ∠*C*

7. *A*, *B* and *C* are 3 towns
    $AC = 65$ km, $\angle CAB = 41°$ and $\angle CBA = 28°$.
    Find the distances *BC* and *AB*.
    How much further is it for a plane to fly
    from *A* to *B* via *C*, than to go directly
    from *A* to *B* ?

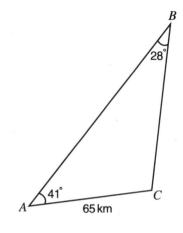

8. In this tetrahedron, $\triangle ABC$ is on a
    horizontal plane and *DB* is a vertical line.
    $DB = 12$ cm, $AB = 16$ cm, $BC = 9$ cm,
    $\angle ABC = 30°$.
    Find
    1   *AC*,
    2   *AD*,
    3   *CD*,
    4   $\angle ADC$.

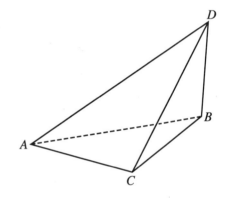

Exercise 23.2   Applications

1. A ship sails from a harbour *A* for 2 miles on a bearing of 065°. It then sails on a bearing
    of 100° until it reaches a landing-stage at a place *B* which is due East of *A*.

    1   Calculate the distance *AB*.
    2   Find how far the ship sailed altogether.

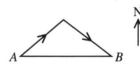

2. In a sailing race the boats go round a triangular
    course *ABC*, with $AB = 4$ km, $BC = 5$ km and
    $CA = 6$ km.
    If the direction of *AB* is due North, on what bearing
    do the boats head from *B* to *C* ?

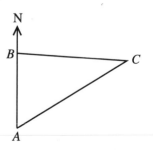

3. *ABC* is a triangular field. *AC* = 400 m and *C* is
    due East of *A*. *BC* = 300 m and ∠*B* = 70°.

    1 Calculate the size of ∠*A*.
    2 Hence find the bearings of *B* from *A*, and
           B from *C*.
    3 Find the area of the field in hectares, to
           1 decimal place.
           (1 hectare = 10 000 m²)

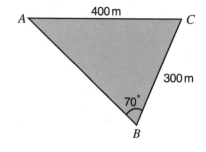

4. The angle of elevation of a balloon due West of an
    observer *A* and 600 m high is 42°.
    How far is the observer from a point on level ground
    vertically below the balloon ?
    A second observer *B* is on ground which is level with the
    first observer and he is due South-east of the balloon.
    He sees the balloon at an angle of elevation of 35°.
    How far is he from the point on the ground vertically
    below the balloon ?
    Find the distance apart of the two observers.

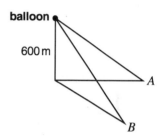

5. *ABCD* is a field with *AB* = 140 m, *AC* = 150 m,
    BC = 120 m, *AD* = 100 m and ∠*DAC* = 70°.

    1 Calculate the size of ∠*BAC*.
    2 Find the area of the field in hectares, to
           1 decimal place.
           (1 hectare = 10 000 m²)

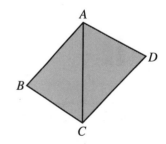

6. A vertical pole *AB* stands on sloping ground which
    rises at 10° to the horizontal. At a point *C*, 50 m
    directly downhill from the foot of the pole, the angle
    of elevation of the top of the pole is 18°.
    Calculate the height of the pole.

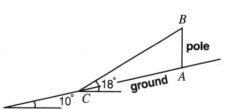

7. An explorer walks 1000 m on a bearing of 070° and then he walks 2000 m on a bearing
    of 150°. Draw a sketch diagram of his route.
    Find how far he has to go to return directly to his starting point, and the bearing he
    must follow.

8.   If $AB = 8$ cm, $BC = 5$ cm and $\angle ABC = 50°$, find

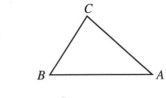

   1   the area of $\triangle ABC$, to the nearest cm^2,

   2   the length of AC, to the nearest mm,

   3   the size of $\angle BAC$, in degrees, to 1 decimal place.

9. ABC is a triangular field on horizontal ground, in
which $AB = 28$ m, $AC = 92$ m and $\angle BAC = 80°$.
BD is a tree, and the angle of elevation of the top D
of the tree from C is $7°$.

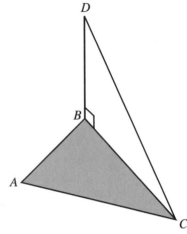

Find

   1   the length of BC,

   2   the height BD of the tree.

Practice test 23

1.   The sides of a triangle are 5 cm, 7 cm and 10 cm. Find the size of the largest angle.

2.   In $\triangle ABC$, $\angle B = 30°$, $AB = 3$ cm and $AC = 4$ cm. Find the size of $\angle C$ and hence find
the size of $\angle A$.

3.   Two lookout stations A and B are 1600 m apart.
B is due East of A.
A ship S is seen out at sea. The bearing of the ship
from A is $042°$ and its bearing from B is $328°$.
Find the distance of the ship from A.

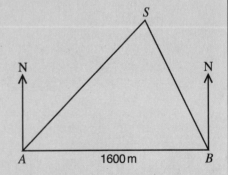

4.   In a triangular field ABC, $AB = 50$ m, $AC = 60$ m and $\angle BAC = 70°$.

Find

   1   the length of fencing needed to totally enclose the field,

   2   the area of the field, in m^2.

5. Two vertical posts *AD* and *BE* are each 12 m high, and they are 24 m apart. From a point *C* on ground which is level with *A* and *B* the angle of elevation of *D* is 38° and the angle of elevation of *E* is 42°.

Find
1 *AC*,
2 *BC*,
3 ∠*ACB*.

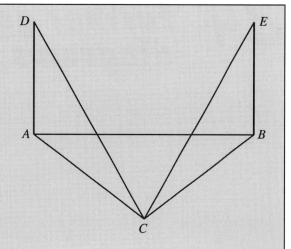

PUZZLES

47. Write the numbers from 100 to 200 as the sum of consecutive integers.
e.g. $100 = 18 + 19 + 20 + 21 + 22$
$101 = 50 + 51$
$102 = 33 + 34 + 35$
$104 = 2 + 3 + 4 + \cdots + 13 + 14$
It is possible to do this for every number except one of them. Which number is this ?

48. In a dress shop there were six dresses in the window, marked for sale at £15, £22, £30, £26, £16 and £31. Five of the dresses were sold to two customers, the second customer spending twice as much as the first one. Which dress was unsold ?

49. If it takes 5 men 5 days to plough 5 fields, how long does it take 1 man to plough 1 field, working at the same rate ?

50. Practical maths. Fold a piece of paper in half, then in half again, and again, ... , 9 times altogether.

51. Nine people, Andrew, Bilkish, Craig, Dhiren, Edith, Faruk, Graham, Helen and Iqbal share a prize of £450 amongst themselves.
Bilkish gets £1 more than Andrew, Craig gets £1 more than Bilkish, Dhiren gets £1 more than Craig, and so on. How much does Iqbal get ?

24 Further graphs and diagrams

The topics in this chapter include:

- sketching and comparing graphs of functions,
- using coefficients in quadratics,
- interpreting diagrams used in linear programming,
- interpreting critical path analysis diagrams.

Sketch graphs of functions

A sketch graph should show the main shape of the graph and perhaps also the coordinates of a few important points on it, such as where it crosses the axes, and any maximum or minimum points.

It may be helpful to make a table of values to get an idea of the general shape of the graph, but do not plot unimportant points for just a few values of x near the origin. Consider what happens to the graph when x is a very big positive or negative number.

If you can use a computer graph plotting program, or a graphics calculator, you can investigate the shape of a graph and other related graphs quite quickly.

Example

Sketch the graph of the function $y = 5 + 4x - x^2$.

It is of the form $y = ax^2 + bx + c$ with $a = -1$, $b = 4$, $c = 5$.
a is negative so the graph has a maximum point.
The graph cuts the x-axis at the points where $5 + 4x - x^2 = 0$.
i.e. $x^2 - 4x - 5 = 0$
$(x + 1)(x - 5) = 0$
$x + 1 = 0$ or $x - 5 = 0$
$x = -1$ or $x = 5$

The graph cuts the y-axis at (0, 5).

The line of symmetry is the line
$$x = -\frac{b}{2a} = -\frac{4}{-2} = 2$$

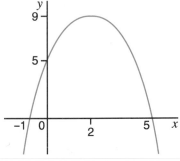

When $x = 2$, $y = 5 + 4 \times 2 - 2^2 = 9$, so the maximum point has coordinates (2, 9).

Some special functions

See also page 294.

The graph of $y = \dfrac{1}{x^2}$

Look at the graph of $y = x^2$ and you will see that y is always positive, except when $x = 0$, where $y = 0$.

So $\dfrac{1}{x^2}$ will always be positive, except when $x = 0$, where there is no value, since dividing by 0 is not possible.

As x gets very large, x^2 is larger and so $\dfrac{1}{x^2}$ gets very small and approaches 0.

When x is between 0 and 1, x^2 is less than 1 and is very small when x is near 0. So $\dfrac{1}{x^2}$ is greater than 1 and is very large when x is near 0.

The graph of $y = x^2$ is symmetrical about the y-axis, and so is the graph of $y = \dfrac{1}{x^2}$.

Using this information here is a sketch graph of $y = \dfrac{1}{x^2}$.

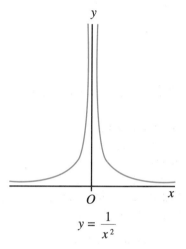

$$y = \frac{1}{x^2}$$

The graphs of $y = x^4$ and $y = \dfrac{1}{x^4}$

These can be sketched in a similar way.

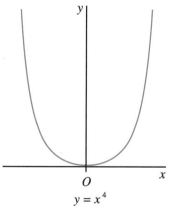

$$y = x^4$$

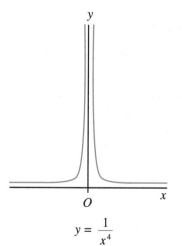

$$y = \frac{1}{x^4}$$

$y = x^4$ is flatter near the origin, so is more U-shaped than $y = x^2$.

Compare this graph with that of $y = \dfrac{1}{x^2}$.

The graphs of $y = \dfrac{1}{x}$ and $y = \dfrac{1}{x^3}$

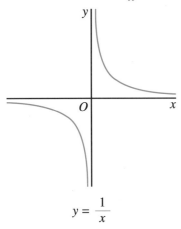

$$y = \frac{1}{x}$$

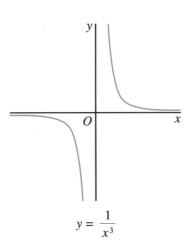

$$y = \frac{1}{x^3}$$

Compare this graph with that of $y = \dfrac{1}{x}$.

Related functions

The relationship between $y = f(x)$ and $y = f(x) + a$

a is a constant number.
The graph of $y = f(x) + a$ will be a translation of the graph of $y = f(x)$, of a units in the y-direction.

$y = x^2$

$y = x^2 + 2$

The 2nd graph is 2 units higher.

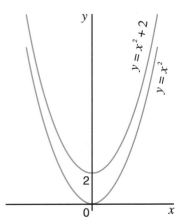

The relationship between $y = f(x)$ and $y = f(x - a)$

The graph of $y = f(x - a)$ will be a translation of the graph of $y = f(x)$, of a units in the x-direction.

$y = x^2$

$y = (x - 3)^2$
(i.e. $y = x^2 - 6x + 9$)

The 2nd graph is 3 units further along.

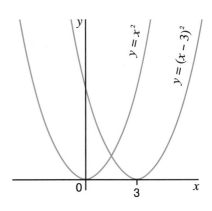

The relationship between $y = f(x)$ and $y = a\,f(x)$

The graph of $y = a\,f(x)$ will have the y-values of the function $y = f(x)$ multiplied by a factor a.

$y = x^3 + 1$

$y = 2(x^3 + 1)$
(i.e. $y = 2x^3 + 2$)

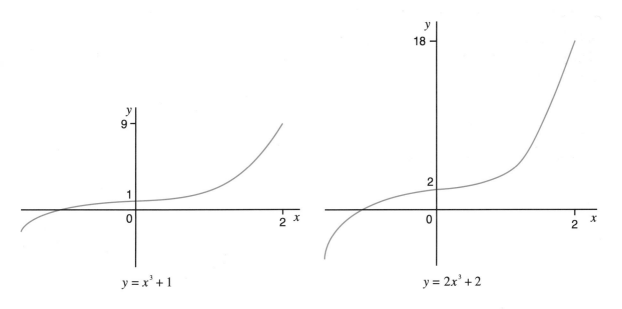

$y = x^3 + 1$ $y = 2x^3 + 2$

The relationship between $y = f(x)$ and $y = f(ax)$

The graph of $y = f(ax)$ will have the x-values of the function $y = f(x)$ divided by a $\left(\text{or multiplied by } \dfrac{1}{a}\right)$.

$y = x^2 - 6x$

$y = (3x)^2 - 6(3x)$
(i.e. $y = 9x^2 - 18x$)

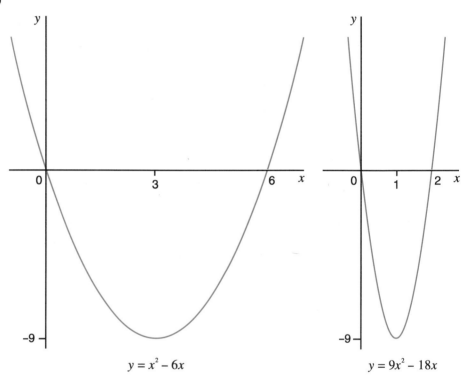

$$y = x^2 - 6x$$ $$y = 9x^2 - 18x$$

If you cannot sketch a graph by discovering its relationship to another graph, remember that you can always make a table of values to get an idea of its general shape.

Exercise 24.1

1. These sketch graphs represent the functions $y = 2$, $y = 2x$, $y = x + 2$, $y = 2x + 2$, $y = 2 - x$, $y = 2 - 2x$. Identify each graph.

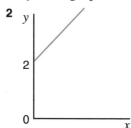

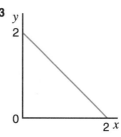

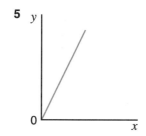

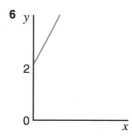

2. This question uses the quadratic function $y = x^2 + x - 20$.
   1 Has the graph of the function got a maximum point or a minimum point ?
   2 Find the coordinates of the points where the graph cuts the x-axis.
   3 Find the coordinates of the point where the graph cuts the y-axis.
   4 Sketch the graph of the function.

3. Repeat question 2 for the quadratic function $y = 3 + 5x - 2x^2$.

4. 1 Make a table of values for the function $y = x^2$, for x from -4 to 4 including $x = -\frac{1}{2}$ and $x = \frac{1}{2}$.
   Sketch the graph of $y = x^2$, not on graph paper.

   2 Make a table of values for the function $y = 4x^2$ for x from -4 to 4, and use this and the sketch graph of $y = x^2$ to sketch the graph of $y = 4x^2$.

   3 Make a table of values for the function $y = x^2 + 4$ for x from -4 to 4, and use this and the sketch graph of $y = x^2$ to sketch the graph of $y = x^2 + 4$.

   4 Copy and complete this table of values for the function $y = (x - 4)^2$.

x	0	1	2	3	4	5	6	7	8
$x - 4$	-4								
$(x - 4)^2$	16								

   Use this and the sketch graph of $y = x^2$ to sketch the graph of $y = (x - 4)^2$.

5. **1** Make a table of values for the function $y = x^3$, for x from -3 to 3, including $x = -\frac{1}{2}$ and $x = \frac{1}{2}$.
Sketch the graph of $y = x^3$.

2 Make a table of values for the function $y = 2x^3$ for x from -3 to 3, and use this and the sketch graph of $y = x^3$ to sketch the graph of $y = 2x^3$.

3 Make a table of values for the function $y = x^3 - 1$, for x from -3 to 3, and use this and the sketch graph of $y = x^3$ to sketch the graph of $y = x^3 - 1$.

4 Copy and complete this table of values for the function $y = (x - 1)^3$.

x	-2	-1	0	1	2	3	4
$x - 1$	-3						
$(x - 1)^3$	-27						

Use this and the sketch graph of $y = x^3$ to sketch the graph of $y = (x - 1)^3$.

6. For each question, sketch the graphs of the two functions, on the same or adjoining sketches, to show the relationship between them.

1 $y = 3x - 2$
$y = 3x + 2$

2 $y = x^2$
$y = (x - 2)^2$

3 $y = x^2(x - 3)$
$y = 2x^2(x - 3)$

4 $y = x^2 - 1$
$y = 4x^2 - 1$

5 $y = x^3$
$y = (x + 5)^3$

6 $y = x(x + 1)$
$y = 3x(3x + 1)$

7 $y = x^3$
$y = x^3 - 8$

8 $y = x^2 + 5x$
$y = 3x^2 + 15x$

9 $y = x^2 - 4$
$y = 4 - x^2$

10 $y = x^3 + 1$
$y = 3x^3 + 1$

7. Sketch these graphs on separate sketches, showing how they are related to each other.

1 $y = x^3$
2 $y = 2x^3$

3 $y = -2x^3$
4 $y = 16 - 2x^3$

8. **1** Make a table of values for the graph of $y = \dfrac{48}{x}$, for x from -6 to 6, including $x = -\frac{1}{2}$ and $x = \frac{1}{2}$ but not including $x = 0$.
Sketch the graph of $y = \dfrac{48}{x}$.

2 Make a table of values for the graph of $y = \dfrac{48}{x^2}$, for x from -6 to 6, including $x = -\frac{1}{2}$ and $x = \frac{1}{2}$ but not including $x = 0$.
Sketch the graph of $y = \dfrac{48}{x^2}$.

8.   3   Sketch the graphs $y = \dfrac{48}{x}$ and $y = \dfrac{48}{x^2}$ for $x > 0$ using the same axes, and label them. Where do the graphs intersect each other ?

Linear Programming

You have already used inequalities and represented them by regions on graphs. This has a practical use in finding the greatest or least values of a particular function which has to satisfy certain conditions.

Example

The shaded area, including the boundary lines, is the region

$x \geqslant 0$
$y \geqslant x$
$y \leqslant 3 - \tfrac{1}{2} x$

Now suppose that we want to find a point in the region which gives the greatest value for $x + y$.
If the greatest value is k, then $x + y = k$.
This equation is represented by the line $y = k - x$.

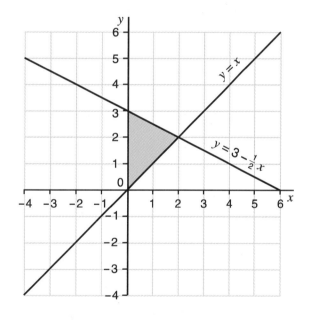

On the graph, we could draw the line $y = 6 - x$.
It passes through (6, 0) and (0, 6). You also know that its gradient is -1.
Put your ruler on the graph, passing through these 2 points.
This line does not pass through the region so $k = 6$ is not a solution.
Try $y = 5 - x$, going through (5, 0) and (0, 5).
You will notice that this line is parallel to the 1st one.
But it, too, does not pass through the shaded region.

Keeping your ruler parallel to this line, move it until it just meets the region, which will be at the point (2, 2).
So $x + y = 2 + 2 = 4$, and this is the greatest value of $x + y$ for a point (x, y) in the region.

We will show the lines $y = 6 - x$, $y = 5 - x$ and $y = 4 - x$ on a diagram.
(Normally you would draw lines on the graph, but do not draw them in the book.)

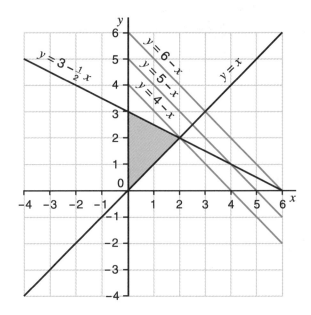

As another example, using the same region, suppose we want to find a point in the region which gives the greatest value for $2y - x$.
If this greatest value is k, then $2y - x = k$.
This equation is represented by the line $2y = x + k$, i.e. $y = \frac{1}{2}x + \frac{1}{2}k$.
This line has gradient $\frac{1}{2}$.

Possible lines are $y = \frac{1}{2}x$, $y = \frac{1}{2}x + 1$, $y = \frac{1}{2}x + 2$, etc.
Since we want the greatest value of k, we want the highest of these lines which passes through the region.

The line $y = \frac{1}{2}x$ passes through $(0, 0)$ and $(6, 3)$. Put your ruler on the graph, passing through these 2 points.
Now keep the ruler parallel to this line and move it upward until it is as far as it will go, but still passing through the shaded region. This is when it passes through the point $(0, 3)$.
So the greatest value of $2y - x$ for a point (x, y) in the region is $2 \times 3 - 0 = 6$.
The diagram shows the lines $y = \frac{1}{2}x$ and $y = \frac{1}{2}x + 3$.

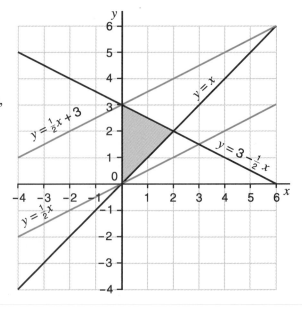

Critical Path Diagrams

These are used to help in the planning of a job which consists of a number of operations. They are network diagrams with a beginning and an end. The operations are represented by the lines of the network and the time each operation takes is also shown.

The critical path shows the route through the network from start to end which takes the longest time. The total job cannot be finished in less time than this.

Critical path diagrams can be used in an industrial situation to make the most efficient use of the workforce and machinery, and keep costs to a minimum.

Example

In this diagram, find the critical path. What is the shortest time in which the job can be completed ?

What is the latest time at which operations C and E must be started, if the job is to be finished in the shortest possible time ? The earliest time the job can start is noon.

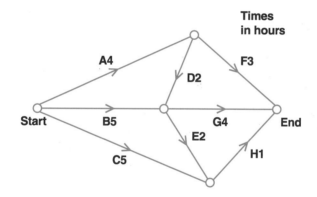

Capital letters have been used to identify the operations.

The first 3 operations are A, 4 hours, B, 5 hours and C, 5 hours.

The other operations are D, E, F, G, H.

D can be started after A is completed, that is, after 4 hours.

Operation E can only be started when all the operations leading to E have been completed. B is completed after 5 hours and operations A and D are completed after 6 hours. So E cannot be started for 6 hours. Similarly, G cannot be started for 6 hours. The end can be reached via G in 10 hours.

F can be started after A is completed, and, via F, the end can be reached in 7 hours.

H can be started after E and C are completed (E 8 hours, C 5 hours), so H cannot be started for 8 hours. Via H the end can be reached in 9 hours.

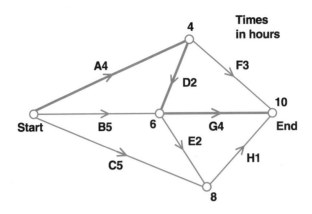

The critical path is ADG, taking 10 hours.
The job cannot be done in less than 10 hours.

Slack time

Since the other routes take less than 10 hours, there is some 'slack time'.
If we let the operations start at noon, the times along the critical path can be noted.

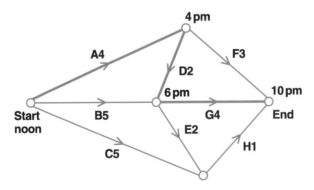

Thus operation B, which takes 5 hours, cannot begin before noon and must finish by
6 pm. Therefore, it could be delayed to start at times up to 1 pm.
The operation F, which takes 3 hours, cannot begin before 4 pm and must finish by
10 pm. Therefore it could be delayed to start at any time up to 7 pm.
The operation H must start at 9 pm at the latest, so the operation E must start at 7 pm
at the latest, and operation C must start at 4 pm at the latest.

Exercise 24.2

1. The lines in the diagram have these equations:
   $AB: 4y = 3x - 5$
   $BC: 6y = 31 - x$
   $AC: y = 7 - 2x$

   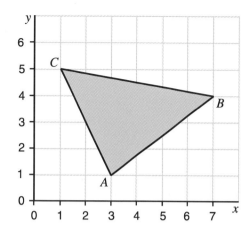

   1 Identify the region of the shaded triangle. The boundary lines are to be included in the region.

   2 Where does the line $3y = 6 - 2x$ meet the axes ?
   Put your ruler along this line and by keeping the ruler parallel to this line, find the least value of $3y + 2x$ for a point (x, y) in the region, and state this value.

   3 Using the same line, find the greatest value of $3y + 2x$ for a point (x, y) in the region, and state this value.

   4 Using another suitable line, find the greatest value of $3y - x$ for a point (x, y) in the region, and state this value.

2. **1** On graph paper, label the x and y axes from 0 to 16, taking a scale of 1 cm to 1 unit on both axes.
   Plot the points A (5, 0), B (10, 6), C (6, 12) and D (1, 10), and join the points to enclose the region $ABCD$. The region includes the boundary lines.

   2 Find the greatest value of $x + y$ for a point (x, y) in the region. What is this greatest value ?

   3 Find the greatest and least values of $5y - 7x$ for points (x, y) in the region. What are these values ?

3. **1** On graph paper, label the x and y axes from 0 to 16, using a scale of 1 cm to 1 unit on both axes.
   Draw the lines $y = x$, $y = 6 - 2x$, $y = 24 - 3x$ and $2y = 3x + 12$, showing as much of the lines as fit on the graph.
   Identify the region
   $y \geqslant x$
   $y \geqslant 6 - 2x$
   $y \leqslant 24 - 3x$
   $2y \leqslant 3x + 12$.

   2 Find the greatest value of $2x + y$ for a point (x, y) in the region.

   3 Find the greatest and least values of $y - 2x$ for points (x, y) in the region.

4.   Copy these diagrams and for each one find the critical path. Show it in colour. State the
      least time needed to complete each job.

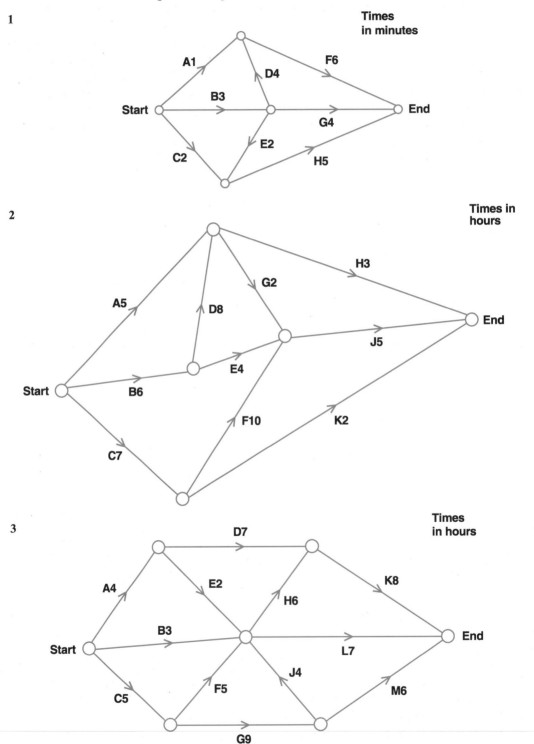

1

Times in minutes

A1   F6   D4   B3   Start   End   G4   E2   C2   H5

2

Times in hours

H3   G2   A5   D8   End   E4   J5   Start   B6   F10   K2   C7

3

Times in hours

D7   A4   E2   K8   H6   B3   Start   End   L7   J4   C5   F5   M6   G9

5.   For a party, Eileen wants to buy some biscuits. She buys x packets of chocolate biscuits
      and y packets of cream biscuits.
      Write down inequalities if she decides to buy at least 3 packets of each kind, but not
      more than 12 packets altogether.
      Packets of chocolate biscuits cost 60p each and packets of cream biscuits cost 30p each.
      Eileen must not spend more than £4.80 altogether. Write down another inequality.
      On graph paper, draw x and y axes from 0 to 16. Draw lines representing the boundary
      lines of the inequalities and identify the region which satisfies the inequalities.
      Packets of chocolate biscuits contain 15 biscuits and packets of cream biscuits contain 12
      biscuits. Find the number of packets of each kind of biscuit to be bought to give the
      greatest number of biscuits, and say how many biscuits there will be.

Exercise 24.3 Applications

1.   The function f is defined by f: $x \mapsto (x+3)(x-4)$.
      1 Solve the equation $f(x) = 0$.
      2 Solve the equation $f(x) = 18$.
      3 Sketch a graph of the function.
      4 Write down the equation of the line of symmetry of the graph.
      5 Find the value of $f(x)$ at the point on the graph when the function has a minimum
             value.

2.   Identify these graphs from this list:

$$y = x^2 + 4, \quad y = x^2 - 4, \quad y = 4 - x^2, \quad y = 4x^2, \quad y = x^2 - 4x + 4.$$

1 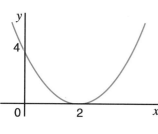   **2** 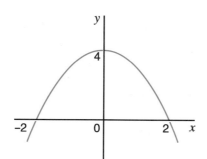   **3**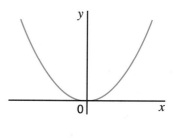

3.   The equation of a curve is $y = x(x-2)(x+3)$.

      1 Write down the coordinates of the points where the curve crosses the x-axis.
      2 What is the value of y when $x = 3$?
      3 What is the value of y when $x = -4$?
      4 Draw a sketch graph of the curve.

4. This sketch graph shows part of the curve defined by $y = x^2 + bx + c$. Find the values of b and c.

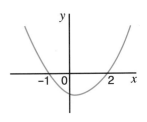

5. Sketch these graphs, on the same or adjoining sketches, to show the relationship between the 1st graph and each of the others.

$$y = x^2, \quad y = 2x^2, \quad y = x^2 + 2, \quad y = (x + 2)^2$$

6. On separate sketches, sketch these graphs, showing the relationship between each one and the next.

$$y = x^2, \quad y = (x - 5)^2, \quad y = 2(x - 5)^2, \quad y = 2(x - 5)^2 + 3.$$

7. Make a table of values for the function $y = \dfrac{1}{x}$ for $x = \frac{1}{2}, 1, 1\frac{1}{2}, 2$.

Repeat for the functions $y = \dfrac{1}{x^2}$, $y = \dfrac{1}{x^3}$.

Sketch the graphs of these three functions using the same axes, for $\frac{1}{2} \leqslant x \leqslant 2$. Label each graph.

8. A coach firm has to carry 500 passengers. Coaches can carry up to 50 passengers and minibuses can carry up to 20 passengers.
If the firm uses x coaches and y minibuses, write down an inequality satisfied by x and y, and simplify it.
The firm has 19 drivers available, and also decides that they will use at least 5 minibuses.
Write down another two inequalities satisfied by x and y.
Draw the x and y axes from 0 to 30 using a scale of 2 cm to 5 units.
Show the inequalities on a graph and identify the region in which the 3 inequalities are satisfied.
To use a coach costs £120 and to use a minibus costs £30.
Write down an expression for the cost of x coaches and y minibuses.
If the total cost is £30k, show that the equation to be satisfied is $y = k - 4x$.
Find the least value of $y + 4x$ satisfied by a point (x, y) in the region. Hence find the number of coaches and minibuses to be used to make the cost least, and state this cost.

9. A builder has a plot of land available on which he can build houses.
He can either build luxury houses or standard houses.
He decides to build at least 15 luxury and at least 5 standard houses, and he cannot build more than 40 houses altogether.
If he builds x luxury houses and y standard houses, write down 3 inequalities satisfied by x and y.
Draw the x-axis from 0 to 40 and the y-axis from 0 to 50, taking a scale of 2 cm to 5 units on both axes.
Draw the boundary lines of the inequalities on the graph.

The luxury houses require 240 m^2 of land each, and the standard houses require 120 m^2 each. The total area of the plot is 7200 m^2. Write down a 4th inequality, simplify it and draw its boundary line on the graph.
Identify the region in which all 4 inequalities are satisfied.

The builder makes a profit of £6000 on each luxury house and a profit of £4000 on each standard house. Write down an expression for the total profit expected.
If this total profit is £2000k, show that the equation to be satisfied is $2y = k - 3x$.

Find the greatest value of $2y + 3x$ satisfied by a point (x, y) in the region. Hence find the number of luxury houses and the number of standard houses that the builder should build to make the greatest profit, and say what this profit will be.

10.   This diagram shows the operations involved in modernising a kitchen, and the time taken to complete each operation.

Times in days

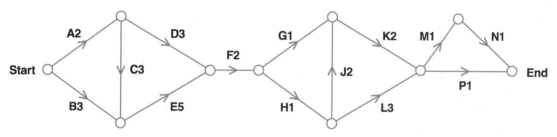

Operations

A	Remove old tiles	H	Fit new sink
B	Install new plumbing	J	Paint woodwork
C	Rewire	K	Walls papered
D	Fit new windows	L	Fit new tiles
E	Install fitted cupboards	M	Fit new carpet
F	Re-plaster where necessary	N	Install appliances
G	Paint the ceiling	P	Replace kitchen equipment

Copy the diagram.
Find the critical path for the complete job, and mark it in colour.
State the least time that the job will take.
If the new windows were not ready when the old tiles were removed, how many extra days are there for them to be made ready if the job is still to be finished in the least time ?

11. A nurseryman takes some flowering shrubs to sell at the market. They are red-flowering
     or yellow-flowering shrubs.
     The man decides to take at least 4 of each kind, but he has only 10 of the red ones and
     18 of the yellow ones ready for sale. There is not room for more than 24 shrubs
     altogether on the stall.
     If he takes x red-flowering shrubs and y yellow-flowering shrubs, write down inequalities
     satisfied by x and y.
     Draw x and y axes labelled from 0 to 24 and draw the lines giving the boundaries of the
     region satisfied by the inequalities. Identify the region.

     If the man plans to sell the red-flowering shrubs at £8 each and the yellow-flowering
     shrubs at £6 each, find the number of each kind he should take to sell, so as to make the
     most money from their sale, and say how much this will amount to.

     If, instead, the man decides that he will sell the red-flowering shrubs at £5 each and the
     yellow-flowering shrubs at £8 each, how many of each kind should he take so as to make
     the most money, and how much will this amount to ?

Practice test 24

1.   If $f(x) = 3(x-1)^2 + 4$, find f(0), f(1), f(2) and f(3). What is the least value of f(x) ?

2.   This question uses the quadratic function $y = x^2 - 2x - 15$.
     1   Has the graph of the function got a maximum point or a minimum point ?
     2   Find the coordinates of the points where the graph cuts the x-axis.
     3   Find the coordinates of the point where the graph cuts the y-axis.
     4   Sketch the graph of the function.

3.   Show on the same sketch the graphs of
     1   $y = x^2$
     2   $y = (x-2)^2$
     3   $y = (x-2)^2 + 4$
     Label each graph.

4.   Make a table of values for the graph of $y = x^3 - 9x$ for x from -4 to 4.
     Sketch the graph of $y = x^3 - 9x$ for $-4 \leqslant x \leqslant 4$.
     From your graph find how many values of x satisfy the equation $x^3 - 9x = 5$.

5.   Show on the same sketch the graphs of
     1   $y = x^3$
     2   $y = 2x^3$
     3   $y = 2x^3 + 6$
     Label each graph.

6. On graph paper, label x and y axes from 0 to 10.
    Draw the lines $y = x - 1$, $y = 9 - x$, $3y = 12 - 2x$ and $x = 1$.
    Identify the region where $y \geqslant x - 1$, $y \leqslant 9 - x$, $3y \geqslant 12 - 2x$ and $x \geqslant 1$.
    Find the greatest and least values of $2x + 5y$ for points (x, y) in the region, and state
    these values.

7. Copy the diagram and find the critical path. Show it in colour. State the least time
    needed to complete the job.
    If the work is begun at 6 am, what is the latest time at which operation D can be
    started, if the work is to be finished in the least time ?

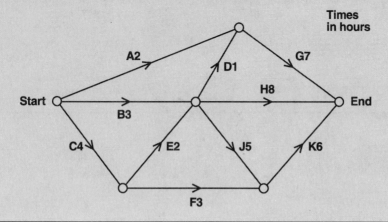

PUZZLES

52. If it takes a clock 6 seconds to strike 6, how long does it take to strike 12 ?

53. How many times in 12 hours do the hands of a clock point in the same direction ?

54. Jill has lost her timetable. She remembers that tomorrow's lessons end with Games,
    but she cannot remember the order of the first 5 lessons. She asks her friends, who
    decide to tease her.
    Alison says, 'Science is 3rd, History is 1st'.
    Brenda says, 'English is 2nd, Maths is 4th'
    Claire says, 'History is 5th, Science is 4th'.
    Denise says 'French is 5th, English is 2nd'.
    Emma says 'French is 3rd, Maths is 4th'
    Naturally, Jill is very confused by all this. Then her friends admit that they have each
    made one true statement and one untrue one.
    When is Maths ?

25 *Transformations*

The topics in this chapter include:

- understanding how transformations are related by combinations and inverses,
- using matrices to define transformations.

Here are details of four kinds of transformation:— translation, reflection, rotation and enlargement.

Examples here use the line AB, where A is (2, 1) and B is (3, 2).

Translation

The translation 4 units in the
x-direction, 1 unit in the y-direction.

A (2, 1) is transformed into A' (6, 2).

B (3, 2) is transformed into B' (7, 3).

The translation can be represented by
the vector $\begin{pmatrix} 4 \\ 1 \end{pmatrix}$.

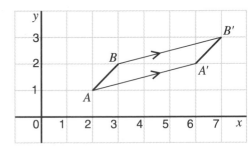

A' is called the image of A, B' is the **image** of B and the line $A'B'$ is the image of the line AB.

Reflection

Reflection in the x-axis

A (2, 1) is transformed into A' (2, −1).
B (3, 2) is transformed into B' (3, −2).

The line AB is reflected into the line $A'B'$.
AB and $A'B'$ are equal in length and the x-axis
is a line of symmetry between AB and $A'B'$.

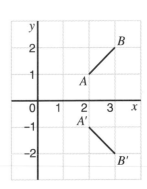

Reflection in the *y*-axis

A (2, 1) is transformed into A' (−2, 1).
B (3, 2) is transformed into B' (−3, 2).

The line AB is reflected into the line $A'B'$.
AB and $A'B'$ are equal in length and the *y*-axis is a line of symmetry between AB and $A'B'$.

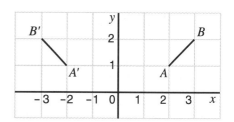

Reflection in the line *y* = *x*

A (2, 1) is transformed into A' (1, 2).
B (3, 2) is transformed into B' (2, 3).

The line AB is reflected into the line $A'B'$.
AB and $A'B'$ are equal in length and the line $y = x$ is an axis of symmetry between AB and $A'B'$.

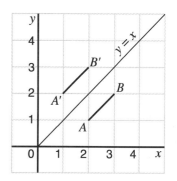

Reflection in the line *y* = −*x*

A (2, 1) is transformed into A' (−1, −2).
B (3, 2) is transformed into B' (−2, −3).

The line AB is reflected into the line $A'B'$.
AB and $A'B'$ are equal in length and the line $y = -x$ is an axis of symmetry between AB and $A'B'$.

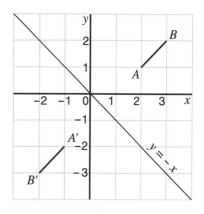

Reflections in other lines
e.g. Reflection in the line $y = 3$.

A (2, 1) is transformed into A' (2, 5).
B (3, 2) is transformed into B' (3, 4).

AB and $A'B'$ are equal in length and $y = 3$ is an axis of symmetry between AB and $A'B'$.

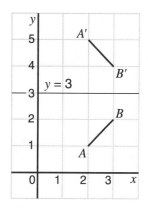

Rotation

3 things are needed to define a rotation.

1   A centre of rotation.
2   An amount of turn.
3   A direction of turn.

Rotation about the origin through 90° anticlockwise ($\frac{1}{4}$ turn)

A (2, 1) is transformed into A' (−1, 2).
B (3, 2) is transformed into B' (−2, 3).

The line AB is rotated into the line $A'B'$.
AB and $A'B'$ are equal in length.

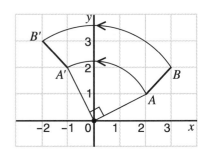

Rotation about the origin through 180° ($\frac{1}{2}$ turn)

A (2, 1) is transformed into A' (−2, −1).
B (3, 2) is transformed into B' (−3, −2).

The line AB is rotated into the line $A'B'$.
AB and $A'B'$ are equal in length.
The origin is a point of symmetry between AB and $A'B'$.

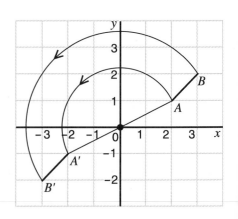

Rotation about the origin through 90° clockwise ($\frac{1}{4}$ turn)

A (2, 1) is transformed into A' (1, −2).
B (3, 2) is transformed into B' (2, −3).

The line AB is rotated into the line $A'B'$.
AB and $A'B'$ are equal in length.

A rotation of 90° clockwise is the
same as a rotation of 270° anticlockwise.

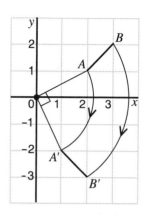

Rotations can be made about other points.
e.g. AB rotated through 90° anticlockwise about point A.

A is unaltered.
B (3, 2) is transformed into B' (1, 2).

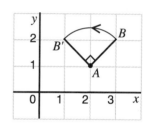

Enlargement

2 things are needed to define an enlargement

   1   A centre of enlargement.
   2   A scale factor.

The centre of enlargement

X is the centre of enlargement and k is
the scale factor of the enlargement.
If the image of A is A' and the image of B
is B', then
$XA' = k \times XA$, with XAA' being a straight line.
$XB' = k \times XB$, with XBB' being a straight line.

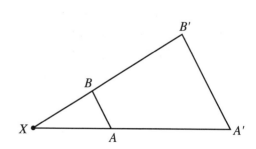

Examples

The dotted lines show the new positions of the triangles when they have been enlarged with the point X as the centre of enlargement.

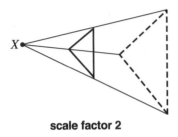

scale factor 2

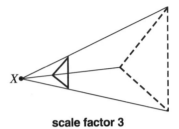

scale factor 3

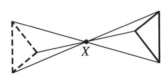

scale factor –1

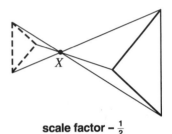

scale factor $-\frac{1}{2}$

Enlargement with scale factor 2, and centre of enlargement O (0, 0).

A (2, 1) is transformed into A' (2 × 2, 2 × 1), i.e. (4, 2).
B (3, 2) is transformed into B' (6, 4).
The line AB is transformed into the line $A'B'$.
AB and $A'B'$ are parallel and
length $A'B' = 2 \times$ length AB.

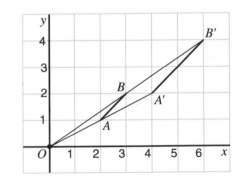

Triangles $OA'B'$ and OAB are similar with lengths in the ratio 2 : 1, and areas in the ratio 4 : 1.

If the scale factor is 3 then
A (2, 1) is transformed into A' (3 × 2, 3 × 1), i.e. (6, 3).
B (3, 2) is transformed into B' (9, 6).
The line AB is transformed into the line $A'B'$.
AB and $A'B'$ are parallel and length $A'B' = 3 \times$ length AB.

Triangles $OA'B'$ and OAB are similar with lengths in the ratio 3 : 1, and areas in the ratio 9 : 1.

Enlargements can have centres of enlargement other than the origin.
e.g. Enlargement with scale factor 2 and centre of
enlargement C (3, 0).

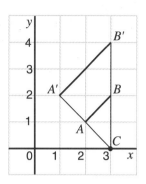

A (2, 1) is transformed into A' (1, 2).
B (3, 2) is transformed into B' (3, 4).

AB and $A'B'$ are parallel and length $A'B' = 2 \times$ length AB.

Triangles $CA'B'$ and CAB are similar with lengths in the
ratio 2 : 1.

Combined transformations

If a first transformation maps points A, B into points A_1, B_1, and a second transformation
maps points A_1, B_1 into points A_2, B_2, then the combined transformation is the single
transformation which would map A, B directly into A_2, B_2.

Example

If A (2, 1) and B (5, 2) are transformed into A_1, B_1 by the transformation, reflect in the
line $y = x$, and then A_1, B_1 are transformed into A_2, B_2 by the transformation, rotate
about the origin through 90° anticlockwise, what is the combined transformation which
maps A, B into A_2, B_2 ?

A (2, 1) is transformed into
A_1 (1, 2), which is transformed
into A_2 (−2, 1).

B (5, 2) is transformed into
B_1 (2, 5), which is transformed
into B_2 (−5, 2).

The combined transformation is,
reflect in the y-axis.
This is shown in the diagram.

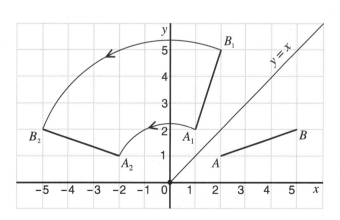

Inverse transformations

If a transformation maps points A, B into points A', B', then the inverse transformation maps points A', B' into points A, B.

Examples

The inverse of the transformation, rotation about the origin through 90° anticlockwise, is rotation about the origin through 90° clockwise.

The inverse of the transformation, enlargement with centre the origin and scale factor 3, is enlargement with centre the origin and scale factor $\frac{1}{3}$.

Exercise 25.1

1.   State which single transformation will map

   1 A into B

   2 A into C

   3 A into D

   4 A into E

   5 A into F

   6 A into G

   7 A into H

   8 B into C

   9 C into F

   10 D into G.

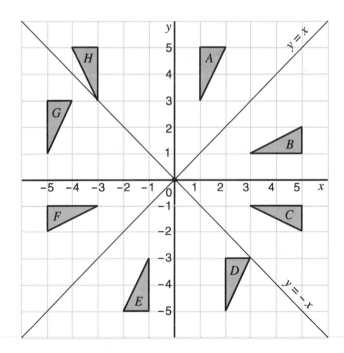

2. In the diagram triangle OAB is
    rotated clockwise about the
    origin through $90°$ into position OA_1B_1.
    Triangle OA_1B_1 is reflected in the
    x-axis into triangle OA_2B_2.
    Draw and label the three triangles
    on your own diagram.

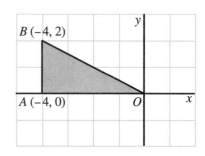

    What single transformation would
    map triangle OAB into triangle OA_2B_2 ?
    What single transformation
    would map $\triangle OA_2B_2$ into $\triangle OAB$?

In questions 3 to 6 draw x and y axes from -8 to 8 using equal scales on both axes.
Draw the triangle ABC where A is $(1, 1)$ B is $(4, 2)$ and C is $(3, 7)$.

3. Reflect triangle ABC about the y-axis. What are the coordinates of the image points
    A_1, B_1, C_1 ?
    Rotate triangle $A_1B_1C_1$ about the origin through $180°$. What are the coordinates of the
    image points A_2, B_2, C_2 ?
    What single transformation would map triangle ABC into triangle $A_2B_2C_2$?
    What single transformation would map $\triangle A_2B_2C_2$ into $\triangle ABC$?

4. Rotate triangle ABC anticlockwise about the origin through $90°$. What are the
    coordinates of the image points A_1, B_1, C_1 ?
    Reflect triangle $A_1B_1C_1$ about the x-axis. What are the coordinates of the image points
    A_2, B_2, C_2 ?
    What single transformation would map triangle ABC into triangle $A_2B_2C_2$?
    What single transformation would map $\triangle A_2B_2C_2$ into $\triangle ABC$?

5. Reflect triangle ABC about the line $y = 1$. What are the coordinates of the image points
    A_1, B_1, C_1 ?
    Reflect triangle $A_1B_1C_1$ about the line $y = x$. What are the coordinates of the image
    points A_2, B_2, C_2 ?
    What single transformation would map triangle ABC into triangle $A_2B_2C_2$?
    What single transformation would map $\triangle A_2B_2C_2$ into $\triangle ABC$?

6. Translate triangle ABC to triangle $A_1B_1C_1$ by moving each point 3 units in the
    x-direction and then -2 units in the y-direction.
    What are the coordinates of the image points A_1, B_1, C_1 ?
    Transform triangle $A_1B_1C_1$ by translating each point by the column vector $\begin{pmatrix} -8 \\ 3 \end{pmatrix}$. What

    are the coordinates of the image points A_2, B_2, C_2 ?
    What single transformation would map triangle ABC into triangle $A_2B_2C_2$?
    What single transformation would map $\triangle A_2B_2C_2$ into $\triangle ABC$?

7.   Draw the *x*-axis from -6 to 6 and the *y*-axis from -6 to 9.
       Take the origin as centre of enlargement.

   1   *A* is (1, 1), *B* is (2, 1) and *C* is (2, 3). Enlarge triangle *ABC* with scale factor 3
           mapping it into triangle $A_1B_1C_1$.
           State the coordinates of $A_1B_1C_1$.
           What is the ratio of areas of triangle $A_1B_1C_1$: triangle *ABC* ?

   2   Enlarge triangle *ABC* with scale factor -2 mapping it into triangle $A_2B_2C_2$.
           State the coordinates of A_2, B_2, C_2.
           What is the ratio of lengths A_2B_2 : *AB* ?
           What transformation would map $\triangle A_2B_2C_2$ into $\triangle ABC$?

   3   *D* is $(-6, 9)$, *E* is $(-6, 3)$, *F* is $\left(-4\frac{1}{2}, 1\frac{1}{2}\right)$ and *G* is $(-3, 6)$.
           Reduce quadrilateral *DEFG* with scale factor $\frac{1}{3}$, mapping it into $D_1E_1F_1G_1$.
           State the coordinates of D_1, E_1, F_1, G_1.
           What is the ratio length F_1G_1 : length *FG* ?
           What is the ratio area $D_1E_1F_1G_1$: area *DEFG* ?
           What transformation would map $D_1E_1F_1G_1$ into *DEFG* ?

Matrices

A matrix is an array of numbers enclosed in a bracket. It is used to store information.

One use of matrices is to define certain transformations.

Column vectors can be used to define translations.
These are 2×1 (2 by 1) matrices. They have 2 rows and 1 column. They can also be called
column matrices.

We can also express the coordinates of a point as a column matrix.

e.g. the point (4, 3) can be expressed as $\begin{pmatrix} 4 \\ 3 \end{pmatrix}$.

Addition or subtraction of column matrices

You have already added or subtracted vectors numerically.
Simply add or subtract the corresponding terms in each position.

e.g. $\begin{pmatrix} 5 \\ 7 \end{pmatrix} + \begin{pmatrix} -6 \\ 3 \end{pmatrix} = \begin{pmatrix} 5 + (-6) \\ 7 + 3 \end{pmatrix} = \begin{pmatrix} 5 - 6 \\ 7 + 3 \end{pmatrix} = \begin{pmatrix} -1 \\ 10 \end{pmatrix}$

$\begin{pmatrix} 4 \\ 9 \end{pmatrix} - \begin{pmatrix} -1 \\ 6 \end{pmatrix} = \begin{pmatrix} 4 - (-1) \\ 9 - 6 \end{pmatrix} = \begin{pmatrix} 4 + 1 \\ 9 - 6 \end{pmatrix} = \begin{pmatrix} 5 \\ 3 \end{pmatrix}$

2 × 2 matrices

We will also use 2 × 2 (2 by 2) matrices. They have 2 rows and 2 columns.

Examples are $\begin{pmatrix} 5 & 4 \\ 7 & 9 \end{pmatrix}$, $\begin{pmatrix} 1 & 0 \\ 0 & 1 \end{pmatrix}$, $\begin{pmatrix} 5 & -7 \\ -2 & 3 \end{pmatrix}$, $\begin{pmatrix} 0.6 & -0.8 \\ -1.4 & 2.2 \end{pmatrix}$.

We need to learn how to multiply two 2 × 2 matrices.

Multiplication of two matrices

This does not follow the same method as addition.

e.g. $\begin{pmatrix} 4 & 9 \\ 5 & 8 \end{pmatrix} \times \begin{pmatrix} 2 & 1 \\ 3 & 7 \end{pmatrix}$ is **NOT** $\begin{pmatrix} 4 \times 2 & 9 \times 1 \\ 5 \times 3 & 8 \times 7 \end{pmatrix}$.

The rule is as follows:
Use the **1st row** of the 1st matrix (4   9) and the **1st column** of the 2nd matrix $\begin{pmatrix} 2 \\ 3 \end{pmatrix}$

and combine them thus: $(4 \times 2) + (9 \times 3) = 8 + 27 = 35$.

This number goes in the 1st row, 1st column of the answer. $\begin{pmatrix} 35 & \cdot \\ \cdot & \cdot \end{pmatrix}$

Now use the **1st row** of the 1st matrix (4   9) and the **2nd column** of the 2nd matrix $\begin{pmatrix} 1 \\ 7 \end{pmatrix}$.

$(4 \times 1) + (9 \times 7) = 4 + 63 = 67$.

This number goes in the 1st row, 2nd column. $\begin{pmatrix} 35 & 67 \\ \cdot & \cdot \end{pmatrix}$

Next use the **2nd row** of the 1st matrix (5   8) and the **1st column** of the 2nd matrix $\begin{pmatrix} 2 \\ 3 \end{pmatrix}$.

$(5 \times 2) + (8 \times 3) = 34$.
This number goes in the 2nd row, 1st column. $\begin{pmatrix} 35 & 67 \\ 34 & \cdot \end{pmatrix}$

Finally, use the **2nd row** of the 1st matrix (5   8) and the **2nd column** of the 2nd matrix $\begin{pmatrix} 1 \\ 7 \end{pmatrix}$.

$(5 \times 1) + (8 \times 7) = 61$.
This number goes in the 2nd row, 2nd column. $\begin{pmatrix} 35 & 67 \\ 34 & 61 \end{pmatrix}$

Note that you only use the **rows** of the 1st matrix and the **columns** of the 2nd matrix.

Two matrices can only be multiplied if there is the same number of columns in the 1st matrix as rows in the 2nd matrix.

The order of multiplication affects the result.

$$\begin{pmatrix} 2 & 1 \\ 3 & 7 \end{pmatrix} \times \begin{pmatrix} 4 & 9 \\ 5 & 8 \end{pmatrix} \quad \text{is not the same as} \quad \begin{pmatrix} 4 & 9 \\ 5 & 8 \end{pmatrix} \times \begin{pmatrix} 2 & 1 \\ 3 & 7 \end{pmatrix}.$$

Check for yourself that $\begin{pmatrix} 2 & 1 \\ 3 & 7 \end{pmatrix} \times \begin{pmatrix} 4 & 9 \\ 5 & 8 \end{pmatrix} = \begin{pmatrix} 13 & 26 \\ 47 & 83 \end{pmatrix}.$

If **A** and **B** are matrices, $\mathbf{A} \times \mathbf{B} \neq \mathbf{B} \times \mathbf{A}$, in general.

The identity matrix

The matrix $\begin{pmatrix} 1 & 0 \\ 0 & 1 \end{pmatrix}$ is denoted by **I** and is called the identity matrix (for 2×2 matrices).

If **A** is any matrix then $\mathbf{A} \times \mathbf{I} = \mathbf{A}$ and $\mathbf{I} \times \mathbf{A} = \mathbf{A}$.

Inverse matrices

If 2 matrices multiplied together give the matrix **I** then they are inverse matrices.

If **A** is one matrix, the other is denoted by $\mathbf{A}^{-1}$ and $\mathbf{A} \times \mathbf{A}^{-1} = \mathbf{I}$, also $\mathbf{A}^{-1} \times \mathbf{A} = \mathbf{I}$.

To find the inverse of the matrix $\begin{pmatrix} a & b \\ c & d \end{pmatrix}.$

If $\mathbf{A} = \begin{pmatrix} a & b \\ c & d \end{pmatrix}$ and $ad - bc = 1$, then the rule for finding $\mathbf{A}^{-1}$ is

1   interchange a and d.
2   change b into $-b$ and c into $-c$.

$$\mathbf{A}^{-1} = \begin{pmatrix} d & -b \\ -c & a \end{pmatrix}$$

e.g. $\mathbf{A} = \begin{pmatrix} 3 & 7 \\ 2 & 5 \end{pmatrix}$

$ad - bc = (3 \times 5) - (7 \times 2) = 1.$

Interchange 3 and 5.
Change 7 into -7 and 2 into -2.

Then $\mathbf{A}^{-1} = \begin{pmatrix} 5 & -7 \\ -2 & 3 \end{pmatrix}$

Check for yourself that $\mathbf{A} \times \mathbf{A}^{-1} = \begin{pmatrix} 1 & 0 \\ 0 & 1 \end{pmatrix}$ and $\mathbf{A}^{-1} \times \mathbf{A} = \begin{pmatrix} 1 & 0 \\ 0 & 1 \end{pmatrix}.$

If $ad - bc$ is not 1, the same rule is used but the new matrix is divided by $ad - bc$.

$ad - bc$ is called the **determinant** of the matrix and can be denoted by $\begin{vmatrix} a & b \\ c & d \end{vmatrix}$.

$$\mathbf{A}^{-1} = \frac{1}{ad - bc} \begin{pmatrix} d & -b \\ -c & a \end{pmatrix}$$

e.g. $\mathbf{A} = \begin{pmatrix} 11 & 4 \\ 7 & 3 \end{pmatrix}$

$ad - bc = (11 \times 3) - (4 \times 7) = 5$.

Then $\mathbf{A}^{-1} = \dfrac{1}{5} \begin{pmatrix} 3 & -4 \\ -7 & 11 \end{pmatrix} = \begin{pmatrix} \frac{3}{5} & -\frac{4}{5} \\ -\frac{7}{5} & \frac{11}{5} \end{pmatrix} = \begin{pmatrix} 0.6 & -0.8 \\ -1.4 & 2.2 \end{pmatrix}$.

Check for yourself that $\mathbf{A} \times \mathbf{A}^{-1} = \begin{pmatrix} 1 & 0 \\ 0 & 1 \end{pmatrix}$ and $\mathbf{A}^{-1} \times \mathbf{A} = \begin{pmatrix} 1 & 0 \\ 0 & 1 \end{pmatrix}$.

If $ad - bc = 0$, the matrix is called a singular matrix and it has no inverse.

$\begin{pmatrix} 0 & 0 \\ 0 & 0 \end{pmatrix}$ is called the zero matrix.

Here is an example of a 2×2 matrix multiplying a 2×1 matrix.

$$\begin{pmatrix} 5 & 2 \\ -1 & 8 \end{pmatrix} \begin{pmatrix} 3 \\ -6 \end{pmatrix} = \begin{pmatrix} 5 \times 3 + 2 \times -6 \\ -1 \times 3 + 8 \times -6 \end{pmatrix} = \begin{pmatrix} 3 \\ -51 \end{pmatrix}$$

These cannot be multiplied in the reverse order since there has to be the same number of columns in the 1st matrix as rows in the 2nd matrix.

Exercise 25.2

1.   Work out these matrices.

1 $\begin{pmatrix} 2 \\ -1 \end{pmatrix} + \begin{pmatrix} 8 \\ 1 \end{pmatrix}$

3 $\begin{pmatrix} 1 \\ 2 \end{pmatrix} - \begin{pmatrix} 2 \\ 4 \end{pmatrix}$

2 $\begin{pmatrix} 5 \\ 0 \end{pmatrix} + \begin{pmatrix} -2 \\ 3 \end{pmatrix}$

4 $\begin{pmatrix} -1 \\ 6 \end{pmatrix} - \begin{pmatrix} 1 \\ -8 \end{pmatrix}$

1. (Work out these matrices.)
   (Note that the multiplication sign can be omitted.)

5 $\begin{pmatrix} 7 \\ -4 \end{pmatrix} + \begin{pmatrix} 0 \\ 3 \end{pmatrix}$

6 $\begin{pmatrix} 2 & 3 \\ 1 & 0 \end{pmatrix} \times \begin{pmatrix} 3 & 1 \\ 6 & -4 \end{pmatrix}$

7 $\begin{pmatrix} 3 & 1 \\ 6 & -4 \end{pmatrix} \times \begin{pmatrix} 2 & 3 \\ 1 & 0 \end{pmatrix}$

8 $\begin{pmatrix} 1 & 1 \\ -2 & -3 \end{pmatrix} \times \begin{pmatrix} 0 & 4 \\ -2 & 1 \end{pmatrix}$

9 $\begin{pmatrix} 5 & -1 \\ 0 & 3 \end{pmatrix} \times \begin{pmatrix} 2 & -1 \\ 1 & 4 \end{pmatrix}$

10 $\begin{pmatrix} 3 & -5 \\ -4 & 7 \end{pmatrix} \times \begin{pmatrix} -1 & 0 \\ 2 & 3 \end{pmatrix}$

11 $\begin{pmatrix} 3 & 1 \\ -1 & 2 \end{pmatrix} \begin{pmatrix} 5 & 0 \\ -4 & 2 \end{pmatrix}$

12 $\begin{pmatrix} -1 & 2 \\ 1 & -3 \end{pmatrix} \begin{pmatrix} 6 & -3 \\ 1 & -1 \end{pmatrix}$

13 $\begin{pmatrix} 1 & 3 \\ -4 & 2 \end{pmatrix} \begin{pmatrix} 0 & -1 \\ -1 & 0 \end{pmatrix}$

14 $\begin{pmatrix} 2 & -3 \\ 1 & 6 \end{pmatrix} \begin{pmatrix} 2 & -4 \\ -1 & 2 \end{pmatrix}$

15 $\begin{pmatrix} 2 & 0 \\ -3 & -1 \end{pmatrix} \begin{pmatrix} 6 & -7 \\ 1 & 2 \end{pmatrix}$

16 $\begin{pmatrix} -1 & 1 \\ 2 & 5 \end{pmatrix} \times \begin{pmatrix} 3 \\ 6 \end{pmatrix}$

17 $\begin{pmatrix} 3 & 1 \\ 8 & 0 \end{pmatrix} \times \begin{pmatrix} 4 \\ -3 \end{pmatrix}$

18 $\begin{pmatrix} 5 & -7 \\ -2 & 3 \end{pmatrix} \begin{pmatrix} 1 \\ 1 \end{pmatrix}$

19 $\begin{pmatrix} 4 & 2 \\ -3 & 1 \end{pmatrix} \begin{pmatrix} 2 \\ -3 \end{pmatrix}$

20 $\begin{pmatrix} -5 & 7 \\ -2 & 3 \end{pmatrix} \begin{pmatrix} 4 \\ 1 \end{pmatrix}$

2. Find the inverse matrices to these matrices. If the matrix is **A** and its inverse is $\mathbf{A}^{-1}$, check that $\mathbf{A} \times \mathbf{A}^{-1} = \mathbf{I}$ and $\mathbf{A}^{-1} \times \mathbf{A} = \mathbf{I}$.

1 $\begin{pmatrix} 4 & -9 \\ -3 & 7 \end{pmatrix}$

2 $\begin{pmatrix} 8 & 5 \\ 3 & 2 \end{pmatrix}$

3 $\begin{pmatrix} 9 & -5 \\ -7 & 4 \end{pmatrix}$

4 $\begin{pmatrix} -1 & 2 \\ 1 & -1 \end{pmatrix}$

5 $\begin{pmatrix} 4 & -6 \\ 3 & -2 \end{pmatrix}$

6 $\begin{pmatrix} 11 & 5 \\ 4 & 2 \end{pmatrix}$

7 $\begin{pmatrix} -13 & 7 \\ 3 & -2 \end{pmatrix}$

8 $\begin{pmatrix} 10 & -3 \\ -3 & 1 \end{pmatrix}$

9 $\begin{pmatrix} -5 & -4 \\ 3 & 2 \end{pmatrix}$

10 $\begin{pmatrix} 0 & -2 \\ 5 & 0 \end{pmatrix}$

3. If $\mathbf{A} = \begin{pmatrix} 2a & a \\ a & -2a \end{pmatrix}$, find the matrix $\mathbf{A}^2$.

Hence find a matrix $\mathbf{B}$ such that $\mathbf{B}^2 = \begin{pmatrix} 20 & 0 \\ 0 & 20 \end{pmatrix}$.

4. If $\mathbf{A} = \begin{pmatrix} -1 & -2 \\ 3 & 2 \end{pmatrix}$, $\mathbf{B} = \begin{pmatrix} 3 & 4 \\ 2 & 3 \end{pmatrix}$, $\mathbf{C} = \begin{pmatrix} 2 & 1 \\ -1 & 0 \end{pmatrix}$, find these matrices, using some results in other questions.

1   $\mathbf{AB}$

2   $\mathbf{C(AB)}$

3   $\mathbf{CA}$

4   $\mathbf{(CA)B}$. Does $\mathbf{C(AB)} = \mathbf{(CA)B}$?

5   $\mathbf{CB}$

6   $\mathbf{C(A+B)}$. Does $\mathbf{C(A+B)} = \mathbf{CA} + \mathbf{CB}$?

7   $\mathbf{B}^{-1}$. (The inverse of $\mathbf{B}$.)

8   $\mathbf{A}^{-1}$.

9   $\mathbf{A}^{-1}\mathbf{(AB)}$. Does $\mathbf{A}^{-1}\mathbf{(AB)} = \mathbf{B}$?

10   $\mathbf{(AB)B}^{-1}$. Does $\mathbf{(AB)B}^{-1} = \mathbf{A}$?

Using matrices to define transformations

Examples here use the line AB, where A is (2, 1) and B is (3, 2).

Translations

e.g. The translation (4, 1) can be represented by the vector $\begin{pmatrix} 4 \\ 1 \end{pmatrix}$.

If each point (a, b) to be translated is represented by the vector $\begin{pmatrix} a \\ b \end{pmatrix}$ then the image point (a', b') is such that $\begin{pmatrix} a' \\ b' \end{pmatrix} = \begin{pmatrix} a \\ b \end{pmatrix} + \begin{pmatrix} 4 \\ 1 \end{pmatrix}$.

If A is (2, 1), then for A', $\begin{pmatrix} 2 \\ 1 \end{pmatrix} + \begin{pmatrix} 4 \\ 1 \end{pmatrix} = \begin{pmatrix} 6 \\ 2 \end{pmatrix}$;

A' is (6, 2).

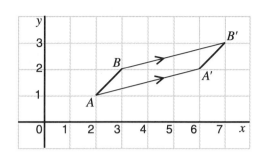

If B is (3, 2), $\begin{pmatrix} 3 \\ 2 \end{pmatrix} + \begin{pmatrix} 4 \\ 1 \end{pmatrix} = \begin{pmatrix} 7 \\ 3 \end{pmatrix}$; B' is (7, 3).

The inverse translation to transform A' to A and B' to B is $\begin{pmatrix} -4 \\ -1 \end{pmatrix}$.

Combined translations

If a point is translated by a vector **a** and the image point is translated by a vector **b**, the combined translation is given by the vector **a** + **b**.

Reflections

Reflection in the x-axis

The matrix giving this transformation is $\begin{pmatrix} 1 & 0 \\ 0 & -1 \end{pmatrix}$.

So for A', $\begin{pmatrix} 1 & 0 \\ 0 & -1 \end{pmatrix}\begin{pmatrix} 2 \\ 1 \end{pmatrix} = \begin{pmatrix} 2 \\ -1 \end{pmatrix}$; A' is (2, −1).

For B', $\begin{pmatrix} 1 & 0 \\ 0 & -1 \end{pmatrix}\begin{pmatrix} 3 \\ 2 \end{pmatrix} = \begin{pmatrix} 3 \\ -2 \end{pmatrix}$; so B' is (3, −2).

For a general point $P(x, y)$, P' is $(x, -y)$.

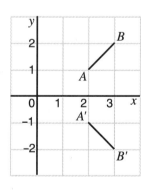

Reflection in the y-axis

The matrix giving this transformation is $\begin{pmatrix} -1 & 0 \\ 0 & 1 \end{pmatrix}$.

For a general point $P(x, y)$, P' is $(-x, y)$.

Reflection in the line $y = x$

The matrix giving this transformation is $\begin{pmatrix} 0 & 1 \\ 1 & 0 \end{pmatrix}$.

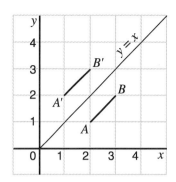

So for A', $\begin{pmatrix} 0 & 1 \\ 1 & 0 \end{pmatrix}\begin{pmatrix} 2 \\ 1 \end{pmatrix} = \begin{pmatrix} 1 \\ 2 \end{pmatrix}$; A' is $(1, 2)$.

For B', $\begin{pmatrix} 0 & 1 \\ 1 & 0 \end{pmatrix}\begin{pmatrix} 3 \\ 2 \end{pmatrix} = \begin{pmatrix} 2 \\ 3 \end{pmatrix}$; B' is $(2, 3)$.

For a general point $P(x, y)$, P' is (y, x).

Reflection in the line $y = -x$

The matrix giving this tranformation is $\begin{pmatrix} 0 & -1 \\ -1 & 0 \end{pmatrix}$.

For a general point $P(x, y)$, P' is $(-y, -x)$.

Rotations

Rotation about the origin through 90° anticlockwise

The matrix giving this transformation is $\begin{pmatrix} 0 & -1 \\ 1 & 0 \end{pmatrix}$.

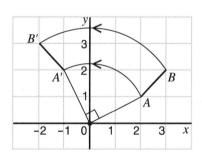

So for A', $\begin{pmatrix} 0 & -1 \\ 1 & 0 \end{pmatrix}\begin{pmatrix} 2 \\ 1 \end{pmatrix} = \begin{pmatrix} -1 \\ 2 \end{pmatrix}$; A' is $(-1, 2)$.

For B', $\begin{pmatrix} 0 & -1 \\ 1 & 0 \end{pmatrix}\begin{pmatrix} 3 \\ 2 \end{pmatrix} = \begin{pmatrix} -2 \\ 3 \end{pmatrix}$; B' is $(-2, 3)$.

For a general point $P(x, y)$, P' is $(-y, x)$.

Rotation about the origin through 180°

The matrix giving this transformation is $\begin{pmatrix} -1 & 0 \\ 0 & -1 \end{pmatrix}$.

For a general point $P(x, y)$, P' is $(-x, -y)$.

Rotation about the origin through 270° anticlockwise (90° clockwise)

The matrix giving this transformation is $\begin{pmatrix} 0 & 1 \\ -1 & 0 \end{pmatrix}$.

For a general point $P(x, y)$, P' is $(y, -x)$.

Enlargements with the origin as centre of enlargement

If the scale factor is k, the matrix giving the transformation is $\begin{pmatrix} k & 0 \\ 0 & k \end{pmatrix}$.

If the scale factor is 2:

For A', $\begin{pmatrix} 2 & 0 \\ 0 & 2 \end{pmatrix}\begin{pmatrix} 2 \\ 1 \end{pmatrix} = \begin{pmatrix} 4 \\ 2 \end{pmatrix}$, A' is (4, 2).

For B', $\begin{pmatrix} 2 & 0 \\ 0 & 2 \end{pmatrix}\begin{pmatrix} 3 \\ 2 \end{pmatrix} = \begin{pmatrix} 6 \\ 4 \end{pmatrix}$, B' is (6, 4).

For a general point $P(x, y)$ and
scale factor k, P' is (kx, ky).

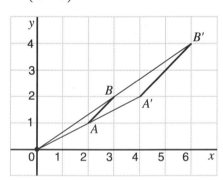

Transformations on the unit square

It is possible to find what transformation results from

any matrix $\begin{pmatrix} a & b \\ c & d \end{pmatrix}$ by investigating the effect on the

unit square $OABC$ where O is the origin, A is (1, 0),
B is (1, 1) and C is (0, 1).

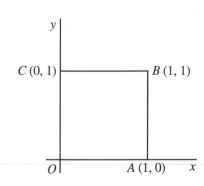

Example

Investigate the transformation

given by the matrix $\begin{pmatrix} 6 & 2 \\ 1 & 4 \end{pmatrix}$.

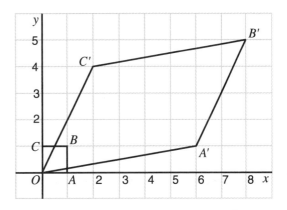

A is mapped into A'.

$\begin{pmatrix} 6 & 2 \\ 1 & 4 \end{pmatrix}\begin{pmatrix} 1 \\ 0 \end{pmatrix} = \begin{pmatrix} 6 \\ 1 \end{pmatrix}$ so A' is (6, 1).

B is mapped into B' (8, 5).
C is mapped into C' (2, 4).
O is mapped into itself.

The unit square $OABC$ is mapped into $OA'B'C'$ which is a parallelogram.

In general the matrix $\begin{pmatrix} a & b \\ c & d \end{pmatrix}$ will transform A into $A'(a, c)$, B into $B'(a+b, c+d)$, C into $C'(b, d)$ and the square is transformed into a parallelogram.

Combined transformations, using matrices

If a figure is transformed using a matrix **A**, and the image is further transformed using a matrix **B**, then the combined transformation is equivalent to a single transformation by the matrix **BA**.
(Notice that the matrix representing the 2nd transformation is written first, before the matrix representing the 1st transformation.)

Inverse transformations

If a figure is transformed using a matrix **A**, then the inverse transformation (to transform the image to the original figure) is given by the inverse matrix $\mathbf{A}^{-1}$.

Exercise 25.3

1.   The image of the point (x, y) under the transformation given by the matrix $\begin{pmatrix} 3 & 0 \\ 0 & 3 \end{pmatrix}$ is (6, −9). Find x and y.

2.   Draw x and y axes from -8 to 8. Plot the points A (1, 1) and B (4, 2) and draw the line
     AB.
     Find the image of the line AB after the following transformations.
     Give the coordinates of the new positions of A and B. Describe the transformations.

     1   Translation represented by $\begin{pmatrix} 2 \\ -3 \end{pmatrix}$

     2   Transformation represented by the matrix $\begin{pmatrix} 2 & 0 \\ 0 & 2 \end{pmatrix}$

     3   Transformation represented by the matrix $\begin{pmatrix} 0 & -1 \\ -1 & 0 \end{pmatrix}$

     4   Transformation represented by the matrix $\begin{pmatrix} 0 & -1 \\ 1 & 0 \end{pmatrix}$

     5   Transformation represented by the matrix $\begin{pmatrix} 1 & 0 \\ 0 & -1 \end{pmatrix}$

3. P is the point (2, 6) and Q is the point $(-2, -6)$. P and Q are transformed by the

     matrix $\begin{pmatrix} 2 & -1 \\ 3 & -2 \end{pmatrix}$. Show P, Q and their images P', Q' on a sketch graph.

     What is the inverse transformation which would transform $P'Q'$ into PQ ?

     What other simple single transformation also maps P into P' and Q into Q' ?

4.   The unit square $OABC$ where O is the origin, A is (1, 0), B is (1, 1) and C is (0, 1)

     is transformed by the matrix $\begin{pmatrix} 3 & 1 \\ 1 & 3 \end{pmatrix}$. Give the coordinates of A', B', C'.

     What kind of quadrilateral is $OA'B'C'$?
     What matrix would transform $OA'B'C'$ into $OABC$?

5.   Draw x and y axes from -8 to 8. Draw the triangle ABC where A is (1, 1), B is (4, 2) and
     C is (3, 7).

     1   A is translated to $A_1(-5, -6)$. What vector represents this translation ? Using this
         vector, translate B and C and draw the new triangle $A_1 B_1 C_1$.

     2   $\triangle ABC$ is transformed under the matrix $\begin{pmatrix} -1 & 0 \\ 0 & 1 \end{pmatrix}$. Draw the new triangle $A_2 B_2 C_2$.

     3   $\triangle ABC$ is transformed under the matrix $\begin{pmatrix} 0 & 1 \\ -1 & 0 \end{pmatrix}$. Draw the new triangle $A_3 B_3 C_3$.

     4   What matrix would transform $\triangle A_3 B_3 C_3$ into $\triangle A_2 B_2 C_2$?

6.   In the diagram, give the matrices or vectors which transform

    1 $\triangle A$ into $\triangle B$
    2 $\triangle A$ into $\triangle C$
    3 $\triangle A$ into $\triangle D$
    4 $\triangle D$ into $\triangle E$
    5 $\triangle F$ into $\triangle G$
    6 $\triangle G$ into $\triangle H$.

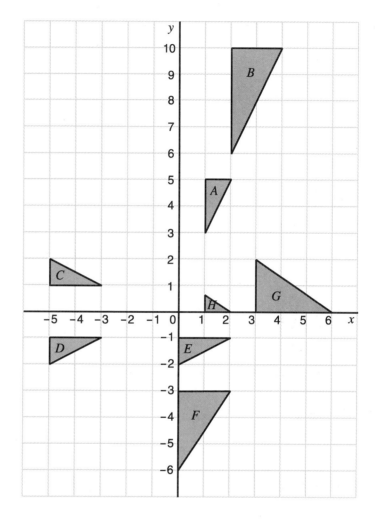

Exercise 25.4 Applications

1.   The design shows 8 congruent triangles arranged
in a rectangle. State the transformation which
would map
    1 triangle (1) into triangle (2),
    2 triangle (1) into triangle (3),
    3 triangle (1) into triangle (4),
    4 triangle (1) into triangle (5),
    5 triangle (1) into triangle ACG.

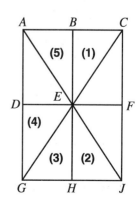

2. Draw the x-axis from 0 to 6 and the y-axis from -3 to 5.
    Taking C (1, 2) as centre of enlargement, A (3, 0) is mapped into A_1 (6, -3). What is the scale factor of the enlargement ?
    Using this same transformation B (2, 3) is mapped into B_1. What are the coordinates of B_1 ?
    What is the ratio length A_1B_1 : length AB ?
    With the same centre of enlargement, what is the scale factor which maps A_1 into A ?

3. An operation is described as, translate 4 units parallel to the x-axis then reflect the image point in the line $y = x$.

    1   What is the final position of the point (3, 4) ?
    2   What is the point whose final position is (3, 4) ?

4. Find the square of the matrix $\begin{pmatrix} 2 & -1 \\ 1 & 0 \end{pmatrix}$.

5. If $\mathbf{A} = \begin{pmatrix} 3 & -5 \\ 1 & 2 \end{pmatrix}$ and $\mathbf{B} = \begin{pmatrix} 2 & -1 \\ -3 & 1 \end{pmatrix}$, find   1 $\mathbf{AB}$,   2   the inverse matrix of $\mathbf{B}$.

6. If $\begin{pmatrix} a & 2a \\ 3b & b \end{pmatrix}\begin{pmatrix} 1 \\ 7 \end{pmatrix} = \begin{pmatrix} 60 \\ -10 \end{pmatrix}$, find a and b.

7. If $\mathbf{A} = \begin{pmatrix} 3 & -1 \\ 2 & 0 \end{pmatrix}$ write down the inverse $\mathbf{A}^{-1}$ of $\mathbf{A}$ and find the matrix $\mathbf{A} + \mathbf{A}^{-1}$.

8. If $\mathbf{A} = \begin{pmatrix} 2 & 0 \\ 0 & -2 \end{pmatrix}$, $\mathbf{B} = \begin{pmatrix} 0 & 1 \\ -1 & 0 \end{pmatrix}$ and $\mathbf{C} = \begin{pmatrix} -3 & 0 \\ 0 & 3 \end{pmatrix}$, find the matrices $\mathbf{A}(\mathbf{BC})$ and

    $(\mathbf{AB})\mathbf{C}$. Are these equal ?

9. In $\triangle ABC$, A is (2, 1), B is (4, 3) and C is (7, 0). Use a transformation matrix to find the coordinates of the image points A_1, B_1, C_1 when $\triangle ABC$ is rotated about the origin through 180°. If $\triangle A_1B_1C_1$ is then reflected in the x-axis, find the coordinates of the image points A_2, B_2, C_2.
    If the 1st transformation matrix used is $\mathbf{T}_1$ and the 2nd one is $\mathbf{T}_2$ find the matrix product $\mathbf{T}_2\mathbf{T}_1$.
    What single transformation would map $\triangle ABC$ into $\triangle A_2B_2C_2$?
    What transformation would map $\triangle A_2B_2C_2$ into $\triangle ABC$?

10. P is the point (2, 5). Q is the image of P under the translation $\mathbf{T}$ given by the

    vector $\begin{pmatrix} 3 \\ 1 \end{pmatrix}$.

    The enlargement, centre at the origin, scale factor 2 is carried out on points P and Q giving points P' and Q'. Say how the point P' can be mapped into Q', expressing this in terms of $\mathbf{T}$.

11. The square $OABC$ where O is the origin, A is (1, 0), B is (1, 1) and C is (0, 1) is transformed into $OA_1B_1C_1$ by the matrix $\begin{pmatrix} 3 & 0 \\ 0 & 3 \end{pmatrix}$.

State the area of $OA_1B_1C_1$.

The figure $OA_1B_1C_1$ is now transformed into $OA_2B_2C_2$ by the matrix $\begin{pmatrix} 0 & -1 \\ -1 & 0 \end{pmatrix}$.

The figure $OA_2B_2C_2$ is then transformed into $OA_3B_3C_3$ by the matrix $\begin{pmatrix} -\frac{1}{3} & 0 \\ 0 & -\frac{1}{3} \end{pmatrix}$.

Give the matrix of the single transformation which would transform square $OABC$ into $OA_3B_3C_3$.

12. The transformation **T** is given by $\begin{pmatrix} x \\ y \end{pmatrix} \rightarrow \begin{pmatrix} -2\frac{1}{2} & 3 \\ 0 & 1 \end{pmatrix} \begin{pmatrix} x \\ y \end{pmatrix}$. P is the point (2, 3) and

Q is the point (0, 2). Find the images P' and Q' of the points P and Q and show the points P, Q, P' and Q' on a sketch.

What simple geometrical operation would map P into P' and Q into Q' ?

Practice test 25

1. Describe the transformations which map the triangles

    1   A into B,
    2   A into C,
    3   A into D,
    4   B into C,
    5   C into D.

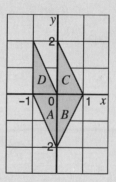

2. On graph paper draw x and y axes from -6 to 6.

    1   Plot the points $A(3, 1)$, $B(3, 2)$, $C(6, 1)$, $D(6, 5)$. Join AB and CD.
    What is the scale factor of the enlargement which maps AB into CD ?
    Let E be the centre of this enlargement. What are the coordinates of E ?

    2   With origin as centre of enlargement map triangle EAB into a triangle FGH, using
    a scale factor of -2. What are the coordinates of F, G, H ?
    What is the ratio of areas of triangles $EAB : FGH$?
    What is the transformation which maps $\triangle FGH$ into $\triangle EAB$?

    [Turn over]

3.   On graph paper draw x and y axes from -8 to 8.
      Plot points $K(-7, -6)$, $L(-4, -8)$, $M(-1, -6)$, $N(-4, -4)$.
      Join KL, LM, MN, NK.
      What sort of quadrilateral is $KLMN$?
      What are the equations of its axes of symmetry?

      Rotate this quadrilateral about the origin through $90°$ anticlockwise.
      Draw it in its new position $K_1L_1M_1N_1$.
      What are the coordinates of K_1, L_1, M_1, N_1?

      Reflect the quadrilateral $K_1L_1M_1N_1$ in the x-axis.
      Draw it in its new position $K_2L_2M_2N_2$.
      What are the coordinates of K_2, L_2, M_2, N_2?

      What single transformation would map $KLMN$ into $K_2L_2M_2N_2$?
      What single transformation would map $K_2L_2M_2N_2$ into $KLMN$?

4.   If $\mathbf{A} = \begin{pmatrix} 3 \\ -5 \end{pmatrix}$, $\mathbf{B} = \begin{pmatrix} -2 \\ 1 \end{pmatrix}$, $\mathbf{C} = \begin{pmatrix} 4 & -2 \\ 1 & 0 \end{pmatrix}$, $\mathbf{D} = \begin{pmatrix} 3 & 1 \\ 7 & 4 \end{pmatrix}$,

      find the matrices representing

      1    $\mathbf{A} + \mathbf{B}$ 6 $\mathbf{C}^{-1}$, the inverse of $\mathbf{C}$
      2    $\mathbf{CD}$ 7 $\mathbf{D}^{-1}$
      3    $\mathbf{DC}$ 8 $\mathbf{C}^2$
      4    $\mathbf{CA}$ 9 $\mathbf{C}^2\mathbf{A}$, using the result of 8
      5    $\mathbf{DB}$ 10 $\mathbf{C}^{-1}(\mathbf{C}^2\mathbf{A})$, using the result of 9.

5.   What is the image of the point $(3, -4)$ after the transformation given by the matrix
      $\begin{pmatrix} 5 & 0 \\ 2 & -1 \end{pmatrix}$?

6.   The points $O\,(0, 0)$, $A\,(1, 0)$, $B\,(1, 1)$, $C\,(0, 1)$ are transformed by the matrix
      $\mathbf{M} = \begin{pmatrix} -2 & 0 \\ 0 & -2 \end{pmatrix}$ into $OA_1B_1C_1$.

      The points $OA_1B_1C_1$ are transformed by the matrix $\mathbf{N} = \begin{pmatrix} 0 & \frac{1}{2} \\ -\frac{1}{2} & 0 \end{pmatrix}$ into $OA_2B_2C_2$.

      What single transformation will transform $OABC$ into $OA_2B_2C_2$? What is its matrix?

7.   In the diagram, state the transformation matrices or vectors which are used to map

1   △A into △B
2   △A into △C
3   △A into △D
4   △A into △E
5   △A into △F.

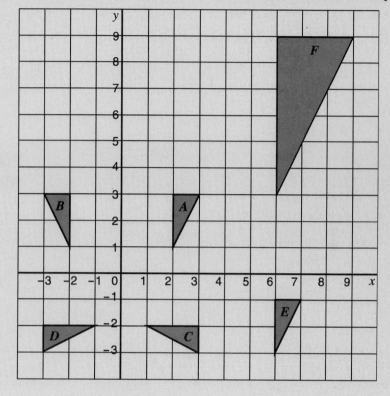

PUZZLES

55.   How many squares are there on a chessboard ?

56.   Each evening Grandfather and little Ian play ludo. They are evenly matched at this game, but Ian insists on playing until he wins a game. What is the average number of games played in an evening ?

57.   Bill, the shepherd and Shep, his dog, are going home after a day on the hills. Bill walks at a steady 4 miles per hour. When they are half a mile from his cottage, Bill sends Shep on ahead to warn his wife that he is on his way. Shep races to the cottage, barks, immediately returns back to his master and continues to run back and forth between the cottage and Bill until Bill reaches home. Shep's running speed is 16 miles per hour. How far did he run altogether, from when he was sent on ahead ?

Miscellaneous Section E

Exercise E1   Revision

1. State whether it is a reflection, rotation or translation which transforms

    1 AB into CD
    2 AB into DC
    3 AB into ED
    4 AB into EF
    5 CD into ED
    6 CD into FE.

    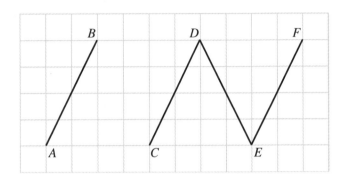

    On sketch diagrams show the centres of rotation or axes of reflection for each transformation.

2. Find the range of values of x if

    1 $\frac{2}{3}(5x + 4) > 2x - 1$
    2 $12 + x > 5 - x > 1$

3. Five people measured the length of a field, each to the nearest m, and the lengths were 53 m, 55 m, 56 m, 52 m, 55 m.
    What are the lower and upper bounds for the average of the measurements ?

4. **1** Explain what is meant by a **random** sample.

    There are 60 teenagers in a Youth club, 38 boys and 22 girls. A sample of 6 of them has to be chosen to form a committee to discuss the next term's programme.
    2 How could a random sample be chosen ?
    3 Why might this sample not be fully representative of the members ?
    4 State a different way of selecting a sample, which might be more representative.

5. Two boats leave a harbour at the same time. One sails at 12 km/h on a bearing of 010° and the other sails at 15 km/h on a bearing of 340°. How far are they apart half-an-hour later, to the nearest 0.1 km ?

6. On the same diagram, sketch the graphs of
    1 $y = 4 - x^2$
    2 $y = 4x - x^2$.
    Label each graph and the points where they cut the axes.

7. O is the centre of the circle and TP is a
    tangent touching the circle at P.
    Find the sizes of the angles a, b and c.

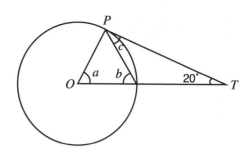

8. In the formula $s = ut + \frac{1}{2}at^2$, s metres is the distance travelled in a straight line in
    t seconds by a particle whose initial velocity is u m/s and whose acceleration is a m/s^2.
    Calculate, to 2 decimal places, the number of seconds taken by a particle to travel 9 m
    with initial velocity 3 m/s and acceleration 2 m/s^2.

9. A boy, John, goes jogging and leaves his home A at 6 pm on a straight run of 8 km to a
    village B, which he reaches at 6.45 pm. Assuming that he jogs at a steady speed, draw a
    distance-time graph to represent his journey.
    Another boy, Ken, leaves B at 6 pm, cycling towards A, at a steady speed of 24 km/h.
    Draw on the same graph a line to represent his journey.
    When and where do the two boys pass each other ?

10. With centre of enlargement A, P is mapped into B and
    Q is mapped into C.

    1 What is the scale factor of the enlargement ?
    2 What is the ratio of lengths $BC : PQ$?
    3 What is the ratio of areas $\triangle ABC : \triangle APQ$?
    4 Hence find the ratio of areas trapezium $PQBC : \triangle APQ$.

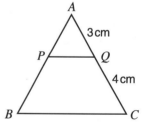

11. Draw a rectangle $ABCD$ with $AB = 12$ cm and $BC = 8$ cm. Join BD.
    Construct the locus of points inside the rectangle which satisfy the following conditions.
    (Label each locus clearly.)

    (1) 2 cm from the side AB,
    (2) 5 cm from the corner B,
    (3) equidistant from B and D,
    (4) equidistant from the lines AD and DB.

    Mark a point S which is 2 cm from AB and 5 cm from B.
    Mark a point T on AB which is equidistant from B and D.
    Mark a point U which is equidistant from AD and DB, and 2 cm from AB.

12. Here is a flow diagram which multiplies two numbers by halving and doubling.

Use the flow diagram to multiply 278 by 92.
Write down *a*, *b*, *c* in columns to keep a record of them.
What is the answer ?

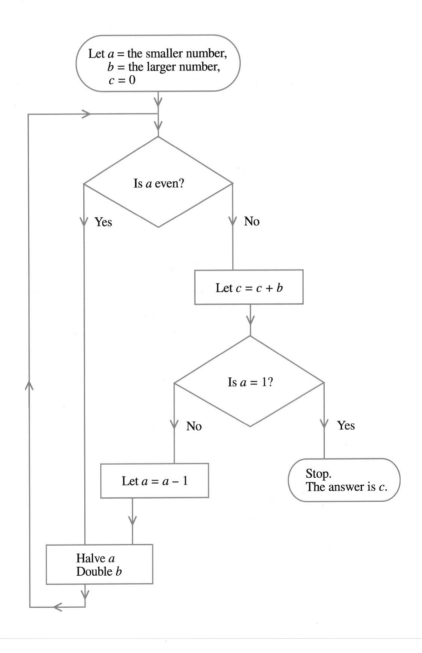

13. Mrs Parmer wants to buy some biscuits for a children's party. She does not want to spend more than £3.
The brand X packets cost 40p and the brand Y packets cost 20p. She decides to get at least 4 packets of each, but not more than 10 packets altogether.
If she buys x packets of Brand X, and y packets of Brand Y, write down the inequalities satisfied by x and y.

On graph paper, draw the x-axis from 0 to 10 and the y-axis from 0 to 15, and draw the lines giving the boundaries of these inequalities.
Identify the region containing the set of points (x, y) satisfying all these inequalities.
List the possible combinations of packets she could buy, e.g. 4 of Brand X and 4 of Brand Y.
If Brand X packets contain 20 biscuits and Brand Y packets contain 25 biscuits, consider the possible combinations and decide which combination will give most biscuits.

14. If 10% of a large batch of electronic components manufactured by a certain firm are defective, and a sample of 5 components is chosen from the batch at random, what is the probability that

   1 all 5 components are defective,
   2 there will be no defective components in the sample,
   3 there will be at least one defective component ?

15. **1** If $v^2 = u^2 + 2as$, find a in terms of u, v, s.

   2 If $V = \frac{1}{3}\pi r^2 h$, find h in terms of V, r and π.

   3 If $S = 4\pi r^2$, and r is positive, find r in terms of S and π.

Exercise E2 Revision

1. If $f(x) = 3^x$, find
   1 $f(4)$,
   2 the value of x if $f(x) = \frac{1}{3}$.

2.   Copy the diagram and
     1   reflect ■ in the line *AB*,

     2   reflect ■ in the line *CD*,

     3   rotate ■ through 90° clockwise
         about the point *E*,

     4   rotate ■ through 180° about the point *G*.

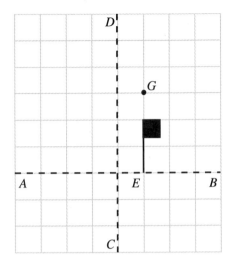

3.   A box contains 12 discs. 3 are red, 4 are yellow and 5 are green. A disc is drawn out and
     replaced, then a second disc is drawn out.
     Show the results of the two drawings on a tree-diagram.
     What is the probability that
     1   both discs are red,
     2   both discs are the same colour ?

4.   The edges of a cube are all increased in length by 10%. By what percentage is the volume
     increased ?
     The edges of a second cube are all decreased in length by 10%. By what percentage is the
     volume decreased ?

5.   *AB*, *AC* and *AD* are 3 lines at right angles
     to each other. *AB* = 16 cm, *AC* = 9 cm
     and *AD* = 12 cm.

     Find
     1   the lengths of *BC*, *BD* and *CD*,
     2   the size of ∠*BDC*.

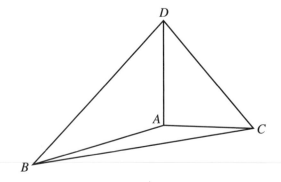

6. The age distribution of the population of the Isle of Man in 1961 and 1971 is given in the table.
    Draw frequency polygons for both years on the same diagram. Assume the last age-group is 80–89 years.
    Comment about the data.

Age (years)	Population (in 100's) 1961	1971
0–9	60	77
10–19	64	70
20–29	43	68
30–39	54	54
40–49	62	63
50–59	76	73
60–69	66	85
70–79	41	53
80 and over	15	19

7. *BC* is a tangent touching the circle, centre *A*, at *B*.

    1 Explain why triangles *ADE*, *ABC* are similar.
    2 Find the value of *x*.
    3 Find the lengths of *DE* and *BC*.

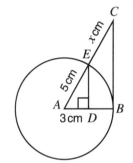

8. The area of this rectangle is 80 cm². Write down
    an equation, simplify it, and solve it.
    State the sizes of the length and breadth
    of the rectangle.

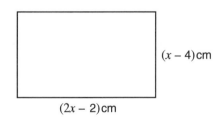

$(x - 4)$ cm

$(2x - 2)$ cm

9. Copy and complete the table of values for the graph of $y = 2\cos x° + \sin x°$.

x	0	10	20	30	40	50	60	70	80	90
$2\cos x°$	2	1.97								
$\sin x°$	0	0.17								
y	2	2.14								

Draw the graph of $y = 2\cos x° + \sin x°$, taking a scale of 2 cm to 10 units on the *x*-axis and labelling *y* from 0 to 3 taking a scale of 2 cm to 1 unit.
Use the graph to find the maximum value of *y* in this range, and the value of *x* for which this maximum value occurs.
Also use the graph to find the solution of the equation $4\cos x° + 2\sin x° = 3$.

10. The diagram shows the operations for doing a job, and the time each operation takes.
     Copy the diagram, find the critical path and mark it on your diagram.
     What is the least time needed to complete the job ?
     What is the latest time after starting the job that operation E can be started, if the job is
     to be finished in the least time ?

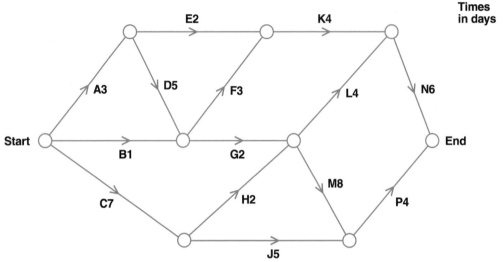

11. The graph shows the rate of gas consumption recorded in an area between 6 am and
     6 pm on one Saturday.
     By counting squares, find the amount of gas used in this time.

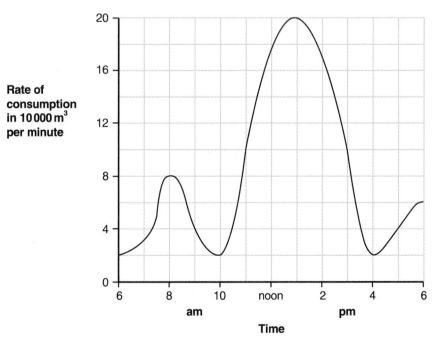

12. In each diagram, the angle marked x is $52°$. Find the size of the angle marked y.
O is the centre of the circle.

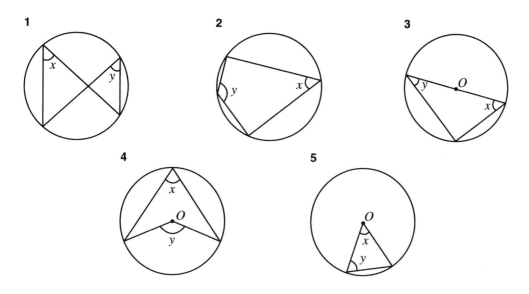

13. Calculate
    1 the length of AC
    2 the area of $\triangle ABC$.

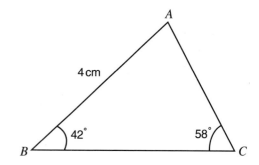

14. Find the equation which will be given by the limiting value of the iteration formula
$x_{n+1} = \dfrac{10}{3} - \dfrac{2}{x_n}$, in the form $ax^2 + bx + c = 0$.

Solve the equation using the iteration formula, starting with $x_1 = 2$, finding the solution correct to 2 decimal places.

15. If $A = \begin{pmatrix} 2 & 3 \\ 5 & 8 \end{pmatrix}$, $B = \begin{pmatrix} 3 & -4 \\ 1 & 0 \end{pmatrix}$, find $A + B$, AB, BA, A^{-1} and B^{-1}.

Show that $A^{-1}(AB) = B$.

Exercise E3 Revision

1. Two similar solid cylinders have radii 4 cm and 6 cm. They are made of similar material and the first one weighs 2 kg. What is the weight of the second one ?

2. Write down the reciprocal of 54
    1 as a recurring decimal,
    2 correct to 3 decimal places,
    3 correct to 3 significant figures.

3. $\triangle ABC$ is isosceles with $AB = AC$ and $BC = 4$ cm. X is the mid-point of BC. The triangle is inscribed in a circle, centre O, radius 7 cm. Calculate
    1 $\angle XOB$,
    2 $\angle BOC$,
    3 $\angle BAC$.

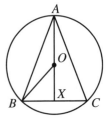

4. Below are sketch graphs of $y = 3x^2$, $y = 2x^3$, $y = \dfrac{3}{x}$, $y = 3^x$ and $y = x^2 + 3$. Identify each one.

1   **2**   **3**   **4**   **5**

5. The points $A(1,2)$, $B(3,-2)$, $C(-4,-1)$ and $D(-2,4)$ are transformed by the transformations **Q, R, S, T, U**.

    Q is 'reflect the point in the y-axis'.
    R is 'rotate the point about the origin through $180°$'.
    S is 'move the point until it is twice as far from the origin in the same direction'.
    T is 'translate the point 2 units parallel to the x-axis'.
    U is 'reflect the point in the line $y = x$'.

    Copy the table below and fill in the coordinates of the new positions of A, B, C and D, and by deducing the pattern give the coordinates of the general point $E(h,k)$.

	Q	R	S	T	U
$A(1,2)$	$(-1,2)$	$(-1,-2)$			
$B(3,-2)$					
$C(-4,-1)$					
$D(-2,4)$					
$E(h,k)$					

6. Parallelogram $ABCD$ has sides a cm and b cm and $\angle B = x°$.
   Find an expression for the area of the parallelogram.

   If the area is 24 cm^2, $a = 5$ and $b = 9.6$, find the size of
   the (acute) angle B.

   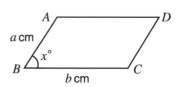

7. A rectangular block has height h cm and a square base of side x cm.

   1 If the total surface area is A cm^2, find a formula for A in terms of x and h.
   2 Find the value of A when $x = 5$ and $h = 3$.
   3 Find h in terms of A and x.
   4 Find the length of a side of the base, when the total surface area is 440 cm^2 and the
     height is 6 cm.

8. Factorise the following.

   1 $2x^2 + 8xy$ 4 $x^2 - 12x + 32$
   2 $pr - ps + 2qr - 2qs$ 5 $2x^2 - 5x - 3$
   3 $16x^2 - 81y^2$

9. A rectangular poultry run of area 300 m^2 is to be made.

   If one side is x m long, show that the length of fencing, y m, needed is $2\left(x + \dfrac{300}{x}\right)$ m.

   Draw a graph to show the relationship between x and y, taking values of x from 10 to
   30, values of y from 60 to 80, and plotting at least six points.

   1 Is it economical to make the run long and narrow ? (Give a reason.)

   Use your graph to find the length and width of the run
   2 if 75 m of fencing is just sufficient,
   3 if the amount of fencing needed is a minimum.

10. Instead of using a more accurate value for π, the value 3 was used in calculating the area
    of a circle of radius 10 cm. Use your calculator to find the percentage error in the result.
    (Use the value given by the π key on your calculator as the more accurate value of π.)

11. The data gives the marks of 10 students in Papers 1 and 2 of an examination. Show the
    data on a scatter diagram and draw a line of best fit.

Student	A	B	C	D	E	F	G	H	I	J
Mark on Paper 1	56	52	45	53	51	67	64	58	69	56
Mark on Paper 2	68	61	53	57	62	74	79	73	81	70

Another student gained 60 marks for Paper 1 but was absent through illness for Paper 2.
Use your line of best fit to estimate the mark she might have gained on Paper 2.

12. Draw a graph to convert gallons into litres.
Draw the 'gallons' axis horizontally, label from 0 to 10.
Draw the 'litres' axis vertically, label from 0 to 50.
10 gallons is equivalent to 45.5 litres.
Plot this point on the graph and join it to the origin $(0,0)$ with a straight line.

Use your graph to convert 6.5 gallons into litres, and to convert 10 litres into gallons.

13.

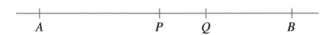

A man makes the journey between two cities A and B, 960 km apart, by a direct route.
He can either fly by plane to airport P, which takes 2 hours, and then complete the
journey with a 6-hour train ride, or he can fly to airport, Q, which takes 3 hours, and
then complete the journey with a 1-hour train ride.
If the speed of the plane is x km/h and the speed of the train is y km/h, write down two
equations connecting x and y.
Solve these equations to find x and y.
How far is Q from B ?

14. A, B and C are 3 points on horizontal ground.
A is South-west of B and C is due East of B.

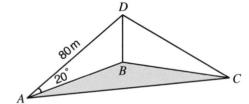

A kite attached to A by a string 80 m long
is at D, vertically above B, and its angle of
elevation from A is 20°.

  1 Find the height of the kite above the ground,
and the distance AB.
  2 The angle of elevation of the kite from C is 12°. Find the distance BC.
  3 Find the length of AC.
(Give all lengths to the nearest metre.)

15. In the diagram, AB is a diameter of the
semicircle and C is any point on the
circumference. AP and BQ are perpendicular
to the tangent at C.
Prove that
  1 $\triangle ABC$, $\triangle ACP$ and $\triangle CBQ$ are similar,
  2 area $\triangle ABC =$ area $\triangle ACP +$ area $\triangle CQB$.

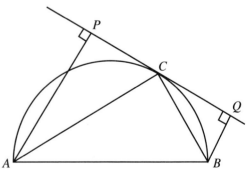

Exercise E4   Revision

1. The following numbers were written on pieces of paper, put into a hat, and drawn out at random.

    10,   13,   16,   17,   21,   25,   30,   36,   39,   49,   110,   121.

    What is the probability of drawing out
    1   a number greater than 100,
    2   a number less than 20,
    3   a prime number,
    4   a number which is not a square number ?
    5   If an odd number is drawn out and not replaced, what is the probability of drawing out a second odd number ?

2. The circles are concentric, with centre O and radii 10 cm and 6 cm. Chord AB touches the smaller circle at C.

    1   What is the size of $\angle OCA$?
    2   Find the length of AC, and hence find the length of AB.

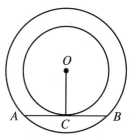

3. Identify these sketch graphs. The first quantity named is measured on the horizontal axis.

    1   The relationship between the radius and the volume of a cylinder with constant height.

    2   The relationship between speed and the time taken to travel a fixed distance.

    3   The relationship between money invested and Simple Interest gained per year, when the rate of interest is constant.

    4   The relationship between children present and children absent in a class of 30 pupils on different days.

4. If an object is thrown straight upwards with a speed of 50 m/s, its height above the ground after t seconds is approximately $(50t - 5t^2)$ metres. Find the two times at which the height above the ground is 45 m.

5. 1   Explain why triangles PDC and PBA are similar.
    2   Find the ratio area $\triangle PDC$: area $\triangle PBA$

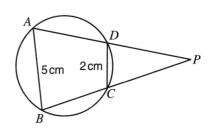

6. If $\mathbf{A} = \begin{pmatrix} 2 & 3 \\ 3 & 5 \end{pmatrix}$ and $\mathbf{B} = \begin{pmatrix} 4 & 0 \\ 1 & 2 \end{pmatrix}$, find

   1 $\mathbf{A} + \mathbf{B}$ **2** $\mathbf{AB}$ **3** $\mathbf{BA}$ **4** $\mathbf{A}^{-1}$ **5** $\mathbf{B}^{-1}$

7. The weights of 8 eggs were, in grams,

   47, 53, 53, 57, 48, 57, 55, 46.

   Find the mean and the standard deviation of the weights.

8. In the diagram, B is due North of A and the bearing of C from B is 057°. $AB = 8$ km and $BC = 6$ km. Calculate the distance AC, to the nearest 0.1 km.

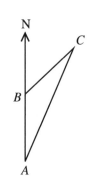

9. A farmer has to enclose a rectangular paddock on three sides, (a wall bounds the fourth side). The length of fencing he has available is 50 m.

   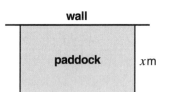

   If the width of the paddock is x m, write down expressions for
   1 the length of the paddock,
   2 the area of the paddock.

   3 If this area is 288 m², find 2 possible values of x.

10. Sketch the graphs of

    1 $y = x - 3$ **2** $y = x(x - 3)$ **3** $y = x^2(x - 3)$

11. The radius of a circle, measured to the nearest metre, is 11 m.
    Find
    1 the largest possible length of the circumference,
    2 the smallest possible length of the circumference,
    3 the largest possible area of the circle.
    4 the smallest possible area of the circle.
    Give answers correct to 3 significant figures.

12.   *ABCD* is a rectangle and *ABEFG* is a regular pentagon.
      Prove that $\triangle ADG$ and $\triangle BCE$ are congruent and
      hence that $DG = CE$.

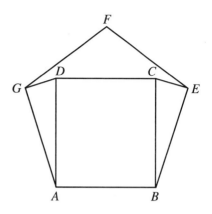

13.   **1**   If $0.02345 = 2.345 \times 10^n$, what is the value of n ?

      2   If $4970 = 4.97 \times 10^n$, what is the value of n ?

      3   Express 0.852 and 19.7 in standard index form.

14.   Find the volume of metal needed to make 1000 spherical ball-bearings of diameter 3 mm.

15.   The diagram shows the speed-time graph
      of a train as it travels between two stations.
      Find

      1   the acceleration of the train over
              the first 800 seconds (in m/s^2),

      2   the total distance travelled, in km,

      3   the average speed over the whole journey,
              in km/h.

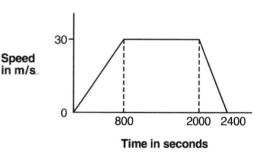

Exercise E5   Revision

1.   A man bought 600 eggs for £48 and planned to sell them at £1.20 per dozen. What
     percentage profit would he have made on his cost price ?
     However, 60 of the eggs were broken and he could not sell them. What was his
     percentage profit after he had sold the rest ?

2.   *P* is a point on the rim of a bicycle wheel,
     initially touching the ground at *A*.
     The bicycle is moved forward until *P*
     touches the ground at *B*, the wheel having
     moved through one revolution.

     Copy the drawing and sketch the
     locus of *P*.
     If the diameter of the wheel is 35 cm,
     find the length of *AB*.
     How many metres will a cyclist have travelled when the wheel has made 100 revolutions ?

3. The probability of Amy winning the prize in a raffle is $\frac{7}{100}$, the probability of Barbara winning it is $\frac{1}{20}$ and the probability of Charles winning it is $\frac{2}{25}$. What is the probability that none of them will win it ?

4. AB, which is 18 cm long, is 2 cm from the centre O of the circle. How long is chord DC, which is 6 cm from O ?

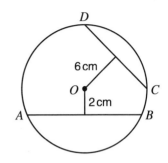

5. Copy the figure except for triangles E and F, and add these triangles:
    Triangle B, in the position of triangle A reflected in the line $y = 1$.
    Triangle C, in the position of triangle A rotated about the origin through 90° clockwise.
    Triangle D, in the position of triangle A when it is reflected in the line $x = 0$.

    Describe in a similar way how triangle A can be transformed into the position of triangle E, and into triangle F.

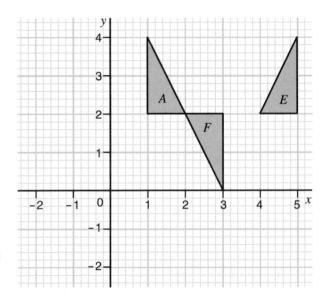

6. PT is a tangent touching the circle centre O at T.
    $PD = 15$ cm, $TD = 6$ cm.

    1   Name two triangles similar to triangle PTD.
    2   Find the length of OD.

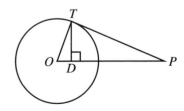

7. The heights of two hills are 160 m and 230 m, and the horizontal distance between their summits is 280 m.
    Find the angle of elevation of the line joining the summits.

8. A path x m wide goes round a rectangular lawn which
    measures 10 m by 8 m.
    Find a formula for y where y m^2 is the area of the path.
    Draw the graph of y against x for values of x from 0 to 6.
    (Draw the y-axis from 0 to 400.)
    Use the graph to find the width of the path when its area
    is 240 m^2.
    Check your answer by solving an equation using
    the quadratic equation formula.

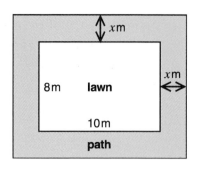

9. The distribution of the percentage yield of 112 top shares, quoted on a day in March,
    1993, was as follows:

Percentage yield	0–1	1–2	2–3	3–4	4–5	5–6	6–7	7–8
f	2	3	14	23	44	18	5	3

    1 Draw a histogram of the distribution and describe its shape.
    2 Make a cumulative frequency table and draw a cumulative frequency graph. From
       the graph find the median percentage yield and the interquartile range of yields.
       Estimate how many of the shares had a yield of over 4.5%.

10. Draw a line AB of length 10 cm.
    Construct accurately points P_1, P_2, P_3, ... such that $\angle PAB = x°$ and $\angle PBA = (90 - x)°$,
    taking x in turn to be 10°, 20°, 30°, ..., 80°.

    If A and B are fixed and P is a movable point such that $\angle APB = 90°$, what is the locus
    of P?

11. The table gives the distance, s m, travelled by a train, starting from rest, in t seconds.
    Draw a distance-time graph and use it to find the speed of the train 1 minute after the
    start.

t	10	15	20	30	40	60	80	100	120	140	160
s	15	35	65	135	230	480	785	1110	1440	1745	1990

12. A to H are operations involved in building a garage. Copy the diagram and label it to show a critical path diagram of these operations, assuming that there are several workmen to do the work.

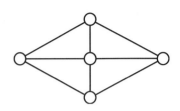

Operation	Time taken (days)	Preceding activity
A	3	–
B	4	–
C	5	–
D	1	B
E	2	B
F	4	A, D
G	4	B
H	1	C, E

Show the critical path on your diagram.
State the least time the complete job will take.

13. The transformation **T** is given by the matrix $\begin{pmatrix} -1 & 1 \\ 2 & 1 \end{pmatrix}$. The triangle ABC has vertices $A(1,1)$, $B(2,1)$, $C(1,2)$. Under the transformation **T**; A, B and C are transformed to A_1, B_1, C_1. Find the coordinates of A_1, B_1, C_1.
Under the transformation **T**; A_1, B_1 and C_1 are transformed to A_2, B_2 and C_2. Find the coordinates of A_2, B_2, C_2.
Plot the triangles ABC, $A_1B_1C_1$, $A_2B_2C_2$ on graph paper and find their areas. State the ratio of their areas.
What single transformation would map $\triangle ABC$ into $\triangle A_2B_2C_2$? Give the geometrical description, and the matrix.

14. The following values of x and y satisfy a relation of the form $y = ax^2 + b$. By plotting y against x^2, show that the points lie on a straight line $y = a(x^2) + b$.

x	0	1	2	$2\frac{1}{2}$	3
y	-5	-4	-1	$1\frac{1}{4}$	4

(Take the x^2-axis from 0 to 9 and the y-axis from -5 to 4.)
Find a and b from the graph and thus find the equation for y in terms of x.

15. A and B are two harbours 15 km apart on a straight coastline running West–East. A ship, C, out at sea is seen from A on a bearing of 056° and from B on a bearing of 288°.
Find the distance of the ship from B, to the nearest 0.1 km.

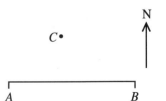

Exercise E6   Revision

1. Use your calculator to find the answers to these questions.

    1 Which is larger, $\sqrt{225} + \sqrt{64}$ or $\sqrt{225 + 64}$, and by how much ?

    2 Which is larger, 2^{11} or 3^7, and by how much ?

    3 Find a prime factor of 69 961 between 30 and 50.

2. In a bag there are 3 red and 2 blue marbles. Gill and Helen take turns to draw out marbles, until a blue one is drawn. Whoever draws the first blue marble wins the game. (The marbles are not replaced during a game.)

    Find the probability that
    1 Gill draws out a blue marble on her first turn,
    2 Gill draws out a red one and then Helen draws out a blue one on her first turn,
    3 both girls draw red ones, then on her second turn Gill draws out a blue one,
    4 Helen gets a second turn, and then draws out a blue one.
    5 What is the probability of Gill winning the game ?
    6 What is the probability of Helen winning the game ?

3. Solve the equations, giving the answers correct to 1 decimal place.
    1 $x^2 - 8x + 1 = 0$, using the method of completing the square,
    2 $2x^2 + 3x - 4 = 0$, using the general formula.

4. A road slopes at a steady angle of 17° to the horizontal. Calculate the increase in height of the road over a distance of 2 km.

    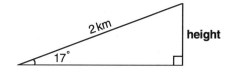

5. $\triangle ABC$ is isosceles with $AB = AC$ and $BC = 6$ cm. O is the centre of the circle and the radius is 5 cm. Find OD, AD and the area of $\triangle ABC$.

    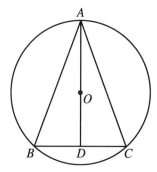

6. **a** and **b** are two vectors not in the same direction. $\overrightarrow{OA} = \mathbf{a}$, $\overrightarrow{OB} = \mathbf{b}$, $\overrightarrow{OC} = \frac{1}{4}(\mathbf{a} + \mathbf{b})$ and $\overrightarrow{OD} = \frac{3}{4}(\mathbf{a} + \mathbf{b})$. Show that $ACBD$ is a parallelogram.

7.   Here is a list of formulae. a and b are lengths.

$$W = \tfrac{1}{2}\sqrt{a^2 + b^2}$$

$$X = \tfrac{2}{3}\pi a b^2$$

$$Y = \pi\left(a^2 - b^2\right)$$

$$Z = 2\pi a + b^2$$

Which letter, W, X, Y or Z represents
1   a length,   **2**   an area,   **3**   a volume ?

8.   A boat owner runs pleasure cruises. His boat will carry 24 passengers, but of the passengers at least half of them, but not more than three-quarters of them, must be children.
The fares charged are £3 for an adult and £2 for a child. To cover expenses the fares on any trip must be at least £30.
If there are x children and y adults on a particular trip, write down 4 inequalities satisfied by x and y.

Draw a graph showing the region satisfying all these inequalities. (Label the x and y axes from 0 to 24.)
Use the graph to find the greatest possible amount that could be taken in fares on the trip.

9.   Find the smallest angle of a triangle whose sides are 7 cm, 10 cm and 13 cm.

10.   On the same diagram sketch the graphs of
$$y = x^3, \quad y = x^3 - 8, \quad y = (x - 8)^3.$$

Label where each graph cuts the x-axis, and label the graphs.

11.   In the diagram, PT is a tangent touching the circle at T.
Find the size of angle a.

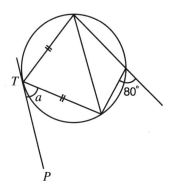

12.   Draw the x-axis from -3 to 4 and the y-axis from -6 to 6. Draw the graphs of $y = 2 - x$ and $2y = 3x - 2$.
Use the graphs to solve the simultaneous equations $y = 2 - x$, $2y = 3x - 2$.

13. Draw a histogram to represent this distribution of times, taken by 50 students to complete a piece of work.

Time (minutes)	f
0–10	7
10–15	10
15–20	9
20–30	14
30–50	10
	50

14. Simplify the expression $\dfrac{5}{x-3} - \dfrac{4x+18}{(x+3)(x-3)}$.

15. A is $(-2, 2)$, B is $(-3, 3)$ and C is $(-1, 6)$. The triangle ABC is translated by the vector $\begin{pmatrix} 7 \\ 2 \end{pmatrix}$ to form the triangle $A_1B_1C_1$. State the coordinates of A_1, B_1 and C_1.

The triangle $A_1B_1C_1$ is transformed by the matrix $\begin{pmatrix} 1 & 0 \\ 0 & -1 \end{pmatrix}$ into triangle $A_2B_2C_2$. State the coordinates of A_2, B_2 and C_2.

The triangle $A_2B_2C_2$ is transformed by a translation which maps A_2 into A, with B_2 into B_3 and C_2 into C_3. State the vector giving this translation.

Draw a diagram on graph paper showing the triangles ABC, $A_1B_1C_1$, $A_2B_2C_2$ and AB_3C_3. Give a geometrical description of a single transformation which maps triangle ABC into triangle AB_3C_3.

Exercise E7 Activities

1. **Sevenths**

   Work out the recurring sequences of decimals for $\frac{1}{7}, \frac{2}{7}, \frac{3}{7}, \frac{4}{7}, \frac{5}{7}, \frac{6}{7}$.
   Investigate the patterns formed.
   Also try adding the 1st and 4th figures, the 2nd and 5th, the 3rd and 6th.
   Add the 1st 2 figures as a 2-figure number, with the 3rd and 4th, and 5th and 6th.
   Add the 1st 3 figures as a 3-figure number with the last 3 figures as a 3-figure number.

   Investigate the decimals for the thirteenths, $\frac{1}{13}, \frac{2}{13}$, etc.
   You could also investigate the seventeenths, but the sequence is too long to get it all displayed on your calculator. You can find it in stages, however.

2.   **Number chains**

You can invent your own rules for number chains.

Here is one idea using 2-digit numbers and their squares.
e.g.
$77 \rightarrow 7^2 + 7^2 = 98 \rightarrow 9^2 + 8^2 = 145 \rightarrow 1^2 + 4^2 + 5^2 = 42 \rightarrow 4^2 + 2^2 = 20 \rightarrow 2^2 + 0^2 = 4$
Stop when you reach a 1-digit number.
The chain here is $77 \rightarrow 98 \rightarrow 145 \rightarrow 42 \rightarrow 20 \rightarrow 4$
Investigate for other 2-digit numbers. To which 1-digit number do most of them lead ?
Which are the exceptions, and which other 1-digit numbers are possible ?

You can do a similar investigation with 2-digit multiples of 3 and their cubes.

e.g. $36 \rightarrow 3^3 + 6^3 = 243 \rightarrow 2^3 + 4^3 + 3^3 = \ldots$
What happens ?

Here is a chain using 2 or 3 digit multiples of 7.
Multiply the hundreds digit by 2, the tens digit by 3, add them together and add on the units digit.
e.g. $854 \rightarrow 8 \times 2 + 5 \times 3 + 4 = 35 \rightarrow 3 \times 3 + 5 = \ldots$
What happens ?

Another rule you can investigate using 2-digit numbers is:
If the number is odd, multiply it by 3 and add 1, if it is even, divide it by 2. Stop when you get to 1.
e.g. $22 \rightarrow 11 \rightarrow 34 \rightarrow 17 \rightarrow 52 \rightarrow \ldots$

3.   **Matrices**

If $\mathbf{A} = \begin{pmatrix} 1 & 0 \\ 0 & -1 \end{pmatrix}$, $\mathbf{B} = \begin{pmatrix} -1 & 0 \\ 0 & -1 \end{pmatrix}$, $\mathbf{C} = \begin{pmatrix} -1 & 0 \\ 0 & 1 \end{pmatrix}$ and $\mathbf{I} = \begin{pmatrix} 1 & 0 \\ 0 & 1 \end{pmatrix}$ show that
$\mathbf{AB} = \mathbf{C}$. You also know that $\mathbf{IA} = \mathbf{AI} = \mathbf{A}$.
These results are shown in this table.

		2nd matrix		
		I	A	B	C
	I		A		
1st	**A**	A		C	
matrix	**B**				
	C				

Work out the other products. Copy and fill in the rest of the grid.
Do you notice any patterns in the results ?

You can extend this table to include the matrices

$\mathbf{D} = \begin{pmatrix} 0 & -1 \\ -1 & 0 \end{pmatrix}$, $\mathbf{E} = \begin{pmatrix} 0 & 1 \\ 1 & 0 \end{pmatrix}$, $\mathbf{F} = \begin{pmatrix} 0 & -1 \\ 1 & 0 \end{pmatrix}$, $\mathbf{G} = \begin{pmatrix} 0 & 1 \\ -1 & 0 \end{pmatrix}$.

4. Proving statements

Here are some statements to be proved. Hints are given in some cases.

1 In the quadrilateral $ABCD$, $AB = DC$ and $AD = BC$.
Prove that $ABCD$ is a parallelogram. (i.e. Prove that AB is parallel to DC and AD is parallel to BC.)

2 In the quadrilateral $ABCD$, AC and BD intersect at X and $AX = XC$, $BX = XD$.
Prove that $ABCD$ is a parallelogram.

3 Prove that, in a circle, the angle at the centre is twice as big as the angle at the circumference. (In the diagrams, prove that $\angle AOB = 2\angle ACB$.)

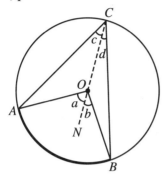 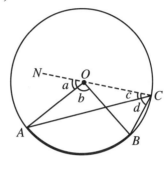

4 Using the result of **3**, prove the other angle properties of circles, shown on pages 423 and 424.

5 Prove that, if in a quadrilateral $ABCD$, $\angle B + \angle D = 180°$, the quadrilateral is a cyclic quadrilateral.
(Only one circle can be drawn to pass through A, B and C. Suppose D is outside this circle, and let CD cut the circle at E. Prove that this is not possible, and then prove that it is not possible for D to be inside the circle. What does this prove ?)

6 **The converse of Pythagoras' theorem**
If in $\triangle PQR$, $PR^2 = PQ^2 + QR^2$, prove that $\angle Q$ is a right angle.
(Draw $\triangle ABC$ with $AB = PQ$, $BC = QR$ and $\angle B = 90°$. Prove that $PR = AC$. Hence prove that $\triangle PQR$, $\triangle ABC$ are congruent, so $\angle Q = 90°$.)

7 Prove that the solution of the general quadratic equation $ax^2 + bx + c = 0$ is
$$x = \frac{-b \pm \sqrt{b^2 - 4ac}}{2a}.$$
(Begin by dividing by a, and solve the equation by completing the square.)

8 If $\theta°$ is an acute angle, prove that $(\sin \theta°)^2 + (\cos \theta°)^2 = 1$.

(This equation is also true if $\theta°$ is an angle of any size.)

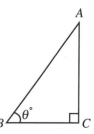

9 Prove that the product of any 5 consecutive numbers is exactly divisible by 120.

5.   **Matrices and trigonometry**

Investigate the transformation given by the matrix $\begin{pmatrix} \cos\theta° & -\sin\theta° \\ \sin\theta° & \cos\theta° \end{pmatrix}$ where $0 \leqslant \theta < 360$.

(You may like to begin by considering $\theta = 0, 90, 180$ and 270.)

6.   **Regular polygons**

1   Investigate the number of diagonals for polygons with 3, 4, 5, ... sides. Find a formula for the number of diagonals of an n-sided polygon.

2   When all the diagonals are drawn, how many regions are there inside the polygon ?

3   Paper knots. Use strips of paper of uniform width. Practise with narrow strips first. Tie an ordinary knot to get a pentagon. Go round an extra turn to get a heptagon. Tie a reef knot in two strips of paper for a hexagon. By bending the paper in a different way you get an octagon.

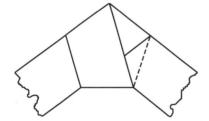
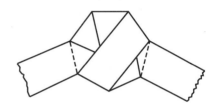

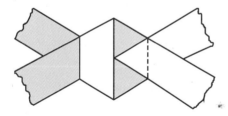
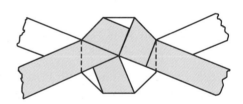

4   You probably can construct a hexagon using ruler and compasses. Here is how to find the arc length to construct a regular pentagon or decagon, without measuring the angles. Draw a circle centre C, radius r and mark a point A on the circumference. Construct a tangent at A. Mark a point D on the tangent such that $AD = \frac{1}{2}r$. (Measure or bisect AC to get this length.) With centre D, radius DC, mark a point E on the tangent on the other side of A to D. Then AE is the radius you need to step out arcs on the circle to make the vertices of a regular decagon. Joining alternate arcs will give a pentagon.

5   Draw a regular pentagon and join its diagonals. Find in the figure an acute-angled isosceles triangle, an obtuse-angled isosceles triangle, an isosceles trapezium, a rhombus, a kite, a pentagon. Find non-regular polygons with different numbers of sides. How many triangles are there altogether in the figure ?

Do a similar investigation for a regular hexagon and a regular octagon.

6   Find a general trig. formula for the area of a regular polygon of n sides with length of side l cm. Verify that this is correct for an equilateral triangle and a square. Represent the sequence of areas for $n = 3, 4, 5, \ldots$ on a graph and say whether the sequence is convergent or divergent. If it is convergent, state the limit.

Find a general trig. formula for the area of a regular polygon which is inscribed in a circle of radius r cm. Verify that this is correct for an equilateral triangle and a square. Represent the sequence of areas for $n = 3, 4, 5, \ldots$ on a graph and say whether the sequence is convergent or divergent. If it is convergent, state the limit.

7.   Centres of a triangle

It is easy to find the centre of an equilateral triangle because there is only one. Investigate triangles of different shapes and find the following centres.
We are considering a triangle ABC.

1   O. Bisect AB and BC. These bisectors intersect at O. Can you prove that the bisector of AC will also pass through O ?

2   I. Bisect angles A and B (internally). These bisectors intersect at I. Can you prove that the bisector of angle C will also pass through I ?

3   G. Let the mid-points of BC, CA and AB be D, E and F respectively. Join AD and BE. These lines intersect at G. Show on your drawing that CF also passes through G. Can you discover any connection between the lengths of AG and GD (or BG and GE, or CG and GF) ?

4   H. Draw the perpendicular line from A to BC, and the perpendicular line from B to AC. These lines meet at H. Show on your drawing that the perpendicular line from C to AB also passes through H.

5   Of the centres O, I, G and H, which centre is the incentre, the centre of the inscribed circle ? Draw the inscribed circle of the triangle showing this centre.

6   Which centre is the circumcentre, the centre of the circumcircle ? Draw the circumcircle of the triangle showing this centre.

7   Which centre is the centre of gravity (the balancing point) of the triangle ? Draw triangles on thick cardboard, draw this centre on them, cut them out and try to balance them at this point on the flat end of a pencil.

8   Find points O, G and H in the same triangle. What do you notice about these points ?

9   **The 9-point circle**
In one diagram, repeat part 1 to find O, and draw all three bisectors. Repeat part 4 to find H, and draw all three perpendiculars. Mark the mid-points of AH, BH and CH. Find N, the mid-point of OH.
There is a circle, centre N, which passes through 9 special points of the triangle. Can you decide which points it should pass through ? If so, find the required radius and draw the circle.

8.   **Mean and standard deviation**

Here is a set of numbers:

8,   11,   12,   15,   16,   18,   19,   20,   25,   26.

1   Find the mean and the standard deviation of the numbers.

2   If every number has 10 added to it, state or find the mean and standard deviation of the new numbers.

3   If every (original) number is doubled, state or find the new mean and standard deviation.

4   Investigate with other numbers, and then copy and complete these statements:

If a set of numbers has a mean $\bar{x}$ and standard deviation s, then if each number is increased by a constant number a, the new mean is ... and the new standard deviation is ...

If each original number is multiplied by a number b, the new mean is ... and the new standard deviation is ...

9.   **Simultaneous equations**

Linear simultaneous equations can be solved using matrices.

e.g. $\begin{array}{l} 3x + 4y = 7 \\ x + 2y = 1 \end{array}$.

These can be written as $\begin{pmatrix} 3 & 4 \\ 1 & 2 \end{pmatrix} \begin{pmatrix} x \\ y \end{pmatrix} = \begin{pmatrix} 7 \\ 1 \end{pmatrix}$.

Pre-multiply both sides by the inverse matrix of $\begin{pmatrix} 3 & 4 \\ 1 & 2 \end{pmatrix}$, which is $\frac{1}{2} \begin{pmatrix} 2 & -4 \\ -1 & 3 \end{pmatrix}$

$$\frac{1}{2} \begin{pmatrix} 2 & -4 \\ -1 & 3 \end{pmatrix} \begin{pmatrix} 3 & 4 \\ 1 & 2 \end{pmatrix} \begin{pmatrix} x \\ y \end{pmatrix} = \frac{1}{2} \begin{pmatrix} 2 & -4 \\ -1 & 3 \end{pmatrix} \begin{pmatrix} 7 \\ 1 \end{pmatrix}$$

Multiplying these gives $\begin{pmatrix} 1 & 0 \\ 0 & 1 \end{pmatrix}$

$$\begin{pmatrix} 1 & 0 \\ 0 & 1 \end{pmatrix} \begin{pmatrix} x \\ y \end{pmatrix} = \frac{1}{2} \begin{pmatrix} 10 \\ -4 \end{pmatrix}$$

$$\begin{pmatrix} x \\ y \end{pmatrix} = \begin{pmatrix} 5 \\ -2 \end{pmatrix}$$

so $x = 5$, $y = -2$.

Solve some of the equations of Exercise 8.3, using this method. You can then decide which method you prefer to use.

10. Packaging problems

1 A square piece of cardboard has sides of length 30 cm. Out of each corner a square of side x cm, where $x < 15$, is cut, and the flaps remaining are turned up to form an open box.
Find an expression for the volume of the box.
By trial, find the value of x for which this volume is a maximum, and state this volume.

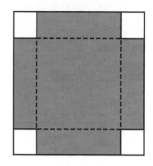

2 A modelling material is made in rods of length 15 cm and diameter 4 cm, and they are packed in sixes, in cardboard boxes with open ends. The cross-section is shown.
Find the perimeter of this cross-section and hence the area of cardboard needed.
(Ignore any overlap.)

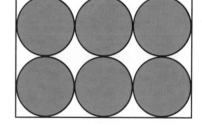

Two ways of using less cardboard are to be investigated.
(a) Making a new design of open box, with cross-section shown below.
(b) Making the modelling material with a square cross-section instead of a circular cross-section but with the same cross-sectional area, and then enclosing the bars in a rectangular box.

(a)

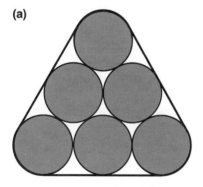

(b)

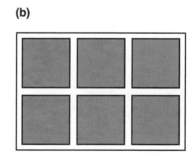

For each way, what is the new perimeter of the cross-section and hence what area of cardboard is needed?
Which method uses the least cardboard and what percentage of cardboard is saved, compared with the original method?

You can think of other packaging problems to solve.

Formula checklist

This list should remind you of the more important formulae. There are some notes about learning formulae on page 421.

Indices

1. $a^m \times a^n =$
2. $a^m \div a^n =$
3. $(a^m)^n =$
4. $a^0 =$
5. $a^{-n} =$
6. $a^{\frac{1}{n}} =$
7. $a^{\frac{m}{n}} =$

Standard index form

8. The form of the number is

Difference of 2 squares:

9. $a^2 - b^2 =$
10. 4 methods for factorising:

Completing the square:

11. $x^2 + 2kx + \ldots = \ldots$

Quadratic equations

12. Solution of $ax^2 + bx + c = 0$ is

Variation

Formulae for:
13. y is directly proportional to x
14. y varies as the square of x
15. y is inversely proportional to x
16. y varies inversely as the square of x

Surds

17. $\sqrt{ab} =$

18. $\sqrt{\dfrac{a}{b}} =$

19. The reciprocal of $x =$

Lengths, areas and volumes

20. Perimeter of a rectangle $=$
21. Circumference of a circle $=$
22. Length of arc $=$

Areas of:

23. Rectangle $=$
24. Square $=$
25. Triangle $=$
26. Parallelogram $=$
27. Trapezium $=$
28. Circle $=$
29. Sector of a circle $=$

Volumes of:

30. Cuboid $=$
31. Cube $=$
32. Prism, solid of uniform cross-section $=$
33. Pyramid $=$
34. Cylinder $=$
35. Cone $=$
36. Sphere $=$

Curved surface areas of:

37. Cylinder $=$
38. Cone $=$
39. Sphere $=$

40. Pythagoras' theorem:
41. 4 conditions for congruent triangles:
42. 3 conditions for similar triangles:

Similar figures

43. Ratio of areas:
44. Ratio of volumes:
45. Scale factor $=$

Vectors

46. If $\overrightarrow{OA} = \mathbf{a}$ and $\overrightarrow{OB} = \mathbf{b}$, $\overrightarrow{AB} =$

Statistics

47.   Mean of a set of numbers =

48.   Mean of a frequency distribution =

49.   Definition of the median:

50.   Definition of the mode:

51.   Range =

52.   Interquartile range =

53.   Standard deviation of a set of numbers, $s =$

54.   Alternative formula for standard deviation, $s =$

55.   Standard deviation of a frequency distribution, $s =$

56.   Frequency density =

Probability

57.   Probability of a successful outcome =

58.   Probability (relative frequency) =

Mutually exclusive events:

59.   P(A or B) =

Independent events:

60.   P(A and B) =

Conditional probability:

61.   P(A and B) =

62.   Error (absolute error) =

63.   Percentage error =

64.   Density =

Travel

65.   Speed =

66.   Average speed =

67.   Acceleration =

Graphs

68.   Gradient of a line =

69.   Gradient of the line $y = mx + c$ is

70.   Point where $y = mx + c$ cuts the y-axis is

Trapezium rule for area under curve

71.   Area =

Trig. in right-angled triangles

72. $\sin A =$

73. $\cos A =$

74. $\tan A =$

Trig. in general triangles

75.   Sine rule:

76.   Cosine rule: $a^2 =$

77.   Cosine rule: $\cos A =$

78.   Area of triangle =

Matrices (2×2)

79.   The identity matrix, **I** is

80.   The determinant of $\begin{pmatrix} a & b \\ c & d \end{pmatrix} =$

81.   The inverse matrix of $\begin{pmatrix} a & b \\ c & d \end{pmatrix}$ is

Matrices and transformations

Matrices for

82.   Enlargement with scale factor k and centre of enlargement (0, 0)

83.   Reflection in the x-axis

84.   Reflection in the y-axis

85.   Reflection in the line $y = x$

86.   Reflection in the line $y = -x$

87.   Rotation about the origin through 90° anticlockwise

88.   Rotation about the origin through 180°

89.   Rotation about the origin through 90° clockwise

Sketch graphs of

90. $y = mx + c$

91. $y = x^2$

92. $y = x^3$

93. $y = \dfrac{1}{x}$

94. $y = \sin x°$

95. $y = \cos x°$

96. $y = \tan x°$

To the student: 6

The day before the examination

Get all your equipment ready:
Pen (and spare cartridges),
Pencil and sharpener,
Rubber,
Ruler,
Compasses, protractor, set square,
Calculator,
Watch.

For your calculator, buy new batteries and make sure they work. Spend a few minutes playing with your calculator to recall which functions you can get with the various keys. How do you find $\sqrt{40}$, $\sqrt[3]{64}$, 40^2, $\frac{1}{40}$, $\sin 40°$ and x where $\cos x° = 0.4$? Remove the instruction booklet which you must not take into the examination room.

Although there should be a clock in the examination room, you may not be able to see it from where you are sitting so it is advisable to wear your watch. Does it also need new batteries ? If you have not got a watch, then borrow one or buy a cheap one.

You want to be comfortable in the exam room so plan to wear a jacket or pullover to keep you warm if it is cold, but which you can take off if you get too hot. (If it gets very stuffy during the exam, ask the invigilator if a window can be opened. If you are in a chilly draught, ask him if it can be closed.)

Check your exam timetable. If you think the exam is in the **afternoon**, check very carefully, because you will be too late if you turn up in the afternoon for an exam that actually took place that morning. Check with someone else in your class to make sure.

Have a last-minute glance at last year's paper or a practice paper. See what instructions were given on that. Plan ahead as to how you will allocate your time. Have a final look at your revision checklist and maybe do just a little more revision, but not too much, as this should be a time for relaxation. Get out into the fresh air and have some exercise. Then go to bed at a reasonable time.

The day of the examination

Get to the exam room in good time, with all your equipment, and have nothing on your desk or in your pockets which you are not supposed to have with you.

When the exam begins, make a note of the time shown on your own watch, and note the time it is due to end.

Check the instructions at the beginning of the paper so that you know whether you must answer all the questions or whether you have to make a choice from one section. Note any other important points.

Do not rush into the first question too quickly. Read it very carefully. Decide how to answer it, then do so. If you have to show your working, set it down neatly. You have plenty of time. It is so easy to make a mistake at this stage as you have not settled down, so do not be in too much of a rush.

When you have finished this question, and this applies to all the other questions as well, read the printed question again. Have you done what you were asked to do ? Have you answered all of it ? Is the answer reasonable ? (Should you check your calculations again ?) Is the answer given to the accuracy required, e.g. to 3 significant figures, and have you given the units, e.g. cm^2 ?

Continue answering questions carefully until you have done a few. Then check the time. If you are going very slowly it might be sensible to leave out any long questions so as to do a few quick ones at this stage. Remember it is the marks which count so spend the time on what will gain you the most marks.

If you cannot do a question, read it again carefully. What is it about ? Are you using all the information given ? Is there a diagram ? Is there any other information you could deduce from the diagram ? If there is not a diagram, would a sketch diagram help ? If so, draw one. What facts or formulae do you know about this topic ? Do they help ? If the question is in several parts, often an answer to an earlier part may be needed in working out a later part. Even if you cannot finish the question, put something down on paper because your attempt might be worth some marks and it cannot be marked if it is not written down. If you cannot do part (1) of a question but can do part (2), then do part (2) so that you will get the marks for that. You can always go back to thinking about part (1) later if you want to, and have the time. If you cannot get any further on any part of the question then abandon it and try a different one.

If the numbers in a question turn out to be complicated it is possible that you have made a simple mistake. Check that you have copied the numbers or expression correctly, and check the signs in your working.

Keep your writing clear. Show all necessary working with your answer as you cannot gain marks for it if it is in a jumbled mess at the bottom of the page. You can do rough work at the side of the page near the answer, and then cross it out if you wish, but cross it out neatly so that it can still be read, in case it is worth some marks.

Do not use white paint correction fluid to blot out your mistakes. Some Examination Boards do not allow you to use this, but even if allowed, it wastes time, and if you write over it the new writing might get soaked up and be illegible by the time your script has reached the examiner.

Once the examination is over, forget it, until the results come out. You have done your best and that is all that matters. We hope you will be satisfied with your final grade. GOOD LUCK!

Index

Answers

Some answers have been given corrected to reasonable degrees of accuracy, depending on the questions. There may be variations in answers where questions involve drawings or graphs. Sometimes it will not be possible to give answers to the same degree of accuracy, depending on the scale used.

Page 3 **Exercise 1.1**

1. 56   120   15   72   20

   24   15   6   0   106

   20   121   600   8   0

   60   8   12   13   144

2. 8   3   11   6   3

   6   12   8   5   7

   8   10   12   7   9

   7   12   5   12   9

3. **1** 3   **4** 0
   2 4   **5** 4
   3 2

4. **1** 4   **.4** 3
   2 8   **5** 19
   3 5

5. **1** 15   **5** 250   **8** 12
   2 0   **6** 188   **9** 190
   3 19   **7** 36   **10** 36
   4 8000

6. **1** 2   **4** 9, 10
   2 4   **5** 3, 4, 5
   3 5, 6

7. **1** 44, 9, 4, 7, 30, 12, 21, 26, 45, 48
   2 6, 33, 20, 8, 15, 9, 1, 7, 13, 25
   3 2, 7, 20, 25, 13, 11, 1, 6, 40, 9
   4 12, 4, 9, 2, 20, 3, 7, 15, 11, 40
   5 4, 10, 16, 6, 20, 40, 22, 60, 50, 12

8. **1** 4, 9   **5** 4, 12   **8** 8, 9
   2 5, 6   **6** 2, 3, 6   **9** 3, 8
   3 2, 50   **7** 3, 4, 5   **10** 7, 11
   4 1, 15

9. **1** 4   **4** 106
   2 1024   **5** 105
   3 8

10. **1** 8   **2** 4   **3** 10

Page 9 **Exercise 1.2**

1. 23, 29

2. **1** 31, 37   **2** 83, 89

3. **1** 16   **5** 4   **8** 88
   2 343   **6** 72   **9** 2700
   3 100 000   **7** 140   **10** 650
   4 11

4. **1** $2^4 \times 3$ **9** 2^6
   2 $3^2 \times 11$ **10** $2^2 \times 5^2$
   3 $2^2 \times 13$ **11** 3×13
   4 $2^2 \times 3 \times 5$ **12** $2^4 \times 5$
   5 $2^2 \times 3^2 \times 5$ **13** 11^2
   6 $2^3 \times 3$ **14** 3^4
   7 $2 \times 5 \times 7$ **15** $2 \times 3 \times 5^2$
   8 $2^5 \times 3$

5. **1** $3^2 \times 5^2$, 15   **4** 2^8, 16
   2 $2^2 \times 3^2 \times 7^2$, 42   **5** $3^2 \times 5^4$, 75
   3 $3^2 \times 11^2$, 33

6. **1** $2^2 \times 7$, 2^4, (1) 4, (2) 112
   2 2×5, $3^2 \times 5$, (1) 5, (2) 90
   3 $2 \times 3 \times 11$, $2^3 \times 11$, (1) 22, (2) 264
   4 $2 \times 3 \times 5 \times 7$, $2 \times 3^2 \times 5 \times 7$,
   (1) 210, (2) 630
   5 $2^4 \times 3^2$, $2^3 \times 3^3$, (1) 72, (2) 432

7. 1 3^6 5 3^4 8 6^{-4}
   2 5^3 6 2^{-2} 9 3^2
   3 7^8 7 5^4 10 5^2
   4 2^{20}

8. 1 $\frac{1}{49}$ 6 7 11 27
   2 1 7 100 12 8
   3 $\frac{1}{8}$ 8 2 13 $\frac{1}{3}$
   4 3 9 $\frac{1}{2}$ 14 $\frac{1}{4}$
   5 $1\frac{1}{3}$ 10 4 15 $\frac{1}{100}$

9. 1 81 4 91 7 81
   2 8 5 8 8 50
   3 37, 73 6 360

10. $2^6 \times 3^3$, 12

Page 15   Exercise 1.3

1. 1 $\frac{3}{11}$ 5 $\frac{4}{9}$ 8 $\frac{7}{12}$
   2 $\frac{2}{5}$ 6 $\frac{5}{7}$ 9 $\frac{1}{10}$
   3 $\frac{1}{4}$ 7 $\frac{5}{8}$ 10 $\frac{2}{3}$
   4 $\frac{3}{8}$

2. 1 $\frac{7}{4}$ 5 $\frac{22}{7}$ 8 $\frac{77}{10}$
   2 $\frac{7}{3}$ 6 $\frac{77}{12}$ 9 $\frac{47}{8}$
   3 $\frac{29}{6}$ 7 $\frac{67}{20}$ 10 $\frac{42}{5}$
   4 $\frac{100}{11}$

3. 1 $4\frac{3}{5}$ 5 $33\frac{1}{3}$ 8 $6\frac{1}{9}$
   2 $3\frac{7}{10}$ 6 $2\frac{5}{6}$ 9 $3\frac{7}{11}$
   3 $2\frac{3}{4}$ 7 $3\frac{1}{8}$ 10 $8\frac{3}{4}$
   4 $2\frac{3}{5}$

4. 1 $1\frac{1}{12}$ 5 $4\frac{3}{4}$ 8 $3\frac{1}{3}$
   2 $\frac{19}{24}$ 6 $7\frac{17}{24}$ 9 $4\frac{11}{20}$
   3 $4\frac{3}{10}$ 7 $5\frac{13}{18}$ 10 $5\frac{17}{24}$
   4 $5\frac{7}{40}$

5. 1 $\frac{11}{24}$ 5 $\frac{11}{20}$ 8 $\frac{2}{3}$
   2 $2\frac{1}{24}$ 6 $1\frac{1}{2}$ 9 $2\frac{4}{5}$
   3 $1\frac{7}{12}$ 7 $\frac{1}{9}$ 10 $3\frac{33}{40}$
   4 $1\frac{19}{36}$

6. 1 $\frac{1}{4}$ 5 $1\frac{1}{2}$ 8 $3\frac{3}{4}$
   2 $\frac{35}{48}$ 6 $\frac{3}{4}$ 9 $8\frac{1}{4}$
   3 $\frac{3}{4}$ 7 $11\frac{3}{7}$ 10 40
   4 $4\frac{1}{5}$

7. 1 $\frac{20}{21}$ 5 $\frac{5}{8}$ 8 $\frac{16}{21}$
   2 $\frac{9}{35}$ 6 $\frac{2}{5}$ 9 $\frac{10}{27}$
   3 $1\frac{1}{2}$ 7 $1\frac{9}{16}$ 10 $5\frac{1}{7}$
   4 4

8. 1 $5\frac{1}{12}$ 5 $2\frac{3}{5}$ 8 1
   2 $\frac{2}{3}$ 6 $\frac{1}{2}$ 9 $4\frac{11}{12}$
   3 $7\frac{1}{3}$ 7 2 10 $1\frac{1}{7}$
   4 8

9. 1 1 5 $25\frac{1}{6}$ 8 $2\frac{1}{5}$
   2 $3\frac{2}{3}$ 6 $\frac{1}{4}$ 9 $1\frac{13}{20}$
   3 $3\frac{1}{2}$ 7 $\frac{5}{16}$ 10 7
   4 3

10. 1 4 : 5
   2 5 : 12
   3 5 : 8

11. 1 90p, £1.35
   2 56p, 98p
   3 42p, 18p

12. 1 £450
   2 £67.50
   3 £160

13. 8 : 27

14. 40°, 60°, 100°, 160°

15. 2.7 cm

16. £7.70

17. 81 lb

18. £12

19. 16 days

20. 15 days

21. £300

22. 100 kg

23. 10 days

24. 2

25. 10 lb

26. yes

27. 42 km/h

28. 95 km/h

29. 4.5 ℓ

30. 8.9 g/cm^3

31. 3 h 48 min

32. **1** £2437.50
    2 £1600, £2800, £3600
    3 4.5 (ℓ)

Page 23   **Exercise 1.4**

1. **1** $\frac{9}{25}$ **4** $\frac{1}{30}$

   2 $\frac{9}{20}$ **5** $\frac{2}{3}$

   3 $\frac{7}{40}$

2. **1** 0.47   **4** 0.0625
   2 0.95   **5** 0.999
   3 0.225

3. **1** 75%   **4** $33\frac{1}{3}$%
   2 62.5%   **5** 87.5%
   3 15%

4. **1** 1.44 m   **4** 1.5 cm
   2 600 g   **5** £4.60
   3 5 min

5. **1** 72%   **4** $37\frac{1}{2}$%
   2 8%   **5** $66\frac{2}{3}$%
   3 60%

6. **1** £6.24   **4** £60
   2 £2.90   **5** £336
   3 £108

7. **1** 20%   **2** $16\frac{2}{3}$%   **3** 12%

8. **1** £700   **4** £150
   2 £4.00   **5** £9000
   3 300 ml

9. **1** £60   **2** £264   **3** £168

10. **1** £64.93   **2** £310.84   **3** £176.40

11. £28.20

12. £360, £63

13. £1350, £112.50

14. £17 150

15. 9%, 10%, 7.5%

16. 12%

Page 25   **Exercise 1.5**

1. **1** 19, 23   **4** 27
   2 25   **5** 19, 25
   3 18, 27

2. $2^3 \times 3^3 \times 5$; $a = 3$, $b = 3$, $c = 1$; 30

3. $360 = 2^3 \times 3^2 \times 5$, $405 = 3^4 \times 5$, $145\,800 = 2^3 \times 3^6 \times 5^2$

4. **1** $7^2 \times 11$ **2** $7^3 \times 11^3 \times 13 \times 17$

5. 1, 81, 3, $\frac{1}{9}$, $\frac{1}{27}$

6. **1** 729   **2** 9

7. **1** 60   **2** 13   **3** 17

8. $\frac{1}{9}$

9. $5\frac{1}{4}$ feet

10. £750

11. **1** $\frac{3}{5}$ **2** $1\frac{1}{5}$

12. £60.50

13. £146.20, 48 h

14. A £240, B £300, C £360; 96°, 120°, 144°

15. £120.25

16. 49 min

17. £1155

18. **1** 48 mph   **3** 38 miles/gallon
    2 36 mph

19. 3.8%

20. £75

21. £2700, none, £435, £8.37

22. 8%, £1819.58

Page 27   **Practice test 1**

1. **1** 19   **4** 12
   2 16   **5** 16, 20
   3 20   **6** 8, 19

2. $378 = 2 \times 3^3 \times 7$, $441 = 3^2 \times 7^2$

    1 21   **2** 63   **3** $2 \times 3^3 \times 7^2$

3. £160

4. **1** $5:6$ **2** $6:5$

5. 0.8 g/cm^3

6. £3630

Page 32   Exercise 2.1

1. the perpendicular bisector of the line joining the rocks
2. a line parallel to the slide
3. an arc of a circle, centre at the top of the rope
4. a circle, centre at the centre of the fixed disc, radius 8 cm
5. $PA = 3.2$ cm
6. $PB = 3.6$ cm
8. 49 m

Page 37   Exercise 2.2

1. **1** $\mathbf{a} = \begin{pmatrix} 4 \\ 6 \end{pmatrix}$, $\mathbf{b} = \begin{pmatrix} 4 \\ 2 \end{pmatrix}$, $\mathbf{c} = \begin{pmatrix} 0 \\ -4 \end{pmatrix}$, $\mathbf{d} = \begin{pmatrix} -4 \\ 2 \end{pmatrix}$, $\mathbf{e} = \begin{pmatrix} 6 \\ -4 \end{pmatrix}$, $\mathbf{f} = \begin{pmatrix} -4 \\ 2 \end{pmatrix}$, $\mathbf{g} = \begin{pmatrix} 8 \\ 4 \end{pmatrix}$

    2 d, f   **3** e   **4** g

2. $\overrightarrow{AB} = \begin{pmatrix} 3 \\ 2 \end{pmatrix}$, $\overrightarrow{BC} = \begin{pmatrix} 1 \\ -4 \end{pmatrix}$,

    $DE = 2$ units

3. **1** $\begin{pmatrix} 6 \\ 4 \end{pmatrix}$ **3** $\begin{pmatrix} 4 \\ 1 \end{pmatrix}$ **2** $\begin{pmatrix} 6 \\ 1 \end{pmatrix}$ **4** $\begin{pmatrix} 3 \\ 3 \end{pmatrix}$

4. **1** $\begin{pmatrix} 8 \\ 3 \end{pmatrix}$ **3** $\begin{pmatrix} 3 \\ 0 \end{pmatrix}$ **2** $\begin{pmatrix} 3 \\ -5 \end{pmatrix}$ **4** $\begin{pmatrix} -4 \\ -3 \end{pmatrix}$

5. **1** $\begin{pmatrix} 2 \\ -2 \end{pmatrix}$ **3** $\begin{pmatrix} 4 \\ -5 \end{pmatrix}$ **2** $\begin{pmatrix} -4 \\ 5 \end{pmatrix}$ **4** $\begin{pmatrix} 7 \\ -1 \end{pmatrix}$

6. **1** $\begin{pmatrix} 2 \\ -3 \end{pmatrix}$ **3** $\begin{pmatrix} -5 \\ 4 \end{pmatrix}$ **2** $\begin{pmatrix} -5 \\ 1 \end{pmatrix}$ **4** $\begin{pmatrix} -4 \\ 3 \end{pmatrix}$

8. $\mathbf{a} + \mathbf{b} = \begin{pmatrix} 5 \\ 3 \end{pmatrix}$, $\mathbf{a} - \mathbf{b} = \begin{pmatrix} 1 \\ 5 \end{pmatrix}$, $3\mathbf{a} = \begin{pmatrix} 9 \\ 12 \end{pmatrix}$, $\mathbf{a} + 4\mathbf{b} = \begin{pmatrix} 11 \\ 0 \end{pmatrix}$, $2\mathbf{a} - 3\mathbf{b} = \begin{pmatrix} 0 \\ 11 \end{pmatrix}$

9. $\overrightarrow{AD} = \overrightarrow{BC} = \begin{pmatrix} -5 \\ -2 \end{pmatrix}$, parallelogram

10. $B\,(1, 5)$, $C\,(5, 4)$; $\overrightarrow{CE} = \begin{pmatrix} 2 \\ 3 \end{pmatrix}$, C is mid-point of line AE

Page 42   Exercise 2.3

1. **1** $\mathbf{a} + \mathbf{b}$ **2** $\mathbf{a} + \mathbf{b} + \mathbf{c}$
2. $\mathbf{a} + \frac{1}{2}\mathbf{b}$
4. $1 : 2 : 1$

Page 44   Exercise 2.4

1. **1** $\triangle ABX \equiv \triangle ADX$
        $\triangle CBX \equiv \triangle CDX$
        $\triangle ABC \equiv \triangle ADC$
    2 $\angle ADC$
    3 DX
2. **1** $BC = DC$, $AB = ED$
    2 $\angle CDE$
3. **1** yes
       $\triangle ABC \equiv \triangle DEF$ (SAS)
       $BC = EF$
       $\angle B = \angle E$
       $\angle C = \angle F$

3. **2** yes
   $\triangle ABC \equiv \triangle HJG$ (AAS)
   $AB = HJ$
   $AC = HG$
   $\angle A = \angle H$

  3 yes
   $\triangle ABC \equiv \triangle NML$ (AAS)
   $BC = ML$
   $AC = NL$
   $\angle A = \angle N$

  4 no

  5 yes
   $\triangle ABC \equiv \triangle STU$ (RHS)
   $BC = TU$
   $\angle A = \angle S$
   $\angle B = \angle T$

  6 no

  7 yes
   $\triangle ABC \equiv \triangle EGF$ (SSS)
   $\angle A = \angle E$
   $\angle B = \angle G$
   $\angle C = \angle F$

  8 yes
   $\triangle ABC \equiv \triangle KJH$ (SAS)
   $AC = KH$
   $\angle A = \angle K$
   $\angle C = \angle H$

  9 yes
   $\triangle ABC \equiv \triangle NMP$ (SAS)
   $AC = NP$
   $\angle A = \angle N$
   $\angle C = \angle P$

  10 no

5. **1** (SSS)

6. **1** (SSS)   **2** $\angle BXZ$ **3** (SAS)

Page 45   Exercise 2.5

3. 420 m

5. 100 m

6. an arc of a circle, centre at the point where the wall meets the ground

8. **1** $\begin{pmatrix} -3 \\ -5 \end{pmatrix}$ **2** $\begin{pmatrix} 2 \\ -3 \end{pmatrix}$ **3** $\begin{pmatrix} -\frac{1}{2} \\ -4 \end{pmatrix}$

9. $(17, 9)$

10. $a = 2, b = -3$

11. $\overrightarrow{AB} = \begin{pmatrix} 3 \\ -3 \end{pmatrix}, \ \overrightarrow{BC} = \begin{pmatrix} 1 \\ 5 \end{pmatrix}$

12. $\overrightarrow{AB} = \begin{pmatrix} 9 \\ 3 \end{pmatrix}, \ \overrightarrow{BC} = \begin{pmatrix} -12 \\ -4 \end{pmatrix}$

13. **1** $\mathbf{b} - \mathbf{a}$ **2** $\frac{1}{2}\mathbf{b} - \frac{1}{2}\mathbf{a}; \ DE = \frac{1}{2}AB$

14. $\overrightarrow{SP} = \overrightarrow{RQ} = \frac{1}{2}\mathbf{d}; \ SP, RQ$ are parallel,
   $SP = RQ$; parallelogram

15. 17 km/h, 28°

16. 17.4 N

17. **1** $\triangle ADN \equiv \triangle AEN, \triangle ABN \equiv \triangle ACN,$
    $\triangle ABE \equiv \triangle ACD$
  2 $BE = CD, AD = AE$
  3 $\angle ACN$

18. $\triangle ABC \equiv \triangle DEF$ (SSS or other), $\angle DFE$

19. **1** (SAS)
  2 $\triangle BDC$
  3 $\angle FAE = \angle BCE, \angle GAD = \angle CBD$
  4 sum of angles $= 180°$
  5 $GA = AF = BC$

Page 49   Practice test 2

1. 14 m

3. **1** $\begin{pmatrix} 3 \\ -2 \end{pmatrix}$ **2** $\begin{pmatrix} -1 \\ 5 \end{pmatrix}$ **3** $\begin{pmatrix} -2 \\ -3 \end{pmatrix}$

4. $\overrightarrow{AB} = \begin{pmatrix} 4 \\ 3 \end{pmatrix}, \ \overrightarrow{BC} = \begin{pmatrix} -4 \\ -5 \end{pmatrix},$

   $\overrightarrow{AD} = \begin{pmatrix} -4 \\ -5 \end{pmatrix}, \ \overrightarrow{DC} = \begin{pmatrix} 4 \\ 3 \end{pmatrix}$

5. $\overrightarrow{OE} = \frac{1}{3}\mathbf{a}, \quad \overrightarrow{EB} = \mathbf{b} - \frac{1}{3}\mathbf{a}, \overrightarrow{OF} = 3\mathbf{b},$

   $\overrightarrow{AF} = 3\mathbf{b} - \mathbf{a}; \quad EB : AF = 1 : 3$

6. **1** (SAS)
  2 DE
  3 $\angle EDC$
  4 they are equal and parallel

7. (AAS), 80 m

Page 57   Exercise 3.1

1. **1** $5a$ pence   **3** $(3e + 2f)$ pence
  2 $120b$ (min)   **4** $(100 - gh)$ pence

2. **1** $C = \dfrac{k^2}{100}$ **2** $e = \frac{1}{3}m$ **3** $m = \dfrac{n}{20}$

3.
1 c
2 0
3 $8e$
4 $3g - 4h$
5 a^2
6 b^3
7 1
8 d^2
9 e^5
10 f^4
11 $45a^2$
12 $16bc$
13 $20e^3$
14 $3f$
15 $9g^2$
16 $5h$
17 $\dfrac{4m}{n}$
18 $1\frac{1}{2}$
19 $2ab$
20 $2c^3$
21 $8d^2$
22 $2ef$
23 $6a^2$
24 $9g^4h^6$
25 $4jk^2$

4.
1 $3a$
2 $-b$
3 $5c$
4 $-3d$
5 $9e$
6 $-2f$
7 0
8 $7h$
9 $-3x$
10 $5x$

5.
1 $16xy$
2 $-28xy$
3 $-\frac{2}{3}$
4 $27x^2$
5 -1
6 $-6xy$
7 $-24x^2$
8 $\dfrac{1}{x}$
9 $4x^2$
10 0

6.
1 $3a + 3b$
2 $c - 10d$
3 $8e - f$
4 $-3g - 9h$
5 $j + 6k$
6 $8p - 13q + r$
7 $44 - 5s$
8 $x^2 - x - 6$
9 $2x^2 - 9x + 4$
10 $x - x^2$

7.
1 $x^2 + 7x + 6$
2 $x^2 - 10x + 21$
3 $x^2 + 2x - 15$
4 $x^2 + 8x + 16$
5 $2x^2 + 7x + 5$
6 $6x^2 + 7x - 5$
7 $2x^2 - 5x + 3$
8 $4x^2 - y^2$
9 $60 + 11x - x^2$
10 $x^2 - 2xy + y^2$
11 $3x^2 + 14xy - 24y^2$
12 $2x^2 + 3xy - 5y^2$
13 $9x^2 + 6xy + y^2$
14 $4x^2 + 8xy - 21y^2$
15 $4x^2 + xy - 3y^2$
16 $9x^2 + 12x + 4$
17 $16x^2 - 9$
18 $4x^2 - 4xy + y^2$
19 $x^2 - 16y^2$
20 $9x^2 + 3xy - 2y^2$

8.
1 $4a$
2 $\dfrac{c}{9d}$
3 $\dfrac{5e^2f}{3}$

9.
1 $\dfrac{13a}{24}$
2 $\dfrac{28b}{9}$
3 $\dfrac{d}{2}$

10.
1 $\dfrac{5a+1}{6}$
2 $\dfrac{b-3c}{4}$
3 $\dfrac{9d+2}{12}$

11.
1 $\dfrac{2c}{3b}$
2 $\dfrac{2b}{5}$
3 $\dfrac{ce^2}{15df}$

12.
1 23
2 34
3 50
4 3
5 100

13.
1 $1\frac{1}{6}$
2 0
3 $\frac{7}{12}$
4 $3\frac{1}{3}$
5 $6\frac{1}{2}$
6 $\frac{3}{4}$
7 3
8 $4\frac{11}{12}$
9 $\frac{3}{8}$
10 $1\frac{1}{2}$

14.
1 $-4\frac{1}{2}$
2 12
3 2
4 5
5 25

15.
1 $5(2x - 3y)$
2 $3y(x - 4z)$
3 $4\pi(a - b)$
4 $5(4abc + 2a - b + 5c)$
5 $7xy(2x - 3y)$
6 $a^2(1 + a)$
7 $a(a + 2b - c)$
8 $7(7 + x^3)$
9 $2\pi r(r + h)$
10 $xy(x - y)$

16.
1 $-\frac{2}{5}$ **2** $-\frac{1}{3}$

17. 650

Page 66   Exercise 3.2

1.
1 $a = 3$
2 $b = 4$
3 $c = 5$
4 $d = 4$
5 $e = 10$
6 $f = 4$
7 $g = 26$
8 $h = 13$
9 $j = 70$
10 $k = 8$

2.
1 $x = 28$
2 $x = -\frac{1}{6}$
3 $x = 10$
4 $x = \frac{3}{4}$
5 $x = 2$

3.
1 $x = 4$
2 $x = 13$
3 $x = -15$
4 $x = 2\frac{1}{2}$

4.
1 $x = \pm 12$
2 $x = 7$
3 $x = \pm 0.24$
4 $x = 49$
5 $x = 216$
6 $x = \pm 1.9$
7 $x = 2.20$
8 $x = 1.01$
9 $x = 0.81$
10 $x = \pm 3.16$

5.
1 $y = \dfrac{c - ax}{b}$
2 $v = \sqrt{\dfrac{2E}{m}}$
3 $a = \dfrac{v - u}{t}$
4 $F = \dfrac{9C}{5} + 32$
5 $n = \dfrac{2s}{a + \ell}$

6. 2

7. $y = \frac{1}{4}x^2$, $6\frac{1}{4}$

8. 9

9. 8

10. $y = 8x^3$, 8000

11. $\frac{1}{4}$

12. 125

13. 28

14. $y = \frac{36}{x^2}$, $2\frac{1}{4}$

15. $W = \frac{\ell d^2}{105}$, 10 kg

16. 7

Page 70   Example

cube numbers

Page 71   Exercise 3.3

1. **1** a^7 **5** e^2 **8** h
   2 b^{-2} **6** $f^{1\frac{1}{2}}$ **9** 1
   3 c^{10} **7** 1   **10** $k^{-\frac{2}{3}}$
   4 d^2

2. **1** 10^{p+q} **4** 10^{2p}
   2 10^{p-q} **5** 10^{q-2}
   3 10^{p+1}

3. **1** 6   **4** 0
   2 4   **5** $-\frac{1}{2}$
   3 -2

4. 3

5. **1** 19, 23; $4n - 1$ **6** 217, 344; $n^3 + 1$
   2 12, 11; $17 - n$ **7** $-25, -35$;
   $25 - 10n$
   3 22, 25; $3n + 7$ **8** 30, 42; $n(n - 1)$
   4 75, 70; $100 - 5n$ **9** $\frac{5}{7}, \frac{6}{8}$; $\frac{n}{n+2}$
   5 $\frac{1}{5}, \frac{1}{6}; \frac{1}{n}$ **10** 35, 46; $n^2 + 10$

6. **1** 2, 5, 8, 11   **5** 3, 8, 15, 24
   2 90, 80, 70, 60   **6** 3, 9, 27, 81
   3 2, 5, 10, 17   **7** $\frac{1}{2}, \frac{2}{3}, \frac{3}{4}, \frac{4}{5}$
   4 10, 100, 1000,   **8** 0, 7, 26, 63
   10 000

7. 105.8°F

8. 11.6, the mean

9. 1, 1, 2, 3, 5, 8, 13, 21, 34, 55, 89, 144;
   Fibonacci sequence

10. 5^n, $n = 9$

Page 74   Exercise 3.4

1. £ $\frac{k(y - x)}{100}$

2. $T = \frac{1 + c}{3}$

3. **1** $7a^3$ **2** $12a^6$ **3** $\frac{3}{4}$

4. **1** $-\frac{3}{7}$ **2** $\frac{1}{2}$ **3** 58

5. **1** 33   **2** -5

6. 35

7. **1** $12xy$ **2** $\frac{7}{12xy}$ **3** $1\frac{1}{3}$

8. **1** $20a^{13}$ **2** $3b^4$

9. $3\frac{2}{7}$

10. $\frac{3}{5}$

11. $\frac{x - 1}{12x}$

12. 0

13. **1** 24.3   **4** 31.42
    2 169   **5** 6800
    3 9700

14. **1** $2\frac{2}{5}$ **2** 10

15. $\frac{360}{a}^{\circ}, \frac{360}{b}^{\circ}, \left(180 - \frac{360}{c}\right)^{\circ}$; $a = 4$, square

16. 8 years

17. 18

18. **1** $R = 100\left(\frac{A}{P} - 1\right)$ or $\frac{100}{P}(A - P)$

    2 $\ell = \frac{T^2 g}{4\pi^2}$

    3 $\ell = \frac{S - \pi r^2}{\pi r}$ or $\frac{S}{\pi r} - r$

    4 $x = 9a^2 - 2$

    5 $x = (3a - 2)^2$

19. **1** $18\frac{3}{4}$ **2** $x = \sqrt{\frac{6V}{h}}$

20. **1** $c = \frac{b^2}{a}$ **2** $b = \sqrt{ac}$

21. **1** $7\frac{1}{2}$ **2** $r = \frac{s - a}{s}$ or $1 - \frac{a}{s}$

22. 3 ohms

23. 12.5 tonnes

24. **1** a **2** b **3** c **4** $d^2 - 1$

25. **1** $x = 0$ **3** $x = \frac{2}{3}$
    2 $x = -1$ **4** $x = 8$

26. **1** $n = 3$, $y = \frac{3}{4}$, $x = 1.5$
    2 $n = \frac{1}{2}$, $y = 44$, $x = \frac{1}{4}$

27. **1** $6, 3, 1\frac{1}{2}; \dfrac{192}{2^n}$
    2 $-4, -7, -10; 11 - 3n$
    3 $\frac{5}{8}, \frac{6}{9}, \frac{7}{10}; \dfrac{n}{n + 3}$

28. $-9, 27, -81, 243$

29. **1** $120°$ **2** $162°$

30. **1** not prime; no, no, no, yes
    2 prime; no, no, no, no, no, no
    3 not prime; no, yes
    4 not prime; no, no, no, no, no, yes
    5 prime; no, no, no, no, no, no

Page 79   Practice test 3

1. **1** $2a$ **4** 1
   2 0 **5** a
   3 a^2

2. **1** 0 **4** 2
   2 -10 **5** 5
   3 8

3. **1** $\frac{1}{6}$ **2** $\frac{5}{6}$ **3** $\frac{1}{15}$

4. $A = 60 + 25n$; £360

5. $3x^2 + 2x + 16$

6. **1** $x = -8$ **4** $x = -15$
   2 $x = -\frac{2}{3}$ **5** $x = 4$
   3 $x = \frac{1}{2}$

7. $\pi r(\ell + r + 2h)$, 628

8. **1** $x = \dfrac{c - b}{a}$ **3** $x = \frac{5}{3}a$
   2 $x = \sqrt{a^2 - b^2}$ **4** $x = \dfrac{(b - 5)^2}{4}$

9. 5 cm

10. **1** 1 **2** b^2 **3** d^2 **4** e

11. **1** $43, 51, 59; 3 + 8n$
    2 $16, 32, 64; 2^{n-1}$
    3 $5, 1, -3; 25 - 4n$

12. $1, 4, 9, 16, 25, 36$; square numbers

Page 87   Exercise 4.1

1. **1** 7.612   **2** 7   **3** 0.241

2. **1** 21.013   **2** 6.95   **3** 0.0094

3. **1** 15.48   **2** 0.06   **3** 1.456

4. **1** 0.97   **2** 0.0008   **3** 0.0416

5. **1** 0.4   **2** 0.37   **3** 0.16

6. **1** 13.2   **5** 0.0015   **8** 3100
   2 250   **6** 0.02132   **9** 0.0031
   3 0.3792   **7** 2.72   **10** 0.004
   4 1030

7. **1** 15   **4** 32
   2 120   **5** 1400
   3 0.3

8. **1** 0.072   **4** 0.63
   2 0.003   **5** 0.002
   3 0.006

9. **1** 8.792   **2** 0.066417   **3** 198.38

10. **1** 200   **4** 300
    2 300   **5** 0.05
    3 0.02

11. **1** 29.712   **4** 4.680
    2 1.628   **5** 0.004
    3 202.916

12. **1** 29.7   **4** 4.68
    2 1.63   **5** 0.00353
    3 203

13. **1** 56 800   **4** 207
    2 83.0   **5** 1000
    3 253

14. **1** 20   **4** 0.05
    2 3   **5** 40 or 48
    3 0.0009

15. **1**

Page 93   Exercise 4.2

1. **1** 0.667   **4** 0.167
   2 0.714   **5** 0.727
   3 0.444

2.
1	107	**6**	3260
2	0.0000284	**7**	3.67
3	1.33	**8**	0.202
4	0.356	**9**	27.0
5	4720	**10**	3.44

3.
1	137 rem 16	**3**	562 rem 16
2	14 rem 7		

4.   2, 0.5

3, 0.$\dot{3}$, 0.333

4, 0.25

5, 0.2

6, 0.1$\dot{6}$, 0.167

7, 0.$\dot{1}$42857, 0.143

8, 0.125

9, 0.$\dot{1}$, 0.111

10, 0.1

11, 0.0$\dot{9}$, 0.091

12, 0.08$\dot{3}$, 0.083

13, 0.$\dot{0}$7692$\dot{3}$, 0.077

14, 0.0$\dot{7}$14285$\dot{7}$, 0.071

15, 0.0$\dot{6}$, 0.067

16, 0.0625

1	2, 4, 5, 8, 10, 16
2	3, 6, 9, 12, 15
3	11
4	7, 13, 14

5.
1	5.06×10^2	**9**	3.45×10^{-1}
2	2.187×10^3	**10**	2.08×10^{-2}
3	1.507×10	**11**	9.307×10^4
4	2.3×10^3	**12**	1.3×10^{-7}
5	7×10^6	**13**	1.157×10
6	2.7×10^{-2}	**14**	1.157×10^{-1}
7	5.1×10^{-4}	**15**	9.9×10^{-3}
8	6×10^{-6}		

6.
1	105	**9**	293
2	96 000	**10**	1 100 000
3	0.412	**11**	0.043
4	5200	**12**	800 000
5	0.0289	**13**	0.000203
6	750 000	**14**	9900
7	0.004	**15**	0.1072
8	0.611		

7.
1	4.674×10^8	**7**	9.86×10^{-3}
2	7.5×10	**8**	5.8×10
3	2.209×10^7	**9**	3.481×10^{-5}
4	2.2×10^3	**10**	2.5×10^{-7}
5	3×10^{-2}	**11**	1.6×10^{-6}
6	2.64×10^3	**12**	8×10^{-2}

8. 7.35×10^{19} tonnes

Page 96   Exercise 4.3

1.
1	50	**11**	10 000
2	3000	**12**	135
3	1000	**13**	2000
4	50	**14**	150
5	365	**15**	300
6	4000	**16**	52
7	200	**17**	1000
8	6000	**18**	30
9	8000	**19**	1 000 000
10	31	**20**	1000

2.
1	10.64 kg
2	101.4°F
3	1250 g or 1.25 kg
4	4 ml

3.
1	750 g	**6**	1.52 kg
2	12.6 cm	**7**	70 cl
3	260 cm	**8**	78 mm
4	0.4 ℓ	**9**	120 cm
5	1.6 m	**10**	3.04 tonnes

4.
1	metres	**4**	metres
2	grams	**5**	cm
3	litres		

5.
1	6.45 cm, 6.55 cm
2	8.745 kg, 8.755 kg
3	4.15 ℓ, 4.25 ℓ
4	2 h 5 min, 2 h 15 min
5	8 h 4$\frac{1}{2}$ min, 8 h 5$\frac{1}{2}$ min

6.
1	8.7 m	**5**	156.9 cm	**8**	5.44 kg
2	280 g	**6**	4.1 ℓ	**9**	2500 ℓ
3	4200 ℓ	**7**	5.0 m	**10**	47.0 s
4	6 m				

7.
1	4.95 cm, 5.05 cm	**4**	59.5 ml, 60.5 ml
2	195 g, 205 g	**5**	£29.50, £30.50
3	2$\frac{1}{2}$ min, 3$\frac{1}{2}$ min		

8.   (possible answers)

1	nearest cm; 1.615 m, 1.625 m
2	nearest kg; 37.5 kg, 38.5 kg

Page 100   Exercise 4.4

1.
1	rational	**4**	integer
2	irrational	**5**	natural number
3	natural number		

2. $n = 15$

3.   rational: 2.$\dot{7}$, $\dfrac{1}{\sqrt{9}}$, $\sqrt[3]{27}$; irrational $\sqrt{3}$, 3π

4. $\pi + 2$, irrational; 5.1416, rational; $5\frac{1}{7}$,
    rational; 2.268^2, rational; $\sqrt{27}$, irrational

5. **1** $3\sqrt{5}$ **4** $6\sqrt{2}$
    2 $2\sqrt{11}$ **5** $10\sqrt{2}$
    3 $5\sqrt{3}$

6. **1** $\frac{3}{4}$ **5** 2   **8** 30
    2 $\frac{1}{9}$ **6** 5   **9** $3\sqrt{5}$
    3 $2\frac{1}{2}$ **7** 6   **10** $5 - \sqrt{5}$
    4 $\sqrt{13}$

7. **1** irrational   **7** rational
    2 rational   **8** rational
    3 irrational   **9** irrational
    4 rational   **10** rational
    5 irrational   **11** rational
    6 rational   **12** irrational

8. **1** $\frac{1}{5}\sqrt{5}$ **4** $2\sqrt{5} - 2$
    2 $\frac{1}{2}\sqrt{6}$ **5** $6\sqrt{6} + 12$
    3 $4\sqrt{2}$

Page 101   **Exercise 4.5**

1. **1** 30 000   **5** 0.4   **8** 7
    2 14   **6** 90   **9** 11
    3 0.48   **7** 110   **10** 0.6
    4 36

2. 2150

3. 0.4

4. 0.006

5. 28

6. 0.036

7. 0.054

8. 10.688

9. 1

10. $\frac{3}{40}$

11. **1** 22.149   **2** 0.0514   **3** 81.6

12. **1** 9877   **2** 9876.52   **3** 9880

13. 50

14. 7

15. Alan, £1

16. £13.50

17. 6 g, 0.14 mm

18. 52.2

19. **1** 4.9   **2** 4.0

20. (possible answers)
    1 tonnes   **4** km
    2 litres   **5** mm
    3 grams

21. (possible answers)
    nearest 5 min; $17\frac{1}{2}$ min, $22\frac{1}{2}$ min

22. 30, 0.0333   36, 0.0278
    31, 0.0323   37, 0.0270
    32, 0.03125   38, 0.0263
    33, 0.0303   39, 0.0256,
    34, 0.0294   40, 0.025
    35, 0.0286

    1 32, 40   **4** 37
    2 30, 36   **5** 31, 34, 35, 38, 39
    3 33

23. **1** 1.5×10^4 **4** 5.276×10^{-1}
    2 3.64×10^2 **5** 2.32×10
    3 9.52×10^{-4}

24. **1** 1860   **4** 200 000
    2 0.00765   **5** 0.009
    3 12 609

25. 1.5×10^8 km

26. 8.99×10^{-5} g

27. **1** $\sqrt{3}$, $2 + \sqrt{3}$ (or others)
    2 $\sqrt{5}$, $5 - \sqrt{5}$
    3 $\sqrt{3}$, $2 + \sqrt{3}$ (or others)
    4 $\sqrt{3}$, $\sqrt{12}$

28. **1** e.g. 2.1, 2.15
    2 e.g. π, $\sqrt{8}$

29. irrational

30. **1** $\frac{7}{8}$ **5** 15   **8** $10\sqrt{2}$
    2 $1\frac{1}{3}$ **6** 12   **9** 1
    3 $\sqrt{2}$ **7** 20   **10** 1
    4 4

Page 104   **Practice test 4**

1. **1** 1800   **5** 1   **8** 300
    2 0.07   **6** 6   **9** 0.6
    3 36   **7** 7   **10** 100
    4 4.8

2.   **1** 0.04$\dot{5}$ **2** 0.0455   **3** 0.045

3.   0.281

4.   **1** $n = -3$ **2** $n = 3$

5. 1.08×10^2

6.   **1** 55 kg, 65 kg   **4** 4.55 m, 4.65 m
   2 55.5 kg, 56.5 kg   **5** £650, £750
   3 245 ml, 255 ml

7. $\dfrac{9\pi}{20}$, irrational; 1.4$\dot{1}$, rational;

   1.4142, rational; $\sqrt{2}$, irrational;
   1.19², rational

8.   68 (francs)

Page 122   Exercise A1

1.   £7.56

2.   **1** $\frac{1}{8}$ **2** $\frac{1}{4}$ **3** 0   **4** $2\frac{1}{3}$

3.   **1** 150°   **2** 15°   **3** 45°

4.   32 min

5.   Wages £22 500, food £18 000, fuel £6000, extras £7500; new cost £56 730

7.   8 amps

8.   **1** $6\frac{7}{12}$ **4** $1\frac{2}{3}$
   2 $\frac{1}{2}$ **5** $5\frac{1}{2}$
   3 5

9. $\triangle ABD$, BD

10. 2.59 (km²)

11. **1** $x = \dfrac{y-c}{m}$ **3** $x = \dfrac{b}{a+c}$

   2 $x = \dfrac{(y+3)^2}{4}$ **4** $x = \sqrt{y-4}$

12. $\overrightarrow{AB} = \overrightarrow{DC} = \begin{pmatrix} 2 \\ 4 \end{pmatrix}$,

   $\overrightarrow{BC} = \overrightarrow{AD} = \begin{pmatrix} -1 \\ -10 \end{pmatrix}$; parallelogram

13. 3200

14. **1** fp (pence)   **4** $(x-2)$ years
   2 $\dfrac{y}{x}$ pence   **5** £$(12x + 52y)$
   3 $12 - x$, $x(12 - x)$

15. £662   (£660)

Page 124   Exercise A2

1.   1000

2. $x = 100$, parallelogram (or rhombus)

3.   **1** 16.55   **3** 25 p
   2 7 h 13 min   **4** 72 km/h
                         70

4.   **1** 255°   **2** 305°   **3** 125°

5.   **1** $2^5 \times 3$ **2** 360   **3** 41, 43, 47

6.   X £49, Y £41

7. $x = 4$ or -4

8.   **1** 532   **4** 500
   2 0.035   **5** 9
   3 0.04

10. 1 h 30 min

12. **1** 116   **4** 6
   2 240   **5** 6
   3 7

13. 64°

14. 5 cm

Page 136   Exercise 6.1

1.   **1** 11.2 cm   **4** 8.1 cm
   2 10 cm   **5** 4 cm
   3 2.2 cm

2.   **1** $c = 15$ cm   **4** $b = 3.3$ cm
   2 $c = 6.7$ cm   **5** $c = 8.5$ cm
   3 $b = 7$ cm

3. $x = 10$ cm, $y = 8$ cm

4.   **1** 5 cm   **2** 16 cm   **3** 21 cm

5.   **1** 11.0 cm   **2** 4.0 cm   **3** 5.0 cm

6.   50 cm

7.   **1** 20 cm   **2** 25 cm

Page 141   Exercise 6.2

1.   **1** 48 cm²   **2** 34 cm²

2.   **1** circumference 88.0 cm, area 616 cm²
   2 37.7 cm, 113 cm²
   3 6.28 cm, 3.14 cm²
   4 28.3 cm, 63.6 cm²

3.   **1** 4.40 cm   **4** 45.2 cm²
   2 9.22 cm   **5** 2.23 cm
   3 6.26 cm²

4. **1** 120 cm^2 **2** 15

5. **1** 11.0 cm   **4** 24.5 cm^2
    2 25.0 cm   **5** 14.0 cm^2
    3 38.5 cm^2

6. **1** 30 cm^2 **3** 36 cm^2
    2 21 cm^2 **4** 57 cm^2

Page 145   Exercise 6.3

1. 180 cm^3

2. **1** 7.5 m^2 **2** 30 m^3

3. **1** 198 cm^3 **4** 3140 cm^2
    2 3770 cm^2 **5** 181 cm^2
    3 246 cm^3

4. **1** 201 cm^3 **4** 6210 cm^3
    2 63.4 cm^3 **5** 9 cm
    3 4190 cm^3

5. 35 m^2

6. **1** 5 m   **4** 15 (m^3)
    2 54 cm^2 **5** 3 (m^3)
    3 (1) 240 cm^3
        (2) 30

7. **1** 7 cm   **2** 1230 cm^3

Page 148   Exercise 6.4

1. **1** volume   **9** length
    2 length   **10** length
    3 area   **11** length
    4 length   **12** length
    5 area   **13** area
    6 volume   **14** length
    7 volume   **15** length
    8 area

2. **1** $b + 2\pi r$ **2** $b^2 + \pi rh$ **3** $\frac{1}{3}b^3 + \pi r^2 h$

3. **1** Dimension 4, should be 3; $V = \pi r^2 h$

    2 Dimension 3, should be 1; $h = \dfrac{2A}{b}$

    3 Dimension 2, should be 1; $r = \sqrt{\dfrac{A}{\pi}}$

    4 Dimension 4, should be 3; $V = Ah$

    5 Dimension 1, should be 2; $S = 2\pi r(h + r)$

Page 148   Exercise 6.5

1. 39 m

2. 17 km

3. 25 feet

4. **1** 150 cm^2 **2** 25 cm   **3** 12 cm

5. **1** 13 cm   **2** 20 cm   **3** 20.6 cm

6. **1** and **3**
    (**5** has an angle which is nearly a right-angle.)

7. $\triangle APS$, 3 cm^2; $\triangle BPQ$, 12 cm^2; $\triangle CQR$, 8 cm^2;
    $\triangle DRS$, 10 cm^2; $PQRS$, 31 cm^2

8. **1** 6π cm   **4** 3 cm
    2 24π cm^2 **5** 24π cm^2, yes
    3 6π cm

9. **1** $\triangle DBC$ **3** 60 cm^2
    2 15 cm   **4** 60 cm^2

10. 239 m^2

11. **1** 15.9 m   **2** 5.64 m

12. $\frac{1}{5}$; **1** 12.6 cm   **2** 62.8 cm^2

13. **1** 45°   **2** 40°

14. 27.6 tonnes

15. 58.3 m^2

16. **1** 50 m^2 **2** 500 m^3

17. vol = 385 cm^3; 12 tins

18. 11.9 cm

19. 2860 cm^3

20. **1** length   **5** length   **8** none
     2 area   **6** area   **9** length
     3 none   **7** length   **10** length
     4 volume

Page 151   Practice test 6

1. **1** 25 cm   **3** 66 cm
    2 15 cm   **4** 234 cm^2

2. 59 cm^2

3. 7.73 cm^2

4. **1** 3.14 cm   **2** 11.8 cm^2

5. radius 3.6 cm, area 40.7 cm^2

6. **1** 21 cm^2 **2** 189 cm^3

7. **1** $\dfrac{pq}{r} + \sqrt{\pi r^2}$

   2 $\dfrac{3pqr}{\sqrt{p^2 + q^2}}$

   3 $\pi p^3 + 2q^2 r$

8. $35\,200\,\mathrm{cm}^3$

Page 156   Exercise 7.1

9. yellow 2, red 1, blue 3

Page 161   Exercise 7.2

1. **1** $\frac{1}{6}$ **2** $\frac{1}{3}$

2. **1** $\frac{3}{10}$ **2** $\frac{1}{5}$ **3** $\frac{1}{10}$

3. **1** $\frac{1}{2}$ **2** $\frac{1}{6}$

4. $\frac{1}{8}$

5. **1** $\frac{1}{13}$ **2** $\frac{1}{4}$ **3** $\frac{5}{26}$

6. **1** $\frac{2}{11}$ **2** $\frac{4}{11}$ **3** $\frac{3}{11}$

7. **1** $\frac{6}{25}$ **2** $\frac{1}{25}$ **3** 0

8. **1** $\frac{4}{9}$ **2** $\frac{2}{9}$

9. **1** $\frac{1}{12}$ **2** $\frac{1}{6}$ **3** $\frac{1}{6}$ **4** $\frac{1}{9}$

10. **1** $\frac{1}{15}$ **2** $\frac{1}{5}$ **3** $\frac{1}{5}$

11. **1** $\frac{1}{25}$ **2** $\frac{2}{25}$ **3** $\frac{1}{20}$, $\frac{1}{10}$

Page 164   Exercise 7.3

1. **1** $\frac{9}{20}$ **2** $\frac{5}{8}$

2. **1** $\frac{3}{10}$ **2** $\frac{1}{2}$ **3** $\frac{7}{20}$

3. $\frac{3}{40}$

4. **1** $\frac{5}{12}$ **2** 49

5. **1** $\frac{3}{8}$ **2** $\frac{1}{4}$

6. **1** 0.35   **2** 0.45   **3** 0.05

7. **1** $\frac{11}{32}$ **2** $\frac{21}{32}$ **3** $\frac{63}{64}$

Page 165   Exercise 7.4

4. $\dfrac{7}{100}$

5. $\dfrac{x}{12}$, 2 red

7. **1** $\frac{11}{100}$ **4** $\frac{3}{100}$
    2 $\frac{1}{10}$ **5** $\frac{41}{50}$
    3 $\frac{9}{50}$

8. **1** $\frac{19}{36}$ **2** $\frac{1}{36}$ **3** $\frac{5}{36}$ **4** $\frac{3}{8}$

9. **1** $\frac{1}{4}$ **2** $\frac{4}{17}$

10. **1** $\frac{1}{16}$ **2** $\frac{5}{16}$ **3** $\frac{3}{8}$

11. **1** $\frac{1}{8}$ **2** $\frac{29}{200}$ **3** $\frac{7}{50}$

12. **1** $\frac{4}{15}$ **2** $\frac{2}{15}$ **3** $\frac{1}{15}$

13. **1** $\frac{1}{3}$ **2** $\frac{1}{6}$ **3** $\frac{5}{36}$ **4** $\frac{2}{9}$

14. $\frac{4}{15}$

15. **1** 0.06   **2** 0.4   **3** 0.7

16. **1** 0.18   **2** 0.02   **3** 0.2

Page 168   Practice test 7

1. **1** $\frac{6}{25}$ **2** $\frac{121}{400}$ **3** $\frac{29}{50}$

2. **1** $\frac{11}{25}$ **2** $\frac{3}{5}$ **3** $\frac{6}{25}$ **4** $\frac{3}{7}$

3. **1** $\frac{1}{16}$ **2** $\frac{3}{16}$ **3** $\frac{3}{16}$

4. **1** 0.2   **2** 0.3

5. **1** 0.01   **2** 0.998   **3** 0.83

Page 172   Exercise 8.1

2. **1** $-2, -1, 0, 1, 2, 3, 4$
    2 $-4, -3, -2$
    3 $0, 1, 2, 3, 4$
    4 $-4, -3, -2, -1, 0, 1, 2, 3$
    5 no values
    6 $-3, -2, -1, 0, 1, 2, 3, 4$
    7 $-4, 3, 4$
    8 $-4, -3, -2, -1, 0, 1, 2, 3, 4$

3. **1** $x < 8$ **4** $x \leqslant -4$ **7** $x \geqslant -1$
    2 $x < -6$ **5** $x \leqslant \frac{3}{4}$ **8** $x \geqslant 12$
    3 $x \geqslant \frac{1}{2}$ **6** $x > 11\frac{1}{2}$

4. 1 $x < -6$ or $x > 6$
    2 $x < -1.5$ or $x > 1.5$
    3 $-10 \leqslant x \leqslant 10$
    4 $-1 < x < 1$
    5 $x \leqslant -\frac{1}{4}$ or $x \geqslant \frac{1}{4}$

5. 1 $-7 \leqslant x \leqslant 7$
    2 $x \leqslant -9$ or $x \geqslant 9$
    3 $-12 < x < 12$

6. 1 7, 8, 9, 10   3 9, 10
    2 1, 2, 3   4 6, 7, 8

7. 1 $9\frac{1}{4}$ 2 $7\frac{1}{3}$ 3 8, 9

8. $x \geqslant 2$, $y \geqslant 3$, $x + y \leqslant 9$, $20x + 24y \leqslant 200$;
    5 lemons

Page 175   Exercise 8.2

1. 1 $x = 6$ 4 $x = 3$ or $x = 5$
    2 $x = 3$ 5 $x = 4$
    3 $x = 1$ or $x = 6$

2. 1 $x = 5$ 4 $x = 5$
    2 $x = 3$ 5 $x = 4$
    3 $x = 2$

3. 1 $x = 5.4$ 5 $x = 3.8$ 8 $x = 6.8$
    2 $x = 1.4$ 6 $x = 1.5$ 9 $x = 2.4$
    3 $x = 4.6$ 7 $x = 4.8$ 10 $x = 9.1$
    4 $x = 4.2$

4. Ann 16, Bobby 12 years old

5. 1.3 s

Page 178   Exercise 8.3

1. $x = 7$, $y = 2$ 8. $x = -\frac{1}{2}$, $y = 0$
2. $x = -1$, $y = -2$ 9. $x = -2$, $y = 3$
3. $x = -2$, $y = 4$ 10. $x = 4$, $y = -3$
4. $x = -3$, $y = 2$ 11. $x = 0$, $y = -\frac{1}{2}$
5. $x = 1$, $y = \frac{1}{2}$ 12. $x = 4$, $y = 1$
6. $x = 5$, $y = 3$ 13. $x = -1$, $y = \frac{1}{2}$
7. $x = 2\frac{1}{2}$, $y = -5$ 14. $x = 8$, $y = -3$

15. tea 25p, coffee 35p

16. $x = 4$, $y = -3$; $AB = CD = 11$ cm,
     $AD = BC = 15$ cm

Page 178   Exercise 8.4

1. 1 $x \leqslant -5$ 2 $1 < x < 10$

2. 7

3. (1, 1), (1, 2), (1, 3), (1, 4), (2, 1), (2, 2), (3, 1)

4. $0 \leqslant x \leqslant 5$, $0 \leqslant y \leqslant 7$, $x + y \leqslant 10$,
    $50x + 20y \geqslant 300$; 5 coaches, 3 minibuses

5. 13 sides

6. $(110 - x)$ m, 70 m

7. 8

8. 2.4

9. adult £1.60, child £1

10. $x = 40$, $y = 25$; $\angle ABD = \angle ACE = 70°$,
     $\angle CBD = 110°$

11. $x = 4$, $y = 3$; perimeter 39 cm

12. $a = 0.05$, $c = 5$

13. 6

14. 28 m at £20, 40 m at £16

15. $a = 3$, $b = -4$

16. 1 8   2 -1; $x = 3\frac{1}{2}$, $y = 4\frac{1}{2}$

17. $a = 3$, $b = -2$; $c = \frac{1}{3}$, $d = -\frac{1}{2}$

Page 181   Practice test 8

1. 1 $x \leqslant -1\frac{1}{2}$ 3 $-7 \leqslant x \leqslant 7$
    2 $x < 5\frac{1}{2}$

2. 1 $x = 10$ 2 $x = 2.2$

3. 1 $x = 3$, $y = -1$
    2 $x = \frac{1}{2}$, $y = -3$

4. rose 25p, carnation 20p

Page 185   Exercise 9.1

1. 1 mean = 9, median = 8, range = 13
    2 mean = 44, median = 39, range = 73
    3 mean = 8, median = 7, range = 12
    4 mean = 40.7, median = 35, range = 76
    5 mean = 1.9, median = 1.95, range = 0.7

2. 1 median = 9, mode = 12, range = 9
    2 median = 28, mode = 27, range = 8
    3 median = $4\frac{1}{2}$, mode = 5, range = 8

3. 1 64.4   4 $2\frac{13}{36}$
    2 £917.40   5 2.9 kg
    3 2 h 1 min

4. 1 mean = 57 kg, median = 55 kg
    2 12 y 2 m
    3 164 g

5. 2.81; more in North-west

6. 32

Page 188   Exercise 9.2

1. **2**   mean = 2.7, median = 2, mode = 2

2. **2**   mean = 1.6, median = 1, mode = 1

3. **2**   mean = 3.8, median = 4, mode = 4

4. **2**   mean = 30.7, median = 30, mode = 30

5. **2**   mean = 5.3, median = 5.5, mode = 7

6. £8.25

7. 8 y 7 m

8. frequencies in order: 2, 4, 7, 10, 14, 15, 8;
    mean = 6.8, median = 7, mode = 8

Page 193   Exercise 9.3

1. **1**   12–14 marks   **3**   11.1 marks

2. **2**   5.6 cm

3. **1**   75–80 kg   **2** 77.5 kg   **4**   74.6 kg

4. **1**   4–6 years   **3**   5.2 years

5. **1**   6.5 cm, 9.5 cm; 8 cm   **2**   13.8 cm

6. **1**   40   **4**   8.5 min
    2   30%   **5**   7.7 min
    3   8–9 min

Page 196   Exercise 9.5

1. 23

2. 10 min 25 s

3. 4.6 kg

4. 14.7, 4

5. 1.5

6. mean = 3.9, median = 4, mode = 3,
    probability = 0.6

7. 62

8. frequencies: 3, 5, 4, 5, 5, 2, 1; 74.8

9. mean £95, modal class £90–£110

10. mean 180.2 cm, modal class 179.5–182.5 cm

11. mean 12.9 years, modal class 12–13 years

12. mean 7.3 cm, modal class 7.25–7.75 cm

13. mean 15.4 min, modal class 15–20 min

14. **1**   75
    2   10.5–11.5 kg
    3   10.9 kg
    4   16%

15. frequencies 4, 8, 8, 6, 3, 1; mean 12.8 hours

22. means (1) 36.3, (2) 13.7

Page 200   Practice test 9

1. 22°C

2. 4 hours

3. frequencies in order: 21, 26, 25, 7, 3, 2;
    mean 1.4, median 1, mode 1, range 5

4. 17.6p

5. **1**   170–174 cm
    2   169.5–174.5 cm
    3   172 cm
    6   171.4 cm

Page 206   Exercise 10.1

1. **1** $y = \frac{1}{2}x$ **2** D (5, 5)   **3** $y = 5$

2. (1) 0.4   (4) −1.2
    (2) 1.1   (5) 0.7
    (3) −0.2

3. −8, −2, 13; gradient 3; (0, −2)

4. $AB : -1$; $CD : 3$

5. **1**   4, (0, −1)   **4**   −5, (0, 2)
    2   −1, (0, 3)   **5** $\frac{1}{3}$, (0, 1)
    3 $\frac{1}{2}$, (0, 7)

6. **1**   25   **2**   13   **3**   15

8. 3.1, $c = 3.1d$ ($c = \pi d$)

9. 4, $-\frac{1}{4}$; −3, $\frac{1}{3}$; $1\frac{1}{2}$, $-\frac{2}{3}$; lines are perpendicular
    to each other; product = −1

Page 210   Exercise 10.2

1. $x = 8$, $y = 2$

2. $x = 8$, $y = 6$

3. $x = -2$, $y = 5$

4. $x = 1.6$, $y = 3.7$

5. $x = 2$, $y = 0.5$

6. **1** $y = 2$, $x = 3$; $x = 2.7$, $y = 3.7$

7. $2x + y = 56$, $x + 2y = 64$; $x = 16$, $y = 24$;
    16 of 10p, 24 of 5p

Page 212   Exercise 10.3

5.   12 points

6. $-2 \leqslant y \leqslant 0,\ y \leqslant 3x + 4,\ x \leqslant 0$

7. $1 \leqslant x \leqslant 5,\ 2 \leqslant y \leqslant 7, x + y \leqslant 9$

Page 214   Exercise 10.4

1. C (8, 4, 0)   2. B (12, 4, 5)
     F (8, 1, 6) C (12, 7, 5)
     G (8, 4, 6) D (1, 7, 5)
     H (2, 4, 6) E (1, 4, 9)
                                    F (12, 4, 9)
                                    H (1, 7, 9)

3. B (9, 3, 4)   4. A $(-8, -4, -3)$
     C (9, 4, 4) B $(7, -4, -3)$
     D (2, 4, 4) C $(7, 9, -3)$
     E (2, 3, 7) D $(-8, 9, -3)$
     F (9, 3, 7) E $(-8, -4, 4)$
     G (9, 4, 7) F $(7, -4, 4)$
     H (2, 4, 7) H $(-8, 9, 4)$

Page 215   Exercise 10.5

1. AB, DC gradient 1; BC, AD gradient $-\frac{2}{3}$

2. $AB = \sqrt{50}$, $AC = \sqrt{160}$, $BC = \sqrt{50}$;
     isosceles (obtuse-angled)

3.   **1** $y = 8 - x$ **3** $3y = x + 1$
     2 $y = 2x - 9$

4. A (2, 0), $y = 4x - 8$

5.   14

6. $y = 2.15\ x + 32$, 161 (approx.)

7. $a = 3.3$

8.   **1** P $(0, -3)$, R $(0, 3\frac{1}{2})$

     2 $5\frac{1}{2}$ units

     3 $y = 2x - 3$, $x + 2y = 7$
     4 T (2.6, 2.2)

9. $x = 2.8$, $y = 10.4$

10. cost $(16x + 32y)$ pence; $x + y = 25$,
     $x + 2y = 40$, 10 packets of sweets, 15 bars of
     chocolate

11. $x > 3$, $y > 2$, $x + 2y < 11$

12. $y \geqslant 2x$, $x \geqslant 2$, $x + y \leqslant 10$;
     (dogs, elephants) $\rightarrow$ (2, 4), (2, 5), (2, 6), (2, 7),
     (2, 8), (3, 6), (3, 7); 3 dogs and 7 elephants
     for most profit, £46

13. C (6, 6, 5),
     F (6, 3, 17),
     G (6, 6, 17),
     H (2, 6, 17),
     AB 4 units,
     BC 3 units,
     AC 5 units,
     CG 12 units,
     $\angle ACG = 90°$,
     $AG = 13$ units

Page 218   Practice test 10

1.   **1** $\frac{1}{4}$ **2** $\sqrt{68}$ $(= 8.2)$ **3** (1, 2)

2. $-\frac{4}{3}$, $3y = 12 - 4x$

3. $y = 1.6x + 4$, $y = 32$ (approx.)

4. $x = 3.5$, $y = -1$

5. B $(9, -4, -2)$ F $(9, -4, 4)$
     C $(9, 5, -2)$ G (9, 5, 4)
     D $(-1, 5, 2)$ H $(-1, 5, 4)$
     E $(-1, -4, 4)$

6. $(-1, 3.5)$, (4, 1);
     isosceles (obtuse-angled) triangle

Page 220   Exercise B1

1.   **1** 47   **4** 34, 51
     2 15, 51   **5** 27, 15
     3 47, 57

3.   11

4.   5 red, 3 yellow, 2 green

5.   **1** 6   **2** 7.5   **3** 8.5   **4** 12

6.   **1** $n = 8$ **2** 1, 2, 3, 4, 5

7. $\overrightarrow{OD} = \begin{pmatrix} 7 \\ 11 \end{pmatrix}$, $\overrightarrow{AD} = \begin{pmatrix} 6 \\ 8 \end{pmatrix}$, length 10 units

8.   **1** 0.12   **2** 0.0035   **3** 1.4

9.   7

10. 7, 1, 4, $\frac{1}{25}$, 27, $\frac{1}{2}$

11. **1** 0.8   **2** 0.2

12. 1.33 m

13. **1** 5 units   **2** $-\frac{4}{3}$

14. 66p

15. **1** $x = 7$ **2** $x = 12$ **3** $x = 10$

Page 222   **Exercise B2**

1. **1** D **2** A

2. 3.5 m

3. 110 ml at 92p

4. 12

5. mean 2.06, median 2, mode 2

6. 6, 5.97

7. 2

8. **1** $y = -x$ **4** $y = 3 - x$
   2 $y = \frac{1}{2}x$ **5** $y = 2x + 1$
   3 $y = x - 1$

9. **1** Pythagoras
   2 11 in (5, 11, 13), correct number 12
   3 (13, 84, 85)

10. $x = 12$, $y = 15$

12. **1** $2\frac{2}{3}$ **2** 4   **3** $2\frac{3}{4}$

13. $W = 62\frac{1}{2}$, $a = 6$

14. **1** $-\frac{2}{3}$ **2** 23   **3** 4

15. **1** 0.16   **3** 0.606 (0.61)
    2 0.498 (0.50)

Page 232   **Exercise 11.1**

1. 16 cm by 12 cm

2. **1** 4.5   **2** 13.5 cm   **3** 2 cm

4. **1** $\frac{2}{3}$ **2** 48 cm

Page 235   **Exercise 11.2**

1. **1** $9 : 5$; $x = 14.4$ cm, $y = 12.5$ cm
   2 $3 : 5$; $x = 44$ cm, $y = 10$ cm
   3 $7 : 3$; $x = 0.9$ cm, $y = 4.2$ cm
   4 $4 : 5$; $x = 20$ cm
   5 $5 : 8$; $x = 5.6$ cm

2. **1** $81 : 25$ **4** $16 : 25$
   2 $9 : 25$ **5** $25 : 64$
   3 $49 : 9$

3. **1** $3 : 5$; $d = 10.5$ cm
   2 $5 : 7$; $y = 21$ cm
   3 $7 : 5$; $x = 6$ cm, $y = 4.9$ cm
   4 $4 : 7$; $x = 2$ cm
   5 $5 : 2$; $x = 35$ cm, $y = 28$ cm

4. **1** surface areas, $9 : 25$; volumes, $27 : 125$
   2 $25 : 49$; $125 : 343$
   3 $49 : 25$; $343 : 125$
   4 $16 : 49$; $64 : 343$
   5 $25 : 4$; $125 : 8$

5. $1 : 50\ 000$, 4.2 km

6. 8 cm by 5.4 cm

7. **1** $3 : 4$ **2** $9 : 16$ **3** $\frac{7}{16}$

8. $3.2\ \ell$

Page 240   **Exercise 11.3**

1. **1** equiangular; $\dfrac{AB}{FD} = \dfrac{BC}{DE} = \dfrac{AC}{FE}$, $\angle A = \angle F$

   2 3 sides in proportion; $\dfrac{AB}{LK} = \dfrac{BC}{KM} = \dfrac{AC}{LM}$,
   $\angle A = \angle L$, $\angle B = \angle K$, $\angle C = \angle M$

   3 equiangular; $\dfrac{AB}{PQ} = \dfrac{BC}{QR} = \dfrac{AC}{PR}$, $\angle C = \angle R$

   4 2 sides in proportion and included angles equal;
   $\dfrac{AB}{TS} = \dfrac{BC}{SU} = \dfrac{AC}{TU}$, $\angle B = \angle S$, $\angle C = \angle U$

2. **1** 2 sides in proportion and included angles equal
   2 $2 : 5$
   3 $4 : 25$
   4 $\angle F$

3. **1** 3 sides in proportion
   2 $\angle E$
   3 $9 : 4$

4. **1** $\frac{2}{3}$ **5** $4 : 9$
   2 yes   **6** 13.5 cm^2
   3 $\angle C$ **7** 7.5 cm^2
   4 $2 : 3$

5. **1** yes   **2** 4.5 cm   **3** $9 : 4$

6. 80 m

7. 3, 1.5 cm, 66°

Page 242   **Exercise 11.4**

2. $6 : 7$; 11.9 cm; $36 : 49$; $216 : 343$

3. 8 m, 200 m^2, 1600 m^3

4. 15 cm

5.   3.5 km, 0.2 km^2

6. $\frac{1}{4}$

7.   **1**   3 : 5   **2**   9 : 25

8.   12.8 m

9.   **1**   20 cm   **3**   7.5 cm

10. **1** $\frac{9}{25}$ **2** $\frac{4}{25}$ **3** $\frac{12}{25}$

11. **1** $\triangle ADX$, $\triangle CBX$
     2   3 : 4
     3   3 : 4
     4   9 : 16

Page 244   Practice test 11

1.   **1** $1\frac{2}{3}$ **2**   3 cm

2.   **1**   yes   **2**   2 : 5

3.   2 km

4.   **1**   3 : 4   **2**   9 : 16   **3**   27 : 64

5.   **1**   equiangular
     2   3 : 4
     3   3 : 4
     4   9 : 16
     5   6 cm
     6   areas 6.75 cm^2, 12 cm^2

6.   2 sides in proportion and included angles
     equal; $\angle A = \angle D$, $\angle B = \angle E$, $\angle ACB = \angle DCE$;
     AB and ED are parallel

Page 246   Example

     walks: 6 km/h,
     cycles: $1\frac{1}{4}$ hours, 27 km, 21.6 km/h,
     rest: 30 km from P
     bus: 2.15 pm, $\frac{1}{2}$ hour, 60 km/h

Page 247   Exercise 12.1

1.   30 km/h

2.   **1**   (1) and (4), 67 km/h
     2   (2) 33 km/h
     3   30 min

3.   **1** $\frac{1}{2}$ hour   **4**   16 km/h
     2   15 km/h   **5**   10 km
     3   1.40 pm, 9 km

5.   9.51 am, 26 miles

6.   **1**   20 min   **4**   10 min
     2   1 h 4 min   **5**   20 km/h
     3   2 km

7.   **1**   1200 km   **3**   5 h 13 min
     2 $\frac{1}{2}$ hour   **4**   900 km/h

8.   **1**   7.5 m   **2**   5.8 s

Page 251   Exercise 12.2

1.   **1**   £108   **2** $4\frac{1}{2}$ hours

2.   **1**   48 g   **2**   48°C

3.   70°F = 21°C, 80°C = 176°F, 98.4°F = 37°C

Page 255   Exercise 12.3

1.   **1 D**   **2 A**   **3 B**   **4 C**

Page 257   Exercise 12.4

1.   **1**   15 min   **2**   28 km/h   **3**   2 km

2.   **1**   33 km   **2**   12 km, 2.01 pm

3.   2.55 pm, 115 km

4.   **1**   27 km   **2**   17 min

5.   length 90 miles
     1   5 min   **2**   7 miles   **3**   78 mph

6.   12.39 pm, 13 km

7.   **1**   20 cm   **2**   20 s

8.   **1**   0.16 kg   **2**   22.7 cm   **3**   20.3 cm

10. **1**   6 am, 6 pm
     2   12 am, 12 noon, 12 am
     3   6 am

12. **1 C**   **2 A**   **3 B**   **4 D**

Page 261   Practice test 12

1.   **1**   2.45 pm
     2   30 mph
     3   2.05 pm, 28 miles from A
     4   6 miles
     5   34 mph

2.   9.36 am, 48 miles

3.   **1**   1125 m
     2   4.5 s and 25.5 s
     3   13 s

4.   17 articles

5. **1** 47 km/h **2** 28 m/s
6. **1** 18°C, 4 am **2** 4 pm, 37°C
7. **1 B** **2 A** **3 D** **4 C**

Page 267 Exercise 13.1

1. 27
2. 21
3. 31
4. 17
5. 33
7. 57
8. 1.67 m

Page 273 Exercise 13.2

1. cum. freq: 0, 2, 6, 14, 27, 41, 50, 57, 60
    median 180.1 cm
    quartiles 183.8 cm, 176.7 cm
    interquartile range 7.1 cm
    taller than 1.8 m, 31

2. cum. freq: 0, 8, 18, 24, 28, 30
    median 12.7 years
    quartiles 13.8 y, 11.9 y
    interquartile range 1.9 y

3. cum. freq: 0, 1, 6, 13, 24, 28, 30
    median 7.3 cm
    quartiles 7.7 cm, 6.8 cm
    interquartile range 0.9 cm

4. cum. freq: 0, 3, 18, 45, 79, 98, 100
    median 15.7 min
    quartiles 19.4 min, 11.3 min
    interquartile range 8.1 min

5. cum. freq: 0, 2, 12, 30, 50, 66, 75
    median 10.9 kg
    quartiles 11.9 kg, 9.9 kg
    interquartile range 2.0 kg
    less than 10 kg, 21

Page 274 Exercise 13.3

1. £64 000
2. 72 kg
3. 66
5. 60

6. cum. freq. in order: 0, 1, 8, 18, 30, 38, 40
    median 5.7 cm
    quartiles 6.5 cm, 4.7 cm
    interquartile range 1.8 cm

7. cum. freq: 0, 4, 22, 58, 108, 118, 120
    median 75.2 kg
    quartiles 78.2 kg, 71.1 kg
    interquartile range 7.1 kg

8. cum. freq: 0, 16, 39, 63, 80, 92, 99, 100
    median 4.9 years
    quartiles 7.4 y, 2.8 y
    interquartile range 4.6 y

9. cum. freq: 0, 4, 20, 44, 57, 60
    median 13.8 cm
    quartiles 15.7 cm, 11.6 cm
    interquartile range 4.1 cm

10. cum. freq: 0, 3, 12, 22, 35, 40
    median 7.8 min
    quartiles 8.6 min, 6.8 min
    interquartile range 1.8 min

11. median 6.9 min
    quartiles 12.9 min, 2.8 min
    interquartile range 10.1 min

12. cum. freq: 0, 10, 22, 49, 86, 108, 120
    median £26
    quartiles £44, £13
    interquartile range £31

Page 276 Practice test 13

1. 41

2. cum. freq: 0, 6, 16, 33, 57, 72, 77, 80
    median 5.6 min,
    upper quartile 6.1 min, lower quartile 5.1 min,
    interquartile range 1.0 min,
    17.5% of the workers

Page 281 Exercise 14.1

1. **1** 2.55 cm **6** 8.67 cm
    2 8.39 cm **7** 14.6 cm
    3 2.24 cm **8** 5.23 cm
    4 5.07 cm **9** 15.6 cm
    5 7.47 cm

2. 7.73 cm

3. **1** 37.9° **4** 40.5°
    2 53.1° **5** 33.6°
    3 58.0°

4. $\frac{12}{13}, \frac{5}{13}, \frac{12}{5}, \frac{5}{13}, \frac{12}{13}, \frac{5}{12}$

5. 74.9 m

6. 201°

7. $BD = 108$ m, $CD = 78$ m, distance 30 m

8. $AC = 6$ km, angle 7.1°

Page 287   Exercise 14.2

1. **1** $AC = 58.3$ cm, $AG = 61.6$ cm
    2 21.8°
    3 18.9°

2. **1** 9.4 cm   **3** 10.7 cm
    2 58.0°   **4** 48.5°

3. **1** 2 cm   **3** 2.8 cm
    2 2.4 cm   **4** 40.1°

4. **1** 12.1 cm   **2** 24.4 cm   **3** 29.8°

5. **1** 60 m   **2** 12.8 m   **3** 14.9°

6. $DB = 246$ m, $DC = 143$ m, distance $= 285$ m

Page 289   Exercise 14.3

1. 246 m

2. 12.2 km, 260°

3. 11.8 cm, 58.9 cm^2

4. **1** 21.3 m   **2** 44.5 m   **3** 6.6°

5. **1** 63.0 km   **2** 70.1 km

6. **1** $h = 9.5$ cm, area $= 47.6$ cm^2
    2 area of sector $= 62.8$ cm^2,
        shaded area $= 15.3$ cm^2

7. **1** 4.2 cm   **2** 55.5 cm^2

8. **1** 60 m   **3** 104.6 m
    2 85.7 m   **4** 29.8°

9. height $= 156$ m, 250 m, 32.0°

Page 291   Practice test 14

1. 65.4°

2. 75.0 m

3. 16.7°

4. **1** 90°   **3** 851 m
    2 293 m   **4** 277 m

5. **1** 20 cm   **4** 53.1°
    2 17.0 cm   **5** 62.1°
    3 18.1 cm

Page 296   Example 2

axis of symmetry, $x = \frac{1}{2}$; maximum point $(\frac{1}{2}, 6\frac{1}{4})$

Page 298   Exercise 15.1

1. $x = 1\frac{1}{2}$; $x = -1.4$ or 4.4

2. 12; 3.5

3. (1, 9); $x = -1.45$ or 3.45

4. $x = 0.7$, $x = 4.3$

5. $x = -2.45$ or 2.45; $x^2 = 6$

7. $x = 0.3$, 1.5 or 4.2

8. $x = 3.3$

10. $x^2 + 12x - 80 = 0$; 4.8 cm

Page 305   Exercise 15.2

1. $f(0) = 1$, $f(45) = 3$, $f(135) = -1$, $f(180) = 1$

3. **2** -2.82
    3 62.2 or 297.8

4. $A(0, 1)$, $B(90, 0)$, $C(180, 1)$, $D(270, 2)$

5. 1, 0.5, 0, -1, 0, 0.5, 1

6. **1** $x = 24$ or 156
    2 $x = 124$

7. 10 m, 2 hours

Page 306   Exercise 15.3

1. $x = 0.3$ or 6.7; $x = 1.55$ or 6.45

2. $x = -1$, 0.6 or 3.4

3. $x = 2.1$

4. $x = 1.7$

5. $x = 1.3$

6. $x = -0.7$ or 2.7; $x = -3.7$ or 2.7

7. $x = 2.4$ or 4.1

8. $x = 30$

9. **1** $x = 45$ **2** $y = 1.41$

10. values: 1, 0.93, 0.75, 0.5, 0.25, 0.07, 0

11. h: 0, 0.5, 0.87, 1, 0.87, 0.5, 0, -0.5, -0.87, -1, -0.87, -0.5, 0; $h = \sin t°$; $k = \cos t°$, $90 < t < 270$

Page 309   Practice test 15

1. $x = \frac{1}{2}$; $x = -1.8$ or 2.8

3. **2** 1, -1
   3 $y = 0.985$
   4 $x = 30, 150$
   5 $x = 210, 330$

4. 2 m, 30 s

Page 310   Exercise C1

1. **1** 14   **2** 0.88

2. **1** 24 cm   **2** 1230 cm^3

3. **1** $-6 \leqslant x \leqslant 6$ **2** $x \leqslant -5$ or $x \geqslant 5$

4. **1** 5.4 cm   **2** 8.4 cm   **3** 45.7 cm^2

5. **1** 41   **2** 66   **3** 45

6. **1** $x = 5, y = 3$ **2** $x = 3, y = -2$

8. 3 : 4

9. £3.60

10. **B**

11. **1** 0.1   **2** 0.4

12. $m = -2, c = 4$

13. B (3, 1), C (5, 6); E is the mid-point of BF

14. **1** $6x^5 + 2x^3$
    2 $x^2 - 8x + 7$
    3 $2x^2 + 11x + 15$
    4 $6x^2 - 13xy - 5y^2$
    5 $4x^2 + 4xy + y^2$

15. $x = 2.45$

Page 312   Exercise C2

1. $AB = 12$ cm; $\sin A = \frac{5}{13}$, $\cos A = \frac{12}{13}$, $\tan A = \frac{5}{12}$

2. $1\frac{1}{2}$ sq. miles

3. **1** 5 cm   **2** 5.2 cm   **3** 13.1 cm^2

4. 3rd month

5. $x = 4.4$

6. 270 m

7. **1** 81, 121, $(2n - 1)^2$
   2 21, 28, $\frac{1}{2}n(n + 1)$
   3 32, 64, 2^n
   4 65, 58, $107 - 7n$
   5 $\frac{1}{6}, \frac{1}{7}, \frac{1}{n}$

8. **1** 72 cm^2 **2** 10 cm   **3** 53.1°   **4** 50.0°

9. **1** 1.9×10^3 **2** 7.6×10^5

10. $\frac{25}{37}$ (0.68)

11. $x = 7$, $y = 3$; $PQ = 21$ cm, $QR = 26$ cm, $PR = 13$ cm

12. **1** £60   **2** 3

13. **1** $x = 1$
    2 $x = -0.7$ or 2.7
    3 $x = -1.6$ or 3.6

14. $2x^2$ cm^2; $x = 3$; 41.0 cm

15. cum. freq: 0, 13.7, 27.4, 44.3, 58.3, 71.5, 82.2, 92.1, 97.8, 100;
    median 34 years
    interquartile range 36 years
    over 65, 13%

Page 315   Exercise C3

1. **1** 4, $\sqrt{25}$
   2 4, $\sqrt{25}, -5$
   3 $0.\dot{3}, \frac{3}{4}, 3\frac{1}{7}$, 3.142
   4 $\sqrt[3]{6}, \pi$

4. $\frac{1}{4}, \frac{1}{2}, 1, 2, 8$

5. 6.75 ℓ

6. **1** 48 min   **2** 12 km/h   **3** 15 km/h

7. **1** $\frac{4}{7}$ **2** $\frac{2}{7}$

8. **1** $\dfrac{x - 7}{6}$ **2** $x = -15$

10. A and E, B and F, C and D

11. $y = \dfrac{600}{x}$; 47 m by 13 m

12. 122°

13. area 616 cm^2, height 16.2 cm, total surface area 2660 cm^2

14. 6 m

15. frequencies in order: 6, 6, 7, 8, 3
    modal class 16–20 hours (15.5–20.5 hours)
    mean 12.3 hours

Page 326   Exercise 16.1

1. $\frac{9}{64}$

2. **1** $\frac{8}{75}$ **2** $\frac{11}{25}$

3. **1** $\frac{1}{216}$ **2** $\frac{1}{36}$

4. **1** $\frac{1}{7}$ **2** $\frac{1}{42}$

5. $\frac{37}{40}$

6. 68%

7. **1** $\frac{1}{16}$ **2** $\frac{9}{16}$ **3** $\frac{3}{8}$

8. **1** 0.3   **2** 0.343   **3** 0.441   **4** 0.784

9. **1** $\frac{1}{4}$ **2** $\frac{7}{24}$

Page 330   Exercise 16.2

1. $\frac{3}{11}$

2. **1** $\frac{1}{17}$ **2** $\frac{19}{34}$ **3** $\frac{15}{34}$

3. $\frac{5}{63}$

4. **1** $\frac{5}{42}$ **2** $\frac{1}{21}$ **3** $\frac{1}{84}$

5. $\frac{2}{63}$

6. **1** $\frac{1}{45}$ **2** $\frac{16}{45}$ **3** $\frac{28}{45}$

7. **1** $\frac{1}{3}$ **2** $\frac{2}{3}$

8. $\frac{19}{66}$

9. **1** $\frac{1}{35}$ **2** $\frac{12}{35}$ **3** $\frac{18}{35}$ **4** $\frac{4}{35}$

10. **1** $\frac{1}{22}$ **2** $\frac{7}{22}$ **3** $\frac{21}{44}$ **4** $\frac{7}{44}$

Page 331   Exercise 16.3

1. **1** $\frac{1}{16}$ **2** $\frac{1}{676}$ **3** $\frac{15}{169}$

2. **1** $\frac{1}{12}$ **2** $\frac{5}{12}$ **3** $\frac{1}{2}$

3. $\frac{1}{21}$

4. **1** $\frac{2}{15}$ **2** $\frac{1}{40}$ **3** $\frac{1}{60}$

5. **1** $\frac{1}{1728}$ $(= 0.00058)$ **2** $\frac{55}{96}$ $(= 0.573)$

6. $\frac{3}{5}$

7. **1** $\frac{1}{169}$ **2** $\frac{1}{221}$

8. **1** 0.54   **2** 0.375

9. **1** $\frac{10}{153}$ **2** $\frac{46}{153}$

10. **1** $\frac{1}{15}$ **2** $\frac{7}{15}$ **3** $\frac{8}{15}$

11. All $\frac{1}{6}$

12. **1** $\frac{27}{64}$ **2** $\frac{27}{64}$ **3** $\frac{9}{64}$ **4** $\frac{1}{64}$

13. **1** $\frac{1}{12}$ **2** $\frac{5}{12}$ **3** $\frac{1}{3}$

14. **1** $\frac{1}{32}$ **2** $\frac{3}{32}$ **3** $\frac{3}{16}$

15. **1** $P(2) = P(12) = \frac{1}{36}$,

     $P(3) = P(11) = \frac{1}{18}$,

     $P(4) = P(10) = \frac{1}{12}$,

     $P(5) = P(9) = \frac{1}{9}$,

     $P(6) = P(8) = \frac{5}{36}$,

     $P(7) = \frac{1}{6}$

 2 7

 3 $\frac{1}{216}$

16. **1** $\frac{4}{9}$ **2** $\frac{1}{6}$ **3** $\frac{7}{18}$

17. **1** $\frac{12}{25}$ **2** $\frac{13}{80}$ **3** $\frac{1}{16}$

18. **1** $\frac{1}{12}$ **2** $\frac{7}{12}$

Page 334 Practice test 16

1. 0.0576

2. **1** $\frac{1}{10}$ **2** $\frac{1}{40}$

3. $\frac{9}{50}$

4. **1** 0.81 **2** 0.19

5. $\frac{22}{703}$ $(= 0.031)$

6. **1** $\frac{6}{55}$ **2** $\frac{21}{55}$

7. **1** $\frac{31}{105}$ **2** $\frac{74}{105}$

8. **1** $\frac{125}{216}$ **2** $\frac{25}{72}$ **3** $\frac{5}{72}$ **4** $\frac{1}{216}$

Page 337 Exercise 17.1

1. $y = 4x - 3$

2. $y = x^3$

3. $y = 10^x$

4. $y = \dfrac{48}{x}$

5. $y = 5 - 4x$

6. $y = 4^x$

7. $y = x^2 - 2$

8. $y = \dfrac{x + 2}{x + 3}$

9. $\ell = 10 + 1.6w$

10. $s = 4.9t^2$

Page 342 Exercise 17.2

1. **1** $5(x + 3y)$ **4** $6(x^3 + 2)$
    2 $3x(x - 2)$ **5** $x(x^2 + y)$
    3 $4b(a - 3c)$

2. **1** $(3x + y)(3x - y)$
    2 $(x + 4y)(x - 4y)$
    3 $(x + 1)(x - 1)$
    4 $(5x + 7y)(5x - 7y)$
    5 $(1 + 6x)(1 - 6x)$
    6 $(10x + 3)(10x - 3)$
    7 $(x + 13)(x - 13)$
    8 $(8 + x)(8 - x)$
    9 $3(x + 2y)(x - 2y)$
    10 $(x + 10)(x - 10)$

11 $x(x + 1)(x - 1)$
12 $(9x + 5)(9x - 5)$
13 $\pi(a + b)(a - b)$
14 $5(x + 5)(x - 5)$
15 $4(x + 3y)(x - 3y)$

3. **1** $(x + y)(p + q)$ **6** $(2y - 1)(x + 3)$
    2 $(x - y)(a + b)$ **7** $(a - 2)(3y - 1)$
    3 $(1 + y)(1 + x)$ **8** $(p - 2)(q + 2)$
    4 $(x - 2y)(2a - 3b)$ **9** $(1 + x^2)(1 + x)$
    5 $(a + 2b)(3x + y)$ **10** $(a - c)(a + b)$

4. **1** $(x + 10)(x + 1)$ **11** $(x + 4)^2$
    2 $(x - 6)(x - 2)$ **12** $(x + 18)(x + 1)$
    3 $(x + 6)(x - 2)$ **13** $(x + 3)(x - 2)$
    4 $(x + 3)(x - 5)$ **14** $(x - 6)(x - 1)$
    5 $(x + 6)(x - 5)$ **15** $(x + 5)(x + 3)$
    6 $(x - 15)(x - 2)$ **16** $(x - 1)^2$
    7 $(x + 5)(x + 4)$ **17** $(x - 7)(x - 3)$
    8 $(x + 4)(x - 2)$ **18** $(x + 4)(x - 6)$
    9 $(x + 1)(x - 8)$ **19** $(x + 11)(x - 3)$
    10 $(x + 7)(x - 2)$ **20** $(x + 7)^2$

5. **1** $3(x + 3)(x - 1)$ **11** $(2x - 5)(x + 1)$
    2 $(2x + 7)(x + 1)$ **12** $(2x + 3)(x - 3)$
    3 $(2x - 1)(x - 5)$ **13** $2(x + 5)(x - 3)$
    4 $(2x - 3)(x - 4)$ **14** $(3x + 1)(x - 6)$
    5 $2(x + 2)(x - 3)$ **15** $2(x + 1)(x - 3)$
    6 $(3x + 4)(x - 5)$ **16** $2(x + 5)(x + 1)$
    7 $(3x - 1)(x + 1)$ **17** $(2x - 3)(x + 1)$
    8 $(3x + 11)(x + 1)$ **18** $(3x - 8)(x + 1)$
    9 $(3x - 1)(x - 10)$ **19** $4(x + 3)(x - 1)$
    10 $3(x + 10)(x + 1)$ **20** $4(x + 2)(x - 2)$

6. **1** $ab(a - 4b)$ **10** $(a + 2b)(4x - y)$
    2 $(x + 4)(x - 3)$ **11** $(2 + x)(1 - 3x)$
    3 $4\pi(a + b)(a - b)$ **12** $5(3x + y)(3x - y)$
    4 $(p - 5)(a + 2b)$ **13** $(x + 3)(x - 8)$
    5 $(1 - 3x)(1 - 2x)$ **14** $(x - 3y)(3x - a)$
    6 $(1 + 3x)(1 - 3x)$ **15** $(2x + 9)(x - 2)$
    7 $(x + y)(x - 15y)$ **16** $(x + 20)(x + 3)$
    8 $2(x - 3)(x - 2)$ **17** $(1 + 4x)(1 - 5x)$
    9 $x(x + 6)(x - 5)$ **18** $(x + 3)^2$
    19 $(x^2 + 9)(x + 3)(x - 3)$
    20 $6(x + 1)^2$

7. $4(2x + 5)\,\mathrm{cm}$

8. $n(n + 1),\ n(n + 1)(n - 1)$

Page 345 Exercise 17.3

1. **1** $64,\ (x + 8)^2$ **4** $\frac{1}{4},\ \left(x + \frac{1}{2}\right)^2$
    2 $144,\ (x - 12)^2$ **5** $30\frac{1}{4},\ \left(x - 5\frac{1}{2}\right)^2$
    3 $2\frac{1}{4},\ \left(x + 1\frac{1}{2}\right)^2$

2. 1   minimum, -32 2   maximum, 7

3. 4

4. 1 $\dfrac{3a}{2b}$ 3 $\dfrac{e-2}{2(f-3)}$

    2   $\dfrac{c}{c-d}$ 4 $\dfrac{h-2}{h+3}$

5. 1 $\dfrac{3}{(x-3)(2x-3)}$ 3 $\dfrac{x-4}{(x-1)(x-2)}$

    2   $\dfrac{2x^2+3}{x(2x+3)}$ 4 $\dfrac{1}{x-2}$

6. 1 $\dfrac{b}{2(2a-b)}$ 2 $\dfrac{1}{(x+1)^2}$

7. 1 $x=\frac{5}{6}$ 2 $x=-5\frac{1}{2}$

8. £$\dfrac{40}{x}$, £$\dfrac{40}{x-2}$, £$\dfrac{80}{x(x-2)}$

Page 349   Exercise 17.4

1. 1   24, 28; divergent
    2   -11, -14; divergent
    3   $\frac{1}{64}$, $\frac{1}{256}$; convergent to 0
    4   32, 64; divergent
    5   $\frac{8}{10}$, $\frac{9}{11}$; convergent to 1
    6   27, 81; divergent
    7   30.375, 22.78125; convergent to 0
    8   -96, 192; divergent
    9   $3-\frac{1}{64}$, $3+\frac{1}{128}$; convergent to 3
    10 0.00005, 0.000005, convergent to 0

2. 1   3, 7, 23, 87, 343, 1367, 5463, 21 847;
        divergent
    2   1, 5, 3.4, 3.5882, 3.5574, 3.5622, 3.5614,
        3.5616; convergent to 3.56
    3   2.5, 3, 3.1623, 3.2132, 3.2290, 3.2339,
        3.2354, 3.2359; convergent to 3.24
    4   2, 2.25, 2.1176, 2.1857, 2.1502, 2.1686,
        2.1590, 2.1640; convergent to 2.16
    5   7, 3, -4, -14, -27, -43, -62, -84;
        divergent
    6   80, 80, 40, 13.3333, 3.3333, 0.6667,
        0.1111, 0.0159; convergent to 0
    7   2, 5, 14, 41, 122, 365, 1094, 3281;
        divergent
    8   4, 3, 3.5, 3.25, 3.375, 3.3125, 3.3438,
        3.3281; convergent to (approx) 3.33

3. 8.9443

Page 350   Exercise 17.5

1. 1 $W=12r^2$

    2   $d=\dfrac{30}{W}$

    3   $t=12-0.006\,h$

    4   $W=\dfrac{1}{10}\,h^3$

2. 1 $(x+3)(x-3)$, 17×23
    2   $(3x+1)(x+2)$; 31×12, $2^2\times 3\times 31$

3. $(c+b)(c-b)$,
    1   7   2   12   3   12

4. $(x+3)$ cm

5. $3x-2$

6. $2(x+2y)(x-2y)$

7. 1   minimum, 4
    2   maximum, $6\frac{1}{4}$
    3   minimum, -17

8. $\dfrac{x}{(x-6)^2}$

9. $x=6$

10. $\dfrac{140x+600}{x(x+10)}$ hours

11. 1 $\frac{36}{5}$, $\frac{36}{6}$; convergent to 0
    2   $\frac{25}{6}$, $\frac{29}{7}$; convergent to 4
    3   $81+1$, $243+1$; divergent
    4   $\frac{1}{4}$, $\frac{1}{2}$; divergent

12. 0.1, 0.9091, 0.5238, 0.6563, 0.6038, 0.6235,
    0.6159, 0.6188; convergent to 0.62

13. $x=0.66$

Page 352   Practice test 17

1. $w=14d^2$

2. 1 $3a(a-4b)$ 4 $(3x+2)(x-7)$
    2   $(x-15)(x-1)$ 5 $(2a+3)(4b-3c)$
    3   $\pi h(x+y)(x-y)$

3. 100, $(x-10)^2$

4. 1 $\frac{3}{4}$ 2 $\dfrac{xy}{6}$ 3   3

5. $\dfrac{x^2 + 16}{(x+4)(x-4)}$

6. $x = 6$

7. 1, 3, 6, 10, 15, 21, 28, 36, 45, 55; divergent; triangular numbers

8. 6.037

Page 356　　　Exercise 18.1

1. **1** 2.0, 2.4, 2.7, 1.85, 1.1, 0.3

2. **1** 0.7, 0.6, 2.4, 3.4, 3.8, 3.0, 2.1, 0.6

4. frequencies in order: 19, 25, 46, 34, 39, 20; total 183

Page 362　　　Exercise 18.2

1. $\bar{x} = 25\,\text{kg}$, $s = 2.16\,\text{kg}$

2. $\bar{x} = 42$, $s = 13.52$

3. $\bar{x} = 161\,\text{cm}$, $s = 7.07\,\text{cm}$

4. $\bar{x} = 53.5\,\text{m}$, $s = 7.37\,\text{m}$

5. $\bar{x} = £9700$, $s = £569$

6. $\bar{x} = 8.0$ miles/litre, $s = 1.129$ miles/litre

7. $\bar{x} = 59.1°\text{F}$, $s = 9.00$ deg F

8. $\bar{x} = 42.7$, $s = 14.27$

9. $\bar{x} = 48.9\,\text{s}$, $s = 1.42\,\text{s}$

10. $\bar{x} = 315\,\text{kg}$, $s = 63.18\,\text{kg}$

11. $\bar{x} = 2.7$, $s = 1.39$

12. $\bar{x} = 188.3\,\text{cm}$, $s = 12.22\,\text{cm}$

13. $\bar{x} = 4.2$ years, $s = 2.96$ years

14. $\bar{x} = 164.9\,\text{cm}$, $s = 5.24\,\text{cm}$

Page 368　　　Exercise 18.3

7. **1** 50%　**2** 68%　**3** 95%　**4** 16%

8. **1** 30 to 78 (48 marks)
   2 1900
   3 50

Page 370　　　Exercise 18.4

2. heights, men: 4.8, 29.5, 24, 10.2, 4.9, 2.0, 1.1; women: 13.8, 35, 18.2, 7.4, 3.7, 1.5, 0.6

3. frequencies in order: 20, 22, 17, 25, 39, 12; total 135

4. $\bar{x} = 1.02\,\text{kg}$, $s = 0.015\,\text{kg}$

5. $\bar{x} = 39\,\text{mm}$, $s = 11.73\,\text{mm}$

6. $\bar{x} = 50.2$, $s = 2.86$

7. $\bar{x} = 60.4\,\text{min}$, $s = 9.60\,\text{min}$

8. $\bar{x} = £166.80$, $s = £27.46$

9. $\bar{x} = 0.92$, $s = 0.93$

10. $\bar{x} = 7.79\,\text{cm}$, $s = 0.641\,\text{cm}$

11. $\bar{x} = 29.3\,\text{min}$, $s = 10.89\,\text{min}$

15. heights: 0.55, 1.8, 3.8, 5.2, 4.2, 1.3; $\bar{x} = 47\,300\,\text{km}$

16. **1** 16%
    2 $97\frac{1}{2}\%$
    3 996 kg and 1044 kg

Page 373　　　Practice test 18

1. heights: 0.15, 0.8, 1.6, 1.5, 1.7, 0.95, 0.75, 0.45, 0.36

2. frequencies: 16, 28, 48, 5; total 97

3. $\bar{x} = 27$, $s = 1.73$

4. $\bar{x} = 95.5\,\text{kg}$, $s = 6.83\,\text{kg}$

5. $\bar{x} = 1.4$, $s = 1.39$

7. **1** 1360　　**2** 1900　　**3** 950

Page 382　　　Exercise 19.1

1. gradients 4, 8, 12; gradient 10 at (5, 25)

2. gradients for $x = 2, 3, 4, 5, 6$: $-4, -2, 0, 2, 4$; at $x = 7$, gradient $= 6$

3. gradients in the table: 12, 3, 0, 3, 12, 27, 48

4. height 31 m; times 0.4 s, 4.6 s; speed 10 m/s

5. **2** 2 s and 4 s　　**3** 2.3 m/s

6. **1** 20 km　　**2** 25 km/h, 17.75 s

7. **1** 22 m/s
   2 20 s, 105 s from the start
   3 0.6 m/s^2

8. values for y: 73, 22, 17, 20.5, 27.9, 38; $x = 3.3$; length and width 3.3 m, height 1.7 m

9. 7.7 deg. per min, 14 deg. per min

10. population (1000's): 1, 2, 4, 8, 16, 32; time 3.3 h; rates: 2800 per hour, 11 000 per hour

Page 391   Exercise 19.2

1.   900 m

2.   **1**   160 m   **2**   16 m/s   **3**   5 m/s^2

3. $5\frac{1}{2}$ m

4.   **1**   20 m/s^2 **2**   173 m

5.   speed 16 m/s, distance 24 m

6.   2200 m^2

7.   values: $3\frac{1}{2}$, 4, $3\frac{1}{2}$, 2;
     1   4 m   **2**   13 m^2

8.   **2**   140 ml/s   **4**   1.25 ℓ
     3   22 s   **5**   2.25 ℓ

Page 393   Exercise 19.3

1.   **2**   26 m/s   **3**   2.5 s, 4.9 s

2.   **2**   3.7 min
     3   2.8 min, 4.7 min
     4   6 gallons/minute

3.   **1**   90%   **2**   53 000   **3**   4000 people/year

4.   **1**   0.4 km/min^2 **2**   5.4 km

5.   **1**   14 s   **3**   150 m
     2   9.5 s, 17.5 s   **4**   128 m

6.   **2**   0.35 cm/s   **4**   2.22 cm
     3   10 s   **5**   17.5 cm

7.   5325 m^2

Page 395   Practice test 19

1.   At A, gradient −0.2; at B, −0.6; at C, −1.5

2.   27.6 unit^2, $9\pi = 28.3$ unit^2, slightly less

3.   **2**   1 s and 3 s   **3**   −3 cm/s

4.   **1**   3 m/s^2 **2**   20 m/s   **3**   1275 m

Page 400   Exercise 20.1

1.   **1**   1.62 m   **4**   234 000 miles
     2   2 h 45 min   **5**   40 ℓ
     3   2600

2.   **1**   2.955, 2.965   **6**   615, 625
     2   0.6065, 0.6075   **7**   20.95, 21.05
     3   5.2255, 5.2265   **8**   8650, 8750
     4   62.5, 63.5   **9**   23.995, 24.005
     5   2.045, 2.055   **10**   8295, 8305

3.   **1**   8.77; 8.76, 8.78
     2   2.39; 2.38, 2.40
     3   598.66; 598.27, 599.04
     4   117.74; 117.56, 117.93
     5   43.69; 43.63, 43.76

4.   **1**   61; 60, 62   **4**   0.46; 0.45, 0.47
     2   50; 49, 51   **5**   5.1; 4.9, 5.3
     3   78; 69, 88

5.   **1**   69.2; 69.1, 69.3   **4**   38.2; 37.4, 39.0
     2   66.3; 66.2, 66.4   **5**   2.40; 2.38, 2.42
     3   34.1; 33.2, 35.0

6.   **1**   15.2; 15.2, 15.3   **4**   0.840; 0.839, 0.841
     2   1.63; 1.62, 1.63   **5**   4760; 4750, 4770
     3   3.10; 3.10, 3.11

7.   363 000, 370 000

8.   **1**   1619 g, 1623 g   **2**   404.8 g, 405.8 g

Page 403   Exercise 20.2

1.   **1**   0.05 cm, 0.9%   **3**   £5, 1.6%
     2   0.005 kg, 0.3%   **4**   0.5 month, 7.1%

2.   **1**   2.1%   **2**   3.5%   **3**   1.3%

3.   5 m, 1.4%; 12 m, 0.17 m, 1.4%

4.   71 600 ℓ, 79 200 ℓ

Page 404   Exercise 20.3

1.   **1**   106 m, 110 m   **2**   702 m^2, 756 m^2

2.   385 g, 387 g

3.   3.10, 3.17

4.   83.6 cm, 83.8 cm

5.   12.45 cm, 12.75 cm

6.   0.77, 0.83

7.   0.05 g, 1.3%; 76 g, 1 g, 1.3%

8.   1.9%

9.   **1**   14.8 m, 15.4 m   **3**   54.7 m, 56.9 m
     2   12.5 m, 13.1 m   **4**   186 m^2, 201 m^2

Page 405   Practice test 20

1.   **1**   50 kg   **4**   4830 m
     2   717 ℓ **5**   300 000 km/s
     3   262 000

2.   0.944; 0.942, 0.945

3. 586 g, 588 g

4. 29.0 g, 29.4 g

5. **1** 20.6 cm, 21.0 cm   **2** 25.3 cm², 26.4 cm²

6. 0.8%

Page 406   Exercise D1

1. **1** 4 : 7   **2** 16 : 49

2. **1** $x(x + 16)$
    2 $(x + 4)(x - 4)$
    3 $(x + 20)(x - 4)$
    4 $(x - 10)(x - 6)$

3. $5.2 \times 10^{-3} \text{ m}^2$

4. 2.7 cm

6. £141.50

7. **2** cum freq: 0, 14, 48, 70, 100, 118, 120;
    median 5.1 cm, interquartile range 4.4 cm

8. **1** 22 cm
    2 18 cm
    3 29.25 cm²
    4 19.25 cm²

9. y-values: $\frac{1}{16}, \frac{1}{8}, \frac{1}{4}, \frac{1}{2}$, 1, 2, 4, 8, 16;

    gradients: 0.09, 0.35, 1.39, 5.55;

    $\dfrac{\text{gradient}}{y} \approx 0.7$

10. **1** $\frac{4}{15}$ **2** $\frac{1}{30}$ **3** $\frac{7}{15}$

11. **1** 3.5 cm   **2** 63.2°   **3** 70.3°

12. **1** rational   **3** rational
    2 irrational   **4** irrational

13. mean 8, median 7, mode 2,
    standard deviation 6.27

14. 2, 2.236, 2.288, 2.300, 2.302, 2.303, 2.303,
    2.303; limit 2.30

15. orange 13p, lemon 20p

Page 408   Exercise D2

1. 62 kg, 70 kg

2. C (18, 14, 0)
    F (18, 2, 15)
    G (18, 14, 15)
    H (2, 14, 15)
    $AC = 20$ units
    $AG = 25$ units

3. **1** $\frac{11}{24}$ **2** $\frac{2}{3}$ **3** $\frac{3}{4}$

4. 190 m

5. **1** $y = x^2 + x$ **2** $y = x^3 + x$

6. **1** 50 s   **2** 1100 m

7. **1** −3.25   **2** $x = -2.3$ or 1.3

8. heights: 1, 4, 12.5, 27, 31, 35, 28, 16, 2, 1.5

9. 5.29 tonnes, 5.51 tonnes

10. **1** $x = 8$ **2** $x = 2$

11. **1** $\frac{1}{15}$ **2** $\frac{14}{45}$ **3** $\frac{31}{45}$

12. **1** $\frac{1}{3}\pi\ell$ cm

13. $DE = 13.5$ cm, $DF = 12$ cm; areas 4 : 9

14. sizes 90°, 108°, 120°, 135°, 140°; 7-sided, 129°

15. £725, £75

Page 412   Exercise D3

1. 75 cm²

3. **1** x^3 **4** 8
    2 x^2 **5** $\frac{1}{7}$
    3 3

4. $x = 2, y = 1$

5. mean 4.5 min, standard deviation 2.76 min

6. **1** $\dfrac{x + 6}{12}$ **2** 1

7. $\overrightarrow{BC} = 3\mathbf{a} + 2\mathbf{b}$, $\overrightarrow{CD} = 9\mathbf{a} + 6\mathbf{b}$;
    $BC : CD = 1 : 3$

8. 3.89 m, 4.06 m

9. $\frac{1}{6}, \frac{5}{9}$

10. **1** 8 km/h
    2 30 km/h
    3 5.05 pm, 33 km from A

11. $x = 5, y = 1$; $AB = 7$ cm, $BC = 12$ cm,
    $AC = 9$ cm

12. **1** 6 cm   **2** 24 cm²   **3** 4.8 cm

13. $y = 50 \sin x°$

14. 36.0 unit², 37.7 unit²

15. **1** $\frac{8}{15}$ **2** $\frac{7}{15}$ **3** 60

Page 425   Exercise 21.1

1. 8 cm

2. **1** The line through A, B **2**   14 cm

3. 7.5 cm

4. **1** $a = 48°$
   2 $b = 17°$, $c = 23°$, $d = 40°$
   3 $d = 33°$
   4 $e = 140°$, $f = 220°$, $g = 110°$
   5 $h = 85°$, $j = 104°$
   6 $k = 92°$, $m = 110°$

5. **1** $a = 70°$, $b = 35°$
   2 $c = 40°$, $d = 50°$, $e = 80°$

6. **1** $a = 80°$, $b = 50°$
   2 $c = 25°$, $d = 50°$
   3 $e = 25°$, $f = 130°$, $g = 50°$
   4 $j = 50°$, $k = 130°$

7. $\angle P = 63°$, $\angle Q = 55°$, $\angle R = 62°$

8. **1** $f = g = h = 65°$
   2 $k = 90°$, $m = p = 35°$, $n = 55°$

9. $\angle AXO = 90°$, $AB = 19.2$ cm

10. **1** $\angle TAB = 28°$, $\angle TBA = 62°$,
         $\angle TPB = 34°$, $\angle TQR = 45°$

Page 428   Exercise 21.2

1. **1** 9 cm
   2 circle centre O, radius 9 cm

2. 7 cm

3. **2** 26°

4. 44°

5. **1** 70   **4** 36
   2 60   **5** 26, $a = 102°$
   3 20

6. 50°

7. 30°

8. **1** $(180 - 2x)°$ **2** $(90 - x)°$

10. **1** 72°   **2** 36°   **3** $\frac{1}{3}$

11. **2** 10 cm

12. **1** $\angle XDC$ **3** 6.6 cm

Page 431   Practice test 21

1. 28°

2. $OP = 17$ cm, $AP = 9$ cm

3. $\angle A = 70°$, $\angle B = 65°$, $\angle C = 45°$

4. $\angle BAC = \angle ADE = 38°$, $\angle AEB = 71°$,
   $\angle DAE = 33°$

Page 435   Exercise 22.1

1. **1** $x = -1$ or 2 **4** $x = -1\frac{1}{3}$ or $1\frac{1}{2}$
   2 $x = -2$ or $-\frac{1}{3}$ **5** $x = -\frac{1}{4}$ or $\frac{2}{3}$
   3 $x = \frac{1}{2}$ or 3

2. **1** $x = -5$ or -2 **11** $x = 0$ or 5
   2 $x = 1$ or 12 **12** $x = -12$ or 3
   3 $x = -4$ or 3 **13** $x = -8$ or -5
   4 $x = -2$ or 15 **14** $x = -6$ or 0
   5 $x = 3$ or 10 **15** $x = 2$ or 10
   6 $x = 4$ (or 4)   **16** $x = 0$ or 1
   7 $x = -2$ or 4 **17** $x = -3$ (or -3)
   8 $x = -6$ or 7 **18** $x = -3$ or 11
   9 $x = -25$ or 1 **19** $x = -25$ or -4
   10 $x = 3$ or 8 **20** $x = 6$ or 8

3. **1** $x = \pm 1$ **4** $x = \pm \frac{1}{2}$
   2 $x = \pm 5$ **5** $x = 1$ or 3
   3 $x = \pm \frac{2}{3}$ **6** $x = -8$ or 2

4. **1** $x = \frac{1}{2}$ or 7 **6** $x = -\frac{1}{2}$ or 3
   2 $x = -2\frac{1}{2}$ or -1 **7** $x = -2$ or $1\frac{2}{3}$
   3 $x = -1$ or $\frac{1}{3}$ **8** $x = -4$ or $-1\frac{1}{2}$
   4 $x = \frac{2}{3}$ or 4 **9** $x = \frac{1}{3}$ or 3
   5 $x = -2$ or $2\frac{1}{2}$ **10** $x = 4$ or 5

5. **1** 0.59, 3.41
   2 -2.12, -0.38
   3 -2.08, 1.08

6. **1** $x = -5.61$ or 1.61
   2 $x = 0.22$ or 2.28
   3 $x = -1.65$ or 3.65
   4 $x = -1.79$ or 1.12
   5 $x = -2.37$ or -0.63
   6 $x = -0.88$ or 1.88
   7 $x = 0.18$ or 2.82
   8 $x = -0.54$ or 5.54
   9 $x = -4.41$ or -1.59
   10 $x = 0.43$ or 11.57

7. $x = -2\frac{1}{2}$ or 11

8. $3x^2$ m^2, $x = 20$

9. $x = -1\frac{1}{2}$, 0 or 1

Page 439   Exercise 22.2

1.   **1**   real, rational
     2   real, rational (equal)
     3   real, irrational
     4   no real roots
     5   real, rational

2.   **1** $x = -0.48$ or 12.48
     2 $x = -3.83$ or 1.83
     3 $x = 0.57$ or 17.43
     4 $x = 1.63$ or 7.37
     5 $x = -0.19$ or 2.69

3.   0 or 16

4.   **1** $x = -1.76$ **4** $x = 0.18$
     2 $x = 1.70$ **5** $x = 3.14$
     3 $x = 0.55$

5.   **3**   path 4 m wide

Page 440   Exercise 22.3

1.   **1** $x = -6$ or 3   **3** $x = 0$
     2 $x = 4$ or 11   **4** $x = 0$ or 5

2.   **1** $x = -2$ **3** $x = 1$ or 3
     2 $x = -2$ or 5

3. $PB = (13 - 2x)$ cm, $x = 5$, area 46 cm^2

4. $\left(\dfrac{80}{x} + \dfrac{45}{x - 10}\right)$ hours, $x = 40$

5.   width $\dfrac{160}{x}$ m; $x + \dfrac{160}{x} = 30$; length 23.1 m, width 6.9 m

6. $x = 1$ or 27, $y = 1$ or 3

7. $x = 0.721$

Page 441   Practice test 22

1.   **1** $x = \pm 3$ **4** $x = 1.17$ or 6.83
     2 $x = 0$ or 9   **5** $x = -0.82$ or 9.82
     3 $x = -1$ or 9

2.   20 m by 15 m

3.   4.2 cm

4. $x = 2.78$

Page 447   Exercise 23.1

1.   **1**   3.97 cm   **4**   6.84 cm
     2   8.49 cm   **5**   5.86 cm
     3   3.76 cm

2.   **1**   36.1°   **4**   27.4°
     2   16.2°   **5** $\angle C = 51.2°$, $\angle A = 68.8°$
     3   39.0°

3.   **1** $BC = 8.67$ cm   **4** $AB = 10.1$ cm
     2 $AC = 7.20$ cm   **5** $AC = 7.39$ cm
     3 $BC = 4.18$ cm

4.   **1**   57.1°   **4**   132.2°
     2   127.2°   **5**   95.7°
     3   48.7°

5.   **1**   19.7 cm^2 **4**   41.3 cm^2
     2   8.83 cm^2 **5**   7.36 cm^2
     3   12.0 cm^2

6.   **1**   8.75 cm   **7**   26.8°
     2   13.5 cm   **8**   78.5°
     3   4.71 cm   **9** $AC = 7.56$ cm,
     4   10.5 cm $\angle A = 54.4°$
     5   11.4 cm   **10** $\angle A = 110.2°$,
     6   58.4° $\angle B = 51.0°$,
                                          $\angle C = 18.8°$

7. $BC = 91$ km, $AB = 129$ km, 27 km further

8. $AC = 9.36$ cm, $AD = 20$ cm, $CD = 15$ cm, $\angle ADC = 26.4°$

Page 450   Exercise 23.2

1.   **1**   6.6 miles   **2**   6.9 miles

2.   097°

3.   **1**   44.8°   **2**   135°, 205°   **3**   5.4 ha

4.   (A) 670 m, (B) 860 m, $AB = 610$ m

5.   **1**   48.7°   **2**   1.5 ha

6.   7.3 m

7.   2390 m, 306°

8.   **1**   15 cm^2 **2**   6.1 cm   **3**   38.7°

9.   **1**   91 m   **2**   11 m

Page 452   Practice test 23

1.   111.8°

2. $\angle C = 22.0°$, $\angle A = 128.0°$

3.   1410 m

4.   **1** 174 m   **2** 1410 m^2

5.   **1** 15.4 m   **2** 13.3 m   **3** 113°

Page 459   Exercise 24.1

1.   **1** $y = 2 - 2x$ **4** $y = 2$
     2 $y = x + 2$ **5** $y = 2x$
     3 $y = 2 - x$ **6** $y = 2x + 2$

2.   **1** minimum point
     2 $(-5, 0)$, $(4, 0)$
     3 $(0, -20)$

3.   **1** maximum point
     2 $(-\frac{1}{2}, 0)$, $(3, 0)$
     3 $(0, 3)$

8.   **3** $(1, 48)$

Page 465   Exercise 24.2

1.   **1** $4y \geqslant 3x - 5$ **2** $(3, 0)$, $(0, 2)$, 9
          $6y \leqslant 31 - x$ **3** 26
          $y \geqslant 7 - 2x$ **4** 14

2.   **2** 18   **3** 43, −35

3.   **2** 20   **3** 6, −6

4.   **1** Path B, D, F; 13 min
     2 Path C, F, J; 22 hours
     3 Path C, G, J, H, K; 32 hours

5. $x \geqslant 3$, $y \geqslant 3$, $x + y \leqslant 12$,
     $60x + 30y \leqslant 480$ $(2x + y \leqslant 16)$;
     4 chocolate, 8 cream; 156 biscuits

Page 467   Exercise 24.3

1.   **1** $x = -3$ or 4   **4** $x = \frac{1}{2}$
     2 $x = -5$ or 6   **5** $-12\frac{1}{4}$

2.   **1** $y = x^2 - 4x + 4$
     2 $y = 4 - x^2$
     3 $y = 4x^2$

3.   **1** $(-3, 0)$, $(0, 0)$, $(2, 0)$
     2 18
     3 −24

4. $b = -1$, $c = -2$

8. $5x + 2y \geqslant 50$, $x + y \leqslant 19$, $y \geqslant 5$;
     £$(120x + 30y)$; 5 coaches, 14 minibuses;
     £1020

9. $x \geqslant 15$, $y \geqslant 5$, $x + y \leqslant 40$, $2x + y \leqslant 60$;
     £$(6000x + 4000y)$; 20 luxury, 20 standard;
     profit £200 000

10. Path A, C, E, F, H, J, K, M, N, 19 days;
     5 days

11. $4 \leqslant x \leqslant 10$, $4 \leqslant y \leqslant 18$, $x + y \leqslant 24$;
     10 red, 14 yellow-flowering, £164;
     6 red, 18 yellow-flowering, £174

Page 470   Practice test 24

1. $f(0) = 7$, $f(1) = 4$, $f(2) = 7$, $f(3) = 16$;
     least value is 4

2.   **1** minimum point
     2 $(-3, 0)$, $(5, 0)$
     3 $(0, -15)$

4.   3 values

6.   greatest 42, least 16

7.   Path C, E, J, K; 17 hours; 3 hours

Page 478   Exercise 25.1

1.   **1** reflection in $y = x$
     2 rotation about the origin through 90°
          clockwise
     3 translation by vector $\begin{pmatrix} 1 \\ -8 \end{pmatrix}$
     4 rotation about the origin through 180°
     5 reflection in $y = -x$
     6 translation by vector $\begin{pmatrix} -6 \\ -2 \end{pmatrix}$
     7 reflection in $x = -1$
     8 reflection in the x-axis
     9 reflection in the y-axis
     10 translation by the vector $\begin{pmatrix} -7 \\ 6 \end{pmatrix}$

2.   reflection in $y = x$, reflection in $y = x$

3. $A_1 (-1, 1)$, $B_1 (-4, 2)$, $C_1 (-3, 7)$;
     $A_2 (1, -1)$, $B_2 (4, -2)$, $C_2 (3, -7)$;
     reflection in the x-axis, reflection in the x-axis

4. $A_1 (-1, 1)$, $B_1 (-2, 4)$, $C_1 (-7, 3)$;
     $A_2 (-1, -1)$, $B_2 (-2, -4)$, $C_2 (-7, -3)$;
     reflection in $y = -x$, reflection in $y = -x$

5. A_1 (1, 1), B_1 (4, 0), C_1 (3, −5);
    A_2 (1, 1), B_2 (0, 4), C_2 (−5, 3);
    rotation about A through 90° anticlockwise,
    rotation about A through 90° clockwise

6. A_1 (4, −1), B_1 (7, 0), C_1 (6, 5);
    A_2 (−4, 2), B_2 (−1, 3), C_2 (−2, 8);

    translation by vector $\begin{pmatrix} -5 \\ 1 \end{pmatrix}$, translation by

    vector $\begin{pmatrix} 5 \\ -1 \end{pmatrix}$

7. 1 A_1 (3, 3), B_1 (6, 3), C_1 (6, 9); areas 9 : 1
    2 A_2 (−2, −2), B_2 (−4, −2), C_2 (−4, −6);
       2 : 1; enlargement centre the origin scale
       factor $-\frac{1}{2}$
    3 D_1 (−2, 3), E_1 (−2, 1), F_1 $(-1\frac{1}{2}, \frac{1}{2})$,
       G_1 (−1, 2); $F_1G_1 : FG = 1 : 3$; areas 1 : 9;
       enlargement centre the origin scale factor 3

Page 483   Exercise 25.2

1. 1 $\begin{pmatrix} 10 \\ 0 \end{pmatrix}$ 11 $\begin{pmatrix} 11 & 2 \\ -13 & 4 \end{pmatrix}$

    2 $\begin{pmatrix} 3 \\ 3 \end{pmatrix}$ 12 $\begin{pmatrix} -4 & 1 \\ 3 & 0 \end{pmatrix}$

    3 $\begin{pmatrix} -1 \\ -2 \end{pmatrix}$ 13 $\begin{pmatrix} -3 & -1 \\ -2 & 4 \end{pmatrix}$

    4 $\begin{pmatrix} -2 \\ 14 \end{pmatrix}$ 14 $\begin{pmatrix} 7 & -14 \\ -4 & 8 \end{pmatrix}$

    5 $\begin{pmatrix} 7 \\ -1 \end{pmatrix}$ 15 $\begin{pmatrix} 12 & -14 \\ -19 & 19 \end{pmatrix}$

    6 $\begin{pmatrix} 24 & -10 \\ 3 & 1 \end{pmatrix}$ 16 $\begin{pmatrix} 3 \\ 36 \end{pmatrix}$

    7 $\begin{pmatrix} 7 & 9 \\ 8 & 18 \end{pmatrix}$ 17 $\begin{pmatrix} 9 \\ 32 \end{pmatrix}$

    8 $\begin{pmatrix} -2 & 5 \\ 6 & -11 \end{pmatrix}$ 18 $\begin{pmatrix} -2 \\ 1 \end{pmatrix}$

    9 $\begin{pmatrix} 9 & -9 \\ 3 & 12 \end{pmatrix}$ 19 $\begin{pmatrix} 2 \\ -9 \end{pmatrix}$

    10 $\begin{pmatrix} -13 & -15 \\ 18 & 21 \end{pmatrix}$ 20 $\begin{pmatrix} -13 \\ -5 \end{pmatrix}$

2. 1 $\begin{pmatrix} 7 & 9 \\ 3 & 4 \end{pmatrix}$ 6 $\begin{pmatrix} 1 & -2\frac{1}{2} \\ -2 & 5\frac{1}{2} \end{pmatrix}$

    2 $\begin{pmatrix} 2 & -5 \\ -3 & 8 \end{pmatrix}$ 7 $\begin{pmatrix} -0.4 & -1.4 \\ -0.6 & -2.6 \end{pmatrix}$

    3 $\begin{pmatrix} 4 & 5 \\ 7 & 9 \end{pmatrix}$ 8 $\begin{pmatrix} 1 & 3 \\ 3 & 10 \end{pmatrix}$

    4 $\begin{pmatrix} 1 & 2 \\ 1 & 1 \end{pmatrix}$ 9 $\begin{pmatrix} 1 & 2 \\ -1\frac{1}{2} & -2\frac{1}{2} \end{pmatrix}$

    5 $\begin{pmatrix} -0.2 & 0.6 \\ -0.3 & 0.4 \end{pmatrix}$ 10 $\begin{pmatrix} 0 & 0.2 \\ -0.5 & 0 \end{pmatrix}$

3. $\mathbf{A}^2 = \begin{pmatrix} 5a^2 & 0 \\ 0 & 5a^2 \end{pmatrix}$

    $\mathbf{B} = \begin{pmatrix} 4 & 2 \\ 2 & -4 \end{pmatrix}$ $\left[\text{or} \ \begin{pmatrix} -4 & -2 \\ -2 & 4 \end{pmatrix} \right]$

4. 1 $\begin{pmatrix} -7 & -10 \\ 13 & 18 \end{pmatrix}$ 6 $\begin{pmatrix} 9 & 9 \\ -2 & -2 \end{pmatrix}$, yes

    2 $\begin{pmatrix} -1 & -2 \\ 7 & 10 \end{pmatrix}$ 7 $\begin{pmatrix} 3 & -4 \\ -2 & 3 \end{pmatrix}$

    3 $\begin{pmatrix} 1 & -2 \\ 1 & 2 \end{pmatrix}$ 8 $\begin{pmatrix} \frac{1}{2} & \frac{1}{2} \\ \frac{3}{4} & -\frac{1}{4} \end{pmatrix}$

    4 $\begin{pmatrix} -1 & -2 \\ 7 & 10 \end{pmatrix}$, yes   9 $\begin{pmatrix} 3 & 4 \\ 2 & 3 \end{pmatrix}$, yes

    5 $\begin{pmatrix} 8 & 11 \\ -3 & -4 \end{pmatrix}$ 10 $\begin{pmatrix} -1 & -2 \\ 3 & 2 \end{pmatrix}$, yes

Page 489   Exercise 25.3

1. $x = 2, \ y = -3$

2. 1 A' (3, −2), B' (6, −1); (translation)
    2 A' (2, 2), B' (8, 4); enlargement centre
       the origin scale factor 2
    3 A' (−1, −1), B' (−2, −4); reflection in
       $y = -x$
    4 A'(−1, 1), B' (−2, 4); rotation about the
       origin through 90° anticlockwise
    5 A' (1, −1), B' (4, −2); reflection in the
       x-axis

3. P' (−2, −6), Q' (2, 6), $\begin{pmatrix} 2 & -1 \\ 3 & -2 \end{pmatrix}$;

    rotation about the origin through 180°

4. A' (3, 1), B' (4, 4), C' (1, 3);

    rhombus, $\begin{pmatrix} \frac{3}{8} & -\frac{1}{8} \\ -\frac{1}{8} & \frac{3}{8} \end{pmatrix}$

5. **1** $\begin{pmatrix} -6 \\ -7 \end{pmatrix}$ **4** $\begin{pmatrix} 0 & 1 \\ 1 & 0 \end{pmatrix}$

6. **1** $\begin{pmatrix} 2 & 0 \\ 0 & 2 \end{pmatrix}$ **4** $\begin{pmatrix} 5 \\ 0 \end{pmatrix}$

    2 $\begin{pmatrix} 0 & -1 \\ 1 & 0 \end{pmatrix}$ **5** $\begin{pmatrix} 0 & -1 \\ 1 & 1 \end{pmatrix}$

    3 $\begin{pmatrix} 0 & -1 \\ -1 & 0 \end{pmatrix}$ **6** $\begin{pmatrix} \frac{1}{3} & 0 \\ 0 & \frac{1}{3} \end{pmatrix}$

Page 491   Exercise 25.4

1. **1** reflection in the line DF
    2 rotation about E through 180°
    3 translation in distance and direction CE
    4 reflection in the line BH
    5 enlargement centre C scale factor 2

2. $2\frac{1}{2}$; B_1 $(3\frac{1}{2}, 4\frac{1}{2})$; 5 : 2; $\frac{2}{5}$

3. **1** (4, 7)   **2** (0, 3)

4. $\begin{pmatrix} 3 & -2 \\ 2 & -1 \end{pmatrix}$

5. **1** $\begin{pmatrix} 21 & -8 \\ -4 & 1 \end{pmatrix}$ **2** $\begin{pmatrix} -1 & -1 \\ -3 & -2 \end{pmatrix}$

6. $a = 4$, $b = -1$

7. $\begin{pmatrix} 0 & \frac{1}{2} \\ -1 & 1\frac{1}{2} \end{pmatrix}$, $\begin{pmatrix} 3 & -\frac{1}{2} \\ 1 & 1\frac{1}{2} \end{pmatrix}$

8. Both $\begin{pmatrix} 0 & 6 \\ -6 & 0 \end{pmatrix}$, yes

9. A_1 (−2, −1), B_1 (−4, −3), C_1 (−7, 0);
    A_2 (−2, 1), B_2 (−4, 3), C_2 (−7, 0);

    T_2T_1 $\begin{pmatrix} -1 & 0 \\ 0 & 1 \end{pmatrix}$; reflection in the y-axis;

    reflection in the y-axis

10. translation 2**T**

11. area 9 unit², $\begin{pmatrix} 0 & 1 \\ 1 & 0 \end{pmatrix}$

12. P' (4, 3), Q' (6, 2); reflection in $x = 3$

Page 493   Practice test 25

1. **1** reflection in the y-axis
    2 rotation about the origin through 180°
    3 rotation about $(-\frac{1}{2}, 0)$ through 180°
    4 reflection in the x-axis
    5 translation by the vector $\begin{pmatrix} -1 \\ 0 \end{pmatrix}$

2. **1** 4, E (2, 1)
    2 F (−4, −2), G (−6, −2), H (−6, −4);
    areas 1 : 4; enlargement centre origin scale factor $-\frac{1}{2}$

3. rhombus; $x = -4$, $y = -6$;
    K_1 (6, −7), L_1 (8, −4), M_1 (6, −1),
    N_1 (4, −4);
    K_2 (6, 7), L_2 (8, 4), M_2 (6, 1), N_2 (4, 4);
    reflection in $y = -x$; reflection in $y = -x$

4. **1** $\begin{pmatrix} 1 \\ -4 \end{pmatrix}$ **6** $\begin{pmatrix} 0 & 1 \\ -\frac{1}{2} & 2 \end{pmatrix}$

    2 $\begin{pmatrix} -2 & -4 \\ 3 & 1 \end{pmatrix}$ **7** $\begin{pmatrix} 0.8 & -0.2 \\ -1.4 & 0.6 \end{pmatrix}$

    3 $\begin{pmatrix} 13 & -6 \\ 32 & -14 \end{pmatrix}$ **8** $\begin{pmatrix} 14 & -8 \\ 4 & -2 \end{pmatrix}$

    4 $\begin{pmatrix} 22 \\ 3 \end{pmatrix}$ **9** $\begin{pmatrix} 82 \\ 22 \end{pmatrix}$

    5 $\begin{pmatrix} -5 \\ -10 \end{pmatrix}$ **10** $\begin{pmatrix} 22 \\ 3 \end{pmatrix}$

5. (15, 10)

6. rotation about the origin through 90°
    anticlockwise, $\begin{pmatrix} 0 & -1 \\ 1 & 0 \end{pmatrix}$

7. **1** $\begin{pmatrix} -1 & 0 \\ 0 & 1 \end{pmatrix}$ **4** $\begin{pmatrix} 4 \\ -4 \end{pmatrix}$

    2 $\begin{pmatrix} 0 & 1 \\ -1 & 0 \end{pmatrix}$ **5** $\begin{pmatrix} 3 & 0 \\ 0 & 3 \end{pmatrix}$

    3 $\begin{pmatrix} 0 & -1 \\ -1 & 0 \end{pmatrix}$

Page 496   Exercise E1

1. **1** translation   **4** translation
    2 rotation   **5** reflection
    3 reflection   **6** rotation

2. **1** $x > -2\frac{3}{4}$ **2** $-3\frac{1}{2} < x < 4$

3. 53.7 m, 54.7 m

5. 3.8 km

7. $a = 70°$, $b = 55°$, $c = 35°$

8. 1.85 s

9. 6.14 pm, 2.5 km from A

10. **1** $2\frac{1}{3}$ **2** $7:3$ **3** $49:9$ **4** $40:9$

12. 25 576

13. $2x + y \leqslant 15$, $x \geqslant 4$, $y \geqslant 4$, $x + y \leqslant 10$;
    $(X, Y) \to (4, 4), (4, 5), (4, 6), (5, 4), (5, 5)$;
    4 of X, 6 of Y

14. **1** 0.00001   **2** 0.59   **3** 0.41

15. **1** $a = \dfrac{v^2 - u^2}{2s}$ **3** $r = \sqrt{\dfrac{S}{4\pi}}$

    2 $h = \dfrac{3V}{\pi r^2}$

Page 499   Exercise E2

1. **1** 81   **2** $x = -1$

3. **1** $\frac{1}{16}$ **2** $\frac{25}{72}$

4. 33.1%, 27.1%

5. **1** $BC = 18.4$ cm, $BD = 20$ cm, $CD = 15$ cm
    2 61.3°

7. **2** $3\frac{1}{3}$ **3** $DE = 4$ cm, $BC = 6\frac{2}{3}$ cm

8. $x = 9$; 16 cm, 5 cm

9. y-values: 2.22, 2.23, 2.17, 2.05, 1.87, 1.62,
    1.33, 1. Maximum $y = 2.24$ when $x = 27°$;
    $x = 74°$

10. Path B, G, M, P; 22 days, 10 days

11. 60 000 000 m³ (approx)

12. **1** 52°   **4** 104°
    2 128°   **5** 64°
    3 38°

13. **1** 3.2 cm   **2** 6.2 cm²

14. $3x^2 - 10x + 6 = 0$, $x = 2.55$

15. $\mathbf{A} + \mathbf{B} = \begin{pmatrix} 5 & -1 \\ 6 & 8 \end{pmatrix}$

    $\mathbf{AB} = \begin{pmatrix} 9 & -8 \\ 23 & -20 \end{pmatrix}$

    $\mathbf{BA} = \begin{pmatrix} -14 & -23 \\ 2 & 3 \end{pmatrix}$

    $\mathbf{A}^{-1} = \begin{pmatrix} 8 & -3 \\ -5 & 2 \end{pmatrix}$

    $\mathbf{B}^{-1} = \begin{pmatrix} 0 & 1 \\ -\frac{1}{4} & \frac{3}{4} \end{pmatrix}$

Page 504   Exercise E3

1. 6.75 kg

2. **1** $0.0\dot{1}8\dot{5}$ **2** 0.019   **3** 0.0185

3. **1** 16.6°   **2** 33.2°   **3** 16.6°

4. **1** $y = \dfrac{3}{x}$ **3** $y = 3^x$

    2 $y = 3x^2$ **4** $y = 2x^3$

                              5 $y = x^2 + 3$

5. new coordinates of E:
    $Q(-h, k)$; $R(-h, -k)$; $S(2h, 2k)$;
    $T(h + 2, k)$; $U(k, h)$

6. area $= ab \sin x°$, $\angle B = 30°$

7. **1** $A = 2x^2 + 4xh$
    2 110
    3 $h = \dfrac{A - 2x^2}{4x}$ $\left(\text{or } \dfrac{A}{4x} - \dfrac{x}{2}\right)$
    4 10 cm

8. **1** $2x(x + 4y)$ **4** $(x - 8)(x - 4)$
    2 $(r - s)(p + 2q)$ **5** $(2x + 1)(x - 3)$
    3 $(4x + 9y)(4x - 9y)$

9. **2** 26.0 m by 11.5 m   **3** 17.3 m square

10. 4.5%

11. 71

12. 29.5 ℓ, 2.2 gallons

13. $2x + 6y = 960$, $3x + y = 960$;
    $x = 300$, $y = 60$; 60 km

14. **1** height 27 m, $AB = 75$ m
    2 130 m
    3 190 m

Page 507 **Exercise E4**

1. **1** $\frac{1}{6}$ **4** $\frac{7}{12}$

   2 $\frac{1}{3}$ **5** $\frac{6}{11}$

   3 $\frac{1}{6}$

2. **1** $90°$ **2** 8 cm, 16 cm

3. **1** B **2** D **3** A **4** C

4. 1 s, 9 s

5. **1** equiangular **2** $4 : 25$

6. **1** $\begin{pmatrix} 6 & 3 \\ 4 & 7 \end{pmatrix}$ **4** $\begin{pmatrix} 5 & -3 \\ -3 & 2 \end{pmatrix}$

   2 $\begin{pmatrix} 11 & 6 \\ 17 & 10 \end{pmatrix}$ **5** $\begin{pmatrix} \frac{1}{4} & 0 \\ -\frac{1}{8} & \frac{1}{2} \end{pmatrix}$

   3 $\begin{pmatrix} 8 & 12 \\ 8 & 13 \end{pmatrix}$

7. mean 52.0 g, standard deviation 4.15 g

8. 12.3 km

9. **1** $(50 - 2x)\,\text{m}$
   2 $(50x - 2x^2)\,\text{m}^2$
   3 $x = 9$ or 16

11. **1** 72.3 m **3** $415\,\text{m}^2$
    2 66.0 m **4** $346\,\text{m}^2$

13. **1** -2
    2 3
    3 8.52×10^{-1}, 1.97×10

14. $14.1\,\text{cm}^3$

15. **1** $\frac{3}{80}\,\text{m/s}^2$ $(0.038\,\text{m/s}^2)$
    2 54 km
    3 81 km/h

Page 509 **Exercise E5**

1. 25%, 12.5%

2. 110 cm, 110 m

3. $\frac{4}{5}$

4. 14 cm

5. *E*, reflected in $x = 3$;
   F, rotated through $180°$ about $(2, 2)$

6. **1** $\triangle POT, \triangle TOD$ **2** 2.4 cm

7. $14.0°$

8. $y = 4x^2 + 36x$, 4.46 m

9. cum. freq: 0, 2, 5, 19, 42, 86, 104, 109, 112;
   median 4.3%, interquartile range 1.6%;
   48 shares

10. circle on *AB* as diameter

11. 14 m/s

12. Path B, D, F; 9 days

13. $A_1 (0, 3)$, $B_1 (-1, 5)$, $C_1 (1, 4)$;
    $A_2 (3, 3)$, $B_2 (6, 3)$, $C_2 (3, 6)$;
    areas $\frac{1}{2}$, $1\frac{1}{2}$, $4\frac{1}{2}$, ratio $1 : 3 : 9$;
    enlargement centre origin scale factor 3;
    $\begin{pmatrix} 3 & 0 \\ 0 & 3 \end{pmatrix}$

14. $a = 1$, $b = -5$; $y = x^2 - 5$

15. 10.6 km

Page 513 **Exercise E6**

1. **1** $\sqrt{225} + \sqrt{64}$, 6
   2 3^7, 139
   3 43

2. **1** $\frac{2}{5}$ **4** $\frac{1}{10}$
   2 $\frac{3}{10}$ **5** $\frac{3}{5}$
   3 $\frac{1}{5}$ **6** $\frac{2}{5}$

3. **1** $x = 0.1$ or 7.9
    2 $x = -2.4$ or 0.9

4. $585 \, \text{m}$

5. $OD = 4 \, \text{cm}$, $AD = 9 \, \text{cm}$; area $= 27 \, \text{cm}^2$

7. **1** W **2** Y **3** X

8. $x + y \leqslant 24$, $y \leqslant x$, $y \geqslant \frac{1}{3}x$, $3y + 2x \geqslant 30$;
    £60

9. $32.2°$

11. $50°$

12. $x = 1.2$, $y = 0.8$

13. frequency densities: 0.7, 2.0, 1.8, 1.4, 0.5

14. $\dfrac{1}{x + 3}$

15. A_1 (5, 4), B_1 (4, 5), C_1 (6, 8);